PRAISE FOR MARY MACLANE

"Anyone who reads her will **never forget her voice**." - *Biographile* "Mary MacLane comes off the page quivering with life. **Moving**." - *London Times* "She reminds us of the **power of personal narrative**, honestly told." - *The Atlantic* "In a pre-sound-bite age she already knew **how to draw blood in one direct sentence**." - *The Awl* "She had a short but fiery life of writing and misadventure, and her writing was **a template for the confessional memoirs that have become ubiquitous**." - *The New Yorker* "One of the **most fascinatingly self-involved personalities of the 20th century**." - *The Age* "Confessional journalists have **people like Mary Mac-Lane** to thank." - *Flavorwire* "Her diaries ignited a **national uproar**, ushering in a **new era** for women's voices. Her elegant, ambitious embrace of **full-disclosure opened a door to what was possible for women**." - *The Atlantic* "**Fiery frankness** made her a pioneer." - *Time Out Chicago* "Her poetry is one of extremes: **lust for happiness, despair for life**." - *Hairy Dog Review* "Riveting." - New Hampshire Public Radio "*I Await the Devil's Coming* is a small **masterpiece, full of camp and swagger**." - Parul Sehgal, NPR "First of the self-expressionists, and **the first of the Flappers**." - *Chicagoan*

*

PRAISE FOR PREVIOUS EDITION

"A **girl wonder**." - *Harper's* (two-page exclusive spread) "A **pioneering feminist - a sensation**." - *Feminist Bookstore News* "From now on it must take **a prominent place in any discussions of American women's writing and the literature of the West**." - Dr Peter Donahue, Oklahoma State University - "A **pioneering newswoman** and later a **silent-screen star**, considered **the veritable spirit of the iconoclastic Twenties**, 'the **Joan of Arc** of the Red-Hot Mamas.' 'How did it happen,' declared one of her eulogists, 'that **a revolution in manners started, or seemed to start, with an unruly young woman** who couldn't bear the sight of the toothbrushes hanging up in the family bathroom at **Butte, Montana**?'" - Robert Taylor, Chief Critic, *Boston Globe*

*

Michael R. Brown is the foremost MacLane researcher in the world today. He published the acclaimed MacLane anthology *Tender Darkness* and more recently authored the well-reviewed experimental memoir *She and I: A Fugue*. He is completing a multi-volume series on MacLane's life, career, and influence for publication in 2015. He lives in Northern California.

Bojana Novakovic, an Australian Film Inst. Award-winning film/stage/television actress, is co-Artistic-Director of Ride On Theatre and a director, translator, and playwright. She recently toured Australia in her original stage interpretation *The Story of Mary MacLane - by Herself*, playing the title role. She makes her home in Melbourne, Australia.

By the Editor:

Tender Darkness: A Mary MacLane Anthology (with Elisabeth Pruitt)

She and I: A Fugue (Petrarca Press)

   http://fuguewriter.com

*

Coming in 2015:

Mary in The Press: Miss MacLane and Her Fame

A Quite Unusual Intensity of Life: The Lives, Works and Influence of Mary MacLane

   (with Chiara di Benedetto)

HUMAN DAYS

A Mary MacLane Reader

*

Edited, With an Introduction & Notes,
by Michael R. Brown

Foreword by Bojana Novakovic

Petrarca Press
Austin · Texas
October · 2014

1st US ed., 1st prntg. Printed in the USA.

This paper is PH-balanced.
It should undergo lessened crumbling,
yellowing, or other deterioration over time.

BIBLIOGRAPHIC DATA

MacLane, Mary, 1881-1929
Human days: a Mary MacLane reader
1st ed. / p. cm.
Includes bibliographic references (p.).
Lib. of Congress Control No. PENDING
1. Feminism - United States - Literary collections
2. Women - United States - Literary collections
ISBN 978-1-883304-03-4 - Paperbound
ISBN 978-1-883304-04-1 - Casebound

Table of Contents

Introduction

FROM NOWHERE KNOWN, Mary MacLane - from the earliest time we know of her - founded her life on the closest thing there is to a formula for the creative life: passionate extremism. The unique public sensation her work immediately created - remembered today, yet still to be documented and fully comprehended - became very rapidly the artistic material of her later work. At the height of fame she disdained it, and when the crest of that fame had broken several years previous, she admitted a fondness for it (nothing more) and said what only she could say: "It's fun to be Mary MacLane, a set-apart individuality in any gathering." Set-apart and individual she was, and remains, and the fun she had with it is one of her continuing relevancies to our time: when we are wont either to deny our individuality (and thus risk the contradiction of saying we do not exist) or to express it joylessly and reactively (and thus give it the lie).

Born in 1881 in Winnipeg, she and her three siblings followed the fortunes of their deep-chested frontier entrepreneur father, whose death at age fifty when MacLane was eight haunted her for longer than she would ever admit. The young tomboy was moved from Minnesota, where her father had retired after making a fortune, to Montana on the occasion of her mother's rather rapid remarriage. After some time in Great Falls, her stepfather moved the family to Butte in about 1897, in whose uproaring mining heyday MacLane would sharpen her wits, strengthen her opposition to most things conventional, and - before the age of twenty - would craft the book that made her famous, infamous, loved, hated, and most of all attended-to.

In an age when even Butte citizens observed certain proprieties - one of their great whorehouses offered the wealthiest patrons a private tunnel so that they would not be seen entering or exiting at street level - MacLane did what was more remarkable than simply breaking the rules. She played with customs and morals, scrutinized them, largely ignored them - to the point of seeming almost normal. Then she would be off on another adventure, which could take the form of living off a single lucky throw of the dice in a St. Augustine casino, or shutting herself away for years to work on books that never saw print. In 1918, at the climax of her career, in a nod to the future, she wrote and starred in a ninety-minute silent movie - playing herself. It was probably the first to unify writer, narrator, and star - and one of the first, if not the first, to entirely break the fourth wall by a star's facing the camera and, in sustained scenes, addressing the audience directly.

And, for all this, she was not fundamentally a controversialist or attention-seeker and was decidedly not an extrovert. Indeed, her career - of which her public appearances and actings-out were only a derivative manifestation - possesses a deep unity through an uncompromising, sometimes precipitous introversion and self-scrutiny. The piercing moral inspection of her Scottish Presbyterian forebears never ended - she decoupled it from morality, and explored where it led. Her career, seen in its totality (which has been impossible until very recently), is a sustained performance in transcending what were and usually are held to be necessary dichotomies, which yet retains all the electric tension of very earnestly believing in those dichotomies. When she brands herself as decadent or perverse, she believes it, is perplexed by it, is making art of it, and is experimenting with how it feels.

Her career testifies to the power of writing as the organizing principle of an entire life. Whatever else she was - and years of research have only begun to disclose the full trajectory of even her written life - she *lived* writing.

In 1913, the then-famous California novelist Gertrude Atherton visited Butte. The pen-sketch in her memoirs twenty years later is one of the most vivid.

"When [MacLane] called on me she remained for several hours, talking all the time, and with exceeding brilliance. She was very nervous, pacing the room for the most part, for she led a wild life down on 'The Flat,' that resort of all the wild spirits in Butte ... [S]he read constantly, the best that was written, had been well drilled in the classics from childhood. Her criticisms of current authors were acute, unbiased, and everything she said was worth listening to."

And yet, Atherton gives a facile history of MacLane as recklessly deteriorating decadent *sans* creative talent - which the leonine novelist (whose heroines conquer ardent men through age-defying beauty) felt was best expressed through - writing novels. "She had the genius of personality," concluded Atherton, but "could only write of herself."

It must be said that this was not an uncommon judgment around the time of MacLane's death in August 1929, two years short of her father's death-age. She was remembered in obituaries across the nation - in pieces that showed almost no comprehension of the extent or the meaning of her work. Obituarists and editorialists spoke of comets, star-bursts, called her "the lovely pagan" and the pioneer of the Flapper era, all in a hectic confusion which got the titles of her books and movie wrong and had nothing to do with the craft of her work. She was made an instance of, as the *New York Times* put it, "the paths of glory" which lead over an obscure horizon to dissolution, a warning of life's brevity and the transience of fame. At times there was a sad kind of pity, at times an esteem, sometimes mockery, at points an elegiac regret that did not quite know why it was sad. Every so often, someone understood.

But for the most part, what was before the eye was missed.

It is to bring before new minds this author's progress, and invite a full survey of a sophisticated, highly-crafted œuvre, that this book is offered. A recent spate of mechanically-assembled reprints of her three books has shed no light; indeed, a comprehensive examination of MacLane - despite several worthy doctoral dissertations on specific aspects - is sorely overdue. The editor intends to complete two detailed studies - *Mary in The Press: Miss MacLane and her Fame* and *A Quite Unusual Intensity of Life: The Lives, Works and Influence of Mary MacLane* - in 2015.

First, however: Mary MacLane, as she spoke. Not a museum piece, not a sensation of long ago, but a sharp blade of self-knowing that shows us of today and tomorrow how much is possible through the descent within, the adventure without, and exact expression that flows out at the line between.

*

Many through the years have contributed to our knowledge of MacLane. Some are many decades beyond anyone's ability to thank. This edition was enriched by - to name but a few - Vicky Anderson's Minnesota research, Tim Blue's film-sharing, Nola Cassady's flame-keeping, Len Chester's unexpected generosity, Arlene Copeland's and Nicolas Gosse's Europe research, Chiara di Benedetto's wise counsel, John Emeigh's expert reportage, Suzanne Hahn's rapid responsiveness, Jonathan Ned Katz's decades' bravery, Jerry Kilmer's kind aid, Shoshana Milgram Knapp's long inspiration, Philip Lipson's and Virginia R. Terris' and Leslie Wheeler's path-clearing scholarship, Ada McAllister's bright friendship, William A. Mays' archive-keeping, Joan Melcher's creative ways, Cheree Miller's dedicated labors, Haley Anne Nelson's confident artistry, Bojana Novakovic's unfailing energy, Lee Phillips' literary safeguarding, Sharon Presley's history-devotion, Marthe Séguin-Muntz's Canada research, Zoe Ann Stoltz's Montana research, and Ken Storie's Manitoba research.

It is dedicated to the memory of Elisabeth Pruitt, who in the first MacLane anthology introduced to new generations a deeply-woven body of work, and of Martha Finnerty and John Hughes, who sent me the keys that opened the first doors.

Michael R. Brown
Butte County, California

Foreword

I STUMBLED UPON HER writings accidentally one wintry morning, when I was bemusing my own wanton state by reading a collection of contemporary ramblings by outsiders: people we refer to as being depressed or mad.

My first encounter was a brief one: a small segment from her first book. But it was enough to leave me struck with adoration, awe, and an odd sense of kinship. Her name was Mary MacLane and she was raw, honest and surreal. I wished that I had written her words, would never have admitted that to anyone, and did not think her mad at all.

I wanted to know more about her, so I took to the (newly discovered) World Wide Web for research. What I found shocked and delighted me. I was reading the ramblings of a woman from over a hundred years ago. A teenager from 1902 was writing of things that mattered to me (a woman barely out of my teens), in 2004.

I shared it with my girlfriends and they too were in love. Mary MacLane had tapped into something that mattered to us: an incessant yearning for self-discovery: something which my generation was on the verge of exploiting (for better or for worse) on the Internet over the next decade. Mary was doing it, in style, over 100 years ago. If she had a blog today, she would be a superstar.

Mary knew nothing of Freud, yet the sense of self-discovery in her writing contains an instinctively psychoanalytic perspective. Her observations of herself and her environment are free of social constraint and psychobabble. Her use of language is original and startlingly contemporary, her ideas universal and timeless.

A host of contemporary definitions have been applied to her through time. But Mary's own diagnosis is the most relevant: that of a Genius. It was a unique branding. She was a genius of The Self. Her emotional intelligence was prodigious. She was unparalleled in the world of acute, over-analytical self-knowledge.

Today we witness a metastasizing strain of humanity searching for meaning through superficial communication where content is irrelevant: a cultural addiction to expressing every arbitrary feeling to anyone via Facebook updates and Twitter tweets. This adrenaline-driven, anxiety-stricken quest for validation has urged fame for fame's sake, where it is not what you say, but how many people hear it, that matters. Mary MacLane wills us, even from the grave, to draw parallels and comparisons between her time and the wayward manifestations of self-discovery in our digital age.

Like those utilizing today's social networks, Mary wrote with a sense of audience, a knowledge of the existence of the reader. But she did so without quest for validation. Hers was a yearning to express herself and be understood, *not* to be validated. I am convinced that were she alive now, her contribution to the virtual public sphere would revolutionize it with *class*.

While she was proclaimed as the first of the Flappers by one of the Jazz Age's big magazines, I would like to suggest that Mary was not only decades, but well over a century ahead of her time. If you ask me, she was the first of the Grungers and now Emos: a generation of contemporary teenagers and "tweens," walking around lost in their own unfathomable sense of self, willing each other to look at and talk about the dark side of life, writing poetry, wearing black, and feeling things very deeply ...

All jokes aside, I found Mary's writing fundamentally theatrical, yearning to be shared with an audience or read out loud. So I dug her up from the grave and set out to write her a play ...

This started me on a search for materials, facts, and artifacts. I trawled through the Net and found an incredibly comprehensive website, made by this book's editor. I called people, emailed, wrote letters, and asked questions. I went to Butte and scanned the archives, one by one, year by year, hoping to find more answers.

The world of Mary was available but it was scattered. Annoyingly so. If I were not so keen, I would have given up. All this information was hard to track down and (even more) difficult to explain to people.

But now there is this book, compiled, annotated, and edited by Michael R. Brown. It not only makes Mary accessible to those of us who have been searching for her material over the years, but it makes her available to the new reader. Here she is as comprehensible as she will ever be. The book is carefully thought out, categorized, and annotated in a way that puts the pieces of the puzzle back together delightfully. From someone who has traveled the world looking for all things Mary, I promise you, there is no need to look further than this anthology. Michael R. Brown, thank you.

*

A little feverish thrill runs through my veins as I, merely a humble fan, sit by and read this night after night. *A spell of silent human-music glows and burns upon me like gentle fire. Often is God thus capriciously kind to me* ...

So please, ladies and gentlemen, take this time to uncork your favourite bottle of red, find an apple tree to sit under, put away your fob watches, forget for an hour or so about all those splendid little wars the world is always in, and join us in saluting the collected works of the greatest genius you've never heard of: The One, the only Miss Mary MacLane ...

Bojana Novakovic
Melbourne, Australia

MacLane wrote at least five books: three published, two she is known to have destroyed. Her first - a journal of three months in utter obscurity in Butte - brought international fame. Written in a cool, precise, almost faultless style, I Await established her persona to the present day. Everything she wrote after, and almost all later interest in her, would be founded on this book.

Her prediction at age twenty-one that "fifty years after I am dead they will say, 'Her first book was her masterpiece'" proved correct. It has been adapted for the stage, reprinted around the world, made the subject of academic study, and is quoted on and off the Internet.

More than a century before what Anna Saunders has called "Generation Exhibition," MacLane created a proto-blog and populated it with entries that sum to a portrait of a time, a place, and the talent they are seen through.

The text given here removes the original publisher's expurgations and edits.

I AWAIT THE DEVIL'S COMING

(Pub. as "The Story of Mary MacLane")

- 1902 -

To The Devil
Of the Steel-Gray Eyes, Who One
Day may Come - Who knows? -
I Dedicate, with the Mad Love of
A Young Weary Wooden Heart,
This, My Book.

*

Butte, Montana
November, 1901.

I, of womankind and of nineteen years, will now begin to set down as full and frank a Portrayal as I am able of myself, Mary MacLane, for whom the world contains not a parallel.

I am convinced of this, for I am odd.

I am distinctly original innately and in development.

I have in me a quite unusual intensity of life.

I can feel.

I have a marvelous capacity for misery and for happiness.

I am broad-minded.

I am a genius.

I am a philosopher of my own good peripatetic school.

I care neither for right nor for wrong - my conscience is nil.

My brain is a conglomeration of aggressive versatility.

I have reached a truly wonderful state of miserable morbid unhappiness.

I know myself, oh, very well.

I have attained an egotism that is rare indeed.

I have gone into the deep shadows.

All this constitutes oddity. I find therefore that I am quite, quite odd.

I have hunted for even the suggestion of a parallel among the several hundred persons that I call acquaintances. But in vain. There are people and people of varying depths and intricacies of character, but there is none to compare with me. The young ones of my own age - if I chance to give them but a glimpse of the real workings of my mind - can only stare at me in dazed stupidity, uncomprehending; and the old ones of forty and fifty - for forty and fifty are always old to nineteen - can but either stare also in stupidity, or else, their own narrowness asserting itself, smile their little devilish smile of superiority which they reserve indiscriminately for all foolish young things. - The utter idiocy of forty and fifty at times! -

These to be sure are extreme instances. There are among my young acquaintances some who do not stare in stupidity, and yes, even at forty and fifty there are some who understand some phases of my complicated character, though none to comprehend it in its entirety.

But, as I said, even the suggestion of a parallel is not to be found among them.

I think at this moment, however, of two minds famous in the world of letters between which and mine there are certain fine points of similarity. These are the minds of Lord Byron and of Marie Bashkirtseff. It is the Byron of *Don Juan* in whom I find suggestions of myself. In this sublime outpouring there are few to admire the character of Don Juan, but all must admire Byron. He is truly admirable. He uncovered and exposed his soul of mingled good and bad - as the terms are - for the world to gaze upon. He knew the human race. And he knew himself.

As for that strange notable, Marie Bashkirtseff, yes, I am rather like her in many points, as I've been told. But in most things I go beyond her.

Where she is deep, I am deeper.

Where she is wonderful in her intensity, I am still more wonderful in my intensity.

Where she had philosophy, I am a philosopher.

Where she had astonishing vanity and conceit, I have yet more astonishing vanity and conceit.

But she, forsooth, could paint good pictures, - and I - what can I do?

She had a beautiful face, and I am a plain-featured insignificant little animal.

She was surrounded by admiring, sympathetic friends, and I am alone - alone, though there are people and people.

She was a genius, and still more am I a genius.

She suffered with the pain of a woman, young, and I suffer with the pain of a woman, young and all alone.

And so it is.

Along some lines I have gotten to the edge of the world. A step more and I fall off. I do not take the step. I stand on the edge, and I suffer.

Nothing, oh, nothing on the earth can suffer like a woman young and all alone!

- Before proceeding farther with the portraying of Mary MacLane, I will write out some of her uninteresting history.

I was born in 1881 at Winnipeg, in Canada. - Whether Winnipeg will yet live to be proud of this fact is a matter for some conjecture and anxiety on my part. - When I was four years old I was taken with my family to a little town in western Minnesota, where I lived a more or less vapid and lonely life until I was ten. We came then to Montana.

Whereat the aforesaid life was continued.

My father died when I was eight.

Apart from feeding and clothing me comfortably and sending me to school - which is no more than was due me - and transmitting to me the MacLane blood and character, I can not see that he ever gave me a single thought.

Certainly he did not love me, for he was quite incapable of loving any one but himself. And since nothing is of any moment in this world without the love of human beings for each other, it is a matter of supreme indifference to me whether my father, Jim MacLane of selfish memory, lived or died.

He is nothing to me.

There are with me still a mother, a sister, and two brothers.

They also are nothing to me.

They do not understand me any more than if I were some strange live curiosity, as which I dare say they regard me.

I am peculiarly of the MacLane blood which is Highland Scotch. My sister and brothers inherit the traits of their mother's family which is of Scotch Lowland descent. This alone makes no small degree of difference. Apart from this the MacLanes - these particular MacLanes - are just a little bit different from every family in Canada, and from every other that I've known. It contains and has contained fanatics of many minds - religious, social, whatnot. And I am a true MacLane.

There is absolutely no sympathy between my immediate family and me. There can never be.

My mother, having been with me during the whole of my nineteen years, has an utterly distorted idea of my nature and its desires, if indeed she has any idea of it.

When I think of the exquisite love and sympathy which might be between a mother and daughter, I feel myself defrauded of a beautiful thing rightfully mine, in a world where for me such things are pitiably few.

It will always be so.

My sister and brothers are not interested in me and my analyses and philosophy, and my wants. Their own are strictly practical and material. The love and sympathy between human beings is to them, it seems, a thing only for people in books.

In short, they are Lowland Scotch and I am a MacLane.

And so, as I've said, I carried my uninteresting existence into Montana. The existence became less uninteresting, however, as my versatile mind began to develop and grow and know the glittering things that are. But I realized as the years were passing that my own life was at best a vapid, negative thing.

A thousand treasures that I wanted were lacking.

I graduated from the High School with these things: very good Latin; good French and Greek; indifferent Geometry and other mathematics; a broad conception of History and Literature; peripatetic philosophy that I acquired without any aid from the High School; genius of a kind, that has always been with me; an empty heart that has taken on a certain wooden quality; an excellent strong young woman's-body; a pitiably starved soul.

With this equipment I have gone my way through the last two years. But my life, though unsatisfying and warped, is no longer insipid. It is fraught with a poignant misery - the misery of Nothingness.

I have no particular thing to occupy me. I write every day. Writing is a necessity - like eating. I do a little housework, and on the whole am rather fond of it - some parts of it. I dislike dusting chairs, but I have no aversion to scrubbing floors. Indeed, I have gained much of my strength and gracefulness of body from scrubbing the kitchen floor - to say nothing of some fine points of philosophy. It brings a certain energy to one's body and to one's brain.

But mostly I take walks far away in the open country. Butte and its immediate vicinity present as ugly an outlook as one could wish to see. It is so ugly indeed that it is near the perfection of ugliness. And anything perfect, or nearly so, is not to be despised. I have reached some astonishing subtleties of conception as I have walked for miles over the sand and barrenness among the little hills and gulches. Their utter desolateness is an inspiration to the long, long thoughts and to the nameless wanting. Every day I walk over the sand and barrenness.

And so then my daily life seems an ordinary life enough, and possibly, to an ordinary person, a comfortable life.

That's as may be.

To me it is an empty damned weariness.

I rise in the morning; eat three meals; and walk; and work a little, read a little, write; see some uninteresting people; go to bed.

Next day, I rise in the morning; eat three meals; and walk; and work a little, read a little, write; see some uninteresting people; go to bed.

Again I rise in the morning; eat three meals; and walk; and work a little, read a little, write; see some uninteresting people; go to bed.

Truly an exalted, soulful life!

What it does for me, how it affects me, I am now trying to portray.

January 14

I have in me the germs of intense life. If I could live, and if I could succeed in writing out my living, the world itself would feel the heavy intensity of it.

I have the personality, the nature, of a Napoleon, albeit a feminine translation. And therefore I do not conquer; I do not even fight. I manage only to exist.

- Poor little Mary MacLane, - what might you not be? What wonderful thing might you not do? But held down, half-buried, a seed fallen in barren ground, alone, uncomprehended, obscure - poor little Mary MacLane! -

Weep, world, - why don't you - for poor little Mary MacLane.

Had I been born a man I would by now have made a deep impression of myself on the world - on some part of it. But I am a woman, and God, or the Devil, or Fate, or whosoever it was, has flayed me of the thick outer skin and thrown me out into the midst of Life - has left me a lonely damned thing filled with the red, red blood of ambition and desire, but afraid to be touched, for there is no thick skin between my sensitive flesh and the world's fingers.

But I want to be touched.

Napoleon was a man and though sensitive his flesh was safely covered.

But I am a woman, awakening, and upon awakening and looking about me, I would fain turn and go back to sleep.

There is a pain that goes with these things when one is a woman, young and all alone.

- I am filled with an ambition. I wish to give to the world a naked Portrayal of Mary MacLane: her wooden heart, her good young woman's-body, her mind, her soul.

I wish to write, write, write!

I wish to acquire that beautiful benign gentle satisfying thing - Fame. I want it - oh, I want it! I wish to leave all my obscurity, my misery, - my weary unhappiness behind me forever.

I am deadly, deadly tired of my unhappiness.

I wish this Portrayal to be published and launched into that deep salt sea - the world. There are some there surely who will understand it and me.

Can I be that thing which I am - can I be possessed of a peculiar rare genius, and yet drag my life out in obscurity in this uncouth warped Montana town!

It must be impossible! If I thought the world contained nothing more than that for me - oh, what should I do! Would I make an end of my dreary little life now? I fear I would. I am a philosopher - and a coward. And it were infinitely better to die now in the high-beating pulses of youth than to drag on, year after year, year after year, and find oneself at last a stagnant old woman, spiritless, hopeless, with a declining body, a declining mind, - and nothing to look back on except the visions of things that might have been - and the weariness.

I see the picture. I see it plainly. Oh, kind Devil, deliver me from it!

Surely there must be in a world of manifold beautiful things something among them for me.

And always while I am still young, there is that dim light, the Future. But it is indeed a dim, dim light, and ofttimes there's a treachery in it.

So then yes. I find myself at this stage of womankind and nineteen years, a genius, a thief, a liar - a general moral vagabond, a fool more or less, and a philosopher of the peripatetic school. Also I find that even this combination can not make one happy. It serves, however, to occupy my versatile mind, to keep me wondering what it is a kind Devil has in store for me.

A philosopher of my own peripatetic school - hour after hour I walk over the desolate sand and dreariness among tiny hills and gulches on the outskirts of this mining town; in the morning, in the long afternoon, in the cool of the night. And hour after hour, as I walk, through my brain some long, long pageants march: the pageant of my fancies, the pageant of my unparalleled egotism, the pageant of my unhappiness, the pageant of my minute analyzing, the pageant of my peculiar philosophy, the pageant of my dull, dull life, - and the pageant of the Possibilities.

We three go out on the sand and barrenness: my wooden heart, my good young woman's-body, my soul. We go there and contemplate the long sandy wastes, the red, red line on the sky at the setting of the sun, the cold gloomy mountains under it, the ground without a weed, without a grass-blade even in their season - for they have years ago been killed off by the sulphur smoke from the smelters.

So this sand and barrenness forms the setting for the personality of me.

I feel about forty years old.

Yet I know my feeling is not the feeling of forty years. These are the feelings of miserable, wretched youth.

Every day the atmosphere of a house becomes unbearable, so every day I go out to the sand and the barrenness. It is not cold, neither is it mild. It is gloomy.

I sit for two hours on the ground by the side of a pitiably small narrow stream of water. It is not even a natural stream. I dare say it comes from some mine among the hills. But it is well enough that the stream is not natural - when you consider the sand and barrenness. It is singularly appropriate.

And I am singularly appropriate to all of them. It is good, after all, to be appropriate to something - to be in touch with something, even sand and barrenness.

The sand and barrenness is old - oh, very old. You think of this when you look at it.

What should I do if the earth were made of wood, with a paper sky!

I feel about forty years old.

And again I say I know my feeling is not the feeling of forty years. These are the feelings of miserable, wretched youth.

Still more pitiable than the sand and barrenness and the poor unnatural stream is the dry, warped cemetery where the dry, warped people of Butte bury their dead friends. It is a source of satisfaction to me to walk down to this cemetery, and contemplate it, and revel in its utter pitiableness.

"It is more pitiable than I and my sand and barrenness and my poor unnatural stream," I say over and over, and take my comfort.

Its condition is more forlorn than that of a woman young and alone. It is unkempt. It is choked with dust and stones. The few scattered blades of grass look rather ashamed to be seen growing there. A great many of the headstones are of wood and are in a shameful state of decay. Those that are of stone are still more shameful in their hard brightness.

The dry, warped friends of the dry, warped people of Butte are buried in this dusty dreary wind-havocked waste. They are left here and forgotten.

The Devil must rejoice in this graveyard.

And I rejoice with the Devil.

It is something for me to contemplate that is more pitiable than I and my sand and barrenness and my unnatural stream.

I rejoice with the Devil.

The inhabitants of this cemetery are forgotten. I have watched once the burying of a young child. Every day for a fortnight afterward I came back, and I saw the mother of the child there. She came and stood by the small new grave. After a few days more she stopped coming.

I knew the woman and went to her house to see her. She was beginning to forget the child. She was beginning to take up again the thread of her life where she had let it go. The thread of her life is involved in the divorces and fights of her neighbors.

Out in the warped graveyard her child is forgotten. And presently the wooden head-stone will begin to decay. But the worms will not forget their part. They have eaten the small body by now, and enjoyed it. Always worms enjoy a body to eat.

And also the Devil rejoiced.

And I rejoiced with the Devil.

They are more pitiable, I insist, than I and my sand and barrenness - the mother whose life is involved in divorces and fights, and the worms eating at the child's body, and the wooden headstone which will presently decay.

And so the Devil and I rejoice.

But no matter how ferociously pitiable is the dried-up graveyard, the sand and barrenness and the sluggish little stream have their own persistent individual damnation. The world is at least so constructed that its treasures may be damned each in a different manner and degree.

I feel about forty years old.

And I know my feeling is not the feeling of forty years. They do not feel any of these things at forty. At forty the fire has long since burned out. When I am forty I shall look back to myself and my feelings at nineteen - and I shall smile.

Or shall I indeed smile?

January 17

As I have said, I want Fame. I want to write - to write such things as compel the admiring acclamations of the world at large; such things as are written but once in years, things subtly but distinctly different from the books written every day.

I can do this.

Let me but make a beginning, let me but strike the world in a vulnerable spot, and I can take it by storm. Let me but win my spurs, and then you will see me - of womankind and young - valiantly astride a charger riding down the world, with Fame following at the charger's heels, and the multitudes agape.

But oh, more than all this I want to be happy!

Fame is indeed benign and gentle and satisfying. But Happiness is something at once tender and brilliant beyond all things.

I want Fame more than I can tell.

But more than Fame I want Happiness. I have never been happy in my weary young life.

Think, oh *think* of being happy for a year - for a day! How brilliantly blue the sky would be; how swiftly and joyously would the green rivers run; how madly, merrily triumphant the four winds of heaven would sweep round the corners of the fair earth!

What would I not give for one day, one hour, of that charmed thing Happiness! What would I not give up?

How we eager fools tread on each other's heels, and tear each other's hair, and scratch each other's faces, in our furious gallop after Happiness. For some it is embodied in Fame, for some in Money, for some in Power, for some in Virtue - and for me in something very much like love.

None of the other fools desires Happiness as I desire it. For one single hour of Happiness I would give up at once these things: Fame, and Money, and Power, and Virtue, and Honor, and Righteousness, and Truth, and Logic, and Philosophy, and Genius. The while I would say, What a little,

little price to pay for dear Happiness.

I am ready and waiting to give all that I have to the Devil in exchange for Happiness. I have been tortured so long with the dull, dull misery of Nothingness - all my nineteen years. I want to be happy - oh, I want to be happy -

The Devil has not yet come. But I know that he usually comes, and I await him eagerly.

I am fortunate that I am not one of those burdened with an innate sense of virtue and honor which must come always before Happiness. They are but few who find their Happiness in their Virtue. The rest of them must be content to see it walk away. But with me virtue and honor are nothing.

I long unspeakably for Happiness.

And so I await the Devil's coming.

January 18

And meanwhile - as I wait - my mind occupies itself with its own good odd philosophy, so that even the Nothingness becomes almost endurable.

The Devil has given me some good things - for I find that the Devil owns and rules the earth and all that therein is. He has given me, among other things - my admirable young woman's body, which I enjoy thoroughly and of which I am passionately fond.

A spasm of pleasure seizes me when I think in some acute moment of the buoyant health and vitality of this fine young body that is feminine in every fiber.

You may gaze at and admire the picture in the front of this book. It is the picture of a genius - a genius with a good strong young-woman's body, - and inside the pictured body is a liver, a MacLane liver, of admirable perfectness.

Other young women and older women and men of all ages have good bodies also, I doubt not - though the masculine body is merely flesh, it seems, flesh and bones and nothing else. But few recognize the value of their bodies; few have grasped the possibilities, the artistic graceful perfection, the poetry of human flesh in its health. Few have even sense enough indeed to keep their flesh in health, or to know what health is until they have ruined some vital organ, and so banished it forever.

I have not ruined any of my vital organs, and I appreciate what health is. I have grasped the art, the poetry of my fine feminine body.

- This at the age of nineteen is a triumph for me. -

Sometime in the midst of the brightness of an October I have walked for miles in the still high air under the blue of the sky. The brightness of the day and the blue of the sky and the incomparable high air have entered into my veins and flowed with my red blood. They have penetrated into every remote nerve-center and into the marrow of my bones.

At such a time this young body glows with life.

My red blood flows swiftly and joyously - in the midst of the brightness of October.

My sound sensitive liver rests gently with its thin yellow bile in sweet content.

My calm beautiful stomach silently sings as I walk a song of peace, the while it hugs within itself the chyme that was my lunch.

My lungs, saturated with mountain ozone and the perfume of the pines, expand in continuous ecstasy.

My heart beats like the music of Schumann, in easy graceful rhythm with an undertone of power.

My very intestine even basks contentedly in its place like a snake in the hot dust, vibrating with conscious life.

My strong and sensitive nerves are reeking and swimming in sensuality like drunken little Bacchantes, gay and garlanded in mad revelling.

The entire wonderful graceful mechanism of my woman's-body has fallen at the time - like the wonderful graceful mechanism of my woman's-mind - under the enchanting spell of a day in October.

"It is good," I think to myself, "oh, it is good to be alive! It is wondrously good to be a woman young in the fullness of nineteen springs. It is unutterably lovely to be a healthy young animal living on this charmed earth."

After I have walked for several hours I reach a region where the sulphur smoke has not penetrated, and I sit on the ground with drawn-up knees and rest as the shadows lengthen. The shadows lengthen early in October.

Presently I lie flat on my back and stretch my lithe slimness to its utmost like a mountain lioness taking her comfort. I am intensely thankful to the Devil for my two good legs and the full use of them under a short skirt, when, as now, they carry me out beyond the pale of civilization away from tiresome dull people. There is nothing in the world that can become so maddeningly wearisome as people, people, people!

- And so Devil, accept, for my two good legs, my sincerest gratitude. -

I lie on the ground for some minutes and meditate idly. There is a worldful of easy indolent beautiful sensuality in the figure of a young woman lying on the ground under a warm setting sun. A man may lie on the ground - but that is as far as it goes. A man would go to sleep, probably, like a dog or a pig. He would even snore, perhaps - under the setting sun. But then, a man has not a good young feminine body to feel with, to receive into itself the spirit of a warm sun at its setting, on a day in October. - And so let us forgive him for sleeping, and for snoring.

When I again rise to a sitting posture all the brightness has focused itself to the west. It casts a yellow glamor over the earth, a glamor not of joy, nor of pleasure, nor of happiness - but of peace.

The young poplar trees smile gently in the deathly still air. The sage brush and the tall grass take on a radiant quietness. The high hills of Montana, near and distant, appear tender and benign. All is peace - peace. I think of that beautiful old song -

Sweet vale of Avoca! how calm could I rest
In thy bosom of shade -.

But I am too young yet to think of peace. It is not peace that I want. Peace is for forty and fifty. I am waiting for my Experience.

I am awaiting the coming of the Devil.

And now, just before twilight, after the sun has vanished over the edge, is the red, red line on the sky.

There will be days wild and stormy, filled with rain and wind and hail; and yet nearly always at the sun's setting there will be calm - and the red line of sky.

There is nothing in the world quite like this red sky at sunset. It is Glory, Triumph, Love, Fame!

Imagine a life bereft of things, and fingers pointed at it, and eyebrows raised; tossed and bandied hither and yon; crushed, beaten, bled, rent asunder, outraged, convulsed with pain; and then, into this life while still young, the red, red line of sky!

- Why did I cry out against Fate, says the line; why did I rebel against my term of anguish! I now rather rejoice at it; now in my Happiness I remember it only with deep pleasure. -

Think of that wonderful, most admirable, matchless man of steel, Napoleon Bonaparte. He threw himself heavily on the world, and the world has never since been the same. He hated himself, and the world, and God, and Fate, and the Devil. His hatred was his term of anguish.

Then the sun threw on the sky for him a red, red line - the red line of triumph, glory, fame!

And afterward there was the blackness of Night, the blackness that is not tender, not gentle.

But black as our Night may be, nothing can take from us the memory of the red, red sky. "Memory is possession," and so the red sky we have with us always.

Oh Devil, Fate, World - Someone, bring me my red sky! For a little, brief time and I will be satisfied. Bring it to me intensely red, intensely full, intensely alive! Short as you will, but red, red, red!

I am weary - weary, and oh, I want my red sky!

Short as it might be, its memory, its fragrance would stay with me always - always. Bring me, Devil, my red line of sky for one hour and take all, *all* - everything I possess. Let me keep my Happiness for one short hour and take away all from me forever. I will be satisfied when Night has come and everything is gone.

Oh, I await you, Devil, in a wild frenzy of impatience!

And as I hurry back through the cool darkness of October, I feel this frenzy in every fiber of my fervid woman's-body.

January 19

I come from a long line of Scotch and Canadian MacLanes. There are a great many MacLanes, but there is usually only one real MacLane in each generation. There is but one who feels again the passionate spirit of the Clans, those barbaric dwellers in the bleak but well-beloved Highlands of Scotland.

I am the real MacLane of my generation. The real MacLane in these later centuries is always a woman. The men of my family never amount to anything worth naming - if one excepts the acme, the zenith, of pure Selfishness, with a large letter S.

Life may be easy enough for the innumerable Canadian MacLanes who are not real. But it is certain to be more or less a Hill of Difficulty for the one who is. She finds herself somewhat alone. I have brothers and a sister and a mother in the same house with me - and I find myself somewhat alone. Between them and me there is no tenderness, no sympathy, no binding ties. Would it affect me in the least - do you suppose - if they should all die tomorrow? If I were not a real MacLane perhaps it would have been different, or perhaps I should not have missed these things.

How much, Devil, have I lost for the privilege of being a real MacLane.

But yes. I have also gained much.

January 20

I have said that I am quite alone.

I am not quite, quite alone.

I have one friend - of that Friendship that is real and is inlaid with the beautiful thing Truth. And because it has the beautiful thing Truth in it, this my one Friendship is somehow above and beyond me; there is something in it that I reach after in vain - for I have not that divinely beautiful thing Truth. Have I not said that I am a thief and a liar? But in this Friendship nevertheless there is a rare, ineffably sweet something that is mine. It is the one tender thing in this dull dreariness that wraps me round.

Are there many things in this cool-hearted world so utterly exquisite as the pure love of one woman for another woman?

My one friend is a woman some twelve or thirteen years older than I. She is as different from me as day from night. She believes in God - that God that is shown in the Bible of the Christians. And she carries with her an atmosphere of gentleness and truth. The while I am ready and waiting to dedicate my life to the Devil in exchange for Happiness - or some lesser thing. But I love Fannie Corbin with a peculiar and vivid intensity, and with all the sincerity and passion that is in me. Often I think of her, as I walk over the sand in my Nothingness, all day long. The Friendship of her and me is a fair, dear benediction upon me, but there is something in it - deep within it - that eludes me. In moments when I realize this, when I strain and reach vainly at a thing beyond me, when indeed I see in my mind a vision of the personality of Fannie Corbin, it is then that it comes on me with force that I am not good.

But I can love her with all the ardor of a young and passionate heart.

Yes, I can do that.

For a year I have loved my one friend. During the eighteen years of my life before she came into it I loved no one, for there was no one.

It is an extremely hard thing to go through eighteen years with no one to love, and no one to love you - the first eighteen years.

But now I have my one friend to love and to worship.

I have named my friend the "anemone lady," a name beautifully appropriate.

The anemone lady used to teach me Literature in the Butte High School. She used to read poetry in the class room in a clear sweet voice that made one wish one might sit there forever and listen to it.

But now I have left the High School, and the dear anemone lady has gone from Butte. Before she went she told me she would be my friend.

Think of it - to live and have a friend!

My friend does not fully understand me; she thinks much too well of me. She has not a correct idea of my soul's depths and shallows. But if she did know them she would still be my friend. She knows the heavy weight of my unrest and unhappiness. She is tenderly sympathetic. She is the one in all the world who is dear to me.

Often I think, if only I could have my anemone lady and go and live with her in some little out-of-the-world place high upon the side of a mountain for the rest of my life - what more would I desire? My Friendship would constitute my life. The unrest, the dreariness, the Nothingness of my existence now is so dull and gray by contrast that there would be Happiness for me in that life, Happiness softly radiant, if quiet - redolent of the fresh, thin fragrance of the dear blue anemone that grows in the winds and rains of spring.

But Miss Corbin would doubtless look somewhat askance at the idea of spending the rest of her life with me on a mountain. She is very fond of me, but her feeling for me is not like mine for her, which indeed is natural. And her life is made up mostly of sacrifices - doing for her fellow-creatures, giving of herself. She never would leave this.

And so then the mountainside and the solitude and the friend with me are, like every good thing, but a vision.

"Thy friend is always thy friend; not to have, nor to hold, nor to love, nor to rejoice in: but to remember."

And so do I remember my one friend, the anemone lady - and think often about her with passionate love.

January 21

Happiness, don't you know, is of three kinds - and all are transitory. It never stays, but it comes and goes.

There is that happiness that comes from newly-washed feet, for instance, and a pair of clean stockings on them, particularly after one has been upon a tramp into the country. Always I have identified this kind of happiness with a Maltese cat dipping a hungry, stealthy sensual tongue into a bowl of fresh, thick cream.

There is that still happiness that has come to me at rare times when I have been with my one friend - and which does very well for people whose feelings are moderate. They need wish for nothing beyond it. They could not appreciate anything deeper.

And there is that kind of happiness which is of the red sunset sky. There is something terrible in the thought of this indescribable mad Happiness. What a thing it is for a human being to be *happy* - with the red, red Happiness of the sunset sky!

It's like a terrific storm in summer with rain and wind, beating quiet water into wild waves, bending great trees to the ground, - convulsing the green earth with delicious pain.

It's like something of Schubert's played on the violin that stirs you within to exquisite torture.

It's like the human voice divine singing a Scotch ballad in a manner to drag your soul from your body.

But there are no words to tell it. It is something infinitely above and beyond words. It is the kind of Happiness the Devil will bring to me when he comes, - to me, to *me*! Oh, why does he not come now when I am in the midst of my youth! Why is he so long in coming?

Often you hear a dozen stories of how the Devil was most ready and willing to take all from some one and give him his measure of Happiness. And sometimes the person was innately virtuous and so could not take the Happiness when it was offered. But Happiness is its own justification, and it should be eagerly grasped when it comes.

A world filled with fools will never learn this.

And so here I stand in the midst of Nothingness waiting and longing for the Devil, and he doesn't come. I feel a choking, strangling, frenzied feeling of waiting - oh, why doesn't my Happiness come! I have waited so long - so long! -

There are persons who say to me that I ought not to think of the Devil, that I ought not to think of Happiness - Happiness for me would be sure to mean something wicked (as if Happiness could ever be wicked!); that I ought to think of being good, - I ought to think of God. These are persons who help to fill the world with fools. At any rate their words are unable to affect me. I can not distinguish between right and wrong in this scheme of things. It is one of the lines of reasoning in which I have gotten to the edge, the end. I have gotten to the point to which all logic finally leads. I can only say, What is wrong? What is right? What is good? What is evil? The words are merely words, with word-meanings.

Truth is Love and Love is the only Truth, and Love is the one thing out of all that is Real.

God is less than nothing to me. The Devil is really the only one to whom we may turn, and he exacts payment in full for every favor.

But surely he will come one day with Happiness for me.

Yet, oh, how can I wait!

To be a woman, young and all alone, is hard - *hard!* - is to want things, is to carry a heavy, heavy weight.

Oh, damn! damn! damn! Damn every living thing, the world! - the universe be damned!

Oh, I am weary, weary! Can't you see that I am weary and pity me in my own damnation?

January 22

It is night. I might well be in my bed taking a needed rest. But first I shall write.

To-day I walked far away over the sand in the teeth of a bitter wind. The wind was determined that I should turn and come back, and equally I was determined I would go on. I went on.

There is a certain kind of wind in the autumn to walk in the midst of which causes one's spirits to rise ecstatically. To walk in the midst of a bitter wind in January may have almost any effect.

To-day the bitter wind swept over me and around me and into the remote corners of my brain and swept away the delusions, and buffeted my philosophy with rough insolence.

The world is made up mostly of nothing. You may be convinced of this when a bitter wind has swept away your delusions.

What is the wind?

Nothing.

What is the sky?

Nothing.

What do we know?

Nothing.

What is Fame?

Nothing.

What is my heart?

Nothing.

What is my soul?

Nothing.

What are we?

We are nothing.

We think we progress wonderfully in the arts and sciences as one century follows another. What does it amount to? It does not teach us the All-Why. It does not let us cease to wonder what it is that we are doing, where it is that we are going. It does not teach us why the green comes again to the old, old hills in the spring; why the benign balm-o'-Gilead shines wet and sweet after the rain; why the red never fails to come to the breast of the robin, the black to the crow, the gray to the little wren; why the sand and barrenness lies stretched out around us; why the clouds float high above us; why the moon stands in the sky, night after night; why the mountains and valleys live on as the years pass.

The arts and sciences go on and on - still we wonder. We have not yet ceased to weep. And we suffer still in 1901, even as they suffered in 1801, and in 801.

To-day we eat our good dinners with forks.

A thousand years ago they had no forks.

Yet, though we have forks, we are not happy. We scream and kick and struggle and weep just as they did a thousand years ago - when they had no forks.

We are "no wiser than when Omar fell asleep."

And in the midst of our great Wondering, we wonder why some of us are given faith to trust without question, while the rest of us are left to eat out our life's vitals with asking.

I have walked once in summer by the side of a little marsh filled with mint and white hawthorn. The mint and white hawthorn have with them a vivid, rare delicious perfume. It makes you want to grovel on the ground - it makes you think you might crawl in the dust all your days, and well for you. The perfume lingers with you afterward when years have passed. You may scream and kick and struggle and weep right lustily every day of your life, but in your moments of calmness sometimes there will come back to you the fragrance of a swamp filled with mint and white hawthorn.

It is meltingly beautiful.

What does it mean?

What would it tell?

Why does the marsh, and the mint and white hawthorn, freeze over in the fall? And why do they come again voluptuous, enticing in the damp spring days - and rack the souls of wretches who look and wonder?

- You are superb, Devil! You have done a magnificent piece of work. I kneel at your feet and worship you. You have wrought a perfection, a pinnacle of fine, invisible damnation. -

The world is like a little marsh filled with mint and white hawthorn. It is filled with things likewise damnably beautiful. There are the green, green grass-blades and the Gray Dawns; there are swiftly-flowing rivers and the honking of wild geese, flying low; there are human voices and human eyes; there are stories of women and men who have learned to give up and to wait; there is the poetry of James Whitcomb Riley; there is Charity; there is Truth.

The Devil has made all of these things, and also he has made human beings who can feel.

Who was it that said, long ago, "Life is always a tragedy to those who feel?"

In truth the Devil has constructed a place of infinite torture - the fair green earth, the world.

But he has made that other infinite thing - Happiness. I forgive him for making me wonder since possibly he may bring me Happiness. I cast myself at his feet. I adore him.

The first third of our lives is spent in the expectation of Happiness. Then it comes, perhaps, and stays ten years, or a month, or three days, and the rest of our lives is spent in peace and rest - with the memory of the Happiness.

Happiness - though it is infinite - is a transient emotion.

It is too brilliant, too magnificent, too overwhelming to be a lasting thing. And it is merely an emotion. But, ah - *such* an emotion! Through it the Devil rules his domains. What would one not do to have it!

I can think of no so-called vile deed that I would scruple about if I could be happy. Everything is justified if it gives me Happiness. The Devil has done me some great favors: he has made me without a conscience, and without Virtue.

For which I thank thee, Devil, profoundly.

At least I shall be able to take my Happiness when it comes - even though the piles of nice distinctions between it and me be mountains high.

But meanwhile, the world, I say, and the people are nothing, nothing, nothing. The splendid castles, the strong bridges, that we are building are of small moment. We can only go down the wide roadway wondering and weeping, and without where to lay our heads.

January 23

I have eaten my dinner.

I have had, among other things, a fine, rare-broiled porterhouse steak from Omaha, and some fresh, green young onions from California. And just now I am a philosopher, pure and simple - except that there's nothing very pure about my philosophy, nor yet very simple.

Let the Devil come and go; let the wild waters rush over me; let nations rise and fall; let my favorite theories form themselves in line suddenly and run into the ground; let the little earth be bandied about from one belief to the other; but, I say in the midst of my young peripatetic philosophy, I need not be in complete despair - the world still contains things for me, while I have my fine rare porterhouse steak from Omaha - and my fresh green young onions from California.

Fame may pass over my head; money may escape me; my one friend may fail me; every hope may fold its tent and steal away; Happiness may remain a sealed book; every remnant of human ties may vanish; I may find myself an outcast; good things held out to me may suddenly be withdrawn; the stars may go out, one by one; the sun may go dark; yet still I may hold upright my head, if I have but my steak - and my onions.

I may find myself crowded out from many charmed circles; I may find the ethical world too small to contain me; the social world may also exclude me; the professional world may know me not; likewise the worlds of the arts and the sciences; I may find myself superfluous in literary haunts; I may see myself going gladly back to the vile dust from whence I sprung - to live in a green forest like the melancholy Jacques; but fare they well, I will say with what cheerfulness I can summon, while I have my steak - and my onions.

Possibly I may grow old and decrepit; my hair may turn gray; my bones may become rheumatic; I may grow weak in the knees; my ankle-joints which have withstood many a peripatetic journey may develop dropsical tendencies; my heart may miss a beat now and then; my lungs may begin to fight shy of wintry blasts; my eyes may fail me; my figure that is now in its slim gracefulness may swathe itself in layers of flesh, or worse, it may wither and decay and stoop at the shoulders; my red blood may flow sluggishly; but if I still have teeth left to eat with, why need I lament, while I still have my steak - and my onions?

I am obscure; I am morbid; I am unhappy; my life is made up of Nothingness; I want everything and have nothing; I have been made to feel the "lure of green things growing," and I have been made to feel also that something of them is withheld from me; I have felt the deadly tiredness that is among the birthrights of a human being; but with it all the Devil has given me a philosophy of my own - the Devil has enabled me to count, if need be, the world well lost for a fine rare porterhouse steak - and some green young onions.

For which I thank thee, Devil, profoundly.

Who says the Devil is not your friend? Who says that the Devil does not believe in the all-merciful Law of Compensation?

And so it is, do you see, that all things look different after a satisfying dinner, that the color of the world changes, that life in fact resolves itself into two things: a fine rare-broiled porterhouse steak from Omaha, and some fresh green young onions from California.

January 24

I am charmingly original. I am delightfully refreshing. I am startlingly Bohemian. I am quaintly interesting - the while in my sleeve I may be smiling and smiling - and a villain. I can talk to a roomful of dull people and compel their interest, admiration, and astonishment. I do this sometimes for my own amusement. As I have said, I am a rather plain-featured, insignificant-looking genius, but I have a graceful personality. I have a pretty figure. I am well set up. And when I choose to talk in my charmingly original fashion, embellishing my conversation with many quaint lies, I have a certain very noticeable way with me, an "air."

- It is well, if one has nothing, to acquire an air. -

And an air taken in conjunction with my charming originality, my delightfully refreshing candor, is something powerful and striking in its way.

I do not, however, exert myself often in this way; partly because I can sometimes foresee, from the character of the assembled company, that my performance will not have the desired effect - for I am a genius, and genius at close range at times carries itself unconsciously to the point where it becomes so interesting that it is atrocious, and can not be carried farther without having somewhat mildly disastrous results; and then again, the facial antics of some ten or a dozen persons possessed more or less of the qualities of the genus fool - even they become tiresome after a while.

Always I talk about myself on an occasion of this kind. Indeed, my conversation is on all occasions devoted directly or indirectly to myself.

When I talk on the subject of ethics, I talk of it as it is related to Mary MacLane.

When I give out broad-minded opinions about Ninon de l'Enclos, I demonstrate her relative position to Mary MacLane!

When I discourse liberally on the subject of the married relation, I talk of it only as it will affect Mary MacLane.

An interesting creature, Mary MacLane.

- As a matter of fact, it is so with every one, only every one is far from realizing and acknowledging it. -

And I have not lacked listeners, though these people do not appreciate me. They do not realize that I am a genius.

I am of womankind and of nineteen years. I am able to stand off and gaze critically and dispassionately at myself and my relation to my environment, to the world, to everything the world contains. I am able to judge whether I am good and whether I am bad. I am able indeed to tell what I am and where I stand. I can see far, far inward. I am a genius.

Charlotte Brontë did this in some degree, and she was a genius; and also Marie Bashkirtseff, and Olive Schreiner, and George Eliot. They are all geniuses.

And so then I am a genius - a genius in my own right.

I am fundamentally, organically egotistic. My vanity and self-conceit have attained truly remarkable development as I've walked and walked in the loneliness of the sand and barrenness.

Not the least remarkable part of it is that I know my egotism and vanity thoroughly - thoroughly, and plume myself thereon.

These are the ear-marks of a genius - and of a fool. There is a finely drawn line between a genius and a fool. Often this line is overstepped and your fool becomes a genius, or your genius becomes a fool.

It is but a tiny step.

There's but a tiny step between the great and the little, the tender and the contemptuous, the sublime and the ridiculous, the aggressive and the humble, the Paradise and the perdition.

And so it is between the genius and the fool.

I am a genius.

- I am not prepared to say how many times I may overstep the finely drawn line, or how many times I have already overstepped it. 'Tis a matter of small moment. -

I have entered into certain things marvelously deep. I know things, I know that I know them, and I know that I know that I know them. Which is a fine psychological point.

It is magnificent of me to have gotten so far, at the age of nineteen, with no training other than that of the sand and barrenness. Magnificent - do you hear?

Very often I take this fact in my hand and squeeze it hard like an orange, to get the sweet, sweet juice from it. I squeeze a great deal of juice from it every day, and every day the juice is renewed, like the vitals of Prometheus. And so I squeeze and squeeze, and drink the juice, and try to be satisfied.

Yes, you may gaze long and curiously at the portrait in the front of this book. It is of one who is a genius of egotism and analysis, a genius who is awaiting the Devil's coming, - a genius, with a wondrous liver within.

I shall tell you more about this liver, I think, before I have done.

January 25

I can remember a time long, oh, very long ago. That is the time when I was a child. It is ten or a dozen years ago.

Or is it a thousand years ago?

It is when you have but just parted from your friend that he seems farthest from you. When I have lived several more years the time when I was a child will not seem so far behind me.

Just now it is frightfully far away. It is so far away that I can see it plainly outlined on the horizon.

It is there always for me to look at. And when I look I can feel the tears deep within me - a salt ocean of tears that roll and surge and swell bitterly in a dull, mad anguish, and never come to the surface.

I do not know which is the more weirdly and damnably pathetic: I when I was a child, or I when I am grown to a woman, young and all alone. I weigh the question coldly and logically, but my logic trembles with rage and grief and unhappiness.

When I was a child I lived in Canada and in Minnesota. I was a little wild savage. In Minnesota there were swamps where I used to wet my feet in the spring, and there were fields of tall grass where I would lie flat on my stomach in company with lizards and little garter snakes. And there were poplar-leaves that turned their pale green backs upward on a hot afternoon, and soon there would be terrific thunder and lightning and rain. And there were robins that sang at dawn. - These things stay with one always. - And there were children with whom I used to play and fight.

I was tanned and sunburned and I had an unkempt appearance. My face was very dirty. The original pattern of my frock was invariably lost in layers and vistas of the native soil. My hair was braided or else it flew about, a tangled maze, according as I could be caught by some one and rubbed and straightened before I ran away for the day. My hands were little and strong and brown, and wrought much mischief. I came and went at my own pleasure. I ate what I pleased; I went to bed all in my own good time; I tramped wherever my stubborn little feet chose. I was impudent; I was contrary; I had an extremely bad temper; I was hard-hearted; I was full of infantile malice.

Truly I was a vicious little beast.

I was a little piece of untrained Nature.

And I am unable to judge which is the more savagely forlorn: the starved-hearted child, or the woman, young and all alone.

The little wild stubborn child felt things and wanted things. She did not know that she felt things and wanted things.

Now I feel and I want things and I know it with burning vividness.

The little vicious Mary MacLane suffered, but she did not know that she suffered. Yet that did not make the suffering less.

And she reached out with a little sunburned hand to touch and take something.

But the sunburned little hand remained empty. There was nothing for it. No one had anything to put into it.

The little wild creature wanted to be loved; she wanted something to put in her hungry little heart.

But no one had anything to put into a hungry little heart.

No one said "dear."

The little vicious child was the only MacLane, and she felt somewhat alone. But there, after all, were the lizards and the little garter snakes.

The wretched, hardened little piece of untrained Nature has grown and developed into a woman, young and alone. For the child there was a Nothingness, and for the woman there is a great Nothingness.

Perhaps the Devil will bring me something in my lonely womanhood to put in my wooden heart.

But the time when I was a child will never come again. It is gone - gone. I may live through some long, long years, but nothing like it will ever come. For there is nothing like it.

It is a life by itself. It has naught to do with philosophy, or with genius, or with heights and depths, or with the red sunset sky, or with the Devil.

These come later.

The time of the child is a thing apart. It is the Planting and Seed-time. It is the Beginning of things. It decides whether there shall be brightness or bitterness in the long after-years.

I have left that time far enough behind me. It will never come back. And it had a Nothingness - do you hear, a *Nothingness*! Oh, the pity of it! The pity of it -

Do you know why it is that I look back to the horizon at the figure of an unkempt, rough child, and why I feel a surging torrent of tears and anguish and despair?

I feel more than that indeed, but I have no words to tell it.

I shall have to miss forever some beautiful, wonderful things because of that wretched lonely childhood.

There will always be a lacking, a wanting - some dead branches that never grew leaves.

It is not deaths and murders and plots and wars that make life tragedy.

It is Nothing that makes life tragedy.

It is day after day, and year after year, and Nothing.

It is a sunburned little hand reached out and Nothing put into it.

January 26

I sit at my window and look out upon the housetops and chimneys of Butte. As I look I have a weary, disgusted feeling.

People are abominable creatures.

Under each of the roofs live a man and woman joined together by that very slender thread - the marriage ceremony, - and their children, the result of the marriage ceremony.

How many of them love each other? Not two in a hundred, I warrant. The marriage ceremony is their one miserable petty paltry excuse for living together.

This marriage rite, it appears, is often used as a cloak to cover a world of rather shameful things.

How virtuous these people are, to be sure, under their different roof-trees. So virtuous are they indeed that they are able to draw themselves up in the pride of their own purity, when they happen upon some corner where the marriage ceremony is lacking. So virtuous are they that the men can afford to find amusement and diversion in the woes of the corner that is without the marriage rite; and the women may draw away their skirts in shocked horror and wonder that such things can be, in view of their own spotless virtue.

And so they live on under the roofs, and they eat and work and sleep and die; and the children grow up and seek other roofs, and call upon the marriage ceremony even as their parents before them - and then they likewise eat and work and sleep and die; and so on world without end.

This also is life - the life of the good, virtuous Christians.

I think, therefore, that I should prefer some life that is not virtuous.

I shall never make use of the marriage ceremony. - I hereby register a vow, Devil, to that effect. -

When a man and a woman love one another that is enough. That is marriage. A religious rite is superfluous. And if the man and woman live together without the love, no ceremony in the world can make it marriage. The woman who does this need not feel the tiniest bit better than her lowest sister in the streets. Is she not indeed a step lower since she pretends to be what she is not - plays the virtuous woman? While the other unfortunate pretends nothing. She wears her name on her sleeve.

If I were obliged to be one of these I would rather be she who wears her name on her sleeve. I certainly would. The lesser of two evils, always.

I can think of nothing in the world like the utter littleness, the paltriness, the contemptibleness, the degradation, of the woman who is tied down under a roof with a man who is really nothing to her; who wears the man's name, who bears the man's children - who plays the virtuous woman. There are too many such in the world now.

May I never, I say, become that abnormal merciless animal, that deformed monstrosity - a virtuous woman.

Anything, Devil, but that.

And so, as I look over the roofs and chimneys I have a weary, disgusted feeling.

January 27

This is not a diary. It is a Portrayal. It is my inner life shown in its nakedness. I am trying my utmost to show everything - to reveal every petty vanity and weakness, every phase of feeling, every desire. It is a remarkably hard thing to do, I find, to probe my soul to its depths, to expose its shades and half-lights.

Not that I am troubled with modesty or shame. Why should one be ashamed of anything?

But there are elements in one's mental equipment so vague, so opaque, so undefined - how is one to grasp them? I have analyzed and analyzed, and I have gotten down to some extremely fine points - yet still there are things upon my own horizon that go beyond me.

There are feelings that rise and rush over me overwhelmingly. I am helpless, crushed and defeated, before them. It is as if they were written on the walls of my soul-chamber in an unknown language.

My soul goes blindly seeking, seeking, asking. Nothing answers. I cry out after some unknown Thing with all the strength of my being; every nerve and fiber in my young woman's-body and my young woman's-soul reaches and strains in anguished unrest. At times as I hurry over my sand and barrenness all my life's manifold passions culminate in utter rage and woe. Waves of intense, hopeless longing rush over me and envelop me round and round. My heart, my soul, my mind go wandering - wandering; ploughing their way through darkness with never a ray of light; groping with helpless hands; asking, longing, wanting things: pursued by a Demon of Unrest.

I shall go mad - I shall go mad, I say over and over to myself.

But no. No one goes mad. The Devil does not propose to release any one from a so beautifully wrought, artistic damnation. He looks to it that one's senses are kept fully intact, and he fastens to them with steel chains the demon of Unrest.

It hurts, - oh, it tortures me in the days and days! But when the Devil brings my Happiness I will forgive him all this.

When my Happiness is given me, the Unrest will still be with me, I doubt not, but the Happiness will change the tenor of it, will make it an instrument of joy, will clasp hands with it and mingle itself with it, - the while I, with my wooden heart, my woman's-body, my mind, my soul, shall be in transports. I shall be filled with pleasure so deep and pain so intense that my being's minutest nerve will reel and stagger in intoxication, will go drunk with the fullness of Life.

When my Happiness is given me I shall live centuries in the hours. And we shall all grow old rapidly, - I and my wooden heart, and my woman's-body, and my mind, and my soul. Sorrow may age one in some degree. But Happiness - the real Happiness - rolls countless years off from one's finger-tips in a single moment, and each year leaves its impress.

It is true that life is a tragedy to those who feel. When my Happiness is given me life will be an ineffable, a nameless thing.

It will seethe and roar; it will plunge and whirl; it will leap and shriek in convulsion; it will quiver in delicate fantasy; it will writhe and twist; it will glitter and flash and shine; it will sing gently; it will shout in exquisite excitement; it will vibrate to the roots like a great oak in a storm; it will dance; it will glide; it will gallop; it will rush; it will swell and surge; it will fly; it will soar high - high; it will go down into depths unexplored; it will rage and rave; it will yell in utter joy; it will melt; it will blaze; it will ride triumphant; it will grovel in the dust of entire pleasure; it will sound out like a terrific blare of trumpets; it will chime faintly, faintly like the remote tinkling notes of a harp; it will sob and grieve and weep; it will revel and carouse; it will shrink; it will go in pride; it will lie prone like the dead; it will float buoyantly on air; it will moan, shiver, burst, - oh, it will reek of Love and Light!

The words of the English language are futile. There are no words in it, or in any other, to express an idea of that thing which would be my life in its Happiness.

The words I have written describe it, it is true - but confusedly and inadequately.

But words are for every-day use.

When it comes my turn to meet face to face the unspeakable vision of the Happy Life I shall be rendered dumb.

But the rains of my feeling will come in torrents!

January 28

I am an artist of the most artistic, the highest type. I have uncovered for myself the art that lies in obscure shadows. I have discovered the art of the day of small things.

And that surely is Art with a capital A.

I have acquired the art of Good Eating. Usually it is in the gray and elderly forties and fifties that people cultivate this art - if they ever do; it is indeed a rare art.

But I know it in all its rare exquisiteness at the young slim age of nineteen. Which is one more mark of my genius, do you see?

The art of Good Eating has two essential points: one must eat only when one is hungry, and one must take small bites.

There are persons who eat for the sake of eating. They are gourmands and partake of the natures of the pig and the buzzard. There are persons who take bites that are not small. These also are gourmands and partake of the natures of the pig and the buzzard. There are persons who can enjoy nothing in the way of eating except a luxurious, well-appointed meal. These, it is safe to say, have not acquired the art of anything.

But I - I have acquired the art of eating an olive.

Now listen and I will tell you the art of eating an olive.

I take the olive in my fingers, and I contemplate its green oval richness.

It makes me think at once of the land where the green citron grows - where the cypress and myrtle are emblems; of the land of the Sun where human beings are delightfully, enchantingly wicked, - where the men are eager and passionate, and the women gracefully developed in mind and in body - and their two breasts show round and full and delicately veined beneath fine drapery.

The mere sight of the olive conjures up this charming picture in my mind.

I set my teeth and my tongue upon the olive, and bite it. It is bitter, salt, delicious. The saliva rushes to meet it, and my tongue is a happy tongue. As the morsel of olive rests in my mouth and is crunched and squeezed lusciously among my teeth, a quick temporary change takes place in my character. I think of some adorable lines of the Persian poet:

> *Give thyself up to Joy, for thy Grief will be infinite.*
> *The stars shall again meet together*
> *At the same point in the firmament,*
> *But of thy body shall bricks be made*
> *For a palace wall.*

"Oh, dear, sweet, bitter olive," I say to myself.

The bit of olive slips down my red gullet, and so into my Stomach. There it meets with a joyous welcome. Gastric juices leap out from the walls and swathe it in loving embrace. My Stomach is fond of something bitter and salt. It lavishes flattery and endearment galore upon the olive. It laughs in silent delight. It feels that the day it has long waited for has come. The philosophy of my Stomach is wholly Epicurean. Let it receive but a tiny bit of olive and it will reck not of the morrow, nor of the past. It lives, voluptuously, in the present. It is content. It is in Paradise.

I bite the olive again. Again the bitter salt crisp ravishes my tongue. "If this be vanity, - vanity let it be." The golden moments flit by and I heed them not. For am I not comfortably seated and eating an olive? - Go hang yourself, you who have never been comfortably seated and eating an olive! - My character evolves farther in its change. I am now bent on reckless sensuality, let happen what will. The fair earth seems to resolve itself into a thing oval and crisp and good and green and deliciously salt. I experience a feeling of fervent gladness that I am a female thing living, and that I have a tongue and some teeth, and salivary glands.

Also this bit slips down my red gullet, and again the festive Stomach lifts up a silent voice in psalms and rejoicing. It is now an absolute monarchy with the green olive at its head. The kisses of the gastric juice become hot and sensual and convulsive and ecstatic. "Avaunt, pale shadowy ghosts of dyspepsia!" says my Stomach. "I know you not. I am of a brilliant shining world. I dwell in Elysian fields."

Once more I bite the olive. Once more is my tongue electrified. And the third stage in my temporary transformation takes place. I am now a gross but supremely contented sensualist. An exquisite symphony of sensualism and pleasure seems to play somewhere within me. My heart purrs. My brain folds its arms and lounges. - I put my feet up on the seat of another chair. - The entire world is now surely one delicious green olive. My mind is capable of conceiving but one idea: that of a green olive. Therefore the green olive is a perfect thing - absolutely a perfect thing.

Disgust and disapproval are excited only by imperfections. When a thing is perfect, no matter how hard one may look at it, one can only see itself - itself, and nothing beyond.

And so I have made my olive and my art perfect.

Well then, this third bit of olive slides down the willing gullet into my Stomach. "And then my heart with pleasure fills." The play of the gastric secretions is now marvelous. It is the meeting of the waters! It were well, ah, how well if the hearts of the world could mingle in peace, as the gastric juices mingle at the coming of a green olive into my Stomach! "Paradise, Paradise!" says my Stomach.

Every drop of blood in my passionate veins is resting. Through my Stomach - my *Stomach*, do you hear - my soul seems to feel the infinite. The minutes are flying. Shortly it will be over. But just now I am safe. I am entirely satisfied. I want nothing, nothing.

My inner quiet is infinite. I am conscious that it is but momentary, and it matters not. On the contrary the knowledge of this fact renders the present quiet - the repose more limitless, more intense.

Where now, Devil, is your damnation? If this be damnation, damnation let it be! If this be the human fall, then how good it is to be fallen! At this moment I would fain my fall were like yours, Lucifer, "never to hope again."

And so, bite by bite, the olive enters into my body and soul. Each bite brings with it a recurring wave of sensation and charm.

No. We will not dispute with the brilliant mind that declared life a tragedy to those who feel. We will let that stand. However there are parts of the tragedy that are not tragic. There are parts that admit of a turning aside.

As the years pass, one after another, I shall continue to eat. And as I eat I shall have my quiet, my brief period of aberration.

This is the art of Eating.

I have acquired it by means of self-examination, analyzing - analyzing - analyzing. Truly my genius is analytical. And it enables me to endure - if also to feel bitterly - the heavy, heavy weight of life.

What a worm of misery I should be were it not for these bursts of philosophy, these turnings aside!

If it please the Devil, one day I may have Happiness. That will be all-sufficient. I shall then analyze no more. I shall be a different being.

But meanwhile I shall eat.

When the last of the olive vanishes into the Stomach, when it is there reduced to animated chyme, when I play with the olive-seed in my fingers, when I lean back in my chair and straighten out my spinal column, - oh, then do you not envy me, you fine, brave world, who are not a philosopher, who have not discovered the art of the small things, who have not conscious chyme in your stomach, who have not acquired the art of Good Eating!

January 29

As I read over now and then what I have written of my Portrayal I have alternate periods of hope and despair. At times I think I am succeeding admirably, - and again, what I have written compared to what I have felt seems vapid and tame. Who has not felt the futility of words when one would express feelings?

I take this hope and despair as another mark of genius. Genius, apart from natural sensitiveness, is prone equally to unreasoning joy and to bitterest morbidness.

I am more than fond of writing, though I have hours when I can not write any more than I could paint a picture, or play Wagner as it should be played.

I think my style of writing has a wonderful intensity in it, and it is admirably suited to the creature it portrays. What sort of Portrayal of myself would I produce if I wrote with the long elaborate periods of Henry James, or with the pleasant ladylike phrasing of Howells? It would be rather like a little tin phonograph trolling out flowery poetry at breakneck speed, or like a deep-toned church organ pouring forth "Goo-Goo Eyes" with ponderous feeling.

When I read a book I study it carefully to find whether the author *knows things*, and whether I could, with the same subject, write a better one myself.

The latter question I usually decide in the affirmative.

A writer who charms me is Maria Louise Pool with her novels of New England. She is fascinating and she knows things. If she had written seventy years ago she would doubtless now be standard literature. One thing I have noticed about her books is that as I read them I find myself thinking not particularly of the characters therein, but of the author who somehow appears between the lines. And I find this very interesting. I have spent a great many half-hours thinking and conjecturing about Maria Louise Pool. Always

I wonder what she likes to eat, and what she does on a pleasant Saturday afternoon when she has nothing else to do, and what kind of clothes she wears, and if she can possibly be as uninteresting at that stout, gray-haired age as most women are. I hope I may see her some day.

The highest thing one can do in literature is to succeed in saying that thing which one meant to say. There is nothing better than that - to make the world see your thoughts as you see them. Eugene Field and Edgar Allan Poe and R. Louis Stevenson and Charles Dickens, among others, have succeeded in doing this. They impress the world with a sense of their courage and realness.

There are people who have written books which did not impress the world in this way, but which nevertheless came out of the feeling and fullness of zealous hearts. Always I think of that pathetic, artless little old-fashioned thing *Jane Eyre* as a picture shown to a world seeing with distorted vision. Charlotte Brontë meant one thing when she wrote the book and the world after a time suddenly understood a quite different thing, and heaped praise and applause upon her therefor. When I read the book I was not quite able to see just what the message was that the Brontë intended to send out. But I saw that there was a message - of bravery, perhaps, or of that good which may come out of Nazareth. But the world that praised and applauded and gave her money seems totally to have missed it.

It takes centuries of tears and piety and mourning to move this world a tiny bit.

But still, it will give you praise and applause and money if you will prostitute your sensibilities and emotions for the gratification of it.

I have no message to hide in a book and send out. I am writing a Portrayal.

But a Portrayal is also a thing that may be misunderstood.

January 30

An idle brain is the Devil's workshop, they say. It is an absurdly incongruous statement. If the Devil is at work in a brain it certainly is not idle. And when one considers how brilliant a personage the Devil is, and what very fine work he turns out, it becomes an open question whether he would have the slightest use for most of the idle brains that cumber the earth. But, after all, the Devil is so clever that he could produce unexcelled workmanship with even the poorest tools.

My brain is one kind of Devil's-workshop, and it is as incessantly hard-worked and always-busy a one as you could imagine.

It is a Devil's workshop, indeed, only I do the work myself. But there is a mental telegraphy between the Devil and me, which accounts for the fact that many of my ideas are so wonderfully groomed and perfumed and colored. I take no credit to myself for this, though, as I say, I do the work myself.

I try always to give the Devil his due - and particularly in this Portrayal. There are very few who give the Devil his due in this world of hypocrites.

I never think of the Devil as that atrocious creature in red tights, with cloven hoofs and a tail and a two-tined fork. I think of him rather as an extremely fascinating, strong, steel-willed person in conventional clothes - a man with whom to fall completely, madly in love. I rather think, I believe, that he is incarnate at times. Why not?

Periodically I fall completely, madly in love with the Devil. He is so fascinating, so strong - so strong, exactly the sort of man whom my wooden heart awaits. I would like to throw myself at his head. I would make him a dear little wife. He would love me - he would love me. I would be in raptures. And I would love him, oh, madly, madly!

"What would you have me do, little MacLane?" the Devil would say.

"I would have you conquer me, crush me, know me," I would answer.

"What shall I say to you?" the Devil would ask.

"Say to me, 'I love you, I love you, I love you,' in your strong, steel, fascinating voice. Say it to me often, always - a million times."

"What would you have me do, little MacLane?" he would say again.

I would answer: "Hurt me, burn me, consume me with hot love, shake me violently, embrace me hard, *hard* in your strong steel arms, kiss me with wonderful burning kisses - press your lips to mine with passion, and your soul and mine would meet then in an anguish of joy for me!"

"How shall I treat you, little MacLane?"

"Treat me cruelly, brutally."

"How long shall I stay with you?"

"Through the life everlasting - it will be as one day; or for one day - it will be as the life everlasting."

"And what kind of children will you bear me, little MacLane?" he would say.

"I will bear wonderful, beautiful children - with great pain."

"But you hate pain," the Devil will say, "and when you are in your pain you will hate me."

"But no," I will answer. "Pain that comes of you will be ineffable exaltation."

"And how will you treat me, little MacLane?"

"I will cast myself at your feet; or I will minister to you with divine tenderness; or I will charm you with fantastic deviltry; when you weep, I will melt into tears; when you rejoice, I will go wild with delight; when you go deaf I will stop my ears; when you go blind I will put out my eyes; when you go lame I will cut off my legs. Oh, I will be divinely dear, unutterably sweet!"

"Indeed you are rarely sweet," the Devil will say. And I will be in transports.
Oh, Devil, Devil, Devil!

Oh, misery, *misery* of Nothingness!

The days are long - long and very weary as I await the Devil's coming.

To-day as I walked out I was impressed deeply with the wonderful beautiful-
ness of Nature even in her barrenness. The far-distant mountains had that
high pure transparent look, and the nearer ones were transformed completely
with a wistful beseeching attitude that reminded me of my life. It was late
in the afternoon. As the sun lowered, the pure lavender of the far-away hills
was tinted with faint-rose, and the gray of the nearer ones with sun-color.
And the sand - my sand and barrenness - almost flushed consciously in its
wide, mysterious magnitude. In the sky there was a white cloud. The sky was
blue - blue almost as when I was a child. The air was very gentle. The earth
seemed softened. There was an indefinite caressing something over all that
went into my soul and stirred it, and hurt it. There was that in the air which
is there when something is going to happen. - Only nothing ever happens. - It
is rare, I thought, that my sand and barrenness looks like this. I crouched on
the ground, and the wondrous calm and beauty of the natural things awed
and moved me with strange, still emotions.

I felt, and gazed about me, and felt again. And everything was very still.
Presently my eyes filled quietly with tears.

I bent my head into the breast of a great gray rock. Oh, my soul, my
soul, I said over and over, not with passion. It is so divine - the earth is so
beautiful, so untainted - and I, what am I? It was so beautiful that now as
I write, and it comes over me again, I can not restrain the tears.

Tears are not common.

I felt my wooden heart, my soul, quivering and sobbing with their unknown wanting. This is my soul's awakening. Ah, the pain of my soul's
awakening! Is there nothing, *nothing* to help this pain? I am so lonely, so
lonely - Fannie Corbin, my one friend, my dearly-loved anemone lady, I
want you so much - why aren't you here! I want to feel your hand with mine
as I felt it sometimes before you went away. You are the only one among a
worldful of people to care a little - and I love you with all the strength and
worship I can give to the things that are beautiful and true. You are the
only one, the only one - and my soul is full of pain, and I am sitting alone
on the ground, and my head lies on a rock's breast. -

Strange, sweet passions stirred and waked somewhere deep within me as

HUMAN DAYS - 48

I sat shivering on the ground. And I felt them singing far away, as if their faint voices came out of that limitless deep, deep blue above me; and it was like a choir of spirit-voices, and they sang of love and of light and of dear tender dreams, and of my soul's awakening. Why is this - and what is it that is hurting so? Is it because I am young, or is it because I am alone, or because I am a woman?

Oh, it is a hard and bitter thing to be a woman! And why - why? Is woman so foul a creature that she must needs be purged by this infinite pain?

The choir of faint, sweet voices comes to me incessantly out of the blue. My wooden heart and my soul are listening to them intently. The voices are trying hard to tell me, to help me, but I can not understand. I know only that it is about pure, exalted things, and about the all-abiding love that is somewhere; and it is about the earth-love, and about Truth, - but I can not understand. And the voices sing of me the child - a song of the unloved, starved little being; and a song of the unloved, half-grown creature; and a song of me, a woman and all alone - awaiting the Devil's coming.

Oh, my soul - my soul!

A female snake is born out of its mother's white egg, and lives a while in contentment among weeds and grass, and dies.

A female dog lives some years, and has bones thrown at her, and sometimes she receives a kick or a blow, and a dog-house to sleep in, and dies.

A female bird has a nest, and worms to eat, and goes south in the winter, and presently she dies.

A female toad has a swamp or a garden, some bugs and flies, contentment - and then she dies.

And each of these has a male thing with her for a time, and shortly there are little snakes or little dogs for her to love as much as it is given her to love - she can do no more.

And they are fortunate with their little snakes and little dogs.

A female human being is born out of her mother's fair body, branded with a strange, plague-tainted name, and let go; and lives awhile, and dies. But before she dies she awakes. There is a pain that goes with it.

And the male thing that is with her for a time is unlike a snake or a dog. It is more like a man, and there is another pain for this.

And when a little human being comes with a soul of its own there must be another awakening, for she has then reached the best and highest state that any human being can reach, though she is a female human being, and plague-tainted. And here also there is heavy soul-pain.

The name - the plague-tainted name branded upon her - means woman.

I lifted my head from the breast of the gray rock. The tears had been falling, falling. Tears are so strange! Tears from the dried-up fountain of nineteen years are like drops of water wrung out of stone. Suddenly I got up from the ground and ran quickly over the sand for several minutes. I did not dare look again at the hilltops and the deep blue, nor listen again to the voices.

Oh, with it all, I am a coward! I shrink and cringe before the pain of the dazzling lights. Yet I am waiting - longing for the most dazzling light of all: the coming of the Devil.

February 1

Oh, the wretched bitter loneliness of me!

In all the deep darkness, and the silence, there is never a faint human light, never a voice!

How can I bear it - how can I bear it!

February 2

I have been looking over the confessions of the Bashkirtseff. They are indeed rather like my Portrayal, but they are not so interesting, nor so intense. I have a stronger individuality than Marie Bashkirtseff, though her mind was probably in a higher state of development than mine, even when she was younger than I.

Most of her emotions are vacillating and inconsistent. She worships a God one day and blasphemes him the next. She never loves her God. And why, then, does she have a God? Why does she not abandon him altogether? He seems to be of no use to her - except as a convenient thing on which to fasten the blame for her misfortunes. - And, after all, that is something very useful indeed. - And she loves the people about her one day, and the next day she hates them.

But in her great passion - her ambition - Marie Bashkirtseff was beautifully consistent. And what terrific storms of woe and despair must have enveloped her when she knew that within a certain period she would be dead - removed from the world, and her work left undone! The time kept creeping nearer - she must have tasted the bitterness of death indeed. She was sure of success, sure that her high-strained ambition would be gratified to its last vestige - and then, to die! It was certainly hard lines for the little Bashkirtseff.

My own despair is of an opposite nature.

There is one thing in the world that is more bitter than death - and that is life.

Suppose that I learned I was to die on the twenty-seventh of June, 1903, for instance. It would give me a soft warm wave of pleasure, I think. I might be in the depths of woe at the time; my despair might be the despair of despair; my misery utterly unceasing, - and I could say, "Never mind, on the twenty-seventh of June, 1903, all will be over - dull misery, rage, Nothingness, obscurity, the unknown longing, every desire of my soul, all the pain - ended inevitably, completely on the twenty-seventh of June, 1903." I might come upon a new pain, but this, my long old torture, would cease.

You may say that I might end my life on that day, that I might do so now. I certainly shall if the pain becomes greater than I can bear - for what else is there to do? But I shall be far from satisfied in doing so. What if I were to end everything now - when perhaps the Devil may be coming to me in two years' time with Happiness?

Upon dying it might be that I should go to some wondrous fair country where there would be trees and running water, and a resting-place. Well - oh, well! But I want the earthly Happiness. I am not high-minded and spiritual. I am earthly, human - sensitive, sensuous, sensual, and, ah, dear, my soul wants its earthly Happiness!

I can not bring myself to the point of suicide while there is a possibility of Happiness remaining. But if I knew that irrevocable, inevitable death awaited me on June twenty-seventh, 1903, I should be satisfied. My Happiness might come before that time, or it might not. I should be satisfied. I should know that my life was out of my hands. I should know, above all, that my long, long, old, old pain of loneliness would stop, June twenty-seventh, 1903.

I shall die naturally some day - probably after I have grown old and sour. If I have had my Happiness for a year or a day, well and good. I shall be content to grow as old and as sour as the Devil wills. But having had no Happiness - if I find myself growing old and still no Happiness - oh, then I vow I will not live another hour, even if dying were rushing headlong to damnation!

I am, do you see, a philosopher and a coward - with the philosophy of cowardice. I squeeze juice also from this fact sometimes - but the juice is not sweet juice.

The Devil - the fascinating man-Devil - it may be, is coming, coming, coming.

And meanwhile I go on and on, in the midst of sand and barrenness.

February 3

The town of Butte presents a wonderful field to a student of humanity and human nature. There are not a great many people - seventy thousand perhaps - but those seventy thousand are in their way unparalleled. For mixture, for miscellany - variedness, Bohemianism - where is Butte's rival?

The population is not only of all nationalities and stations, but the nationalities and stations mix and mingle promiscuously with each other, and are partly concealed and partly revealed in the mazes of a veneer that belongs neither to nation nor to station, but to Butte.

The nationalities are many, it is true, but Irish and Cornish predominate. My acquaintance extends widely among the inhabitants of Butte. Sometimes when I feel in the mood for it I spend an afternoon in visiting about among divers curious people.

At some Fourth of July demonstration, or on a Miners' Union day, the heterogeneous herd turns out - and I turn out, with the herd and of it, and meditate and look on. There are Irishmen - Kelleys, Caseys, Calahans, staggering under the weight of much whiskey, shouting out their green-isle maxims; there is the festive Cornishman, ogling and leering, greeting his fellow-countrymen with alcoholic heartiness, and gazing after every feminine creature with lustful eyes; there are Irish women swearing genially at each other in shrill pleasantry, and five or six loudly-vociferous children for each; there are round-faced Cornish women likewise, each with her train of children; there are suave sleek sporting men just out of the bath-tub; insignificant lawyers, dentists, messenger-boys; "plungers" without number; greasy Italians from Meaderville; greasier French people from the Boulevarde Addition; ancient miners - each of whom was the first to stake a claim in Butte; starved-looking Chinamen here and there; a contingent of Finns and Swedes and Germans; musty, stuffy old Jewish pawn-brokers who have crawled out of their holes for a brief recreation; dirt-encrusted Indians and squaws in dirty-gay blankets, from their flea-haunted camp below the town; "box rustlers" - who are as common in Butte as bar-maids in Ireland; swell, flashy-looking Africans; respectable women with white aprons tied around their waists and sailor-hats on their heads, who have left the children at home and stepped out to see what was going on; innumerable stray youngsters from the dark haunts of Dublin Gulch; heavy restaurant-keepers with tooth-picks in their mouths; a vast army of dry-goods clerks - the "paper-collared" gentry; miners of every description; representatives from Dog Town, Chicken Flats, Busterville, Butchertown, and Seldom Seen - suburbs of Butte; pale thin individuals who sing and dance in beer-halls; smart society people in high traps and tally-hos; impossible women - so-called (though in Butte no one is more possible), in vast hats and extremely plaid stockings; persons who take things seriously and play the races for a living; "beer-jerkers"; "biscuit-shooters"; soft-voiced Mexicans and Arabians; - the dregs, the élite, the humbly respectable, the off-scouring - all thrown together, and shaken up, and mixed well.

One may notice many odd bits of irony as one walks among these. One may notice that the Irish men are singularly carefree and strong and comfortable - and so jolly! While the Irish women are frumpish and careworn and borne earthward with children. The Cornishman who has consumed the greatest amount of whiskey is the most agreeable, and less and less inclined to leer and ogle. The Cornish woman whose profanity is the shrillest and most genial and voluble, is she whose life seems the most weighted and downtrodden. The young women whose bodies are encased in the tightest and stiffest corsets are in the most wildly hilarious spirits of all. The filthy little Irish youngsters from Dublin Gulch are much brighter and more clever in every way than the ordinary American children who are less filthy. A delicate aroma of cocktails and whiskey-and-soda hangs over even the four-in-hands and automobiles of the upper crust. Gamblers, news-boys, and Chinamen are the most chivalrously courteous among them. And the modest-looking "plunger" who has drunk the greatest number of high-balls is the most gravely, quietly polite of all. The rolling, rollicking, musical profanity of the "ould sod" - Bantry Bay, Donegal, Tyrone, Tipperary - falls much less limpidly from the cigaretted lips of the ten-year-old lad than from those of his mother, who taught it to him. One may notice that the husband and wife who smile the sweetest at each other in the sight of the multitudes are they whose countenances bear various scars and scratches commemorating late evening orgies at home; that the peculiar solid, block-shaped appearance of some of the miners' wives is due quite as much to the quantity of beer they drink as to their annual maternity; that the one grand ruling passion of some men's lives is curiosity; - that the entire herd is warped, distorted, barren, having lived its life in smoke-cured Butte.

A single street in Butte contains people in nearly every walk of life - living side by side resignedly, if not in peace.

In a row of five or six houses there will be living miners and their families, the children of which prevent life from stagnating in the street while their mothers talk to each other - with the inevitable profanity - over the back-fences. On the corner above there will be a mysterious widow with one child, who has suddenly alighted upon the neighborhood, stealthily in the night, and is to be seen at rare intervals emerging from her door - the target for dozens of pairs of eager eyes and half as many eager tongues. And when the mysterious widow, with her one child, disappears some night as suddenly and as stealthily as she appeared, an outburst of highly-colored rumors is tossed with astonishing glibness over the various back-fences - all relating to the mysterious widow's shady antecedents and past history, to those of her child, and to the cause of her sudden departure, - no two of which rumors agree in any particular. Across on the opposite corner there will be a company of strange people who also descended suddenly, and upon whom the eyes of the entire block are turned with absorbing interest. They consist of half-a-dozen men and women seemingly bound together only by ties of conviviality. The house is kept closely-blinded and quiet all day, only to burst forth in a blaze of revel in the evening, which revel lasts all night. This goes on until some momentous night, at the request of certain proper ones, a police officer glides quietly into the midst of a scene of unusual gaiety - and the festive company melts quietly into oblivion, never to return. They also are then discussed with rapturous relish and in tones properly lowered, over the back-fences. Farther down the street there will live an interesting being of feminine persuasion who has had five divorces and is in the course of obtaining another. These divorces, the causes therefor, the justice thereof, and the future prospects of the multi-grass widow, are gone over, in all their bearings, by the indefatigable tongues. Every incident in the history of the street is put through a course of sprouts by these same tireless members. The Jewish family that lives in the poorest house in the neighborhood, and that is said to count its money by the hundred thousand; the aristocratic family with the Irish-point curtains in the windows - that lives on the county; the family whose husband and father gains for it a comfortable livelihood - forging checks; the miner's family whose wife and mother wastes its substance in diamonds and seal-skin coats and other riotous living; the family in extremely straitened circumstances into which new babies arrive in great and distressing numbers; the strange lady with an apoplectic complexion and a wonderfully foul and violent flow of invective - all are discussed over and over and over again. No one is omitted.

And so this is Butte, the promiscuous - the Bohemian. And all these are the Devil's playthings. They amuse him, doubtless.

Butte is a place of sand and barrenness.

The souls of these people are dumb.

February 4

Always I wonder, when I die will there be any one to remember me with love?

I know I am not lovable.

That I want it so much only makes me less lovable, it seems. But - who knows? - it may be there will be some one.

My anemone lady does not love me. How can she - since she does not understand me? But she allows me to love her - and that carries me a long way. There are many - oh, a great many - who will not allow you to love them if you would.

There is no one to love me now.

Always I wonder how it will be after some long years when I find myself about to die.

February 7

In this house where I drag out my accursed, devilishly weary existence, upstairs in the bath-room, on the little ledge at the top of the wainscoting, there are six tooth-brushes: an ordinary white bone-handled one that is my younger brother's; a white twisted-handled one that is my sister's; a flat-handled one that is my older brother's; a celluloid-handled one that is my stepfather's; a silver-handled one that is mine; and another ordinary one that is my mother's. The sight of these tooth-brushes day after day, week after week, and always, is one of the most crushingly maddening circumstances in my fool's life.

Every Friday I wash up the bath-room. Usually I like to do this. I like the feeling of the water squeezing through my fingers, and always it leaves my nails beautifully neat. But the obviousness of those six tooth-brushes signifying me and the five other members of this family and the aimless emptiness of my existence here - Friday after Friday - makes my soul weary and my heart sick.

Never does the pitiable barren contemptible damnable narrow Nothingness of my life in this house come upon me with a so intense force as when my eyes happen upon those six tooth-brushes.

Among the horrors of the Inquisition, a minute refinement of cruelty was reached when the victim's head was placed beneath a never-ceasing falling of water, drop by drop.

A convict sentenced to solitary confinement, spending his endless days staring at four blank walls, feels that had he committed every known crime he could not possibly deserve his punishment.

I am not undergoing an Inquisition, nor am I a convict in solitary confinement. But I live in a house with people who affect me mostly through their tooth-brushes - and those I should like, above all things, to gather up and pitch out the bath-room window - and oh, damn them, *damn* them!

You who read this, can you understand the depth of bitterness and hatred that is contained in this for me? Perhaps you can a little if you are a woman and have felt yourself alone.

When I look at the six tooth-brushes a fierce, lurid storm of rage and passion comes over me. Two heavy leaden hands lay hold of my life and press, press, press. They strike the sick, sick weariness to my inmost soul.

Oh, to leave this house and these people, and this intense Nothingness - oh, to pass out from them, forever! But where can I go, what can I do? I feel with mad fury that I am helpless. The grasp of the stepfather and the mother is contemptible and absurd - but with the persistence and tenacity of narrow minds. It is like the two heavy leaden hands. It is not seen - it is not tangible. It is felt.

Once I took away my own silver-handled tooth-brush from the bathroom ledge, and kept it in my bed-room for a day or two. I thought to lessen the effect of the six.

I put it back in the bath-room.

The absence of one accentuated the significant damnation of the others. There was something more forcibly maddening in the five than in the six tooth-brushes. The damnation was not worse, but it developed my feeling about them more vividly.

And so I put my tooth-brush back in the bath-room.

This house is comfortably furnished. My mother spends her life in the adornment of it. The small square rooms are distinctly pretty.

But when I look at them seeingly I think of the proverb about the dinner of stalled ox.

Yet there is no hatred here, except mine and my bitterness. I am the only one of them whose bitter spirit cries out against things.

But there is that which is subtler and strikes deeper. There is the lack of sympathy - the lack of everything that counts: there is the great deep Nothing.

How much better were there hatred here than Nothing!

I long hopelessly for will-power, resolution to take my life into my own hands, to walk away from this house some day and never return. I have nowhere to go - no money, and I know the world quite too well to put the slightest faith in its voluntary kindness of heart. But how much better and wider, less damned, less maddening, to go out into it and be beaten and cheated and fooled with, than *this*! - this thing that gathers itself easily into a circle made of six tooth-brushes with a sufficiency of surplus damnation.

I have read about a woman who went down from Jerusalem to Jericho and fell among thieves. Perhaps she had a house at Jerusalem with six tooth-brushes and Nothingness. In that case she might have rushed gladly into the arms of thieves.

I think of crimes that would strike horror and revulsion to my maid-senses. And I think of my Nothingness, and I ask myself were it not better to walk the earth an outcast, a solitary woman, and meet and face even these, than that each and every one of my woman-senses should wear slowly, painfully to shreds, and strain and break - in this unnameable Nothing?

Oh, the dreariness - the hopelessness of Nothing!

There are no words to tell it. And things are always hardest to bear when there are no words for them.

However great one's gift for language may be there is always something that one can not tell.

I am weary of self - always self. But it must be so.

My life is filled with *self.*

If my soul could awaken fully perhaps I might be lifted out of myself - surely I should be. But my soul is not awake. It is awakening, trying to open its eyes; and it is crying out blindly after something, but it can not *know*. I have a dreadful feeling that it will stay always like this.

Oh, I feel everything - everything! I feel what might be. And there is Nothing. There are six tooth-brushes.

Would I stop for a few fine distinctions, a theory, a natural law even, to escape from this into Happiness - or into something greatly less?

Misery - misery! If only I could feel it less!

Oh, the weariness, the weariness - as I await the Devil's coming.

February 8

Often I walk out to a place on the flat valley below the town, to flirt with Death. There is within me a latent spirit of coquetry, it appears.

Down on the flat there is a certain deep dark hole with several feet of water at the bottom.

This hole completely fascinates me. Sometimes when I start out to walk in a quite different direction, I feel impelled almost irresistibly to turn and go down on the flat in the direction of the fascinating, deep black hole.

And here I flirt with Death. The hole is so narrow - only about four feet across - and so dark, and so deep! I don't know whether it was intended to be a well, or whether it is an abandoned shaft of some miner. At any rate it is isolated and deserted, and it has a rare loving charm for me.

I go there sometimes in the early evening and kneel on the edge of it, and lean over the dark pit, with my hand grasping a wooden stake that is driven into the ground near by. And I drop little stones down and hear them splash hollowly, and it sounds a long way off.

There is something wonderfully soothing, wonderfully comforting to my unrestful, aching wooden heart in the dark mystery of this fascinating hole. Here is the End for me, if I want it - here is the Ceasing, when I want it. And I lean over and smile quietly.

"No flowers," I say to myself, "no weeping idiots, no senseless funeral, no oily undertaker fussing over my woman's-body, no useless Christian prayers. Nothing but this deep dark restful grave."

No one would ever find it. It is a mile and a half from any house.

The water - the dark still water at the bottom - would gurgle over me and make an end quickly. Or if I feared there was not enough water, I would bring with me a syringe and some morphine and inject an immense quantity into one white arm, and kneel over the tender darkness until my youth-weary, waiting-worn senses should be overcome, and my slim light body should fall. It would splash into the water at bottom - it would follow the little stones at last. And the black muddy water would soak in and begin the destroying of my body, and murky bubbles would rise so long as my lungs continued to breathe. Or perhaps my body would fall against the side of the hole, and the head would lie against it out of the water. Or perhaps only the face would be out of the water, turned upward to the light above - or turned half-down, and the hair would be darkly wet and heavy, and the face would be blue-white below it, and the eyes would sink inward.

"The End, the End -" I say softly and ecstatically. Yet I do not lean farther out. My hand does not loosen its tight grasp on the wooden stake. I am only flirting with Death now.

Death is fascinating - almost like the Devil. Death makes use of all his arts and wiles, powerful and alluring, and flirts with deadly temptation for me. And I make use of my arts and wiles - and tempt him.

Death would like dearly to have me, and I would like dearly to have him. It is a flirtation that has its source in mutual desire. We do not love each other, Death and I, - we are not friends. But we desire each other sensually, lustfully.

Sometime I suppose I shall yield to the desire. I merely play at it now - but in an unmistakable manner. Death knows it is only a question of time.

But first the Devil must come. First the Devil, then Death: a deep dark soothing grave - and the early evening, "and a little folding of the hands to sleep."

February 12

I am in no small degree, I find, a sham - a player to the gallery. Possibly this may be felt as you read these analyses.

While all of these emotions are written in the utmost seriousness and sincerity, and are exactly as I feel them, day after day - so far as I have the power to express what I feel - still I aim to convey through them all the idea that I am lacking in the grand element of Truth - that there is in the warp and woof of my life a thread that is false - false.

I don't know how to say this without the fear of being misunderstood. When I say I am in a way a sham, I have no reference to the truths as I have given them in this Portrayal, but to a very light and subtle thing that runs through them.

Oh, do not think for an instant that this analysis of my emotions is not perfectly sincere and real, and that I have not felt all of them more than I can put into words. They are my tears - my life-blood!

But in my life, in my personality, there is an essence of falseness and insincerity. A thin, fine vapor of fraud hangs always over me and dampens and injures some things in me that I value.

I have not succeeded thoroughly in analyzing this - it is so thin, so elusive, so faint - and yet not little. It is a natural thing enough viewed in the light of my other traits.

I have lived my nineteen years buried in an environment at utter variance with my natural instincts, where my inner life is never touched, and my sympathies very rarely, if ever, appealed to. I never disclose my real desires or the texture of my soul. - Never, that is to say, to any one except my one friend, the anemone lady. - And so every day of my life I am playing a part; I am keeping an immense bundle of things hidden under my cloak. When one has played a part - a false part - all one's life, for I was a sly, artful little liar even in the days of five and six, then one is marked. One may never rid oneself of the mantle of falseness, charlatanry - particularly if one is innately a liar.

A year ago when the friendship of my anemone lady was given me, and she would sometimes hear sympathetically some long-silent bit of pain, I felt a snapping of tense-drawn cords, a breaking away of flood-gates - and a strange new pain. I felt as if I must clasp her gentle hand tightly and give way to the pent-up surging tears of eighteen years. I had wanted this tender thing more than anything else all my life, and it was given me suddenly.

I felt a convulsion and a melting, within.

But I could not tell my one friend exactly what I felt. There was no doubt in my own mind as to my own perfect sincerity of feeling, but there was with it and around it this vapor of fraud, a spirit of falseness that rose and confronted me and said "hypocrite," "fool."

It may be that the spirit of falseness is itself a false thing - yet true or false, it is with me always. I have tried, in writing out my emotions, to convey an idea of this sham element while still telling everything faithfully true. Sometimes I think I have succeeded, and at other times I seem to have signally failed. This element of falseness is absolutely the very thinnest, the very finest, the rarest of all the things in my many-sided character.

It is not the most unimportant.

I have seen visions of myself walking in various pathways. I have seen myself trying one pathway and another. And always it is the same: I see before me in the path, darkening the way and filling me with dread and discouragement, a great black shadow - the shadow of my own element of falseness.

I can not rid myself of it.

I am an innate liar.

This is a hard thing to write about. Of all things it is the most liable to be misunderstood. You will probably misunderstand it, for I have not succeeded in giving the right idea of it. I aimed at it and missed it. It eluded me completely.

You must take the idea as I have just now presented it for what it may be worth. This is as near as I can come to it. But it is something infinitely finer and rarer.

It is a difficult task to show to others a thing which, though I feel and recognize it thoroughly, I have not yet analyzed for myself.

But this is a complete Portrayal of me - as I await the Devil's coming - and I must tell everything - everything.

February 13

So then yes. As I have said, I find that I am quite, quite odd. My various acquaintances say that I am *funny*. They say, "Oh, it's that May MacLane, Dolly's younger sister. She's funny." But I call it oddity. I bear the hall-mark of oddity.

There was a time, a year or two since, when I was an exceedingly sensitive little fool. Sensitive in that it used to strike very deep when my young acquaintances would call me funny and find in me a vent for their distinctly unfriendly ridicule. My years in the High School were not years of joy. Two years ago I had not yet risen above these things. I was a sensitive little fool.

But that sensitiveness, I rejoice to say, has gone from me. The opinion of these young people, or of these old people, is now a thing that is quite unable to affect me.

The more I see of conventionality, it seems, the more I am odd.

Though I am young and feminine - very feminine - yet I am not that quaint conceit, a *girl*: the sort of person that Laura E. Richards writes about, and Nora Perry, and Louisa M. Alcott, - girls with bright eyes, and with charming faces - (they always have charming faces), - standing with reluctant feet where the brook and river meet, - and all that sort of thing.

I missed all that.

I have read some girl-books, a few years ago - *Hildegarde Graham*, and *What Katy Did*, and all, - but I read them from afar. I looked at those creatures from behind a high board fence. I felt as if I had more tastes in common with the Jews wandering through the Wilderness, or with a band of fighting Amazons. I am not a girl. I am a woman, of a kind. I began to be a woman at twelve, or more properly, a genius.

And then, usually, if one is not a girl one is a heroine - of the kind you read about. But I am not a heroine, either. A heroine is beautiful - eyes like the sea, shoots opaque glances from under drooping lids, walks with undulating movements, her bright smile haunts one still, falls methodically in love with a man - always with a man, - eats things (they are always called "viands") with a delicate appetite, and on special occasions her voice is full of tears. I do none of these things. I am not beautiful. I do not walk with undulating movements - indeed, I have never seen any one walk so, except, perhaps, a cow that has been overfed. My bright smile haunts no one. I shoot no opaque glances from my eyes, which are not like the sea by any means. I have never eaten any viands, and my appetite for what I do eat is most excellent. And my voice has never yet, to my knowledge, been full of tears.

No. I am not a heroine.

There never seem to be any plain heroines, except Jane Eyre, and she was very unsatisfactory. She should have entered into marriage with her beloved Rochester in the first place. I should have, let there be a dozen mad wives up-stairs. But I suppose the author thought she must give her heroine some desirable thing - high moral principles, since she was not beautiful. Some people say that beauty is a curse. It may be true, but I'm sure I should not have minded being cursed a little. And I know several persons who might well say the same. But anyway, I wish some one would write a book about a plain, bad heroine so that I might feel in real sympathy with her.

So far from being a girl or a heroine, I am a thief - as I have before suggested.

I mind me of how, not long since, I stole three dollars. A woman whom I know rather well, and lives near, called me into her house as I was passing and asked me to do an errand for her. She was having an ornate gown made, and she needed some more applique with which to festoon it. The applique cost nine dollars a yard. My trusting neighbor gave me a bit of the braid for a sample and two twenty-dollar bills. I was to get four yards. I did so, and came back and gave her the braid and a single dollar. The other three dollars I kept myself. I wanted three dollars very much, to put with a few that I already had in my purse. My trusting neighbor is of the kind that throws money about carelessly. I knew she would not pay any attention to a little detail like that - she was deeply interested in her new frock; or perhaps she would think I had got thirty-nine dollars' worth of applique. At any rate, she did not need the money, and I wanted three dollars, and so I stole it.

I am a thief.

It has been suggested to me that I am a kleptomaniac. But I am sure my mind is perfectly sane. I have no such excuse. I am a plain, down-right thief.

This is only one of my peculations. I steal money, or anything that I want, whenever I can, nearly always. It amuses me - and one must be amused.

I have only two stipulations: that the person to whom it belongs does not need it pressingly, and that there is not the slightest chance of being found out. (And of course I could not think of stealing from my one friend.)

It would be extremely inconvenient to be known as a thief, merely.

When the world knows you are a thief it blinds itself completely to your other attributes. It calls you a thief, and there's an end. I am a genius as well as a thief - but the world would quite overlook that fact. "A thief's a thief," says the world. That is very true. But the mere fact of being a thief should not exclude the consideration of one's other traits. When the world knows you are a Methodist minister, for instance, it will admit that you may also be a violinist, or a chemist, or a poet, and will credit you therefor. And so if it condemns you for being a thief, it should at the same time admire you for being a genius. If it does not admire you for being a genius, then it has no right to condemn you for being a thief.

- And why the world should condemn any one for being a thief - when there is not within its confines any one who is not a thief in some way - is a bit of irony upon which I have wasted much futile logic. -

I am not trying to justify myself for stealing. I do not consider it a thing that needs to be justified, any more than walking or eating or going to bed. But, as I say, if the world knew that I am a thief without being first made aware with emphasis that I am some other things also, then the world would be a shade cooler for me than it already is - which would be very cool indeed.

And so in writing my Portrayal I have dwelt upon some other things at some length before touching on my thieving propensities.

None of my acquaintances would suspect that I am a thief. I look so respectable, so refined, so "nice," so inoffensive, so sweet, even!

But, for that matter, I am a great many things that I do not appear to be.

The woman from whom I stole the three dollars, if she reads this, will recognize it. This will be inconvenient. I fervently hope she may not read it. It is true she is not of the kind that reads.

But after all, it's of no consequence. This Portrayal is Mary MacLane: her wooden heart, her young woman's-body, her mind, her soul.

- The world may run and read. -

I will tell you what I did with the three dollars. In Dublin Gulch, which is a rough quarter of Butte inhabited by extremely Irish people, there lives an old world-soured, wrinkle-faced woman. She lives alone in a small untidy house. She swears frightfully like a parrot, and her reputation is bad - so bad indeed that even the old woman's compatriots in Dublin Gulch do not visit her lest they damage their own. It is true that the profane old woman's morals are not good - have never been good - judged by the world's standards. She bears various marks of cold, rough handling on her mind and body. Her life has all but run its course. She is worn out.

Once in a while I go to visit this old woman. - My reputation must be sadly damaged now. -

I sit with her for an hour or two and listen to her. She is extremely glad to have me here. Except me she has no one to talk to but the milk man, the grocery man, and the butcher. So always she is glad to see me. There is a certain bond of sympathy between her and me. We are fond of each other. When she sees me picking my way toward her house, her hard sour face softens wonderfully and a light of distinct friendliness comes into her green eyes.

Don't you know, there are few people enough in the world whose hard sour faces will soften at the sight of you and a distinctly friendly light come into their green eyes. For myself I find such people few indeed.

So the profane old woman and I are fond of each other. No question of morals, or of immorals, comes between us. We are equals.

I talk to her a little - but mostly she talks. She tells me of the time when she lived in County Galway, when she was young - and of her several husbands, and of some who were not husbands, and of her children scattered over the earth. And she shows me old tin-types of these people. She has told me the varied tale of her life a great many times. I like to hear her tell it. It is like nothing else I have heard. The story in its unblushing simplicity, the sour-faced old woman sitting telling it, and the tin-types, - contain a thing that is absurdly, grotesquely, tearlessly sad.

Once when I went to her house I brought with me six immense heavy fragrant chrysanthemums.

They had been bought with the three dollars I had stolen.

It pleased me to buy them for the profane old woman. They pleased her also - not because she cares much for flowers, but because I brought them to her. I knew they would please her, but that was not the reason I gave her them.

I did it purely and simply to please myself.

I knew the profane old woman would not be at all concerned as to whether they had been bought with stolen money or not, and my only regret was that I had not had an opportunity to steal a larger sum so that I might have bought more chrysanthemums without inconveniencing my purse.

But as it was they filled her dirty little dwelling with perfume and color.

Long ago when I was six I was a thief - only I was not then, as now, a graceful, light-fingered thief - I had not the philosophy of stealing.

When I would steal a copper cent out of my mother's pocket-book I would feel a dreadful suffocating sinking in my bad heart, and for days and nights afterwards - long after I had eaten the chocolate mouse - the copper cent would haunt me and haunt me, and oh, how I wished it back in that pocket-book with the clasp shut tight and the bureau-drawer locked!

And so is it not fine to be nineteen and a thief, with the philosophy of stealing - than to be six and haunted day and night by a copper cent?

For now always my only regret is, when I have stolen five dollars, that I did not steal ten while I was about it.

It is a long time ago since I was six.

February 17

To-day I walked over the hill where the sun vanishes down in the afternoon.

I followed the sun so far as I could, but two even very good legs can do no more than carry one into the midst of the sunshine - and then one may stand and take leave, lovingly, of it.

I stood in the valley below the hill and looked away at the gold-yellow mountains that rise into the cloudy blue, and at the long gray stretches of rolling sand. It all reminded me of the Devil and the Happiness he will bring me.

Some day the Devil will come to me and say: "Come with me."

And I will answer: "Yes."

And he will take me away with him to a place where it is wet and green - where the yellow, yellow sunshine falls on heaven-kissing hills, and misty, cloudy masses float over the valleys.

And for days I shall be happy - happy - happy!

For *days*! The Devil and I will love each other intensely, perfectly - for days! He will be incarnate but he will not be a man. He will be the man-Devil, and his soul will take mine to itself and they will be one - for days.

Imagine me raised out of my misery and obscurity, dullness and Nothingness, into the full, brilliant life of the Devil - for days!

The love of the man-Devil will enter into my barren, barren life and melt all the cold, hard things, and water the barrenness, and a million little green growing plants will start out of it; and a clear, sparkling spring will flow over it - through the dreary, sandy stretches of my bitterness, among the false stony roadways of my pain and hatred. And a great rushing, flashing cataract of melting love will flow over my weariness and unrest and wash it away forever. My soul will be fully awakened and there will be a million little sweet new souls in the green growing things. And they will fill my life with everything that is beautiful - tenderness, and divineness, and compassion, and exaltation, and uplifting grace, and light, and rest, and gentleness, and triumph, and truth, and peace. My life will be borne far out of self, and self will sink quietly out of sight - and I shall see it farther and farther away, until it disappears.

"It is the last - the *last* - of that Mary MacLane," I will say, and I will feel a long, sighing, quivering farewell.

A thousand years of misery - and now a million years of Happiness.

When the sun is setting in the valley and the crests of those heaven-kissing hills are painted violet and purple, and the valley itself is reeking and swimming in yellow-gold light, the man-Devil - whom I love more than all - and I will go out into it.

We will be saturated in the yellow light of the sun and the gold light of Love.

The man-Devil will say to me: "Look, you little creature, at this beautiful picture of Joy and Happiness. It is the picture of your life as it will be while I stay with you - and I will stay with you for days."

Ah, yes, I will take a last long farewell of this Mary MacLane. Not one faint shadow of her weary wretched Nothingness will remain.

There will be instead a brilliant, buoyant, joyous creature - transformed, adorned, garlanded by the love of the Devil.

My mind will be a treasure-house of Art, swept and garnished and strong and at its best.

My barren hungry heart will come at last to its own. The red flames of the man-Devil's love will burn out forever its pitiable distorted wooden quality, and he will take it and cherish it - and give me his.

My young woman's-body likewise will be metamorphosed, and I shall feel it developing and filled with myriads of little contentments and pleasures. Always my young woman's-body is a great and important part of me, and when I am married to the Devil its finely-organized nerve-power and intricate sensibility will be culminated to marvelous completeness.

My soul - upon my soul will descend consciously the light that never was on land or sea.

This will be for days - for days.

No matter what came before, I will say; no matter what comes afterward. Just now it is the man-Devil, my best-beloved, and I, living in the yellow light.

Think of living with the Devil in a bare little house, in the midst of green wetness and sweetness and yellow light - for days!

In the gray dawn it will be ineffably sweet and beautiful, with shining leaves and the gray unfathomable air, and the wet grass, and all.

"Be happy now, my weary little wife," the Devil will say.

And the long, long yellow-gold day will be filled with the music of Real Life.

My grandest possibility will be realized. The world contains a great many things - and this is my grandest possibility realized!

And in the soft black night I will lie by the side of the man-Devil - and my head will rest in the hollow of his shoulder, and my hand will be clasped in his hand.

I will weep rapturous tears. -

When I think of all this and write it there is in me a feeling that is more than pain.

Perhaps the very sweetest, the tenderest, the most pitiful and benign human voice in the world could sing these things and this feeling set to their own wondrous music, - and it would echo far - far, - and you would understand.

February 19

- Am I not intolerably conceited? -

February 20

At times when I walk among the natural things - the barren natural things - I know that I believe in Something. Why can I not call it God and pray to it?

There is Something - I do not know it intellectually, but I feel it - I *feel* it - with my soul. It does not seem to reach down to me. It does not pity me. It does not look at me tenderly in my unhappiness.

My soul feels only that it is there.

No. It is not all-loving, all-gracious, all-pitying. It hurts me - it hurts me always as I walk over the sand. But even while it hurts me it seems to promise - ah, those beautiful things that it promises me!

And then the hurting is anguish - for I know that the promises will never be fulfilled.

There is within me a thing that is aching, aching, aching always as the days pass.

It is not my pain of wanting, nor my pain of unrest, nor my pain of bitterness, nor of hatred. I know those in all their own anguish.

This aching is another pain. It is a pain that I do not know - that I feel ignorantly but sharply, and oh, it is torture, torture!

My soul is worn and weary with pain. There is no compassion - no mercy upon me. There is no one to help me bear it. It is just I alone out on the sand and barrenness. It is cruel anguish to be always alone - and so long - oh, so long!

Nineteen years are as ages to you when you are nineteen.

When you are nineteen there is no experience to tell you that all things have an end.

This aching pain has no end.

- I feel no tears now, but I feel heavy sobs that shake my life to its center. -

My soul is wandering in a wilderness.

There is a great Light sometimes that draws my soul toward it. When my soul turns toward it, it shines out brilliant and dazzling and awful - and the worn sensitive thing shrinks away, and shivers, and is faint.

Shall my soul have to know this Light, inevitably? Must it, some day, plunge into this?

Oh, it may be - it may be. But I know that I shall die with the pain.

There are times when the great Light is dim and beautiful as the star-light - the utter agony of it - the cruel ineffable loveliness!

- Do you understand this? That I am telling you my young passionate life-agony? Do you listen to it indifferently? Has it no meaning for any one? For me it means everything. For me it makes life old long weariness.

It may be that you know. And perhaps you would even weep a little with me if you had time. -

It is as if this Light were the light of the Christian religion - and the Christian religion is full of hatred. It says, Come unto me - you that are heavy laden, and I will give you rest. But when you would go, when you reach up with your weary hands, it sends you a too-brilliant Light - it makes you fair, wondrous promises - it puts you off. You beseech it in your suffering -

> *While the waters near me roll,*
> *While the tempest still is high -*

but it does not listen - it does not care. Worship me, worship me, it says, but after that let me alone. There is a bookful of promises. Take it and thank me and worship me.

It does not care.

If I obey it, it looks on indifferently. If I disobey it, it looks on indifferently. If I am in woe, it looks on indifferently. If I am in a brief joy, it looks on indifferently.

I am left all alone - all alone.

The Light is shown me and I reach after it, but it is placed high out of my reach.

I see the promises in the Light. Oh, why - *why* does it promise these things! Is not the burden of life already greater than I can bear? And there is the story of the Christ. It is beautiful. It is damningly beautiful. It draws the tears of pain and soft anguish from me at the sense of beauty. And when every nerve in me is melted and overflowing, then suddenly I am conscious that it is a lie - a *lie*.

Everywhere I turn there is Nothing - Nothing.

My soul wails out its grief in loneliness.

My soul wanders hither and thither in the dark wilderness and asks, asks always in blind, dull agony: How long? - how long?

February 22

Life is a pitiable thing.

February 23

I stand in the midst of my sand and barrenness and gaze hard at everything that is within my range of vision - and ruin my eyes trying to see into the darkness beyond.

And nearly always I feel a vague contempt for you, fine brave world, - for you and all the things that I see from my barrenness. But, I promise you, if some one comes from among you over the sunset hill one day with love for me, I will fall at your feet.

I am a selfish, conceited, impudent little animal it is true, but, after all, I am only one grand conglomeration of Wanting - and when some one comes over the barren hill to satisfy the Wanting, I will be humble, humble in my triumph.

It is a difficult thing - a most difficult thing - to live on as one year follows another, from childhood slowly to womanhood, without one single sharer of your life - to be alone, always alone, when your one friend is gone. Oh, yes, it is hard! Particularly when one is not high-minded and spiritual, when one's near longing is not a God and a religion, when one wants above all things the love of a human being - when one is a woman, young and all alone. Doubtless you know this. After all, fine brave world, there are some things that you know very well. Whether or not you care is a quite different matter.

You have the power to take this wooden heart in a tight, suffocating grasp. You have the power to do this with pain for me, and you have the power to do it with ravishing gentleness. But whether or not you will is another matter.

You may think evil of me before you have finished reading this. You will be very right to think so - according to your standards. But sometimes you see evil where there is no evil, and think evil when the only evil is in your own brains.

My life is a dry and barren life. You can change it.

> *Oh, the little more, and how much it is!*
> *And the little less, and what worlds away.*

Yes, you can change it. Stranger things have happened. Again, whether you will - that is a quite different thing.

No doubt you are the people and wisdom will die with you. I do not question that. I will admit and believe anything you may assert about yourselves. I do not want your wisdom, your judgment. I want some one to come up over the barren sunset hill. My thoughts are the thoughts of youth, which are said to be long, long thoughts.

Your life is multi-colored and filled with people. My life is the gray of sand and barrenness, and consists of Mary MacLane, the longing for Happiness, and the memory of the anemone lady.

This Portrayal is my deepest sincerity, my tears, my drops of red blood. Some of it is wrung from me - wrung by my ambition to tell *everything*. It is not altogether good that I should give you all this, since I do not give it for love of you. I am giving it in exchange for a few gaily-colored things. I want you to know all these passions and emotions. I give them with the utmost freedom. I shall be furious indeed if you do not take them. At the same time, the fact that I am exchanging my tears and my drops of red blood for your gaily-colored trifles is not a thing that thrills me with delight.

But it's of little moment. When the Devil comes over the hill with Happiness I will rush at him frantically headlong - and nothing else will matter.

February 25

Mary MacLane - what are you, you forlorn, desolate little creature? Why are you not of and in the galloping herd? Why is it that you stand out separate against the background of a gloomy sky? Why can you not enter into the lives and sympathies of other young creatures? There have been times when you have strained every despairing nerve to do so - before you realized that these things were not for you, that the only sympathy for you was that of Mary MacLane, and the only things for you were those you could take yourself - not which were given you. And your things are few, few, you starved, lean little mud-cat - you worn, youth-weary, obscure little genius!

Oh, it is a wearisome waiting - for the Devil.

To-day when I walked over my sand and barrenness I felt Infinite Grief.

Everything is beyond me.

Nothing is mine.

My single friendship shines brightly before me, and is fascinating - and always just out of my reach.

I want the love and sympathy of human beings and I repel human beings.

Yes, I repel human beings.

There is something about me that faintly and finely and unmistakably repels.

When my Happiness comes, shall I be able to have it? Shall I ever have anything?

This repellant power is not an outward quality. It is something that comes from deeply, deeply within. It is something that was there in the Beginning. It is a thing from the Original.

There is no ridding myself of it. There is no ridding myself of it. There is no ridding myself of it.

Oh, I am damned - damned!

There is not one soul in the world to feel for me and with me - not one out of all the millions. No one can understand me - *no one.*

You are saying to yourself that I imagine this.

What right have you to say so? You don't know anything about me. I know all about me. I have studied all the elements and phases in my life for years and years. I do not imagine anything. I am even fool enough to shut my eyes to some things until, inevitably, I know I must meet them. I am racked with the passions of youth, and I am young in years. Beyond that I am mature - old. I am not a child in anything but my passions and my years. I feel and recognize everything thoroughly. I have not to imagine anything. My inner life is before my eyes.

There is something about me that no one can understand. Can there ever be any one to understand? Shall I not always walk my barren road alone?

This follows me incessantly. It is burning like a smouldering fire every hour of my life.

Oh, deep black Despair!

How I suffer, how I suffer - just in being alive.

I feel Infinite Grief.

Oh, Infinite Grief -

Often in the early morning I leave my bed and get me dressed and go out into the Gray Dawn. There is something about the Gray Dawn that makes me wish the world would stop, that the sun would never come up over the edge, that my life would go on and on and rest in the Gray Dawn.

In the Gray Dawn every hard thing is hidden by a gray mantle of charity, and only the light, vague, caressing fancies are left.

Sometimes I think I am a strange, strange creature - something not of earth, nor yet of heaven, nor of hell. I think at times I am a little thing fallen on the earth by mistake: a thing thrown among foreign, unfitting elements, where there is nothing in touch with it, where life is a continual struggle, where every little door is closed - every Why unanswered, and itself knows not where to lay its head. I feel a deadly certainty in some moments that the wide world contains not one moment of rest for me, that there will never be any rest, that my woman's-soul will go on asking long, long centuries after my woman's-body is laid in its grave.

I felt this in the Gray Dawn this morning, but the gray charitable mantle softened it. Always I feel most acutely in the Gray Dawn, but always there is the thing to soften it.

The gray atmosphere was charged. There was a tense electrical thrill in the cold soft air. My nerves were keenly alive. But the gray curtain was mercifully there. I did not feel too much.

How I wished the yellow beautiful sun would never come up over the edge to show me my nearer anguish!

"Stay with me, stay with me, soft Gray Dawn," implored every one of my tiny lives. "Let me forget. Let the vanity, the pain, the longing sink deep and vanish - all of it, all of it! And let me rest in the midst of the Gray Dawn."

I heard music - the silent music of myriad voices that you hear when all is still. One of them came and whispered to me softly: "Don't suffer any more just now, little Mary MacLane. You suffer enough in the brightness of the sun and the blackness of the night. This is the Gray Dawn. Take a little rest."

"Yes," I said, "I will take a little rest."

And then a wild swelling chorus of voices whispered in the stillness: "Rest, rest, rest little Mary MacLane. Suffer in the brightness, suffer in the blackness - your soul, your wooden heart, your woman's-body. But now a little rest - a little rest."

"A little rest," I said again.

And straightway I began resting lest the sun should come too quickly over the edge.

When I have heard in summer the wind in a forest of pines, blowing a wondrous symphony of purity and truth, my varied nature felt itself abashed and there was a sinking in my wooden heart. The beauty of it ravished my senses, but it savored crushingly of the virtue that is far above and beyond me and I felt a certain sore despairing grief.

But the Gray Dawn is in perfect sympathy. It is quite as beautiful as the wind in the pines and its truth and purity are extremely gentle, and partly hidden under the gray curtain.

Almost I can be a different Mary MacLane out in the Gray Dawn. Let me forget all the mingled agonies of my life. Let me walk in the midst of this gray softness and drink of the waters of Lethe.

The Gray Dawn is not Paradise; it is not a Happy Valley; it is not a Garden of Eden; it is not a Vale of Cashmere. It is the Gray Dawn - soft, charitable, tender. "The brilliant, celestial yellow will come shortly," it says. "You will suffer then to your greatest extent. But now I am here - and so, rest."

And so in the Gray Dawn I was forgetting for a brief period. I was submerged for a little in Lethe, river of oblivion. If I had seen some one coming over the near horizon with Happiness I should have protested, Wait, wait until the Gray Dawn has passed.

The deep, deep blue of the summer sky stirs me to a half-painful joy. The cool green of a swiftly-flowing river fills my heart with unquiet longings. The red, red of the sunset sky convulses my entire being with passion. But the dear Gray Dawn brings me Rest.

Oh, the Gray Dawn is sweet - sweet!

Could I not die for very love of it!

The Gray Dawn can do no wrong. If those myriad voices suddenly had begun to sing a voluptuous evil song of the so great evil that I could not understand, but that I could feel instantly, still the Gray Dawn would have been fine and sweet and beautiful.

Always I admire Mary MacLane greatly - though sometimes in my admiration I feel a complete contempt for her. But in the Gray Dawn I love Mary MacLane tenderly and passionately.

I seem to take on a strange calm indifference to everything in the world but just Mary MacLane and the gray dawn. We two are identified with each other and joined together in shadowy vagueness from the rest of the world.

As I walked over my sand and barrenness in the Gray Dawn a poem ran continuously through my mind. It expressed to me in my gray condition an ideal life and death and ending. Every desire of my life melted away in the Gray Dawn except one good wish that my own life and death might be short and obscure and complete like them. The poem was this beautiful one of Charles Kingsley's:

"Oh, Mary, go and call the cattle home,
And call the cattle home,
And call the cattle home,
Across the sands of Dee!"
The western wind was wild and dank with foam,
And all alone went she.

The creeping tide came up along the sand,
And o'er and o'er the sand,
And round and round the sand,
As far as eye could see;
The blinding mist came up and hid the land -
And never home came she.

Oh, is it weed, or fish, or floating hair? -
A tress of golden hair,
Of drowned maiden's hair,
Above the nets at sea.
Was never salmon yet that shone so fair
Among the stakes on Dee.

They rowed her in across the rolling foam,
The cruel, crawling foam,
The cruel, hungry foam,
To her grave beside the sea;
But still the boatmen hear her call the cattle home
Across the sands of Dee.

This is a poem perfect. And in the Gray Dawn it expresses to me a most desirable thing - a short eventless life, a sudden ceasing, and a forgotten voice sometimes calling. This Mary, in the Gray Dawn, would wish nothing else. If the waters rolled over me now - over my short eventless life - there would be the sudden ceasing, - and the anemone lady would hear my voice sometimes, and remember me - the anemone lady and one or two others. And after a short time even my pathetic, passionate voice would sound faint and be forgotten, and my world of sand and barrenness would know me and my weary little life-tragedy no more.

And well for me, I say, - in the Gray Dawn.

It is different - oh, very different - when the yellow bursts through the gray. And the yellow is with me all day long, and at sunset - the red, red line!

Yet - oh, sweet Gray Dawn -

Sometimes I am seized with nearer, vivider sensations of love for my one friend, the anemone lady.

She is so dear - so beautiful!

My love for her is a peculiar thing. It is not the ordinary woman-love. It is something that burns with a vivid fire of its own. The anemone lady is enshrined in a temple on the inside of my heart that shall always only be hers.

She is my first love - my only dear one.

The thought of her fills me with a multitude of feelings, passionate yet wonderfully tender, - with delight, with rare, undefined emotions, with a suggestion of tears.

- Oh, dearest anemone lady, shall I ever be able to forget your beautiful face! There may be some long crowded years before me; it may be there will be people and people entering and departing - but oh, no - no, I shall never forget! There will be in my life always - always the faint sweet perfume of the blue anemone: the memory of my one friend.

Before she went away, to see her, to be near her, was an event in my life - a coloring of the dullness. Always when I used to look at her there would rush a train of things over my mind, a vaguely glittering pageant that came only with her, and that held an always-vivid interest for me.

There were manifold and varied treasures in this train. There were skies of spangled sapphire, and there were lilies, and violets wet with dew. There was the music of violins, and wonderful weeds from the deep sea, and songs of troubadours, and gleaming white statues. There were ancient forests of oak and clematis vines; there were lemon-trees, and fretted palaces, and moss-covered old castles with moats and draw-bridges and tiny mullioned windows with diamond panes. There was a cold glittering cataract of white foam, and a little green boat far off down the river, drifting along under drooping willows. There was a tree of golden apples, and a banquet in a beautiful house with the melting music of lutes and harps, and mulled orange-wine in tall thin glasses. There was a field of long fine grass, soft as bat's-wool, and there were birds of brilliant plumage - scarlet and indigo with gold-tipped wings.

All these and a thousand fancies alike vaguely glittering would rush over me when I was with the anemone lady. Always my brain was in a gentle delirium. My nerves were unquiet.

- It was because I love her. -

Oh, there is not - there can never be - another anemone lady!

My life is a desert - a desert, but the thin, clinging perfume of the blue anemone reaches to its utter confines. And nothing in the desert is the same because of that perfume. Years will not fade the blue of the anemone, nor a thousand bitter winds blow away the rare fragrance.

I feel in the anemone lady a strange attraction of sex. There is in me a masculine element that, when I am thinking of her, arises and overshadows all the others.

"Why am I not a man," I say to the sand and barrenness with a certain strained, tense passion, "that I might give this wonderful, dear, delicious woman an absolutely perfect love!"

And this is my predominating feeling for her.

So then it is not the woman-love, but the man-love, set in the mysterious sensibilities of my woman-nature. It brings me pain and pleasure mingled in that old, old fashion.

Do you think a man is the only creature with whom one may fall in love?

- Often I see coming across the desert a long line of light. My soul turns toward it and shrinks away from it as it does from all the lights. - Some day, perhaps, all the lights will roll into one terrible white effervescence and rush over my soul and kill it. - But this light does not bring so much of pain, for it is soft and silvery, and always with it is the Soul of Anemone.

March 8

There are several things in the world for which I, of womankind and nineteen years, have conceived a forcible repugnance - or rather, the feeling was born in me; I did not have to conceive it.

Often my mind chants a fervent litany of its own that runs somewhat like this:

From good Catholics and virtuous Christians: kind Devil deliver me.

From women and men who dispense odors of musk; from little boys with long curls; from the kind of people who call a woman's figure her "shape": kind Devil deliver me.

From all sweet girls; from "gentlemen"; from feminine men: kind Devil deliver me.

From black under-clothing - and any color but white; from hips that wobble as one walks; from persons with fishy eyes; from the books of Archibald C. Gunter and Albert Ross: kind Devil deliver me.

From the soft, persistent, maddening glances of water-cart drivers: kind Devil deliver me.

From lisle-thread stockings; from round tight garters; from brilliant brass belts: kind Devil deliver me.

From insipid sweet wine; from men who wear moustaches; from the sort of people that call legs "limbs"; from bedraggled white petticoats: kind

Devil deliver me.

From unripe bananas; from bathless people; from a waist-line that slopes up in the front: kind Devil deliver me.

From an ordinary man; from a bad stomach, bad eyes, and bad feet: kind Devil deliver me.

From red note-paper; from a rhinestone-studded comb in my hair; from weddings: kind Devil deliver me.

From cod-fish balls; from fried-eggplant, fried beef-steak, fried pork-chops, and fried French toast: kind Devil deliver me.

From wax-flowers off a wedding-cake, under glass; from thin-soled shoes; from tape-worms; from photographs perched up all over my house: kind Devil deliver me.

From soft old bachelors and soft old widowers; from any masculine thing that wears a pale blue neck-tie; from agonizing elocutionists who recite "Curfew Shall Not Ring To-night," and "The Lips that Touch Liquor Shall Never Touch Mine"; from a Salvation Army singing hymns in slang: kind Devil deliver me.

From people who persist in calling my good body "mere vile clay"; from idiots who appear to know all about me and enjoin me not to bathe my eyes in hot water since it hurts their own; from fools who tell me what I "want" to do: kind Devil deliver me.

From a nice young man; from tin spoons; from popular songs: kind Devil deliver me.

From pleasant old ladies who tell a great many uninteresting, obvious lies; from men with watch-chains draped across their middles; from some paintings of the old masters which I am unable to appreciate; from side-saddles: kind Devil deliver me.

From the kind of man who sings "Oh, Promise Me!" - who sings *at* it; from constipated dressmakers; from people who don't wash their hair often enough: kind Devil deliver me.

From a servant girl with false teeth; from persons who make a regular practice of rubbing oily mixtures into their faces; from a bed that sinks in the middle: kind Devil deliver me.

And so on and on and on. And in each petition I am deeply sincere. But, kind Devil, only bring me Happiness and I will more than willingly be annoyed by all these things. Happiness for two days, kind Devil, and then, if you will, languishing widowers, lisle-thread stockings - anything, for the rest of my life.

And hurry, kind Devil, pray - for I am weary.

It is astonishing to me how very many contemptible, petty vanities are lodged in the crevices of my genius. My genius itself is one grand good vanity - but it is not contemptible. And even those little vanities - though they are contemptible I do not hold them in contempt by any means. I smile involuntarily at their absurdness sometimes, but I know well that they have their function.

They are peculiarly of my mind, my humanness, and they are useful therein. When this mind stretches out its hand for things and finds only wilderness and Nothingness all about it, and draws the hand back empty, then it can only turn back - like my soul - to itself. And it finds these innumerable little vanities to quiet it and help it. - My soul has no vanity, and it has nothing, nothing to quiet it. My soul is wearing itself out, eating itself away. - These vanities are a miserable substitute for the rose-colored treasures that it sees a great way off and even imagines in its folly that it may have, if it continues to reach after them. Yet the vanities are something. They prevent my erratic, analytical mind from finding a great Nothing when it turns back upon itself.

If I were not so unceasingly engrossed with my sense of misery and loneliness my mind would produce beautiful, wonderful logic. I am a genius - a genius - a genius. Even after all this you may not realize that I am a genius. It is a hard thing to show. But, for myself, I feel it. It is enough for me that I feel it.

I am not a genius because I am foreign to everything in the world, nor because I am intense, nor because I suffer. One may be all of these and yet not have this marvelous perceptive sense. My genius is because of nothing. It was born in me as germs of evil were born in me. And mine is a genius that has been given to no one else. The genius itself enables me to be thoroughly convinced of this.

It is hopeless, never-ending loneliness!

My ancestors in their Highlands - some of them - were endowed with second sight. My genius is not in the least like second sight. That savors of the supernatural, the mysterious. My genius is a sound sure earthly sense, with no suggestion of mystery or occultism. It is an inner sense that enables me to feel and know things that I could not possibly put into thought, much less into words. It makes me know and analyze with deadly minuteness every keen tiny damnation in my terrible lonely life. It is a mirror that shows me myself and something in myself in a merciless brilliant light, and the sight at once sickens and maddens me and fills me with an unnamed woe. It is something unspeakably dreadful. The sight for the time deadens all thought in my mind. It freezes my reason and intellect. Logic can not come to my aid. I can only feel and know the thing as it analyzes itself before my eyes.

I am alone with this - alone, alone, alone! There is no pitiful hand extended from the heights - there is no human being - ah, there is Nothing.

How can I bear it! Oh, I ask you - how can I bear it!

My genius is an element by itself and it is not a thing that I can tell in so many words. But it makes itself felt in every point of my life. This book would be a very different thing if I were not a genius - though I am not a literary genius. Often people who come in contact with me and hear me utter a few commonplace remarks feel at once that I am extraordinary.

I am extraordinary.

I have tried longingly, passionately, to think that even this sand and barrenness is mine. But I can not. I know beyond the shadow of a doubt that it, like all good things, is beyond me. It has something that I also have. In that is our bond of sympathy.

But the sand and barrenness itself is not mine.

Always I think there is but one picture in the world more perfect in its art than the picture of me in my sand and barrenness. It is the picture of the Christ crucified with two thieves. Nothing could be more divinely appropriate. The art in it is ravishingly perfect. It is one of the few perfect pictures set before the world for all time. As I see it before my mind I can think only of its utter perfectness. I can summon no feeling of grief at the deed. The deed and the art are perfect. Its perfectness ravishes my senses.

And within me I feel that the picture of me in my sand and barrenness - knowing that even the sand and barrenness is not mine - is only second to it.

Sometimes when I go out in the barrenness my mind wanders afar.

To-day it went to Greece.

Oh, it was very beautiful in Greece!

There was a wide long sky that was vividly, wonderfully blue. And there was a limitless sea that was gray and green. And it went far to the south. The sky and the sea spread out into the vast world - two beautiful elements, and they fell in love with each other. And the farther away they were the nearer they moved together until at last they met and clasped each other in the far distance. There were tall dark-green trees of kinds that are seen only in Greece. They murmured and whispered in the stillness. The wind came off from the sea and went over them and around them. They quivered and trembled in shy, ecstatic joy - for the wind was their best-beloved. There were banks of moss of a deep emerald color, and golden flowers that drooped their heavy sensual heads over to the damp black earth. And they also loved each other, and were with each other, and were glad. Clouds hung low over the sea and were dark-gray and heavy with rain. But the sun shone from behind them at intervals with beams of bronze-and-copper. Three white rocks rose up out of the sea, and the bronze-and-copper beams fell upon them, and straightway they were of gold.

Oh, how beautiful were those three gold rocks that came up out of the sea!

Aphrodite once came up out of this same sea. She came gleaming, with golden hair and beautiful eyes. Her skin glowed with hints of carmine and wild rose. Her white feet touched the smooth, yellow sand on the shore. - The white feet of Aphrodite on the yellow sand made a picture of marvelous beauty. - She was flushed in the joy of new life.

But the bronze-and-copper sunshine on the three white rocks was more beautiful than Aphrodite.

I stood on the shore and looked at the rocks. My heart contracted with the pain that beautiful things bring.

The bronze-and-copper in the wide gray and green sea!

"This is the gateway of Heaven," I said to myself. "Behind those three gold rocks there is music and the high notes of happy voices." My soul grew faint. "And there is no sand and barrenness there, and no Nothingness, and no bitterness, and no hot, blinding tears. And there are no little heart-weary children, and no lonely young women - oh, there is no loneliness at all!" My soul grew more and more faint with thinking of it. "And there is no heart there but that is pure and joyous and in Peace - in long, still, eternal Peace. And every life comes there to its own; and every earth-cry is answered, and every earth-pain is ended; and the dark spirit of Sorrow that hangs always over the earth is gone - gone, - beyond the gateway of heaven. And more than all, Love is there and walks among the dwellers. Love is a shining figure with radiant hands, and it touches them all with its hands so that never-dying love enters into their hearts. And the love of each for another is like the love of each for self. And here at last is Truth. There is searching and searching over the earth after Truth - and who has found it? But here is it beyond the gateway of heaven. Those who enter in know that it is Truth at last."

And so Peace and Love and Truth are there behind the three gold rocks. And then my soul could no longer endure the thought of it.

Suddenly the sun passed behind a heavy, dark-gray cloud and the bronze-and-copper faded from the three rocks and left them white - very white in the wide water.

The yellow flowers laid their heads drowsily down on the emerald moss. The wind from off the sea played very gently among the motionless branches of the tall trees. The blue, blue sky and the wide, gray-green sea clasped each other more closely and mingled with each other and became one vague, shadowy element - and from it all I brought my eyes back thousands of leagues to my sand and barrenness.

The sand and barrenness is itself an element, and I have known it a long, long time.

March 12

Everything is so dreary - so dreary.

I feel as if I should like to die to-day. I should not be the tiniest bit less unhappy afterward - but this life is unutterably weary. I am not strong. I can not bear things. I do not want to bear things. I do not long for strength. I want to be happy.

When I was very little, it was cold and dreary also, but I was certain it would be different when I should grow and be ten years old. It must be very nice to be ten, I thought, - and one would not be nearly so lonesome. But when the years passed and I was ten it was just exactly as lonesome. And when I was ten everything was very hard to understand.

But it will surely be different when I am seventeen, I said, - I will know so much when I am seventeen. But when I was seventeen it was even more lonely, and everything was still harder to understand.

And again I said - faintly - everything will become clearer in a few years more, and I will wonder to think how stupid I have always been. But now the few years more have gone and here I am in loneliness that is more hopeless and harder to bear than when I was very little. Still, I wonder indeed to think how stupid I have been - and now I am not so stupid. I do not tell myself that it will be different when I am five-and-twenty.

For I know that it will not be different.

I know that it will be the same dreariness, the same Nothingness, the same loneliness.

It is very, very lonely.

It is hope deferred and maketh the heart sick.

It is more than I can bear.

Why - *why* was I ever born!

I can not live, and I can not die - for what is there after I am dead? I can see myself wandering in dark and lonely places.

Yet I feel as if I would like to die to-day.

March 13

If it were pain alone that one must bear, one could bear it. One could lose one's sense of everything but pain.

But it is pain with other things. It is the sense of pain with the sense of beauty and the sense of the anemone. And there is that mysterious pain.

Who knows the name of that mysterious pain?

It is these mingled senses that torture me.

March 14

I have been placed in this world with eyes to see and ears to hear, and I ask for Life. Is it to be wondered at? Is it so strange? Should I be content merely to see and to hear? There are other things for other people. Is it atrocious that I should ask for some other things also?

Is thy servant a dog?

March 15

In these days of approaching emotional Nature even the sand and barrenness begins to stir and rub its eyes.

My sand and barrenness is clothed in the awful majesty of countless ages. It stands always through the never-ending march of the living and the dead. It may have been green once - green and fertile, and birds and snakes and everything that loves green growing things may have lived in it. It may have sometime been rolling prairie. It may have been submerged in floods. It changed and changed in the centuries. Now it is sand and barrenness and there are no birds and no snakes; only me. But whatever change came to it, whatever its transfiguration, the spirit of it never moved. Flood, or fertility, or rolling prairie, or barrenness - it is only itself. It has a great self, a wonderful self.

I shall never forget you, my sand and barrenness.

Some day, shall my thirsty life be watered, my starved heart fed, my asking voice answered, my tired soul taken into the warmth of another with the intoxicating sweetness of love?

It may be.

But I shall remember the sand and barrenness that is with me in my Nothingness. The sand and barrenness and the memory of the anemone lady are all that are in any degree mine.

And so then I shall remember it.

As I stand among the barren gulches in these days and look away at the slow-awakening hills of Montana, I hear the high, swelling, half-tired, half-hopeful song of the world. As I listen I know that there are things, other than the Virtue and the Truth and the Love, that are not for me. There is beyond me, like these, the unbreaking, undying bond of human fellowship - a thing that is earth-old.

It is beyond me and it is nothing to me.

In my intensest desires - in my widest longings - I never go beyond *self.* The ego is the all.

Limitless legions of women and men in weariness and in joy are one. They are killing each other and torturing each other, and going down in sorrow to the dust. But they are one. Their right hands are joined in unseen sympathy and kinship.

But my two hands are apart, and clasped together in an agony of loneliness.

I have read of women who have been strongly, grandly brave. Sometimes I have dreamed that I might be brave. The possibilities of this life are magnificent.

To be saturated with this agony, I say at times, and to bear with it all; not to sink beneath it but to vanquish it, and to make it the grace and comeliness of my entire life from the Beginning to the End!

Perhaps a woman - a real woman - could do this.

But I? - No. I am not real - I do not seem *real* to myself. In such things as these my life is a blank.

There was Charlotte Corday - a heroine whom I admire above all the heroines. And more than she was a heroine she was a woman. And she had her agony. It was for love of her fair country.

To suffer and do and die for love of something! It is glorious! What must be the exalted ecstasy of Charlotte Corday's soul now!

And I - with all my manifold passions - I am a coward.

I have had moments when, vaguely and from far off, it seemed as if there might be bravery and exaltation for me, - when I could rise far over myself. I have felt unspeakable possibilities. While they lasted - what wonderful emotion was it that I felt?

But they are not real.

They fade away - they fade away.

And again come the varied phenomena of my life to bewilder and terrify me.

Confusion! Chaos! Damnation! They are not moments of exaltation now. Poor little Mary MacLane!

If to do were as easy as to know what were good to do,
Chapels had been churches, and poor men's cottages
Princes' palaces.

I do not know what to do.

I do not know what were good to do.

I would do nothing if I knew.

I might add to my litany this: Most kind Devil deliver me - from myself.

To-day I walked over the sand and it was almost beautiful. The sun was sinking and the sky was filled with roses and gold.

Then came my soul and confronted me. My soul is wondrous fair. It is like a young woman. The beauty of it is too great for human eyes to look upon. It is too great for mine. Yet I look.

My soul said to me: "I am sick."

I answered: "And I am sick."

"We may be well," said my soul. "Why are we not well?"

"How may we be well?" I asked.

"We may throw away all our vanity and false pride," said my soul. "We may take on a new life. We may learn to wait and possess ourselves in patience. We may labor and overcome -"

"We can do none of these things," I cried. "Have I not tried all of them sometime in my short life? And have I not waited and waited until you have become faint with pain? Have I not looked and longed? Dear soul, why do you not resign yourself? Why can you not stay quiet and trouble yourself and me no more? Why are you always straining and reaching? There isn't anything for you. You are wearing yourself out."

My soul made answer: "I may strain and reach until only one worn nerve of me is left. And that one nerve may be scourged with whips and burned with fire. But I will keep one atom of faith. I may go bad, but I will keep one atom of faith in Love and in the Truth that is Love. You are a genius, but I am no genius. The years - a million of years - may do their utmost to destroy the single nerve. They may lash and beat it. I will keep my one atom of faith."

"You are not wise," I said. "You have been wandering and longing for a time that seems a thousand years - through my cold dark childhood to my cold dark womanhood. Is that not enough to quiet you? Is that not enough to teach you the lesson of Nothing? You are not a genius, but you are not a fool."

"I will keep my one atom of faith," said my soul.

"But lie and sleep now," I said. "Don't reach after that Light any more. Let us both sleep a few years."

"No," said my soul.

"Oh, my soul," I wailed, "look away at that glowing copper horizon - and beyond it. Let us go there now and take an infinite rest. Now! We can bear this no longer."

"No," said my soul. "We will stay here and bear more. There would be no rest yet beyond the copper horizon. And there is no need of going anywhere. I have my one atom of faith."

I gazed at my soul as it stood plainly before me, weak and worn and faint, in the fading light. It had one atom of faith, it said, and tried to hold its head high and to look strong and triumphant. Oh, the irony - the pathos of it!

My soul, with its one pitiful atom of faith, looked only what it was - a weeping, hunted thing.

March 17

In some rare between-whiles it is as if nothing mattered. My heart aches, I say; my soul wanders; this person or that person was repelled to-day; but nothing matters.

A great inner languor comes like a giant and lays hold of me. I lie fallow beneath it.

Someone forgot me in the giving of things. But it does not matter. I feel nothing.

Persons say to me, don't analyze any more and you will not be unhappy.

When Something throws heavy clubs at you and you are hit by them, don't be hurt. When Something stronger than you holds your hands in the fire, don't let it burn you. When Something pushes you into a river of ice, don't be cold. When Something draws a cutting lash across your naked shoulders, don't let it concern you - don't be conscious that it is there.

This is great wisdom and fine clear logic.

It is a pity that no one has ever yet been able to live by it.

But after all it's no matter. Nothing is any one's affair. It is all of no consequence.

And have I not had all my anguish for nothing? I am a fool - a fool.

A handful of rich black mud in a pig's yard - does it wonder why it is there? Does it torture itself about the other mud around it, and about the earth and water of which it is made, and about the pig? Only fool's-mud would do so. And so then I am fool's-mud.

Nothing counts. Nothing can possibly count.

Regret, passion, cowardice, hope, bravery, unrest, pain, the love-sense, the soul-sense, the beauty-sense - all for nothing! What can a handful of rich black mud in a pig's yard have to do with these? I am a handful of rich black mud - a fool-woman, fool's-mud.

All on earth that I need to do is to lie still in the hot sun and feel the pig rolling and floundering and slushing about. It were folly to waste my mud-nerves on wondering. - Be quiet, fool-woman, let things be. Your soul is a fool's-mud soul and is governed by the pig; your heart is a fool's-mud heart, and wants nothing beyond the pig; your life is a fool's-mud life and is the pig's life.

Something within me shrieks now, but I do not know what it is - nor why it shrieks.

It groans and moans.

There is no satisfaction in being a fool - no satisfaction at all.

March 18

But yes. It all matters, whether or no. Nature is one long battle and the never-ending perishing of the weak. I must grind and grind away. I have no choice. And I must know that I grind.

Fool, genius, young lonely woman - I must go round and round in the life within, for how many years the Devil knows. After that my soul must go round and round, for how many centuries the Devil knows.

What a master-mind is that of the Devil! The world is a wondrous scheme. For me it is a scheme that is black with woe. But there may be in the world some one who finds it beautiful Real Life.

I wonder as I write this Portrayal if there will be one person to read it and see a thing that is mingled with every word. It is something that you must feel, that must fascinate you, the like of which you have never before met with.

It is the unparalleled individuality of me.

I wish I might write it in so many words of English. But that is not possible. If I have put it in every word and if you feel it and are fascinated, then I have done very well.

I am marvelously clever if I have done so.

I know that I am marvelously clever. But I have need of all my peculiar genius to show you my individuality - my aloneness.

I am alone out on my sand and barrenness. I should be alone if my sand and barrenness were crowded with a thousand people each filled with melting sympathy for me - though it would be unspeakably sweet.

People say of me, "She's peculiar." They do not understand me. If they did, they would say so oftener and with emphasis.

And so I try to put my individuality in the quality of my diction, in my method of handling words.

My conversation plainly shows this individuality - more than shows it indeed. My conversation hurls it violently at people's heads. My conversation - when I choose - makes people turn around in their chairs and stare and give me all of their attention. They admire me, though their admiration is mixed decidedly with other feelings.

I like to be admired.

It soothes my vanity.

When you read this Portrayal you will admire me. You will surely have to admire me.

And so this is life and everything matters.

But just now I will stop writing and go down-stairs to my dinner. There is a porterhouse steak, broiled rare, and some green onions. Oh, they are good! And when one is to have a porterhouse steak for one's dinner - and some green young onions - one doesn't give a tuppenny damn whether anything else matters or not.

March 19

On a day when the sky is like lead and a dull, tempestuous wilderness of gray clouds adds a dreariness to the sand, there is added to the loneliness of my life a deep bitterness of gall and wormwood.

Out of my bitterness it is easy for bad to come.

Surely Badness is a deep black pool wherein one may drown dullness and Nothingness.

I do not know Badness well. It is something material that seems a great way off now but that might creep nearer and nearer as I became less and less young.

But now when the day is of the leaden dullness I look at Badness and long for it. I am young and all alone, and everything that is good is beyond my reach. But all that is bad - surely that is within the reach of every one.

I wish for a long pageant of bad things to come and whirl and rage through this strange leaden life of mine and break the spell.

Why should it not be Badness instead of Death? Death, it seems, will bring me but a change of agony. Badness would perhaps so crowd my life with its vivid phenomena that they would act as a narcotic to the racked nerves of my Nothingness. It would be an outlet - and possibly I could forget some things.

I think just now of a woman who lived long ago and in whom the world at large seems not to have found anything admirable. I mean Messalina Valeria, the wife of the stupid emperor Claudius. I have conceived a profound admiration for this historic wanton. She may not indeed have had anything to forget; she may not have suffered. But she had the strength of will to take what she wanted, to do as she liked, to live as she chose to live.

It is admirable and beautiful beyond expression to sacrifice and give up and wait for love of that good that gives in itself a just reward. And only next to this is the throwing to the winds of all restraint when the good holds itself aloof and gives nothing. We are weak, contemptible fools who do not grasp the resources within our reach when there is no just reward for our restraint. Why do we not take what we want of the various temptations? It is not that we are virtuous. It is that we are cowards.

And is it worth while to remain true to an ideal that offers only the vaguest hopes of realization? It is not philosophy. When one has made up one's mind that one wants a dish of hot stewed mushrooms, and set one's heart on it, should one scorn a handful of raw evaporated apples, if one were starving, for the sake of the phantom dish of hot stewed mushrooms? Should one say, "Let me starve, but I will never descend to evaporated apples; I will have nothing but a dish of hot stewed mushrooms"? If one is sure one will have stewed mushrooms finally, before one dies of starvation, then very well. One should wait for them and take nothing else.

But it is not in my good peripatetic philosophy to pass by the Badness that the gods provide for the sake of a far-away, always-unrealized ideal, however brilliant, however beautiful, however golden.

When the lead is in the sky and in my life, a vision of Badness looms up on the horizon and looks at me and beckons with a fascinating finger. Then I say to myself: What is the use of this unsullied, struggling soul; this unbesmirched, empty heart; this treasureless, innocent mind; this insipid maid's-body? There are no good things for them. But here, to be sure, are fascinating, glittering bad things - the goods that the gods provide, the compensation of the Devil.

Comes Death, some day, I said - but to die, in the sight of glittering bad things - and I only nineteen! These glittering things appear fair.

There is really nothing evil in the world. Some things appear distorted and unnatural because they have been badly done. Had they been perfect in compensation and execution they would strike one only with admiration at their fine, iridescent lights. You remember Don Juan and Haidee. That to be sure was not evil in any event - they loved each other. But if they had had only a passing, if intense, fancy for one another, who would call it evil? Who would call it anything but wonderful, charming, enchanting? The Devil's bad things - like the Devil's good things - may gleam and glisten, oh, how they may gleam and glisten! I have seen them do so, not only in a poem of Byron's - but in the life that is.

Always when the lead is in the sky I would like to cultivate thoroughly this branch of the vineyard. Now doesn't it make you shiver to think of this dear little Mary MacLane wandering unloved through dark by-ways and deadly labyrinths? It makes me shiver. But it needn't. If I am to wander unloved, why not as well wander there as through Nothingness?

I fancy it must be wonderfully easy to become used to the many-sided Badness. I have lived my nineteen years in the midst of Nothingness, and I have not yet become used to it. It has sharp knives in it, has Nothingness. Badness may have some sharp knives also - but there are other things. Yes, there are other things.

Kind Devil, if you are not to fetch me Happiness, then slip from off your great steel key-ring a bright little key to the door of the glittering, gleaming bad things, and give it me, and show me the way, and wish me joy.

I would like to live about seven years of judicious Badness, and then Death, if you will. Nineteen years of damnable Nothingness, seven years of judicious Badness - and then Death. A noble ambition! But might it not be worse? If not that, then nineteen years of damnable Nothingness, and then Death. No. When the lead is in the sky that does not appeal to me. My versatile mind turns to the seven years of judicious Badness.

There is nothing in the world without its element of Badness. It is in Literature; it is in every art - in pictures - sculpture - even in music. There are certain fine, deep, minute passages in Beethoven and in Chopin that tell of things wonderfully, sublimely bad. Chopin one can not understand. - Is there any one in the world who can understand him? - But we know at once that there is the Badness - and it is music!

There is the element of Badness in me.

I long to cultivate my element of Badness.

Badness compared to Nothingness is beautiful.

And so, then, I wait also for some one to come over the hill with things other than Happiness.

But whatever I wait for, nothing comes.

March 20

There were pictures in the red sunset sky to-day. I looked at them and was racked with passions of desire. I fancied to myself that I could have any of the good things in the pictures for the asking and the waiting. The while I knew that when the sunset should fade from the sky I would be overwhelmed by my heaviest woe.

There was a picture of intense peace. There were stretches of flat, green country, and oak-trees and aspens, and a still, still lake. In the dim distance you could see fields of wheat and timothy-grass that moved a little as if in the wind. You could fancy the cows feeding just below the brow of the near hills, and a hawk floating and wheeling among the clouds. A rainbow arched over the lake. There is nothing lacking here, I thought. "Life and health and peace possessing." Give me this, kind Devil.

There was a picture of endless, limitless strength. There were the oak-trees again but bereft now of every leaf, and the bristling, jagged rocks back of them were not more coldly staunch. The sun poured brilliantly bright upon them. A river flowed unmoved and quiet between yellow clay banks. A tornado might sweep over this and not one twig would be disturbed, not one ripple would come to the river. "Is it not fine!" I said to myself. No feeling, no self-analysis, no aching, no pain - and the strength of the Philistines. Oh, kind Devil, I entreat you, let me have that!

There was a picture of untrammeled revel and forgetfulness. There were fields of swaying daffodils and red lilies. The young shrubs tossed their heads and were joyous. Lambs gamboled and the happy meadow-lark knew whereof she sang.

The winds with wonder whist
Smoothly the waters kissed.

Be carefree, be light-hearted, be wicked, - above all, forget. The deeds are what you will; the time is now; the aftermath is nothing; the day of reckoning is never. Love things lightly, take all that you see, and to the winds with regret! Gracious Devil, I whispered intensely, give me this and no other!

There was a picture of raging elements. "The winds blew, and the rains descended and the floods came." The sky was overcast with rolling clouds. The air was heavy with unrest. There was a gray stone house set upon a rocky point, and I had momentary glimpses of an unquiet sea below it. Back on the surface of the land slender trees were waving wildly in the gale. The wind and the rain were saying, "Damn you, little earth, I have you now, - I will rend and ruin you." They whipped and raged in frenzied joy. The little earth liked it. The elements whirled and whistled round the gray stone house. A lurid light came from a ghastly moon between clouds. The entire scene was desolately savage and forlorn, but attractive. As I listened in fancy to that shrieking wailing wind, and saw green branches jerked and twisted asunder in the storm, my barren, defrauded heart leaped and exulted. If I could live in the midst of this and be beaten and shaken roughly, would not that deep sense forget to ache? Kind Devil, pray send me some storms. It is Nothingness that bears down heavy.

There was a picture of an exalted spiritual life. There was that strange bright Light. And the things in the picture were those things alone in this world that are real, and the only things that count. The old soft green of the old, old rolling hills was the green of love - the earth-love and the love that comes from beyond the earth. The air and the blue water and the sunshine were so beautifully real and true that except for their deep-reaching, passionate tenderness human strength could not endure them. There were lanes of climbing vines and white violets. Was it my fancy that brought their thin fragrance to me over piles of billowy clouds? There was something there that was old - old as the race. Those green valleys were the same as when the mists first lifted from the earth. As I looked my life stood still. My soul shivered faintly. As I looked I felt nearer my God to thee - though I have no God and everything is away from me, nothing tender comes to me.

Still it was nearer my God to thee.

A voice came out of the far, far distant ages and said very gently: "All these shadows are falling in vain. You are blinded and bewildered in the darkness - the darkness is deep - deep. There is not one dim ray of light. Your feet falter and stumble. You can not see. But the shadows are falling in vain."

I ask you, why is this life not mine?

I implore and wring my hands in agonized entreaty, and almost it seems sometimes my fingers can grasp these things - but there is something cold and strong between them and me. Oh, what is it!

There was a picture of various castles in Spain. They were most beautiful, were those castles. The lights that shone on the battlements were soft bright lights. For one thing, I fancied I saw myself and Fame with me. Fame is very fine. The sun and moon and stars may go dark in the heavens. Bitter rain may fall out of the clouds. But never mind. Fame has a sun and moon and gently brilliant stars of her own, and these, shining once, shine always. The green river may run dry in the land. But Fame has a green river that never runs dry. One may wander over the face of the earth. But Fame is herself a refuge. One may be a target for stones and mud. Yes - but Fame stands near with her arm laid across one's shoulders - as no other arm can be laid across one's shoulders. Fame would fill several empty places. Fame would continue to fill them for some years.

Fame, if you please, Devil.

There was a picture of Death. I saw a figure lying in the midst of a desert that was rather like my sand and barrenness. Not far off a wolf sat on his haunches and waited for the end. A buzzard perched near and waited also. They both appeared hungry. It seemed as though the end might come quickly.

Let it come, kind Devil.

And a wolf and a buzzard are better than an undertaker and some worms. Although that doesn't much matter.

And oh, there again was the dearest picture of all - the red, red picture of Happiness for me, Happiness with the sunshine falling on the Heaven-kissing hills! There was I, and I loved and was loved. I - out of loneliness into perfect Happiness! The yellow-gold of the glorious hot sun melted and poured over the earth and over everything that was there. The river ran and rippled and sang the most sweetly glad song that ever river sang. Winged things sparkled in the gold light and flew down the sky.

> *The wonderful air was over me;*
> *The wonderful wind was shaking the tree.*

The silent voices in the air rang out like flutes and clarionets. And the love of the man-Devil for me was everywhere - above me, around me, within me. It would last for a number of beautiful yellow-gold days. I - out of the anguish of loneliness into this!

My heart is filled with desire.

My soul is filled with passion.

My life is a life of longing.

All pictures fade before this picture. They fade completely. When the sun itself faded I gazed over my sand and barrenness with blurred, unseeing eyes and wished only with a heavy, desolate spirit for the coming of the Devil.

March 21

Some people think, absurdly enough, that to be Scotch or descended from the Scottish clans is to be rather strong, rather conservative, firm in faith, and all that. The idea is one that should be completely exploded by this time. I think that the Scotch as a nation are the most difficult of all to characterize. Their traits and tendencies cover a wider field than those of any other. To be Scotch is to be anything. There is no man so narrow as a Scotchman. There is no man so broad as a Scotchman. There is no mind so versatile as a Scotch mind. At the same time only a Scotch mind is capable of clinging with bull-dog tenacity to one idea. A Scotch heart, out of all, and through all, can be as true as death. A Scotch heart - the same one - can be as cunning and treacherous as false human hearts are made. To be English is to have limits; the Germans, the French, the Russians - they have all some inevitable attributes to modify their genius.

But one may be anything - anything, if one is Scotch.

Always I think of the cruel, hardened, ferocious, weather-beaten, kilted Clan MacLean wandering over the bleak winter hills, fighting the powerful MacDonalds and MacGregors - and generally wiping them from the earth, - marching away with merrily shrieking pipes from fields of withered, blood-soaked heather - and all this merely to gather intensified life for me. I feel that the causes of my tragedy began long, long ago from remote germs.

My Scotch blood added to my genius sense has made me into a dangerous chemical compound.

By analyzing I have brought an almost clear portrait of myself up before my mind's eyes.

When I was a child I did not analyze knowingly, but the child was this same genius, though I am one of the kind that changes widely and decidedly in the years. This weary unhappiness is not a matter of development.

When I was a child I felt dumbly what I feel now less dumbly. At the age of five I used sometimes to weep silently in the night - I did not know why. It was that I felt my aloneness, my foreignness to all things. I felt the heavy, heavy weight of life - and I was only five.

I was only five, and it seems a thousand years ago. But sometimes back through the long, winding unused passages of my mind I hear that silent sobbing of the child and the unnamed wailing of a tiny, tired soul.

It mingles with the bitter Nothingness of the grown young woman, and oh, with it all - with it all I am so unhappy!

There is something subtly *Scotch* in all this.

But Scotch or Indian or Japanese, there is no stopping of the pain.

March 22

I fear, do you know, fine world, that you do not yet know me really well - particularly me of the flesh. Me of the peculiar philosophy and the unhappy spirit you know rather well by now, unless you are stupider than I think you are. But you might pass me in the street - you might spend the day with me and never suspect that I am I. Though for the matter of that, even if I had set before you a most graphic and minutely drawn portrait of myself, I am certainly clever enough to act a quite different role if I chose - when you came to spend the day. Still, if the world at large is to know me as I desire it to know me without ever seeing me, I shall have to bring myself into closer personal range with it - and you may rise in your seats and focus your opera glasses, stare with open mouths, stand on your hind-legs and gape - I will myself turn on glaring green and orange lights from the wings.

I believe that it's the trivial little facts about anything that describe it the most effectively. In *Vanity Fair*, when Becky Sharpe was describing young Crawley in a letter to her friend Amelia, she stated that he had hay-colored whiskers and straw-colored hair. And knowing this you feel that you know much more about the Crawley than you would if Miss Sharpe had not mentioned these things. And yet it is but a mere matter of color!

When you think that Dickens was extremely fond of cats you feel at once that nothing could be more fitting. Somehow that marvelously mingled humor and pathos and gentle irony seem to go exceeding well with a fondness for soft, green-eyed purring things. If you had not read the pathetic humor but knew about Dickens and his warm feline friends you might easily expect such things from him.

When you read somewhere that Dr. Johnson is said never to have washed his neck and his ears, and then go and read some of his powerful, original philosophy, you say to yourself, "Yes, I can readily believe that this man never troubled himself to wash his neck and his ears." I, for my part, having read some of the things he has written, can not reconcile myself to the fact that he ever washed any part of his anatomy. I admire Dr. Johnson - though I wash my own neck occasionally.

When you think of Napoleon amusing himself by taking a child on his knee and pinching it to hear it cry, you feel an ecstatic little wave of pleasure at the perfect fitness of things. You think of his hard, brilliant, continuous victories, and you suspect that Napoleon Bonaparte lived but to gratify Napoleon Bonaparte. When you think of the heavy, muscular man smilingly pinching the child, you are quite sure of it. Such a method of amusement for that king among men is so exquisitely appropriate that you wonder why you had not thought of it yourself.

So then yes. I believe strenuously in the efficacy of seemingly trivial facts as portrayers of one's character - one's individual humanness.

Now I will set down for your benefit divers and varied observations relative to me - an interesting one of womankind and nineteen years, and curious and fascinating withal.

Well then.

Nearly every day I make me a plate of hot rich fudge, with brown sugar, - (I should be an entirely different person if I made it with white sugar - and the fudge would not be nearly so good) - and take it up-stairs to my room, with a book or a newspaper. My mind then takes in a part of what is contained in the book or the newspaper, and the stomach of the MacLane takes in all of what is on the plate. I sit by my window in a miserable uncomfortable stiff-backed chair, but I relieve the strain by resting my feet on the edge of the low bureau. Usually the book that I read is an old dilapidated bound volume of that erstwhile periodical *Our Young Folks*. It is a thing that possesses a charm for me. I never grow tired of it. As I eat my nice brown little squares of fudge I read about a boy whose name is Jack Hazard and who, J.T. Trowbridge informs the reader, is doing his best, and who seems to find it somewhat difficult. I believe I could repeat pages of J.T. Trowbridge from memory, and that ancient bound volume has become a part of my life. I stop reading after a few minutes but I continue to eat - and gaze at the toes of my shoes which need polishing badly, or at the conglomeration of brilliant pictures on my bed-room wall, or out of the window at the children playing in the street. But mostly I gaze without seeing, and my versatile mind is engaged either in nothing or in repeating something over and over, such as, "But the sweet face of Lucy Gray will never more be seen." Only I am not aware that I have been repeating it until I happen to remember it afterward. Always the fudge is very good, and I eat and eat with unabated relish until all the little squares are gone. A very little of my fudge has been known to give some people a most terrific stomach-ache - but my own digestive organs seem to like nothing better. It's so brown - so rich!

I amuse myself with this for an hour or two in the afternoon. Then I go down-stairs and work a while. -

There are few things that annoy me so much as to be called a young lady. I am no lady - as any one could see by close inspection, and the phrase has an odious sound. I would rather be called a sweet little thing, or a fallen woman, or a sensible girl - though they would each be equally a lie. -

Always I am glad when night comes and I can sleep. My mind works busily repeating things while I divest myself of my various dusty garments. As I remove a dozen or two of hair-pins from my head I say within me:

> You are old, father William, one would hardly suppose
> That your eye is as steady as ever;
> Yet you balanced an eel on the end of your nose -
> What made you so awfully clever?

Always I take a little clock to bed with me and hang it by a cord at the head of my bed, for company. I have named the clock Little Fido because it is so constant and ticks always. It is beginning to stand in the same relation to me as J.T. Trowbridge's magazine. If I were to go away from here I should take Little Fido and the magazine with me. -

Every morning, being beautifully hungry after my walk, I eat three boiled eggs out of the shell for my breakfast. The while I mentally thank the kind Providence that invented hens. Also I eat bits of toast. I have my breakfast alone - because the rest of the family are still sleeping, - sitting at a corner of the kitchen table. I enjoy those three eggs and those bits of toast. Usually when I am eating my breakfast I am thinking of three things: the varying prices of any eggs that are fit to eat; of what to do after I've finished my house-work and before lunch; and of my one friend. And I meditatively and gently kick the leg of the table with the heel of my right foot. -

I have beautiful hair. -

In the front of my shirt-waist there are nine cambric handkerchiefs cunningly distributed. My figure is very pretty, to be sure, but not so well developed as it will be in five years - if I live so long. And so I help it out materially with nine cambric handkerchiefs. You can see by my picture that my waist curves gracefully out. Only it is not all flesh - some of it is handkerchief. It amuses me to do this. It is one of my petty vanities. -

Likewise by an ingenious arrangement of my striped moreen petticoat I contrive to display a more evident pair of hips than Nature seems to have intended for me at this stage. Doubtless they also will take on fuller proportions when some years have passed. Still I am not dissatisfied with them as they are. It is not as if they were too well developed - in which case I should have need of all my skill in arranging my moreen petticoat so as to lessen their effect. It is easy enough to add on to these things, but one would experience serious difficulty in attempting to take from them. I hate that heavy, aggressive kind of hips. Moreover small graceful ones are desirable when one is nineteen. The world at large judges you more leniently on that account - usually. Narrow shapely hips may give one an effect of youth and harmlessness which is a distinct advantage, when, for instance, one is writing a Portrayal and so will be at the world's mercy. I believe I should not think of attempting to write a Portrayal if I had hips like a pair of saddle-bags. Certainly it would avail me nothing. -

Sometimes I look at my face in a mirror and find it not plain but ugly. And there are other times when I look and find it not pretty but beautiful with a Madonna-like sweetness. -

I told you I might say more about the liver that is within me before I have done. Well then, I will say this: that the world, if it had a liver like mine, would be very different from what it is. The world would be many-colored and mobile and passionate and nervous and high-strung and intensely alive and poetic and romantic and philosophical and egotistic and pathetic, and oh, racked to the verge of madness with the spirit of unrest - if the world had a liver like mine. It is not all of these now. It is rather stupid. Gods and little fishes! would not the world be wonderful if all in it were like me? And it would be if it had a liver like mine. For it is my liver mostly that makes me what I am - apart from my genius. My liver is fine and perfect, but sensitive, and, well - it's a dangerous thing to have within you.

It is the liver of the MacLanes.

It is the foundation of the curious castle of my existence.

And after all, fine brave stupid world, you may be grateful to the Devil that yours is not like it. -

I have seventeen little engraved portraits of Napoleon that I keep in one of my bureau-drawers. Often late in the evening, between nine and ten o'clock, when I come in from a walk over the sand and barrenness, I take these pictures from the drawer and gaze at them carefully a long time and think of that man until I am stirred to the depths.

And then easily and naturally I fall in love with Napoleon.

If only he were living now, I think to myself, I would make my way to him by whatever means and cast myself at his feet. I would entreat him with the most passionate humbleness of spirit to take me into his life for three days. To be the wife of Napoleon for three days - that would be enough for a life-time! I would be much more than satisfied if I could get three such days out of life.

I suppose a man is either a villain or a fool, though some of them seem to be a judicious mingling of both. The type of the distinct villain is preferable to a mixture of the two, and to a plain fool. I like a villain anyway - a villain that can be rather tender at times. And so then as I look at the pictures I fall in love with the incomparable Napoleon. The seventeen pictures are all different and all alike. I fall in love with each picture separately.

In one he is ugly and unattractive - and strong. I fall in love with him.

In another he is cruel and heartless and utterly selfish - and strong. I fall in love with him.

In a third he has a fat, pudgy look, and is quite insignificant - and strong. I fall in love with him.

In a fourth he is grandly sad and full of despair - and strong. I fall in love with him.

In the fifth he is greasy and greedy and common-looking - and strong. I fall in love with him.

In the sixth he is masterly and superior and exalted - and strong. I fall in love with him.

In the seventh he is romantic and beautiful - and strong. I fall in love with him.

In the eighth he is obviously sensual and reeking with uncleanness - and strong. I fall in love with him.

In the ninth he is unearthly and mysterious and unreal - and strong. I fall in love with him.

In the tenth he is black and sullen-browed and ill-humored - and strong. I fall in love with him.

In the eleventh he is inferior and trifling and inane - and strong! I fall in love with him.

In the twelfth he is rough and ruffianly and uncouth - and strong. I fall in love with him.

In the thirteenth he is little and wolfish and vile - and strong. I fall in love with him.

In the fourteenth he is calm and confident and intellectual - and strong. I fall in love with him.

In the fifteenth he is vacillating and fretful and his mouth is like a woman's - and still he is strong. I fall in love with him.

In the sixteenth he is slow and heavy and brutal - and strong. I fall in love with him.

In the seventeenth he is rather tender - and strong. I fall vividly in love with him.

Napoleon was rather like the Devil, I think as I sit in the straight-backed chair with my feet on the bureau and gaze long and intently at the seventeen pictures, late in the evening.

Then I wearily put them away, maddened with the sense of Nothingness, and take Little Fido and go to bed. -

Sometimes early in the evening just before dinner I sit in the stiff-backed chair with my elbows on the window-sill and my head resting on one hand, and I look out of the window at a Pile of Stones and a Barrel of Lime. These are in the vacant lot next to this house.

I fix my eyes intently on the Pile of Stones and the Barrel of Lime. And I fix my thoughts on them also. And some of my widest thoughts come to me then.

I feel an overwhelming wave of a kind of pantheism which, at the moment I feel it, begins to grow less and less and continues in this until finally it dwindles to a Pile of Stones and a Barrel of Lime.

I feel at the moment that the universe is a Pile of Stones and a Barrel of Lime. They alone are the Real Things.

Take anything at any point and deceive yourself into thinking that you are happy with it. But look at it heavily; dig down underneath the layers and layers of rose-colored mists and you will find that your Thing is a Pile of Stones and a Barrel of Lime.

A struggle or two, a fight, an agony, a passing - and then the only Real Things: a Pile of Stones and a Barrel of Lime.

Damn everything, beginning with that fool-God that you have set up for yourself and ending with the Devil. Afterward you will find that you have done all your damning for naught. For there is nothing worthy of damnation except a Pile of Stones and a Barrel of Lime - and they are not damnable. They have never harmed you, and moreover they alone are the Real Things.

Julius Caesar made many wars. Sir Frances Drake went sailing over the seas. It was all child's play and counts for nothing. Here are a Pile of Stones and a Barrel of Lime.

And so this is how it is early in the evening just before dinner, when I sit in the uncomfortable chair with my elbows on the window-sill and my head resting on one hand. -

I have two pictures of Marie Bashkirtseff high upon my wall. Often I lean my head on the back of the chair with my feet on the bureau - always with my feet on the bureau - and look at these pictures.

In one of them she is eighteen years old and wears a green frock which is extremely becoming - of which fact the person inside seems fully aware. The other picture is taken from her last photograph, when she was twenty-four.

Marie Bashkirtseff is a very beautiful creature. And evidently *she* is not obliged to arrange a moreen petticoat over her plumpness. She has a wonderfully voluptuous look for a woman of eighteen years. In the later picture vanity is written in every line of her graceful form and in every feature of that charming face. The picture fairly yells: "I am Marie Bashkirtseff - and, oh, I am splendid!"

And as I look at the pictures I am glad. For though she was admirable and splendid, and all, she was no such genius as I. She had a genius of her own it is true. But the Bashkirtseff, with her voluptuous body and her attractive personality, is after all a bit ordinary. My genius though not powerful is rare and deep and no one has ever had or ever will have a genius like it.

- Mary MacLane, if you live - if you live, my darling, the world will one day recognize your genius. And when once the world has recognized such genius as this - oh, then no one will ever think of profaning it by comparing it with any Bashkirtseff! -

But I would give up this genius eagerly, gladly - at once and forever - for one dear, bright day free from loneliness.

The portraits of the Bashkirtseff are certainly beautiful but there is something about them that is - well, not common, but bourgeois at least, as if she were a German waitress of unusual appearance, or an aristocratic shop-girl, or a nurse with good taste who would walk out on pleasant forenoons wheeling a go-cart - something of that sort. Perhaps it is because her neck is too short, or because her wrists are too muscular-looking. I thank a gracious Devil as I look at the pictures that I have not these particular points and that particular bourgeois air. I am bound to confess that I have one of my own, but mine is Highland Scotch - and anyway, I am Mary MacLane.

Marie Bashkirtseff is beautiful enough, however, that she can easily afford to look rather second-rate.

I like to look at my two pictures of her. -

I value money literally for its own sake. I like the feeling of dollars and quarters rubbing softly together in my hand. Always it reminds me of those lovely chestfuls of gold that Captain Kidd buried - no one seems to know just where. Usually I keep some fairly-clean dollars and quarters to handle. "Money is so nice!" I say to myself. -

If you think, fine world, that I am always interesting and striking and admirable, always original, showing up to good advantage in a company of persons, and all - why then you are beautifully mistaken. There are times to be sure when I can rivet the attention of the crowd heavily upon myself. But mostly I am the very least among all the idiots and fools. I show up to the poorest possible advantage.

Of several ways that are mine there is one that gives me a distinct and hopeless air of insignificance. I have seen people, having met me for the first time, glance carelessly at me as if they were quite sure I had not an idea in my brain - if I had a brain; as if they wondered why I had been asked here; as if they were fully aware that they had but to fiddle and It would dance. Sometimes before this highly intellectual gathering breaks up I manage to make them change their minds with astonishing suddenness. But nearly always I don't bother about it at all. I go among people occasionally because it amuses me. It may be a literary club where they talk theosophy, or it may be a Cornish dance where they have pastry and saffron cake and the chief amusement is sending beer-bottles at various heads, or it may be a lady-like circle of married women with cerise silk drop-skirts and white kid gloves, drinking chocolate in the afternoon and talking about something "shocking!"

And often, as I say, I am the least of them.

Genius is an odd thing. -

When certain of my skirts need sewing, they don't get sewed. I simply pin the rents in them together and it lasts as long or longer than if I had seated myself in my stiff-backed chair with a needle and thread and mended them - like a sensible girl. (I hate a sensible girl.)

Though I have never yet hurriedly pinned up a torn flounce or several inches of skirt-binding without saying softly to myself, using a trite, expressive phrase, "Certainly it's a hell of a way to do." Still I never take a needle and mend my garments. I couldn't anyway. I never learned to sew, and I don't intend ever to learn. It reminds me too much of a constipated dress-maker.

And so I pin up the torn places - though, as I say, I never fail to make use of the quaint, expressive phrase.

All of which a reasonably astute reader will recognize as an important point in the portraying of any character - whether mine or the queen of Spain's. -

I had for my dinner to-day some whole-wheat bread, some liver-and-bacon, and some green, green early asparagus. While I was eating these the world seemed a very nice place indeed. -

I never see people walking along on the opposite side of the street, as I sit by my window, without wondering who they are, and how they live, and how ugly they would look if their bodies were not adorned with clothes. Always I feel certain that some of them are bow-legged. -

And sometimes I see a woman in a fearful state of deshabille walk across the vacant lot next to this: "A plague on me," I say then to myself, "if I ever become middle-aged and if my entire being seems to tip up in the front, and if I go about with no stays so that when I tie an apron around my waist my upper fatness hangs over the band like a natural blouse." -

And so - I could go on writing all night these seemingly trivial but really significant details relating to the outer genius. But these will answer. These to any one who knows things will be a revelation.

Sometimes you know things, fine brave world.

You must know likewise that though I do ordinary things, when *I* do them they cease to be ordinary. I make fudge - and a sweet girl makes fudge, but there are ways and ways of doing things. This entire affair of the fudge is one of my uniquest points.

No sweet girl makes fudge and eats it, as I make fudge and eat it.

So it is.

But oh - who is to understand all this? Who will understand any of this Portrayal? My unhappy soul has delved in shadows far, far beyond and below.

March 23

My philosophy, I find after very little analysis, approaches precariously near to sensualism.

It is wonderful how many sides there can be to just one character.

Nature with all those suns, and all those hill-tops, and all those rivers, and all those stars, is inscrutable - intangible - maddening. It affects one with unutterable joy and anguish, but no one can ever begin to understand what it means.

Human nature is yet more inscrutable - and nothing appears on the surface. One can have no idea of the things buried in the minds of one's acquaintances. And mostly they are fools and have no idea themselves of what germs are in themselves - of what they are capable. And in most minds it is true the dormant devils never awaken and never are known.

It is another sign of my analytical genius, that I, aged nineteen, recognize the devils in my character. I have not the slightest wish, since things are as they are with me, to rid myself of them. There is in me much more of evil than of good. Genius like mine must needs have with it manifold bad. "I have in me the germ of every crime." I have no desire to destroy these germs. I should be glad indeed to have them develop into a ravaging disease. Something in this dreadful confusion would then give way. My wooden heart and my soul would cry out in the darkness less heavily, less bitterly.

They want something - they know not what.

I give them poison.

They snatch it and eat it hungrily.

Then they are not so hungry. They become quieter.

The ravaging disease soothes them to sleep - it descends on them like rain in the autumn. And so.

When I hurry over my sand and barrenness my vivid passions come to me - or when I sit and look at the horizon. When I walk slowly I consider calmly the question of how much evil I should need to kill off my finer feelings, to poison thoroughly this soul of unrest and this wooden heart so that they would never more be conscious of too-brilliant Lights, and to make myself over into a quite different creature.

A little evil would do - a little of a fine, good quality.

I should like a man to come (it is always a man, have you ever noticed? - whatever one contemplates when one is of womankind and young). I should like a man to come, I said calmly to myself to-day as I walked slowly over my barrenness - a perfect villain to come and fascinate me and lead me with strong gentle allurements to what would be technically termed my ruin. And as the world views such things it would be my ruin. But as I view such things it would not be ruin. It would be a new lease on life.

Yes. I should like a man to come - any man so that he is strong and thoroughly a villain, and so that he fascinates me. Particularly he must fascinate me. There must be no falling in love about it. I doubt if I could fascinate him but I should ask him quite humbly to lead me to my ruin.

I have never yet seen the man who would not readily respond to such an appeal.

This villain would be no exception.

I would then jerk my life out of this Nothingness by the roots. Fare-well, a long farewell, I would say. Then I would go forth with the man to my ruin. The man would be bad to his heart's core. And after living but a short time with him my shy, sensitive soul would be irretrievably poisoned and polluted. The defilement of so sacred and beautiful a thing as marriage is surely the darkest evil that can come to a life. And so everything within me that had turned toward that too-bright Light would then drink deep of the lees of death.

The thirst of this incessant unrest and longing, this weariness of *self*, would be quenched completely.

My life would be like fertile soil planted thickly with rank wild mustard. On every square inch of soil there would be a dozen sprouts of wild mustard. There would be no room - no room at all - for an anemone to grow. If one should start up, instantly it would be choked and overrun with wild mustard.

- But no anemone would start up. -

My life now is a life of pain and revolt.

My life darkened and partly killed would be more than content to drift along with the current.

Oh, it would be a rest!

The Christians sing, there is rest for the weary, on the other side of Jordan, where the tree of life is blooming. But that rest of course is for the Christians. My rest will have to come on this side of Jordan. Let the impress of a thoroughly evil and strong man be stamped upon my inner life and I am convinced there would come a wonderful settled quiet over it. Its spirit would be broken. It would rest. Why not? I have no virtue-sense. Nothing to me is of any consequence except to be rid of this unrest and pain. Yes, surely I might rest.

The coming of the man-Devil would bring rest. But am I fool enough to think that marriage - the real marriage - is possible for me?

This other thing is within the reach of every one - of fools and geniuses alike - and of all that come between.

And so I want a fascinating wicked man to come and make me positively, rather than negatively, wicked. I feel a terrific wave of utter weariness. My life lies fallow. I am tired of sitting here. The sand and barrenness is gray with age. And I am gray with age.

Happiness - the red of the sunset sky - is the intensest desire of my life. But I will grasp eagerly anything else that is offered me - *anything*.

The poisoning of my soul - the passing of my unrest - would rouse my mental power. My genius would receive a wonderful impetus from it. You would marvel, good world, at the things I should write. Not that they would be exalted - not that they would surge upward. Do men gather grapes of thorns or figs of thistles? But they would be marvels of fire and intensity. I should no longer exhaust much of my energy in grinding, grinding within. The things that would come of the thorns and thistles would excite your astonishment and admiration, though they be not grapes and figs.

And as for me - the real me - the creature imbued with a spirit of intense femininity, with a spirit of an intense sense of Love - with a spirit like that of the Magdalene who loved too much, with the very soul of unrest and Nothingness - this thing would vanish swiftly into oblivion, and I, a despoiled animal, should go down a dark world and feel not.

March 25

One of the remarkable points about my life is that it is so completely, hopelessly alone - a lonely, lonely life. This book of mine contains but one character - myself.

There is also the Devil - as a possibility.

And there is also the anemone lady - my dearest beloved - as a memory.

I have read books that were written to portray but one character and there were various people brought in to help in the portraying. But my one friend is gone, and there is no person who enters into my inner life in the very least. I am always alone. I might mingle with people intimately every hour of my life - still I should be alone.

Always alone - alone.

Not even a God to worship.

How do I bear this! How do I get through the days and days!

And oh, when it all comes over me, what frightful rage - what long agony of my breaking heart - what utter woe!

When the stars shine down upon me with cold hatred; when miles and miles of barrenness stretch out around me and envelop me in its weary, weary Nothingness; when the wind blows over me like the breath of a vicious giant; when the ugly, ugly sun radiates centuries of hard, heavy bitterness around me from its stinging rays; when the sky maddens me with its cold careless blue; when the rivers that are flowing over the earth send echoes to me of their hateful voices; when I hear wild geese honking in bitter wailing melody; when bristling edges of jagged rocks cut sharply into my tired life; when drops of rain fall on me and pierce me like steel points; when the voices in the air shriek little-minded malice in my ears; when the green of Nature is the green of spitefulness and cruelty; when the red, red of the setting sun burns and consumes me with its horrid feverish effervescence; when I feel the all-hatred of the Universe for its poor little earth-bugs: then it is that I approach nearest to Rest.

The softnesses are my Unrest.

I do not want those bitter things.

But I must have them if I would rest.

I want the softnesses and I want Rest!

Oh, dear faint soul, it is hard - hard for us.

We are sick with loneliness.

Now and again I have torturing glimpses of a Paradise. And I feel my soul in its pain every moment of my life. Otherwise, how gladly would I deny the existence of a soul and a life to come!

For my soul is beset with Nothingness, and the Paradise that shows itself is not for me.

Hatred, after all, is the easiest thing of all to bear.

If you have been forgotten by the one who must have made you, and if you have been left alone of human beings all your life - all your nineteen years, - then, when at last you see some one looking toward you with beautiful eyes, and extending to you a beautiful hand, and showing you a beautiful heart wherein is just a little of beautiful sympathy for you - for you - oh, that is harder than anything to bear. Harder than the loneliness and the bitterness - and the tears are nearer and nearer.

But one would be hurt often, often for the sake of the beautiful things. Yes, one would gladly be hurt long and often.

I shall never forget how it was with me when I first saw the beautiful eyes of the dearest anemone lady when they were looking gently - at me, - and the beautiful hand, and the beautiful heart. The awakening of my racked soul is hardly more heavily laden with passion and pain. I shall never forget.

Though I feel away from her also, she is the only one out of all to look gently at me.

- Let me writhe and falter with pain; let me go mad - but oh, worldful of people - for the love of your God - give me out of this seething darkness only one beautiful human hand to touch mine with *love*, one beautiful human heart to know the aching sad loneliness of mine, one beautiful human soul to mingle with mine in long, long Rest. -

Oh, for a human being, my soul wails - a human being to love me!

Oh, to know - just once - what it is to be loved!

Nineteen years without one faint shadow of love is mouldy, crumbling age - is gray with the dust of centuries.

How long have I lived!

How long must I live!

I am shrieking at you, cold stupid world.

Oh, the long, long waiting -

The millions of human beings -

I am a human being and there is no one - no one - no one.

Who can know this that has not felt it? You do not know - you can not know.

Surely I do not ask too much. But whether or not it is too much I can not go through the years without it - oh, I can not!

You have lived your nineteen years, fine world, and you have lived through some after years.

But in your nineteen years there was some one to love you.

It is that that counts.

Since you have had that some one, in your nineteen years, can you understand what life is to me - me - in my loneliness?

My wailing, waiting soul burns with but one desire: *to be loved - oh, to be loved.*

March 29

I am making the world my confessor in this Portrayal. My mind is fairly bursting with egotism and pain and in writing this I find a merciful outlet. I have become fond of my Portrayal. Often I lay my forehead and my lips caressingly upon the pages.

And I wish to let you know that there is in existence a genius - an unhappy genius, a genius starving in Montana in the barrenness - but still a genius. I am a creature the like of which you have never before happened upon. You have never suspected that there is such a person. I know that there is not such another. As I said in the beginning, the world contains not my parallel.

I am a fantasy - an absurdity - a genius!

Had I been one of the beasts that perish I had been likewise a fantasy. I think I should have been a small animal composite of a pig, a leopard, and a skunk: an animal that I fancy would be uncanny to look upon but admirable for a pet.

However I am not one of the beasts that perish.

I am human.

That is another remarkable point.

I have heard persons say they can hardly believe I am quite human.

I am the most human creature that ever was placed on the earth. The geniuses are always more human than the herd. Almost a perfection of humanness is reached in me. This by itself makes me extraordinary. The rarest thing in the world, I find, is the quality of humanness.

Humanity and humaneness are much less rare.

"It is a brave thing to understand something of what we see." Indeed it is. An exceeding brave thing. The one who said that had surely gone out on the highways and byways and found how little he could understand.

To understand oneself is not so brave a thing. To go in among the hidden gray shadows of the deep things is a fool's errand. It is not from choice that I do it. No one carries a mill-stone around her neck from choice. When I see what is among the hidden gray shadows - when I see a vision of *Myself* - I am seized with a strange sick terror.

A fool's errand - but one on which I must need go.

- And for that matter I myself am a fool. -

Yet to know oneself well is a rare fine art.

I analyze myself now. I analyzed myself when I was three years old.

The only difference is that at the age of three I was not aware that I analyzed. - It is true, that is a great difference. - Now I know that I am analyzing at nineteen, and now I know that I analyzed at three.

And at the age of nineteen I know that I am a genius.

A genius who does not know that he is a genius is no genius. A drunken man might stagger up to a piano and accidentally play music that vibrates to the soul - that touches upon the mysteries. But he does not know his power and he is no genius though men awaken and go mad therefrom.

I know I am a genius more than any genius that has lived.

I have a feeling that the world will never know this.

And as I think of it I wonder if angels are not weeping somewhere because of it.

March 31

> *She only said: "My life is dreary,*
> *He cometh not," she said;*
> *She said, "I am weary, aweary.*
> *I would that I were dead."*

All day long this heart-sickening song of Mariana has been reeling and swimming in my brain. I awoke with it early in the morning and it is still with me now in the lateness. I wondered at times during the day why that very gentle and devilishly persistent refrain did not drive me insane or send me into convulsions. I tried vainly to fix my mind on a book. I began reading *The Mill on the Floss*, but that weird poem was not to be foiled. It bewitched my brain. Now as I write I hear twenty voices chanting it in a sad minor key - twenty voices that fill my brain with sound to the bursting point. "He cometh not - he cometh not - he cometh not." "That I were dead" - "I am aweary, aweary," - "that I were dead - that I were dead." "He cometh not - that I were dead."

It is maddening in that it is set sublimely to the music of my own life.

Now that I have written it I can hope that it may leave me. If it follows me through the night and if I awake to another day of it the cords of my overworked mind will surely break.

But let me thank the kind Devil.

It is leaving me now!

It is as if tons were lifted from my brain.

How can any one bring a child into the world and not wrap it round with a certain wondrous tenderness that will stay with it always!

- There are persons whose souls have never entered into them. -

My mother has some fondness for me - for my body because it came of hers. That is nothing - nothing.

A hen loves its egg.

A hen!

This evening in the slow-deepening dusk I sat by my window and spent an hour in passionate conversation with the Devil. I fancied I sat, with my hands folded and my feet crossed, on an ugly but comfortable red velvet sofa in some nondescript room.

And the fascinating man-Devil was seated near in a frail willow chair.

He had willingly come to pass the time of day with me. He was in a good-humored mood and I amused and interested him. And for myself, I was extremely glad to see the Devil sitting there and felt vividly as always. But I sat quietly enough.

The fascinating man-Devil has fascinating steel-gray eyes, and they looked at me with every variety of glance - from quizzical to tender.

- It were easy - oh, how easy - to follow those eyes to the earth's ends. -

The Devil leaned back in the frail willow chair and looked at me.

"And now that I am here, Mary MacLane," he said, "what would you?"

"I want you to marry me," I replied at once. "And I want it more than ever anything was wanted since the world began."

"So? I am flattered," said the Devil, and smiled gently, enchantingly.

At that smile I was ravished and transported and a spasm of some rare emotion thrilled all the little nerves in me from my heels to my forehead. And yet the smile was not for me but rather somewhat at my expense.

"But," he went on, "you must know it is not my custom to marry the women."

"I am sure it is not," I agreed, "and I do not ask to be peculiarly favored. Anything that you may give me, however little, will constitute marriage for me."

"And would marriage itself be so small a thing?" asked the Devil.

"Marriage," I said, "would be a great, oh, a wonderful thing, the most beautiful of all. I want what is good according to my lights, and because I am a genius my lights are many and far-reaching."

"What do your lights tell you?" the man-Devil inquired.

"They tell me this: that nothing in the world matters unless love is with it, and if love is with it and it seems to the virtuous a barren and infamous thing, still - because of the love - it partakes of the very highest."

"And have you the courage of your convictions?" he said.

"If you offered me," I replied, "that which to the blindly virtuous seems the worst possible thing, it would yet be for me the red, red line on the sky, my heart's desire, my life, my rest. You are the Devil. I have fallen in love with you."

"I believe you have," said the Devil. "And how does it feel to be in love?"

Sitting composedly on the ugly red velvet sofa, with my hands folded and my feet crossed, I attempted to define that wonderful feeling.

"It feels," I said, "as if sparks of fire and ice crystals ran riot in my veins with my blood; as if a thousand pin-points pierced my flesh, and every other point a point of pleasure, and every other point a point of pain; as if my heart were laid to rest in a bed of velvet and cotton-wool but kept awake by sweet violin arias; as if milk and honey and the blossoms of the cherry flowed into my stomach and then vanished utterly; as if strange beautiful worlds lay spread out before my eyes, alternately in dazzling light and complete darkness with chaotic rapidity; as if orris-root were sprinkled in the folds of my brain; as if sprigs of dripping wet sweet-fern were stuck inside my hot linen collar; as if - well, you know," I ended suddenly.

"Very good," said the Devil. "You are in love. And you say you are in love with me."

"Oh, with you!" I exclaimed with suppressed violence. The effort to suppress this violence cost me pounds of nerve-power. But I kept my hands still quietly folded and my feet crossed, and it was a triumph of self-control. "I want you to marry me," I added despairingly.

"And you think," he inquired, "that apart from the opinion of the wise world, it would be a suitable marriage?"

"A suitable marriage!" I exclaimed. "I hate a suitable marriage! No, it would not be suitable. It would be Bohemian, outlandish, adorable!"

The Devil smiled.

This time the smile was for me. And oh, the long, old overpowering enchantment of the smile of steel-gray eyes! - the steel-gray eyes of the Devil!

It is one of those things that one remembers.

"You are a beautifully frank little feminine creature," he said. "Frankness is in these days a lost art."

"Yes, I am beautifully frank," I replied. "Out of countless millions of the Devil's anointed I am one to acknowledge myself."

"But withal you are not true," said the man-Devil.

"I am a liar," I answered.

"You are a liar, surely," he said, "but you stay with your lies. To stay with anything is Truth."

"It is so," I replied. "Nevertheless I am as false as woman can be."

"But you know what you want."

"Oh, yes," I said, "I know what I want. I want you to marry me."

"And why?"

"Because I love you."

"That seems an excellent reason, certainly," said the Devil.

"I want to be happy for once in my life," I said. "I have never been happy. And if I could be happy once for one gold day I should be satisfied, and I should have that to remember in the long years."

"And you are a strangely pathetic little animal," said the Devil.

"I am pathetic," I said. I clasped my hands very tightly. "I know that I am pathetic: and for this reason I am the most terribly pathetic of all in the world."

"Poor little Mary MacLane," said the Devil. He leaned toward me. He looked at me with those strange, wonderfully tender, divine steel-gray eyes. "Poor little Mary MacLane," he said again in a voice that was like the Gray Dawn. And the eyes - the glance of the steel-gray eyes entered into me and thrilled me through and through. It frightened and soothed me. It racked and comforted me. It ravished me with inconceivable gentleness so that I bent my head down and sobbed as I breathed.

"Don't you know, you little thing," said the man-Devil, softly-compassionate, "your life will be very hard for you always - harder when you are happy than when you go in Nothingness?"

"I know - I know. Nevertheless I want to be happy," I sobbed. I felt a rush of an old thick heavy anguish. "It is day after day. It is week after week. It is month after month. It is year after year. It is only time going and going. There is no joy. There is no lightness of heart. It is only the passing of days. I am young and all alone. Always I have been alone: when I was five and lay in the damp grass and tortured myself to keep back tears; and through the long cold lonely years till now - and now all the torture does not keep back the tears. There is no one - nothing - to help me bear it. It is more than pathetic when one is nineteen in all young new feeling and sees Nothing anywhere - except long dark lonely years behind her and before her. - No one that loves me and long, long years. -"

I stopped. The gray eyes were fixed on me. Oh, they were the steel-gray eyes! - and they had a look in them. The long bitter pageant of my Nothingness mingled with this look and the coming together of these was like the joining of two halves.

I do not know which brings me the deeper pain - the loneliness and weariness of my sand and barrenness, or the look in the steel-gray eyes. But as always I would gladly leave all and follow the eyes to the world's ends. They are like the sun's setting. And they are like the pale beautiful stars. And they are like the shadows of earth and sky that come together in the dark.

"Why," asked the Devil, "are you in love with me?"

"You know so much - so much," I answered. "I think it must be that. The wisdom of the spheres is in your brain. And so then you must understand me. Because no one understands all these smouldering feelings my greatest agony is. You must need know the very finest of them. - And your eyes! Oh, it's no matter why I'm in love with you. It's enough that I am. And if you married me I would make you happier than you are."

"I am not happy at all," said the man-Devil. "I am merely contented."

"Contentment," I said, "in place of Happiness, is a horrid feeling. Not one of your countless advocates loves you. They serve you faithfully and well, but with it all they hate you. Always people hate their tyrant. You are my tyrant but I love you absorbingly, madly. Happiness for me would be to live with you and see you made happy by the overwhelming flood of my love."

"It interests me," he said. "You are a most interesting feminine philosopher - and your philosophy is after my own heart, in its lack of *virtue*. It is to be hoped that you are not 'intellectual,' which is an unpardonable trait."

"Indeed I am not," I replied. "Intellectual people are detestable. They have pale faces and bad stomachs and bad livers, and if they are women their corsets are sure to be too tight, and probably black, and if they are men they are *soft*, which is worse. And they never by any chance know what it means to walk all day in the rain, or to roll around on the ground in the dirt. And above all, they never fall in love with the Devil."

"They are tiresome," the Devil agreed. "If I were to marry you how long would you be happy?"

"For three days."

"You are wise," he said. "You are wonderfully wise in some things though you are still very young."

"I am wise," I answered. "Being of womankind and nineteen years I am more than ready to give up absolutely everything that is good in the world's sight, though they are contemptible things enough in my own, for love. All for love. Therefore I am wise. Also I am a fool."

"Why are you a fool?"

"Because I am a genius."

"Your logic is good logic," said the Devil.

"My logic - oh, I don't care anything about logic," I said with sudden complete weariness. I felt buried and wrapped round and round in weariness. Everything lost its color. Everything turned cold.

"At this moment," said the Devil, "you feel as if you cared for nothing at all. But if I chose I could bring about a transfiguration. I could kiss your soul into Paradise."

I answered "Yes," without emotion.

"An hour," said the Devil, "is not very long. But we know it is long enough to suffer in, and go mad in, and live in, and be happy in. And the world contains a great many hours. Now I am leaving you. It is likely that I may never come again, and it is likely that I may come again."

It all vanished. I still sat by my window in the gloom. "It is dreary," I said.

But yes. The world contains a great many hours.

April 4

I have asked for bread, sometimes, and I have been given a stone.

Oh, it is a bitter thing - oh, it is piteous, piteous!

I find that I am not far apart from human beings. I can still be crushed, wounded, stunned - by the attitude of human beings.

To-day I looked for human-kindness, and I was given coldness. I repelled human beings.

I asked for bread and I was given a stone.

Oh, it is bitter - bitter.

Oh, is there a thing in the wide world more bitter?

God, where are you! I am crushed, wounded, stunned - and oh, - I am alone!

April 10

I have a sense of humor that partakes of the divine in life - for there are things even in this chaotic irony that are divine. My genius is not divine. My patheticness is not divine. My philosophy is not divine, nor my originality, nor my audacity of thought. These are peculiarly of the earth. But my sense of humor -

It is humor that is far too deep to admit of laughter. It is humor that makes my heart melt with a high, unequaled sense of pleasure and ripple down through my body like old yellow wine.

A rare tone in a person's voice, a densely wrathful expression in a pair of slate-colored eyes, a fine, fine shade of comparison and contrast between a word in a conversation and an angle-worm pattern in a calico dressing-jacket - these are the things that make me conscious of divine emotion.

One day last summer an Italian peddler-woman stopped at the back door and rested herself. I stood in the doorway and the peddler-woman and I talked. She had a dirty white handkerchief tied over her head - as all Italian peddler-women do - and she had a telescope valise filled with garters, and hair-pins, and soap, and combs, and pencils, and china buttons on blue cards, and bean-shooters, and tacks, and dream-books, and mouth-organs, and green glass beads, and jew's-harps. - There is something fascinating about a peddler-woman's telescope valise. - This peddler-woman wore a black satine wrapper and an ancient cape. She said that she would like to stop and rest a while, and I told her she might. I had always wanted to talk to a peddler-woman, and my mother never would allow one in the house.

"Is it nice to be a peddler?" I asked her.

"It ain't bad," replied the peddler-woman.

"Do you make a great deal of money?" I next inquired.

"Sometime I do, and sometime I don't," said the woman. She spoke with an accent that, while it sounded Italian, still showed unmistakably that she had lived in Butte.

"Well, do you make just enough to live on, or have you saved some money?" I asked.

"I got four hundred dollar in the bank," she replied. "I been peddlin' eight year."

"Eight years of tramping around in all kinds of weather," I said. "Your philosophy must be peripatetic, too. Haven't you ever had rheumatism in your knees?"

"I got rheumatism in every joint in my body," said the woman. "I have to lay off, sometime."

"Have you a husband?" I wished to know.

"I had a man - oh, yes," said the peddler-woman.

"And where is he?"

"Back home - in Italy."

"Why doesn't he come out here and work for you?" I asked.

"Yes, w'y don't he?" said the woman. "Dat-a man, he's dem lucky w'en he can git enough to eat - he is."

"Why don't you send him some money to pay his way out, since you've saved so much?" I inquired.

"Holy God!" said the peddler-woman. "I work hard for dat-a money. I save ev'ry cent. I ain't go'n now to t'row it away - I ain't. Dat-a man, he's all right w'ere he is - he is."

"What did you marry him for?" I asked.

The peddler-woman looked at me with that look which seems to convey the information that curiosity once killed a cat.

"What for?" I persisted - "for love?"

"I marry him w'en I was young girl. And he was young, too."

"Yes - but what did you do it for? Was he awfully nice, and did he say awfully sweet things to you?"

"He was dem sweet - oh, yes," said the peddler-woman. She grinned. "And I was young."

"And you liked it when you were young and he was sweet, didn't you?"

"Yes, I guess so. I was young," she answered.

The fact that one is young seems to imply - in the Italian peddler mind - a lacking in some essential points.

"And don't you like your man now?" I asked.

"Dat-a man, he's all right, in Italy - he is," replied the woman.

"Well," I observed, "if I had a man who had been dem sweet once, when I had been young, but who was not sweet any more, I think I should leave him in Italy, too."

"You'll git a man some day soon," said the peddler-woman.

I was interested to know that.

"They all do - oh, yes," she said. "But you likely to be better off peddlin', I tell you."

"Yes, I think it would be amusing to be a peddler for a while," I said. "But I should want the man, too, as long as he was dem sweet."

The peddler-woman picked up the telescope valise.

"Yes," she remarked, "a man, he's sweet two days, t'ree days, then - holy God! he never work, he git-a drunk, he make-a rough house, he raise hell."

The peddler-woman nodded at me and limped out of the yard. The telescope valise was heavy. When she walked every muscle in her body seemed pressed into the service. She had a heavy solid look. She seemed as though she might weigh three hundred pounds though she was not large. The afternoon sun shone down brightly on her dirty white handkerchief, on her brown comely face, on her brown brass-ringed hands, on her black satine wrapper, on her ancient cape.

As I watched her walk out of sight I thought to myself: "Two days, t'ree days, then - holy God! he never work, he git-a drunk, he make-a rough house, he raise hell."

I was conscious of an intense humor that was so far beyond laughter that it was too deep even for tears. But I felt tears vaguely as I watched the peddler-woman limping up the road.

It was not pathos. It was humor - humor. My emotion was one of vivid pleasure - pleasure at the sight of the woman, and at the telescope valise, and at her conversation supplemented by my own.

This emotion is divine and I can not grasp it.

As I looked after the Italian peddler-woman it came to me with sudden force that the earth is only the earth, but that it is touched here and there brilliantly with divine fingers.

Long and often as I've sat in intense silent passion and gazed at the red, red sunset sky I have never felt this sense of the divine.

It comes only through humor.

It comes only with things like an Italian peddler-woman in a black satine wrapper and an ancient cape.

My soul - how heavily it goes.

Life is a journeying up a spring-time hill. And at the top we wonder why we are there. Have mercy on me, I implore in a dull idea that the journey is so long - so long, and a human being is less than an atom.

The solid heavy figure of an Italian peddler-woman with a telescope valise, limping away in the afternoon sunshine, is more convincing of the Things that Are than would be the sound of the wailing of legions of lost souls, could it be heard.

- For the world must be amused. -

And the world's wind bloweth as it listeth.

April 11

I write a great many letters to the dear anemone lady. I send some of them to her and others I keep to read myself. I like to read letters that I have written - particularly that I have written to her.

This is a letter that I wrote two days ago to my one friend:

To you: -

And don't you know, my dearest, my friendship with you contains other things. It contains infatuation, and worship, and bewitchment, and idolatry, and a tiny altar in my soul-chamber whereon is burning sweet incense in a little dish of blue and gold.

Yes, all of these.

My life is made up of many outpourings. All the outpourings have one point of coming-together. You are the point of coming-together. There is no other.

You are the anemone lady.

You are the one whom I may love.

To think that the world contains one beautiful human being for me to love! It is wonderful.

My life is longing for the sight of you. My senses are aching for lack of an anemone to diffuse itself among them.

A year ago when you were in the High School often I used to go over there when you would be going home, so that my life could be made momentarily replete by the sight of you. You didn't know I was there - only a few times when I spoke to you.

And now it is that I remember you.

Oh, my dearest, - you are the only one in the world!

We are two women. You do not love me, but I love you -

You have been wonderfully-beautifully kind to me.

You are the only one who has ever been kind to me.

There is something delirious in this - something of the nameless quantity.

It is old grief and woe to live nineteen years and to remember no person ever to have been kind. But what is it - do you think? - at the end of nineteen years, to come at last upon one who is wonderfully-beautifully kind!

Those persons who have had some one always to be kind to them can never remotely imagine how this feels.

Sometimes in these spring days when I walk miles down into the country to the little wet gulch of the sweet-flags, I wonder why it is that this thing does not make me happy. "She is wonderfully-beautifully kind," I say to myself - "and she is the anemone lady. She is *wondrously* kind and though she's gone, nothing can ever change that."

But I am not happy.

Oh, my one friend - what is the matter with me? What is this feeling? Why am I not happy?

But how can you know?

You are beautiful.

I am a small vile creature.

Always I awake to this fact when I think of the anemone lady.

I am not good.

But you are kind to me - you are kind to me - you are kind to me.

You have written me two letters.

The anemone lady came down from her high places and wrote me two letters.

It is said that God is somewhere. It may be so.

But God has never come down from his high places to write me two letters.
Dear, - do you see, you are the only one in the world.

Mary MacLane

Oh, the dreariness, the Nothingness!

Day after day - week after week, - it is dull and gray and weary. It is *dull*, DULL, DULL!

No one loves me the least in the world.

"My life is dreary - he cometh not."

I am unhappy - unhappy.

It rains. The blue sky is weeping. But it is not weeping because I am unhappy.

I hate the blue sky, and the rain, and the wet ground, and everything. This morning I walked far away over the sand and these things made me think they loved me - and that I loved them. But they fooled me. Everything fools me. I am a fool.

No one loves me. There are people here. But no one loves me - no one understands - no one cares.

It is I and the barrenness. It is I - young and all alone.

Pitiful Heaven! - but no, heaven is not pitiful.

Heaven also has fooled me, more than once.

There is something for every one that I have ever known - some tender thing. But what is there for me? What have I to remember out of the long years?

The blue sky is weeping, but not for me. The rain is persistent and heavy as damnation. It falls on my mind and maddens my mind. It falls on my soul and hurts my soul. - Everything hurts my soul. - It falls on my heart and it warps the wood in my heart.

Of womankind and nineteen years, a philosopher of the peripatetic school, a thief, a genius, a liar, and a fool - and unhappy, and filled with anguish and hopeless despair. What is my life? Oh, what is there for me!

There has always been Nothing. There will always be Nothing.

There was a miserable, damnable, wretched lonely childhood. Itself has passed, but the pain of it has not passed. The pain of it is with me and is added to the pain of now. It is pain that never lets itself be forgotten. The pain of the childhood was the pain of Nothing. The pain of now is the pain of Nothing. Oh, the pathetic burlesque-tragedy of Nothing!

It is burlesque but it is none the less tragedy. It is tragedy that eats its way inward.

It is only I and the sand and barrenness.

I have never a tender thing in my life. The sand and barrenness has never a grass-blade.

I want a human being to love me. I have need of it. I am starving to death for lack of it.

Bitterest salt tears surge upward - sobs are shaking themselves out from the depths. Oh, the salt is bitter. I might lay me down and weep all day and all night - and the salt would grow more bitter and more bitter.

But life in its Nothingness is more bitter still.

It is burlesque-tragedy that is the most tragic of all.

It is an inward dying that never ends. It is the bitterness of death added to the bitterness of life.

What hell is there like that of one weak little human being placed on the earth - and left *alone*?

There are people who live and enjoy. But my soul and I - we find life too bitter, and too heavy to carry alone. Too bitter, and too heavy.

Oh, that I and my soul might perish at this moment, forever!

April 13

I am sitting writing out on my sand and barrenness. The sky is pale and faded now in the west, but a few minutes ago there was the same old-time always-new miracle of roses and gold, and glints and gleams of silver and green, and a river in vermilions and purples - and lastly the dear, the beautiful: the red, red line.

There also are heavy black shadows.

I have given my heart into the keeping of this.

And still as always I look at it - and feel it all with thrilling passion - and await the Devil's coming.

*

L'Envoi

October 28, 1901

And so there you have my Portrayal. It is the record of three months of Nothingness. Those three months are very like the three months that preceded them, to be sure, and the three that followed them - and like all the months that have come and gone with me, since time was. There is never anything different; nothing ever happens.

Now I will send my Portrayal into the wise wide world. It may stop short at the publisher; or it may fall still-born from the press; or it may go farther indeed and be its own undoing.

That's as may be.

I will send it.

What else is there for me, if not this book?

And, oh, that some one may understand it!

- I am not good. I am not virtuous. I am not sympathetic. I am not generous. I am merely and above all a creature of intense passionate *feeling*. I feel - everything. It is my genius. It burns me like fire. -

My portrayal in its analysis and egotism and bitterness will surely be of interest to some. Whether to that one alone who may understand it; or to some who have themselves been left alone; or to those three whom I, on three dreary days, asked for bread, and who each gave me a stone - and whom I do not forgive (for that is the bitterest thing of all): it may be to all of these.

But none of them, nor any one, can know the feeling made of relief and pain and despair that comes over me at the thought of sending all this to the wise wide world. It is bits of my wooden heart broken off and given away. It is strings of amber beads taken from the fair neck of my soul. It is shining little gold coins from out of my mind's red leather purse. It is my little old life-tragedy.

It means everything to me.

Do you see, it means *everything* to me.

It will amuse you. It will arouse your interest. It will stir your curiosity. Some sorts of persons will find it ridiculous. It will puzzle you.

But am I to suppose that it will also awaken compassion in cool indifferent hearts? And will the sand and barrenness look so unspeakably gray and dreary to coldly critical eyes as mine? And shall my bitter little story fall easily and comfortably upon undisturbed ears, and linger for an hour, and be forgotten?

Will the wise wide world itself give me in my outstretched hand a stone -

*

Publication at the end of April in 1902 brought a pandemonium which lasted until fall. Headlines referred simply to "Mary." Some reporters traveled to Butte, others investigated the family's past in Great Falls, and in time the rumors died that she was a publisher's fiction.

Within weeks, she had made a fortune. By early July she had left Butte and traveled first to Chicago, where she met her editor, Lucy Monroe, and Lucy's sister, Harriet, who would become a great unrequited love of her life.

Solicited by Hearst's and Pulitzer's New York papers, she signed for a month's articles with the latter's sensationalizing, populist World. Thus began an expressive opening parallel but different to the books: feature articles, often widely distributed, for everyday papers - all done with no hint of talking down. Her early pieces likely were many Americans' first brush with proto-Surrealism.

Before New York, she visited Massachusetts to see Frances Corbin, now known from I Await. Reporters knocked at the door, but for the most part were not admitted. Then came a reporter with an appointment, who sparred with, observed, and understood the young author - and whom, MacLane later telegraphed her Chicago publishers, MacLane would come to love.

FEATURES

- 1902 -

"The Real Mary MacLane"

by Zona Gale · *New York World* · 17 August 1902

Mary MacLane, of Butte, Montana, wrote the story of herself and committed it to the "wise, wide world." She told everything she knew about herself, and everything she thought and felt - but not everything she is.

For last week, as I sat with her for three hours at the home of Miss Corbin, her "Anemone Lady," in Cambridge, and as we two lunched together next day, I believe I saw her as she is, and I believe I know the real Mary MacLane. And so this is the story of Mary MacLane, which her book does not tell.

Inasmuch as I did not go to Cambridge to pass judgment on Mary MacLane, or to find out whether she poses or whether she is a genius, or whether she is good, or she loves her mother, or steals - or indeed whether any of her book is really herself - I shall not say what I thought about any of these things.

I will simply tell what she did and said in the time we were together, prefaced by two statements which ought to be taken into consideration at every step.

First: she is exceedingly pretty - far prettier than her pictures.

Second: nobody can repeat what she says verbatim and at the same time be perfectly fair to her. For her manner and her voice and her pretty ripply laugh are extra-illustrations not to be reproduced.

When I heard her steps on the stair at the home of the "Anemone Lady," they came tapping out a little refrain, the burden of her portrayal of herself: "I am not good," they said, singing from her book; "I am not virtuous; I am not generous. I am awaiting the coming of the Devil and I know that he usually comes. I am a genius."

"And, oh dear," I thought, "you are not pretty. For only otherwise unattractive people give out that they are not good."

She came in and took my hand in her own warm and firm and rather large hand. She sat down in a big leather chair and waited for me to begin. The little refrain her tan boots had tapped out died in my head as I looked at her.

*

Mary MacLane, alert for the coming of the Devil, looks like a Madonna, and a pot of sweet lavender and a fall of old lace. Mary MacLane is not little. She is tall - 5 feet and 6 inches, really - and she has a pretty figure and a well-set head.

Her hair, which is her chief glory, is all ripples and brown shadows, and in tendrils about her face.

Her eyes are blue and direct and old and sad. Her chin is round and petulant and faintly dimpled like a child's.

Her mouth is nearly perfect.

Her nose is straight and delicate, and all her features are small.

She looks both child and woman. She has a ready, merry little laugh, like a child's, and a frequent, only partly-suppressed yawn, like a child's, and a quick nod of understanding that is some way childlike, too.

Her eyes alone are old, and "her eyelids are a little weary." Yet, curiously enough, her sudden far-away look, the droop of her mouth sometimes, and even her direct gaze, are more childish tiredness than ennui.

*

When she makes the most *outre* statements you feel a quick impulse to have her learn her lesson better; but the next minute she may be teaching you.

She was wearing a little pale-blue muslin frock, flowery and trailing, with something dainty and tucked and white for a yoke, and little clusters of baby-blue ribbons. She looked like a Dresden shepherdess, or like Phyllis at a spinning-wheel, and far, far less wise than either ingenue or debutante.

Yet for that matter she herself had written: "None of my acquaintances would suspect I am a thief. I look so respectable, so refined, so 'nice,' so inoffensive, so sweet, even!"

And yet she had also written: "The world is like a little marsh filled with mint and white hawthorn."

At all events, I decided she should have the benefit of the mint and white hawthorn side of her. And I straightway tried to forget everything her book had said and to start afresh on the story of Mary MacLane.

*

"Do you wish you hadn't published your book?" I asked. For she so little resembled her book that her answer seemed inevitable, and my question pardonable.

"No," she said, "because when I wrote it I was only nineteen. Now I am twenty-one."

"Is it the true story of yourself as you were then?" I said, "and don't you mind the 'wise, wide world' knowing all about it?"

"It is the true story of myself," she answered. "Why should I have written untruly? The only joy I had was writing what was. That book was. It no longer amuses me to be all the things I was when I wrote that. But it is my story as I was then.

"I am a genius. Then it amused me to keep saying so, but now it does not. I expected to be happy sometime. Now I know I shall never be."

I looked at the dimple in her chin.

"Why not?" I said.

"The only time I could ever be happy," said Mary MacLane, "would be not when I was really happy, but just the instant before that happiness. And that I am sure I shall never have.

"When I wrote my book I wanted to love someone. I wanted to be in love. Now I know that I shall never be in love - and I no longer wish to be.

"I don't like men. I met a man in Chicago with whom I should like to have been in love," she added, "but I couldn't fall in love with him. I was born to be alone, and I always shall be; but now I want to be.

"When I wrote my book," she went on, "I hated Butte. I hated the sand and the barrenness. I hated the people and the life.

"Now I know I should love to go back there and live there. I know that I love Butte. I didn't at nineteen. I do at twenty-one."

*

It began to look as if these two years had made a woman out of the child who laid bare her soul to the "wide, wise world." Here was no self-assertive being breathing invectives at home and the universe. Here was a girl with shadow hair and a blue flowered gown who said she longed for her home.

"And the Devil," I asked her; "you are not waiting for him?"

"Oh, yes, I am," she said, simply.

So there we were back two full years.

"Such a mountain has been made of that," she said, "hasn't there? I don't want the Devil particularly, but I do want experience. So does every one. Every one keeps quite still about it and goes softly along to meet the Devil, quite silently. I said I was going to meet him, and the rest didn't know I spoke for them too. But I knew. Don't let's talk of that."

"There are two things in your book," I said, "that I wish you hadn't written. One was that your mother is nothing to you."

"Of course," she answered, without surprise, "I don't expect you to approve of that. I don't approve of it myself. Only it was true, so I said it. Oh!" she exclaimed, "don't think that I approve of what I say in my book. I don't - of much of it. I don't approve of myself.

"I know I am unworthy, through and through, and I don't approve of that, but it is all true.

"I was writing about myself as I knew myself. And so I put in everything. What was the other thing you didn't like?"

"I wish," I said, "that you had not said that you are a thief."

"Oh!" said Mary MacLane, laughing, "but I'm not now. It doesn't amuse me any longer. It used to then. But I really haven't stolen anything now in some months."

"Now see," I said, "never mind for a minute about the morality of stealing. Suppose that we set that aside. Do you think it is good breeding to steal?"

"Why," she said, "if it amuses you, and the people you steal from are not inconvenienced, I don't see why it is any worse than half the diversions of society, and just as honest too. I did steal eight spoons on the dining-car, but they were to give away. Besides, every one steals dining-car things.

"I do think," she added, "that the point you make about good breeding is an important one. All the Ten Commandments that really need be kept and that are not now outworn, are those that offend good taste only. There is really no right and wrong. I recognize no right and wrong."

"Why did you say a moment ago that you were unworthy, then?" I asked. "Don't you want to speak quite frankly for a minute and let us talk about whichever is not the pose?"

It is curious when you begin to be frank how hopelessly rude you have to be. A perfectly truthful world would be intensely bad-mannered.

"But I pose all the time," said Mary MacLane. "I never give my real self. I have a hundred sides, and I turn first one way and then the other. I am playing a deep game. I have a number of strong cards up my sleeve. I have never been myself, excepting to two friends."

I laughed and took her hand.

"Your real self was in every sentence just then," I said, "don't you see?"

"But," she exclaimed, "why shouldn't everybody pose? Most people are stupid unless they do. I wouldn't be, but it is so amusing to pose. Besides, unless you aren't clever enough to select poses, why ever be yourself to any one? You have a right to yourself for yourself and a few friends. Why should I give myself to you? You are nothing to me."

"That motorman," I said, "looks better in his uniform than in silver armor or doublet and hose. But you and I take it for granted. We don't say it to the motorman, especially when the motorman is our guest."

The blue figure flashed across the room and put out its hand.

"I know," she said, with a pretty gesture. "I beg your pardon."

"See the ink," she observed presently, looking at her finger, "but don't look at my hands. They are large. I don't like my hands, but I do like my feet. Don't you?" she added.

*

She pointed forward a prettily shaped buckled shoe.

"When people say I have pretty hair," she went on, "I always correct them by saying at once, 'I have beautiful hair.' It is so funny. I did that several times in Chicago. Oh," she said, "the people at the teas in Chicago - you should have seen me caper for them.

"I dislike myself far less for capering than those for wanting to see me. 'How do you do, Miss MacLane? I am so interested in you,' they all said. Many of them didn't know how to be interested in me. Oh, but there were a few," she said, "whom I did love."

Her face was very tender for a minute, until she recalled something.

"One woman," she said, "said to me, 'Oh, you haven't found yourself yet. That's all. You will.' How I hated her. Don't they suppose I know I'm not the way I will be? Why can't they see I am the way I am, and I say so; that's all."

"Don't you think you will be different in two years?" I asked her.

"Yes," she said, "I know I shall. I shall write three more books - four in all. I shall do these before I am twenty-five. After that I shall be nothing. We MacLanes all go down after twenty-five.

"My other books will be very different from this. I don't know whether they will be novels or not. But people are going to say, 'Oh, that is her real self now.' They will say that of each book.

"But fifty years after I am dead they will say, 'Her first book was her masterpiece.' Not only that, but it *is* a masterpiece."

"And what will become of you after you are twenty-five?" I asked her.

"I don't care. But I shall not be forgotten."

*

She leaned back in the deep leather chair and let the lace ruffles fall over her hands.

"I am," she said simply, "one of the great ones of earth."

"Tell me," I said, "whom of the other great ones of earth you are most fond of. What do you read?"

"I don't read," she said.

"They say you are a feminine Walt Whitman," I suggested, "who began younger."

"I have never read a line of Walt Whitman," she declared.

"They say," I went on, "that you are, now and then, like Elbert Hubbard."

"I never read him," she said. "I have seen a copy or two of *The Philistine*, that is."

"They say," I concluded, "that you are like Marie Bashkirtseff. Do you think that?"

"I am greater than she," she said. "I have only read two or three entries in her journal, but I know that."

Then she told me what she had read.

"I don't care at all about Browning," she began. "I hold Mrs. Browning far more of a poet than he. No, I haven't read all he wrote, of course. I don't know Christina Rossetti, but I know a few of Dante Rossetti's. And Longfellow I don't care for.

"Of poets I put Virgil first - he was greatest. Poe next, and the greatest thing he wrote was 'Annabel Lee.' And Chaucer third. 'Annabel Lee' is the greatest poem ever written.

"I have read Stevenson - I like him. And some of Dickens, and *Jane Eyre*, and Albert Ross."

"In your book," I said, "you quoted 'The lure of green things growing.' You evidently liked that. Wouldn't you like to read Keats and Pater and Dante and Shakespeare and find more like that?"

"No," she said, "I don't have to do that. I have all those beautiful things in myself."

There was a pause.

"Read me something from my book," she said, finally. "Read me the chapter I like best - the one about the Gray Dawn. That has all my soul in it. I will tell you if I don't like the way you read it."

I read it, and when I misplaced a word she told me just what was wrong.

"Now read the entry about Greece," she said, "and then the one about asking for bread and receiving a stone. The last is the most intense in the book. In the first a Chicago woman emphasized the word 'music' as she read. I could have murdered her."

"When I wrote my book," she said after I finished, "I wrote from nine or ten at night until four in the morning. Then I would be too exhausted to undress and I would throw myself on the bed and sleep. But at six the next morning I was up again and out in the sand to see the Gray Dawn. All of myself is in that book - myself, as I was then."

"'Why should I give myself?'" I quoted from her words. "Why did you give yourself?"

"I wished to, then," she answered. "No," she answered me in a moment, quite simply. "I do not see any beauty in self-restraint. Give something. If not yourself, then a pose. I gave myself."

Then she read to me - the chapter about her sense of humor and the Italian woman-peddler.

"' - an angle-worm pattern in a calico dressing-jacket,'" she read. "Wasn't that clever of me to select just that?" she looked up to say.

"' - and tacks and dream-books and mouth-organs,'" she read. "Mouth-organs, do you fancy?" she broke off again. "Wasn't that a fine streak of mine to say mouth-organs?

"' - on her brown brass-ringed hands, on her black satine wrapper' - wasn't that wonderful detail to say black satine wrapper?" she interrupted herself. "Yes, that is where I am great - in my use of detail."

It was growing dark in the drawing-room of the Anemone Lady. Outside the window a group of curious girls stood, pointing out the house.

Mary MacLane read on, her voice vibrating with real feeling and notable for its complete lack of emphasis. There is a curious levelness in her voice. She reads and talks as one pronounces French words.

Often she turned her face to the window and read on as faultlessly as Cyrano read his letter. She knows every word of her story of herself.

In the half light her blue gown and lace ruffles and her hair looked so newly inconsistent that I could not resist reassuring myself, at the door, that it was she.

"What would you rather do with your life than anything in the world - honestly?" I asked her.

"I would rather be a fairly happy wife and mother," she said simply. "There is nothing better in the world. But I never shall be. I am not worthy to be. You see, all the tastes and instincts with which I was born are not high. I am not good at heart."

So I said good-night to her, standing in the vine-set doorway of the old Cambridge house, looking like a pot of lavender and a fall of old lace.

The next day we lunched together.

I talked with her about Radcliffe, about Boston, about Butte, about frankness, about Chicago people, about a book or two, about those at the other tables. Of all these it was naturally the personal aspect and its relation to her which interested her.

"Indeed," runs one paragraph in Mary MacLane's book, "my conversation is at all times devoted, directly or indirectly, to myself."

Over luncheon she never for a moment ceased to do her part.

"One must always say things that aim to interest," she said, "because in the world one must after all pay for one's keep."

These two things happened -

From the little dish of cracked ice Miss MacLane took half a dozen olives and dropped them deliberately in the blouse of her shirt-waist.

"I love them so!" she explained. "They are wonderful to eat - in very small bites."

And when the waiter was bowing over his tip she addressed him -

"Waiter," said Miss MacLane, "will you match me for the tip?"

"Madam?" said the waiter.

"Will you match me for the tip?" she asked.

"But yes, Madam," he complied. The first quarter he lost; the second time he won them both.

"Do you think I am crazy, waiter?" asked Miss MacLane, as she rose.

"No, madam," said the waiter, "I have seen many others many times."

"And yet," I said to Mary MacLane, "you wrote well indeed about the three gold rocks that came up out of the sea."

She crossed Tremont Street to the Common, and her lithe, athletic figure and erect head were those of any healthy-minded girl, only a bit more attractive than most. As she walked she ate an olive delicately.

"Mary MacLane at Newport"

New York World · 24 August 1902

I am come down out of Butte-Montana into the mysterious East. I go here and there in trains in the mysterious East and gaze at things.

In very truth, the mysterious East is not so greatly different from Butte-Montana, and a person is a person, I find, east or west.

But there are differences.

For instance it's a far and exceeding confounding cry from Butte-Montana to Newport - Newport with a very large N.

Upon occasion I have read in the well-filled Bible about the pomps and vanities of this wicked world. And I have wondered what it meant - it hath indeed a glittering sound. The pomps and vanities must need be of always-vivid interest and this wicked world, as we all know, is fascinating.

And always when I have seen the phrase in the well-filled Bible I have thought within me: "Until I have really come upon the pomps and vanities of this wicked world my life is not complete." There are, to be sure, a great many things in Butte-Montana which relate quite directly to this wicked world - but not just what one might call pomps and vanities. They're a trifle too heavy for that.

In Chicago I happened upon a friendly gaiety, and some fine and good impressions that will last. In Boston, if you please, I happened upon something so still, so cold, so unrelenting - so utterly intolerant of anything that may come down out of Butte-Montana - that my thanks for the strength that must come of it died instantly upon my lips. In New York I came upon a strenuous thing, to be sure, but mostly commercial as yet, and it glittered little. But all upon a fine bright summer morning I anchored my bark at Newport and lo - I, of Butte-Montana, straightaway walked into the midst of the pomps and vanities of this wicked world!

Only think, now. 'Tis a most grotesque conceit.

Newport is a little lovely restful town in itself. There are few things new, and the old things are earth-old. The stars and the dust and the wild weeds are there, as in the beginning. And in the gray morning a pale, pale sky hangs over wonderful wide water - a sky so pale that one half-expects a Raphael virgin's head to emerge slowly, sleepily from it. And the sea - the sea runs on always, in weariness, in joy - the gray, the blue, the gray, the blue - world with no end. Far away in Butte-Montana I had fancied the sea, and here is it. And the sea has a sister in Newport - a fascinating seductive sloe-eyed sister with soft long hair and magic finger-tips. She is the Air, and she is incomparable. After the first look into the sloe-eyes you close your own and lift your face and feel the sweep of the long soft locks of hair upon your chin and forehead. You feel the touch of those finger-tips upon your shoulder-blades, and straightaway you give your quiet heart into her hands to keep for a season.

The perfume of her long hair is of sea-weed and salt and of moss and decayed wood, and of half-sunk islands over the sea. In the plains of heaven is there any more exquisite thing? Round and about Newport there are bits of rude country that, after the shaven lawns of other parts, rest the nerves and senses. There are places where long dry yellow grass grows confusedly, and tiny rocks, and spaces between that are like the sand and barrenness of Butte-Montana, - but a long, long way apart. Here and there is a fresh-water pond and some lilies and wet, wet leaves. The wild grasses grow tall by the pond, and are also wet and very sweet. Back from the sea I looked long at a prospect that was fair and exceeding good. It was of smiling farms and rolling country and dark-colored trees and fields of corn. And all was green, green, green. It is gray in Butte-Montana, and my mind then opened and took in a new color. And all was green. The flowers bloomed in plenty, and the farms - and Jersey cows fed from the land. To my mind there came a bit of very old poetry from that same well-filled Bible, which seemed to tell it all in a serene voice saying: "My well-beloved hath a vineyard in a very fruitful hill." All this is the background. In the foreground there are people, and there is life: in truth, the pomps and vanities of this wicked world.

How glittering, to be sure, is the pageant at Newport, - how the women and men reek with The Money, how unreal - how like phantoms do they seem to one who has thus far been wont to take a few things seriously and has lived a small, narrow life in Butte-Montana. I gazed at this glittering pageant until my senses were strained and a faint sickening influence came to them. As I looked there came a feeling of deadly weariness and sickness of heart. For through this false brilliant procession, the infinite - life itself - shows in poignant bitter intensity. There is a thing in the life of the women and men that one can not grasp. The stars and the dust and the wild weeds give at once of their deepest and the pain that they send is soft. The vision of the pageant at Newport tells of something so false, so distorted, so sharply cruel, that all of life - all of the past and all of the present - becomes useless. The Universe shrinks into a damnable little thing, and the souls - there are no souls.

Well, then.

At Newport I looked at a wedding. I looked very hard at that wedding. I had been told that I must, and so I did. It seemed excessively like every other little extravaganza in B-flat that I have seen, but it did have a few distinctive points. All the women and men were thoroughly sated, thoroughly steeped. Their bodies were the much-indulged, much-groomed kind - some of The Money certainly buys them the flesh-pots. And a few of the feminine bodies were truly exquisite - the few that were not overdone. The heads and hands had been worked at minutely with little ivory implements until Nature was obliterated and art - albeit with a painfully small "a" - reigned supreme. There were hands of alabaster - a very old simile but still good - with nails delicately wrought as miniature paintings. Each nail meant hours of work and more of The Money. The frocks that adorned these persons were equally exquisite - they represented labor and capital. Physically the women were pieces of fine workmanship - excellent products of skill. Except those that were overdone. They were sadly grotesque indeed.

Some of the bodies that were driven to the wedding were groomed to the nearly annihilation point - just a little more, one thought involuntarily, and they were surely mummified. Certainly no more skilful work could ever have been put on the body of a long-since Egyptian king than that on those nervous American persons. And Solomon in all his glory was not arrayed like one of these. A single bright stone on one of those patrician fingers would have purchased sea air for a very great number of the little bare-footed New York populace - which, however, is entirely without the question and an entirely impertinent idea. These are the pomps and vanities of this wicked world. Let them go down as such.

- When one sees a face - even a wrought Newport summer face at a wedding - one looks at once for the soul - well, no, not the soul. Impossible! But the mind. And one finds - what does one find?

One finds a once beautiful and vital thing dead or dying in the faces of women and men. One finds something subtly imbecile - a strange, weird, and tragic thing. There is surely nothing like unto this in Butte-Montana. It has come from generations of indulgence at the flesh-pots, and years of disuse and reckless wasting of nerves; and too much perfume, and too much music, and too much food. And it has come from the mad straining after pleasure, the devising of ways to spend The Money, the petty rivaling of one another, the utter futility. -

And so it was a very pretty wedding indeed. There was something quite distracting in the way those equipages pulled up at the church, and in the way the high-heeled occupants tottered up the walk to the door. And there was something more distracting still in the way the populace - for Newport boasts a very well-assorted populace likewise - lined up on the opposite street and gazed almost as hard as if they had every one of them just come down out of Butte-Montana to contemplate the pomps and vanities of this wicked world. And the most distracting thing of all, I assure you, was when a goodly carriageful of bridesmaids and things rolled neatly down upon a fat little dog in the street and rolled him over and over and over - a bunch of ruined and feebly-yelping hair. Oh, it was very distracting - hard on the dog, doubtless, but the lace on the gowns of those bridesmaids was worth many thousands of good American dollars with Liberty-heads on one side and eagles on the other.

And when every one had finally arrived the bride tottered up to the altar on the arm of somebody and her own high white heels, and met the groom and they were married and lived happily ever after.

A very charming wedding, to be sure.

And another time I went to see the powers at play - the people of The Money soaking their persons in salt water at Bailey's Beach. 'Twas very interesting and these people ran about and disported themselves and skipped like young lambs just exactly as if they hadn't a cent of money in the world.

Only it was here that I had explained to me the names and the Cottages and the numbers of millions and the Divorces - particularly the Divorces.

I beheld a striped lady with quite the best shoulders I have ever seen emerge from a bunch of waves - she had a figure and a laugh and several high spirits of her own. "That, surely, now, is real," I observed. "That?" responded my guide with elevated brows. "That? Only last year her conduct was scandalous, and her husband - that man in the blue pajamas - obtained a Divorce. She lives in the swell little place I pointed out to you, and her Money is - ." I find that I've forgotten the large number. They have larger ones in Butte-Montana.

And I saw a bright red lady with a pair of eyes - a very good looker, she was. She knew things, moreover. "What is that?" I inquired of the guide. "That," the guide replied, "has the prettiest Cottage in Newport. She has no Divorce as yet, but is getting one as fast as ever she can. Her husband - the man with the green tennis-shoes - went somewhere with that heavy purple lady, and so it is all off." "And what will the red lady do after she has procured her Divorce?" I asked. "She will marry that pretty little thing with the freshness of youth still upon him," answered my guide with remarkable promptness and accuracy. "Her Money is estimated at - ." I find that I've forgotten the large number. They have larger ones in Butte-Montana.

And I saw a brilliant small pink lady leap joyously into the wild waves. She was not much of anything to look at, but she had a way with her.

"Whom is that divorced from?" I said. "Oh, that," said the guide. "She is not married. Her mother is working to obtain that simple figure in black. He has good horses, and his Money is - ." I find that I've forgotten the large number. They have larger ones in Butte-Montana.

And I saw a tall man in a fine plain bathing-suit walking by the sad sea waves, with melancholia on his forehead and a tennis-racquet in his hands. "Wherefore?" said I to my guide. "Oh, that is an old, old story," she murmured. "He married somebody, and no one ever speaks to them. They have that big pile on the hill. They are left alone. There's a Scandal with it." "What's a Scandal?" I asked eagerly. "A Scandal's a reason and a back-thought," said the guide, and went on. "His yacht is immense and his Money is - ." I find that I've forgotten the large number. They have larger ones in Butte-Montana.

And I saw two young creatures - a pale-blue-and-white lady and a reddish-grayish man. The pale-blue-and-white lady was attending the reddish-grayish man with the utmost solicitude. "What of them?" I inquired - (I was there to inquire, don't you know). "They are engaged," answered the guide. "And are they quite happy?" I asked, in the innocence of my heart.

"Well, she ought to be," said the guide, cold-bloodedly. "She has worked hard for two years to get it. And now she works harder to keep it. And certainly she's done well for herself. None but the brave deserve the fair. His house is the one with all the gables and his Money is - ." I find that I've forgotten the large number. They have larger ones in Butte-Montana.

So then these, too, are the pomps and vanities - bathing-dresses, salt water, Divorces, and all.

'Tis most awfully interesting.

And another day I looked at a polo game. I have seen polo several times - polo is much the same everywhere. But there were some fine contrasts about the setting of this game. The horses were good to look at - and some of the women who looked at them wore blue or white or black shoes with very red heels! Those red heels taken with polo made a delicate little incongruity that is quite rare and appeals directly to the artistic sense. The horses were so very good, do you see, and the heels were so very red.

Newport teems, bristles, with just such delicate little incongruities. Set down among small quaint ramshackle houses and new staring red brick buildings, and surrounded farther away by the Cottages - some of which resemble one's idea of a Venetian palace more than anything else - is a church which is a really fine thing. It is small and old - it is of the days of the Revolution, and the air in it is true. The architecture is the simplest and plainest, and inside the wood-work and upholstering are plain and poor to ugliness. George Washington sat in this place on Sundays, when time was. And - it rings utterly true. And now, likewise on Sundays, the sated Newport pageant assembles in it - the dear knows what for - to pray, it may be: a delicate little incongruity.

There is one thing in Newport that is absolutely and quite its own, which suits every element and everything there, and fits in as it surely could not elsewhere. This is the hydrangea bloom - a grafted and artificially colored shrub. The tints of the large round flower bunches are indescribably delicate and lovely, and they grow in the utmost lavishness. The color comes from the application of salt water to the roots and is a blending of the pale sea and the paler sky with a brief vivid gleam of sun.

Also the sea's sloe-eyed sister gives of herself to this flower and rests her magic finger-tips on the stems. Straightaway they bloom delicately, gracefully, immensely, with astonishing and delicious recklessness.

They are fascinating and false - like many, many other things in Newport-by-the-sea.

There is here indeed the little rift that sometime, somehow, inevitably must widen, and - as always - ever widening, slowly silence all.

And thus it is that one receives an Impression, having come down out of Butte-Montana in the days of her youth, and having lo! - walked into the midst of the pomps and vanities of this wicked world.

"Mary MacLane at Coney Island"

New York World · 31 August 1902

Well, and by this time, having been in the mysterious East days and weeks, I have gazed at several things, as you may imagine. I have not come into the mysterious East to learn and live, but rather to gaze and inquire. And so I gaze and inquire, and gaze and inquire, sometimes perfunctorily, sometimes quite desperately, sometimes very heavily. But always with dogged persistence and the fresh candor of youth. (I don't know just what the fresh candor of youth is, but I like the look of it - when written.) And in so doing I have come upon some rather good things - some very good things, in fact.

By far the best thing yet is Coney Island.

One bright, pretty day I - of Butte-Montana - in company with a Little Chaperone-person went out to Coney Island to gaze and inquire. Coney Island leaves nothing to be desired. Everything is there. God is in his heaven and all's right with the world. It is delicious.

The first thing one gazes at is the beach and the humanity thereupon - especially the children. Little Billy and little Alice and little Katie and little Henry dig and splash and shovel and kick and burrow in the sand. And their legs are bare - it is here indeed that one realizes the glory of bare legs.

"They have no stockings and no shoes," I said to the Little Chaperone-person, wistfully.

"They have not," murmured the Little Chaperone-person, with a note of envy in her voice.

"They have knees - knees of their own. My dear, do you realize that they have knees of their own?" I exclaimed.

The Little Chaperone-person nodded.

And we thought straightaway of the time when we had also been six - the Little Chaperone-person and I. There were all kinds of children on the beach at Coney Island. I thought that I had seen in Butte-Montana all the kinds of children that the world contains. But no. Here upon the beach at Coney Island I found worlds unknown. There was a little girl lying buried in the sand - only a tousled head, a tanned flat little face, and two hard brown fists were visible. I felt a distinct pleasure in gazing at this. There seemed something fine and desirable about the figure of the tiny girl in the sand.

"Look," I said to the Little Chaperone-person.

"Yes," she made answer. The Little Chaperone-person is an extremely appreciative one.

We walked over to the child.

"Do you like the sand, little girl?"

"Yes, ma'am," replied the child. The child's eyes were the common yet lovely eyes of a real child. She looked out of them as always a child looks.

"Why do you like it?" I went on.

"'Cause it's sand," she replied.

"What is your name?" I ventured.

"Gertrude," replied the child. The wind and the water were mixed in Gertrude's hair. Gertrude's little life was full of weather. "I am six," she added hastily to forestall any questions upon that point.

"Does it feel good to be six?" I inquired.

"I dunno," said Gertrude.

"You are extremely fortunate in not knowing," I observed. "It's hell - just hell - to know, sometimes."

"Huh!" said Gertrude, with wide startled eyes.

"Yes, it is," I repeated, "but never mind. Good-by."

"Good-by," replied the child. She sat up in the sand and stared, stared, stared as always a child stares.

Dear little Gertrude -

"Isn't it very well," I said, "to be six, and not to know it?"

"Oh, very well," assented the Little Chaperone-person.

"And look at this beach," I added, "and all the people on it who are only six."

"They will always be six," said the Little Chaperone-person.

Just then there came a heavy masculine individual of the whiskey-drinking kind and interrupted us.

"Lady-could-you-give-me-a-few-cents-for-the-love-of-God?-I'm-dead-broke-and-" We gave him the few cents - not for the love of God, however. Rather because we wished him to go and get drunk. He was already half-seas over.

"That was not six, certainly," said the Little Chaperone-person.

"No, I think that was about five," I replied with my most positive intonation.

And also upon the beach we came upon a stout old lady who was sitting upright while another packed sand about her in a damp heavy bank. These were not wearing bathing suits, but were in ordinary clothes. The stout old lady sat stiff for this process as she would have sat for a shoe polish or a shampoo.

Often as I've gazed and inquired in my life I have never before beheld anything quite like this.

"What would you call that?" I asked the Little Chaperone-person.

"That is a bit of scenic effect," she replied, meaninglessly.

"Doubtless," I rejoined idiotically.

We both enjoyed the moment thoroughly.

The entire beach was picturesquely infested with humanity.

A man and a girl in their scant flannel garments were sitting side by each, in the sand. They ogled. They coquetted. They languished. They were two lovers. We agreed - the Little Chaperone-person and I - that it did not require a brilliant intellect to divine that.

"Don't speak to them," said the Little Chaperone-person.

Much as I wished to gaze and inquire, we avoided them as if they had had a grievous plague.

And a lone girl sat with her back to the sounding sea.

"What on earth -" I began. "Don't ask me," said the Little Chaperone-person. "Let it go - it's perfect as it is." Which was true enough.

And the most delicate little incongruity of all was the very slim figure of a young lad stretched out on the sand reading - would you believe it, *Villette* by Charlotte Brontë. "Did you suppose," I said to the Little Chaperone-person, "that any one ever read that now - particularly a boy!" "I am not thinking of that so much," she made answer, "as of that book plate on this beach, Coney Island, New York."

After which we walked on in ruminating silence.

Then we went to gaze at that steeplechase arrangement. There are some things at Coney Island that are altogether delightful, but there are two things at least that are simple monstrosities. So much so indeed that it gives one thrills and spasms of pleasure to gaze at them and to talk about them.

The steeplechase arrangement is one of them. The grown persons who went in for that were very young. Their shoulders moved and their necks curved exactly as if they were six years old, and the short detached sentences that came from their lips were very well done. "Happy childhood," we said.

And the other monstrosity is that loop-the-loop affair. To merely gaze at this gives one a decided sensation. To make the brief, frantic little journey one must be like a thing that never was on land or sea. The Little Chaperone-person and I stared in rapture at a young woman who had either misjudged her powers or else had been told that the proper thing to do was yell. She yelled. Her mouth opened and emitted loud whoops at irregular intervals on the frantic journey. Her facial expression was a marvel, a caution, a symphony.

"Now, what do you think of," I inquired, "when you see a thing like that?"

"Oh," mused the Little Chaperone-person, "I think of a pink parasol - and a little green bottle of cucumber pickles. What do you think of?"

"Of the world, the flesh, and the devil," I replied instantly with another of my most positive intonations.

For a moment we enjoyed life.

Then we came upon a succession of interesting and heterogeneous things.

There was a box that was labeled "Drop in a cent and see twelve - astounding pictures of the war in South Africa - twelve." We dropped in a cent. The pictures were very astounding - the most astounding I have ever seen. And what I liked was the expression of the Little Chaperone-person's face as she looked at them - the delicate incongruity of the two.

And we came to another box labeled "Drop in a cent and hear twelve - popular songs - twelve." We dropped in a cent. The songs were extremely popular - and it was evident that the entire twelve were given out at one and the same time.

"Lovely," said the Little Chaperone-person and I. And we came to a building where one might eat things if one's stomach were good and one's digestion strong. We watched a man consume an egg, and then we turned hastily and walked away. And we came to a barn-like structure labeled "The Johnstown Flood." We ventured inside and looked at it. "There is almost too much striking stage effect," I remarked. "And almost too many foamy billows," added the Little Chaperone-person.

Then we peered into a room where all the machinery in Coney Island was plainly situated. It smelled of steam and grease. And in the midst of pipes and boilers a hand-made peacock with a glass tail was perched. He was a delicate incongruity. "That glass tail," we said with one voice. It alone was well worth the price of admission.

And we came to a dry-goods box where a man with a soiled but angelic countenance expressed a great willingness to make tin-type photographs of you provided you gave him two dimes in advance. I gave him two dimes in advance and he made two tin-type photographs. I suppose they were of me. At any rate I had no reliable information to the contrary. I looked healthy in those pictures. A young person of feminine persuasion brought them to us hot from the camera. The Little Chaperone-person accidentally drew her tiny thumb across one of them, leaving a mark. "Now look what you did!" said the young person in a tense, strained, heavy voice. The Little Chaperone-person recoiled with a sudden serpentine movement. "Oh, let's get out of here," she whispered. We got out. Then we came to a platform scales that was labeled "Your weight and your fortune told for one cent." This was an opportunity that we could not afford to lose. The Little Chaperone-person weighed one hundred and three pounds and I weighed one hundred and seven. Our fortunes were the same. The four pounds difference in weight made no difference it seemed. Our fortune was: "The person you love is waiting for you in advance. Don't fail to have courage." "Isn't it an astonishing thing that the person we love is waiting for us in advance?" I said, wonderingly. She agreed absolutely.

Even out in Butte-Montana I had never heard of anything to equal that. It seemed to require a great deal of gazing and inquiring.

By this time the shades of night had made tracks over the beach, and the Little Chaperone-person and I wandered over to the Bowery. My recollection of the Bowery takes the form of a hall where you must drink beer and gaze at a brilliantly-colored semi-circle of persons with legs who sit around on a stage and sing, one after another, desperately, frantically, loudly, and with amazing voices. These, to be sure, are not so uncommon in vaudeville but everything has a newness in Coney Island.

"Which of these persons do you like best?" I asked the Little Chaperone-person.

"I like them all so well," she replied, "it's hard to choose any one."

It was so with me also - where they were all so nearly perfect of their kind it was difficult to find a favorite.

But finally we selected a gem - a gem who wore eyeglasses and walked the stage with the air of being in merely temporary durance vile. Also she had a look of some high fine respectable matron of a Girl's School in Massachusetts. She was stout and heavy and held her head high and triumphantly, and her eyeglasses had a long gold chain to them. The chain taken together with her ridiculous short frock, her green legs and the song that issued from her lips, made an incongruity so delicate that it seemed like to vanish momentarily. The words of the song could not be heard - even with that voice - in the general din and uproar, and seeing this dignified creation pacing up and down the stage you might have thought it the sleep-walking scene from *Macbeth* or the court-room scene in *The Merchant of Venice*. You might have, only instinctively you didn't.

We gazed at this astonishing vision until our brains seemed paralyzed.

"Come," said the Little Chaperone-person, "that is the limit. Let us leave Coney Island."

So we left Coney Island - a lovable unconscious pathetic thing - and departed into the night.

But as we went we turned, like Lot's wife, and looked back.

We saw a swift picture of the beach in the afternoon: the sweet common world-old faces of the happy children; the lovely eyes of little Gertrude in the sand; the very young babies and the tired work-worn mothers; the salt air from the water, and the water itself in long, long palish-blue waves and lines; the sweep and curl of white foam; the gray shadows on the sky; the dull heavy sun looking through mists; the flying wild clouds - and then a deserted beach in the dusk with water silently moving and vague mysterious phantoms coming up out of the sea.

"Everything," responded the Little Chaperone-person, sleepily.

"Mary MacLane on Wall Street"

New York World · 7 September 1902

I have been a day in Wall Street.

To one who is in Wall Street day after day it doubtless is something peculiarly of now. To one who stands without the whirl an age-worn line of life shows plain-written upon those modern brick walls.

There is a soft monotonous ancient choir that sounds low and deep in the midst of the noise.

There is an old dull gray shadow that shows pale yet marked in the midst of glaring tones.

There is the spirit of an old, old fashion that is as old, older far than the avarice of the money-changers in the temple.

There are human beings grasping, straining madly after treasure, each for himself.

A human being changes not from the long ago till now. In a human being there is the one long old undying element of treasure for himself. There is the first drop of blood that never changes and is transmitted from father to son unto the ten-thousandth generation, and again unto the ten-thousandth generation, and still again.

Wall Street is short and dark and irregular, and the buildings are tall and narrow, and the ground is closely crowded and paved with cobble-stones - so there is no ground.

There is something to loathe and something to worship in the buildings. Some of them have stood for many a good year, and still they stand, and will stand. They are of brick and of stone with touches of marble and bronze. They are strong. They say: "We are the seats of the mighty. These dark walls shelter the millions. Many, many go down in the depths - and never rise. But we stand. The dust of countless yesterdays is gathered in our cracks and crannies. Before the end there will be more dust. More than this, our tall grim stone pinnacles stand out against the vast shadowy sky at dusk - and our mysterious strength is more fearsome than the shadowy sky."

Inside the Stock Exchange the stream of money goes its way. Men shout with lungs of leather, and their mouths and eyes are strained. The atmosphere of this building is of a greenish-grayish and copper-colored hue, and if one is standing aside and looking one imagines it plainly enough.

The men who are shouting are surely thinking of nothing but the shouting. My mind stops and marvels at this. My own mind wanders at will to the times of the Crusades, to the Ptolemys in Egypt, to Darius, to the Philistines, and to the far countries. But here are minds that stay all day long, all month long, all year long between four high narrow walls. And they are minds that go wild at times in that tiny space, in agony of suspense and anxiety for paltry reasons enough, that are aching in unrest which is more than pitiful in its utter unconsciousness.

These minds are they that mourn. Whether or not they reach their desire - whether they grow rich or poor - they are among the most unfortunate ones of earth. They mourn, mourn, mourn always and unconsciously for what is not theirs - each over his condition in life, over the money of his fellows, over the real want of anything vital in his life. For there is nothing vital in all this straining.

A sometime promise to those that mourn is that they shall be comforted. Blessed are they that mourn - but these seem most utterly accursed.

Still it may be that in a day of far reckoning they shall be comforted.

These buildings are peculiarly places of men. There are no feminine elements, no feminine colorings, no feminine hands. Everything is abrupt and unyielding and masculine. One can be sure, as one contemplates them, that these men have no thought of women in this mad whirling. There is no far faint echo of that soft tale within the gray high walls. To be sure, there are but few large human ways of living, such as this, in the world where there is no looking of man to woman. It is one of many outside elements lacking in Wall Street. It is well doubtless that it is lacking. All desires are distorted there - and so that also, were it present.

One knows as little as possible about the buying and selling in the Stock Exchange, or the varying conditions of the money market, or the going up or going down of stocks, or the panics, or indeed any of it. But to look at it from afar it seems utterly absurd. It is obviously one-sided and the profits are so surely with the middle-man. And yet men have no greater pleasure in life than to risk their fortunes in this bottomless pit. And the brokers seemingly ask no greater pleasures than to gratify them. It is one of those mills of the gods that are said to grind slow but exceeding fine.

The great mournful spirit of unrest has come and made this her abiding place. She lays her cold hand upon the eyes of these men and brushes their forms with her somber gray garments as she walks. She leaves naught but rage and woe behind her in her path, and the hearts that she touches are heavy. And men thereafter know not one moment's peace. A tragic vision looms before one's eyes as this thought comes - a vision of two things: one of the wondrous fair green earth, of rapid rushings of water, of the bend of weeping willows, of the white necks of swans upon a lake, of a steep hillside, of the green bay-tree that flourisheth, and of the balm-o'-Gilead: and another and present vision of minds that have wandered far from truth, that are passing by the real things, that seem fallen and lost, that are fighting, struggling, raging in a torrid glare of greenish lights in the company of ghoulish phantoms, that have forgotten the first old lessons, and go on and on with deaf ears and blinded eyes, and hearts eternally bowed down. The more so that they are unconscious and even imagine themselves content.

The life of the street, equally mad as it is, is preferable to the inside of the buildings. The street seethes with life. I have never seen so many different kinds of men as I saw during my day in Wall Street. There were men who knew values, and men who didn't know anything. There were men with murder in their eyes, and men with fair good-tempered faces. There were men in white duck, and men in clerical cloth, and men in unquiet plaids, and men in nondescript clothes, and men in rags, and men in shabby-genteel garments - and a fruit-vender on the curb in a dubious red jacket and waistcoat, with brass rings in his ears. And there were as many young boys plying various extremely small trades - mostly selling the newspapers, but there was also the festive boot-black, and the vender of shoe-strings, and the dealer in pies and gum-drops. And there was a morose individual who displayed fascinating little mechanical toys on the pavement - a strange contrast to the mighty tide of Wall Street.

The cobble-stones of Wall Street have also a voice of their own. They say: "We lie under the feet of the men. We are infinitely wiser than they are. We have been here more years than have passed over their heads. Their gigantic choruses of still voices sometimes cry out together in unanalysed misery: 'My god, why hast thou forsaken me!' But we lie here strong and content. We do not cry; we do not rave; we do not moan. Our name is Strength-and-Patience. We are merely waiting for the end."

Ah, yes - a strong, strong voice comes up from the dark-gray cobblestones, a strong and somehow hateful voice. But it sounds most true.

Often, often in this long journeying it is the hateful thing that is true.

At high noon the sun shines heavy and hot upon Wall Street and all that therein is. The faces of the tall buildings appear all threatening in the thick air, and the faces and the voices of the people are heated to the crackling point. The hoarse yelling of the curb-brokers becomes hoarser and louder. The news-boys frantically cry their papers in the harsh voices of their kind. The shoe-string dealers become agonizingly persistent with their line of goods, which certainly at high noon seem somewhat of a drug on the market. The gum-drop vender gazes in heated despair at his melting delicacies but increases his efforts to dispose of them. The morose individual with his gaily-colored little toys winds them up and sets them going with two-fold velocity until they seem to dance before one's eyes like motes and beams in mid-air. The fruit man in the dingy red garments and the brass ear-rings regards his goods with extreme solicitude and raises a pathetic discordant voice in praise of them. The entire boiling mass of humanity surges and sweeps in every direction, and pushes and jostles and becomes profane. It is an inevitable rule that all must hate each other in a crowd on a hot day, and this seemed particularly evident in Wall Street. Torrid as it was, the look in some of the faces expressed, plainly, desires to see some other faces in yet warmer climes - and different kinds of hatred radiated from eyes and finger-tips.

One's brain seems to ferment in that atmosphere. One thinks vaguely to one's self that hell and damnation must be like this. One looks at the buildings and the cobble-stones and the people and wonders if these are things of the moment or things of all time. Then one is sure that they are things only of the moment - that one, with one's own eyes, can see them all passing, passing, passing in one long dead march to their damp black graves. But still as at first one sees that vague vacillating vanishing, but true, shadow of a thing out of the long ago - that human beings are always human beings and have, each of them, a soul.

These things are mingled but they are kept markedly separate also.

The men move and mourn with their minds of unrest.

The high gray walls stand always, passionless, baffling - and the cobble-stones.

The spire of Trinity rises high in the direction of the stars.

Then render unto Caesar that which is Caesar's, and also unto God that which is God's - and so likewise unto Wall Street that which is Wall Street's.

Two Days Later - Post Scriptum

Having written the foregoing I leaned back in my chair and contemplated it with mixed feelings.

One of them was of profound astonishment that I should have written it at all - considering how and with whom I had visited Wall Street. (I was chaperoned by a man, that time.) And it happens that it is my real, genuine, bona-fide impression of the place. But - will you believe it? - when the Atrocious Editor read it he leaned back in his chair and said: "Mary MacLane, what do you mean by all this? This isn't what I want. Look here." And he wrote me out the following questions to answer in as quiet, pleasant, sane, and ladylike a fashion as is customary in Butte-Montana. And so now I'll answer them - out of the kindness of my heart and to earn my salary - particularly to earn my salary.

Well, then.

The Atrocious Editor's First Question: How did the men you saw in Wall Street compare with the men of Butte-Montana?

My Little Answer: They seemed about alike. I couldn't, for my life, see any difference, - except - ah, yes - their manners. On that point the odds were heavily in favor of Butte-Montana.

The Atrocious Editor's Second Question: Do you regard Wall Street as compatible with personal righteousness?

My Little Answer: I have not the least idea what personal righteousness is. But if it is what I - upon second thoughts - think it is, then I should say: Don't on any account take any of it into Wall Street. 'Twould be a drug on that market.

The Atrocious Editor's Third Question: Do you approve of gambling?

My Little Answer: To be sure. Life is one long gamble, don't you know.

The Atrocious Editor's Fourth Question: How would you define gambling?

My Little Answer: A plunge and a holding of one's breath - and a tinge of profanity.

The Atrocious Editor's Fifth Question: What are your views on other people's money?

My Little Answer: Now, did you ever hear anything like that! Other people's money, indeed!

The Atrocious Editor's Sixth Question: What should you do with a million dollars?

My Little Answer: I should spend it - what else, pray? That's not so large a number. They have larger ones in Butte-Montana.

The Atrocious Editor's Seventh Question: If you received such a legacy in the form of stock would you try Wall Street?

My Little Answer: Certainly not. I might as well go out on the highways and byways and make presents of it to the lame, the halt, and the blind. There is no reason in the world why I should make such presents to Wall Street brokers with whom I have not fallen in love.

The Atrocious Editor's Eighth and Last Question: Do you think that views of money have changed since ancient times?

My Little Answer: No, I really don't think so. They all seem to have had two purposes for things - one for ornamental purposes and the other to earn their salaries - particularly to earn their salaries - from Rome in Nero's time to Butte-Montana in Senator Clark's.

"Mary MacLane in Little Old New York"

New York World · 14 September 1902

August 8

Butte-Montana is behind me and I am living in New York for some days and some more days. I do not know whether New York likes me - and I can't say that I care particularly. But I like it.

I like Butte-Montana better than anything I have known. But I find I also like some things outside of it.

I am fond of delicate little incongruities and of quaint fancies, and, to be sure, New York is a full measure heaped up, pressed down, and running over with both of them.

Also there are things fine and fair that rush over one, times, in great wide waves.

In New York they show me things and show me things, as one day follows another, but I prefer the things that I find for myself.

My favorite quaint fancy about New York is when I sit by a window in the cafe at the top of the hotel and gaze long and fascinatedly far out and down upon a vision of manifold things. Usually it is at dinner time, when the earth and sky are between the lights and shadow.

I see forests of trees of all names in the park - some with great sweeping branches of the green that may be worshiped, and slender tops with narrow leaves, and magnificent weeping willows - crowded together, they all are, in gorgeous joyous confusion - and, oh, the wealth and treasure of green! What is there in the wide world like the fair, fine charm of the natural green?

One thinks of the gardens of Babylon, of vineyards in Spain, of the Cedars of Lebanon - of what not?

Down among the trees is a long, narrow bit of water that in the dusk is of ebony and silver. The ebony says: "Sleep low and soft in these black shadows - and do not venture to breathe. Think and dream silently - live ages in utter solitude - and sleep, sleep, sleep." And the silver says: "The moon is my well-beloved and I shall rise and go. She sends long, delicate, shining ribbons to me that I may reach her quickly. I am rising, flying, floating to the pale white heights, and soon I shall be clasped by my well-beloved."

And so, when I look down from the high window into the park it is still and damp.

Then I look off and away to where the lights of the Wicked City shine

- beckoning, scintillating, fascinating, and in infinite numbers. Always my fertile fancy changes the hotel into a tall, lone tower of gray stone - a moated grange - where I am imprisoned. And I fancy that my two eyes are grown weary with watching and my wooden heart despairs of ever escaping. And then I look out at the lights of the Wicked City - the lights of New York - in mingled fear and desire. These lights shine from countless - limitless - windows: from windows of misery, and windows of [content], and windows of fair good living; from windows of dying and of new life; from windows of song and merry-making, of mystery, of brilliant evil, of everything that is. They say: "Come, little MacLane, come and mingle with this madness - this great many-colored whirlpool - and let your life be wrought and inlaid with red alluring forgetfulness - and then perish and be lost." One wishes to go, oh, one wishes to go, but one is afraid, and sits always in her lone gray tower, and waits.

One thinks withal how very tiny she is, how many, many souls are going, going, going like her own - some to the depths, some over and beyond the horizon, some down gray still pathways, some to the stars.

There are times when one's own soul stands out in high relief from vague backgrounds, and one can see nothing beyond it. But when I look from my tower window far out and down upon the Wicked City I see the vital vision - multitudes of faces and eyes and hands: this world - all this terrible tragic world.

The march is endless - torturing, but the sky and the sun and the winds are with us always.

So this is my favorite picture of little old New York - a picture of trees and windows.

It is fascinating.

Also there are many more things that interest me exceedingly, that I shall not forget.

There are some things that one forgets in one's little life - and with no regrets.

There are other things so beautifully and bitterly true that they grind inward, and one remembers them years and years again.

August 12

To-day I left my gray tower and went down into the crowded, teeming streets of the Wicked City. As I've said, people have a well-meant but vicious habit of showing me things, which has a stultifying effect upon my brain. So this time I made good my escape and went out alone.

I really wanted to see and to hear and to know.

I found many things of vital interest in the humming thoroughfare between the hours of 11 and noon.

Life is exhibited there.

Life is a most curious thing.

What I noticed, first, is - and what I have since noticed always with new futile feelings for the pity of it - are the children and the old women who sell papers in the hot, hot sun.

It seems impossible that they can earn a livelihood by this. One is but comfortable when one pays dollars every day for enough of food and a lodging place. How then can human beings live upon a few stray copper cents each four and twenty hours? Surely their eating is vile, like their garments, and where have they indeed to lay their heads? And always they sell papers in the hot, hot sun.

These people are human beings, but what is their life? What do they think about all day long? What do things mean to them? And when all things come rushing together at nightfall, and the infinite must need manifest itself even, dully, to them, how do their hearts and souls become?

One looks at the faces and the hands of the children, and if one has tears one prepares to shed them then. Still they are children. That is the tragic thing.

Their foreheads are low and narrow. Their eyes are of dull mature colors. Their voices are hoarse and heavy and sound gratingly upon one's hearing with an unspeakable note of pathos.

Their hands are likewise mature, but tiny, and strain and grapple with life - hands that are only seven years old.

The lines of their faces tell of no love given them, no care, no teaching, no thought for them. They are born in the ignorance of their parents - natural laws even go indefinitely against them. There are many, many weights bearing down on their tiny bodies. These little creatures struggle with heaviness that themselves wot not of.

And they shout and sell their papers in the hot, hot sun.

And closely next to them are the figures of the broken old women. They have always been old. They have grown old without ever having been young.

I stopped and spoke to a middle-aged old woman in the City Hall park. The mere act of sitting seemed everything, everything in life to this woman.

"Do you like this?" I said. (It is always my first question.) "Yes, I like it," she answered. "If you had had a great deal less, when you were younger, than you have now, or if you had had a great deal more, would you still like sitting here and working?" I said.

"There's nothin' doing, lady," she replied. And I felt exceeding well answered.

There was but one expression upon the woman's face - and in her yellow eyes. There had never been another - there will never be another as long as she lives.

It was the expression of Nothing Doing.

It is the key-note of her narrowed ways - expressed with a perfection of poetry and truth.

Also it is the key-note of the ways of all her kind. Their life is Nothing Doing.

And always they [sit] and sell their papers in the hot, hot sun.

August 13

I have been to the sea.

I love the sea - I love the sea - I love the sea. The sea is pale and green and gray and white. And it beckons to you in gay humors of purple and sun color. This Wicked City is situate in extremely pleasant ways. The best things of earth are gathered together here. If one lived and died here one still might taste and enjoy all things.

And so there is the salt sea. Down the coast at Long Branch the salt of the sea came into my consideration, and now it will never leave.

One is missing some vital things if the salt of the sea has not entered one's consideration. The mountains about Butte-Montana are well, oh, very well - and here is the sea. They cannot be compared, and they cannot be loved together, but they may be loved separately, with deep long respirations of rest.

Seen from the deck of a boat the line of shore by the bay shows with stunning effect. The tall buildings appear mysterious and beautiful through the mists, and here again the picture is of countless thousands - the inconceivable vastness of the Wicked City. It fascinates me, and I fall in love with it over again.

New York, shining purple and gray through the mists of the morning, might be anything, anything in the long, long vista of living.

It might be Salamis, on the Greek Sea, with its legions of men and myriad fleets, and I fancy the ferocious Persians descending upon it and laying waste those fine buildings, ravaging the coast with fire and pillage and slaying thousands of men. And I fancy the wail of women's voices ascending to upper air.

And it might be some vague ancient town in Egypt where there were palm trees and the thin, high music of stringed instruments sounded in the streets, and where the buildings were all of fine, strong, solid architecture, and the people of a firm Hebraic race.

The view of Staten island is equally striking. One seems to see castles with dazzling white battlements rising from among profusions of dark-green treetops. And one sees grays of every possible tone in the sky above it. Together with the charm of the natural green, the adorable softness and seduction of the gray shadows make a prospect so fair that one's two eyes feel a sudden blur and one half closes them and rests.

This Wicked City is so much - so very much.

The coming home in the night is equally good - and delicately incongruous. In prosaic reality one is coming from a little New Jersey village back to New York in August, 1902. But one might easily be sailing down a black, uncanny stretch of water, in any long-since age in the far-off regions of the North. The boat passes great, silent, dark hulks that rise suddenly, fearsomely beside her, and then vanish forever in the mists.

A rugged, irregular outline of trees and dwellings stands out against the ghastly sky on the island and brings to one's mind visions of menacing fortresses and walled cities with a thousand guns. Also there looms up suddenly - but while yet far off - the Liberty Statue that, in this light at least, stands in utmost majesty and with infinite calmness and strength. Coming toward it and looking at it from out at sea it sends out fine gleams of peace and a vague, quieting radiance that charms. One sees something most pathetic in that heavy, weather-beaten figure. Moreover, thus she, too, in a somewhat subdued voice: "I am grown old in the years, and grotesque, and men mention me, times, with half-smiles of ridicule, and glance up with quizzical eyes. But I stand always, not ashamed, and my torch burns brightly - and the end is not yet."

Is not the Liberty Statue a really fine thing? There is something in that immovable attitude that suggests - "May my right hand forget its cunning if I forget thee, Oh, Jerusalem." And there again are the lights of the Wicked City glowing redly, and alluring, enticing, beckoning - always beckoning.

If these lights beckon much more I shall go to them - I am sure I shall go to them.

August 15

Again I escaped from my tower and went out alone. This time I saw everything.

I saw the streets of New York being reduced to hollow mockeries - the digging of the tunnel for the subway trolleys. If some brilliant inventor had spent days in the devising of means to increase the confusion in the midst of this Wicked City he could not have hit upon a more effective plan than this tunneling process. In the strenuous hour between 11 and noon the uproar becomes chaotic. The heavy traffic wagons, the cabs and hansoms, the delivery carts, the trolley cars, the omnibuses, the automobiles, the pedestrians rush pell-mell, seemingly to luncheon - all these things appear to become suddenly very hungry at that hour. At least I can imagine nothing else that could produce so exciting a rate of speed - though, to be sure, it does not require much to make an automobile look hungry. And all this rushing together with the torn-up streets surpasses one's idea of Bedlam.

In one way this scheme of excavating seems a very good thing - in giving work to so large a number of men. In that it becomes admirable.

I found a fascination in watching the men work. They were burned deep browns and reds from being day after day in the merciless sun, and their hair was faded until in many cases it resembled straw matting cut to fit heads. Their hands seemed made of leather, and it strains one's imagination to think they could ever have been white, as they must have been when their owners were infants.

I have always had a vague idea that workmen are very skillful when they work, but in the course of my watching I changed my mind somewhat.

I observed three men occupied in hoisting a quite large rock - they have larger ones in Butte-Montana - from the bottom of the excavation to the surface of the street. It was a height of perhaps four feet, but seeing the elaborate movements of those three men one might have thought it forty at the very least. There were two men at the bottom and one on the surface. They were lifting the rock with a lever aided by a wire rope in the hands of the man on the surface. This man engineered the proceedings. Of the two men at the bottom one had tow-colored hair and the other was gray-headed. The gray-headed one steadied the rock while the tow-headed one worked the lever. When the man with the wire rope gave the signal the tow-headed man pressed down the weight on the lever and the gray-headed man pushed forward on the rock while the man with the wire rope pulled backward. These two rival forces exerted on the rock rendered quite futile the pressure of the tow-headed person - who thereupon ceased pressing and swore softly, though audibly enough, in measured terms. In the second attempt he evidently deemed it not worth while to exert himself at all, so when the man with the rope gave the signal and pulled diagonally backward, the gray-headed man who steadied the rock found himself suddenly closely embracing its entire weight, owing to the lack of pressure at the other end - a position which he did not seem to find altogether enchanting, for he speedily relieved himself, and, in his turn, swore softly in measured terms, and favored the tow-headed one with his fiery regards. At the third attempt the tow-headed one seemed to repent of his negligence, and when the man on the surface gave the signal and pulled diagonally forward at the rope, he weighted the lever with mighty impetus. But now the gray-haired individual failed to do his part: instead of keeping the rock steady with his arms, he folded them and stood aside with the air of a disinterested spectator. The rock, lifted suddenly on the narrow steel bar and pulled forward by the wire rope, swayed for an instant in mid-air, then, for lack of the steadying arms, plunged all at once off and down, narrowly escaping the toes of the gray headed man - the disinterested spectator. The man on the surface with the rope grasped in his hand thus all at once found himself running forward with astounding rapidity - and he now took his turn, and swore, not softly, but very loudly, and in terms by no means measured - terms in which the stupidity of his two co-workers and the word "damn" occurred with rhythmic and musical frequency. When I turned away from this interesting little drama they had begun a fourth trial - and let us hope it was successful. I should not be surprised, however, to learn that the rock is still lying at the bottom of the excavation.

From this scene of activity I went into that great mingling-place of the unemployed - the City Hall Park. There are men, men, men of many descriptions who are sitting on the benches waiting for the Fates to bring them a change of fortune. Humanity does not seem to be in a state of either mental or moral excitation on these benches. The men sleep while they wait. They consider probably that the Fates will bring them a change of fortune as quickly either sleeping or waking. So they sleep. They look very ugly as they sleep. Their heads fall forward and their jaws drop and their shoulders droop. And their clothes are maddeningly ugly. They have no collars and their shirts are nearly always black or gray with pale blue and yellowish spiders and angleworms scattered about upon them. Their other garments have an ancient, dusty, musty, uncanny appearance that gives one a strong desire to edge away, and edge away.

In the City Hall Park, then, are two kinds of pitiable things - the children and the old women who work, and the benches filled with the men who do not work. They are all touched with a certain sharp pathos - but the two are different. The men are ugly, but the children and the old women are not ugly.

Well, and then my attention went to other things. To my mind there is no more delicate little incongruity in the streets of the Wicked City than that quaint atrocity, the omnibus. It is so manifestly a relic of days long past, and is so heavy and lumbering a vehicle to be carrying people about at this late day. The drivers, and in many cases the horses, seem to date equally far back, and the general decrepitude of the whole is as quaint a fancy as anything one might meet upon a Sabbath day's journey. Likewise the signs that are hung up inside - "No passenger can ride free." There is something so obvious about that rule. One wonders whether, in the days when omnibuses began, every public accommodation was so plain in its speech - whether in the restaurants one's eyes were greeted by "You will have to pay for the things you eat"; or in the shops, "You cannot have anything in this place without paying for it"; or in a livery stable, "Don't think of attempting to hire a horse without the wherewithal"; or in a barroom, "Gentlemen will not be served with drams unless they can show at least four shillings." And so on until the citizen felt himself hedged about by a scheme of things that required money before all else. As a matter of fact, that is exactly the case, and, after all, one cannot in these days enter any of those places without feeling the unwritten rules, in glowing lettering, to the effect that one's money alone is the Open Sesame. The public places shout in a poignant chorus, "We love you, animals, for the money that you will pay." The little old omnibus alone is the only thing that has the courage of its convictions, and it, to be sure, is long out of date. There is nothing so quaintly old-fashioned in Butte-Montana.

I walked down Fifth avenue in the middle of the cloudy-clear afternoon, when the air was soothingly fresh, and the world looked bright. Fifth avenue in the afternoon is one of the most attractive places in the Wicked City. It has a gay, well-dressed, well-groomed, prosperous air with it, and the shops are most fascinating. Many of the buildings are overrun with vines that grow in wild green confusion.

The shop windows gleam with fine things. One has glimpses of Tiffany glass and burnished copper vessels, and of old thin china and wrought leather and pearls, and of stunning pattern frocks, and of brasses and bronzes, of fascinating books and of hot-house blossoms, and of Indian earthenware, and of pictures, and all little articles good to look upon.

And there is no turmoil in Fifth avenue. Its tastes do not descend to anything so plebeian.

I do not find myself lost in admiration for the frightfully tall stone structures that adorn this Wicked City. Doubtless they are extremely convenient and necessary, but they are sadly grotesque to look at. That Flatiron affair seems a strikingly appropriate monument to the headlong spirit of the Wicked City and to some man's vanity.

Always when I look at these buildings there comes a vague idea to my mind that they are all going to tumble over, either to-morrow or the next day after.

That is one of the quaint fancies.

Also I am not lost in admiration for some of the ratty old statues that are placed in the different squares. They are images of good men enough, one doubts not, but certainly shocking bad workmanship. Except a few. There is one of Nathan Hale that leaves naught to be desired.

After dodging horses and cars in several of the ways of uproar, I came upon a beautiful old church with crumbling eighteenth century grave-stones in the yard and green all about.

It was near the hour for closing the shops, and oh, the turmoil became all at once maddening - horrible.

If in the midst of crowded places one's mood changes suddenly - and one finds one still in the crowded places - one suffers sharp lurid anguish, a terrible soul's perdition.

This sensation came to me, and so I escaped and went into the church. Surely this church must have been set there for such reasons. The air is of softnesses - of dead leaves - of damp earth-mould. It quiets one into vague instant peace.

I sat for minutes gazing at nothing. Presently I opened a little black book and read, "Abide with me - fast falls the eventide - oh, Thou Who changest not, abide with me."

Then straightway the Wicked City vanished utterly and the world went into twilight.

August 16

In the freshness of the morning a person came with a horse and took me away from my Tower for a drive. And I saw that really wonderful place, Central Park, in an adorable light, shining and dripping after a heavy rain.

There are a hundred things to interest one.

There are carefully kept green lawns on one side of the drive and the dense forest primeval on the other. There is the civilization of now and the fair wildwood of two hundred years ago. There are artificial lakes with conventional swans swimming or standing on one leg, on the bank - and there is a natural spring that dashes down little hillsides and rests in quiet pools, and shoots over moss-grown rocks with gleaming sprays. The trees and the variety of them are legion - and there is one vision of intense sensuous beauty. It is of the pond with the water lilies. The soft charm of those wide leaves and the pale, pale color of green - the curious old-world shape - the strange, immense flowers, of the tints of the sun fading away on the sea - the immense numbers of them crowded there - what is a vision more fair! The water is dark green from the reflection of the heavy foliage above it, and this shade is contrasted with the pale green of the lilies - the green of the spring-time hills - and one's thrilled senses rejoice. Back of this the land slopes suddenly and is set with the trees and overhanging rocks. It is the wild greenwood. One fancies this the home of Nymphs and Dryads.

And then I looked at the Obelisk.

The Obelisk had a peculiar effect on me. I found my mind asking it questions and vaguely arguing. And the Obelisk was maddening.

"What are you doing here, you heavy thing?" asked the mind.

"I am an Obelisk," it answered.

"For how long?" asked the mind.

"I am an Obelisk," it answered.

"You are old," said the mind.

"I am an Obelisk," it answered.

"You have strange, heathenish letters upon your faces," said the mind.

"I am an Obelisk," it answered.

"You are so ancient, so dusty. Do your nerves suffer and aren't you worried at the noise in this Wicked City?" asked the mind.

"I am an Obelisk," it answered.

"There is music coming from the house by the roadside. Does it go to your heart?" asked the mind.

"I am an Obelisk," it answered.

"Have you a heart?" asked the mind.

"I am an Obelisk," it answered.

"Long ago in Egypt there must have been heavy red flowers and sweet, heavy air and languid, heavy purple dreams; and how do you live without them?"

"I am an Obelisk," it answered.

"I have left my soft gray barrenness in Butte-Montana - but also I have it with me. Have you, then, your heavy purple dreams and your heavy red flowers with you?" asked the mind.

"I am an Obelisk," it answered.

"Are you thinking of what has been or what is to come in the long, long times?" asked the mind.

"I am an Obelisk," it answered.

"Your wisdom is wisdom," said the mind with a terrible sinking and sense of futility. What is anything - what - what - oh, what?

The Obelisk answers with one answer. There is no other. It is old - old, and knows the utter ignorance.

August 18

To-day I sat and ate my little breakfast of cantaloupe and fish in the Claremont place by the side of the Hudson.

The Palisades - the blue, blue water.

Then these thoughts ran in my brain:

I left my good sand and barrenness in Butte-Montana, and Butte-Montana is far - oh, very far away. There is nothing in the mysterious East so fair, so tender as that sand and barrenness - and some things here are hard, hard and glitter like a serpent's eyes. But just now 'tis a trifle - I am sitting and eating my little breakfast of cantaloupe and fish in this Claremont place by the side of the Hudson.

When my eyes look off and away in search of the mountains as in Butte-Montana they see only flat, flat land and a distance. The tall, ugly buildings rise where one looks for the high hills, and the air is dull Eastern air and one suffers a longing. But just now 'tis a trifle - I am sitting and eating my little breakfast of cantaloupe and fish in this Claremont place by the side of the Hudson.

In Butte-Montana at the sun's setting there comes a red, red line to the sky - the air is high and thin and clear - and it shows so red - and the clouds are like nothing that is in the mysterious East. I love those things the best of all and they are not here. But just now 'tis a trifle - I am sitting and eating my little breakfast of cantaloupe and fish in this Claremont place by the side of the Hudson.

In Butte-Montana there was a Gray Dawn, such a Gray Dawn as there is not elsewhere in the wide world. It was a thing that made all things possible - and now I have left it. But just now 'tis a trifle - I am sitting and eating my little breakfast of cantaloupe and fish in this Claremont place by the side of the Hudson.

Since I have come into the mysterious East many worrisome things have beset me and I find little complications and bitternesses by the roadside as I go. But just now 'tis a trifle - I am sitting and eating my little breakfast of cantaloupe and fish in this Claremont place by the side of the Hudson.

August 29

To-day I looked down from the dome of the Pulitzer Building upon New York - my Wicked City.

Looking down upon it the bigness of it is hurled violently at one's eyes and the manifold kinds of life appear - vivid, lurid.

Oh, 'tis a mad world, my masters.

Cars and persons and wagons and dogs and wires and the buildings roar and yell - the church spires rise from the smoke - the park fades and the leaves curl up for lack of rain - the "L" train rushes along frantically in mid-air - and smoke and fumes come sickeningly upward. The roofs of buildings show for miles and miles again - and one's strained eyes cannot see the end. The masts of the boats quiver in the varying light - the water lies still - still. Through it all the inner voice of the Wicked City calls over its domes and pinnacles: Come - come.

And so -

No more.

Her contract at an end, MacLane moved north. She lived in a Massachusetts shore hotel, watched it go near-empty as autumn went on, then - the day she was to move back to Butte - met Caroline Branson, Maria Louise Pool's lover until the authoress' death four years earlier. MacLane and the much-older Branson would live - if as lovers, it is not known - in Pool's ancestral home, travel together, and share a summer house in St. Augustine, until 1908.

MacLane would call her second book - written reluctantly, at her publisher's urge - a sell-out. If so, it was uniquely done. In place of the expected curses and sex, readers found a composed voice, no patent theme, and long horizontals in uncolored thread. I Await *incised a single if complex personality ambitiously held against inimical environments;* Annabel *withdraws from the social world and all chance of bodily action to unfold two auctorial personae in dialogue throughout: the gnomic, declarative, unflappable Annabel Lee and the depressive, credulous, clingy narrator, "Mary MacLane." No hours-long walks, teeming towns, or soul's trips to Greece. Nature is as if non-existent. We hardly ever leave the tomb-apartment, and then only to return to the scene of psychic tension.*

The editor's sense at earlier readings - that Annabel *was a disintegral, at times tiresome, decline from* I Await *- has given way to appreciation of its beauties and constant focus on style. A close reading discloses her most finished book and the purest exhibition of her proto-Surrealism.*

The alleged sell-out may be the book she most wrote for, to, and by herself.

MY FRIEND ANNABEL LEE

- 1903 -

To
Lucy Gray, in Chicago
This book
And one pale-lavender flower of amaranth.

*

Montreal
July 1903

1. The Coming of Annabel Lee

But the only person in Boston town who has given me of the treasure of her heart, and the treasure of her mind, and the touch of her fair hand in friendship, is Annabel Lee.

Since I looked for no friendship whatsoever in Boston town, this friendship comes to me with the gentleness of sun-showers mingled with cherry-blossoms, and there is a human quality in the air that rises from the bitter salt sea.

Years ago there was one who wrote a poem about Annabel Lee - a different lady from this lady, it may be, or perhaps it is the same - and so now this poem and this lady are never far from me.

If indeed Poe did not mean this Annabel Lee when he wrote so enchanting a heart-cry, I at any rate shall always mean this Annabel Lee when Poe's enchanting heart-cry runs in my mind.

Forsooth Poe's Annabel Lee was not so enchanting as this Annabel Lee.

I think this as I gaze up at her graceful little figure standing on my shelf; her wonderful expressive little face; her strange white hands; her hair bound and twisted into glittering black ropes and wound tightly around her head.

Were you to see her you would say that Annabel Lee is only a very pretty little black and terra-cotta and white statue of a Japanese woman. And forthwith you would be greatly mistaken.

It is true that she had stood in extremely dusty durance vile, in a Japanese shop in Boylston street, for months before I found her. It is also true that I fell instantly in love with her, and that on payment of a few strange dollars to the shop-keeper, I rescued her from her surroundings and bore her out to where I live by the sea - the sea where these wonderful, wide, green waves are rolling, rolling, rolling always. Annabel Lee hears these waves, and I hear them, at times holding our breath and listening until our eyes are strained with listening and with some haunting terror, and the low rushing goes to our two pale souls.

For though my friend Annabel Lee lived dumbly and dustily for months in the shop in Boylston street, as if she were indeed but a porcelain statue, and though she was purchased with a price, still my friend Annabel Lee is exquisitely human.

There are days when she fills my life with herself.

She gives rise to manifold emotions which do not bring rest.

It was not I who named her Annabel Lee. That was always her name - that is who she is. It is not a Japanese name, to be sure - and she is certainly a native of Japan. But among the myriad names that are, that alone is the one which suits her; and she alone of the myriad maidens in the world is the one to wear it.

She wears it matchlessly.

I have the friendship of Annabel Lee; but for her love, that is different.

Annabel Lee is like no one you have known. She is quite unlike them all. Times I almost can feel a subtle, conscious love coming from her finger-tips to my forehead. And I, at one-and-twenty, am thrilled with thrills.

Forsooth, at one-and-twenty, in spite of Boston and all, there are moments when one can yet thrill.

But other times I look up and perchance her eyes will meet mine with a look that is cold and penetrating and contemptuous and confounding.

Other times I look up and see her eyes full of indifference, full of tranquillity, full of dull deadly quiet.

Came Annabel Lee from out of Boylston street in Boston. And lo, she was so adorable, so fascinating, so lovable, that straightway I adored her; I was fascinated by her; I loved her.

I love her tenderly. For why, I know not. How can there be accounting for the places one's loves will rest?

Sometimes my friend Annabel Lee is negative and sometimes she is positive.

Sometimes when my mind seems to have wandered infinitely far from her I realize suddenly that 'tis she who holds it enthralled. Whatsoever I see in Boston or in the vision of the wide world my judgment of it is prejudiced in ways by the existence of my friend Annabel Lee - the more so that it's mostly unconscious prejudice.

Annabel Lee's is an intense personality - one meets with intense personalities now and again, in children or in bull-dogs or in persons like my friend Annabel Lee.

And I never tire of looking at Annabel Lee, and I never tire of listening to her, and I never tire of thinking about her.

And thinking of her, my mind grows wistful.

*

2. The Flat Surfaces of Things

"There are moments," said my friend Annabel Lee, "when, willy-nilly, they must all come out upon the flat surfaces of things.

"They look deep into the green water as the sun goes down, and their mood is heavy. Their heart aches, and they shed no tears. They look out over the brilliant waves as the sun comes up, and their mood is light-hearted and they enjoy the moment. Or else their heart aches at the rising and their mood is light-hearted at the setting. But let it be one or the other, there are bland moments when they see nothing but flat surfaces. If they find all at once, by a little accident, that their best-loved is a traitor friend, and they go at the sun's setting and gaze deep into the green water, and all is dark and dead as only a traitor best-beloved can make it, and their mood is very heavy - still there is a bland moment when their stomach tells them they are hungry, and they listen to it. It is the flat surface. After weeks, or it may be days, according to who they are, their mood will not be heavy - yet still their stomach will tell them they are hungry, and they will listen. If their best-loved cease to be, suddenly - that is bad for them, oh, exceeding bad; they suffer, and it takes weeks for them to recover, and the mark of the wound never wears away. But with time's encouraging help they do recover. But if," said my friend Annabel Lee, "their stomach should cease to be, not only would they suffer - they would die - and whither away? That is a flat surface and a very truth. And when they consider it - for one bland moment - they laugh gently and cease to have a best-loved, entirely; they cease to fill their veins with red, red life; they become like unto mice - mice with long slim tails.

"For one bland moment.

"And, too, the bland moment is long enough for them to feel restfully, deliciously, but unconsciously, thankful that there are these flat surfaces to things and that they can thus roll at times out upon them.

"They roll upon the flat surfaces much as a horse rolls upon the flat prairie where the wind is.

"And when for the first time they fall in love, if their belt is too tight there will come a bland moment when they will be aware that their belt is thus tight - and they will not be aware of much else.

"During that bland moment they will loosen their belt.

"When they were eight or nine years old and found a fine, ripe, juicy-plum patch, and while they were picking plums a balloon suddenly appeared over their heads, their first delirious impulse was to leave all and follow the balloon over hill and dale to the very earth's end.

"But even though a real live balloon went sailing over their heads, they considered this: that *some other kids would get our plums that we had found.* A balloon was glorious - a balloon was divine - but even so, there was a bland moment, in which the thought of some vicious, tow-headed Swede children from over the hill who would rush in on the plums, came just in time to make the balloon pall on them.

"But," said my friend Annabel Lee, "by the same token, in talking over the balloon after it had vanished down the sky, there would come another bland moment when the plums would pall upon them - pall completely, and would appear hateful in their eyes for having kept from them the joy of following the divine balloon. That is another aspect of the flat surfaces of things. And they must all come out upon the flat surfaces, willy-nilly.

"And," said Annabel Lee, glancing at me as my mind was dimly wistful; "not only must they come out upon the flat surfaces of things, but also you and I must come, willy-nilly.

"And since we *must* come, willy-nilly," added the lady, "then why not stay out upon the flat surfaces? Certainly 'twill save the trouble of coming next time. Perhaps, however, it's all in the coming."

*

3. My Friend Annabel Lee

My friend Annabel Lee never fails to fascinate and confound me.

Much as she gives, there is in her infinitely more to get.

My relation with her never goes on, and it never goes back. It leads nowhere. She and I stop together in the midst of our situation and look about us. And what we see in the looking about is all and enough to consider.

And considering, I write of it.

*

4. Boston

Yesterday the lady was in her most amiable mood, and we talked together - about Boston, it so happened.

"Do you like Boston?" she asked me.

"Yes," I replied; "I am fond of Boston. It fascinates me."

"But not fonder of it than of Butte, in Montana?"

"Oh, no," said I, hastily. "Butte in Montana is my first love. There are barren mountains there - they are with me always. Boston doesn't go to my heart in the least, but I like it much. I like to live here."

"I am fond of Boston - sometimes," Annabel Lee observed. "Here by the sea it is not quite Boston. It is everything. This sea washes down by enchanted purple islands and touches at the coast of Spain. But if one can but turn one's eyes from it for a moment, Boston is a fine and good thing, and interesting."

"I think it is - from several points of view," I agreed.

"Tell me what you find that interests you in Boston," said my friend Annabel Lee.

"There are many things," I replied. "I have found a little corner down by the East Boston wharf where often I sit on cold days. The sun shines bright and warm on a narrow wooden platform between two great barrels, and I can be hidden there, but I can watch the madding crowd as it goes. The crowd is very madding down around East Boston. And I do not lack company - sometimes brave, sharp-toothed rats venture out on the ground below me. They can not see the madding crowd, but they can enjoy the sunshine and hunt mice among the rubbish.

"The dwellers in East Boston - they are the poor we have always with us. They are not the meek, the worthy, the deserving poor. They are the devilish, the ill-conditioned - one with the wharf rats that hunt for mice. Except that the rats do occasionally try to clean their soft, gray coats by licking them with their little red tongues; whereas, the poor - But why should the poor wash? Are they not the poor?

"As I rest me between my two great barrels and watch this grewsome pageant, I think: It seems a quite desperate thing to be poor in Boston, for Boston is said to be of the best-seasoned knowledge and to carry a lump of ice in its heart. From between my two barrels in East Boston I have seen humanity, oh, so brutal, oh, so barbarous as ever it could have been in merrie England in the reign of good old Harry the Eighth. -

"And so then that is very interesting."

"In truth it is so," said my friend Annabel Lee. "Boston is fair, and very fair. - Tell me more."

"And times," I said, "I sit in one of the window-seats on the stairway of the Public Library. And I look at the walls. A Frenchman with a marvelous fancy and great skill in his finger-ends has worked on those walls. He painted there the emblems of all the world's great material things of all ages. And over them he painted a thin gray veil of those things that are not material, that come from no age, that are with us, around us, above us - as they were with the children of Israel, with the dwellers in Pompeii, with the fair cities of Greece and the inhabitants thereof.

"I have looked at the paintings and I have been dazzled and transported. What is there not upon those walls!

"I have seen, in truth, 'the vision of the world and all the wonder that shall be.'

"I have seen the struggling of the chrysalis-soul and its bursting into light; I have seen the divinity that doth sometime hedge the earth; I have looked at a conception of Poetry and I have heard the thin, rhythmic sounds of shawms and stringed instruments; and I have heard low, voluptuous music from within the temple - human voices like sweet jessamine; I have seen the fascinating idolatry of pagans - and I have seen, pale in the evening by the light of a star, the wooden figure of the Cross; I have leaned over the edge of a chasm and beheld the things of old - the army of Hannibal before Carthage - the Norsemen going down to the sea in ships - the futile, savage fighting of Goths and Vandals; I have seen science and art within the walled cities, and I have seen frail little lambs gamboling by the side of the brook; I have seen night-shades lowering over occult works, and I have seen bees flying heavy-laden to their hives on a fine summer's morning; I have heard a lute played where a tiny cataract leaps, and the pipes of Pan mingled with the bubbling notes of a robin in mint meadows; I have seen pages and pages of printed lines that reach from world's end to world's end; I have seen profound words written centuries ago in inks of many colors; I have seen and been overwhelmed by the marvels of scientific things bristling with the accurate kind of knowledge that I shall never know; withal, I have seen the complete serenity of the world's face, as shown by the brush of the Frenchman Chavannes.

"And over all, the nebulous conception of the long, ignorant silence.

"What is there not upon those wonderful walls!

"I sit in semi-consciousness in the little window-seat and these things swim before my two gray eyes. My mind is full of the vision of murmuring, throbbing life.

"But what a thing is life, truly - for marvelous as are these pictures, those that I have seen, times, down where the rats forage among the rubbish, are more marvelous still."

"Truly," said my friend Annabel Lee, "there is much, much, in Boston. Tell me more."

"Well, and there is the South Station," I went on. "Oh, not until one has ambled and idled away a thousand hours in that place of trains and varied peoples can one know all of what is really to be found within its waiting-rooms.

"I have found Massachusetts there - not any Massachusetts that I had ever read about, but the Massachusetts that comes in from Braintree and Plymouth and Middleboro carrying a Boston shopping-bag; the Massachusetts that is intellectual and thrusts its forefinger through the handle of its tea-cup; the Massachusetts that eats soup from the end of its spoon; the Massachusetts that is good-hearted but walks funny; the Massachusetts that takes all the children and goes down to Providence for a day - each of the children with a thick, yellow banana in its hand; the Massachusetts that has its being because the world wears shoes - for it is intellectual and can make shoes.

"And in the South Station, furthermore, there are people from the wide world around. Actors and authors and artists are to be seen coming in and going out and sitting waiting in the waiting-rooms. Some mightily fine and curious persons have sat waiting in those waiting-rooms, as well as dingy Italians with strings of beads around their necks.

"And in the South Station there are so many, many people, that, once in a long while, one can meet with some of those tiny things that one has waited for for centuries. In among a multitude of faces there may be a young face with lines of worn and vivid life in it, and with alert and much-used eyes, and with soft dull hair above it. In a flash one recognizes it, and in a flash it is gone. It is a face that means beautiful things and one has known it and its divineness a long, long time. And here in the South Station in Boston came the one gold glimpse of it.

"And I have seen in the South Station a strange scene: that of a mild Jew man bearing the brunt of caring for his large family of small children, while their child-weary mother was allowed for once in her life to rest completely, sitting with her eyes closed and her hands folded. She might well rest tranquil in the thought that in giving birth to that small Hebraic army she had done her share of this dubious world's penance.

"And in the South Station, as much as anywhere, one feels the air of Boston.

"The air of Boston, too, is wonderful - and 'tis not free for all to breathe. 'Tis for the anointed - the others must content them with the untinted, unscented air that blows wild from mountain-tops and north seas. But for me, I have eyes wherewith to see - and since the air of Boston has color, I can see it. And I have ears wherewith to hear - and since the air of Boston has musical vibrations, I can hear it. And I have sensibility - wherefore all that is pungent in the air of Boston, and all that is fine, and all that is art, and all that is beautiful, and all that is true, and all that is benign, and particularly all that is very cool and all that is bitterly contemptuous - are not wholly lost upon me.

"If all the persons who go to and fro at the South Station were heroes and breathed the air there and left their dim shadows behind them - as they do - I presume the South Station would be hallowed ground. They all are not heroes, but they breathe the air and leave their dim shadows, whatever they may be, and ever after the air of the South Station is tinctured. And since more than a half of these people are of Boston, the air is tinctured therewith.

"If you are civilized and conventional you may know and breathe this air. If you are not - well, at least you may stand and contemplate it. And always one can bide one's time.

"My contemplation of it has interested me.

"The air of Boston is a mingling of very ancient and very modern things and ways of thinking that are picturesque and at times lead to something. The ancient things date back to Confucius and others of his ilk - and the modern ones are tinted with Lilian Whiting and newspapers and the theater.

"One is half-conscious of this as one contemplates, and one's thought is, 'Woe is me that I have my habitation among the tents of Kedar!' One exclaims this not so much that one considers oneself benighted, but that one is very sure that the air of Boston considers one so. To be sure, it ought to know, but, somehow, as yet one is content to bide one's time.

"But yes. There is a beatified quality in the air of Boston. It is tinted with rose and blue. It sounds, remotely, of chimes and flutes. You feel it, perchance, when you sit within the subdued, brilliant stillness of Trinity church - when you walk among the green and gold fields about Brookline and Cambridge, where orchids are lifting up their pale, soft lips - when you are in the Museum of Fine Arts and see, hanging on the wall, a small dull-toned picture that is old - so old!

"Music is in the air of Boston. It pours into the heart like fire and flood - it awakens the soul from its dreaming - it sends the human being out into the many-colored pathways to see, to suffer, it may be - yes, surely to suffer - but to live, oh, to live!

"One can see in the mists the slender, gray figure of one's own soul rising and going to mingle with all these. In spite of the clouds about it, one knows its going and that it is well. It was long since said: 'My beloved has gone down into her garden to the bed of spices, to feed in the gardens and to gather lilies.' And now again is the beloved in the garden, and in those moments, oh, life is fair" -

My friend Annabel Lee opened her lips - her lips like damp, red quince-blooms in the spring-time - and told me that there were times when I interested her, times when I amused her mightily, and times when in me she made some rare discoveries.

But which of the three this time was, she has not told.

*

5. A Small House in the Country

But Boston - or even Butte in Montana - is not to be compared to a lodging-place far down in the country: a tiny house by the side of a fishy, mossy pond, in summer-time, with the hot sun shining on the door-step, and a clump of willows and an oak-tree growing near; on the side of the house where the sun is bright in the morning, some small square beds of radishes, and pale-green heads of lettuce, and straight, neat rows of young onions, with the moist earth showing black between the rows; and a few green peas growing by a small fence; and on the other side of the little house grass will grow - tall rank grass and some hardy weeds, and perhaps a tiger-lily or two will come up unawares. The fishy pond will not be too near the house, nor too far away - but near enough so that the singing of the frogs in the night will sound clear and loud.

Rolling hills will be lying fair and green at a distance, and cattle will wander and graze upon them in the shade of low-hanging branches. On still afternoons a quail or a pheasant will be heard calling in the woods.

The air that will blow down the long gentle uplands will be very sweet. The message that it brings, as it touches my cheeks and my lips and my forehead, will be one of exceeding deep peace.

I would live in the little house with a friend of my heart - a friend in the shadows and half-lights and brilliances. For if the hearts of two are tuned in accord the harmony may be of exquisite tenor.

In the very early morning I would sit on the doorstep where the sun shines, and my eyes would look off at the prospect. Life would throb in my veins.

In the middle of the forenoon I would be kneeling in the beds of radishes and slim young onions and lettuce, pulling the weeds from among them and staining my two hands with black roots.

In the middle of the day I would sit in the shade, but where I could see the sunshine touching the brilliant greenness, near the house and afar. And I could see the pond glaring with beams and motes.

In the late afternoon I, with the friend of my heart, would walk down among the green valleys and wooded hills, by fences and crumbling stone walls, until we reached a point of vantage where we could see the sea.

In the night, when the sun had gone and the earth had cooled and the dark, dark gray had fallen over all, we would sit again on the doorstep. It would be lonesome there, with the sound of the frogs and of night-birds - and there would be a cricket chirping. We would speak to each other with one or two words through long stillnesses.

Presently would come the dead midnight, and we would be in heavy sleep beneath the low, hot roof of the little house.

Mingled with the dead midnight would be memories of the day that had just gone. In my sleep I would seem to walk again in the meadows, and the green of the countless grass-blades would affect me with a strange delirium - as if now for the first time I saw them. Each little grass-blade would have a voice and would shout: *Mary MacLane, oh, we are the grass-blades and we are here! We are the grass-blades, we are the grass-blades, and we are here!*

And yes. That would be the marvelous thing - that they were *here*. And would not the leaves be upon the trees? - and would not tiny pale flowers be growing in the ground? - and would not the sky be over all? Oh, the unspeakable sky!

In the dead midnight sleep would leave me and I would wake in a vision of beauty and of horror, with fear at my heart, with horrible fear at my heart.

Then frantically I would think of the little radish-beds outside the window - how common and how satisfying they were. Thus thinking, I would sleep again and wake to the sun's shining.

"You would not," said my friend Annabel Lee, "stay long in such a place."

I looked at her.

"Its simplicity and truth," said my friend Annabel Lee, "would deal you deep wounds and scourge you and drive you forth as if you were indeed a money-changer in the temple."

*

6. The Half-Conscious Soul

Annabel Lee leaned her two elbows on the back of a tiny sandalwood chair and looked down at me.

We regarded each other coldly, as friends do, times.

"You," said Annabel Lee, "have a half-conscious soul. Such a soul that when it hears a strain of music can hear away to the music's depths but can understand only one-half of its meaning; but because it is half-conscious it knows that it understands only the half, and must need weep for the other half; such a soul that when it wanders into the deep green and meets there a shadow-woman, with long, dark hair and an enchanting voice, it feels to its depths the spirit of the green and the voice of the shadow-woman, but can understand only one-half of what they tell: but because it is half-conscious it knows that it understands only the half, and must need weep for the other half; such a soul that when it is bound and fettered heavily, it knows since it is half-conscious, that it is bound and fettered, but knows not why nor wherefore nor whether it is well, which is the other half - and it must need weep for it; such a soul that when it hears thunderings in the wild sky will awaken from sleep and listen - listen, but since it is half-conscious it can only hear, not know - and it sounds like an unknown voice in an unknown language, telling the dying speech of its best loved - it is frantic to know the translation which is the other half; such a soul that when life gathers itself up from around it and stands before it and says, Now, contemplate life, it contemplates, since it is half-conscious, but it for that same reason strains its eyes to look over life's shoulders into the dimness - which is an impossible thing, and the other half; such a soul that when it finds itself mingling in love for its friend, and all, it enjoys, oh, vividly in all moments but the crucial moments, when it aches in torment and doubt - for it is half-conscious and so knows its lacking.

"Desolate is the way of the half-conscious soul," said Annabel Lee.

"The wholly conscious soul receives into itself things in their entirety without question or wonder: the half-conscious soul receives the half of things, and knowing that there is another half, it wonders and questions till all's black.

"The wholly conscious soul is different from the wholly unconscious soul in that the former is positive whilst the latter is negative - and they both in their nature can find rest: but the half-conscious soul knows that it is half-conscious, still it knows not at what points it is conscious and at what points unconscious - for when it thinks itself conscious, lo, it is unconscious, and when it thinks itself unconscious it is heavily, bitterly conscious - and nowhere can it find rest.

"The wholly conscious soul holds up before its eyes a mirror and gazes at itself, its color, its texture, its quality, its desires and motives, without flinching, in the strong light of day; the wholly unconscious soul knows not that it is a soul, and never uses a mirror: but the half-conscious soul looks into its glass in the gray light of dusk - it sees its color, its texture, its quality, its desires - but its motives are hidden. Its eyes are wide in the gray light to learn what those, its own motives, are. It can not know, but it can never rest for trying to know.

"The wholly conscious soul knows its love, its sorrow, its bitterness, its remorse.

"The half-conscious soul knows its love - and wonders why it loves, and wonders if it really can love any but itself, and wonders that it cares for love; the half-conscious soul knows its sorrow - and marvels that it should have sorrow since it can grasp not truth; the half-conscious soul knows its bitterness, and realizes at once its right to and its reason for bitterness - but, thinking of it, the arrow is turned in the wound; the half-conscious soul knows its remorse, but it is convinced that it has no right to remorse, since it does its unworthy acts with infinite forethought.

"The wholly conscious soul is a chastened spirit and so has its measure of happiness; the wholly unconscious soul is an unchastened spirit, for it deserves no chastisement - neither has it any happiness, for it knows not whether it is happy or otherwise: but the half-conscious soul is chastised where it is not deserving of it, and goes unchastised where it is richly deserving of it - and so has no happiness, but instead, unhappiness.

"Woe to the half-conscious soul," said Annabel Lee.

"How brilliantly does the emerald sea flash in the sunshine before the eyes of the half-conscious soul! - but burns it with mad-fire.

"How melting-sweet is the perfume of the blue anemone to the sense of the half-conscious soul! - but burns it with mad-fire.

"How beautiful are the bronze lights in the eyes of its friend to the half-conscious soul! - that burn it with mad-fire.

"How joyous is the half-conscious soul at the sounds of singing voices on water! - that burn it with mad-fire.

"How surely come the wild, sweet meanings of the outer air into the depths of the half-conscious soul! - but burn it with mad-fire.

"How madly happy is the half-conscious soul in still hours at sight of a solitary pine-tree upon the mountain-top! - that burns it with mad-fire.

"How tenderly comes Truth to the half-conscious soul in the dead watches of the night! - but burns it with mad-fire.

"Life is vivid, alert, telling to the half-conscious soul," said Annabel Lee.

"You," said Annabel Lee, "with your half-conscious soul, when you sit where the gray waves wash the sea-wall at high-tide, when you sit listening with your head bent and your hands dead cold, you think you realize your life - you think you know its hardness - you think you have measured the cruelty they will give you; but you do not know. You know but half - you weep for the other half, though it be horror.

"Still, though you are but half-conscious, though you weep for the other half, when you sit listening with your head bent and your hands dead cold, where the gray waves wash the sea-wall at high-tide - yet you know some of each one of the things that are around you.

"Wonderful in conception is the half-conscious soul," said Annabel Lee. -

I looked hard at my friend Annabel Lee. Was she teasing me? Was she laughing at me? For she does tease me and she does laugh at me. And was she at either of these pastimes, with all this about a half-conscious soul?

But here again she left me ignorant of her thought, and there is no way of knowing.

*

7. The Young-Books of Trowbridge

There are two writers, among them all, to whom I owe thanks for countless hours of complete pleasure. Not the pleasure that stirs and fires one, but the pleasure which enters into the entire personality, and rests and satisfies a common, unstrained mind. 'Tis the same pleasure that comes with eating all by myself - eating peaches and a fine, tiny lamb chop in the middle of the day.

One of these two writers is J.T. Trowbridge who has written young-books.

Often I have thought, Life would be different, and duller colored, and less thickly sprinkled with marigolds-and-cream, had I never known my Trowbridge.

Often I have thanked the happy fate that put into my hands my first young-book of Trowbridge. 'Twas when I was fourteen - one day in October, when I lived in a flat, windy town that was named Great Falls, in Montana. Since that time I have never been without the young-books of J.T. Trowbridge. There have but seven years passed since then, but when seven years more, and seven years again, up to threescore, have gone, I still shall spend one-half my rest-hours, my pleasure-hours, my loosely-comfortable, unstrained hours with the young-books of Trowbridge.

When I go to a theater I enjoy it thoroughly. A theater is a good thing, and the actor is a stunning person - but how eagerly and gladly I come back into my own room where there is a faithful, little, tan deer standing waiting, all so pathetic and sweet, upon the desk.

When I go out into two crowded rooms among some fascinating persons that I have heard of before - women with fine-wrought gowns - I like that, too, and I wouldn't have missed it - but how utterly restful and adorable it is to come back to my own room where there is my comfortable quiet friend in a rusty black flannel frock, sitting waiting - and her hands so soft and good to feel.

When I read gold treasures of literature - Vergil, it may be, or a Browning, or Kipling - I am enchanted and enthralled. I marvel at these people and how they can write. I think how marvelous is writing, at last - but how gladly and thankfully, after two hours or three, I return back to these my young-books of Trowbridge.

They are about people living on farms, and they are written so that you know that red-root grows among wheat-spears, and must be weeded out, and that the farmer's boys have to milk the cows mornings before breakfast and evenings after supper. For they have supper in the Trowbridge books - and it is even attractive and tastes good.

When the lads go to gather kelp to spread on the land, and are gone for the day by the seashore, they eat roasted ears of corn, and cold-boiled eggs, and bread-and-butter, and three bottles of spruce beer - and if you really know the Trowbridge books you can eat of these with them, and with a wonderful appetite.

When a slim boy of sixteen goes to hunt for his uncle's horse that had been stolen in the night (because the boy left the stable door unlocked), along pleasant country roads and smiling farms in Massachusetts - if you really know the Trowbridge books - the slim boy of sixteen is not more anxious to find the horse than you are. When the boy and the reader first start after the horse they are far too wretched and anxious to eat - for the crabbed uncle told them they needn't come back to the farm without that horse. But long before noon they are glad enough that they have a few doubled slices of buttered bread to eat as they go. When at last they come upon the horse calmly feeding under a cattle-shed at a county fair twenty miles away, they are quite hungry, and in their joy they purchase a wedge of pie and some oyster crackers, so that they needn't be out of sight of the horse while they eat. And the reader - if he really knows the Trowbridge books - would fain stop here, for there is trouble ahead of him. He would fain - but he can not. He must go on - he must even come in crucial contact with Eli Badger's hickory club - he must go with the boy until he sees him and the horse at last safely back at Uncle Gray's farm, the horse placidly munching oats in his own stall, and the boy eating supper once more with appetite unimpaired, and the crabbed uncle once more serene. And - if you know Trowbridge's books - you can eat, too, tranquilly.

When a boy is left alone in the world by the death of his aunt and starts out to find his uncle in Cincinnati - if you know Trowbridge's books - you prepare for hardship and weariness, but still occasional sandwiches and doughnuts (but not the greasy kind). And always you know there must be a haven in the house of the uncle in Cincinnati. Only - if you know the Trowbridge books - you are fearful when you get to the uncle's door, and you would a little rather the boy went in to meet him while you waited outside. Trowbridge's uncles are apt to be so sour as to heart, and so bitter as to tongue, and so sarcastic in their remarks relating to boys who come in from the country to the city in order that they - the uncles - may have the privilege of supporting them. Though you know - if you know the Trowbridge books - that Trowbridge's boys never come into the city for that purpose. The heavy-tempered uncles, too, are made aware of this before long, and change the tenor of their remarks accordingly - and after some just pride on the part of the nephews, all goes well. Whereupon your feeling of satisfaction is more than that of the boy, of the uncle, of Trowbridge himself.

But these roasted ears of corn and cold-boiled eggs are among the lesser delights of the young-books of Trowbridge. The most fascinating things in them are the conversations. They are so real that you hear the voices and see the expressions of the faces.

Trowbridge is one of the kind that listens twice and thrice to persons talking, so that he hears the key-note and the detail, and his pen is of the kind that can write what he hears. It is never too much, never too little; it is not noticeable at all, because it is all harmony.

It is entirely and utterly common.

And it is real.

In the young-books of Trowbridge, and nowhere else, I have heard boys talking together so that I knew how their faces looked, and how carelessly and loosely their various collars were worn, and their dubious hats. I have heard a grasping, grouty old man pound on the kitchen floor with his horn-headed cane - he had come over while the family were at breakfast to inform them that their dog had killed five of his sheep, and to demand the dog's life. I have heard the lessons and other things they said in a country school-room sixty years ago, where boys were sometimes obliged, for punishment, to sit on nothing against the door. I have heard the extreme discontent in the voice of another grouty, grasping farmer when it became evident to him that he would be obliged to give up a horse that had been stolen before he bought him. But here I must quote, as nearly correctly as I can without the book:

"And sold him to this Mr. Badger" (said Kit) "for seventy dollars."

"Seventy gim-cracks!" exclaimed Uncle Gray, aghast. "I should think any fool might know he's worth more than that."

He was thinking of Brunlow, but Eli applied the remark to himself.

"I did know it," he growled. "That's why I bought him. And mighty glad I am now I didn't pay more."

"'Sartin!" replied Uncle Gray; "but didn't it occur to you 't no honest man would want to sell an honest hoss like that for any such sum?"

"I didn't know it," said Eli, groutily. "He told a pooty straight story. I got took in, that's all."

"Took in!" repeated Uncle Gray. "I should say, took in! I know the rogue and I'm amazed that any man with common sense and eyes in his head shouldn't 'a' seen through him at once."

"Maybe I ain't got common sense, and maybe I ain't got eyes in my head," said Eli, with a dull fire in the place where eyes should have been if he had had any. "But I didn't expect this."

Kit hastened to interpose between the two men.

Always I have been sorry that the boy interposed just there.

I have read the book surely seven-and-seventy times. Each time this talk over the horse comes exceeding pungent to my ears. How impossible it is to weary of Trowbridge, because there is no effort in the writing, and no effort in the reading, and because of a deep-reaching, never-failing sense of humor. -

How flat seem these words!

The young-books of Trowbridge can not be set down in words. What with the simplicity, what with the quality of naturalness, what with a delicate tenderness for all human things, what with the rare, rare quality of commonness that is satisfying and quieting as the vision of a little green radish-bed, what with an inner sympathy between Trowbridge and his characters and, above all, an inner sympathy with his readers, what with Truth itself and the sweet gift of portraying the sunshiny days as they are - why talk of Trowbridge?

Is it not all there written?

Can one not read and rest in it?

*

8. "Give Me Three Grains of Corn, Mother"

"No," said my friend Annabel Lee, "I can't really say that I care for Trowbridge. All that you have said is true enough, but he fails to interest me."

"What do you like in literature?" I asked, regarding her with interest, for I had never heard her say. It must need be something characteristic of herself.

"I like strength, and I like simplicity, and I like emotion, and I like vital things always. And I like poetry rather than prose. Just now," said Annabel Lee, "I am thinking of an old-fashioned bit of verse that to me is all that a poem need be. To have written it is to have done enough in the way of writing, because it's real - like your Trowbridge."

"Oh, will you repeat it for me!" I said.

"It is called, 'Give Me Three Grains of Corn, Mother.' It is of a famine in Ireland a great many years ago - a lad and his mother starving."

And then she went on:

> Give me three grains of corn, mother,
> Give me three grains of corn,
> 'Twill keep the little life I have
> Till the coming of the morn.

I am dying of hunger and cold, mother,
Dying of hunger and cold,
And half the agony of such a death
My lips have never told.

It has gnawed like a wolf at my heart, mother,
A wolf that is fierce for blood,
All the livelong day and the night, beside -
Gnawing for lack of food.
I dreamed of bread in my sleep, mother,
And the sight was heaven to see -
I awoke with an eager, famishing lip,
But you had no bread for me.

How could I look to you, mother,
How could I look to you
For bread to give to your starving boy,
When you were starving, too?
For I read the famine in your cheek
And in your eye so wild,
And I felt it in your bony hand,
As you laid it on your child.

The queen has lands and gold, mother,
The queen has lands and gold,
While you are forced to your empty breast
A skeleton babe to hold -
A babe that is dying of want, mother,
As I am dying now,
With a ghastly look in its sunken eye
And the famine upon its brow.

What has poor Ireland done, mother,
What has poor Ireland done,
That the world looks on and sees us die,
Perishing one by one?
Do the men of England care not, mother,
The great men and the high,
For the suffering sons of Erin's isle, -
Whether they live or die?

There's many a brave heart here, mother,
Dying of want and cold,
While only across the channel, mother,
Are many that roll in gold.
There are great and proud men there, mother,
With wondrous wealth to view,
And the bread they fling to their dogs to-night
Would bring life to me and you.

Come nearer to my side, mother,
Come nearer to my side,
And hold me fondly, as you held
My father when he died.
Quick, for I can not see you, mother,
My breath is almost gone.
Mother, dear mother, ere I die,
Give me three grains of corn!

"What do you think," said my friend Annabel Lee, "is it not full of power and poetry and pathos?"

"Yes, it could not in itself be better," I replied. "And it has the simplicity."

"And pretends nothing," said Annabel Lee.

"And who wrote it?" I asked.

"Oh, some forgotten Englishwoman," said Annabel Lee. "I believe her name was Edwards. She perhaps wrote a poem, now and then, and died."

"And are the poems forgotten, also?" I inquired.

"Yes, forgotten, except by a few. But when they remember them, they remember them long."

"Then which is better, to be remembered, and remembered shortly, by the multitudes; or to be forgot by the multitudes and remembered long by the one or two?"

"It is incomparably better to be remembered long by the one or two," said Annabel Lee. "To be forgotten by any one or anything that once remembered you is sorely bitter to the heart."

*

9. Relative

"Do you think, Annabel Lee," I said to her on a day that I felt depressed, "that all things must really be relative, and that those which are not now properly relative will eventually become so, though it gives them acute anguish?"

The face of Annabel Lee was placid, and also the sea. The one glanced down upon me from the shelf, and the other spread away into the distance.

Were that face and that sea relative? Surely they could not be, since those two things in their very nature might go ungoverned. Do not universal laws, in extreme moments, give way?

"Relative!" said Annabel Lee. "Nothing is relative. I tell you nothing is relative. I am come out of Japan. In Japan, when I was very new to everything, there was an ugly frog-eyed woman who washed me and anointed me and dressed me in silk, the while she pinched my little white arms cruelly, so that my little red mouth writhed with the pain. Also the frog-eyed woman looked into my suffering young eyes with her ugly frog-eyes so that my tiny young soul was prodded as with brad-nails. The frog-eyed woman did these things to hurt me - she hated me for being one of the very lovely creatures in Japan. She was a vile, ugly wretch.

"That was not relative. I tell you that was not relative," said Annabel Lee.

"If I had been an awkward, overgrown, bloodless animal and that frog-eyed woman had pinched my little white arms - still *she* would have been a vile, ugly wretch.

"If I had been a vicious spirit and that frog-eyed woman had looked into my vicious eyes with her ugly frog-eyes - still *she* would have been a vile, ugly wretch.

"If I had been a hateful little thing, instead of a gently-bred, gently-living, pitiful-to-the-poor maiden, and that frog-eyed woman had hated me with all her frog-heart - still *she* would have been a vile, ugly wretch.

"If that frog-eyed woman had stood alone in Japan with no human being to compare her to - still the frog-eyed woman would have been a vile, ugly wretch.

"She has left her horrid frog-mark on my fair soul. Not anything beneath the worshiped sun can ever blot out the horrid frog-mark from my fair soul. A thousand curses on the ugly, frog-eyed woman," said Annabel Lee, tranquilly.

"Then that, for one thing, is not relative," I said. "But perhaps that is because of the power and the depth of your eyes and your fair soul. Where there are no eyes and no fair souls - at least where the eyes and the fair souls can not be considered as themselves, but only as things without feeling for life - then are not things relative?"

"Nothing is relative," said Annabel Lee. "If your dog's splendid fur coat is full of fleas and you caress your dog with your hands, then presently you may acquire numbers of the fleas. You love the dog, but you do not love the fleas. You forgive the fleas for the love of the dog, though you hate them no less. So then that is not relative. If that were relative you would love the fleas a little for the same reason that you forgive them: for love of your dog. Forgiveness is a negative quality and can have no bearing on your attitude toward the fleas."

Having said this, Annabel Lee gazed placidly over my head at the sea.

When her mood is thus tranquil, she talks graciously and evenly and positively, and is beautiful to look at.

My mind was now in much confusion upon the subject in question. But I felt that I must know all that Annabel Lee thought about it.

"What would you say, Annabel Lee," said I, "to a case like this: If a soul were at variance with everything that touches it, everything that makes life, so that it must struggle through the long nights and long days with bitterness, is not that because the soul has no sense of proportion, and has not made itself properly relative to each and everything that is? - relative, so that when one hard thing touches it, simultaneously one soft thing will touch it; or when it mourns for dead days, simultaneously it rejoices for live ones; or when its best-loved gives it a deep wound, simultaneously its best enemy gives it vivid pleasure."

"Nothing is relative," again said Annabel Lee. "Nothing can be relative. Nothing need be relative. If a soul is wearing itself to small shreds by struggling days and nights, that is a matter relating peculiarly to the soul, and to nothing else, *nothing* else. If a soul is wearing itself to small shreds by struggling, the more fool it. It is struggling because of things that would never, *never* struggle because of it. In truth, not one of them would move itself one millionth of an inch because of so paltry a thing as a soul."

I looked at Annabel Lee, her hair, her hands, and her eyes. As I looked, I was reminded of the word "eternity."

A human being is a quite wonderful thing, truly - and great - there's none greater.

Annabel Lee is a person who always says truth, for, for her, there is nothing else to say.

She has reached that marvelous point where a human being expects nothing.

"If the days of a life, Annabel Lee," I said, "are made bright because of two other lives that are dear to it, and if the life happens upon a day when the thought of the two whom it loves makes its own heart like lead, then what can there be to smooth away its weariness, in heaven above, in the earth beneath, or in the waters under the earth?"

"Foolish life," said my friend Annabel Lee. "There is no pain in Japan like what comes of loving some one or some thing. And if the some one or the some thing is the only thing the life can call its own, then woe to it. The things it needs are three: a Lodging Place in heaven above; a Bit of Hardness in the earth beneath; a Last Resort in the waters under the earth. These three - but no life has ever had them."

"In the end," I said, "when all wide roadways come together, and all heavy hearts are alert to know what will happen, then will there not indeed be one grand adjustment, and life and all become at once magnificently relative?"

"Never; it can't be so. Nothing is relative," said Annabel Lee, on a day that I felt depressed.

*

10. Minnie Madern Fiske

To-day my friend Annabel Lee and I went to the theater and we saw a wonderful and fascinating woman with long, dark-red hair upon the stage.

She is attractive, that red-haired woman - adorably attractive. And she reminds one of many things.

Annabel Lee was greatly interested in her acting, and was charmed with herself - and so was I.

"Do you suppose she finds life very delightful?" I said to my friend.

"I don't suppose," my friend replied, "she is of the sort that considers whether or not life is delightful. Probably her work is hard enough to keep her out of mischief of any kind."

Whereupon we both fell to thinking how fortunate are they whose work is hard enough to keep them out of mischief of any kind.

"But there must be," I said, "some months, perhaps in the summer, when she doesn't work. I have heard that some actors take houses among the mountains and do their own housework for recreation."

"I," said Annabel Lee, "can not quite imagine this woman with the red hair making bread and scouring pans and kettles for pleasure. But very likely she sometimes goes into the country for vacations, and I can fancy her doing the various small enjoyable things that celebrities can afford to do - like wading barefooted in a narrow brooklet, or swinging high and recklessly in a barrel-stave hammock."

"And since she is so adorable on the stage," I exclaimed, "how altogether enchanting she would be wading in the brooklet or swinging in the barrel-stave hammock - she with the long, red hair! Perhaps it would even be braided down her back in two long tails."

It is a picture that haunts me - Mrs. Fiske in the midst of her vacation doing the small enjoyable things.

"Of course," said my friend Annabel Lee, "we don't *know* that she doesn't spend her vacations in a fine, conventional, stupid yacht, or at some magnificent, insipid American or English country house. We can only give her the benefit of the doubt."

"Yes, the benefit of the doubt," I replied.

How fascinating she was, to be sure, with her personality merged in that of Mary Magdalene!

The Magdalene is no longer a shadowy ideal with a somewhat buxom body, scantily draped, with indefinite hair and with the lifeless beauty that the old masters paint. Nor is she quite the woman of the scriptures who is presented to one's mind without that quality which is called local coloring, and with too much of the quality that is ever present with the women in the scriptures - a something between uncleanness and final complete redemption.

No, Mary Magdalene is Mrs. Fiske, a slight woman still in the last throes of youth, with two shoulders which move impatiently, expressing indescribable emotions of aliveness and two lips which perform their office - that of coloring, bewitching, torturing, perfuming, anointing the words that come out of them. Apart from these lips, Mary Magdalene's face has a wonderfully round and childish look, and her two round eyes at first sight give one an idea of positive innocence. In the Magdalene's face - and in that of an actor of Mrs. Fiske's range - these are a beautifully delicate incongruity.

And my friend Annabel Lee has told me that the strongest things are the delicate incongruities - the strongest in all this wide world. Because they make you consider - and considering, you wait.

With such a pair of round, innocent eyes of some grayish color - who can blame Mary Magdalene?

In the latter acts of the play these eyes go one step farther than innocence: they do hunger and thirst after righteousness. And, ah, dear heaven (you thought to yourself), how well they did it! To hunger and thirst after righteousness - not herself, but her eyes. That was this Mary Magdalene's art.

This Mary Magdalene, though she is indeed in the last throes of youth - without reference to the years she may know - has yet beneath her chin a very charming roundness of flesh which one day obviously will become a double chin. Just now it is enchanting. There are feminine children of seven and eight with round faces, who have just that fullness beneath the chin, and beneath the chin of Mary Magdalene - and added to her eyes - it carries on the idea of innocence and inexperience to a rare good degree. Any other woman actor would have long since massaged this fullness away.

Forsooth, perhaps this is the one woman actor who could wear such a thing with beauty.

Mary Magdalene's hair in its deep redness is scornful and aggressive in the first acts of the play. In the latter acts it assumes a marvelous patheticness. And, if you like, there is a world of patheticness in red hair.

If Mary Magdalene's hair were of a different color - if the bronze shadows were yellow, or gray, or black, or brown shadows - her lips and her shoulders were in vain.

On the stage Mary Magdalene stands with her back to her audience - she stands, calm and placid, for three or four minutes before the rising and falling curtain, graciously permitting all to admire and feast their eyes upon the red of her hair.

"She knows," said my friend Annabel Lee, "that she can make her face bewitching - and she knows also that her hair is bewitching without being so made. And she chooses that the world at large shall know it, too."

She has will-power, has Mary Magdalene. It is her will, her strength, her concentration of all her power to herself that makes her thus bewitching - and that seduces the brains of those who sit watching her as she moves upon the stage.

She controls all her mental and physical features with metallic precision - except her hair, and that she leaves uncontrolled to do its own work. It does its work well.

She has cultivated that mobileness of her lips, probably with hard work and infinite patience - and she makes them damp and brilliant with rouge. She rubs the soft, thick skin of her face with layers of grease. She loads her two white arms with limitless powder. And the two childish eyes are exceeding heavy-laden as to lid and lash with black crayon. One experiences a revulsion as one contemplates them through a glass. Her voice in the days of her youth had drilled into it the power to thrill and vibrate, and to become exquisitely tender upon occasion, and now it does the bidding of its owner with docility and skill. Since its owner has forcefulness and a power of selfish concentration, the voice is mostly magnetic and cold and strong. It is magnetic and cold and strong and contemptuous when its owner says, "My curse upon you!" When its owner's eyes do hunger and thirst after righteousness the voice brings a miserable, anguished feeling to the throats of those who sit listening. Every emotion that the voice betrays is transmitted to the seduced brains of those who sit listening. The red-haired woman works her audience up to some torturing pitches - the while herself blandly and cold-bloodedly earning an honest livelihood by the sweat of her brow.

Forsooth, it's always so.

If all the red-haired woman's scorn and anguish were real, the audience would sit unmoved. If the red-haired woman's scorn and anguish were real it would strike inward - instead of outward toward the audience - and the audience would not know. If the red-haired woman's scorn and anguish were real, it would not seem real and would be very uninteresting. And that very likely is the reason why the scorn and anguish of other red-haired women - and of black-haired, and brown-haired, and yellow-haired, and gray-haired, and pale-haired women, who are not working on the stage - is so uninteresting and ineffectual. It is real, and they can not act it out, and so it doesn't seem real - and you don't have to pay money to see it done.

To make it seem real they must need go at it cold-bloodedly, and work it up, and charge you a round price for it.

Mary Magdalene isn't here to do this, but Mrs. Fiske takes her place and does it for her.

She does it exquisitely well.

Could Mary Magdalene herself - she of the Bible - be among those who sit watching, she would surely marvel and admire.

Meanwhile, for myself, I have two visions of this Mary Magdalene.

One - in one of the acts wherein her eyes do hunger and thirst after righteousness - when she sits before a small table and lifts her pathetic, sweet voice with the words, "When the dawn breaks, and the darkness shall flee away"; and then she stands and the red hair is equally pathetic and twofold bewitching, and she says again, "When the dawn breaks, and the darkness shall flee away." And the other vision is of her in the country in the midst of a summer day, under a summer sky, swinging high and recklessly in a barrel-stave hammock.

*

11. Like a Stone Wall

My friend Annabel Lee has told me there are bitterer things in store for me than I have known yet.

Times I have wondered what they can be.

"When you have come to them," said my friend Annabel Lee, "they will be so bitter and will fit so well into your life that you will wonder that you did not always know about them, and you will wonder why you did not always have them."

"The bitterest things I have known yet," I said, "have had to do with the varying friendship of one or another whom I have loved."

"Varying friendship?" said Annabel Lee. "But friendship does not vary."

"No, that is true," I rejoined. "I mean the varying deception I have had from some whom I have loved."

"In time," said my friend Annabel Lee, "you will love more, and your deceiving will be all at once, and bitterer. It will be a rich experience."

"Why rich?" I inquired.

"Because from it," said my friend Annabel Lee, "you will learn to not see too much, to not start out with faith, in fact, to take the goods that the gods provide and endeavor to be thankful for them. Your other experiences have been poverty-stricken in that respect. They leave you with rays of hope, without which you would be better off. They are poor and bitter. What is to come will be rich and bitterer. Their bitterness will prevent you from appreciating the richness of them - until perhaps years have come and taken them from immediately before your eyes. As soon as they are where you can not see them, you can consider them and appreciate their richness."

"Whatever they may be," I made answer, "I do not think I shall ever be able to appreciate their richness."

"Then you will be very ungrateful," said my friend Annabel Lee.

I looked hard at her - and she looked back at me. There are times when my friend Annabel Lee is much like a stone wall.

"Yes," said my friend Annabel Lee, "if you ever feel to express proper gratitude for the good things of this life, be sure that you express your gratitude for the right thing. Very likely you will not have a great deal of gratitude, and you must not waste any of it - but what you do have will be of the most excellent quality. For it will accumulate, and the accumulation will all go to quality. And the things for which you are to be grateful are the bitternesses you have known. If you have had it in mind ever to give way to bursts of gratitude for this air that comes from off the salt sea, for that line of pearls and violets that you see just above the horizon, for the health of your body, for the sleep that comes to you at the close of the day, for any of those things, then get rid of the idea at once. Those things are quite well, but they are not really given to you. They are merely placed where any one can reach them with little effort. The kind fates don't care whether you get them or not. Their responsibility ends when they leave them there. But the bitternesses they give to each person separately. They give you yours, Mary MacLane, for your very own. Don't say *they* never think of you."

"I've no intention of saying it," said I.

"You will find," said my friend Annabel Lee - without noticing my interruption, and with curious expressions in her voice and upon her two red lips - "you will find that these bitternesses come from time to time in your life, like so many milestones. They are useful as such - for of course you like to take measurements along the road now and again, to see what progress you have made. Along some parts of the road you will find your progress wonderful. If you are appreciative and grateful, at the last milestone you have come to thus far you will express your measure of gratitude to the kind fates. That is, no -" said my friend Annabel Lee, "you will not do this *at* the milestone, but after you have passed it and have turned a corner, and so can not see it even when you look back."

"But why shall I express gratitude there?" I inquired in a tone that must have been rather lifeless.

"Why?" repeated my friend Annabel Lee. "Because you will have grown in strength on account of these milestones; because you will have learned to take all things tranquilly. Why, after the very last milestone I daresay you would be able to sit with folded hands if a house were burning up about your ears!"

"Which must indeed be a triumph," said I.

"A triumph? - a victory!" said my friend Annabel Lee - with still more curious expressions. "And the victories are not what this world sees" - which reminded me of things I used to hear in Sunday-school ever so many years ago. "You remember the story of the Ten Virgins? Taking the story literally," said my friend Annabel Lee, "the lot of the five Foolish Virgins is much the more fortunate. There was a rare measure of bitterness for them when they found themselves without oil for their lamps at a time when oil was needed. They gained infinitely more than they lost. As for the five Wise Virgins - well, *I* wouldn't have been one of them under *any* circumstances," said my friend Annabel Lee. "Fancy the miserable, mean, mindless, imagi-nationless, selfish natures that could remain unmoved by the simplicity of the appeal, 'Give us of your oil, for our lamps are gone out.' It must now," said my friend Annabel Lee, "be a hundred times bitterer for them to think of being handed down in endless history as demons of selfishness - and they are now where they can not, presumably, measure their bitterness by milestones of progress."

"So then, yes," said my friend Annabel Lee - "whatever else you may do as you go through life, remember to save up your gratitude for the bitternesses you have known - and remember that for *you* the bitterest is yet to come."

"Have *you*, Annabel Lee," I asked, "already known the bitterest that can come - and can *you* sit with your hands folded in the midst of a burning house?"

"Not I!" said my friend Annabel Lee, and laughed gayly. Again I looked hard at her - and she looked back at me.

Certainly there are times when my friend Annabel Lee is like a stone wall.

12. To Fall in Love

"I loved madly," said my friend Annabel Lee. "There came one down out of the north country that was dark and strong and brave and full of life's fire. All my short life had been bathed in summer. I had dreamed my thirteen years beneath cherry-blossoms upon a high hill.

"But at the coming of this man from the north country I opened my two sloe-eyes, and the world turned white - exquisite, rapturous, divine white.

"And afterward all was heavy gray.

"Away from the high hill of the cherry-blossoms there lay a stretch of red barren waste with towering rocks - and beyond that a quiet, quiet sea that was only blue.

"At the left of the high hill of the cherry-blossoms there was a mountain covered with green ivy - dark green ivy that defined its own green shape against the brilliant yellow sky behind it. Green and yellow, green and yellow, green and yellow, said the sky and the mountain covered with ivy.

"The high hill of the cherry-blossoms was colored with all the colors of Japan.

"I lived there with people - my mother and my father and some others - all with pale faces and sloe-eyes.

"But some of them were very ugly.

"Then came one down out of the north country that was dark and strong and brave and full of life's fire.

"He was ugly, but his face was perfect.

"Straightway I fell in love with this one. Of all things in Japan, what a thing it is to fall in love!

"Where the red barren waste lay spread below me I saw manifold softnesses, like a dove's breast, like a fawn's eyes, like melted lilies, and the towering, gloomy rocks were the home of violet dreams.

"In the deep green of the ivy mountain my soul found rest at nightfall among mystery and shadow. It wandered there in marvelous peace. And the coolness and damp and the low muttering of the wind and the night birds went into it with a stirring, powerful influence. Also the voices out of the very long ago came from among the green, dark ivy, and from the crevices of gray stones beneath it, and they told me true things in the stillness.

"From the deepness of the brilliant yellow sky - the yellow of burnished brass - there came legion earth-old contradictions. And wondrous paradox and parallel that had not been among the cherry-blossoms appeared to me as my mind contemplated these. I said, Am I thus in love because that I am weak, or that I am strong? For I see here that it is both weakness and strength. And I said, Am I myself when I do this thing? or was that I who lived among the cherry-blossoms? I said, Who am I? What am I?

"Below all there was the blue, broad sea. This sea gave out a white mist that rose and spread over the earth. I knew that I was in love, once and for all.

"The world was white. The world was beautiful. The world was divine.

"Life shone out of the mist unspeakable in its countless possibilities. Voices spoke near me and infinite voices called to me from afar - they sounded clear and faint and maddening-soft and tender, and the soul of me answered them with deafening, joyous silent music.

"He from the north country that was dark and strong and brave and full of life's fire came, some days, to the high hill of the cherry-blossoms. He spoke often and of many things. He spoke to people - to my mother and to my father, and to others. And rarely he spoke to me. Rarely he looked at me. He had been in the great world. He knew wonderful women and wonderful men. He had been touched with all things.

"What a human being was he!

"And of all things in Japan, what a thing it is to fall in love!

"When three days had gone my heart knew rapture beyond any that it had dreamed. It knew the mysteries and the fullnesses.

"After three days the world turned to that divine white, and was white for seven days.

"And afterward all was heavy gray.

"The one from the north country returned back to the north country.

"Of all things in Japan, what a thing it is to fall in love!

"I was not in love with this one because he was a man, or because he was strange and fascinating - but because he was a glorious human being.

"My heart was not turned to this one to marry him. Marrying and giving in marriage are for such as are in love unconsciously.

"To see this one from the north country - to hear his voice - that was life and all for me - life and all.

"But he was gone.

"He left a silence and a weariness.

"These came and crowded out the white from my heart, and themselves found lodgment there.

"And all was heavy gray.

"The picture of life and the mystery and shadow that was revealed to me when the world was white has never gone. It has filled me in the days of my youth with an old terror.

"Of all things in Japan, what a thing it is to fall in love!

"To fall in love!" - said my friend Annabel Lee, the while her two eyes and her two white hands, in their expression, their position, told of a thing that is heart-breaking to see.

*

13. When I Went To the Butte High School

"There was a time," I said to my friend Annabel Lee, "when I went to the Butte High School. I think of it now with mingled feelings."

"You were younger then," said my friend Annabel Lee.

"I was younger, and in those days I still looked upon life as something which would one day open wide and display wondrous and beautiful things for me. And meanwhile I went every day to the Butte High School. I found it a very interesting place - much more interesting than I have since found the broad world. I was sixteen and seventeen and eighteen, and things were not brilliantly colored, and so I made much with a vivid fancy of all that came in my path."

"And what do you, now that you are one-and-twenty?" said my friend Annabel Lee.

"I sit quietly," I replied, "and wish not, and wait not - and look back upon the days in the Butte High School with mingled feelings."

"Also unawares," said my friend Annabel Lee, "you still think things relating to that which is one day to open wondrously for you. But, never mind," she added hastily, as I was about to say something, "tell me about the Butte High School."

"'Twas a place," said I, "where were gathered together manifold interesting phenomena, and where I studied Virgil, and grew fond of it, and was good in it; and where I studied geometry, and was fond of it, and knew less about it each day that I studied it; - and always I studied closely the persons whom I met daily in the Butte High School. I recall very clearly each member of the class of ninety-nine. My memory conjures up for me some quaint and fantastic visions against picturesque backgrounds that appeal to my sense of delicate incongruity, especially so since viewed in this light and from this distance."

"What are some of them?" said my friend Annabel Lee.

"There is one," said I, "of a girl whom always in my mind I called The Shad, for that she was so bland, and so flat, and so silent, - and she had a bad habit of asking me to write her Latin exercises, which perhaps was not so much like a shad as like a person; and there is one of a girl who spent the long hours of the day in writing long, long letters to her love, but knew painfully little about the lessons in the class-rooms; and there is one of a girl who brought to school every day a small flask of whiskey to cheer her benighted hours, - she was daily called back and down by the French teacher on account of her excessively bad French, and life had looked dull for her were it not for the flask's pungent contents; there is one of a strange-looking, tawny-headed girl who sat across the narrow aisle from me in the assembly-room during my last year in school, who kept her desk neatly piled with the works (she called them works) of Albert Ross - and after she had read them, very kindly she would lean over and repeat the stories, with quotations verbatim, for my benefit; her standing in her classes was not brilliant, but in Albert Ross she was thorough; there is one of a clever, pretty girl who was malicious - exquisitely malicious in all her ways and deeds, and seemingly no thought entered her head that was not fraught with it, - she was malicious in algebra, malicious in literature, malicious in ancient history, malicious in physical culture, malicious in the writing of short themes - and when it so chanced that I made a failure in a recitation, or was stupid, she would look up at me and smile very sweetly and maliciously; and there is one of a girl whose quaint and voluble profanity haunts me still. And especially there is in my memory a picture of all these on our graduating day, receiving each a fine white diploma rolled up and neatly tied with the class colors - a picture of these and the others, - we were fifty-nine in all. And the diplomas stated tacitly, in heavily engrossed letters, that we had all been good for four years and had fulfilled every requirement of the Butte High School. So we had, doubtless - but how much some of us had done for which in our diplomas we were not given credit! In truth, nothing was stated in them, in engrossed lettering, about courses in love-letters, or profanity, or malice, and Albert Ross was not in the curriculum.

"And the president of the school board doled out those diplomas, with a short, set speech for each, one wet June day - but he was not aware how insignificant they were.

"And my mind likewise conjures up a vision of two with whom I used to take what we called tramps, during our last year in the High School - far down and out of Butte, on Saturdays and other days when school was not. I remember those two and those tramps exceeding well - nor can I think with but four years gone that the two themselves have forgotten. One of these was an individual whose like I have not since known. She reminded me sometimes of Cleopatra and sometimes of Peg of Limmavaddy. She was of Irish ancestry and had a long black mane of hair braided down behind, and two conscious and lurid eyes of the kind that is known as Irish blue. She had brains enough within her head, but did not study overmuch.

Her ways of going through life were often very dubious. She weighed a great many pounds. Her experience of the world was large, and to me she was fascinating. For herself, she was always rather afraid of me - so much afraid, in truth, that if I said a funny thing she must need laugh - with a forced and fictitious merriment; if I told her she had no soul, she must need agree with me abjectly, though she was a good Catholic; if I frowned upon her, she shivered and was silent. Fanciful names and frocks (though this lady's frocks were always fanciful in ways) were selected for these tramping expeditions. This one's fanciful name was called Muddled Maud. For no particular reason, I believe - but she wore it well. The other member of our trio was of a less extraordinary type. She was stout as to figure, and she knew a great deal about some things. She was very good in history, and at home she could make pie and cake and bread. It is true that her cake sometimes stuck, and sometimes sank in the middle, and when she carved a fowl she could not always hit the joints. And she was one of the kind that always pronounces picture, "pitcher." She was also known as a very sensible girl. I can see her now with a purple ribbon around her neck and a brown rain-coat on coming into the High School on a wet morning. When we went tramping she usually wore an immense gray-white, mother-hubbard gown, belted in at the waist, and a wide flat hat, which made her look rather like a toad-stool. Her fanciful name was Emancipated Eva. Emancipated, in truth, she was. In the High School she was dignified and sedate, but on our tramps she would frequently skip like a young lamb, and frisk and gambol down there in the country.

"She who was called Muddled Maud likewise frisked and gamboled - and always she personified my idea of the French noun *abandon*.

"Also I frisked and gamboled in those days far down in the country.

"The fanciful name selected for me was Refreshment Rosanna - and I can not tell why. But it was thought a good name for a lady tramp. We started on these tramps at six in the morning. We would rise from our beds at five, and at ten minutes before six I would meet Muddled Maud at the corner of Washington and Quartz streets, below her house. Together we would go down east Park street to the home of Emancipated Eva. Then we walked seven miles or eight away into the open and the wild.

"We took things along to eat - sometimes a great many things and sometimes a few. Times Muddled Maud would have but a curious-looking jelly-roll, and Emancipated Eva would come laden with hard bits of beef, and I could show but a plate of fudge. But other times there were tarts and meat-pies and turnovers, and deviled ham and deviled chicken and deviled veal and deviled tongue and deviled fish of divers kinds, and some bottles of nut-brown October ale, and sardines *a l'huile*, and green, green olives. Only the more there was, the harder to carry. But, times, Muddled Maud would carry much with little effort - she would adorn herself with the luncheon - a long bit of sausage-link about her neck like a chain, and upon her hat, held securely with bonnet-pins, fat yellow lemons, and two bananas crossed in front like the tiny guns on a soldier's hat, and bunches of Catawba grapes scattered here and there, and pears hanging by their little stems behind.

"The too early morning prevented all from being seen by the inhabitants of Butte, and we did not venture home again until came the friendly darkness.

"Those were fascinating expeditions - and whose was the glory? Mine was the glory. 'Twas I who invented them. 'Twas I who knew there was none so fitted for a so delicate absurdity as she we called Muddled Maud; and after her, none so fitted as the fair, the good-natured, the Emancipated; and together with them both, I. And I led them forth, and I led them back, and I said things should be thus and so, and straightway they were thus and so. And we enjoyed it, and clear air was in our lungs and life was in our veins, for we had each but eighteen years and were full of youth. But most of all 'twas fascinating because we were three of three widely differing manners of living and methods of reasoning. For I was not like Emancipated Eva, nor yet like Muddled Maud; and Emancipated Eva was not like me, nor yet like Muddled Maud; and Muddled Maud was not like Emancipated Eva, nor yet like me.

"To be sure, there were some things in my ordering which neither the one nor the other found enchanting. Why should the MacLane do all the ordering? they murmured between themselves, but they dared not openly revolt, so all went well.

"But now these are gone.

"The three of us were graduated from the Butte High School with the fifty-nine others of ninety-nine, and had each a fine white diploma, and went our ways.

"She who was like Cleopatra and Peg of Limmavaddy is teaching a school, according to the last that I heard, in the north of Montana; and she that was Emancipated Eva has long since gone to California, and is married, and keeps a house; and for me - I am here, far off from Butte, with you, Annabel Lee, some things having been done meanwhile.

"But though the two are gone, I warrant they have not forgotten. They have not forgotten the Butte High School, nor the class of ninety-nine, nor the tramps we went, nor their tyrant, me.

"And I daresay they all remember their Butte High School - she of the love-letters, she of the whiskey-flask, she the student of Albert Ross, she of the profanity, she of the malice, The Shad, - and all the nine-and-fifty, the young feminine persons and the young masculine persons. Some are married, and some are flown, and some of them are grown up and different, 'and some of them in the churchyard lie, and some are gone to sea.'

"But whenever I've a fancy to shut my eyes and look back, I can see them all, a quaint company.

"Also, whenever I've a fancy to shut my eyes and look back to life when it was unspeakably brilliant in possibilities to look forward to, and was marked in parti-colored checks and rings, it fetches me to the days when I went to the Butte High School and studied geometry and Virgil. Only I'm glad I'm not there now."

"What for?" said my friend Annabel Lee.

"It is rather pitiful and dreadful to think of having been seventeen, and to have gone every day to the Butte High School and imagined how wonderful-beautiful life would be some day," said I, and all at once felt very weary.

*

14. "And Mary MacLane and Me"

There are times in a number of days when my friend Annabel Lee and I enjoy a cigarette together.

My friend Annabel Lee, with her cigarette, her petite much-colored form wrapped round in clouds of thin, exquisite gray, is more than all suggestive and inscrutable. She leans her two elbows on something and looks out at me.

I with my cigarette am nothing but I with my cigarette. I enjoy it, but am not beautiful with it, nor fascinating.

But my friend Annabel Lee is all that my imagination can take in. Under the influence of the thin, exquisite gray she grows fanciful, and subtly and indefinitely she meets me somewhere, and extends me her hand for a moment.

"Don't you know," said my friend Annabel Lee, with her cigarette, "that old song that goes:

> *Mary Seaton,*
> *And Mary Beaton,*
> *And Mary Carmichael,*
> *And me?*

I think it is Mary Stuart of Scotland who says that. And a fair good song it is. But just now, for *me*, if I were Mary Stuart of Scotland, you poor miserable little rat, I should say:

Mary MacLane,
And Mary MacLane,
And Mary MacLane,
And me.

For aren't we two together here, calmly smoking - and doesn't the world spin round?"

I was enchanted. How few are the times when my friend Annabel Lee is like this, warm and friendly and lightly contemptuous and inclined to grotesquerie.

'Tis so that she becomes human and someway near to me.

"Yes, I should say Mary MacLane, and Mary MacLane, and Mary Mac-Lane, and me," said my friend Annabel Lee from her gently-puffed clouds. "There are times when you are soft and satisfying as a gray pussy-cat. If I stroke you, you will purr. If I give you cream, you will lap it up. And then you will curl up warmly in my lap and sleep and purr and open and shut your little fur paws.

I will sit by the fire
And give her some food,
And pussy will love me
Because I am good.

What literature is more literature than Mother Goose?" said my friend Annabel Lee. "And will you love me - because I am good? Has it occurred to you that you must love what is good and because it is good, you poor, miserable, little rat, - and that you must hate what is evil? Look at me, look at me! - am I good?"

I looked at her. Certainly she was good. Just then she had a look of angels.

"Do you love me?" said my friend Annabel Lee, with her cigarette.

"Oh, yes," said I.

"Look at me again - am I evil?" said my friend Annabel Lee.

"I presume you are," I replied, for then she looked vindictive and vicious.

"And do you hate me?"

"No," said I.

"Then you are very bad and wicked yourself, you poor, miserable, little rat," said my friend Annabel Lee, with her cigarette, "and the world and all good people will condemn you."

"I fear," said I, with my cigarette, "that the world and all good people already do that."

"Ah, do they!" said my friend Annabel Lee. "Never mind - I will take care of you, you poor, miserable, little rat; I will make all soft for you; I will keep out the cold; I will color the dullness; I will fight off the mob."

"And I," I replied, "if for that reason you do so, will thank the world and all good people for condemning me."

"That was neatly said," said my friend Annabel Lee. "But let me tell you, when the world grows soft, I will grow hard - hard as nails."

"Then let the world stay hard," I said - "hard and bitter as wormwood, if it will, so that you come indeed thus friendly to me through these gray clouds."

"That, too, was very neat," said my friend Annabel Lee; "but mostly it goes to show that a bird in the hand is worth two in the bush. What literature is more literature than the proverbs? What is a bird in the hand worth?" said my friend Annabel Lee.

"Two in the bush," said I.

"Where does charity begin?" said my friend Annabel Lee.

"At home," said I.

"What does it cover?" said my friend Annabel Lee.

"A multitude of sins," said I.

"What's a miss as good as?" said my friend Annabel Lee.

"A mile," said I.

"What makes the mare go?" said my friend Annabel Lee.

"Money," said I.

"Whom does conscience make cowards of?" said my friend Annabel Lee.

"Us all," said I.

"What does a stitch in time save?" said my friend Annabel Lee.

"Nine," said I.

"When are a fool and his money parted?" said my friend Annabel Lee.

"Soon," said I.

"What do too many cooks spoil?" said my friend Annabel Lee.

"The broth," said I.

"What's an idle brain?" said my friend Annabel Lee.

"The devil's workshop," said I.

"What may a cat look at?" said my friend Annabel Lee.

"A king," said I.

"What's truth stranger than?" said my friend Annabel Lee.

"Fiction," said I.

"What's there many a slip betwixt?" said my friend Annabel Lee.

"The cup and the lip," said I.

"How do birds of a feather flock?" said my friend Annabel Lee.

"Together," said I.

"What do fools do where angels fear to tread?" said my friend Annabel Lee.

"Rush in," said I.

"What does many a mickle make?" said my friend Annabel Lee.

"A muckle," said I.

"What will the pounds do if you take care of the pence?" said my friend Annabel Lee.

"Take care of themselves," said I.

"What do curses do, like chickens?" said my friend Annabel Lee.

"Come home to roost," said I.

"What is it that has no turning?" said my friend Annabel Lee.

"A long lane," said I.

"What does an ill wind blow?" said my friend Annabel Lee.

"Nobody good," said I.

"What's a merciful man merciful to?" said my friend Annabel Lee.

"His beast," said I.

"What's better to do than to break?" said my friend Annabel Lee.

"Bend," said I.

"What's an ounce of prevention worth?" said my friend Annabel Lee.

"A pound of cure," said I.

"What's there nothing half so sweet in life as?" said my friend Annabel Lee.

"Love's young dream," said I.

"What does absence make?" said my friend Annabel Lee.

"The heart grow fonder," said I.

"How would a rose by any other name smell?" said my friend Annabel Lee.

"As sweet," said I.

"How did the Assyrian come down?" said my friend Annabel Lee.

"Like a wolf on the fold," said I.

"What were his cohorts gleaming with?" said my friend Annabel Lee.

"Purple and gold," said I.

"What was the sheen of their spears like?" said my friend Annabel Lee.

"Stars on the sea," said I.

"When?" said my friend Annabel Lee.

"When the blue wave rolls nightly on deep Galilee," said I.

"All of which proves," said my friend Annabel Lee, "that I've but to fiddle and you will dance, you poor, miserable, little rat. And my thought is, what is it better to be than second in Rome?"

"First in a little Iberian village," said I.

"But I'm not sure whether it is or not," said my friend Annabel Lee. "Some day you and I will go out into the great, broad world. Then we shall see who will be first and who will be second. The great, broad world is the best place of all wherein to find ourselves. And no matter how we were situated before, we shall certainly be situated differently in the great broad world. In the great broad world there will be apples - apples enough for you and for me. But, who knows? you poor miserable little rat; it may be that your lot will be *all* the sweet, juicy apples, whilst I shall be given the cores. In the great broad world there will be ripe-red-raspberry shortcake - enough for you and for me. But, who knows? you poor miserable little rat; it may be that your lot will be all the ripe red raspberries, whilst I shall be given the crusts. In the great broad world there will be cigarettes - cigarettes enough for you and for me. But, who knows? You poor miserable little rat; it may be that your lot will be *all* the fine Egyptian tobacco and rice paper and clouds and clouds and clouds of pearl gray, soft pearl gray, to wrap you round, whilst I shall go looking in empty boxes all day long, and never a cigarette. In which case mine will be by far the better lot in the end," said my friend Annabel Lee, "according to the law of compensation."

"Oh, dear!" said my friend Annabel Lee, petulantly; "why do you sit there stupidly staring? Talk and amuse me, why don't you? Make me feel sweet and content."

"If I were but that myself, Annabel Lee," said I. "I can not talk interestingly, but if you like I will ask you the proverbs and you may answer them. That amused me much - and it gave me a wonderful feeling of satisfaction, quite as if I were seven years old and knew my lesson perfectly."

"You ask and I answer?" said my friend Annabel Lee. "Very good. But I don't know my lesson perfectly. Begin."

"What's a bird in the hand worth?" said I.

"A pound of cure," said my friend Annabel Lee.

"What does a stitch in time save?" said I.

"Two in the bush," said my friend Annabel Lee.

"Where does charity begin?" said I.

"Betwixt the cup and the lip," said my friend Annabel Lee.

"What may a cat look at?" said I.

"The broth," said my friend Annabel Lee.

"What does many a mickle make?" said I.

"A multitude of sins," said my friend Annabel Lee.

"What do too many cooks spoil?" said I.

"Us all," said my friend Annabel Lee.

"Whom does conscience make cowards of?" said I.

"Dead men and fools," said my friend Annabel Lee.

"What is it that has no turning?" said I.

"A full stomach," said my friend Annabel Lee.

"What fortifies a stout heart?" said I.

"A stitch in time," said my friend Annabel Lee.

"What does money make?" said I.

"An ill wind," said my friend Annabel Lee.

"What will the pounds do if you take care of the pence?" said I.

"Come home to roost," said my friend Annabel Lee.

"Where is there many a slip?" said I.

"Where angels fear to tread," said my friend Annabel Lee.

"What's sharper than a serpent's tooth?" said I.

"The pen," said my friend Annabel Lee.

"What's mightier than the sword?" said I.

"A rich man," said my friend Annabel Lee.

"What makes the mare go?" said I.

"A fool and his money," said my friend Annabel Lee.

"What should they do who live in glass houses?" said I.

"Draw down the blinds," said my friend Annabel Lee.

"What's a man's castle?" said I.

"The devil's workshop," said my friend Annabel Lee.

"What's better to do than to break?" said I.

"Rob Peter," said my friend Annabel Lee.

"What's the wind tempered to?" said I.

"The camel's back," said my friend Annabel Lee.

"What do many hands make?" said I.

"A shorn lamb," said my friend Annabel Lee.

"What can't you make out of a pig's ear?" said I.

"A gift-horse," said my friend Annabel Lee.

"What should you never look in the mouth?" said I.

"A silk purse," said my friend Annabel Lee.

"What's half a loaf better than?" said I.

"Chickens before they are hatched," said my friend Annabel Lee.

"But let's not play this any more," said my friend Annabel Lee. "I'm languid and weary. Can't you talk to me - and talk so that I may feel rested and comfortable? And don't stare!"

"I fear I can't amuse you. I am sorry," said I. "You may envy me, Annabel Lee. You have not Annabel Lee to look at. Would not life look rich and full to you if you could see before you your own vague, purple eyes, and your red, red lips, and those hands of power and romance - you, with your scarlet gown and the gold marguerites coming near and fading away in mist?"

"No, not particularly," said my friend Annabel Lee. "I rather like *your* looks," she added, and her purple eyes became less vague - "sitting there in your small black frock; and you puff at that tobacco much like a toy engine. Come, you amuse me - you please me. Come near me."

She held out one of her hands and the purple eyes changed suddenly into something that was rarely and indescribably friendly.

I felt much from life.

My friend Annabel Lee rested the hand she had held out upon my shoulder.

"When we go into the great, broad world, Mary MacLane," she said, "and you have all the apples, and all the ripe-red-raspberry shortcake, and all the cigarettes, then perhaps will you *share* them with me?"

I said I would.

*

15. A Story of Spoon-Bills

When the mood takes my friend Annabel Lee she will, if I beg her, tell me quaint and fantastic stories, such as are hidden away in the dusty crevices of this world. These tales have lain away there for centuries, and spiders have spun webs over and about them, so that when, perchance, they are brought out, bits of fine gray fiber are to be found among the lines.

Yesterday a pretty, plain story by my friend Annabel Lee that runs through my mind.

"Long ago," said my friend Annabel Lee, "there lived in Egypt a family of well-born but poorly-bred Spoon-bills in a green marsh by the side of the great green river Nile. This family numbered five, and they were united and dwelling in peace. There were the father and mother and two daughters and a son.

"And there had been another son, but he was dead. And their names were Maren Spoon-bill, the mother; and Oliver W. Spoon-bill, the father; and Lilith Spoon-bill, the elder daughter; and Delilah Spoon-bill, the younger daughter. And the son's name was Le Page Spoon-bill.

"The son who had died was named Roland Spoon-bill. He was buried at the edge of the marsh, and his name and the date were carved upon a square, black, wooden tablet to his memory at the head of the grave. There was also this legend upon the tablet: 'Age 15. Gone in the hey-day of youth to his last rest. But his virtues are with us still.'

"And little Delilah Spoon-bill, who was an elementary, fanciful child of nine, used to stand staring at this legend and wondering about it. A weeping willow hung low over the grave, and Delilah would stand near it picking gnats from its branches with her bill, and speculating about the legend. She wondered for one thing what 'hey-day' meant. Was it anything like a birth-day? Or was it, on the contrary, a day when everything went wrong and ended by a person's being shut into a dark bed-room? Or was it, perhaps, a picnic day - with tarts made of red jam? In that case Delilah felt very sorry for her brother that he should have died on such a day, for if there is an article of diet that spoon-bills really like it is tarts of red jam - made the way Canadians make them.

"But she never could decide.

"And another thing about the epitaph that puzzled her was the concluding clause - 'but his virtues are with us still.' What could virtues be? she asked herself. Were they anything like feathers, or were they good to eat, or were they something she had never seen and knew nothing about? But the letters said plainly, his virtues are with us still. Truly, if they were among the family possessions, why had she not seen them? For anything that belonged to any of the Spoon-bill family that was at all out of the ordinary was always placed in an oak cabinet with glass doors that stood in a corner of the hall in their marsh home. Delilah had often looked in this cabinet to see if the virtues of her brother were not there. There were dried snake skins, and curious white stones, and Spanish moss, and devil's snuff-boxes - but no, there were no virtues. Of that she was convinced. She appealed to her older sister. 'Lilith,' said Delilah, 'what *are* virtues, and where do we keep Roland's? Don't you know, on the tombstone it says, 'his virtues are with us still.'

"'Aren't you a silly!' said Lilith, laughing in Spoon-billish derision. Lilith was twelve, and one knows vastly more at twelve than at nine. 'Virtues aren't anything. And as for Roland's - that doesn't mean that he left them with us, any more than that he took them with him.'

"'Then what *does* it mean?' said Delilah. 'I've thought so much about it.'

"'You'll have to think some more,' said Lilith - 'a good deal more, I should say - of *your* kind of thinking!'

"Delilah did not often appeal to her sister in these matters. She did not enjoy Lilith's habit of laughing. In truth, she didn't enjoy being laughed at at all - not the least in the world. She was like a great many other people.

"And so was Lilith.

"But oh, there were many things that Delilah wished to know!

"The Spoon-bill family was, as I have said, well born but poorly bred. Maren Spoon-bill and Oliver W. Spoon-bill both came of very good stock, but they had been the black sheep of their families and had forgotten the traditions and customs of their race. 'They had left no more pride,' Maren Spoon-bill's mother once said, 'than a sand-hill crane - no, nor a duck.'"

"'No, nor a duck,' echoed Maren Spoon-bill and her husband, and gloried in it.

"And the children ran wild.

"But the children, though they ran wild, were not without ambition. On summer evenings, when the family took tea on the back porch and it was too warm for the children to run about much, they used to sit and tell their ambitions.

"'I'm going to be an actress when *I* get big,' declared Lilith. 'I'm going to have a splendid career on the stage, and I shall earn heaps of money. And I shall have magnificent clothes, and every one will look at me and say, "*Isn't* she in stunning form to-night!"'

"And Le Page and Delilah were so overcome by the vision thus presented of their sister that they could but stare, awed and silent.

"And Delilah wondered how it must seem to be so very clever.

"But Le Page, who was eleven years old himself, soon rallied.

"'Well, then,' said he, 'when *I* get big I'm going to be a pirate. I'll lay over all the pirates that ever were, a-firing and a-pillaging - and I'll wear magnificent clothes, and everyone will look at me - and say, "'*Isn't* he in stunning form to-night!"'

"Delilah thought this latter sounded strangely like Lilith - but perhaps in some subtle way a pirate was like an actress, and so must need be described in the same terms.

"'And Delilah,' said her father, 'what shall you be - what kind of clothes are you going to wear?'

"Delilah had before tried the experiment of relating her ambition to the assembled family, and the result had been bad. The high laughter of Lilith and Le Page always rose on the still evening air, and even her father, who was a kind person, would smile. Delilah's ambition was always the same, but she nearly always varied it a little at each telling - and the amusement evinced by her sister and brother varied accordingly.

"Sometimes they even flapped their wings.

"Which was too cruel.

"Forsooth, children are always cruel.

"But while Delilah's ambition was always the same, those of Lilith and Le Page covered an exceeding wide range. Some evenings Lilith would draw a glowing picture of herself as a lecturer of renown with a wonderful personal magnetism and a telling style - she would move the multitudes and draw tears from stony eyes by lifting up her voice. Whereupon Le Page, when he had recovered his breath, would portray himself as a celebrated scientist delving in marvelous chemical mysteries and discovering things of untold benefit to the race. He also would move the multitudes and draw tears from stony eyes.

"And Delilah would wonder what were lecturers and scientists, and how they could do these things.

"And when Lilith would announce her intention of becoming a famous sculptor whose work in the passionate would be the delight of her day, then Le Page would turn his mind to the idea of becoming a noted explorer who would penetrate into Darkest Africa and Farthest North, and whose work in the passionate would be the delight of his day.

"And Delilah would marvel still more.

"Forsooth, children are always like that - and fascinating they are.

"And each summer evening after Lilith and Le Page had related their ambitions, their father would ask Delilah what was hers. Then always Delilah would whisper; 'I'm going to study tombstones, papa! And when I get big perhaps I shall know what every single tombstone in the world means. And perhaps after I've studied a long time and hard I can read Roland's right off and know what it means without thinking. And perhaps I can explain them all to people who don't know about them.'

"Which to Delilah was a daring ambition indeed - quite hitching her wagon to a star.

"Well, then," said my friend Annabel Lee, "this was when the Spoon-bill family was in its youngness.

"The years followed one after another, and the three children grew. And it came about that Lilith was three-and-twenty, and Le Page was two-and-twenty, and Delilah was twenty.

"They were much as they had been when they were children. Lilith, I may say in passing, was not an actress, nor a lecturer, nor yet a sculptor - and Le Page was merely Le Page.

"Also Delilah was Delilah, but had ceased to be elementary in some ways, while in others she was still, and so would be until the finish.

"It so happened that a young spoon-bill of masculine persuasion, from the other side of the great green river Nile, fell in love with Delilah.

"Likewise Delilah fell in love with a young spoon-bill, but not that young spoon-bill.

"It happens frequently so.

"And Delilah did not fancy the spoon-bill from the other side of the river, and the spoon-bill with whom Delilah was in love did not fancy her in just that way.

"Which also happens frequently.

"On a day when the river Nile was very green, and heavy sickening-sweet flowers of dead white color hung from black trees on the banks, and the sky was, oh, so blue, and all was summer, the young spoon-bill from over the river would come to see Delilah. He loved so well - so hopelessly - that young spoon-bill! But Delilah on such a day would walk where the green water was shallow, and her thoughts would be with the young spoon-bill who had gone to her heart.

"And the young spoon-bill from over the river would come and stand a little way from Delilah under a tree with broad thick leaves. How fine was he to look upon, with his white feathers glistening like silver and his eyes of topaz!

"And Delilah was most adorable with feathers of soft, soft gray - a so soft gray that one, if one were human, would wish to rest one's forehead upon the fluffy down of her breast.

"Then he from over the river - his name was Gerald Spoon-bill - would say: 'Delilah, come with me over the river to the damp meadows, where there is a pool with a thousand pond-lilies, and fair blooms the way. We should be happy there, you and I.'

"But Delilah would say: 'Oh, go back over the river, Gerald Spoon-bill! You and I never should be happy together. Why do you stand there by the rubber-tree day after day? And why do you waste your life-nerves and your heart-nerves? Why are you not giving your good heart to some one who can take it?'

"'But you would be happy with me, Delilah,' he under the dark leaves would answer her eagerly. 'We will stand in the midst of a new day and watch the sun come up out of the sand - we will stand in pale shallows at midday - we will feel our hearts beat high when the lightnings come down through branches - we will fly a little in high winds - we will stand still and silent in the midst of golden solitudes when the sun is going off the sand - and in all these things my heart will be yours.'

"'Go back over the river, Gerald Spoon-bill!' said Delilah.

"But Gerald Spoon-bill felt that he loved so well that he could not go back over the river.

"'Tis not possible to go back over the river when one's best-loved is standing by herself in green shallows.

"Then along the bank from the direction of the date palms came Auden Spoon-bill, he who had gone to Delilah's heart. Likewise he was good to see - not from the handsomeness of his feathers or his eyes, but from the strength of his physical being. Though, too, his eyes were of amethyst.

"Auden Spoon-bill went along parallel to the shore of the river until he saw Delilah standing in the pale green water. Then he crossed over and came toward her.

"'There are lotus flowers blooming down below where the steep cataract breaks over stones,' said he. 'Delilah, will you come with me to eat some?'

"'Oh, yes, I will come,' said Delilah, eagerly.

"For she still was elementary enough to say things eagerly.

"So they went down to where the lotus-flowers grew, where the steep cataract broke over stones.

"It so happened that it was almost the time when the great green river Nile flows out over its banks and makes all wet with water for miles around. At such a time it was the custom of Spoon-bills and cranes and adjutant-birds and others of their ilk, and animals of divers kinds, to leave their homes and move away out of reach of the green and purple flood. But no one had thought of moving yet, for it was too early in the season. Maren Spoon-bill and Oliver W. Spoon-bill had not even begun to gather up their household goods, nor had they, as their wont was, removed the black tablet from the head of Roland Spoon-bill's grave, which was on the very edge of the river.

"The river-god is a person of whims like the rest of us. And so that year, on the day that Delilah and Auden Spoon-bill went down the river to eat lotus flowers, he gave vent to one of them.

"He thought to send a premonition of the yearly flood in the shape of one beautiful green and purple and white wave, one which would not go so very far but which should be damaging in its effects.

"'Delilah,' said Auden Spoon-bill, 'since we are here eating lotus flowers, life is very fine, isn't it?'

"'Oh, very fine - yes, very fine,' said Delilah, and was thrilled.

"'You are a so dear friend,' said Auden Spoon-bill.

"'Yes,' said Delilah, and was not thrilled.

"'Life,' said Auden Spoon-bill, 'is pretty fine, no matter how it is arranged.'

"'But life is a very strange thing,' said Delilah. 'I can't begin to tell you how strange I have found it. For one thing, I may have what is not my heart's desire, and what is my heart's desire I may not have.'

"'It is strange,' admitted Auden Spoon-bill. "But why have any heart's desires aside from what is already yours in this fine, fair world?'

"'One can not rule one's heart,' cried Delilah. 'One's heart goes on before one's mind can stop to think. One's heart rushes in before everything. One's heart plays with brilliant-colored things when all else is dead-color. One's heart loves -'

"But Delilah never finished. Before their eyes rose up a magnificent wall - a wall of water that was fire and cloud and silver, and in it were ineffable rainbows of the purple that gathers up the soul in its brilliance and shows it wondrous possibilities; and in it were lines of the pale lavender that caresses the senses - and one breathes from it almost a fragrance of heliotrope; and in it were broad sheets of deep black and dazzling white that were of the seeming of life and death; and in it, last of all, was a world of infinite green: it had come from a place of great things; it had come to a place where all went down before it, where lives exulted but shrank from it because of its green.

"An exquisite whim, was that of the river-god.

"Delilah and Auden Spoon-bill gazed for a brief moment. They saw the magnificent things. They saw death in the brilliancies, but nevertheless their spirits rose high. They saw also a wild flight of live things before the wave. Delilah beheld her family - Lilith and the rest - struggling and half-covered with water, and their home made of reeds was loosed from its foundations and borne down the river.

"Presently the flood overtook themselves and the life of Delilah was merged in water. She was borne high on a dark swell, and at the turning was suddenly struck a stunning blow upon the gray of her breast by a square black wooden tablet.

"Before death came to her out of the brilliancies she was conscious of several things. She saw before her eyes for an instant with startling plainness the words on the tablet, 'Gone in the hey-day of youth to his last rest. But his virtues are with us still.'

"She even fancied for the first time that she knew what it meant.

" 'The hey-day of youth,' she murmured to herself, 'is the day I go to eat lotus flowers with my best-beloved - and virtues are two eyes of amethyst that are with me still as I am drowning.'

"Auden Spoon-bill was drowning together with her -

"That's all of the story," said my friend Annabel Lee.

"Thank you," said I. "It is lovely in its quaintness. What does it mean, Annabel Lee?"

"Mean?" said my friend Annabel Lee. "I didn't say it meant anything."

"But I suppose," said I, "everything that's true means something."

"Very likely," said my friend Annabel Lee. "But this story isn't true. I made it up."

Because it isn't true, or for some other reason, the story still runs in my head. How like my friend Annabel Lee it is!

*

16. A Measure of Sorrow

"But though you are equally as beautiful as Poe's Annabel Lee," I said to my friend Annabel Lee - "and half the time I think you are the same one - still when I read over the poem in my mind I find differences."

"You find differences," said my friend Annabel Lee.

I repeated:

> *It was many and many a year ago,*
> *In a kingdom by the sea,*
> *That a maiden there lived whom you may know*
> *By the name of Annabel Lee.*
> *And this maiden she lived with no other thought*
> *Than to love and be loved by me.*

"The first four lines," said I, "do very well, for it doesn't matter how long ago you lived and who can tell? But I fancy you live with other thoughts than that mentioned."

"I fancy I do," said my friend Annabel Lee.

I repeated:

> *I was a child, and she was a child,*
> *In this kingdom by the sea;*
> *And we loved with a love that was more than love,*
> *I and my Annabel Lee -*
> *A love that the wingèd seraphs in heaven*
> *Coveted her and me.*

"The first line might stand," said I, "for you are only fourteen, and I but one-and-twenty - which is quite young youth when compared to the age of the earth. But the third and fourth lines are appalling. And, alas, you are not my Annabel Lee. Always you make me feel, indeed, that nothing is mine. And no, surely the winged seraphs in heaven do not envy you and me for anything."

"If they do," said my friend Annabel Lee, "then heaven must needs be very poorly furnished."

I repeated:

> *And this was the reason that long ago,*
> *In this kingdom by the sea,*
> *A wind blew out of a cloud, chilling*
> *My beautiful Annabel Lee,*

So that her high-born kinsman came
And bore her away from me,
To shut her up in a sepulcher
In this kingdom by the sea.

"I imagine, times," said I, "that chill wind has sometimes come out of a cloud by night and gone over you. No high-born kinsman comes to carry you away - but I shiver at the possibility. Will a high-born kinsman come to carry you away - shall you be shut into a gray stone sepulcher?"

"No kinsman, high- or low-born, is coming to carry me away," said my friend Annabel Lee. "Kinsmen do not carry away things that have no intrinsic value."

"No, I believe they don't," said I, and felt relieved.

I repeated:

The angels, not half so happy in heaven,
Went envying her and me,
Yes! that was the reason, (as all men know
In this kingdom by the sea,)
That the wind came out of the cloud by night,
Chilling and killing my Annabel Lee.

"But no," said I; "the angels in heaven are surely more than half so happy as you and I."

"More than half," said my friend Annabel Lee. "They need not send clouds from heaven on that account."

I repeated:

But our love it was stronger by far than the love
Of those who were older than we,
Of many far wiser than we;
And neither the angels in heaven above,
Nor the demons down under the sea,
Can ever dissever my soul from the soul
Of the beautiful Annabel Lee.

"If you loved anything," said I, "'twould be stronger by far than that of some who are older, and of very many who may be wiser."

"I don't think wisdom and age have to do with it," said my friend Annabel Lee.

"And the angels in heaven would count for very little in it," said I.

"No, certainly, not the angels in heaven," said my friend Annabel Lee.
"Nor the demons down under the sea?" I asked.
"I don't know about *them*," said my friend Annabel Lee.
I repeated:

> *For the moon never beams, without bringing me dreams*
> *Of the beautiful Annabel Lee;*
> *And the stars never rise, but I feel the bright eyes*
> *Of the beautiful Annabel Lee;*
> *And so all the night-tide, I lie down by the side*
> *Of my darling - my darling - my life and my bride*
> *In her sepulcher there by the sea,*
> *In her tomb by the sounding sea.*

"The first lines," said I, "are well-fitting. For you are like to the moon and stars, and they are like to you. You are with them in the shadow-way. And if you were out by the sea in a gray stone sepulcher I should stay there near you, in the night-tide and the day-tide. You would be there - and my heart would set in your direction still."

"More than it had set before," said my friend Annabel Lee. "For everything escheats to the sea at last. Those persons," said my friend Annabel Lee, "who have measures of sorrow which can be joined with the sea are the most fortunate persons of all. Those measures of sorrow will serve them well and will stand them in good stead on days when all other things desert them. If a measure of sorrow is joined with the sea it belongs to the sea - and the sea is always there.

"The sea," said my friend Annabel Lee, "is like a letter from some one whom you have written to after a long silence, who you thought might be dead.

"The sea is the measure of sorrow, and the measure of sorrow is the sea. Having once had a measure of sorrow joined with the sea, your measure of sorrow will never be separated from the sea.

"The measure of sorrow will sink all of its woe deep into the sea, and the sea will be of the same color with it. For a measure of sorrow is sufficient to color a great sea.

"The sea will give to the measure of sorrow a bit of wild joy. There is no joy in the world like that of the sea - for there is enough in it to come out and touch all things in life, and life itself. And the wild joy will stop short only of a scene of death. If a life is joined with the sea, in spite of all the weariness, all the anguish, all the heavy-days of unrest, and all the futile struggling and wasting of nerves, there will yet be a wild joy in it all, and thrill after thrill of triumph in extreme moments.

"Those measures of sorrow that are not joined with the sea must do for themselves.

"And for these reasons, those persons who have measures of sorrow that can be joined with the sea are the most fortunate persons of all."

*

17. A Lute With No Strings

The most astonishing thing about my friend Annabel Lee is that, young as she is, she seems except for some thing in the past to be absolutely in the present. She does not build up for herself things in the future. The future is a thing she looks upon with contempt. She has not a use for it - except perhaps to help form a bitter sentence of words.

The present she finds before her, and she lifts it up and places it upon a table before her and opens it as if it were a book - a book with but two pages. She seems to find symbols and figures and faint suggestions upon these two pages from which she derives a multitude of ideas and fancies and material to make bitter sentences of words.

It seems to interest her, and it interests me to rare degrees.

She dwells upon the present.

She talks of things in the present with inflections of voice that are in sharp contrast to the sentiments she utters. The while the expression of her face is inscrutable. Taken by and large, she is an inscrutable person. I wonder while I listen, does she herself believe these things? - or is she talking to amuse herself? But perforce I feel a vein of truth in each thing that she says. I look hard at her to discover signs of irony or insincerity - but I can but feel a vein of rancorous truth, or a vein of friendly truth, or a vein of ancient truth, or curious.

Then, as she is talking and in the same moment I am wondering, I consider: What matters it whether or not any of it is true, or whether or not she believes it, or whether or not I can understand it - since *she* is saying it. Is she not an exquisite person telling me these things in her exquisite voice?

She carries all before her in the world.

For she and I make up a small world.

If she be not brilliant in her talking, then that is because that set of sentences would be ruined by brilliancy.

If she be not profound in her discoursing, then that is because her fancy at the time dwells in the light fantastic and would be ruined by profoundness.

If she be not logical, that is because she is exquisite, which is quite beyond logic.

Nevertheless, when she says what is simple and plain and stupid the look of her face is more than all the look of one saying brilliant things.

And when she touches lightly upon one thin fancy and another the look of her lily face is above all things profound.

And when her mood and its expression are most reckless of logic the look of her face is the model of one giving out platitudes in all open candor and reasonableness.

I have been led by these looks of her face to see some varying visions of my friend Annabel Lee.

One is a vision of her as a capable, elderly maiden aunt, one who stands ready in sickness and in health to do for me, and cooks little meat pies for me, and tells me when I'm spending too much money, and what to do for a cold.

One is a vision of her as a playful child-companion who is with me in all my summer days, and shares all her quaint thoughts with me, and asks me countless questions and accepts my dictum as gospel.

One is a vision of her as a sister - one of that kind who has the best of all things in life whilst I must take the poor things; one of the kind that is to be married to a count from over the seas, and I must work and hurry to get her frocks ready for the wedding - and then go back to live in a small, dead village all the days of my life.

One is a vision of her as the quiet martyr-sister who comes at my call and retires at my bidding - and in this part my friend Annabel Lee walks with exceeding beauty.

One is a vision of her as a strong elderly friend who stands between me and all icy blasts, who lays out my daily life, who quiets my foolish excitement with her calmness and wisdom.

One is a vision of her as one who knows no law, who leads me in strange highways and byways, and whose mind for me is a labyrinth wherein I walk in piteous confusion.

One is a vision of her as an extremely wicked person whom I regard with fear, whom it behooves me to hate but whom I love.

One is a vision of her as a woman of any age who is, above all, uncompromising and unsympathetic. If I am joyous, she is placid; if I am heavy of heart, she is placid; if I am full of anticipation, she is placid; if I am in despair, she is placid.

One is a vision of her as a shadow among shadows. She is not real, I say to myself. One day I shall awake and find her vanished - without pain and without "sadness of farewell," and as if she had not been.

One is a vision of her as one who is in the world and of the world, and like the rest of the world. And when I contemplate her thus my thought is, the best thing of all is to be in the world and of the world, and like the rest of the world - to have the quality of humanness, to know the world so well as to be able to select the best of its treasures, and to make useful that in it which is useless.

But all these visions are vapory. There is not one of them that is my friend Annabel Lee. 'Tis the expressions of her lily face that give me these visions - not that which she says nor that which she does. In truth she is, in some way, like all the visions, but each is mingled so much with herself that the type is lost.

And my friend Annabel Lee, though she sits with the book of the two pages open before her and seems much interested in all that she finds in it, has yet the look of one who, if any one asked to borrow the book from her, would close it quickly and give it up readily with no regret. And after she had given away the book, it seems as if she would pick up a flower from somewhere near, and twirl the stem in her thumb and finger, and glance out the window.

Not that she has a contempt for the present as for the future, but that it seems she is not dependent on the book of the two pages for her thought of it.

But also there is method in her contempt for the future. For she deigns to consider that the future becomes the present, as one day follows after another. But she touches it not in good faith until it is indeed the present.

My friend Annabel Lee, times, sits playing upon a little, old lute.

"The future," said my friend Annabel Lee, "is like a lute with no strings. You cannot play upon such a lute and fill the long, long corridors in your brain with the thin, sweet, meaningless music. You can but sit stupidly staring into the cavity and thinking how joyous will be the music that shall come forth some day, as from time to time your lute is strung with strings - whereas you might better at that moment go out into your garden and fill the cavity with tomatoes and make haste with them to market. And while you sit dreaming over your stringless lute, in your impatience you press upon the stops and press too much and too often, so that when at last your lute is strung the stops will not work right, but will stick fast in one position. And when your other hand touches the strings there will be horrible discord - always horrible discord.

"I have never," said my friend Annabel Lee, "yet seen any one dreaming over an unstrung lute who did not finger the stops."

Having said this, my friend Annabel Lee gazed out over my head at the flat, green Atlantic sea, and her hand went upon and about her lute-strings, and there came out music. And the stops worked right, like stops that had not been tampered with in the lute's unstrung days.

And the music that came out was like yellow wine to the head, and went not only into the corridors but into the towers as well, and low down by the moat and within and without the outer wall, and into the dungeon where had not been music before.

*

18. Another Vision of My Friend Annabel Lee

And I have a vision of my friend Annabel Lee as a princess in a tall, tall castle by the side of the sea - a castle made of dull red granite that glows a gorgeous crimson in the light of the setting sun.

And all day long there is no sign of life about the dull red castle, and also the winds are low and the blue water is very quiet. Far down the shore are only a few gulls flying, and wild ducks riding on the waves.

There is nothing moving on the jagged rocks for miles about the red castle, but there are growing in crevices some wild green weeds that are full of fair sweet life. And all day the sky is pale blue.

The windows in the red castle are of thick, dark glass and are grated and mullioned and set about with iron. The look of these windows is rigid and bitter and it shuts out everything that is without.

The battlements of the castle are high and narrow and fearsome-looking and dark and very sullen. Were I upon the battlements I would gladly plunge off from them down upon the rocks, some hundreds of feet, and be dashed to pieces - or into the deep sea. But below there is a turret and a belfry, but no bell, and the turret is a sheltered and safe retreat looking out upon all. One who had not been content before in the world might be at last content within the turret of this tall, red castle by the side of the sea.

Away at the meeting of the sea and the sky there is a narrow line that is not pale blue like the sky nor dark blue like the sea, but is only pale thin air. And I look at it expecting to see - But in the bright daylight I never know what I expect to see in the line of thin air at the meeting of the pale and the dark.

And so then all day everything is dead quiet, and my friend Annabel Lee is a princess inside the red castle.

How fair a princess is my friend Annabel Lee!

I fancy her in a beautiful white gown embroidered with gold threads. The gown is long and narrow and fits closely about the waist, and trails on the ground. And upon the left forefinger of the princess a great old silver ring set with an unpolished turquoise.

The rooms inside the red castle are fit rooms for such a princess. They are dark and high and narrow, and are adorned with frescoes and wall-paintings, and the thick windows of dark glass shine with marvelous, myriad coloring where the light shows through. Before some of the windows bits of cut glass are hung, and these catch the sunbeams and straightway countless rainbows fall upon the gown and the hands and the hair of the princess.

When the sun sets a great bar of deep golden light falls from afar upon the red castle, and it becomes magnificent with crimson. The dark glass of the windows glows like old copper. The battlements are tipped with gold, and all is like a great flower that has but just bloomed.

After the sun has set and the crimson has faded once more from the red castle, and the copper from the windows, and before the light of day has gone, the sea and the sky take on different shades and different meanings, and the gulls and the wild ducks come up from far down the shore, and the rocks echo with their wild noises. The sky is full of flying cloud-racks and the water rises high and has crests of white foam.

But the line at the horizon looks still the same.

Then the princess in her white gown opens a door high up in the tall castle and comes out under the turret. She comes forward to the railing and leans upon it with her fair chin resting in her hand.

I see her there across a long stretch of dark water, her white frock gleaming in the pale light - so high up and all - and a multitude of thoughts come upon me.

The princess looks at the thin line of sky opposite her, and looks so steadfastly that I turn my eyes from her and look there also.

And now there are manifold scenes there.

There is a scene of a knight going forth to do battle, with his black charger and his shining steel armor. And he wears an orange plume in his helmet. His going is a brave thing. He is in the rising of his youth and strength. And for this reason I - and the princess on the turret - can see him falling gloriously in a fierce battle, with death in his veins, and the charger wandering off with no rider into the night. And the princess looks with envy upon one who can go forth and fall in battle.

There is a scene of a young woman in a small room working hard and persistently by a dim light at some exquisitely fine needlework upon an immense linen oblong. And her shoulders are bent and her eyes are strained and her hands are weary and her nerves shattered and crying out. But she does not leave off her work. She and her work are like an ant carrying away a desert grain by grain, and like one miserable person building up a pyramid, and like one counting all the stars. One does not know whose is the linen or why she works, or whether money will be given her for it. But one may know that verily she will have her reward. Such people working like that in small rooms, and all, with wearied nerves, always have their reward. And the princess on the turret looked out at the woman as if she with her linen and her needle were the fortunate one.

There is a scene of French Canadians cutting hay and raking it early in the summer afternoon - women and men. The day is so beautifully hot and the perfume of the grass is so sweet that a tall red castle by the side of the sea is the dreariest place of all. The princess looks out from her turret with desolate purple eyes. She looks at the ring upon her forefinger - and together with her I wonder why all people were not made French Canadians making hay in the fields. Over their heads is the air of the green French Canadian country; under their feet is the soft French Canadian hay. And they have appetites for their food.

There is a scene of a child playing in the mud under a green willow. She has a large pewter spoon to dip up great lumps of mud, and she takes up the lumps in her two hands and pats them and shapes them and lays them down in rows on a shingle. Water runs down through the meadow near by where she sits and she dips it up also in the spoon to thin out the mud. The rows of mud-cakes on the shingle are very neat and arranged with infinite care. The princess forgets to envy the child and her mud-cakes in the interest she takes in the making of them. Her face and her purple eyes even take on an indefinite look of contentment in that she is in the same world with so fit a thing.

Having looked long at the visions the princess takes her eyes from the line of thin sky and looks down into the tumbled dark water.

"When all is seen," says the princess, "there is nothing better than wild, dark water that is too vast to be measured and that is good for a thousand of years, and that contains yet as good fish as ever came out of it. It gives up pink shells upon the sand in the kindness of its heart, and it sends wild whistling gales up to the pinnacles of my red castle to sing for me and to tell me many stories. And it has wild winds wandering in and upon the high walls and caves along its rugged coast - and if I knew not that they were winds I would surely think them the voices of sea-maids singing - high, thin, piercing voices mingled with the sound of long, washing waves. And it gives out dreary lonesome cries - a loon calling in the night mists a mile away, and wild geese honking - so that I know there are things in it and upon it a hundred times wilder and lonesomer than I. And it sends good ships driving against these great rocks, and dashes them to pieces, and human beings go down with them to rest for a thousand of years in the depths, so that I know it loves human beings well, and has need of them. In the forenoon of a day in July it melts my heart with its glad, warm sunshine and dazzles my eyes and fills me with comfort - and I know that life is a safe thing. When all is seen," says the princess, "there is nothing better."

Thus I have a vision of my friend Annabel Lee as a princess in a tall, red castle by the side of the sea.

But neither is this my friend Annabel Lee. For she is more fascinating still, and her castle is even taller, and a deeper red - and more than all she is herself.

*

19. The Art of Contemplation

Yesterday my friend Annabel Lee and I sat comfortably opposite each other at a small table, eating our luncheon. She was very fair and good-natured - and we had tiny broiled fish, and some tea with slices of lemon in it, and bread, and green lettuce sprinkled over with vinegar and oil and red pepper, and two mugs of ale.

"Food is a lovely thing, don't you think?" said I.

"One of the best ever invented," said my friend Annabel Lee. "Have you considered how *much* would be gone from life if there were no food, and if we had not to eat three times every day?"

"Yes, I've considered it," I replied, "and it's a pleasure that never palls."

"It is so much more than pleasure," said my friend Annabel Lee. "It is a necessity and an art and a relaxation and an unburdening - and, dear me, it brings one up to the level of kings or of the beasts that perish.

"I have fancied," said my friend Annabel Lee, "a deal table set three times every day under a beautiful yew-tree in a far country. The yew-tree would be in a pasture where cattle are grazing, and always when I sat eating at the deal table the cows would stand about watching me. Sometimes on the deal table there would be brown bread and honey; sometimes there would be salt and cantaloupe; sometimes there would be lettuce with vinegar and pepper and oil; sometimes there would be whole-wheat bread and curds and cream in a brown earthen dish; sometimes there would be walnuts and figs; sometimes there would be two little broiled fish; sometimes there would be peaches; sometimes there would be flat white biscuits and squares of brown fudge; sometimes there would be bread and cheese; sometimes there would be olives and Scotch bannocks; sometimes there would be a blue delft pot of chocolate and an egg; sometimes there would be tea and scones; sometimes there would be plum-cake; sometimes there would be bread and radishes; sometimes there would be wine and olives; sometimes there would be a strawberry tart.

"I should live over the hill from the yew-tree, and I should come there to eat at seven o'clock in the morning, and at one in the afternoon, and at seven in the evening. And meanwhile I should be busy at some work so that my eating would be as if I had earned it."

"What sort of work would you do?" I asked.

"I might wash fine bits of lace," said my friend Annabel Lee, "and lay them out upon a sunny grass-plot to bleach and dry. Or I might pick berries and take them to market. Or I might sit in a doorway making baskets - I should make beautiful little baskets. Or I might care for a small garden, or a flock of geese - to feed them with grains and keep them from straying away. 'So many hours must I tend my flock, so many hours must I sport myself, so many hours must I contemplate.' - I should do all these things while tending my flock, and I should tend my flock well. I should do all my work well, so that the food on the deal table, under the yew-tree, would taste as if it had been earned.

"But would it not be strange," said my friend Annabel Lee, eating daintily of lettuce and fish, "after I had had this way of living in a country of always-summer for six months or seven months - oh, I should grow vastly weary of it! And not only should I grow weary of the garden or the geese or the baskets, and the deal table under the yew-tree, but I should grow weary of everything the fair green world could anyway offer. In the so many hours that I should contemplate I should arrive at this: there can be nothing better in the way of living than caring for a garden or a flock of geese, and going up a hill to a yew-tree to eat three times every day - *nothing*, if I do my work faithfully. So then when the gray dawn should break some morning and I should awaken and find an aching at my heart, I should know that the best had failed me, and I should see the Vast Weariness with me. 'Hast thou found me out, oh, mine enemy!' would run over and over in my mind. And all that day the tending of the flocks would be a hard thing, and the apples on the deal table under the yew-tree would turn to dust in my mouth."

My friend Annabel Lee laid down her small silver fork, and placed her hands one upon another on her knee, and sat silent.

Oh, she was a beautiful, brilliant person sitting there! I wondered hazily as I watched her how much of the day's gold sunshine she made up for me, and how much would vanish were she to vanish.

Presently she talked again.

"Much depends," said my friend Annabel Lee, "upon the amount of contemplation that one does in one's way of living, and upon how one's contemplation runs. Contemplation is a thing that does a great deal of mischief. But I daresay that when it as an art is made perfect it is a rare good thing and a neat, obedient servant, and knows exactly when to enter the mind and when to leave it. And whosoever may have it, thus brought to a state of perfection, is a most fortunate possessor and must needs go bravely down the world.

"Perhaps, now," said my friend Annabel Lee, "when one is a goose-girl and goes to eat at a deal table under a green yew-tree, one should contemplate only kings in gilded palaces. One should begin at the beginning of a king's life, it may be, and follow it step by step through heaviness and strife until one sees, in one's vivid goose-girl fancy, the king at last tottering and white-haired and forsaken toward his lonely grave.

"Or else one should contemplate the life of a laborer who must eat husks all his days, and is not worthy of his hire, and goes from bad to worse and becomes a beggar.

"Or else one should contemplate the being of a sweet maid whose life is a fair, round rose garden, and the thorns safely hidden and the stems pruned, and all. And one should likewise follow her step by step to her grave, or, if one so fancies, to the culmination of all happiness and success.

"For the idea is that in all one's contemplation, when one is a goose-girl, one should contemplate anything and everything except the being and condition of a goose-girl.

"But a better idea still," said my friend Annabel Lee, "would be to not contemplate at all, you know, but eat the radishes and other things, under the yew-tree, and rejoice.

"At any rate," said my friend Annabel Lee, "we need not contemplate *now* - what with these two little fishes and these green, crisp leaves."

She picked up her small silver fork again and went to eating lettuce.

And presently we both lifted our mugs of good ale and drank to that which would be a better idea still.

*

20. Concerning Little Willie Kaatenstein

I had one day given my friend Annabel Lee the bare outline of the facts in a case, and I asked her if she would kindly make a story from it and tell it me.

So my friend Annabel Lee told me a little story that also runs in my mind, someway, in measure and rhythm.

"There lived in a town in Montana," said my friend Annabel Lee, "not very long ago, in a quiet street, a family of that sort of persons which is called Jewish. And it is so short a time ago that they are there yet.

"Their name was Kaatenstein.

"There was Mrs. Kaatenstein and Mr. Kaatenstein and the four young children, Harry Kaatenstein and Leah Kaatenstein and Jenny Kaatenstein and little Willy Kaatenstein.

"And there was the hired girl whose name was Emma.

"And there was Uncle Will, Mrs. Kaatenstein's brother, who lived with them.

"Mrs. Kaatenstein was short and dark and sometimes quite cross, and she always put up fruit in its season, with the help of the hired girl, and the kitchen was then very warm.

"And Mr. Kaatenstein was also dark, but was a tall, slim man, and was kind and fond of the children, especially the two little girls. Mrs. Kaatenstein was fond of the children also, but mostly fond of the two boys.

"And Harry Kaatenstein was much like his mother, only he was not so dark, and he was ten years old.

"And Leah Kaatenstein was ten years old also - the two were twins - and she had an eye for strict economy, and wore plain gingham frocks, and had a long dark braid of hair, and played with very homely dolls.

"And Jenny Kaatenstein was seven years old and was most uncommonly fat, and was rarely seen without a bit of unleavened bread in her hand - for the children were allowed to have all that they wanted of unleavened bread. They did not want very much of it, except Jenny. And they all preferred to eat leavened bread spread with butter and sprinkled with sugar - but they couldn't have as much as they wanted of that.

"And little Willy Kaatenstein was only four and pronounced all his words correctly and seemed sometimes possessed of the wisdom of the serpent. He had very curly hair, and it seemed an unwritten law that whenever a grown-up lady passed by and saw the children playing on the walk in front of their house she must stop and exclaim what a pretty boy little Willy was and ask him for one of his curls. Whereat little Willy would stare up into the grown-up lady's face in a most disconcerting fashion and perhaps ask her for one of *her* curls. Or if the groceryman or the butcher would stop on his way to the kitchen and ask little Willy what was his name and how old was he, little Willy would answer with surprising promptness, and directly would ask the groceryman or the butcher what was *his* name and how old was *he*.

"And Emma, the hired girl, was raw-boned and big-fisted and frightfully cold blooded and unsympathetic. And she had a sister who came to see her and sat in the hot kitchen talking, while Emma pared potatoes or scrubbed the floor.

"The sister's name was Juley, and she sometimes brought strange, green candy to the children, which their mother never allowed them to eat. And sometimes Juley brought them chewing-gum, which they were not allowed to chew.

"And Uncle Will was a short, stout man, with a face that was nearly always flushed. He seemed fond of beer. There were a great many cases of beer in the cellar which belonged to Uncle Will. And there were cases full of beer-bottles that had all been emptied, and the children would have liked to sell the bottles, but they were not allowed to sell bottles. Uncle Will was also fond of little Willy, and on summer evenings when he and Mr. Kaatenstein were at home, and after they had eaten dinner, Uncle Will might have been heard inviting little Willy, in his hoarse, facetious voice, to come and have a glass of beer with him. And when little Willy, with his short curls and his small white suit, would come and just taste of the beer and would make a wry mouth and shed a few abortive tears over its bitterness, Uncle Will would laugh very heartily and jovially indeed.

"Mrs. Kaatenstein had a great many ducks and geese in the back-yard and spent much time among them, fattening them to eat and fussing over them, in the forenoons. So the children never played there in the forenoon.

"There were a great number of things that the Kaatenstein children were not allowed to do - the things they were allowed to do were as nothing by comparison, and the things they were allowed to do were, for the most part, things they did not care about.

"They had each a square iron bank in which were ever so many silver quarters and dimes and half-dollars and nickels and gold pieces, too, for they were a Jewish family. Their father and their Uncle Will kept dropping coins into the little slits in the tops of the banks from time to time, and friends of the family would also kindly contribute, and their uncles and aunts would send money for that purpose all the way from Cincinnati. So there was wealth in these banks, but the children were not allowed to have any of it. And they were never given any money 'to throw away buying things,' as their mother said, except a nickel once in a long while - one nickel for the four of them.

"And there were toys that their father and mother and Uncle Will had bought for them, and others that were sent by the uncles and aunts in Cincinnati, but they were never allowed to play with them. The toys were kept in a large black-walnut bureau in their mother's bed-room. There was a small, tinkling piano that Leah Kaatenstein's Aunt Barbara had sent to her, or that had been sent to her parents in trust for her. And there was a little engine, that would run on a track, which had once been given to Harry Kaatenstein. And there was an immense wax doll which had fallen to Jenny Kaatenstein's lot. And little Willy Kaatenstein was the reputed owner of a small mechanical circus with tiny wooden acrobats and horses and a musical box beneath the platform. And there were other toys of all kinds; for the relatives in Cincinnati had been lavish. But the children were not allowed to make use of them, so they languished in the black-walnut bureau.

"And Harry Kaatenstein had a fine gold watch that his mother had given him, but he was not allowed to wear it or even look at it. It was kept in a jewel-case in her bed-room.

"And Leah Kaatenstein had a fine gold watch that her grandmother in Cincinnati had sent, but she was not allowed to wear it or even look at it. It was kept in her mother's jewel-case.

"And Jenny Kaatenstein had a fine gold watch that her aunt Rebecca had sent, but she was not allowed to wear it or even look at it. It was kept in her mother's jewel-case.

"And little Willy Kaatenstein had a fine gold watch that Uncle Will had bought for him - and Uncle Will, who was a privileged character in the house, would sometimes take little Willy's watch from Mrs. Kaatenstein's jewel-case and give it to little Willy to wear in the evening when the family was gathered in the dining-room. And Uncle Will would drink his beer and ask little Willy what time was it. But before Mrs. Kaatenstein put little Willy to bed she replaced the watch carefully in the jewel-case.

"The children had a great many such possessions, but what they really had to play with was a small, much-battered wagon which they put to many uses in the course of a day. Sometimes it was a fire-engine, and sometimes a hose-cart, and sometimes a motor-car, and sometimes a carriage, and sometimes an ambulance, and sometimes a go-cart for Leah Kaatenstein's homely dolls (which by some strange chance were hers to do with as she would - they were not of excessive value), and sometimes for a patrol wagon, and sometimes for a water-cart. They had also a little rocking chair with which they played house on the porch. Both the chair and the wagon were much overworked and were most pathetic in appearance. The children often grew weary of playing always with these two things and languished for other amusement. Sometimes Leah Kaatenstein subsided into the rocking chair with her homely dolls in her lap and talked to them seriously, telling them many things which would be of use to them all their lives and instilling into them strict rules of economy. And sometimes Harry Kaatenstein sat on the lowest step of the porch with the nozzle of the long, rubber hose, which was attached to the faucet at the side of the house, and with which Mr. Kaatenstein or Uncle Will watered the grass in the evening. The children were not allowed to water the grass, but there was usually water enough trickling from the hose for Harry Kaatenstein to make little whirlpools on the steps, which he did, causing loss of life among bugs of divers kinds. And sometimes Jenny Kaatenstein, with her inevitable bit of unleavened bread, sat on the top step, moon-faced and pudgy, resting from her labors. And sometimes little Willy Kaatenstein climbed up and sat upon the post at the bottom of the stoop and kicked it viciously with his heels. He often sat there kicking, as could be plainly seen by the dents in the post.

"One warm day the Kaatenstein children were thus languishing after having played hard with the wagon, and Emma was ironing in the kitchen. Their mother was away for the afternoon and the children had a delightful sense of freedom, even with the grim, big-fisted Emma in charge. Only they wished they had a nickel. Harry Kaatenstein said that if they had a nickel he should certainly go down to Grove's, a block and a half away, and purchase some brown and white cookies. At which little Willy Kaatenstein and Jenny Kaatenstein - more especially Jenny Kaatenstein - smacked their lips, and Leah Kaatenstein sighed and remarked that Harry's extravagance was very discouraging.

"Presently, wonderful to relate, Emma appeared around the corner, from the kitchen, with four thick slices of bread-and-butter slightly sprinkled with sugar, and the children gazed very eagerly in her direction. Jenny Kaatenstein dropped her piece of unleavened bread and half-started to meet Emma, but thought better of it, knowing Emma's ways. Emma distributed the slices of bread, and fastened little Willy Kaatenstein's hat on more firmly with the elastic under his chin, and informed the children that if they knew what was good for themselves they would not get into any mischief while *she* had charge of them. Then she went back to her ironing.

"The children were delighted with their bread-and-butter, and their imagination played lightly about it.

" 'My bread-and-butter's raspberry ice cream,' said Harry Kaatenstein.

" '*My* bread-and-butter's *choc'late* ice cream,' said Leah Kaatenstein, waxing genial.

" '*My* bread-and-butter's *vanilla* ice cream,' said Jenny Kaatenstein.

"But little Willy Kaatenstein said never a word, for his bread-and-butter seemed very good to him *as* bread-and-butter.

"Their bread-and-butter someway put new life into them and made them more fully awake to the fact that their mother was away for the afternoon. After all, they were not afraid of any one but their mother, and she being gone, should they not enjoy life for once?

"When they had finished eating they had a brilliant idea.

" 'I'm going to shake a nickel out of my bank,' said Harry Kaatenstein.

" '*I'm* going to shake a nickel out of *my* bank,' said Leah Kaatenstein, in surprising luxury of spirit.

" '*I'm* going to shake a nickel out of *my* bank,' said Jenny Kaatenstein.

"And little Willy Kaatenstein said never a word, but ran at the first inkling of the idea immediately to the dining-room where the four banks were standing, on the mantel above the fire-place, and pushed up a chair and took down his own green bank. And then he slid back the little piece of iron that was just under the slot in the top of the bank, and shook, shook, shook, with very little noise, and lo, not a nickel but a five-dollar gold coin rolled out on the floor!

"And then Harry Kaatenstein and Leah Kaatenstein and Jenny Kaatenstein rushed in and seized their banks and began shaking, shaking with much *clank, clank* of silver and gold against iron - for was not their mother far from them? - whilst little Willy Kaatenstein stood by with his gold piece clasped tight in his hand. Even his young intelligence knew its marvelous value, and he thought it wise not to reveal his treasure to Leah Kaatenstein's horrified gaze.

" 'I'm going down to Grove's and buy gum-drops with my nickel,' said Harry Kaatenstein, pounding and shaking, but never a nickel appeared for the reason that he had forgotten the little iron slide, which only once in a while fell away from under the slot and never at the right time.

" '*I'm* going down to Grove's and buy a long licorice pipe with *my* nickel,' said Leah Kaatenstein - a long licorice pipe was the very most she could get for her money - also shaking and pounding fruitlessly, for she too had forgotten the little iron slide.

" '*I'm* going down to Grove's and buy some cookies with *my* nickel,' said Jenny Kaatenstein, likewise pounding and shaking and forgetting the little iron slide.

"And little Willy Kaatenstein said never a word, but when he had learned what to buy with his money he ran out of the front door and down the street to Grove's on the corner.

"Now when Harry Kaatenstein and Leah Kaatenstein and Jenny Kaatenstein considered and rejoiced over the absence of their mother, they forgot at the same time to consider and fear the perilous nearness of Emma ironing in the kitchen - the kitchen being next to the dining-room.

"Suddenly while they were in the midst of their work and were shaking and pounding away for dear life, unconscious of all else, the door leading into the kitchen was pushed open with ominous quiet and the head of Emma appeared. It was an unprepossessing head at all times, and it was a dangerous-looking head at that moment.

"Harry Kaatenstein and Leah Kaatenstein and Jenny Kaatenstein perceived this vision at once, and an appalling silence like the tomb followed the clamor that had been.

"'So this is what you're up to, you young lambs!' said Emma, and swooped down and pounced upon them before they could possibly escape, though they had made for the door with very creditable speed. Emma held them with one hand while she picked up the banks with the other. She remarked, in unmeasured terms, upon the condition of the waxed dining-room floor, upon the vicious qualities of some children whom she mentioned by name, upon what would happen to them when their mother came home, and upon what was going to happen to them right away.

"And she led them upstairs to their mother's bed-room and, after shaking them well, locked them in and went downstairs, carrying the key with her.

"Meanwhile little Willy Kaatenstein had gone upon his interesting errand at Grove's on the corner.

"He went into the shop and stood before a glittering glass case of things.

"'And what'll it be for Master Kaatenstein to-day?' said the man behind the glittering case.

"'I want gum-drops and licorice pipes and cookies - and some watermelons,' said little Willy Kaatenstein and laid the shining gold coin before the grocer's astonished eyes, for the grocer had expected to see the Kaatenstein semi-occasional nickel - nothing more or less.

"'Is this yours, Master Kaatenstein?' said the grocer, eyeing the coin with suspicion.

"'Of course it's mine,' said little Willy Kaatenstein, impatiently. 'And I want the things right away.'

"'Well, I suppose its all right, my boy,' said the grocer. 'If it isn't, *one* of us'll have to suffer, I guess. Now, what did you say you wanted?'

"Little Willy Kaatenstein repeated his order, and added other items.

"'Now, Master Kaatenstein,' said the grocer, 'you never will be able to carry all that. That'll make a pile of stuff. Better run back and get your little wagon' - for he knew the Kaatenstein wagon, having often placed in it a paper of sugar or a sack of salt or three tins of something according to Mrs. Kaatenstein's order - for the children to draw home.

"So little Willy Kaatenstein ran back and got the little wagon from the front yard, and the man loaded the things into it. 'Must be going to have a picnic,' he observed.

"There was certainly a pile of stuff. There were long licorice pipes enough in the wagon to surfeit the appetites of the four Kaatensteins for many a day, and the name of the gum-drops was legion. And there were two watermelons, and cookies enough to satisfy even Jenny Kaatenstein's capacious desire. Also there were nuts and some dyspeptic-looking pies, and a great many little dogs and cats and elephants made of a very tough kind of candy which all the Kaatenstein children thought perfectly lovely. Also there were figs in boxes and chocolate-drops and red and white sticks of candy, flavored with peppermint fit to make one's mouth water. And all these things were in surprising quantity and made so heavy a load that little Willy Kaatenstein was hard put to it to drag it up the street. But little Willy Kaatenstein had strong little arms and he and the wagon made slow and sure progress back to the Kaatenstein home. The grocer stood out in front of his shop gazing after the boy and the boy's wagon and the wagon's contents with a puzzled and somewhat dubious smile.

"Little Willy Kaatenstein proceeded into his front yard with the wagon and around to the back on the side of the house where the kitchen door was not. He dragged the wagon quietly on to the farther end of the back yard and opened the gate of the pen made of laths, where Mrs. Kaatenstein's ducks and geese were kept. He drew the wagon in and back behind the duck-house, and left it.

"Then little Willy Kaatenstein closed the lath gate and ran to find Harry Kaatenstein and Leah Kaatenstein and Jenny Kaatenstein and invite them to the feast.

"But they were nowhere to be found. He hunted about in the house and out of doors, but there was no sign of them, and for some reason he thought he would not ask Emma questions touching on their whereabouts.

"So having hunted for his relatives all that he thought best, little Willy Kaatenstein could but go out on the highways and byways and call in the lame, the halt, and the blind. Accordingly he slipped through the fence and went back into the alley-way to the house immediately behind his own, in search of Bill and Katy Kelly, two Irish friends of the Kaatenstein children - with whom they were not allowed to play. Bill and Katy Kelly, to be sure, were neither lame nor halt nor blind, but were very sound in limb and constitution, and were extremely responsive to little Willy Kaatenstein's invitation to come to the feast. Feasts were things that Bill and Katy Kelly reveled in - when they had opportunity.

"So in company with little Willy Kaatenstein - he in his curls and his white suit, and the two in very dingy raiment - they hied them through the fence to the feast. They reached the duck-yard without being seen by Emma, the arch-enemy, and found the little wagon safe, and the ducks and geese staring and peering and stretching their necks at it and its contents with much curiosity.

"This curiosity, on the part of the fowls, must have changed to amazement when they beheld the attack made on the wagon and the strange things in the way of eating that followed.

"How Bill and Katy Kelly did eat and how they reveled! And little Willy Kaatenstein literally waded in gum-drops and long licorice pipes. They began the feast with pie; from pie they went at figs; from figs they transferred to the tough little animals; and from that to cookies; and from cookies to long licorice pipes. Then they stopped eating consecutively and went at the entire feast hap-hazard.

"They ate fast and furiously for several minutes.

"Then the first ardor of the feast subsided, and little Willy Kaatenstein, for one, seemed to lose all interest not only in feasts but in the world at large. He sat back upon a box, which contained a duck sitting on twelve eggs, and looked at the ground with the air of one who has someway lost his perspective.

"Bill and Katy Kelly still ate, but more, it seemed, from a sense of duty to themselves than from appetite, and presently their eating became desultory, and they began to throw remnants of the feast to the fowls. These at first gazed askance at the extraordinary food thus lavished upon them - but finally went at it madly, as if they, too, reveled in feasts.

"Mrs. Kaatenstein's face must need have been a study could she have seen her cherished ducks and geese stuffing their crops with licorice pipes and gumdrops.

"But Mrs. Kaatenstein was out for the afternoon.

"While these things were happening in her duck-yard, no less interesting ones were taking place up-stairs in her bed-room, where Harry Kaatenstein and Leah Kaatenstein and Jenny Kaatenstein were prisoners of Emma.

"At first they merely sat on the window-seat and discussed the several untoward things that they wished would happen to Emma. Having hanged, drawn, and quartered that liberal-proportioned lady until they could no more, they felt better. Then they looked over their mother's room in search of amusement, with the result that the black-walnut bureau, containing the toys with which they were not allowed to play, was made to give forth the wealth of its treasures. The floor of Mrs. Kaatenstein's bed-room presented a motley appearance. Jenny Kaatenstein even forgot to miss her bit of unleavened bread in her excitement over the fact that she actually was holding her own huge wax doll in her lap. And the circus and the steam-engine and the tinkling piano and the tea-sets and the barking dogs and the picture books and the manifold other things were at last put to those uses for which they had been destined. And they even went to the jewel-case and got out their watches.

"But Harry Kaatenstein and Leah Kaatenstein and Jenny Kaatenstein, though they were pleasantly excited, were yet highly uneasy in their minds. They knew they had yet to render up payment for the day's business. -

"The rest of the tale is obvious enough," said my friend Annabel Lee, laughing gently and changing her tone.

"But please tell it," said I, with much eagerness.

"Well, then," said my friend Annabel Lee: -

"The afternoon waned, and Mrs. Kaatenstein came home. She heard unusual noises in her beloved duck-yard, and fled thither, as fast as her goodly proportions would allow.

"Her eyes met a sight which was maddening to them.

"They beheld little Willy Kaatenstein, looking decidedly pale and puffy, sitting weakly on a box containing a setting-duck - and the two objection-able Kelly children actually at that moment feeding her choicest goose with gum-drops. Scattered all about the once neat duck yard was rubbish in frightful variety, and a half-dozen of her tiny ducklings were busy at an atrocious watermelon. Certainly no one but those Irish young ones could have brought in so much litter. It did not take Bill and Katy Kelly long to gather that they were not wanted there. Mrs. Kaatenstein quite quenched, for the time, their fondness for feasts. As they went, she ordered them to take their vile belongings with them, which they were willing enough to do - as much of them as they could carry. They bestowed an apprehensive glance on little Willy Kaatenstein - but little Willy Kaatenstein's face was only pale, puffy, and very passive. Having dispersed the Kellys, Mrs. Kaatenstein led her son into the house and stopped in the kitchen to demand of Emma why she allowed such things to happen, and ordered her to go at once and clean out the duck-yard. Emma obeyed, first giving up Mrs. Kaatenstein's bed-room key and explaining her own possession of it.

"Then Mrs. Kaatenstein, after doctoring little Willy Kaatenstein's poor little stomach and laying him neatly out on a sofa in a cool, dark room, went on to her own room, whence proceeded unusual noises. Unlocking and opening the door, a sight the like of which she had not of late years known overwhelmed her spirit.

"The short, dead silence that followed her appearance on the threshold was but emphasized by the merry tinkling of the gay little circus which had been wound up and would not stop, even under the dark influence of impending tragedy. -

"Well," said my friend Annabel Lee, "the case of Harry Kaatenstein and Leah Kaatenstein and Jenny Kaatenstein was attended to by their mother. She whipped them all soundly and sent them to bed.

"But as for little Willy Kaatenstein - not looking in the least pale or puffy, he sat that evening, after dinner, on Uncle Will's lap, wearing his own fine gold watch out of the jewel-case, and being continually invited to have a glass of beer.

"But in the kitchen, Emma was telling Juley that though she had once thought a great deal of little Willy Kaatenstein she now honestly believed him to be the very worst one of the four. -

"That story," said my friend Annabel Lee, "was very tiresome. You shouldn't ask me to tell you stories."

"I am sorry if it tired you," I said. "But the story was *entirely* fascinating. It was *exactly* like the Kaatensteins. And you, telling a story of the Kaatensteins, are delicately, oh, delicately incongruous!"

"Were *you* ever at a feast in the Kaatenstein duck-yard?" said my friend Annabel Lee.

"Yes, indeed," said I, "along with Bill and Katy Kelly, at the age of eleven. And I have seen every toy in the black-walnut bureau."

"And which would you," said my friend Annabel Lee, "to be at a feast with the Kaatensteins at the age of eleven, or here, now, with me?"

"When all's said," said I, "here with you, now, by far."

" 'Tis very good of you," said my friend Annabel Lee, and looked at me with her purple eyes.

*

21. A Bond of Sympathy

Having told me stories, my friend Annabel Lee demanded that I should write a bit of verse to read to her.

My verse is rather rotten verse, and I told her so. She replied that the fact of its being rotten had but little to do with the matter, that most verse was rotten, anyway, and usually the more rotten the better it suited the reader.

She was in that mood.

So I wrote some lines and read them to her - there was nothing else to do. She had been kind in telling me stories, though probably she told them because it amused her. When I finished reading, she said that the verse was not rotten at all. She, for her part, would call it not yet quite ripe.

"That's the *verse*," said my friend Annabel Lee. "As for the meaning of the words in it, that betrays many things. The most vivid thing it betrays is your age. It shows that you have passed over the period of nineteen and have arrived at exactly one-and-twenty. And therefore it is a triumphant bit of verse.

"Don't you know," said my friend Annabel Lee, "how much verse there is thrown upon the world that means *nothing* whatsoever? And so when one does happen upon a bit of it that tells even the smallest thing, like the height of the writer, or the color of his hair, then one feels repaid.

"And your verse tells still other things," said my friend Annabel Lee. "One is that you still think, as we've agreed once before, of that which will one day open wondrously for you."

"I did not agree to that, you know," said I.

"Well, then, I agreed to it for both of us," said my friend Annabel Lee. "And your verse betrays that so plainly that one is led to feel that there are persons who grow more hopeful with each bit of darkness that comes to them. If your life were all fire and sunshine you would write very different verse. And if it told anything at all it would tell that while you looked forward to still more fire and sunshine, you would somehow know you were not really to have any more, but that it would grow less and less in the years, and by the time you were an old lady, and still not nearly ready to die, it would give out entirely."

"That would be by the law of compensation," said I. "And it would require a great deal of fire and sunshine in her early life to compensate any one who had grown into an old lady and had run out of it."

"So it would," said my friend Annabel Lee. "Now, when you grow old - though you will never be that which is called an old lady - you will be quite mellow. And probably the less you have to be mellow over, the mellower you will be."

"I don't wish to be that way," said I. "I think that kind of person is pitiful, living year after year."

"You'll not be pitiful," said my friend Annabel Lee. "You can not be mellow and pitiful at the same time. It may be that to be mellow is the best thing, and the most comfortable. It may be that people struggle through a long life with but one object in their minds - to be mellow in their old age. This verse certainly sounds as if *you* were looking forward to it."

"I can't see that it sounds that way, at all," said I.

"Of course you can't," said my friend Annabel Lee. "You wrote the verse, and you are but you."

"And what are some of the other things that it betrays?" I inquired.

"It betrays," said my friend Annabel Lee, "that you are better in detail than you are in the entire. And if that is true of you in one thing it is true of you in everything. I daresay your friends find things in you that they like extremely, but you in the entire they look upon as something that has much to acquire."

"Not my *friends*?" said I.

"Yes, your *friends*," said my friend Annabel Lee.

"That is a bitter thing for a verse to show," I made answer, "and a bitter thing to have in my mind."

"Well, and aren't you wise enough to prefer the bitter things to the sweet things?" said my friend Annabel Lee. "For every sweet thing that you have in your mind, it is yours to pay a mighty bitter price. Whereas the bitter things are valuable possessions. And if it is true about your friends, of course you wish to know it."

"No," said I, "I don't wish to know it."

"But, at least," said my friend Annabel Lee, with a wonderful softening of her voice into something that was sincere and enchanting, "believe what I told you about it, for in that case you and I have that good gift - a bond of sympathy. For if I had friends, of that kind, they would look upon me as something with much to acquire, very sure. But don't," said my friend Annabel Lee, hastily, "consider the bond of sympathy a sweet thing - remember the mighty bitter price."

"I will believe what you said about the friends," said I - "and it is bitter enough to purge my soul for a time. The bond of sympathy is not a sweet thing, anyway. I don't expect to have to pay for it. - And it brings a feeling of restfulness. -"

"A bond of sympathy," said my friend Annabel Lee, "comes already paid for. It does very well. It is not sweet - it tastes more like a cigarette or an olive."

"About the verse" - said my friend Annabel Lee.

"Please let's not talk about that any more," said I.

"Whatever you like," said my friend Annabel Lee.

And we talked of George Sand and her books.

But, anyway, this was my bit of unripe verse:

> *Yesterday my star went down in the deep shadows.*
> *It went lightly*
> *Like the rippling of water;*
> *And many tiny dear things went with it, and I watched them:*
> *I knew that my star would never rise again.*

Yesterday my star went down in the deep shadows.
It went softly
Like the half-lights of evening;
And as it went my frantic thoughts pursued it without hoping:
I knew that my star would never rise again.

Yesterday my star went down in the deep shadows.
It went tenderly
Like my friend who loves me;
But since it's gone the way shows dark - my two eyes are tired watching:
I know that my star will never rise again.

*

22. The Message of a Tender Soul

"The message of a tender soul," said my friend Annabel Lee, "is a thing that will go far, oh, so far, and lose nothing of itself.

"When all things in the world are counted the beautiful things are in the greatest numbers. And when all the things in the world are counted the message of a tender soul counts greatly more than many.

"A tender soul receives back no gratitude for its message, and looks for no gratitude, and does not know what gratitude means. And the tenderness of the message is all unmade and all unknown, but is felt for long, long years.

"The message of a tender soul goes over the sea into the lonesomeness of the night and nothing stops it on the way, for all know what it is and bid it god-speed. And it goes down and around a mountain to a house where there is woe, and if before it came that house had turned away charity and love and friendship and good-will and peace, and had sent a curse after them all, still it opens wide its doors for the message of a tender soul. For its coming is not heralded, and the soul that sends it does not even know its tenderness, and the hearts of all in that house where there is woe - they are deeply, unknowingly comforted. And it goes upon the barrenness of a countryside where there is not one green thing growing, and the barrenness is then more than paradise, had paradise no such message. And it goes where lovely flowers grow in thousands, where sparkling water mingles with sparkling water and quenches thirst, where the long gray moss hangs from birch-trees, where pale clouds float - and itself is more beautiful than all these. Have you felt all those tender things that go down into the depths?

They bring comfort, but also they bring tears into the eyes and pain into the heart. The message of a tender soul - what does it bring but ineffable comfort to the heart? You do not feel that it is a message, you do not feel it to be a divinely beautiful thing. There are no sudden salt tears. Only the message is there - only it does that for which it is sent. Have you gone out and done all the work that you could do, and done it faithfully and asked no reward - and have you come back and cried out in bitterness of spirit? Then, it may be, came wondrously beautiful things from over the way to tell you, Take heart. But there was no 'take heart' for you. Then it may be there came from that way which you were not looking, the message of a tender soul. Then there was comfort, and with no tears of pain and no bitter, bitter tears of joy. There was deep comfort so that you could go out and work again and for no reward. There is work that has no reward. For those that work for no reward there can be no comfort in all the vastness except the message of a tender soul. Have you gone out and done all the evil you could do, in cruel ways, and taken away faith in some one from some one - and have come back and suffered more than any of them? Then it may be there came the message of a tender soul - and many, many other things faded from your heart. And still there were no tears. And if there is too much for you in living, and if the countless things near and far in the world crowd over you and fill you with horrible fear, then, if the message of a tender soul comes, one by one they step backward, and in your heart is comfort for the long, long years.

"There have been those that have had happiness that was more than the world, but in the end there was no comfort, for their happiness brought with it tears of joy and emotion that had limitless source.

"If you have wanted happiness and have hungered and thirsted, after there came the message of a tender soul, you were content with a branch from a green pine-tree.

"If you have felt a thousand tender things and have drunk from a thousand cups and then have been about to write it in black lettering that all, *all* have failed you - if then there came the message of a tender soul, you have written instead that nothing has failed you, and you have turned back your footsteps and have tried it all again.

"If for you and me to-day there should come over frozen hills and green meadows from a far country the message of a tender soul, should we shiver when it is dark and should we dread the coming of the years, and should we consider what would bring weariness and what would bring rest, and should we measure and contemplate? But no. For the message of a tender soul is a message from one that has found the quiet and is absolutely at peace, and has gone so far toward the stars and so far and wide over the green earth that she has indeed reached the truth, and her soul gives of its tenderness without thinking, and without knowing, and all in the dark.

"And when we should feel the message, all without knowing, there would come again that long-since faith, and that fullness of life, and that sense of realness, and the shining of the sun would be of new meaning.

"It may be," said my friend Annabel Lee, "that we will have to go still farther into the wilderness before the message comes, and it may be also that it will not come for many years.

"But it is in all ways comforting to know there is such a thing."

More than I considered the message that might come, I considered the voice with no hardness but with softness, and the lily face of my friend Annabel Lee.

*

23. Me to My Friend Annabel Lee

I wrote the day before yesterday this letter to my friend Annabel Lee:

Montreal. -

Dear Fair Lady:

Since I have come to stay in Montreal for a time, and you still in Boston, I have seen you, times, even more vividly than when I was there. You come into my dreams at dead of night.

Can you imagine what you are in my dreams?

I look forward impatiently to the end of my time here, so that I may go to find you again; - but my impatience grows someway less when I think that if I am with you this vision may vanish from my dreams. -

I will write you of some of the things I have found here.

There is much in Montreal that takes me back into the dim mists - the wonderful days when I had lived only three years. It was not here, but farther west - still what is in Canada is Canadian and does not change nor vary. This Canadian land and water and air awakens shadow-things in my memory and visions and voices of the world as it was when I was three.

It is all exceeding fair to look upon about here. The fields are green, not as they are in Massachusetts, but as they might be in the south of France. There is a beautiful, broad, blue river that can be seen from far off, and it sends out a haze and then all is gray French country, and gray French villages. When you come near you see the French peasants working in the fields - old men and maidens, and very old, strange-looking women, all with no English words in their mouths and no English thing in their lives if they can avoid it. They wear brass rings on their hands and in their ears, and the women wear gay-colored fish-wife petticoats, and in all their faces and eyes is that look that comes from working always among vegetables in the sun, the look of a piteous, useless brain.

And there is the strange, long, tree-covered hill that they call Mount Royal. I have in my mind a picture of it in a bygone century, when an adventurous, brave Frenchman and a few Indians of the wild stood high at its summit - he with the French flag unfurled in the wind, and the Indians shading their eyes and looking off and down into the valley. And there was not one sign of human life in the valley, and all was wild growth and tangled underbrush, and death-like silence, except maybe for the far-off sound of flying wild hoofs in the forest. And now this hill is the lodging-place of many things hidden among the trees - convents set about with tall, thick, solid stone walls, and inside the walls are heavy-swathed nuns who have said their farewells to all things without. And there are hospitals founded and endowed in the name of the Virgin, and Jesuit colleges, and the lodges of priests and brotherhoods.

And in the midst of the St. Lawrence valley where the Indians looked down is this old gray-stone city, and in the Place d'Armes square is a fine, triumphant statue of Maisonneuve with his French flag.

This gray-stone city is builded thick with gray-stone cathedrals, and some of them are very fine, and some of them are parti-colored as rainbows inside, and all of them are Roman Catholic and French.

The Protestant churches are but churches.

And the Notre Dame cathedral, when the setting sun touches its great, tall, gray, twin towers with red, is even more than French and Roman Catholic. The white-faced women in the nunnery at the side of it must need have a likeness of those eternal towers graven on their narrow devout hearts. Within, the Notre Dame is most gorgeous with brilliant-colored saints and Virgins and a passion of wealth and Romanism.

And is it not wonderful to think that many of these gray-stone buildings and dwellings were here in the sixteen hundreds, and that gray nuns walked in these same green gardens two centuries ago? And the same country was about here, and the same blue water.

And when all is said, the country and the blue water have been here always, and are the most wonderful things of all. If the gray-stone buildings were of yellow gold and of emeralds and brilliants, the green country would be no fairer and no less exquisitely fair, and the blue of the water would go no deeper into the heart and no less deep, and the pale clouds would float high and gently with the same old-time mystery. And the centuries they know are countless.

The natural things are the same in Massachusetts - but here they seem someway even older. You feel the breath of the very long-ago among the wildness of green - as if only human beings had come and gone, but it had never changed its smallest twig or grass-blade. It seems but waiting, and its patience in the waiting is without end.

Away on the other side of the tree-covered mountain I have seen a flat, gently-curved country road with the sunshine upon it and a few little English sparrows alighting and flying along it and picking at grains. And the grass by the road-side was tall and rank and sweet to the senses, and the road led to farms and the river and the wildwood. Cows were feeding by a shallow brook, and there were sumach bushes, thick and dark, near by.

For several minutes when my eyes rested upon this I felt absolutely content with all of life.

While I'm telling you this, Annabel Lee, I am not quite sure you are listening - and for myself, I see *you* much more than anything I have talked about. I am wondering how it is possible that you have lived only fourteen years - even the fourteen years of a Japanese woman. And I see again in my mind - your red lips, and your dead-black hair, and your purple eyes, and your wonderful hands, and your forehead with the widow's peak, and the two short side-locks that curve around, and your slimness in the scarlet and gold-embroidered gown.

And most of all I see your eyes when they are full of soft purple shadows, and your lips when they are tender - and your heart as I have seen it before, and its depths which are of the white purity.

Last night there was the vision of you with your purple eyes wide and gazing down at me with the white lids still. And I was horror-struck at the look of world-weariness in them - how that it is terrible, how that it follows one into the darkness and light, how that it is grief and rage and madness, how that it makes the heart ache until all the life-nerves ache with it - and there is no end; how that it is life and death, and one can not escape! - a world of tears and entreating and vows; but no, there is no escape.

And then again I looked up at your purple eyes gazing down at me full of strong, high scorn and triumph. "Do you think we have not conquered life?" they said. "Do you think we can not crush out all the little demons that presume to torture? Do you think we can not conquer *everything*? Who is there that we have not known? Where is there that we have not been? Are there any still, still shadows that we have cringed before? Are there any brilliant lights upon the sky that we have not faced boldly and put aside? And the stones and the stars and the mists on the sea are less - less than we, - *we* are the greatest things of all."

Thus your two eyes when I slept, and when I worked I saw you again as you have looked so many times - the expression of your red lips, and your voice with vague bitterness, and your lily face inscrutable.

I shall see you so again many times, my friend Annabel Lee. -

The fact remains that I am in Montreal and Canada. And as the days run along I am reminded that I have in me the old Canadian instincts. The word "Canadian" has always called up in my mind a confused throng of things, like - porridge for tea, and Sir Hugh MacDonald, and Dominion Day, and my aunt Elizabeth MacLane, and old-fashioned pictures of her majesty the queen, and Orangemen's Day, and "good-night" for good-evening, and "reel of cotton" for spool of thread, and "tin" instead of can, and Canadian cheese, and *rawsberries* in a patent pail, and the Queen's Own in Toronto, and soldiers in red coats, and children in Scotch kilts, and jam-tarts, and barley-sugar, and whitefish from Lake Winnipeg, and the CPR, and the Parliament at Ottawa, and coasting in toboggans, and Lord Aberdeen, and everything-coming-over-from-England-so-much-better-and-cheaper-than-American-ware, - and all that sort of thing. And my mind has always had a color for Canada - a shade of mingled deep green and golden brown.

Even in Montreal, where so much is French, there is enough to stamp it as beyond question Canadian. One still sees marks of her majesty the queen - but shopkeepers assert confidently that "Edward is going to make a good king," and Canadian men are made up as nearly as possible after his pattern, stout and with that short pointed beard.

In the greenness of Dominion Square is the most beautiful piece of sculpture I have seen. All the statues that stand about in Montreal are finer than most of their kind, and there are no such hideous creations as are set up in Boston and New York. The Dominion Square statue is a bronze figure of a Sir John A. MacDonald. The face of the figure is all that is serene and benign, and the lines of the body and of the hands are made with strength and beauty. Whether it is like Sir John A. MacDonald, one does not know - 'tis enough that it's an exquisite piece of workmanship with which to adorn a city. And the Maisonneuve statue is a fine, handsome thing, and is altogether alive. The bronze is no bronze, but has seventeenth-century red blood in its veins, and the arm that is held high and the hand with the flag mean conquest and victory.

I shall see Quebec and the length of the blue river before I see you again, and they, like Montreal, will be mingled with a many-tinted looking-forward to being with you again.

High upon the tower of a gray-stone building that I see from my window is a carved gorgon's head, a likeness of Medusa with snaky locks. She is hundreds of feet above me as I sit here, but I see the expression of her face plainly - it is desolate and discouraging. It says, Do you think you will see that fair lily Annabel Lee again? Well, then, how foolish are you in your day and generation! I in my years have seen the passing of many fair lilies. Always they pass. -

Tell me, Annabel Lee, - always do they pass? But no - I shall find you again. You will make all things many-tinted for a thousand thousands of gold days. And are we not good friends in way and manner? And do we not go the foot-pathway together?

But I wonder always why the gorgon seems so fearfully knowing. -

Always my love to you.

Mary MacLane

*

24. My Friend Annabel Lee to Me

And after some days my friend Annabel Lee wrote me this upon a square of rice paper:

Boston, - Monday.

Dear Mary MacLane:

Don't you know a gorgon is the knowingest thing in the land?

You may believe what your friend says of fair lilies.

But have I ever said that I am a fair lily?

As for my eyes - they are good chiefly to see with. And they are bad for many things. Yes - get thee home soon, child.

I miss you when I come to deck me mornings with my lavender slip and my scarlet frock. And the gold marguerites have not been brushed since you went away.

Naught have I to bear me company except Ellen, the faithful little tan deer - and she can not wait upon me, and she cannot worship me.

What hast done with Martha Goneril the cat?

I would fain you had left her here.

But Mary MacLane - *you*. Do you know about it?

Your Friend Annabel Lee

25. The Golden Ripple

My friend Annabel Lee and I are similar to each other in a few, few ways. Daily we contemplate together a great, blank wall built up of dull, blue stones. It stands before us and we can not get over it, for it is too high; neither can we walk around it, for it is too long; and we can not go through it, for it is solid and very thick. It is directly across the road. We have both come but a short way on the road - so short that we can easily look back over our course to the point where we started. We did not walk together from there, but we have met each other now before the great, blank wall of blue stones.

We have stopped here, for we can not go on.

I wonder and conjecture much about the wall, and my friend Annabel Lee regards it sometimes with interest and sometimes with none.

And, times, we forget all about the wall and merely sit and rest in the shade it casts, or walk back on the road, or in the grass about it, or pluck a few wild sweet berries from the stunted wayside briers.

And, too, when a thunder storm comes up and the air is full of wind and rain slanting and whistling about us, we crouch close against the base of the wall, and we do not become so wet as we should were there no wall.

But that is only when the wind is from beyond it.

When the wind with its flood of rain comes toward us as we crouch by the wall we are beaten and drenched and buffeted and driven hard against that cold, blue surface. And the ragged edges of the rocks make bruises on our foreheads.

Some days we become exceeding weary with looking at the great blank wall - and with having looked at it already for many a day, and many a day.

"It is so high and so thick," I say.

"It is so long," says my friend Annabel Lee.

To all appearances we have gone as far upon the road as we ever can go. We can not get over the wall of blue stones - and we can not walk round - and we can not go through. There is nothing to indicate that it will ever be removed.

The field for conjecture as to what lies on the other side of the road is so vast that we do not venture to conjecture.

But we have talked often and madly of the wall itself.

"Perhaps," I say, "it is that the wall is placed here before our eyes to hide from us our limitations."

"Perhaps," says my friend Annabel Lee, "it is that the wall itself is our limitations."

Which, if it is true, is very damnable.

For though human beings have done some divine things they have never gone beyond their limitations.

The blue of the stones in the wall is not a dark blue, but it is very cold. It is the color that is called stone blue.

It never changes.

The sun and the shade look alike upon it; and the wet rain does not brighten it; neither do thick clouds of dust make it dull.

It is stone blue.

Except for this:

Once in a number of days, in fair weather or foul, there will come upon the wide blankness a rippling like gold.

It lingers a second and vanishes - and appears again. And then it's gone until another time.

How tender, how lovely, how bright is the golden ripple against the cold, cold blue!

It is come and gone in a minute.

We do not know its coming or its going.

But while we see it our hearts beat high and fast.

"It may be," I say when it is gone, "that this golden ripple will show us some way to get beyond the wall where things are divine."

"It may be," says my friend Annabel Lee, "that the golden ripple will show us something divine among these few things on this side of the wall."

*

L'Envoi

My friend, Annabel Lee - with your strong, brave little heart and your two strong little hands, you were with me in my weary, bitter day. You were brave enough for two. It is to you from me that a message will go from out of silences and over frozen hills in the years that are coming.

*

We may see - from the latitude as to subjects and styles given to her - that the news-reading public was intensely curious about what MacLane would make of their places as she arrived and walked through them.

High art was evolving toward Modernism, and popular culture would follow suit after the sustained crisis of the Great War. MacLane's native modernity and her classic, romantic, and realist sensibilities enabled her to provide inimitable impressions of outer settings and inward effects - and a look at what was coming.

What she thought of the East - and what she was doing while there - was much-wondered as she wrote for The World, *and when she went into contract with a Western paper in 1903 and traveled from Massachusetts to write, publish, and depart, the curiosity in Denver was just the same.*

FEATURES

- 1903 -

"A Foreground and a Background"

Denver Post · 4 October 1903

I have come to dwell in Denver for a short season.

The outward seeming of Denver is nothing soft and nothing gentle, and as yet my mind refuses to assimilate it.

For Denver, after Boston, Massachusetts, is hard and bright, and Denver after Butte, Montana, my best-loved, is flat and unfanciful.

But a city, even a new Western city, and the chimneys thereof are full of possibilities - and who knows but Denver, the flat, the unmerciful, may become the city of my dreams? Who knows but I may meet a lightsome fate here? Who knows but I may here find a lump of sunshine in material form to carry back with me under my cloak to the gates of Boston-sur-mer?

'Tis thus you can make a bit of a Paradise out of divers wild places. Well, then, no sooner had I arrived in Denver than lo! - I found I must go down to Colorado Springs to take note of the club women that were gathered there and to receive an impression; an idea I found vastly uninteresting.

However, I hied me to Colorado Springs, and, coming back, I find on closely examining my mind's contents, that I have two vague impressions in it - one a background, and the other a foreground.

I like the background better. It consists of Colorado and all the wonderful pictures on the surface of its land - which my long-suffering and short-nibbed pen will now go to tell.

To tell, not as it is, I dare say, but as it was to me.

*

No, I thought within me as I went down swiftly into the open in a train, there is no country like the Western country; there is nothing in the prettiness of the East that approaches this grandness and majesty. Also there is nothing so baffling to the eyes and to the mind of one as the vision of high, heavy mountains and cattle wandering over the aridness.

There was a picture done in mingled marvelous venetian reds and gold-browns and gold-yellows. The vastness of the mountain was mostly dark and grown over with low shrubs of these colors, and it reached far into the pallid blue and the thin clouds.

Between the mountain and me the plains ran many, many miles of grayish-gold, and there were somber cattle on a thousand low hills. Set about the crest of the mountain were many mansions, built of pale gray stone, like the castles of barons of old.

They were windowless, were the castles, and there was no echoing of voices in silent halls within them, but only a solidness of stone. Still they were castles, and were turreted and battlemented and dungeoned, and were the dwelling places of real things and shadows. In truth an acropolis at Athens is not more wonderful than they, and so vivid and so bright was the sunshine that when once a long-tailed magpie sailed out of the blue across a deep bar of light upon the mountain it glowed for a moment like a golden bird of paradise.

Because of this sunshine all the shadows that would anywhere else be gray are red shadows in Colorado.

The foreground is different, and I have not fallen in love with it. It is of divers women holding a club convention in a varnished sort of hall at Colorado Springs. I have, I find, little patience with women - though I have more patience with women than I have with men.

It was the prospect of going to take note of these women that I found vastly uninteresting. Still there have been times when I have entertained myself by merely looking at people and considering their manner and kind. At Colorado Springs in the varnished hall I looked at women and considered them as was my bounden duty.

There were all sorts there. All the sorts and conditions that go to make up the different types of the genus club-woman.

Club women are about the same all over - in Boston, Massachusetts, and in Denver, and even in Butte, Montana, but these in the varnished hall had an atmosphere which was wrought by Colorado, doubtless, for 'twas different from some others I have seen.

*

It was mostly that they were more intensely club women than the generality of their kind. In the varnished hall I saw six distinct types of the club woman. There was, for one, that kind that has a tendency to gray curled hair and to stoutness of figure, and this kind nearly always wears a silk waist of some pale shade which fits exceeding snug, and she discourses about not much of anything with an air of great profoundness. Placid is the word I have always applied to her. In times past I have wondered whether pinching hard the chubby arm of such a woman would perchance ruffle that placidness. Forsooth I have never seen a club woman thus placid without wishing that I by some means might cause her to become less placid.

And there was that kind of club woman who goes about with intellect set rampant upon her brow. How unattractive, to be sure, is one with intellect so placed! So far from fitting snugly the garments of such a woman have no fit at all, and her hair is drawn tightly back - and if you are cleverer than she is, and she knows it, she sees you and passes by on the other side. And she reads a paper before the club in a manner bristling with a profoundness which throws that of the placid lady completely in the shade. From such, I would fain say, in my trite manner of yore, kind devil deliver me.

*

And there was the tall sort of woman with a set plainness of feature whom popular opinion credits with a keen sense of humor, for some reason - probably because the papers she reads are fraught with astonishing puns. This type of club woman, I noticed in the varnished hall, wears frocks much titivated with frills and furbelows and of a much-worn appearance.

The other club women always laugh conscientiously at all her witticisms. Everything she utters purports to be witty. According to which she in truth pays her way as she goes.

And there was that type of club woman who has the look of having once made a loose and hasty toilet which has been forced to last her for all time. The ends of her hair have long since escaped from their moorings. Her collar never quite fits and is never quite fastened. Likewise her girdle. Likewise her shoe-lacings. She usually has but one glove - the other one having been long lost.

Her papers are loose in construction, and her sentiments are apt to wander off into hazy oblivion. She is the best tempered of them all, and takes life easily. If she has any children at home, they take life easily also, and her household is likewise a thing of loose construction. Those of this type that I saw in the varnished hall appeared light-hearted and happy, as if 'twere for club conventions alone that they lived.

*

And there was the serene-browed, large, quiet type of club woman who wisely refrains from reading her papers or doing anything but vote, when the time for voting comes. Also she refrains from expressing an opinion on any subject until she is quite sure that what she says will be popular; a type which has many exponents in and out of women's clubs. And this type of club woman usually is well-dressed, and is entirely an ornament to any club.

And there was the busy-tongued strenuous type whose high instructive voice can be heard in all parts of a varnished hall. She makes long speeches to the assembled clubs, in which the expressions "general good," "work of the past year," "dignity of the club women," "our faithful co-workers," and all that sort of thing occur with painful frequency. In listening to one of this kind of club women I wondered idly whether there were portions of Colorado Springs where that voice did not penetrate. And the gymnastic performances of her countenance fascinated me, and I knew that such were the making and being of the festive woman's club.

These are the six types that I noticed in the varnished sort of hall at Colorado Springs.

Withal I know that among these types and others there are women - even club women - who are high-minded and unselfish, who do hard work for the good of their fellow creatures, who are brave in the facing of public opinion and unpopularity, who in the club-way - it may be in spite of it - are carrying light into shaded places. They do the work that only their kind can do, and even though they are types, even though they meet in a varnished hall, they shall one day claim a just reward. And so, then, of my two impressions that is the foreground.

*

My foreground and my background together make a quaint picture to dwell upon. Only as I dwell the contrast between the two becomes strained.

The foreground of my picture is prone to fade - varnished hall, club women, types, papers being read, fat gray curls, intellectual brows, the fluttering of hair escaped from its moorings, "the dignity of club women," all gradually vanish and leave my serene mind in possession of the vast dull-toned picture, the cattle on the thousand hills, the silent images in the Garden of the Gods, the pallid Colorado sky, the arid plains, the wonderful dull red shadows, the battlemented castles on crests, the prison-houses of red stone, the momentary flashing of bird's wings in deep gold light - in all a picture of the wonderful great West.

A picture to be seen with dreams and visions, and through salt mists at the eyes. And more than all it is for everyone - club women and unclub women - and for whomsoever liketh.

So it is, I find, that impressions come to me in Colorado, and so it is that a foreground will fade.

"Mary MacLane Discusses the 'Outward Seeming of Denver'"

Denver Post · 11 October 1903

By this time my mind has consented to assimilate Denver in a few indefinite ways.

'Tis true Denver has not yet become the city of my dreams; nor have I up to this time found anything at all resembling a lump of sunshine in material form suitable for carrying away; neither has anything looking in the least like my Fate appeared.

" 'Tis true, 'tis pity, and pity 'tis, 'tis true."

But, anyway, about the city of Denver my fancy plays lightly, and though not indeed the city of my dreams, I people it with a multitude of shadows and visions which come readily enough. In truth, they are already there.

They are not the shadows and visions of Boston, nor of Butte, but of Denver and Mary MacLane.

From Denver and Mary MacLane together you might expect much of one sort or another. But you might be disappointed.

I have of late gone about the place with no tiresome guide to point out the deadly uninteresting "point of interest." I have gone with no one who knows any more about it than I do myself. It's the best way.

*

Niagara Falls was quite ruined for me by having been cut up into points of interest by a canal man. Certainly a man - no other creature could possibly come so near to being The Limit.

Denver, I find, is so wrapped about every day by a wealth of sunshine that it is like a city of gold. The sunshine of Denver is like none that I have ever seen before. It is of beaten brass and old gold, with fringes and hangings of Colorado's pallid blue. It is no sunshine to rest lightly the outside - it strikes inward and touches the shaded places - it storms the dark citadels - it bids all heaviness depart. If you walk in the arid meadows with a bitterness of heart that is somber purple this sunshine touches it and changes its color to beaten brass and old gold, and changes the bitterness into something that can be forgotten. All this can the sunshine of Denver do, and more: it can assure me even more than the sea in the East that all the fairness of the earth is as much mine as yours.

Which is one of the great consolations.

Besides the sunshine there is the wind that blows from off the mountain tops. It is the wind of the baffling Western country.

It is the same wind that long since blew over the plains, and swept the masses of galloping Indian ponies and sent cloud-shadows racing.

It comes from the mountain tops to Denver town and mingles with the sunshine. It makes at once a wildness and a softness - the feeling of the Western country.

Withal at the setting of the sun its shining turns from deep yellow to vermillion, and the wind is still, and the inanity of flat brick buildings is hid.

There could be no better place for setting a city than the place where Denver is set. It is fortified by chains of vast deep-toned hills, and the dry plains stretch off and away from it to rest its eyes with distances.

Moreover, it is in the Western country - not in the prettiness of the East.

Though not in the prettiness of the near East, my fancy sometimes transports Denver town into the mystery of the far East.

Times I think persistently of it as a city of Armenia or Lydia, where instead of painfully new modern brick structures, are fretted palaces with music in the enameled walls, and massive temples, and flimsy thatched dwellings whence come forth the poor. There seems to be no power in Denver - which robs it of a fascinating and picturesque feature.

The look of the surrounding country encourages my mind in its Eastern fancy - as much as if there were asphodels blooming on the plains, and I think of Denver town and its inhabitants as a city walled in with its own life and its own atmosphere, and with temples where some go to worship half-heartedly, and amphitheatres where others rush eagerly to be diverted, and long flat streets where people wander idly or meditatively or with jests upon their tongues.

*

"Wonderful," I say to myself when I can push my mind away to view it from afar, "is a city, taken by and large. It is marvelous and fascinating. It is full of human passion and human emotion, and of art and skill, and of nature untrammeled, and in the lodgment of human life!"

Denver is more a city than most, because it has only the deep-toned hills and the yellow plains to compare it to, instead of a long line of other cities by a seaboard. It is true that Denver is fair looking for a modern new city - it has a multitude of green lawns, and sweet-smelling pine trees, and some of the dwelling houses made of white bricks are even good to look at, and the numerous automobiles are not so very ugly. But for some reason I find the thought of modern new Western people maddening. That good house of deep red bricks set in the midst of trees, I say to myself, that is not the home of some one who came to Denver barefooted about thirty years ago and proceeded at once to dig a fortune out of the ground - and his wife is not the daughter of one who still longer ago also started life without shoes. By no means. This is a city of a far Eastern country, and that house of red bricks is the home of a dark-faced man clad always in gay-colored silk garments, and his wife is the daughter of a tribe of Arabs - and there is a court and a fountain in the midst of the house, and servants set out wine and figs, that they may eat and drink.

*

And certainly those long rows of buildings are not uninteresting business blocks, with offices, and desks in the offices, and revolving chairs, and papers stuck in the pigeon holes.

By no means. Those rooms are occupied by wicked wizards, working day and night with infernal machinations that they may ruin their fellow creatures and that they may become rich.

And when I see what looks like real estate and mining brokers' offices ranged along the streets, with a great many bits of ore in the windows, I know that it is an hallucination. These places are the dwellings of magicians, who fire the minds of the people with a desire to exchange their small, hard-earned fortunes for one of the glittering bits of ore to take home and set upon their mantel shelf.

I like Denver chiefly, I find, because it is so extremely modern, it lends itself more readily than is common to these fond pipe dreams, by force of contrast.

To branch off into another line. There are some persons who never, in writing, use the word "perennial" without using the word "bloom" in connection with it.

But that's not I.

Forsooth if it were, I should by the same token describe Denver as an altogether charming city, and I should also state that my sojourn here is pleasant - even pleasant with "very" before it.

That has naught to do with me writing about it. 'Tis not my long suit to write that a city is charming, nor that anything connected with me is pleasant.

*

My long suit is pipe dreams. Pipe dreams of all colors and some passing devilish; sometimes with fierce oaths scattered in amongst them, and sometimes with mere damns and devils thrown in as from a pitchfork for euphony; sometimes with myself in the center, and sometimes spread broadcast through the universe; sometimes relating to New York, and sometimes relating to Boston, and sometimes relating to Butte-on-the-hill; sometimes with gay laughter and sometimes with passions of tears; sometimes writing as a nice woman; and sometimes as a woman who is not nice - but never as a literary lady; sometimes pleasing the public, and sometimes my friends, and sometimes my foes - but mostly myself, and sometimes writing under great protest; but whatever I write it must be pipe dreams.

There's nothing pays so well or goes so far as a pipe dream, and so Denver town has come - as yet indefinitely - into these, my pipe dreams. I see it with half-shut, sleepy eyes through clouds of my own thick smoke, brilliant-tinted and individual, rushing into the temples to worship half-heartedly, and eagerly at the amphitheatres to be diverted, and lounging in strength, and full of Western wealth and Western arrogance, and grinding some pale-colored things beneath its heel. But mostly I blow aside my pipe smoke and gaze out with very wide-open eyes at the prospect of the everlasting hills and the far fair yellow plain, lit by the sunshine of beaten brass.

"Mary MacLane in Vivid Detail Tells the Transition of her 'Kind Devil' of Old"

Denver Post · 18 October 1903

That Devil that I have long thought of as a fading phantom has once more loomed vivid upon my horizon.

That Devil that jerked me out of dim gray obscurity in Butte, Mont. to a prima donnaship in a dizzy and bewildering chaos of newspaper articles, transported me to Chicago, dropped me like a hot cake in Boston, and gracefully retired, has come again to the front in Denver, Colo. At sight of him I place my hand upon my heart and bow with profound respect in recognition of his scarlet majesty, of his old familiar steel-gray eyes, and of the untold service he has rendered me in times past. And he, at the sight of me, bows but lightly and wafts me a jaunty salute from his lips with his finger tips, not in profoundness or respect, but with an air of delicate camaraderie - as if in memory of the days when he and I had in truth pulled together. "Your majesty - my Devil," I say as I bow.

*

"Mary MacLane once more," says the Devil, and repeats a soft early English oath beneath his breath, not in anger, but from some light, effervescent emotion, and together for the first time we meet to compare notes of our weird, quaint escapade, begun warmly in Butte and Chicago, cooled in Boston, and brought to a fit climax in Denver.

Denver, forsooth!

"You have come through it well, fair Devil," I said to him on the occasion of our first meeting. "Your steel-gray eyes are even more steel-gray."

"I thank you," said my Devil, "but I fear the same cannot be said of you. It is as if the avalanche which came down upon us after the publishing of our first little red book had been too much for you. There is a worn look about your lips and your eyes, which, mayhap, is the work of the *New York Journal* and the *Butte Inter Mountain*, and your shoulders droop as if your little body were indeed weary of this great world."

"To be sure," I replied, "those things are always harder on the lady. Still I had them all pretty well gauged before the little red book went forth. The light fantastic lies of even those papers you mention were not too great a surprise. But I confess it has been wearisome - you've no idea, good Devil, to live always up at the level of 'Mary MacLane,' and to be expected to act devilish when I wanted nothing more than to subside into restful obscurity."

"That is one way of looking at it," said the Devil, "but for me, since Herbert S. Stone *& Co.* of Chicago went sponsor for our little red book how prosperous have I become! Now my fame has increased! W.R. Hearst himself, of the said *New York Journal*, is now no more the scarlet Devil than I. And the *Butte Inter Mountain* has but added to my strength."

*

"Of course we will give credit where credit is due," I made answer. "The *Butte Inter Mountain* has given us some heavy pushes, and Mr. Hearst's New York paper has frequently done itself proud with both 'Mary MacLane' and her 'Devil.'"

"So much so," added the Devil, "that, do you know, I sometimes thought seriously of increasing our firm to three, with 'W.R.' as the third and last number. What do you think - is it not a bright idea?"

"It may be bright enough," I replied, "but I'm inclined to think we had best try to continue as we are for a time."

"But there would be no harm in proposing it to 'W.R.'" urged the Devil.

"There might be considerable harm in it for me," said I, "especially if I had to do the proposing."

Which idea the fascinating Devil, for some reason, appeared to find so extremely funny that he quite reveled in merriment for some moments.

"Pray, what is it that amuses you so?" I inquired in wonderment.

"Nothing - nothing of any consequence," replied the Devil - but still laughed musically and very heartily.

I racked my mind for something thus excruciatingly amusing, but my search resulted only in dim fancies concerning myself, my Devil, and Mr. W.R. Hearst of *New York Journal* fame, which were prosaic enough.

Well, then, this was the conversation at my first meeting with my Devil in Denver.

I have met him once or twice since then, and we have talked severally of the days in Butte, Mont., with reminiscences of Chicago, of the parting of our ways at the gates of Boston, and of our reuniting in Denver. And between whiles I have contemplated these various appearances and non-appearances - the transitions of my Devil.

One day my Devil and I walked together out into the golden Colorado country, talking as we went in fair good companionship.

"It is good to be with you again," said the Devil, flatteringly, albeit patronizingly.

I gazed at him dispassionately.

"The time when you were the most fascinating of all," I said to the Devil, "was when I was writing the little red book, when I sat by my obscure window in Butte, Mont., and no newspaper in the land ever thought of printing interviews with me."

"You did find me fascinating then," mused the Devil.

"All day long, sometimes," I went on, "I sat by my obscure window, looking out from it and writing - writing of my sand and barrenness, and of my pile of stones and barrel of lime, and of my good green olive, and of my fine rare-broiled porterhouse steak from Omaha, and my fresh green young onions from California, and of the manifold things from which, kind Devil, deliver me - and of you, my good Devil, with your steel-gray eyes."

*

"I was so very obscure in those days that I was known chiefly as the sister of Dorothy MacLane - and I was so very obscure that my younger brother even held me in contempt.

"Those were the palmy days! And I would leave my bed in the dark of the morning and take my walk over the sand and barrenness, and come home and eat my breakfast of three boiled eggs, and then I would do my bit of housework, after my sister had gone to her work in the library, and then I would walk again my sand and barrenness; and at night I would eat my dinner and take one more walk and come home and go to my writing. Then would my mind revel in quaint fancies. You were most invaluable to me, kind Devil, you with your steel-gray eyes! Without you and the steel-gray eyes what would the little red book have amounted to? Who would have accepted it?"

"Certainly not Herbert S. Stone & Co. of Chicago," murmured the Devil.

"And I would wonder," I continued, "as I wrote in the silence of my room by the light of a little green lamp - I would wonder if all those green onions and olives and Italian peddlers and steel-gray eyes would ever see the light of day! While I wondered I would go on writing my intense red-blooded fancies, and after I had finished a particularly intense and red-blooded chapter I would lay down my pen and would marvel at my own cleverness - all in the silent dimness of my little room."

"Those were the rum days!" said the Devil.

"And sometimes you of the steel-gray eyes would come and talk to me - me sitting on a red sofa with my hands folded and my feet crossed and you in a wicker chair. Those were the times when I was in love with you," I added.

*

"Yes, you were in love with me then," said the Devil, and laughed lightly as we walked leisurely along the sunshiney Colorado road - he swinging a light cane.

"Those certainly were the rum days," and he laughed more lightly than ever.

"And then," continued the Devil, "Herbert S. Stone & Co. went sponsor for the little red book, and lo! within ten days the newspapers all over the country, from one end to the other, cried aloud with it. Chicago fairly shrieked with it, and Butte, Mont. roasted us to a neat brown finish. Little Mary MacLane could no longer walk the Butte pavements in obscurity - and, most wonderful of all, Dorothy MacLane, in her turn, became known as the sister, and the younger brother quite lost his identity."

"And all on account of you, my good Devil," I said, "and the ubiquitous steel-gray eyes. I realized your value more and more as the days passed - especially when John Maguire and all those other theater managers stood in line offering upwards of several thousand good iron dollars per week if I would lecture for ten minutes each night on any subject whatsoever."

"And the *Butte Inter Mountain*," said the Devil, "quite outdid itself, and the *Butte Miner* published more marvelous atrocities each day, and the *Anaconda Standard* became heavily cynical - and altogether we were much in demand."

"Then," I went on, "one night, we folded our little tent like an Arab and quietly stole away from Butte and landed one morning in Chicago."

"Then," continued the Devil, "Chicago began shrieking again."

"Began?" said I. "Had it ever left off?"

*

"Anyway," said the Devil, "we were received with loud newspaper blasts. Little Mary MacLane and her Devil were run in the same paragraphs with Hobart Chatfield-Chatfield Taylors and De Kovens till our heads spun. And oh triumph! Oh Victory! The manager of the far-famed, much acclaimed Floradora offered us five hundred per to induce us to join his matchless sextet. It's a thousand pities that we never accepted any of those theatrical invitations," said the Devil, regretfully, "though I daresay it would have been fatal."

"In all ways fatal," said I, with emphasis.

"Chicago," said the Devil with an air of retrospect, "was what, on the whole, I might call my busy day. Butte viewed me warily and charily and handled me gingerly, as with tongs - a Devil being without honor, like a prophet, in his own country. But, ah! Chicago was the place! Chicago was the Mecca for a pilgrim Devil! The ten days in Chicago - they were my rum days." And he breathed a gentle sigh to their memory.

"Then," said I, "we went to Boston."

"Yes," said the Devil, "that let me out. That was where I faded." (My Devil, I noticed, had picked up a great many expressive slang phrases since last we met.)

"In Boston," I went on, "I sank breathlessly into the first obscure resting place I could find, and for the first time since my little red book was published I breathed freely. In Boston, since I repaired thither to retire into private life, I had no further use for you my good Devil - or of the steel-gray eyes. There were a few half-starved Boston reporters who sometimes tracked me to my lair, but their stuff when it appeared was free from the vivid tints of my Devil. They wrote chiefly of the texture of my plain little frocks and the color of my gloves. And these subjects soon palled on Boston. I subsided at last into a status I had long despaired of ever again reaching - that of a mere human being."

*

"And I," said the Devil, "practically went out of business. I feared that my vogue as the original and only steel-gray-eyed Mary MacLane Devil was about run out, and I doubted if there was any desirable position for me in the role of myself. However, I did go to New York once, and I called upon the widow of *Town Topics* to see if, haply, she might find an opening for me. I knew the widow was game. I found her even more game than I expected. She informed me that though I would certainly make a picturesque figurehead for any paper in the land, as well as for any little red book, still as a working element in *Town Topics* I would be entirely superfluous. And, to be sure, after carefully reading a recent copy of the paper, I could not but agree that the widow was right. They had more convivial things than steel-gray eyes in theirs. And I realized once and for all that in order to be a real, red, fascinating, steel-gray-eyed Devil I must linger in the vicinity of little Mary MacLane."

"I had long," said I, "felt that you were somewhere lying in wait for me, ready at a moment's notice to resume our old fraternal relations for the edification of the public. Your appearance in Denver is not altogether a surprise."

*

"You see," said the Devil, "I knew that the good citizens of Denver would want, not the later demure little Mary MacLane of Boston, but the original article - the pungent, gingery, devilish utterer of damns, the analyzer of that widely discussed 'good young woman's body' - above all, in connection with little Mary MacLane, they would want her Devil. I, though lacking in some essentials as co-operator with the widow of *Town Topics*, am as a companion piece for little Mary MacLane a gem. We are at once a contrast, a harmony, a combine, a trust."

"You are pleased to flatter me, my Devil," said I, with something of the manner I was wont to use toward him in the obscure days of writing my little red book. By this time we had meandered far upon the roadway in the brightness of Colorado's October. Presently we came to two flat rocks, where we seated ourselves to rest, and the sunshine touched us with brilliant color - me and my Devil.

And presently the Devil, with his delicate and inimitable air of camaraderie, proffered me a tiny box of gun-metal set with pearls. It contained the best of Egyptian cigarettes, for which I have a weakness.

As we rested, we wrapped us round with smoke, me and my Devil - a quaint couple.

"When you first arrived in Denver," said the Devil, lounging in graceful ease and jauntily wafting rings skyward, "and before I came I could hear in fancy the voice of Denver. 'We want the Devil,' said the voice. 'We don't want little Mary MacLane without her Devil. We want little Mary MacLane in the picturesque setting of her first little red book. Otherwise little Mary MacLane may go to the Devil.' Thus," said the Devil, "to prevent little Mary MacLane from going to the Devil, I, the Devil, came to join her in Denver."

And how devilish he looked, to be sure - the steel-gray eyes glittering through smoke. He looked less like my conventional-clad Devil of the little red book and more like the scarlet-garbed one of the *New York Journal*.

He was, in truth, more devilish than ever.

As I watched him, my mind contemplated the interesting fancy of the transition of my Devil.

At first, I thought within me, in the obscure days in Butte, he was the strong and fascinating, the comparatively innocent, the Bohemian, the unworldly. Then he had his first touch of life in Chicago and lost his young bloom. And while I rested tranquil and forgotten in Boston he hobnobbed with widows and the like in New York. I don't know but he even went abroad and became yet more of the world, worldly.

And now he appears in Denver, deeply dyed with the tints of this red, red earth, so that, though I know he is indeed my same Devil, with the same steel-gray eyes, he is yet so developed, so veneered with the brilliant emotions that I pause as I view him. And with a small, still shiver I hide me behind the demure shadow of my second little red book.

Yet at sight of him I place my hand upon my heart and bow with profound respect.

"Your Majesty - my Devil," I say, and am more or less thrilled with the dramaticness and picturesqueness of it all.

"Mary MacLane once more," says the Devil. And how quaint and musical are his early English oaths, and how delicate the camaraderie of him! Thus the transition of my Devil.

Brenda Maddox, author of a comprehensive 1994 biography of D.H. Lawrence (who also corresponded with Harriet Monroe and visited her in Chicago), was asked if she liked the man. "No one," she replied, "could read Lawrence's letters and not like him."

MacLane's letters show her writing-personality in distillation. Intensely focused yet untrammeled, they are small unique ad hoc *verbal worlds that end almost upon being perceived. In little glimmers through the performing - for she always is - they show the friend and lover, and they are unfailing-alive.*

The order is staggeredly chronological: to her publisher ("Mr. Stone", invariably M.E. Stone, Jr., partner with his brother Herbert), to Harriet Monroe, to MacLane's mother, to Japanese poet Yone Noguchi, again to Monroe, and to her by then former publisher. Ed.'s excerptions are indicated by ellipses, which in no case are MacLane's.

SELECT LETTERS & TELEGRAMS

1902 - 1909

Herbert S. Stone *&* Co., - Chicago

Dear Sirs,

Your favor of the 19th inst. is received. I confess that I am annoyed on learning that your title for my MS has been retained. I do not fancy that title at all, and I hoped that my communication might reach you in time to have it changed. However, it is a trivial matter, and since your judgment and experience in such things must be superior to mine, I let it pass - particularly as there is no help for it in any case.

I agree with you that the sale of the book might be promoted by interviews with newspaper writers, and I shall receive any that may come. And I think you may rely on me to use discretion in the matter. I shall grant an interview wherever I can see that it will be an advantage to the book, but I shall try to avoid anything like mere cheap notoriety and sensationalism which can only detract from it.

I think the best possible advertisement for it would be a severe criticism in the *Bookman* or *Book-buyer* or some equally well known reviewer. I believe if any of them could be persuaded to review it at length, my book would be fairly started on a career of sorts. An exhaustive criticism and an attractive binding must need go far toward the success of any book.

I should like to have a signed copy of the contract. Will you oblige me by sending one?

Believe me, sincerely yours,

*

My Dear Mr. Stone -

I have your favor of June 11.

About these absurd letters - I think you have taken unnecessary trouble with them. I receive many of them every day which I never think of reading, not only because of their probable character, but because they do not interest me and I have not time to waste upon them. I usually look at the signatures of some of them, to be sure that they are not from persons I know, and then destroy them. Doubtless there are many kind and sincere ones among them - like the one you enclose - but I do not feel called upon to give any attention to these unsought tributes.

I appreciate your motives in opening them, but it is a matter of indifference to me whether I receive them or not.

*

Cambridge - July - 1902

My Dear Mr. Stone -

Doubtless your natural kindness of heart leads you to intercede for the Boston reporters. Certainly the pathetic appeal in your telegram led me to think twice before refusing the next group that appeared. (They appear in groups - bunches, in fact - they are afraid to come singly.)

Still - -

Always I consider my own physical and mental comfort before most things - things such as reporters, publishers' telegrams, my own writer's-interests, and even pathetic appeals of sorts. My physical and mental discomfort upon arriving in Cambridge made the avoiding of interviews a necessity.

However, when your wire came I had begun to receive a reporter now and again. I have given interviews to the *Herald* and the *Globe*, and have promised one to the *Transcript*.

Nothing will induce me to see a reporter from the *Post*, or from any paper of that ilk. They may make interviews if they will - I shall not be greatly troubled. But, I assure you, it would require a very large number of telegrams from publishers - containing a very large number of pathetic appeals of sorts - to cause me to change my decision.

You, peradventure, are you - whilst I, perforce, am I.

*

Cambridge

My Dear Mr. Stone,

The reporters are now things of the past, so your letters - with the pathetic appeals in their behalf - come like strains of futile music: sweet but meaningless.

Your telegrams, somewhat less musical, were more piquant, and had a certain effect. -

A person has written to you - or will do so - about a French edition of that little book you brought out this Spring - the Mary MacLane book. I do not care about the person - a sort of inexpensive person, whatever kind of publisher he may be, but I believe that I consented to some arrangement. I am not prepared to say just what arrangement it is - I've forgotten. But I have not yet signed anything. I shall, doubtless however, just as soon as I see something to sign. The name Mary MacLane looks so neat and picturesque at the end of a document, I think. -

- Miss Corbin tells me that I can not get in at Radcliffe - (not that she said so to any reporters, however). I have not done anything about it yet, but Miss Corbin's inquiries - made before I came - elicited the information that a special course in chemistry required the passing of ten exams in that and kindred subjects. Also these inquiries elicited the interesting intelligence that Radcliffe is not superlatively anxious to receive Mary MacLane - what a peculiar rare gem this Mary MacLane must be - in any case. This from the secretary of Radcliffe. My decision - to enter Radcliffe if it is possible for me to enter Radcliffe - remains unchanged. I foresaw something of this sort, you will remember.

I have not yet seen the secretary - Miss Corbin says that she is one of the cold, fishy kind. I rather think that it would require more strenuous effort than I care to put forth at present, for me to worm and jolly myself into her good graces.

- And so. If you have some influence to use for me, it had better be used immediately. Charity, which is said to begin at home - and to cover a multitude of sins - can sometimes extend so far as Cambridge, I doubt not. No charity ever begins here, I'm sure.

*

Postal Telegraph-Cable - Collect - Cambridge Mass - July 31
M.E. Stone -
I have been asked by the *World* and *Herald* in New York to go there and write for a month. I think I would like it. The *World* provides a Mrs. Hubbard Ayer as chaperone. Have you a suggestion to make -

*

Postal Telegraph-Cable - Paid - Cambridge Mass - August 1
M.E. Stone Jr -
I have fallen in love with the *World* and the *World* has fallen in love with me. Also I have fallen in love with Miss Gale of the *World*.

I am on the point of going to New York with her. Could you not wire me what you have to say. Beware of Mary MacLane in love.

*

Western Union Telegraph - Paid - New York - 12 Aug 02 -
Mr. M E Stone Jr - 11 Eldredge Ct - Chicago -
I don't wish any chaperone. Just returned from Newport with Mrs. Ayer. We didn't quite hit it off. I get along well enough. The hotel is large.

*

New York - August - 19

My Dear Mr. Stone -
I have just returned from Newport and the pomps and vanities of this

wicked world - and am now at the San Remo Hotel. You must magnani-mously forgive me for not wiring you it, but Mr. Hersh of the *World* is not yet ready to have the snap given away. After Miss Gale's story, however, it will not matter.

I am now in the midst of my Impression of Newport. It has to be turned in by Monday noon for the next Sunday *World*. I am learning what it is to write when one *must* write.

Herewith the agreement.

I am willing enough to sign it - no matter what there etc.

Mrs. Ayer chaperoned me to Newport but I am alone at the hotel. The *World* is giving me very good treatment and I think it's worth my while. I wasn't quite satisfied with the agreement you suggested. I want to write only one month for the paper and that while here in New York. I will write one article per week for $150 each and all my expenses paid. That is my contract with them.

- Mrs. Ayer and I got along very well together. And I saw things and met people. -

I still wish to enter Radcliffe - though as I've said there's a certain un-mistakable prejudice existing there against "Mary MacLane." Miss Corbin advised me not to try it at all - to go to some other college. She thinks the life under those circumstances will be too much. But I can carry that, I think, if I can succeed in getting in. -

Sincerely - and hastily -

*

My Dear Mr. Stone -

... About the chaperone matter - I will *not* have one of the *World*'s ap-pointing. And as the *World* seems in no haste to appoint one, we seem mutually agreed. It is perhaps not the best thing possible for me - or the book - to live here alone. I am sure it will not be as soon as I am advertised broadcast as I shall be soon now. But I do not care for Mrs. Ayer. The visit to Newport was enough for both of us.

If Miss Monroe *can* come and it will not be asking too much, I can not tell you how glad I should be -

About what I write - I am obliged to cheapen myself - a little, which means a great deal, I suppose. In the Newport article I gave of my very best, as I intended before I left Boston. Mr. Hersh liked it very well, but told me plainly that it was not yellow enough. So I added and inserted some inexpensive paragraphs which doubtless will suit the masses. However the good is with the bad. There are some very good things in that Newport article as you may see when it appears, a week from next Sunday. And, good or bad, it's all well done.

I had some pictures taken in Boston - good ones. Will the Herbert-S.-Stone-&-Co. firm have any use for any of them? If not I may send you one to hang somewhere in those dingy offices, anyway. I am sending Miss Monroe one of the only good Butte pictures that I had - the same as that you wasted on the *Bookman*.

Well.

New York is not so cold as Cambridge, at least. It is hard lines for "Mary MacLane" in Cambridge. But this Mary MacLane intends to conquer and live down a few things. Times, it will have a taste of gall and wormwood, however, which is not the point.

Meanwhile, New York.

I am learning to find my way easily, I go about alone, and from here to the *World* building up-town every two days, or three. - Mr. Hersh comes to take me driving sometimes and to lunch with him - with no chaperone, a shocking thing. But I am not yet known. When the storm bursts, next Sunday - 'twill be "good-bye, lunches."

*

[undated]

My reputation be damned.

The old ladies be damned.

The gossip be damned.

And don't *you* write me any more letters of virtuous paternal admonition. Believe me - don't.

I find myself making the best of a bad business - it's enough without letters of virtuous paternal admonition.

Which also be damned.

[unsigned]

*

Tuesday

My Dear Mr. Stone -

I shall make an effort to send you a MS by January - not the first, but perhaps soon after.

I shall make the effort, but I do not expect to succeed.

To produce anything worth while - from any point of view - in two months seems atrocious to me.

But I will see what I can do - and keep you informed as to the book's progress.

But it is more than likely that April only will see it finished.

I am capable of turning out some very rotten work if pressed too hard.

Yet I have done some of my best, under pressure.

My Gray Dawn was done, against time, in an hour and fifty minutes.

But we will see. -

I have the last check for my weekly money - I neglected to acknowledge it.

- Will you please send me three Mary MacLanes? The Boston book-shops are continually sold-out of it.

*

Hotel Bartol - Huntington Avenue - Sunday

My Dear Mr. Stone -

The book goes along - sometimes swiftly, sometimes slowly. But always it goes along.

It will not be ready for you for some months yet.

I do not seem to write so easily in this as in the other book.

There are certain advantages to be derived from sand and barrenness when one would write.

Winthrop Beach is boarded up for the winter and I have found a lodging-place at the Hotel Bartol in Boston.

And so - a change of address.

*

Thursday

Dear Mr. Stone -

Doubtless H.S. Stone & Co. are out of patience with me and my book - and with reason, from their view-point.

I am myself out of patience with it. I should like nothing better in life than to wake some morning and find it finished.

But it will *not* go rapidly, - it is heavy, up-hill work. Some of the chapters I read over with huge dissatisfaction.

Can't we let it go over till fall? Do you think the public will read me with less avidity for having been kept waiting? I confess that I have long harbored the fond hope that the critics would deal less savagely with this book if it didn't come too hard upon the heels of the first.

The purple memory of "Mary MacLane" is not yet so dim but that I can afford to be deliberate with my effusions while we know that I am catering to the public as hard as ever - still I think it would be bad policy to let the public know it. It is infinitely preferable to let the public think I am supremely indifferent. It will then knuckle down all the more.

And "Mary MacLane" is not yet dead. Only last week came two men with a standard play saying they held the rights, and would I kindly claim the authorship that money and fame might be mine? And only last month they ceased "Mary McPaine" at Weber and Fields' in New York.

Still I know I must not stand the public off too long. The public is not to be trusted.

(A change of address - 12 St. James Avenue - Boston.)

*

Monday

Dear Mr. Stone -

... As to the agreement - according to the terms of my last contract with you I should be foolish not to stipulate for a single twenty per cent royalty - that being what your friend McClure offered last spring for my second book. And by the said contract you agree to do as well by me as any other publisher might.

Therefore I hereby strike for twenty per cent. -

I expect always to send you my books - if you continue to want them - and especially if my friend Lucy Gray remains always with you.

And my opinion is that no house would have given me quite the good treatment that always the Stones have given. That has been worth several per cent and upwards.

I trust that I am not exorbitant, - and certainly I would be foolish to overlook the advantage your last agreement with me holds out.

*

["Private Post Card" - imprinted *Greetings from Montreal*]

Dear Mr. Stone -

Take heart of grace.

At present writing I've no good reason to think you may not have it before August fifteenth. And it is some better than I have thought it. I work at it not like a genius inspired - but rather like a beaver building a mud-dam. Greetings from Montreal.

M. MacL.-

*

Sunday - Hotel Metropole - Denver, Colorado

Dear Mr. Stone -

Your letter has just been sent on from Boston, and also a check which would have been useful before I left. -

This is no steady job.

I am here but for five or six weeks.

I was in Chicago for a day on my way here - I believe it was last Monday. I stepped in at Eldredge court, in the midst of a drive, but you were not there.

I am sorry about the indifference of the public over my friend Annabel Lee.

Can it be that in my third I shall be obliged to introduce once more the Devil of yore?

We shall see.

A useful Devil, it was, and picturesque. -

The *Denver Post* does itself proud in its treatment of me and my friend. In some ways it throws the *World* in the shade as a host.

I have gathered from the *Post* that it prefers, if 'tis all the same to me, the Mary MacLane of "Mary MacLane" to her of "Annabel Lee."

A judicious mixture will be its. -

* * *

Dear Harriet Monroe -

I remember you.

I remember you on a summer forenoon.

You were there and I was there.

We went out to walk by the lake-shore.

The lake-shore was very beautiful.

You were so fascinating that day. You were so strong. You were so true.

Particularly you were so true.

I loved you.

I had infinite faith in you.

And you were kind.

You were kind - so that I felt it without knowing it.

Which is a wonderful thing and goes far.

Surely no Pharisee was ever yet kind like that.

For a summer forenoon:

My love to you - oh, my love to you.

Dear Harriet Monroe. -

At any rate - good-by.

- My love to you, always. -

*

Dear Harriet Monroe,

My love reaches out to you. My love reaches you through distance and silence and mystery, and through the inevitable things.

And my love reaches out to you in your dark or your light.

If there is a little dark about you my love will shine clearer to you, but if your light is bright and so fade my love in its reflection, still you will know that it is there. -

Your friend -

*

Hotel San Remo - New York - August 24, 1902

My Dear Harriet Monroe, -

... My self is not fine but I gave of my intense depth of love to you - my intensity of love, the fire and the utter unreasoningness of it, is a thing you can not measure. It is mine and of me. It is like a line of brilliant sun and deep shadow that runs down the sky ...

I do not write these short abrupt letters to any one whom I do not love. They are vivid and illuminating. Are not they vivid and illuminating? ...

I wish I were with you - I wish - -

Little MacLane

* * *

467 Broadway - Cambridge - July

My Dear Mother -

... The weather which you said was so hot in Chicago did not make itself evident while I was there. It would be warm for two days - not warmer than many days in Butte - and then cool - and so on during the summer, I was told.

And it is about the same here in Massachusetts. I feel the different altitude very much, however. I felt it in Chicago and in Buffalo and particularly here where it is not only near the sea-level, but near the sea itself, and the air is consequently heavy and full of moisture ...

Tell Dolly to write me and send on the letters.

My love to you.

- Mary MacLane

*

Crest Hall - Winthrop Beach - Mass.

My Dear Mother -

I have your two letters - sent to the Hotel Touraine.

I am now living at Winthrop Beach which is very near Boston. I gave up the idea of entering any school - it would take up all of my time, and I should have no opportunity to write. But I go to Boston every day to study chemistry. I am living at one of the summer hotels on this coast. It stands only a few feet from the water - and the fragrance of the salt and sea-weed comes on always at my windows. The Hotel is a rather large one and full of life in the summer. It is now nearly empty and is more like a boarding-house. It is rather gloomy and deserted but I like the quiet. I have met so very many people and seen so many varied scenes and other things since I left Butte that I am glad of the rest.

But I miss Miss Monroe so much! At first, when she left me in New York, and I came the next day to Boston, I thought that I should have to give it up and follow her - on to Chicago - as she had suggested. We have become very close friends, and I felt much alone in Boston at that great hotel. But now I have become somewhat used to her absence and am content to stay on here indefinitely. I receive a line from her nearly every day - and both she and Mr. Stone are entirely kind. They take a great interest in whatever I do and I feel a sense of protection in their attitude.

I am glad to know that you are in better health since your rest in the country. You needed the change.

Everything goes on as usual in the neighborhood? - I fancy the firemen always gazing, the young Jewish girls always noisy, Molly Nealy and Mrs. Geiger always the same - and Mrs. Job and the Rewitts, and Mrs. Gancy - and Effie Long -

*

14 Osborne St. - Montreal - Monday

Dearest Mama -

You will be surprised to learn that I am in one of your old visiting-places. I came up here last week with my friend Mrs. Branson. As soon as ever I can finish my work we are going south to Toronto and up the St. Lawrence to Quebec.

Montreal is very beautiful and larger than when you saw it last, I think. The French cathedrals are beautiful - and also the river and Mount Royal. Everything is very French and very Canadian. I presume in Toronto things will be more Canadian than French - but more French still in Quebec. I will write you a letter soon.

My love to you, and to papa *&* Jim
Mary M. -

We were at the Windsor Hotel for a day and night. Isn't that an old land-mark? It is very good and very expensive.

*

Sunday - Oct - 8 -

Dear Mother -

... We have had no frosts here as yet - summer still stays by us. I gathered the apples last week from the trees in this yard, and the pears. They were mostly on the ground - there had been a high wind the night before - so they are right for eating. The apples are Baldwins. There are a few chestnut trees hereabouts, but the nuts won't be ripe until there's a frost ...

I hope papa is well again by this time. Love to you all from -

May

*

Wednesday

My Dear Mother -

... The weather still continues warm here. We had a little rain Monday, but it soon passed. Usually, when once it begins to rain it rains in torrents for forty-eight hours or more - as in all tropical countries. We have had one such storm since we've been here. - I've hardly worn an outside coat since we came, the sun is so warm. And I've never seen so many roses blooming as are here in nearly all the yards. Not even our grounds in Fergus, in June, were so over run with roses. They are pink and white and red and yellow and grow on large bushes. -

Occasionally we see orange-trees in bloom, and I have seen one banana-tree with an immense fragrant blossom. There are plenty of orange-trees with oranges, green and ripe. Oleanders grow wild and also the palms. -

In the early morning we hear the mocking-birds. -

I can't realize that it's nearly Christmas-time and yet summer ...

My love to papa, Jim, and much to you. -

May

*

Sunday -

My Dear Mother -

It's very warm here to-day and we are going to the shore late in the afternoon. We always get cooled off going down there in the cars.

I have been working on my book all this week and shall continue at it until it's finished. I have done little but write with an occasional trolley ride in the evening ...

I eat lettuce and onions from my garden every day. The radishes have all gone to seed. I planted more than I could eat. -

... We have thunder storms here as we used to have in Minnesota. There were no such crashes in Butte as we have here in the storms. I'm not much afraid, but my friend is always frightened though she's lived here all her life. We have a good many trees near the house. There's an electric storm after each hot day we have had. -

Love to you all from your daughter,
May

*

September - 22 -

Dear Mother -

I sent you a tiny gift for your birthday a fortnight ago - which I hope arrived safely. You may not care much about it for itself, but I thought it would do for a remembrance. I like little trinkets like that myself. - It's for smelling-salts, to carry in your wrist-bag or to have on your bureau. I had it filled with salts when I bought it, but I afterwards emptied it as I thought it would travel better. -

I hope you have a good birthday with many gifts ...

As ever -
May

* * *

Rockland - Monday

Dear Mr. Noguchi:

... So you thought I was rude, did you? Well, then I am rude. Rudeness is one of my points, a part of my personality. I don't know why 'tis so, but 'tis so. So you had best steer clear of me. But no. You can't come to see me here. I have long since ceased to meet people and moreover I am living with a friend who objects to having strangers in her house. So there it is. But this will I promise you: if ever you are in Boston when I am there, and I know it, I will ask you to luncheon with me and we will sit eating as if we were the best possible friends. We will have a cocktail together and a tiny bird. But it will probably be a good while from now. Or it may be soon, who knows? Again I thank you for the book. I shall probably send mine this week.

*

Dear Mr. Noguchi -

Haven't you a photograph that you can slip into an envelope with a letter and send to me? I should like to know how you look - unless I am to come see you soon. Are you never in Boston or East Milton? You may come to see me here - if you ever come this way. You didn't tell me whether your friend Mr. Stoddard recovered or not.

I am glad you like the book. I don't care so very much about my second book - except as a truthful expression of my mood. My mood at the time I wrote it had not much of passion or strength, and consequently the book lacks those attributes. - I like my first book far better, for some reasons.

I wonder vaguely about you, times. I wonder whether you are mostly American or mostly foreign. Are you long in America? Aren't you glad it's coming summer? I am - for no reason particularly. But yes - for the season, the warmness of the sun - and because things happen in the summer. If they happen in the winter, it's as if they hadn't happened. Meanwhile write to me again, and tell me when you are in Boston.

Your friend,

P.S. What about your poems - aren't you going to send me them?

* * *

Sunday - Hotel Metropole - Denver

My Dear Harriet Monroe -

... Lucy Gray showed me a letter of yours in which you spoke of writing me - and she would not let you send the letter. She said it was not like you.

Next time, don't consult my friend Lucy Gray. Am I so small that I can't be allowed to read anything which does not praise me?

Perhaps I may see you when I stop in Chicago on my way from here to Boston.

I wish all good things to you. - -

*

10 Bay Street - St. Augustine, Florida

Dear Harriet Monroe -

... When I used to have a letter from you I looked long at it, and I said, "Perchance she wrote me this letter against her Better Judgment." And if it were so it were all the more to be valued.

It outrode prejudice.

Nearly all the good things that have come to me - perhaps quite all of them - have come to me from people against their Better Judgment. They come purged. They come free as air.

Free as air. -

It is one of the tokens by which I value a letter from you. -

- Moreover, in reality, I do love you. - ...

Your books are wonderfully like you - so compact as to personality, so firm as to lips and as to hands, so full of repressed emotions and of subdued brilliances ...

There is a bay before my eyes which is today so pale and vague and light as ever your lake was.

On it are two white, white sails. And beyond the bay is an island, - and so richly-green and so fair and tranquil is it, lying in the sea and the sunshine, that I never cast my eyes on it without wondering if there's indeed no balm in Gilead.

- I should like to walk with you once by the side of this bay.

Above the bay is the sky - so peaceful, so restful is it that it makes me long for the time when I shall be no longer held fast to the earth, but may rest in the sky if I will. -

- I wish you might walk with me once beneath the sky. -

Moreover, in reality I do love you. I send you still other messages. -

*

Box 22 - St. Augustine, Florida

Dear Harriet Monroe -

... I frequently think thoughts of you - thoughts of various colors. - One being a wish that I knew you more intimately than I've yet been permitted to, what with time and distances and things. I feel that there's much of you that I've not seen and heard. The memory of you that I carry since that wonderful ten days that I had in Chicago with you and Lucy Gray is always alluring and picturesque. - If one loved you a great deal but wasn't fascinated by you at all - wouldn't you rather that she'd love you something less and *be* fascinated? I should myself. -

I don't care at all to be loved by anybody for my good and gentle qualities - (if I had any) - but only because I'm I, and in spite of my manifold wickednesses of temperament, - or, too, maybe because of them. - So I feel always vaguely fascinated by the depths of your personality and all your mental lights (there being astonishingly few persons that have either, I find) - and I hope some day to know more of them. But I love you, withal. -

... These days I'm busy writing something to be called "Four Years Later"

- meaning four years after the Mary MacLane book - for some Sunday newspapers. And I'm writing it in the absolute sincerity of my heart - as much as ever I wrote in that first book. I'm very anxious to make it a success - both as literature and as a "human document." It's to be an article of about 12,000 words, and I'm allowed about all the latitude in the world. It's intensely interesting to me and for that reason I often fear for its clearness and convincingness. Possibly some of my frankness in the picturing of emotions may be blue-penciled by the Sunday editors, what time they come to read it - but I hope not. - If I can stand it, why not the public? - I hope to finish it in about a month. I work on it daily ...

Always your friend,

*

December 30 - St. Augustine, Florida

Dear Harriet Monroe -

... You asked me some questions about myself, which certainly I shan't answer at this writing. There is something too chaotic and complex in my mind to admit of short simple answers. I am trying to picture much of me in the bit of writing that I told you of and I think I do. But they are not reassuring and peaceful pictures. I find, as I go on with them, that I'm rather an unpleasant person, - by and large. Only my unrealities, you might say, are real. -

Apart from that however, I wish you many happy New Years. And I'm always your friend.

*

January 14 - St. Augustine

Dear Harriet Monroe -

I was glad to know, in your letter which came New Year's day, that the gift which you sent me is a snuff-bottle. That fact sets it forever beyond the pale of vulgar use and preserves its gifthood intact. Because, you see, I don't take snuff. - It still rests before me serene and useless, as I told you in my other letter, and already I've grown to love it - for your sake and its ...

Mary Shelley has always seemed to me so hopelessly high-souled that I've even preferred Keats' Fanny Brawn to her, - she might have been insane but also she was akin to this wicked world. - Mary Godwin had a relieving fund of romance, however ...

I am thankful that the tiny feather fan was in time to blow away the mists and shadows from your birthday. A larger fan would have shrunk from a task so terrific as rescuing a December-23 birthday from the thick-tangled mazes of Christmas. But I fancied that little one might do it. I was careful to send no Merry Christmases with it - on the long slip of paper. -

But I said Happy New Year to you in the ribald rococo letter that I wrote you. - And your letter brought me one. Your wish was that mine should be "outrageously happy" - which is so inspiring a phrase as to be almost its fulfillment. -

My love to you. -

I hope I can see you some day and before errant and wondrous youth has touched us for the last time and fled away.

- Your friend,

*

May 24 - 71 Irving Place

Dear Harriet Monroe -

... I have the same affection for you that I've always had. I think of you frequently - sometimes every day for days there'll be some little vision, a happening that reminds me of you. And occasionally I come upon some of your writing. I remember seeing a poem of yours a month or two ago in *Life* - reprinted from some other magazine - about the modern hotel and all that makes it. I thought it extremely striking and real, and a wonderful vivid picture. The phraseology and the whole thing were characteristic of you. I have always found New York - any city - seething with poetry, on every sordid street corner, in the shops and subway stations, and all. We wear out our lives rubbing against it all daily - and yet these magazine poets, instead of making pictures of it, persist in doing weak-kneed verses about moons and rivulets and other things infinitely remote. - I say "magazine poets" because you never were one. There is always red blood in your poems, - or, not so much red blood as something suggestive of muscular force and vitality. - I think it's particularly true of this one on the Seasons. And the metre alone has strength ...

*

June 7 - New York

Dear Harriet Monroe -

... I know I'm too self-conscious and too introspective a writer to make my darkness seem light - to make anything but distorted pictures if I live a false and perverted life. - At the same time, if I were to give up writing - I should take up with it.

But, as yet, writing holds a thrall for me. I think it always will ...

*

Dear Harriet Monroe -

... I know you disapprove of me, more or less - but also I know you're too downright to run to cold silences and things. There's Friendship between us - Friendship and friendship - and that never yet throve on cold silences.

- If you ask me, friendships are the most subtle and fascinating things in life. The exchanging of bits of one's personality for bits of some other personality - a personality means such an infinite variety of things *to* exchange, - and the compelling charm of knowing a complicated human being cares for you and is 'square' with you, and the exhilaration of knowing you can be square - even if you're not by nature - that you've got to be or there's no use - all that to me, with my bit of imagination, is vivid-and-subtle Delight ...

*

September 10 - 71 Irving Place - New York

Dear Harriet Monroe -

... I want to make this book so big a thing that I can come back and not merely look at this New York thing but live in it. The book's got to bring me money and make me my place - a notorious one probably, but, all the same, not cheap or tawdry. New York simply enchants and fascinates me, the more for all its terrors. And I know the terrors will always be in it, for me - even when I come back to it with renewed sinews.

But if one has the wit and the will one can grasp even them in one's two hands. -

I'm just now writing a chapter that I think is the biggest I have done thus far - it's about the worn and tired youth which makes about one-third of New York - the unattached young women who work at different things daytime and pursue pleasure by night, phantom pleasures that are always out of reach, and lead them on, and never wait. It's a maddening and futile chase, but one we think we've got to keep up. It's as hard on feminine youth as the pavements and cobblestones and skyscrapers and the shrieking of wheels. It makes for pallid faces and drooping lips and shadowed eyes - how many thousands of them I've seen! And there's a look that goes with it - aged and hardened youngness. And for all their outward grooming and delicately-wrought complexions - it's a look suggestive of inward bleeding and burning - the beginnings of decadence in worn young bodies. I know all about it myself. It's but one of New York's tragic things.

- I think I am making a vital picture of it. I point no morals and draw no conclusions in any of my chapters. I write what I see, and I portray my own fantastic personality. And I keep as much to terse vivid words and brief sentences as may be.

But I really oughtn't to talk about it. I think it diffuses strength to talk about one's work. It is to keep it all within till it's ripe. -

I should like to talk over many things with you. I look forward to it ...

*

Dear Harriet Monroe -

... I'm glad of your hope for my book. It can't be all big - it is too much myself, and I'm aware of many shallows among my depths. Still - my idea is, if a thing is human, in art, it's big even in its pettiness. Indeed, I point out that, to me, there is something informing and illuminating in the trivialities and futilities of my own mentality. It's to me a vast and subtle field of thought, - I mean, just that idea of the futilities. -

But my Tired Youth chapter is still the best ...

* * *

September 14, 1906 - Rockland, Massachusetts

Dear Mr. Stone -

... I am now living ... on a lucky shot I made last winter at rouge-et-noir. I put fifteen dollars on number 12 - (usually I lay mine on the color, for even money) and the little white ball actually rolled into the number 12 when the wheel stopped - and I was rich! It gave me the pleasantest sensation! ... When the lid was finally shut down in St. Augustine I was several hundreds to the good solely as the result of being a Sport and betting at odds of 35 to 1. - ...

*

September 26 - Rockland

Dear Mr. Stone -

... A Good Time, with me, differs from an ordinary time in that in the latter I'm nearly always Heavily Chaperoned and in consequence demoralized and flighty; whereas in a Good Time one is never chaperoned - and in consequence, if hilarious, level-headed. Chaperoned, you can very easily go to the Demnition Bow-wows, if you ask me, but unchaperoned, you're quite Safe - wherever you go. Unchaperoned I could slink around the Streets of a Great City at Nightfall, picking up things, - but Chaperoned, - what can a Poor Girl do?

*

Dear Mr. Stone -

I have delayed answering your letter of 30 November in order that I might have something definite to tell you in regard to the time when you may expect the "Four Years Later" articles ...

As for the "damns and devils," - I am glad that they're not required or expected of me - 'twould be a good deal of a burden to have to work them in willy-nilly at the end of every 7th paragraph, for instance. At the same time I am doing this article in absolute sincerity and for that reason I dislike to be restricted in the very least - by even as much as 2 words. Of course, I don't take you too literally - I see your attitude (or rather, that of the ASMs) - and I don't say that I shall require even one damn-and-devil in the course of the story. But what I do say is that if I come to a place where I seem to need it - in it shall go - even if it's got to be blue-penciled, what time your editors read the articles. - I am writing precisely as I feel in every way - in the sentiment as well as the expression thereof - (it adds incomparably to the value of the story) - and if my emotions prove too lurid for the ASMs you've but to get busy with the blue pencil. - Perhaps it would give the story an added interest, as well as being my best-loved conceit, a Delicate Incongruity - to supplement the title "Four Years Later" with - "Being an Expurgated Sequel to her first Purplish Exploit" - or words to that effect. The word "Expurgated" - in a story of this sort - would land the public about as quick as the word "Unexpurgated."

However, these jests apart, I don't think you will find anything to cut out. I am making it real - which is its first and best point. Its other features are secondary. What I mean is that if I write a sentence that's picturesque, devilish, and true - the picturesqueness and the devilishness are so far subordinate to the trueness that they're quite lost sight of. -

What you suggested in your last letter had already occurred to me - the idea of making notes from the first book and drawing the inevitable 4-years-later comparisons. It's all the more effective for the fact that I hadn't looked into that book for quite 3 years. - What I have done on the articles thus far is rather satisfactory to me but I prefer to say little about its trends and purposes yet. - I've been interrupted by my journey down here and getting settled - but I shall go along with it as steadily as need be now. I'll let you know more about it before very long ... Shall you want photographs with the story? -

*

December 19 - St. Augustine, Fla.

Dear Mr. Stone -

... "Four Years Later" makes progress daily. It begins to sound like the *Story of Mary MacL.*, and I believe it has some of its intensity. It grows intensely interesting to *me* as I write it, and I'm very anxious to make it a success - both as a "human document" and as literature. It's got just one *damn* in it thus far - which is so sincere that it ought to be left in. Won't the public stand it - from me? - I *hope* there'll be no editing. -

- I expect the two articles will be merely one long one - of about 12,000 words, but I'll try to send you half of it before finishing the whole.

*

January 29 - St. Augustine, Fla.

Dear Mr. Stone -

... The "Four Years Later" tale goes along well - but some days slowly, its writer being a person of moods. It will probably come out with something over 2,000 words more than the 12,000 you first mentioned: in consequence of which I shall probably demand another $100 for the extra words. 'Twill be better than cutting it down ...

*

March 22 - St. Augustine

Dear Mr. Stone -

Do spirits of vengeance and things like that animate the Associated Sunday Magazines? - Because I made them wait a long time for the 4-years-later tale, and now they're making *me* wait, not only for the payment therefor, but for any word about it whatsoever. If it's vengeance alone which actuates them I can now freely inform them that it's theirs - without making me wait any longer. I sent off the tale March 6, and it's now March 22. I expected it would bring a little frenzied finance in my direction fully eight days ago. But it didn't ...

*

April 22

Dear Mr. Stone -

I've just received yours of April 20. - I am pleased to know that you're going to use even half of the MS. - As for my approval of your selections from it, don't bother to send *me* any proofs - use whatever you like. I had trouble enough with it once, and unless you want me to proof-read it I want no more of it. - I never read the *Boston Post*, which I hear is to have it - so there's no fear of the tale, in its slashed state, confronting me to my vexation.

*

My Dear Mr. Stone -

If you look me up here at 1 o'clock to-day we'll go, whithersoever you may lead, to some little table where we may eat, drink, and be merry.

On me.

May there be no word spoken between us that's fit for publication.

- Give this raw lad an answer so that I may know you concur in the matter of time and place. If it will be more convenient for you to meet me at some other than what I've named, you've but to say so. -

Let us only hope that you are not out of town, now when at last I find the way clear to redeem my pledge. -

*

21 November - 25 Cortes Street, Suite 5

Dear Mr. Stone -

... I have had more meetings with people and notes of invitation in the last six days than I've ever had before in Boston. One of the papers started a story that I had mysteriously disappeared from Rockland and was hiding in Boston. And that set the reporters to hunting me up - and there have been a great many half-column interviews and photographs since. - Some of the newspaper people were attractive women - and even a cub reporter looks attractive to a woman who has absolutely no one in the whole town to talk to.

*

December 31, 1908 - 25 Cortes St., Suite 5 - Boston

Dear Mr. Stone -

I gladly will make a try at Hearst's *Evening Journal* and his $25 a week ... I should prefer to make the try for a week or two without a salary - merely in order to prove conclusively to Mr. Brisbane and me and the Public whether or not I'm worth that, or nothing, or a hundred a week, to the paper. - I'm by no means sure of making good - but what I am sure of is that I want to and that I'll do my best. I wish I knew what sort of things I'm to do.

I'll come to New York on next Sunday's Fall River boat as you suggest. Owing to the as-yet-uncertain outcome of the *Journal* project I shall not give up my lodging here until it's settled. This will be a warm and *cheap* refuge to flee to in case I fail to "come through" in N.Y. - and besides, it holds my somewhat cumbersome Lares and Penates: consisting of all the boys' books Trowbridge ever wrote, and twelve large photographs of Alice and Marie Lloyd. - When I find myself really on my job in Park Row, or wherever, it'll be time enough to take a Sunday off and come and fetch them ...

I shall be very glad of your chaperonage and advice at the start ... I shan't venture to engage so much as that night's lodging in New York until I've seen the *Journal* people. It *may* be: back to the woods, on the boat that brought me. - But I hope not. -

Thank you for finding me a job, and Happy New Year. -

*

January 19

Dear Mr. Stone -

... I don't expect to have the Bread Line story finished - but you will perhaps have something to tell me about Mr. Brisbane's attitude toward me. Not that I don't know it, as well as one need - I almost foresaw it from Boston, - but I'd like to know what he said. As I never exactly pinned my affections to Mr. Brisbane I can stand his dictum anent me with heroic calm. I shall also be glad to see you, for yourself, because I like you. I have no more affections to pin to anybody - you'll think that sounds *young* - but likes and dislikes certainly cling to one.

*

Friday, January 28

Dear Mr. Stone -

... I have been strictly following your last injunction, namely to Be Good - not, possibly, so much because it's sound advice, as that having had several rough jolts from you, with it, I've had no heart at all for any of my brands of Harmless Idiocy. "Be good and you'll be happy - but you won't have a very good time" - that's me, all over, these days. Not that it matters. And the jolts - stinging lashes is a properer simile - are probably what is called "wholesome." I think I loathe everything wholesome. - Not that *it* matters.

*

March 16

Dear Mr. Stone -

... Writing is a slow process of earning your dinner. You write now and it means your dinner next week, perhaps. But you can't wait a week for your dinner. So you lay down your pen and go and forage. Different kinds of foraging have put me much to the bad - but, *n'importe* ...

May 12 - 71 Irving Place

My Dear Mr. M.E. Stone, Jr. -

... I have a landlady of "New Thought" ideas whose room is hung with illuminated signs such as "Fill your Day with Light" and "Be Sunshine for Somebody," but whose real motto is Pay or <u>Git</u> ...

The sisters Elinore are doing their turn this week at the Orpheum Theater in Brooklyn. You had better go to see them. They are not in the least witty or very clever - they're funny. Lots of people besides me like them.

*

May 17 - 71 Irving Place - N.Y.

Dear Mr. Stone -

... The Elinore sisters are at the Colonial Theatre up at 63rd St. They'll do your head good.

*

June 10 - 71 Irving Place

Dear Mr. Stone -

... I've just had a charming letter from Mr. Metcalfe, of *Life*, in answer to one I wrote him about his vaudeville article. He says he'd like to meet me to talk about it. I really know more about the ethics of vaudeville (it *has* ethics of a subtle sort) than he does, and I fancy he recognizes the fact. But I don't expect to meet him. I haven't myself been in a music-hall for months. Even the Elinore Sisters got by me.

*

June 14

Dear Mr. Stone -

... Three invitations have varied the precariousness of this week. One was for breakfast yesterday morning at the Beaux Arts place with Lucy Gray. She was in town for the Sunday. We had the breakfast together and a conversation, very much at cross-purposes. Another is for luncheon tomorrow with Mr. Metcalfe, of *Life* - which I expect will come off. I haven't yet met him. And the third was from young Mrs. Thaw who called me up to ask if I would like to go with her to Pell street to have an opium-pipe, tonight. I should have liked to try a pipe experience, but I have developed a nice vein of snobbishness which caused me to decline to go. (It's not wholly unlikely that I may be, once more, some day, a subject for the yellow papers. In which case I hope not to be visited with the added indignity of being pals with Evelyn Thaw. Besides, she's not interesting - a sort of mongrel American, - no particular personality. I've met her but twice.) Had the Elinore Sisters invited me to hit a pipe, now - I should have gone hot-foot. But they would be about as likely to smoke opium as they would be to jump over the moon. A black coffee, after dinner, would be heavy dissipation for them. Vaudeville people are that way ...

*

Friday

Dear Mr. Stone -

... I had the luncheon with Mr. Metcalfe last Tuesday. A most amazing person. - I wondered afterwards if I mightn't better have taken a chance with Mrs. Thaw and Pell street.

*

MacLane had hinted almost since her departure in 1902 that she would return to Butte; in late 1909, she did. She would remain for nearly eight years.

Her relation to the mining city would be forever complex. She had developed as a writer in opposition to it, thus needed it to strike against - and to turn from and delve fully inside, as she would in her final book, begun after a colorful spate of syndicated features.

While her New York book was never completed, she would later remark she had used much of what she had written in 1910's articles. With this in mind, we may separate old material and connecting passages; the former show that it would have been her least introspecting, most people-centered book - and her brightest-humored.

FEATURES

1909 - 1911

"The Second 'Story of Mary MacLane'"

Butte Evening News · 31 December 1909

This is an expurgated review of my later impressions of Butte and a few crudely-drawn contrasts between the me that was and the me that is.

I, of womankind and unpleasingly more than nineteen years, will now take the *Evening News* and the hybrid Butte public some three thousand words deep into my confidence. I am the Mary MacLane of purple memory whom, slam me though it did, Butte will never, never forget. I have proofs of that on me - some in my two hands and some in the top of my stocking.

Seven years ago I left this weird little town. I left it while myself in a blaze of notoriety made of tinsel and brass, and yet in its own way deep and far-reaching. It went half across the world, did the thing of brass and tinsel, and, too, it clings to me yet. I love my notoriety more, oh, much more than if it were pale, solid gold. It has given me such a run for my money - it has brought me close, close to human realities. I have sat all these seven years not in a shadowy literary niche, but have gone down into the seething market-places. I have felt the hot pulse and tasted the red blood of the cruel and adorable world. Seven years ago I left little old Butte far behind me. And now that the seven years have slipped away I'm here again and for the first time. It's to me a situation piquant and picturesque. I lived in Butte, but little more than seven years ago, the obscurest of shy maids. Butte now looks upon me as a returned and limelighted prodigal, a woman with a past, and an insolent young jade withal. It is wondering divers things about me as it sees me in its midst - if I've spent all my money, why I put on so much complexion, where I acquired my taste for cocktails, and whether I'm still single-hearted. Butte takes note of all these changes in me and shows a tendency to give me a gladdening hand. Well, though I know Butte for exactly what it is, I have none but a joyous hand for it. Butte is sordid, beastly, and time-serving - but withal full of romance and poetry and the wideness of the West. It is fascinating and picturesque, which is all I ask of anything. Morals are nothing but boresome trifles, and art is too often like a nightgown on a hot August night by the sea - superfluous. But the fascinating and the picturesque are never lost.

The Mary MacLane who rose to a so-sudden and somewhat terrific notoriety in 1902 was pre-eminently a Butte product - a shy and delicate creature born of this convulsive desolation. And when at nineteen my head broke out in brains and I wrote my wail of adolescence, with damns and devils and little knocks at Butte, Butte promptly gave me a curse, a blow upon the heart, also on the point of the jaw - a few surreptitious curses, and saw me slip away into the glooms and terrors of the many-pitfall'd world. I went away eagerly enough, but in all the seven years something in Butte subtly called me. I have heart-feelings for it. These barren hills saw my mind's awakening. I once walked over them in the loneliness of nineteen, or sat on some granite boulder with my hands about my knees, and watched the lights of the horizon, and realized the half-sullen, half-brilliant depths in me. I even thought I had a soul in those days (see the red Mary MacLane book) and a heart, of sorts. But the soul I have since passed up as a bore and an uncertainty (it is buried deep in the said red book), and the heart is now - battered and parched from the salt of dried tears. But the mind of black-and-white brilliance remains - and largely I thank Butte for it. A certain deadly thrall hangs over this little place, which impregnates one's mind, if one happens to possess one - they're rare - and brings to it a reckoning and an *accouchement*.

I had an incomparable thrill at my first glimpse of the town, a week or two ago, when I watched it from the windows of the night train sliding slowly in around the mountainside: a million starry gems scintillated on a black hill as if fallen from the spangled blue, and just above them the large deep-gold evening star hung low with down-dropping, glowing-wire rays. Nothing was there but the black hill and the countless diamonds, the silence and the evening star. It was mysterious and enchanting. "And that," I thought to myself, "is the pungent little place which saw the sudden jerking of me from the quietest obscurities into the glaringest limelights - and itself did it." It added depths to the thrill.

The next day I walked into its narrow highways and looked hard at it. It has an exquisite forlornness on it, with the deadly thrall: it is elementally the same little old Butte.

Since then I have done the highways daily and I've become used to the thrall and the forlornness. I am becoming once more a citizen of Butte.

And I've met most of the people with whom I once went to the Butte High School, and most of the people whom I met just after I developed from me into Mary MacLane, and a few more. I do not think the Butte people have changed any since I last knew them. But my attitude has changed toward them as it has toward everything since I wrote my book. So that they all seem different. Seven years ago I took myself and everybody and everything seriously - with nearly always disastrous results. (Do you remember how I "shocked Butte society"?) Now I take nothing seriously. I meet misfortune with an insolent laugh and the malice of my fellows with light-hearted contempt. What I cannot laugh at I pass up. I'll no more of the small tragedies that come from too much faith. They sear and corrode one's heart - they scar one's brain. And so, I've nothing but plaisance for the Butte people; they're all of that for me. In short, we get along fine.

I left Butte crude, innocent, and inexperienced. I return to it in the role of a frazzled old rounder. New York has been my abiding place these many, many moons, and it's been in some ways my undoing. It's a city of a million treacherous delights-and-horrors, and of a thousand grievous slips 'twixt the cup and the lip. It is vast and cruel - it devours youth, feminine youth, with the jaws and the palate of a monstrous insatiate demon. I and my folly - for I'm very much of a fool, among other things - were an easy prey. And so I come back to the scene of my youthful faiths with half my bloom irrevocably rubbed away. Still, even more than I love Butte I love New York.

I was at first bored stiff, after the fresh thrill of getting home had subsided, by the ghastly lack of things to do. There's no Rector's to go to after the play and sit drinking that which bubbles long; no Knickerbocker wherein to browse amid the Broadway chorus people with a swissesse beneath one's chin, no Tom Sharkey's wherein to drink beer in delicate abandonment amid the ribald revelry of hilarious sailors, no Cafe Martin wherein to mingle with the absinthe drinkers at four in the afternoon. There's no Maria's and no Jack's, no White Way and no Bowery. But I find there's a hybrid Indian-village sort of imitation of them all. They are live imitations. Butte is the one Indian village that could do it. Butte has gone off and down since I last knew it, and languishes in the clutch of a deadlock. But the glamor of its golden days still lingers on and there is an alcoholic haze to its nights. Moreover, a kindly law of contrast helps things along in my case. Certain men of Butte have taken me to the "Brewery" and Browne's, and out to Jack Reagan's and Billy Smith's and some others whose names I heard too late in the night to recall. We stayed very late in the night, and they introduced everybody to me - bartenders and Chinese waiters and the drivers of deep-sea-going cabs. Everybody seemed pleased to meet me. I seemed to be the only woman the night contained. The next day I went to an afternoon tea amid West Side ladies galore - they were few but select. I enjoyed both those functions. Butte people are very much Butte people, whether lined up in front of the bar at Jack Reagan's or drinking tea in West Granite street. They didn't happen to be the same people, though. At the time I wrote the book which we all thought was so wicked I considered it quite an awful thing for a young woman to go out to the "roadhouses," and I looked upon Mercury street as the haunt of the damned. But I've changed those opinions, partly because I've found by long experience that you can be as virtuous in a roadhouse as in a morgue, and partly because my attitude toward people-at-large has changed and I take nothing seriously: even if you aren't virtuous you aren't necessarily damned. I suppose there may be a lightness of heart, as well as of morals, in Mercury street, and, taken by and large, I fancy life is rather more human there than in Granite. I prefer Granite street, though, because there seem to be cockroaches in Mercury street, and of all things, kind Devil, deliver me from cockroaches. Rather even a cab driver for a husband or a waiter for a lover. More than I like the roadhouses and the afternoon teas I like the people I once went to school with. I like meeting them, shocking them, and having ardent friendships with them. It's fun to be Mary MacLane, a set-apart individuality in any gathering, as marked a woman as Evelyn Thaw or Carrie Nation. And it's pleasing to my vanity to reflect that I was as marked in New York as in Butte.

As to the things the massed Butte public seems to be wondering about me - I'll tell you some of them with a blending of audacity and chaste aloofness that's all mine. As to whether I've spent all my money: well, most of it. There was quite a lot forthcoming from the wicked book and, as I said, I've had a bully run for it. As to why I'm wearing so much complexion, not unnaturally I prefer to be good-looking than otherwise. As to where I acquired my taste for the dry Martini: that's an easy one - on the Great White Way. As I once loved the pallid olive so I now love the dry Martini - all melted gold in a cup of glass. The poetry that lurks in it can be written but scantily. It transfigures one's body as the colorful religion of the Buddhist transfigures the soul and the mind. I shall write more about it one day. As to whether I'm still single-hearted: it's too leading a question to answer. 'Twere folly to confess it at this stage, if I were or if I weren't. I maintain many a chaste aloofness that would make very interesting reading if done in plain terms. The best policy to pursue, whether in writing or war or love, is to combine limitless audacity with virginal reserves. I have myself tried it countless times and it never failed me. It is a combine that keeps the human equation perennially guessing. I think it's the policy which God pursues with all of us.

Another thing they're all asking me is what I have done with myself these seven years. I rather like to be asked that because it's so obviously and delightfully none of their business. For which reason I will say a few things about it. I have lived - for one thing, and it's a thing I never did here. I have been in love - or fancied myself so, which is exactly the same thing - not with vapid shadows, but with men. I am thinking at this moment of the little London Jew with whom I plighted troth and to whom I was engaged for the space of one week. He is now four years in the past, but himself and the memory of him still rouse deep-red poetry and passion in the black-and-rainbowed personality of me. He was tender-souled, beautiful to look at, and absolutely "on the level," which latter counts heavily. He was far too good for me, for I was never quite on the level with him. To me he was to be but a poetic incident, though I intended being married to him by a civil contract. He was seductive, but not the conquering devil of my dreams. But, to him, I was to be his wife till the grave yawned for one of us - and that sort of thing. Upon that we disagreed, so he went back to London beyond the sea - after a week of delicate and delicious cross-purpose. No other woman has yet got him for her own, which thought gives me a savage pleasure, and at times, as now, he glows warm in my memory. He was but one of several, but incomparably the most alluring and the only one to whom I waft still-born regrets through fast-darkening distance.

The Devil I once wanted never arrived - him of the steel-gray eyes - but so many imitations of him presented themselves, all with the one crude purpose, that he and his sometimes charm grew a bore and a monotony.

But I've not confined myself entirely to efforts to be gaily led adown the primrose path these seven years. I have gone everywhere and seen everything on the island of Manhattan. I have met fascinating people galore, from Ann O'Delia Dis Debar to Elinor Glyn - and back again, and from Mark Twain to Tom Sharkey in his native gin palace, the odds, as an interesting character, being heavily in favor of Tom. More than prize-fighters and literary people, both of whom I do like, I like vaudeville people on and off the stage. I fall the quickest of all for the people from the London music halls. They are artists on the stage, in their own lines of business - people like Cecilia Loftus, Marie Lloyd, Alice Lloyd, and Vesta Victoria - and off the stage, sitting in Rector's, with a pint of 'alf-and-'alf, they prove to be traditional British types of a most delectable brand. They combine a high-colored and high-seasoned domesticity with the thick local-color of the halls. They earn fabulous salaries over here, for they have a charm we cannot duplicate in America, and as they sit in the gilded thick-padded splendor of New York cafes they'll tell you how they started twenty years ago in the Shoreditch hall at "ten-and-six the night." There is nothing introspective about vaudeville people, nothing shadowy and sinister. They have brains of the sanest and simplest. In short, they are so satisfyingly different from myself, of whom, at times, I'm deadly weary, that I find a deep restfulness in their atmosphere.

Which brings me back to me. The thing I took away with me from Butte seven years ago - a restlessness of spirit, a shadowed and turbulent mentality, a lack of inward peace - is the thing I've brought back with me, and which will follow me to what I trust will be a young grave. I am myself like this little town with its subtle deadly thrall upon it, yet fired with certain headlong madnesses of youth. It is so with many, many others in Butte. Their inward fires glow and smoulder, with a dull personal menace, the more for the outward deadlock of this semi-bewitched Butte.

I have written this article, as I wrote the wicked red Mary MacLane book, as personally, as egotistically, as insolently as it's in me to write - because I know that only so could I picture the human equation. I write as many another feels, as many another is - and with the darksome spirit of Butte-Montana hard and fast upon me.

Because the *Evening News* seems to me more vividly Butte-Montana than any other sheet in this place I write it for the *Evening News*.

I am once more a citizen of Butte.

"Mary MacLane Soliloquizes on Scarlet Fever - And Other Things"

Butte Evening News · 20 March 1910

After a cracking bout with scarlet fever (it really was scarlet fever, believe me), in which the fight was stopped in the fortieth round by that canny referee, the trained nurse, lo, here am I, M. MacLane, once more slinging my purple emotional ink for the benefit of my foes and friends, the citizens of Butte: to whom, as always, my loves and greetings!

I have been quarantined and guarded *ad infinitum* and *nauseam* these many, many days. I have lain for awhile hard upon the borderland of Nirvana, that plain of infinite peace. I have lain passive in the deadly hug of a scarlet terror. For days I felt the things of this world slipping, slipping away, and the cool young happiness of death begin to whisper round me. But the restless fingers of the world woke me, and the restless voices of the world called me, and a thousand magnetic phantom hands beckoned me back. I opened wearied and lack-luster eyes once more upon my cruel and adorable world, and found it good. Its color again gleamed out - at first faintly, then softly aglow, then brilliant, then, as ever before, dazzling and luring me back to be again fascinated and undone by its delectable falsehoods, its luscious lies, its jonquil-grown pitfalls.

So here I am. No matter how much you may say you hate me, citizens of Butte, you're glad it's so; you're tickled to death. For so long as I'm alive and in Butte, and so long as I write for the *Evening News*, I am something to be talked about in tones delicately tinctured with venom, something to be picturesquely traduced by a million-tongued rumor, without which, in Butte, we faint, we stagnate, we languish.

Scarlet fever is a funny thing. After the scarlet and the fever have both left you, you find your slim young body in a condition of infinite weakness and lassitude, and your erratic mind in a state of indescribable alertness and aliveness to all the things in life. Pictures from the childhood-past flit across it with startling vividness. Forgotten details of incidents and events rush into it with the revealing glare of lightning on a pitch-black night. Facts in the present cut into it with the precision of a tempered blade upon one's flesh.

The first picture my unfevered mind became aware of was of the nurse, bending over me, a comely young woman in her white, stiff-starched uniform, not a detail of whose outward seeming failed to instantly record itself upon my brain. Her personality was like a printed page, mine for the reading - or more like a wireless message, mine without even the reading. So alert was my mind that I needed not to analyze her to ascertain whether I was to be bored by a banal and colorless inanity, or buoyed up and charmed by a human being. The fates were kind, I may add - she was what is technically known as a live wire. During the weeks we were caged in together, I worried, harried, and shocked her, which latter is said to be a difficult feat to perform with a trained nurse - and it was - but her game and light-hearted laughter rings pleasingly yet in my ears. It as much as anything kept me from going down to the darkness and the worms.

There's nothing in all the world so incomparably fascinating as a human personality. And the joyous part of it is, they are all around us - they are thicker than the melting golden stars in a mid-summer night, and I, with an intuition that's a gift from the gods, can find the lilies and the roses and the dead-sea fruits that grow in them all. Countless thousands are there who go down the world in a futile and irrational pursuit of art or literature or science alone with, belike, no results but the dryness of dust and ashes upon their lips - whilst all about them are the red-blooded realities, the warmth of flesh, the beating of hearts, the infinite intricacies of human equations. Thus it was that even my scarlet fever, itself a bitter curse, meant to me yet another human experience, and a trained nurse (I once thought them ghastly inventions) and I became friends and pals. Allah go with her for the light-hearted laugh that penetrated my most fevered dreams!

One's slim young body being kept in its lassitude on a deadly diet of milk, with the occasional addition of an innocent egg, aided and abetted by brackish mixtures out of bottles, one's erratic mind continues to be abnormally and electrically alive. And then it was in my case that million-tongued rumor began to sift in through the quarantine and I, prone upon my narrow bed, began to realize the powerful inventive imagination, the rich verbal ferulity of the citizens of Butte. Yes, though I grieve to have to confess it, it really was scarlet fever. I recognize that by every tenet of romance and gay adventure, I should have been beaten and cut into ribbons by a broken bottle - or was it a horsewhip? - in the hands of some lady of undoubted female persuasion and vivid reputation, at her domicile among the hop-fiends - or was it the Three-and-a-Half-Mile House? But grim reality will step in and rob this sordid world of its romance. The hands of what's-her poetic name have never been raised against me, nor even clasped mine in the throes of friendship. And my brief sojourn in the Three-and-a-Half-Mile House was notable chiefly for its deadly peace and quietude. Also it touched my proper pride that the Butte public would so readily believe me worsted. Should any lady, be she bantam, feather, light, or welter, become so blind to her own interests as to set upon me with a bottle used in the way, shape, manner, or form of a club, believe me, in but a brief interval of time she would e'en be taking the count.

"Such a gorgeous, glitt'ring time," said I to the nurse, "as all these wild tales depict of my life since I've been in Butte - and how bored I've been in reality." And I musingly considered what a happy idea 'twould be for me to sit tight and let the citizens of Butte plan out my amusements for me - they whose vivid fancy and deep-reaching invention so far out-strip mine, they in whose hands a drab mole-hill becomes a scarlet mountain.

Why should I ever do such inane things as spend evenings with a former schoolmate of palpable virtue, eating chocolates out of a box and dealing in airy nothings, when I might be in a gilded haunt of sin being smashed up by some lady or ladies unknown? Why should I ever find fun to sit at home with one foot under me and a volume of Wordsworth or Balzac in my lap, several evenings a week, when I might be tipsily wandering around the backstairs of the "Brewery" (where "the nights shall be filled with music"), astounding the lady orchestra and the hefty *chanteuses* with my ribald quips? Why should I ever go up the hill to play with my plump and youthful nephews, when I might be in the back rooms of beer-stores, playing with fire?

I have indeed let a lot get by me. 'Tis true, 'tis pity, and pity 'tis, 'tis true. Despite all which, the citizens of Butte are not nearly so much interested in me and my alleged lack of morals as I am fascinated by them and all their traits and attributes. There's something so thoroughly characteristic of Butte in their attitude toward me, and in all their other attitudes - something so subtle and still so crude, so incontinently barbarian and still so New-York-ish. I had the citizens of Butte analyzed to my own satisfaction seven years ago, when every malicious rag of a newspaper in the place was tearing me limb from limb. But in my cold young scorn I failed to do them justice. I could not then quite grasp them in the hollow of my hand. I left out of account their many-hued imagination as well as their incomprehensible softnesses of heart. For they have a heart, have the citizens of Butte, and marvelous to tell, even I am not without its pale. When the scarlet terror was at its worst the telephone bell rang twenty times a day and revealed the human consideration of not just friends and acquaintances, but of strangers - the citizens of Butte. Equally they sent boxes of pale, deep-scented blossoms (so many that had they come in the form of broken columns and gates ajar the body might have been then and there laid out). And there were other evidences. There is more to me in the heart-feeling of Butte than in that of all the other dwelling-places on the hither and thither sides of Manhattan. I know how rare and precarious are the softnesses in the hearts of Butte citizens - and besides that, Butte-Montana is my first if not my last love.

Mild mirth mixed itself with my deadly milk diet at the quaintly para-doxical idea of the citizens of Butte letting their astounding imagination and inventive faculty play lightly around my personality alternately with ringing my telephone bell to leave kindly messages and strewing my germ-laden path with flowers. It was all characteristic of the place, with its delicate incongruities, its utter unthinking youthfulness. It's as if the citizens rose *en masse* and said, "Kindly refrain from dying yet, Mary - we sadly need something to talk about, and for the present you're it." And such is the het-erogeneous nature of my popularity that the message came not from just one caste or class. Oh, no! There was a delightful lack of sameness about the sources whence it came. Milliners and Christian Science people, bartenders (with whom I seem to have suddenly and mysteriously become a popular idol - such is fame!) and grocery clerks, hair-dressing ladies - the kind that sell you switches and are called Madam - and bank clerks, butchers and telephone girls, the entire strength of the glove, shoe, corset, toilet-article, and linen departments at Symons', vegetable Chinamen, dress-makers, an assortment of amalgamated washerwomen, one cab-driver, three lawyers, a notary public - and many, many more. Every vocation in Butte, I think, with the exception of two: the Proscribed of Mercury street and the members of the Butte press, gave evidence that its followers were true citizens of Butte, mixing caresses with curses in a way that's all theirs.

That they should give me either is also as characteristic of their unrecking emotionalism as anything they have done. Butte is astonishingly young. Several weeks ago I coldly sat down and coldly wrote, for the *Evening News*, a bit of frank portraiture of what's to me the most interesting thing in the world, my own personality. Did the citizens of Butte take it as coldly, and judge it for what it was, as mere writing? Oh no! The citizens of Butte took it very warmly indeed. They looked on it, not as writing, but, as nearly as one can judge, as something in the nature of a large package of scandal, and they rose like gudgeons to that bait. They rushed at it, tooth and nail, hammer and tongs, and tore, not it, but me, to shreds. Did they credit me with being clever enough to make my portrait so vivid that they couldn't differenti-ate between the reality and the picture? Oh, no, again! They slammed me for having no morals, or something like that. I have written the same sort of things for New York newspapers, and New York, being a cold worthy old head with a century or two of civilization and ethics behind it, merely bought it and read it and only slammed it where it failed as literature. They know in New York that a revelation of the human equation must reveal something weak, something reckless, something passionate, something full of foibles, and with the very old-fashioned tendency to want what it's supposed not to have - there being about four million of such on and hard-by Broadway - and they would contemn a portrait which lacked them. But Butte in its crass youngness would make a virtue of concealment and would seem, by what one may observe in it, to have for its motto: *Go as far as you like, as long as nobody knows it.* Be immoral and even degenerate, up to the limit, but keep it hid. It is a juvenile attitude, and Butte has truly all the unreasoning cruelty that goes with juvenility. It would be difficult, even if I took anything seriously, to take seriously the irrational javelin thrusts of the citizens of Butte. To do that were to place oneself on Butte's level and thereby to become infinitely vulnerable.

Once in New York I said to a woman of much heart, much sensitiveness, and much money, who was herself not long ago a citizen of Butte, "Do you never expect to return to Butte to live?" And she replied, with concentrated bitterness, "I left my youth and much of my money there, and had my heart broken in the vile little place, and that's enough for it. It repaid me with slander and lies, and I've done with it forever."

It does have those results, now and then. But for me, to stay in Butte and write things for the *News*, for the citizens to run and read, has all the charm of playing with matches, or nibbling at forbidden fruit. I never know what they're going to say about my articles, or how they're going to take them, or what brand of little one-ring row their marvelous imagination is going to concoct. It's dull in Butte at best, and if one can so easily stir things up and make things lively - why, how nice it'll be! And what a temptation it's going to be to be very frank, now and then, to be very human, to picture the warm flesh and the beating hearts, and the red blood as they are. The citizens of Butte are themselves as warm of flesh as they of New York, if not warmer (which I'm inclined to think), and as red of blood, if not redder (which, too, I'm inclined to think), but they're shocked to death, or they say they are - it's not quite the same thing - if it's suggested to them in cold print that the world is inhabited by real live people.

If there's an impression prevailing among the citizens of Butte that I advocate immorality and laud the vices, I write it here, with contempt and impatience, that I do no such thing. I have written, and I expect to write many times yet, that morals are of comparatively little moment, and vice, let who will defend or condemn it, will last as long as the race. It touches the highest-browed of us with at least the tips of its fingers. If we cannot rid the world of physical immorality and vice - and why should we, since, if we do, they crop out in some form of mental abscess or other? - let us at least make them poetic and romantic. They're but trifles, anyway. It is not they that count.

But there are such potent things as sincerity, loyalty, and truth - there are such things as charity and kindness of heart - things which do count heavily in the long, long pathway of woe and shadow. Beside them the ethics of the body are but an atom.

But the citizens of Butte open their youthful eyes wide at such heresy - merely because it's written. They stare like amazed children at axioms that held good before Omar's day, before Chaucer's, before Homer's - and beyond that. Yet it's partly for that that they're fascinating.

Meanwhile they do not deter me. The dry Martini still shines goldenly in its cup of glass -

The cup that clears
Today of past regret and future fears.

It is not wise to dwell upon it - it is not wise to drink it. It is only delectable, enchanting, seductive, and bewitching. That for mine always. And to the citizens of Butte I waft, with the blue diaphanous rings from my cigarette, again my loves and greetings. They're a subtle joy. They appeal to half of my senses and all of my brains. They're my own kind, for I, too, am a citizen of Butte. They keep me guessing more than I can possibly keep them. Their curses and caresses lend my days a piquant charm and my nights a thin temptation - incongruous, incontinent, inconsistent, delightful, and adorable citizens of Butte!

"Mary MacLane Meets the Vampire on the Isle of Treacherous Delights"

Butte Evening News · 27 March 1910

It is close upon the witching hour of midnight. I, of womankind and some-thing-and-twenty years, sit alone in my little blue and white room, fallow and eke somewhat forlorn. I am surrounded by the silence of West Park street, than which the vast stillnesses of the everlasting hills to the southwest are not more profound. It sets somberly upon me for I, who imagined myself built for si-lences, solitudes, sunsets, still gray dawns - I am longing for little old New York.

New York - oh, New York - the mere thought of it fills me with a subtle restlessness, a half-insane emotion of far desire. Its name calls up a throng of turbulent memories, of mingled mournfulness and the utter reckless joy of living such as nothing but a dweller in New York can know.

All - all that is in the soul, the body, the mind, the heart of a human being, New York, the vampire, the cruel and much-loved, drags out. It demands the last fluttering gasp of breath, the last drop of blood, the last thrill of the worn nerves. While there's left one glimmer of light in one's mind, or one conscious nerve in one's body, the lips of the vampire are pressed close upon one's human lips, passionate, insatiate, mad until all is over and one lies abandoned, cold and dead.

There's nothing, nothing, nothing that New York gathers in and holds as it does youth. The mind and the body in the fullness of their youth are the food of the vampire. It devours, but, oh, it gives in exchange - life!

All the life, the youth; all the brain, such as it is, and all the restless heart; all the wild, nameless vitalities that make me human, every treasured thing I have to give, I waft at this moment, over frozen river and snow-clad hill - a thousand leagues - to New York, the exquisite vampire, merciless, bewitching.

I know New York as I know Butte-Montana, for exactly what it is. I have no roseate illusions about it. It has lodged me not as a transient bird of passage, but as one of the four million who call it home. I well know that it is no place to go to gather lilies. Its paving stones are the paving stones of hell. But on them walk people who are more wonderful than lilies. And the lesson it teaches is the adamant truth itself.

I first went to New York in the summer of 1902, at the age of 19, when I was a crude but successful child, guarded and looked-after and chaperoned to the point of atrophy. New York seemed to me then a vast, tiresome Babel, with a mingled atmosphere of skyscrapers and of alcoholic beverages, which latter continually were being offered me and which I did not like. I last went to New York at the age of five-and-twenty, when I was cast into it as into a seething whirlpool, "broke," at the time, heavy-hearted, and alone. My little body, like Juliet's, was already aweary of this great world. But what it and the heart in it had to suffer before they caught the meaning and the pace of the seething whirlpool only the silent gods know. I may one day write it or I may keep it, a black memory, locked fast within me. But this much let me say for myself, that I bore misfortune in solitude and with cold disdain for its slings and arrows, and New York, though it has got everything else out of me that I could give it, wrung not one salt tear from my tired eyes. It gives me infinite satisfaction to be able to say it now and before I left New York, but a little time ago - yet, I remembered even that crucial time as a precious and informing experience. Also before I left I could gauge New York - I could grasp it, as I now grasp Butte, in the hollow of my hand. Nothing in it could faze or frighten me. The skyscrapers had become something attractive and beloved, and the quick fire of the alcoholic things, absinthe, vermouth, chartreuse, had run a thousand times, a negative passion, in my veins. In short, on the altar of the exquisite vampire I had offered up, madly and gladly, what was left of the first half of my youth. I am conscious as I sit here, in the chaste silence of West Park street, in my blue and white room, of but just entering on the second half of my youth - which is a fuller half than the first, if less radiant; light-hearted and care-freer, if less innocent - and by those tokens I fain would haste with it to where the North and East rivers wash the glittering shores of the Isle of Treacherous Delights - to lay it upon the same broad altar, already piled high with a million like gifts.

There is nothing at all in New York that is not fascinating to those who love it. For them there is poetry in every seething subway station, in every low-down Italian, with his banana cart on the Third and Fourth avenue corners, in the Siegel and Macy and Wanamaker department stores, as well as in the wonderful shops on the avenue, in the vaudeville theaters, and even in the piano-organs that awaken the echoes and the dwellers in the apartment buildings on the side streets. To them the look of New York is beautiful. No turreted castle overlooking a desolate sea could show more picturesque than the Flatiron building at sunset, with the dying lights on its battlements, and the Twenty-third street mob, like scurrying insects, at its base. And close to it is another thing of beauty which to me typifies the spirit of all New York - the great bronze Diana of St. Gaudens, which rests a-tiptoe on the Madison Square tower. She suggests youth in its gay and triumphant freedom.

But, however, it's not for those chaste delights alone I'm longing in the midst of West Park street's remote gloom. One can not live on even Flatiron buildings, and Diana, though she's inspiring, is not satisfying to the emotions she rouses. Besides, she's bronze.

But the quality that is so distinctively New Yorkish, and which Butte-Montana conspicuously lacks (having in its place the deadly thrall we all wot of), is the quality of deep and intimate humanness. It is that and not the glitter which makes people, after a half-year of living in it, fall so abandonedly in love with New York; it is that which makes New York people think there's no other town in the world. They may tell you it's the glitter of the gay white way, or the cafes, or the theaters, or the Fifth avenue parade, or what not, but those are only the delectable setting. It's the subtle freemasonry among the millions, the silent recognition and understanding of each other's humanness and the half suggestion of intimacy that one feels toward all or any of the persons one meets and passes on Broadway - it's that that's all the glitter and enchantment of it. And, too, it's that together with the glitter of the white way that is the most alluring and treacherous and annihilating of all the attributes of the vampire. In truth, it is that quality that is the vampire. For it's intimacy with human beings and all that it betokens - the exchanging of bits of one's personality for bits of another's, the idiosyncrasies of friendship, the nerve-racking experience of being in love, the hypnotic effects of one personality upon another, the utter throwing to the winds of all one's reserves of body and soul before the compelling magnetisms of some, and the lesser intoxication of knowing one's domination of others - it is all these things that devour flesh and blood and nerve. They eat their way from the outer wall that guards the crude human being to the inmost keep of the citadel. One's loves and friendships have effects on one's slim young body and one's wayward mind that are more malignant than cocaine and more subtle than absinthe. But it's all so exquisitely and poetically and seductively worth while. Not one affair of the heart - and even friendships with me seem to be affairs of the heart - that New York has given me, though they left me, times, battered, stung, wounded, a bundle of frazzled nerves - not one would I exchange for any non-human treasure that life could bring. If there's one tenet that I cling to with sincerity and faith, it's that which enjoins absolute freedom of action, to follow not the precepts but the impulses, to grasp one's heart's desires, to emulate the surging voice of all New York in its wild cry, "More Life, More Life!" - to turn everything outward, to let slip all one's emotions, all one's glimmering passion, all one's dormant lights-o'-love.

That's what you do in New York. And it's that that makes the deadly thrall of Butte seem deadlier and the stillness of West Park street more deep. No solitary cell at Sing Sing could rival my little blue and white room at this moment for aloofness, for there's no such thing as human intimacy in this young, young town.

I did not know that when I lived in Butte before I had myself no intimate friendships, but I knew that I was entirely abnormal, anyway. But since I've been gone from it I realize that the people in Butte are all abnormal in that they form no real intimacies. They are as shy as wild sea-fowl with each other, and absolutely dead-locked in iron-bound personal isolation. They have what they call friendships, and there are little clubs of women who foregather, and people take drinks together and that - but with it all they are not, they seemingly can't be, intimate with each other. They think they exchange bits of their personalities, when they are really exchanging only talk. They exchange kisses and hand-clasps and even lingering caresses, but all in the deadly thrall way. I idly wonder as I sit here whether there would be anything intimate about even the doing of a murder in Butte. "But no," I think to myself, "there would be more of passion, let loose, in New York in a mere brushing together of finger-tips, or in gazing into eyes across a little table, than in anything that's done in Butte. It's the way you do them in New York."

Butte's way is without doubt the wiser of the two, but what's that to do with it? Butte's way makes for more strength in that since one turns nothing outward, one's resources are husbanded, but what's the use? What do we do with our strength after we husband it? There's no development where there's no intimacy. One barely begins to live only after one has rubbed hard against at least two live people, with nerves in their finger-ends and lights in their eyes.

I have in Butte two deadly, thrall friendships - or are they a love and a friendship, I don't myself quite know - upon which I've been bold enough, since I've been back, to try out the methods in favor on and hard-by the white way. It's fascinating to watch their effects, which are to one-third perplex, one-third frighten, and one-third allure. I get nothing of the kind myself in return, since the wild sea-bird shyness is fast upon them and I have all the advancing to do, but, withal, I have at least the pleasure of making two people writhe at the unusualness, in Butte, of friendship in the nude.

But pungent though it is, it is not a wholly satisfying pursuit and the half-lenient gods, after all, do not limit me to those two. There are one or two people in Butte who have themselves lived on the Isle of Treacherous Delights. I find they know the game as it's played there, and they go to it with a recognizing, if shy, eagerness. But - this is Butte-Montana, where the on-lookers make scarlet mountains of drab mole hills - and when all's said I believe I, M. MacLane, am the one citizen Butte will ever have who is absolutely undisturbed and undeterred by the whispering tongues. Contempt is the word which correctly pictures my attitude toward them. And contempt is the correct attitude to maintain. Why should they judge me? Why should any one judge any one else? Which brings me back to little old New York, where no one judges any one else. How much better to be living than slowly drying up inwardly. How much better to be in New York, where people are really let live. How I long at this witching hour of midnight, with the staid quietness of West Park street oppressing me, and at the threshold of my second half of youth, to feel once more the lips of the vampire very close against mine.

On the corner of Fifth avenue and Twenty-sixth street, close to where the bronze Diana stands, poised against the blue, is the Cafe Martin, where the Dry Martini is more palely golden than anywhere else on the Isle, where the people are more attractive and all the delights more bewitchingly treacherous. It has been the scene of more new and well nigh insane adventures for me - and a million other feminine youths - than probably any cafe could be outside London. It is swagger, extremely French (for America), and cordial in its welcome to unescorted women before the bell tolls six in the evening. The place is so pallidly, prettily decorated, the music is so thin and sensuous, the women such high wrought things. It is consequently crowded with them from lunch-time until then. There are also men to be sure - at about four in the afternoon, when one type of the masculine absinthe-drinker of New York assembles to steep its sodden soul in anise. But the restaurant which looks on the Avenue is mostly filled with women, such a picturesque crowd, with a freedom of mood upon them which is remarkable even in New York. They are nearly all young women - (but New York women are still in the throes of youth at five-and-forty) - there are artists, writers, chorus-girls, vaudeville people, *habitues* of Bohemia, *dilettantes* of all sorts - all the loose young feminine fish in New York. It is the one cafe on the Isle wherein the crowd is not specialized - where that most fascinating, most complex, most unexplainable of human beings, the New York young woman, may be seen in the mixed aggregate. In that the Martin is unlike the Knickerbocker, up at Forty-second street, the center of the Rialto and the haunt of the moneyed but unaristocratic theatrical people, or the Cafe des Beaux Arts, frequented chiefly by the high-browed followers of the arts, or Rector's, beloved of the refined *demimondaines*, or Churchill's, loved of the unrefined ones, or Sherry's, the feeding-place of the swagger, or the Waldorf, where the ungrammatical and heavily upholstered inhabitants of Pittsburgh feel at home, or Maria's, the resort of the not-too-successful *litterateurs*, or Jack's, where the hippodrome ballet nightly grazes. Any or all of those types are to be seen at Martin's, whereas they would be unlikely to find themselves at any two of the others.

What a picture of youth it is at the Martin, at four in the afternoon! - a picture of tired, tired youth, women like crushed lilies or half-wilted jonquils. They are all in the clutch of the vampire. The mark of the vampire is upon their delicately-rouged and faintly-drooping lips, in the glint of their all-knowing eyes, upon their insolent brows and in the movements of their slender hands. Their hearts and bodies are weary from the ceaseless glitter of the world and from their endless pursuit of Pleasure - a Pleasure like an *ignis fatuus* that is always a little way beyond, that never, never waits. I have seen it myself around corners, behind doors, at the top of flights of stairs - always beyond, never in my hands or by my side. I have sat, times, in the Martin, with some delectable companion, twirling the stem of my absinthe glass with my thumb and finger and with my chin on my hand, and looked about at the gay-hearted company and wondered if they knew they had never caught up with the *ignis fatuus* Pleasure, and never would - and if they did that the flavor of the Grape would become wormwood on their lips, and the daylight shadowed, and the music stilled.

But no, assuredly they never think of it at all. The generality of the amblers down the primrose path are happily not given to introspection. That is a seething curse peculiar to those to whom the birth-stars are not kind, with whom it plays perennial mischief. And if one is both lured by the primrose path and, too, given to introspection - so much the more grievous the curse - so much the more.

For as one sits here, in the aforesaid silence, it comes over one like a cold, distracting breath, and the look of all of life makes one but shudder. One's longing for the Isle of Delights falls away like a mantle - that mad utter folly, that dedication of all things to life at its last and utmost tension, that picture of the flower-faces, of tired youth, in the Cafe Martin - float across one's mind with a suggestion of blackness like death itself.

One wants no human intimacy either in the marts of New York or the little by-ways of Butte. One sees one's portion in an aloofness and isolation far beyond what even Butte can give. For the having fed at the flesh-pots in the Isle of the Delights one pays a heavy, heavy reckoning - and to introspection that does it all. It once made the Delights more seductive, and it now makes the heavy reckoning so much the more heavy - so much the more, and -

"The Flower that once has bloomed forever dies."

New York or Butte-Montana, is it worth while - or isn't it? I ask me, with my hands pressed upon my eyes.

"The Autobiography of the Kid Primitive"

Butte Evening News · 3 April 1910

Far be it from me, in the insolent intrepidity of my youth, to make anything like excuse or exculpation to anybody who walks the earth, particularly the citizens of Butte. For I do what I do, and I write what I write, absolutely without let or hindrance, and with naught but high scorn for those who question it. If it's liked or if it's not liked - what boots it? If they line up with the javelins - what's that to me? Inside of me are good and sufficient reasons for what I do and what I write, and that's enough. The public's one privilege anent the matter is to cherish their own opinion. I don't expect them to change it, and a pox o' me, as they say in early English dramas, if they can make me change mine. Still, even that being so, I fain would say here this: If I seem mostly to write about myself for the citizens of Butte to run and read, it is not because of egotism and vanity, or because I'm fond of myself. I have but just my share, my human share, of egotism and no more, and no one who knows me ever saw my thousand faults with a clearer eye or a colder judgment than I do - my word upon it. And as for being fond of myself - Gramercy! (to quote again from the aforesaid dramas) - my chief feelings toward me are exasperation with a large "E," bewilderment with a large "B," and despair with a large "D." But I'm fascinated by myself because I'm always fascinated by live persons, and I am the live person I know most about. Of course, people don't admit it, but it's nonetheless evident that to each person the most fascinating thing in life is herself or himself - and next to that we are interested in other personalities. The pictures I have made of my personality have been the most real writing I have done. It was real. It was alive. And it happens to be a field that I have all to myself. Other writers lack the courage, or the audacity, or the gameness, or something, to turn their search-lights inward and write of what they see - and unless they make their fictional characters very striking and original indeed, the reading public will none of them. There are many, many novels published every year, clever ones, written by clever people, that are still-born or strangled at birth - never heard of - merely because they are fiction after all, and not reality. But the red Mary MacLane book, in some ways a far lesser thing than many of the still-born novels, was simply eaten up from the day it was published until two or three years later - it drew instant blood from the newspapers, the public, Anthony Comstock, and the vaudeville stage - not for its cleverness, or its originality, but because it was no little masquerade of fictional characters, but a live portrayal of one live young woman. I would myself give nearly anything in the world if some one else would write that sort of book - for the enthralling pleasure I should have in reading it, in feeling the heart-beats beneath the words.

Before I have done I shall, perhaps, write for the *Evening News* about such things as the condition of the roads, or the height of the Big Butte, or the look of the highlands, or the color of the sunsets - and lo, the people who condemn me for egotism and all, will be the first to cease reading it. I know human nature and the citizens of Butte well enough to be convinced of that.

Meanwhile, however, I still, in the present page, write of M. MacLane. If you're bored with it, gentle readers, then pray do not read further. Send the papers to the grocer's boy.

Though now I'm indeed of womankind and something-and-twenty years; though I've been cast by the heels out on the hard-paved highways of life; though I've had every possible experience that a young woman can have - except one or two; though I have had all of New York to be reckless in - yet there was a time when they were all far impossibilities, when life was largely mystery and battle, when "green fields and running brooks" were all my surroundings, when the pomps and vanities of this wicked world were all far removed from me; in short, there was a time when I was seven years old.

There are people who will tell you that we do not change with the going of years - we only develop. It might be, and I suppose that I, at seven, was the embryonic M. MacLane of now. But an even half of my character is different as day from night from the character of the hard young villain who was myself at seven, and the other half seems to me the same as it then was, without the development. But you can never tell about those things. The perspective and the view point alter so much that there's no certain comparison.

But my recollections of me at seven, and of the setting of my life, and of my own outlook upon it are as vivid in my memory as if 'twere all yestere'en. And yet so remote am I, a complex young woman, from the Primitive Kid of seven that it's as if I were making a picture of some other child.

The Primitive Kid lived in Minnesota, the land of the little lake, the gopher, the hazel nut, and the Norwegian hired girl. It was on the outskirts of a little town - a large gloomy-looking house, surrounded by oak trees, poplars, and balm-o'-Gileads. I can see the trees now on a sultry August afternoon, with a tense stillness upon them, with not a movement of leaf or whisper of branch, and a mysterious fearsomeness in their presence, and I can see the same trees just before sunset, lashing to and fro in the fury of a thunder squall, now looking like black masses of tangled foliage, and anon, lit up by terrific flashes of lightning in which each leaf-vein seemed picked out in silver-point lightning, such as is hardly known but in that region. And there were hedges of wild roses, pink-blooming in June, and a kitchen garden, and a corn field, and two brackish little ponds on our five acres, and stretches of bird-haunted woods. And the air from the wind-swept hillsides came laden with anemone and was exceeding sweet, and the subtle perfume of the meadows was rosemary, and the wet places in spring-time were a-bloom with blackthorn. Green grew the rushes on the shores of the little ponds and winding and devious were the hidden pathways in the woods. Also there was a great red barn where the wrens built their tiny houses over the sliding door and the swallows their mud nests under the eaves. And there was a horse or two and a cow or two inside it, and two spotted pigs in their pen back of it, and a chicken house at the side. It was full of nooks to play in and its possibilities were greater than if it had been a "fretted palace with music in th'enameled walls."

We were three who played and quarreled frantically together within its red portals. I, aged seven; Jim, my brother and henchman, aged five; and a chronic playmate and neighbor of ours, named Henrietta, aged six. I was a slim, tanned, pig-tailed person in a faded gingham frock reaching not quite to my knees - the same being handed down from my sister, whose cast-off, outgrown, faded summer-before's wardrobe meant tight detestation to me. I looked, on general principles, rather too much like a Shanghai rooster to be quite beautiful. Also I was insufferably arrogant and proud-stomached - a leader and a tyrant. Jim, my henchman, was an equally slim and somewhat freckled individual, plaid-kilted and glengarry-bonneted, a craven soul if ever there was one, whose keeper I seemed to be (very much against my will), whose lickings I had to take, whose business in life was four-flushing. And his sense of humor was a weird and astounding thing. But let me add for him that his four-flushing was done with extreme cleverness, that he was a faithful henchman and in crucial moments a game loser. That he was scared to death of a good, strong mosquito, hawk, or a humming bird in a rampant state, and would turn tail and run like a deer from an infant garter snake, that he had no imagination whatsoever, and was unable to project his mind so much as four minutes into the future, that he believed absolutely everything that was told him, by anybody - these were points in his makeup perhaps more to be pitied than censured. It is not to condemn him now for his defects. Say rather that as a henchman he was perfect. As for Henrietta, she was too oft the scapegoat of us both. She was a smooth, rather plump, yellow-haired fluffy personage, afflicted with a weak will and an erratic mother. She had shapely legs, a round pink and white face, and a quite unholy passion for brown sugar. She was not so craven as the Henchman - she had far more temper and enterprise - what is technically known as "spunk" - but she was by nature a grafter, was Henrietta, with too much the spirit of the genus tight-wad upon her. Still she was a not unfascinating companion and no raid on the pantry, braving the fire of that arch enemy the hired girl, was a real success without Henrietta on picket duty - albeit she did require infinite brown sugar as her reward. Failing that from the raid she would sell out both the Henchman and me to the Arch Enemy for one lump of it.

As we were of the vintage of the late '80s, when Harrison was President, the three of us - Henrietta, the Henchman, and I - wore our hair in a thick breastwork of "bangs" across our foreheads, the feature which would be most noticeable in us could we fare forth now. For the present-day fringe on boys is but the pallid ghost of the amazing bangs of '88. Mine was straw-colored, Henrietta's hay-colored, and the Henchman's a neat chocolate brown.

It remains but to describe the hired girl, who was a poignant factor in our lives. She was a person who chewed gum without ceasing and had teeth which were very, very false - quite the falsest teeth I have seen before or since. She wore her hair in a sort of tight cylinder above her forehead in what was then known as a "French twist" - and she had an arm like a sledge-hammer and a voice like a foghorn. She used to sing a mournful ballad about a butcher's boy whom she had loved not wisely, but too well. Her classic name was Ida, and she concocted strange pies which came out of the oven looking rather black. Her ruling passion was not for brown sugar but for laying out in the barrel-stave hammock under the trees and dozing there, oblivious to pies and all the other mundane things - with the possible exception of woodticks. Follows is a hypothetical bit of a diary such as I might have written at seven had I been able to write at all - which I couldn't, not having been sent to school till eight - and had I possessed a vocabulary. I had plenty of ideas and plenty of analytic introspection in those days, but a limited erudition. So the vocabulary and the diction and the idiom of the hour in the following bits of diary must be more or less those of my present day.

*

Fergus Falls, Minnesota
Aug. 13, 1889

This is Tuesday. The hired girl is ironing in the kitchen. I want my bean blower off the window sill, but I don't dare go after it, and it's no use sending Jim. He would bungle and be sure to let her see him going out with it. She would instantly take it and smash it, because I hit her in the ear with a kidney bean. Besides, she is still mad over the dead toad we dropped in the churn. To pay me for that what does she do but go and gobble up my half of the peach turnover. She is a devil. But I'll be even with her yet. The last time she ate pie off me I had Jim go upstairs and spit in her hat - the one with the gilt bunch grass on it. He did it. No, she doesn't get the start of me. While we are waiting for Henrietta we'll go and play in the barn. It is nice in the barn. I would rather be there than in the house any day. I like to be with the horse. He is a nice horse and we feed him lots of oats. Then we bring him ever so much water, nearly a tubful, in the wooden pail, and he drinks it all up through his nose. Then he makes a noise inside like an engine just starting. And when the hired man comes in he says, "What the deuce've you young brats been feeding this horse today? You want to give 'im the heaves?" I'm sure it's not we that's giving him heaves, if he gets any. We never give him anything but a few oats and a little water. The hired man is crazy. He is a good healthy horse. I wish he would have a colt this summer - a Shetland pony one. So does Jim. But no such luck. We have wished that for years, and he has never had a colt yet. I see Henrietta coming so I guess we'll go over by old man Causs' garden to play. Their melons are getting ripe.

Aug. 14

We had such a delightful time yesterday afternoon. There wasn't much doing over at old man Causs' in the way of melons - old man Causs was at work in his garden. So we came home and I tried to get Henrietta to go and get the bean blower. But no chance. She couldn't see any brown sugar in it, and besides she's even more afraid of Ida than I am. While we stood looking at the Arch Enemy from the wood shed off the kitchen a bright thought came to me. I had a match in my pocket that I had found under the stove, and it came over me in a flash what a dandy idea it would be to light it and set fire to the hired girl, and just burn her up. No sooner said than done. She was standing with her back to us ironing and chewing gum, and I softly lit the match on the doorsill and said to my henchman: "Here, Jim, you take this and slip up behind her and light the bottom of her dress - and don't let her hear you or see you." Jim was delighted. Jim is no good at all in laying plans or bringing them, unaided, to fruition. But as a serving man I think he has no equal. My plans always make an instant hit with him, moreover - he knows by long experience that they seldom fail to furnish prolonged entertainment for him and Henrietta and me. So he took the match and, slipping up on the hired girl, he held it to the bottom of her calico dress. He held it till a little blue blaze was well started, while Ida continued ironing and chewing in happy oblivion, and Henrietta and I watched from the wood shed door. I can see now the little blue blaze turning yellow and getting larger. I can see the Arch Enemy suddenly leave off her ironing - and eke her chewing - and with a flat-iron in her poised hand begin to sniff the air and exclaim: "Something's burning." I can see Jim - Jim, who like the perfect fool he is, knew no more than to first set a hired girl on fire and then go and tell of it - I can see Jim, pleased at being able to convey useful information, pointing out to her the source of the burnt odor. I can see her glance follow the direction of Jim's pointing finger and herself suddenly become aware of the location of the blaze. And I can see her, with the iron in her hand, begin to whirl round and round and round, like a kitten chasing its own tail, in a very vain effort to catch the fire. The heavy flat-iron lent her a momentum which she otherwise lacked, and she spun around like a human teetotum, while the Henchman, with the burnt match still in his fingers, and his eyes popping out of his head, stood back, rooted to the floor with astonishment at the antics he had caused, and Henrietta and I looked on with excitement and pleasure from the wood shed. The hired girl brought matters to a quick terminus by sitting down abruptly in the water pail, which stood beside her table - and, of course, the fun was over. The Henchman made a hurried exit at my behest and we all three retired to a safe sequestered nook to talk it over. For about two minutes, we had one grand time. The Arch Enemy, with a flat-iron at one end of her and a fire at the other, doing a frenzied waltz around the kitchen, with fright writ large on her countenance, was a sight which brought keen delight to us and one we rarely witnessed. Henrietta even forgot to require brown sugar, and she, like me, took an artist's impersonal pleasure in the neat unusual form of our revenge. It was well worth the loss of my half of the peach turnover. She'll think twice before she eats another off me, I guess.

Aug. 15

What do you think of this for news? Today the Frankberg kid, the little one, came and offered to fight me. He shook his fist in my face and called me a low-down blackguard. Now, I don't take that from anybody, and it was hardly a minute before the fight was on. I had only Henrietta, the Henchman, Milly Wessberg, and Georgie Lee lined up behind me, while he was being backed up by the entire Norwegian Sunday school. But I didn't care. I knew what the outcome would be. He had something on me in weight and reach, and that's all. My wallop is known for as much as a mile around here, to say nothing of my left hook, and everybody knows how quick I am on my feet. He came in for punishment and went home, after between two and three rounds, a bloody-nosed and beaten kid. The Norwegian Sunday school, if it had had it in mind to move in an armed phalanx on Henrietta, the Henchman, Milly Wessberg, and Georgie Lee, changed its mind and followed him. The yelling on both sides beat anything that has ever been heard before in this vicinity. Ida put her head - with her gum in it - out the kitchen window and remarked in no uncertain terms that if we didn't all shut up and clear out she'd give us all something to yell for. This may have had a little to do with the retreat of the phalanx and the Frankberg kid - but something tells me that he won't soon call me a low-down blackguard again. I don't know what is a blackguard. It sounds to me like a turnip or something of the sort.

Aug. 16

Life is so dull here. There's positively nothing interesting to do. This afternoon my brother Jack brought home some fish that he had caught, and one was a horned-pout, which Ida and the family rejected as food. So Jim and I and Henrietta took him and put him in the rain barrel in the hope that he would entertain us by coming to life and swimming. But he wouldn't. So we took him out and tied a pink ribbon very tight around his waist - so tight that his eyes looked prominent - and brought him into the house to show the family. But if they were uninterested in him as a fish, they were still less interested in him as the wearer of a sash. Ida was told to take him out and dispose of him. I last saw him in the warm embrace of the cat. His sash was the worse for wear. It's so difficult to find anything amusing to do. Henrietta went home in despair and in search of brown sugar, and the Henchman and I went upstairs by the back way and rummaged awhile in Ida's.

Aug. 17

The Henchman, Henrietta, and I went up the hill back of the barn to play today. We had a good time, though nothing happened. Jim was mad because he had to wear his red suit that's got all the pockets ripped off. If he had to wear what I do he might have something to rew about. Dolly must have used the one I've got on today to play run-sheep-run in the back pasture in. It does not look like a hand-me-down merely - it is more like an heirloom. Henrietta had about a peck of brown sugar that she had lifted off the grocery wagon while it was standing at our gate. And Jim and I took a package of figs that the grocery man had left on our kitchen table. He was busy talking to Ida at the side door. Every time he comes to her and says, "Well, how's my best girl today?" And she says, "Go along with you, you pelican." The grocery man says that to everybody's hired girl. We knew Ida had not missed the figs when we got to the top of the hill because we could hear issuing from the kitchen -

In Jer-sey - town
Where-I-Once-Did-Dwell
Lived a butch - er's-boy
I-Loved-Too-Well.
Oh, what a fool - ish, fool-lish joy
To - wreck—my - life
For-A-Butcher's-Boy!

We sat down on the windy hilltop and had a feast. Henrietta, who would willingly pawn her soul for an ounce of brown sugar, for once had almost as much as she wanted of it. I had some matches and I brought the hatchet and the buggy whip so we could cut it up and smoke it. I cut off a short piece like a cigar, and so did Henrietta, but the Henchman, thinking doubtless that if a short one would taste good a long one would taste better, hacked off a piece about a foot long and smoked it - with very much difficulty. It was manual labor, but Henrietta and I didn't have so far to draw in the smoke, so we got along better. But a buggy whip cigar is rather strong. We laid ours down after about five minutes and filled in the time with conversation. Jim had already laid his down and laid himself down beside it. He keeled over in a pale, red-kilted heap. It was the figs as much as anything, I guess. He looked figgy. But he got over it presently.

"I," said Henrietta, "am going to be a hired girl when I get big." "I'm going to be a pirate," said the Henchman, instantly.

They asked me what I was going to be, but I have no wish except to grow up into a grown woman and to get away - away, to the other side of the horizon, where I'm sure are wonderful things that glitter and dazzle - to break the chrysalis, to be free: the desire of the moth for the star.

*

I have had my wish.

"The bird of time has but a little way to flutter," and alack, the bird even then was "on the wing." I have got to the other side of the horizon and seen and touched the wonderful things. And it's to never, never return. Much farther off now is the day of the Primitive Kid than ever was the horizon at that time. I think of Henrietta as the companion of another life, and wonder where she is. In me rises a hope that the gods have been kind to her, and that their largess included limitless brown sugar. And I wonder what fates gathered in the hired girl, and whether they battered her, and "who's kissing her now." As for the Henchman - vanished, gone. Back of me as I write sits what once was he - with a volume of de Maupassant and a pipe, and a measure of contempt and indifference in his philosophy that rivals even mine. He is not indeed a pirate, but it's possible he is a henchman - of another color.

I mix me a mental cocktail - of the gin of introspect, the vermouth of retrospect, and the subtle bitter of unshed tears - and I drink it to the memory of: Henrietta, the Henchman, the Hired Girl, and me.

"Mary MacLane Wants a Vote - For the Other Woman"

Butte Evening News · 17 April 1910

If the world were not so full of other interesting things and if I hadn't already a lot to occupy my mind, I think I should take up the cause of woman suffrage, to do what I might for it, be it little or much. I believe in sanity and justice and I believe in the honor and integrity of women - my experience has been that they're of far more dependable and less hysterical a quality than those of men - and these United States sadly need such things in their bodies politic. Their bodies politic, beginning with Italian laborers at two dollars a vote and ending with senators in bought seats, are extremely rotten. They couldn't possibly be worse and might be bettered. The franchise for women is the obvious thing needful.

Most men are by nature grafters and parasites. Some women are, not by nature but by training and influence of environment, grafters and parasites. But most of women, when they do turn themselves inside out in the sight of the world, reveal an independence of viewpoint, and a freedom and a bravery of soul that cannot possibly be bought with money. It is all that the politics of the country needs - something that cannot be bought with money. When all women are voting - they will be twenty years from now - that quality will have made itself felt. There is something in the nature of most women which loves to give of itself, and to suffer long, without recompense. It is not too subtle a quality to infuse itself into their politics and to evince itself in the end.

There are men, plenty of men, one observes in passing, who also love to give - but for value received, always for value received.

What I most admire about the suffragists, of forty years ago and now, is their willingness and readiness to suffer for their cause. It is a rare trait in this, the day of the four-flusher. If the cause of woman suffrage had not in itself one merit, or one tottering leg to stand on, or was the tenet of fools, it still would be a fine thing and a poetic thing for the heroic sincerity that gave it birth, and that keeps it living, and that finally will triumph.

What makes woman suffrage interesting to me is not the issue itself - that, if you ask me, is a most weighty bore - but the spirit and the personalities it has brought forth. For what I care personally about them, these United States might go to rack and ruin and I should not miss so much as one stroke of my finger-nail buffer, or one swipe of my powder-rag, to help them out. But to show my belief in such women as Susan Anthony, a hero and a martyr if ever there was one, I enthusiastically and gladly would go in sackcloth. Woman suffrage never before had, and belike never will have again, another such woman for a leader. It's alas! at this restless and crucial near-crisis of it, that she is deep in her quiet grave. Still, her soul, like John Brown's, goes marching on. It stands for strength, nobility, and truth. Those things by themselves hold their own and inevitably win out - and to a person like me, whose life is made up of the picturesque romanticnesses, the fascinating treacheries, the exquisitely cruel slips 'twixt the cup and the lip, the iridescent trivialities - to such as me they have their own deep compelling and enthralling charm. Countless people, through countless ages, though they know it not, have ranged themselves on the side of a cause, not at all for itself or its issues, but for adoration of and belief in a leader. The Coeur de Lion, in his medieval mail, by the potent power of his personality, led a terrific rabble of pagans and heathen soldiers of fortune, not a tenth percent of whom cared a farthing dip about it, into the holy land to retrieve the sepulcher of the Christ. It has been so with many another magnetic leader, from Julius Caesar in his Gallic wars to Theodore Roosevelt at San Juan Hill. The great mass of the suffragettes are interested chiefly in the advancement of suffrage, but there are still many others who, like me, would go into it with what sincerity they might for the sake of the strong-hearts to whom it's vital.

I believe the most fascinating quality of the human mind and the rarest, when all's said, is sincerity - and next after that enthusiasm, that thing of fire and passion which, when given leeway, bids the sleeping soul awake in the dankest clay that breathes.

It's by those two things that the suffragists of forty years ago blazed the trail for those of the present day. Susan Anthony, gently bred and frail of body, went undaunted, *sans* fear and *sans* reproach, to a villainous county jail to live for months, amid a mixed company of prostitutes and drug-tainted women, rather than pay the fine, or let her friends pay it, which was the alternative penalty for her "improper use of the ballot": the casting of her vote for president. The speeches of Mrs. Stanton on the floor of the Senate, as literature, as the expression of a high-wrought, deep-fired mind, and as logical argument for her cause, were recorded among the big things that were heard there, and are so recorded yet. That not-too-sane, but entirely picturesque and delightful woman, Victoria Woodhull, and her almost-as-picturesque sister, Tennessee Claflin, in the hey-day of their youth, of their insolent beauty and good looks, and of their brilliant mentalities, turned their young energies into the channel of the suffrage movement with all the ardor of their hearts, and lent to a somber and half-lost cause a parti-colored impetus. If woman suffrage is not like ever to have another advocate so strong, so loyal, and so noble-minded as Susan Anthony, it is equally unlikely to have one so picturesque, so valiant, so absolutely "game" as the handsome young Woodhull of the veiled star eyes and the goddess brow. She followed up all her enthusiasms with a headlong belief in their rightness and justness, and a scornful regardlessness of the cost to herself, which could make in a day twenty thousand friends for the cause and twenty thousand foes for her. She made countless mistakes, but the honor of her intent redeemed them all. The eloquence of Elizabeth Stanton and Julia Howe, and the example of Susan Anthony and Lucy Stone, meant the enrollment in the ranks of all women whom they reached. But only Victoria Woodhull, though, too, well worshiped by women, ever succeeded, on her lecture platform and off it, in hammering the cold iron of masculine indifference into malleable conversion. It was, of course, mostly her star eyes, and the slender grace of her body, and the rippling dusk of her hair, that brought her the masculine consideration - and she knew it well. She brought every gift and talent and advantage she owned into the woman suffrage game - she knew its need. Her life, set as it was in New York (then as now a city of Treacherous Delights), might have been one of beflowered gaiety. But she cast in her lot with the reformers of her day and found in it, as she made it for others, a toil and a task more enthralling, by reason at once of its humanness and its truth, than even the world-old pursuit of the flying Pleasure. She likewise went to jail in punishment for some of her zeal, but with a high courage, as Marie Antoinette to the guillotine.

All those are of a by-gone day, but the history of their efforts is the most informing and convincing that the cause has yet shown. There was a splendid desolation about them in their battle for what they knew was, and would be while they lived, a hopeless cause.

The latter-day suffragettes are of lesser depth and lesser patriotism and more hysteria - probably only because the political situations of now have an element of complexity and atrocity which was not known forty years ago. For the sincerity and enthusiasm of them equals that of the pioneers, and they are as ready to sacrifice and to suffer. It is not wonderful that they do not reveal much patriotism, for these United States are rapidly becoming a country in which it's difficult to be patriotic, what with the intricate and involved mixing of the races, and what with the blowing off of our fingers and ears on July 4th by way of delicate commemoration of the Signing. The early suffragists worked for patriotism and justice, whereas the modern ones work chiefly for justice. But it's all to the same end.

The chief point at issue is that since all men vote, all women should be allowed to. If the Italian laborers, the kind who work on roads and dig trenches for the water-pipes, a detestable and abysmally ignorant crew - if all those vote, then all the fragile young women who come out of their dark holes, when the electric globes flare on Fourteenth street in New York, to patrol that thoroughfare till dawn, should each have the privilege of selling her vote for the most it will bring. If all the black bell-hops in the apartment hotels - but few are under age - are let to express their political views in the form of votes for president, then equally every chamber-maid should have the same right - e'en though she knows no more of the platforms and their issues than a mermaid at the bottom of the Red Sea. There will be time and room to reform those conditions when the first most glaring injustice is righted.

Having got all which out of my system, as they say on the "vodeville" stage, I feel free to put forth my own private and erratic brand of views anent the subject. Much and sincerely as I admire and feel inspired by the Anthonys and the Woodhulls, and the Ida Harpers, and the Carrie Chapman Catts, and the Mrs. Pankhursts and militant suffragettes in England, as a heroic cult, and much as I'm interested in the cause itself, I, M. Mac-Lane, personally would be an extremely unfit person to hold the ballot. And I'm so well aware of the fact that I never would bother to vote though all my sisters-in-arms were going, loaded and primed, to the polls. I am governed only by my impulses and affections and led on by the fascinations with which life for me is always rife. And I should cast a vote on the same picturesque principles, if I cast one at all, with no regard for such tiresome things as safe, sane conservatism. I should never, for instance, vote for a fat president no matter how much the country needed him or how ripping a chief executive he would make. I should never have voted for Rutherford B. Hayes because I don't like people with beards, nor for Franklin Pierce because he was, from my viewpoint, an uncompromisingly plain-faced man and a dead wire. If by chance I should vote 'twould be, belike, for a picturesque villain with "some class" to him. I don't think I should ever sell my vote, but I should vote for anyone who seemed physically delightful, let the rest of him be what it might. There are - no doubt at all - many, many women who would go to it after the same delirious methods - and equally, though they'll not at all admit it, there are a million men, and then some more, voting now in these United States, whose opinions are formed and whose choice is made on exactly the same basis. Mental hysteria is by no means confined to women, and for crass, unreasoning, pig-headed prejudice, commend me every time to the *genus homo*. Take it from me, the real, twin-screw, double-funneled, copper-bottomed level-headedness of this broad and pit-fall'd world is all in the women. Men are the dreamers and fanatics, the superstitious and the gullible. Their level-headedness has ever some "bug" in it - my word, no, when it comes to voting for president I shouldn't be there - I should find more interest in sitting at home and mending me a pair of blue silk stockings, the while going over in my mind the affairs of the heart I might then be engaged in. I don't much believe in presidents, anyway. They don't seem to change anything, benefit anything, or "start" anything. Patent medicines with wood alcohol in them are still being sold to the public, and white-faced children are still working in mills and mines. Trusts and combines are yet solid with themselves, and the hook-worm remains rampant and triumphant. So, what's the use? But if we were to change our form of government to a monarchy and the women and men were to go forth and elect a king, I for one would be there, as the poets say, with bells on. A monarchy is a sane and level-headed sort of political arrangement, and more than that - it's picturesque - there's class to it. Instead of a small, framed, not-too-well-kept-up house of complicated architecture, with cloth palms sitting around in the main hall, and ratty-looking old portraits on the walls, there'd be a gray stone palace at Washington with a thousand windows reflecting the red glows at sunset, and with lackeys galore inside it, and a court-scene, like those in Shakespeare, two or three times a week. The clothes of the queen and the ladies-in-waiting would be like rainbows and roses and would rival the raiment of Solomon in all his glory - and even those of the lords would be of a stylishness. There would be a royal family that would be dear to the nation merely by reason of its being our own - we should feel a potent personal interest in its births and deaths and educations and marriages. We should each feel that we slightly owned it. A nation can't possibly feel that way about a president that it loses every four years. A president bears the same relation to a king that the modern swift-coming-and-going kitchen mechanic bears to the old-fashioned hired girl who would live in a family nineteen years. There is no such adoration rife in these United States for one president as is apparent to the stranger in the Netherlands, from the Dutch nation to their young sovereign and her tiny heiress - or even as the malcontent Spaniards show to theirs, with his girlish queen and plump princelings. Mr. Taft is probably a very nice man, but we don't adore him yet. And as soon as we begin to get used to him, and maybe fond of him, he'll have to go. What we need is tradition and a sense of permanency and duration. We need more patriotism and fewer presidents. Until we get it, which *certes* will be quite some time, I, for one, am not going to be much interested in the politics of this domain. I am a deal keener for prizefighting - I am strong for the virile heroes of the ring.

But I'm still stronger for the qualities of sincerity and enthusiasm - which brings me back to the suffragists and my deep belief in them. The wide, long, ancient curse upon women includes limitless waiting and limitless durance and an infinite hoping against hope. They will win out, beyond a doubt's shadow, in a dozen or fourteen years, or less. And when women do get the franchise, their work and their battling will have just begun. There will come up, with the achievement of equal rights, a subtle antagonism of the sexes which will wage below the surface like a long love war, and in which women will always, always be worsted. Not that they'll be defeated - very far from it, with their weapons of intuition and finesse. But it will be theirs to take the hurts, and theirs to bear the consequences, theirs to count to reckoning and theirs to pay it. But theirs, too, will be a certain brave bliss - the fruit of long loyalty and long labor. It will be enough: their Reward.

"Men Who Have Made Love to Me"

Butte Evening News · 24 April 1910

This article is going to be very egotistical and MacLanesque and maybe somewhat shocking besides, so I strongly advise divers citizens of Butte not to read it. It occurs to me that some of the things I write do not agree with the constitutions of the said citizens - it seems to be bad for their livers - hence this preliminary note of warning. So now if you go right on and read it and it affects your liver unpleasantly, don't blame me.

To the others I fain would say here this, that I aim not to instruct in these articles, neither do I aim to better people's morals, nor in fact to bore people in any other way. My aim is to write something to entertain those who pay a nickel-a-throw for the Sunday *News* - to entertain them in the vaudeville way, artistically if I can, but, anyway, cheerfully, gayly, after the drive-dull-care-away method. If only the citizens of Butte would regard me as vaudeville and read me, with a patter and kettle-drum chorus, only to be entertained! But no, the stuff comes out on Sunday and so they read it at breakfast and assuage their consciences for not going to church by knocking it and me. And they call me a menace. All right - I'll be a menace, and if they don't look out I'll be "some menace." But at that I'll be a gay menace, a menace bound in red and gold, a menace with hair in little curls, a men-ace with bells on, a menace de luxe. Perhaps I'll come out as the original menace. I'll hit up the menacing business in Butte - I'll let my friends in cheap at the bottom - and we'll all go a-menacing together. It'll be quite fine and dandy. And all owing to the nifty parties who read my stuff at or after their Sunday morning breakfast and don't go to church.

I am herewith going to make a few *genre* pictures of men I have known and loved. I would rather write about women because men are so nearly all alike and are such conventional masculine beasts, anyway. But the editor of this neat sheet said men for this article - (it'll be women in another one) - so what can a poor girl do?

Since the spring of 1902, that lucky time when I ceased to be I and became M. MacLane and left little old Butte to go and fathom the mysteries that lie along the Atlantic seaboard in the depths of cities, when I knew completely nothing about the element masculine - since that time I have met upwards of a thousand men. The women at first fought shy of me for the most part, but the men came and went in my life in a never-ending stream, like a long glittering galaxy of little gods. So I know quite a lot about them. I shan't write everything I know - 'twould hardly bear it - but from the thronged memories within me I'll cull a few types - like as: the Callow Youth, the Literary Man, the Bank Clerk, the Prize-Fighter, the Absinthe Drinker, the Middle-Aged Gambler, the Younger Son, and the Husband of Another.

If all these types seem to make love to me don't be surprised or alarmed. It's the only reason I happen to know anything about them, and besides men always make love to women - always.

The Callow Youth: I knew him first in St. Augustine, Florida, where I used to spend my winters. St. Augustine is a be-palmed and be-poinsettiaed winter resort of wonderful hotels, small in territory and congested in visiting population. One meets a motley moneyed company there - people from darkest Pittsburgh and deepest Indiana. And into my life one winter there blew a Callow Youth, aged but twenty: I being twenty-four. He was not only callow, but was a gilded sort of youth as well, a golden lad. His hair was the color of benedictine, his outlook on life was assured and mostly sanguine, and he looked a dream in white duck without a hat and with his sleeves rolled up over his bronzed biceps. He had a doting mother and an acrid spinster cousin, by way of family, in Stamford, Connecticut, and he himself was a Yale sophomore. But at the time I met him he was out of that institution on an involuntary vacation, the sole information he gave me on the subject being, "Poor mamma! She doesn't know I'm down here. You see it would worry her - and so needlessly - to know I'd got suspended just for wrecking a fire-engine." He had absolutely no sense of humor - his type never has, and the lack is either quite fatal or else the most delicious thing in the world. 'Twas the latter in the case of the Callow Youth - his callow name was Gerald - he took himself and all the world with a seriousness that was colossal, and for some mysterious reason he fancied himself in love with me. And for the time - and *pour passer le temp* - it was not difficult to imagine oneself in love with him. He and I used to amble together at sunset when the bells of the ancient cathedral sent languid chimes out over the sea and the low waves splashed the sea-wall at noon-tide, and the sky was of opals and amethysts. And thus the Callow Youth: "You know, Mary, you're the only woman I've ever known who understood me at all, and you don't know how much it means to a man. You see, a man's got to have sympathy from some woman or nothing's worth while. There are plenty who'll tell you they love you, without really being sympathetic, like poor Fluff, for instance." ("Poor Fluff" was a personage with intensely yellow hair, by surname O'Rourke, who had supported Trixie Friganza in the chorus of "The American Idea.") "Fluff was an uncommon girl in every way, and an awfully good sort, but she always wanted so much sympathy herself, you know - it made it awkward. Now, you're so different. There's just one woman in all the world for me, from now on. Everything and everybody are dead set against me, except you, and if you should fail me now there'd be nothing before me but the grave."

At which point I always looked away at the line of opals and amethysts, whereupon he glanced at me with, "You may not even yet quite comprehend me, Mary - you may think me young and all that rot, but I tell you, truly and really, I'm a devil of a fellow when I get started." Alack, that he never did get "started," whatever that may mean. 'Twas full three weeks before he bored me.

The Literary Man: a type that is rife in New York town, and quite the coldest, hardest, brutalest of all who walk its busy marts, but with a certain scourge-like charm of its own - he was my *bete noir* for a matter of months. I was not happy with him nor away from him. He possessed that pleasant faculty of keeping me in a chronic state of tolerable misery. And this his manner of speech the while he sat in my little den smoking my cigarettes and damaging sundry of my little belongings - pictures or pillows or articles of *vertu* by roughly handling them as he talked: "Mary - Mary, you're such an incomparable idiot! I've known you long enough by this time to cease to expect even ordinary decency and propriety from that twisted concoction you call your personality - but up to now I have given you credit for ordinary intelligence. The things that I impressed upon you as distinctly not to be said, at that tea-fight yesterday, were the very things you said, and now see what's come of it - you utter fool! You have just cost me six useful friends merely by sheer wanton recklessness. I wonder if there can ever be such a thing as keeping a tab on your insanity and reckoning on it, or whether it will always be a little blighting curse on us both." Said I, in extreme discomfort, "That being the case, why don't we just drop things right here?" On my left third finger blazed an oriental stone of deep-toned red, the outward and visible sign that the Literary Man and I had exchanged betrothal vows. The Literary Man: "Oh, I've promised myself to break it off - a hundred times. You've cost me so much in every way! But sometimes, and almost, I think possibly you're worth it. Let's go over to Mouquin's and talk things over." We talked things over infinitely that winter, and a countless number of times - and he called me a liar, and an evil spirit, and an imp of darkness, and various other names, besides tramping rough-shod on my already battered heart. But withal it was I who finally broke it off, quietly and triumphantly, and with the pleasant feeling of knowing that it left him in a carping, dissatisfied mood, and with a set of assorted qualms which I think even yet flit, hornet-like, through his mind.

The Bank Clerk: his temperament may not be typical of bank clerks, and yet I've found it characteristic of men in those clerical positions which occupy them from eight in the morning till six in the evening, working for an employer, and leaving them thereafter time to indulge their poetic dreams. I have never known a magazine poet - and New York teems with them - who really had any romance in him. They are all much more interested in sausages and beer and poker games. But in clerks, from law-readers to bartenders, it runs like a vein of precious metal.

The Bank Clerk: - a tall, slightly consumptive looking, rather ordinary chap of six-and-thirty - I recollect his eyes were set somewhat too close together - I knew him in Boston, a picturesque old town which harbored me five years, a town full of delicate incongruities and as capable, in its way, as New York of being one's undoing - and New York's indeed but five hours away from it. The Bank Clerk: he had made up his mind, years before, that when he happened upon a young woman of ordinary good looks and possessed of an imagination, a soul above beer and skittles, he would straightway fall in love with her and ask the favor of her hand in marriage. Well, he happened upon me, and realizing only that I had an imagination, and not that I was also a perfect devil - he foolishly fell in love with me and asked the favor of my hand in marriage. And I - I never intended to marry him, but for a matter of eleven days my left third finger bore a glittering diamond set between two scintillant sapphires. Because my own name was too ordinary he called me Rosemary; we walked on the Common Sunday noons and week-day evenings, in the teeth of November winds, the while he spoke: "To think that my long dream is realized and She is walking by my side! My dear - my dear, do you know how I look forward to six weeks from today? I have saved up for the last dozen years about six thousand dollars out of my fool salary - and all for my wedding journey! Though I've had none but a phantom bride - still I laid it up against the time when she'd be Living Reality and she and I would make a wedding journey together. Six weeks - think of it! - and you and I will have quitted this frozen New England for Naples - we'll have landed on the shores of fair Italy, where the skies are ever blue. Can you fancy, my Rosemary, the bay of Naples at nightfall, with an indigo sky above it, hung with stars such as Massachusetts will never know - stars like immense yellow daffodils and seeming so near that almost we might reach up with our hands and gather them - stars like golden tears from the tender eyes of some mammoth night goddess - stars that will be blooming there but for us? We'll rest on some rocky promontory between sea and sky, surrounded by the soft black silence, unbroken save for the remote voices of singing fishermen many feet below, and the low music of the orchestras in the little cafes that edge the bay. It will be a soft black world lit but with yellow daffodils, voiced but with far-off music, and melting with the nameless enchantments of only you and me and the feelings in us."

Thus the Bank Clerk, to whom I listened fascinated, for he meant it all. Yet - not for mine. If ever there's a wedding journey for me 'twill be to London, to nowhere but London, that vast mixture of Babylon, Ancient Rome, and itself. As for the Bank Clerk - Boston is full of women - may he have found one, a better one - which might be, easily, and may they have had their day in fair Italy, where the skies are ever blue.

The Prize-Fighter: I met him in New York: a featherweight of local fame, with the lithe grace of a Greek disc thrower, the brows and lips of a demi-god, and the eyes and mind of an unreflective terrier. His succinct name was Red, though his very beautiful hair was of a deep orange color, and though his clothes were well-tailored his taste in neckties was something indeed fierce. With him have I gone many a summer's day down to Coney, and many an evening to Sharkey's, or to Port Arthur or some Chinese restaurant down the Bowery, and many a night have we danced away a half-dozen golden hours in the Third avenue dance-halls. He was a delight to at least three-fourths of my senses - I think he gave me more unmixed pleasure on the little jaunts we took than any man I've yet known. "Kiddo," he said one evening, over a chop-suey, "you sure've got me going. There ain't another skirt on the planet. Jimmy Ryan, frien' o' mine, manager of the Idle Hour, 'e says to me the other night, 'e says, 'Just cast yer lamps over this bunch o' skirts on the floor,' e' says, 'and pick the winner - she's yours.' But I shakes me head an' I says, 'Jimmy, I know a kiddo that's got 'em all skinned forty ways' - and, kiddo, that goes. You don't want me money and y'er the only skirt I ever knowed that was on the level. I was dippy about you the first time we went out to Coney, and I'm dippy about you yet. You may chuck me away any day - I know you ain't in me class - but I'd be dippy still." He himself was one square pal while I knew him, and he never failed to thrill me to my very finger-tips. I'm wondering, with qualms and regrets, if indeed he's dippy still.

The Absinthe Drinker: him, too, I knew in New York. He was good-looking in a pallid sort of way, a slender, tallish young man, a *dilettante* in letters, and a follower - if that can be called following which bothers not even to note the direction of its leader - of an extremely indifferent, light-hearted, indolently-reckless cult. I was fond of him for two reasons - that the light-hearted and reckless always make an appeal to me, and that I felt my conscience in a perpetual state of assuagement (like the citizens of Butte at their Sunday morning breakfasts) by being myself in a state of but half-approval of his tenets. Every time I held back and took exception to his modes of thought, I reflected, "What a good sort I must be, to disapprove of this." It's a pleasant feeling. In the Cafe Martin, Twenty-sixth street and Fifth avenue, at four o'clock, we spent a hundred afternoons, listening to the music, watching the people, desultorily talking, and looking upon the absinthe in its cold, sinister, death-colored seduction. The Drinker drank eight absinthe frappes in the hour, while I ambled through one. "To think," said I in half-sad protest, "that it's slowly killing you, that you've been slowly dying for two years and are slowly dying now!" And said he quickly, "But, my child, what a sweet, sweet death to die! We are all dying, you know, from one cause or another - we are all, in this orchid-decked room, slowly moving toward our graves. So how much better to go with this exquisite poison in our veins, with the taste of it on our lips, and the flavor of it in our hearts! It brings us the flower of life and the music of the spheres - it would bring them to you if you'd give way to it and take it as I do, with ardor and delight. We would then slowly die together - a primrose death. It softens all the heart-breaks of life. My soul and body are dedicated to it and it, like a Green God of Misericorde, giveth me sundry good gifts in high reward. So drink, my child, drink to the primrose death." I drank with him that spring too often, to the primrose death, but always under a protest - a protest not strong enough to let me refuse my one thin glass, and so much the less strong to make his number smaller. Presently an invisible grave began to yawn too near his careless feet. He was a charming thing, the Absinthe Drinker, but my friendship with him blew away in the autumn winds like the scattering of dead leaves.

The Middle-Aged Gambler: the memory of him brings me mirth. He was hard-headed and hard-hearted (except in my direction), with hard-looking iron-gray hair, and hard-looking fishy gray eyes. He had race-horses at Sheepshead and a great deal of money. I liked him because he was one more type of humanity, and it was my plan to crowd all the people and all the experiences I might into my life while living in New York - knowing that some day Butte-Montana, of deadly-thrall fame, would be again my portion. Besides, the Gambler was kind to me, though he was the sort of man who by nature is hard on women - hard on their souls and hearts and bodies, a flinty experience in their lives. He had a penchant for slim sweet feminine youth with an admixture of subtle brain, and he fancied I filled that bill. He came ever and anon to see me in my little green-and-white apartment in Twenty-seventh street, into which he fitted with that aptness proverbially accredited to a bull in a china shop. He would glance contemptuously around at its thin lack of luxury as he walked about in it - he himself lived in apartments of bizarre and barbaric splendor - and would regard me with amorous compassion. "Kid," said he, "I've got to run out to Pittsburgh for a couple of days, and when I come back we must have this thing settled. I've told you before now that I'm crazy about you - and you know I am - I needn't go over that ground again. You can do whatever you like about me, but Kid, I'm damned if I'll go on like this. You need some one to take care of you - and you've got to agree to let me do it. I've thrown that into you fifty times, and I'm going to keep on throwing it into you till you agree to something. After that, whatever you want - I don't care what it is - anything in New York - just hand me the tip and I'll come through with the coin. Whatever I clean up on the ponies - but I've told you all that before. Come, Kid, be nice to me - say something kind." - I liked him better than literary men, anyway.

As for the others, the Younger Son and the Husband of Another - I'm supposed to hold the stage but seventeen minutes in this vaudeville stunt, so it's to dismiss them with cursory glances. The Younger Son was the younger son of a baronet in England, who had been busily engaged since the hour of his birth in doing nothing whatsoever. He wore a monocle. "But I'm frightfully interested in you, Mary," said he, "and New York's a frightfully interesting place - frightfully."

He and I wandered languidly around New York, languidly out to Brighton, languidly up to the Bronx, and languidly down to Coney. Languidly he loved and languidly he rode away. He had filled me with languid laughter while he stayed, then languidly I "ditched" him. A quaint experience was the Younger Son. He had managed to waste a shocking lot of my time, but then - he was so frightfully classy!

The Husband of Another: the most exasperating invention known to civilized man. He railed at his wife and wept on my doorstep four in the morning. Indeed, one never knew just when he wasn't going to burst into tears - otherwise one might have avoided those damp incidents. "If only I had met you thirteen years ago," he wailed, "the tragedy of all this might have been averted." "Thirteen years ago," said I, "I was just twelve years of age. I didn't know a tragedy from a glass of lemonade - and cared considerably less. Now kindly retreat from this, my little abode, for I've got to make a quick change and go uptown for dinner." "Always hard - cold - heartless with me now," said he, gazing at me with a large, heavy, sodden, and most annoying brand of reproach. "Is it because I'm married? Is it? Oh, but had I known you thirteen years ago!" and he managed to change the gay, chaste atmosphere of my little flat into a briny gloom, flavored with what may be termed the juice of forbidden fruit. The Husband of Another - I recall him now, and from this distance, without exasperation - with no feeling at all, in fact, but one of gratitude that the gods did not lead him up to me thirteen years ago.

So there were eight of the little gods. There were more. May there be others! A fascinating, fascinating game. One's loves are so real - while they last. And thereafter - one day later - of what are they made, and where are they?

The nightingale that in the branches sang,
Ah, whence, and whither flown again, who knows?

Yet - how much better to be wondering whither and whence the nightingale than never to have heard its mad trill!

"The Latter-Day Litany of Mary MacLane"

Butte Evening News · 8 May 1910

The psychology of antipathy, if you ask me, is far and away the most subtle and potent branch of all psychology. And in the average mind it's the last and least to be marked and digested. We're far from recognizing that it's the things we don't like, not the things we like, that make up our temperaments. Our personalities and individualities are founded on our hatreds and not on our loves. When you say, "I'm fond of apricots," you're revealing much less of your nature than when you say, "I hate rice pudding." The antipathy is the stronger quality, the combative one - the other is the going with the current. The victorious achievements of the world were conceived and born of dislikes, disagreements, and discontents. The effects of our hatreds on other persons and the effects of other persons' hatreds on us are what set wheels turning and machinery moving in this mooted scheme of things. One might name a thousand instances of that, of a thousand different adaptations, but all to the same purpose. The one which comes to my mind at the moment is this: About thirteen years ago, when I and my family lived over in Great Falls, my sister and I were at the carping half-grown age when sisters, with any spirit in their veins and brains in their heads, some days quarrel long and bitterly for hours over points of the utmost unimportance. My sister and I quarreled with unusual ferocity and tenacity, times - partly because she had more than ordinary brains and imagination, with spit-firey tendencies as well, and partly because I had, at thirteen or thereabouts, what is commonly known as the very-devil-of-a-temper and a contrary self-will which nothing in the world, short of a heavy charge of giant powder - which never was tried on it - could quell. Add to this that we had to wash dishes together three times a day, during those periods between the leaving of one greasy hired girl (all hired girls seem to have been greasy in Great Falls) and the coming of another - and you have more than sufficient data to presuppose many a Brutus-and-Cassius tent scene. My sister has since remarked of us that we were "easily dissatisfied." There was one period when for all of eight months no be-greased slave reigned in our kitchen, and during that time it seemed to us that we washed at least a million dishes. We wished a great many things in those days, but chief among them all was the deep desire that our family might go back to a state of Primeval Man, where dishes were not. We agreed on no other point in life where it was possible to disagree, but over dish-washing our feelings were entirely mutual. My sister washed them and I wiped them - a rule which never varied, a sort of unwritten law. Now the point I wish to make is this: On days when we were friends and pals, and tempers were in a quiescent state, and all was serene, we would go into the kitchen after dinner, at about seven in the evening, to begin on the dinner dishes, and we would amble and linger and dally and wander-at-will through our dish-washing, with the utmost nonchalance and abandon. While we washed and wiped we beguiled the time by ripping our friends up the back, in making very indifferent puns, to each of which we paid the tribute of the wild and spontaneous ha-ha, and in singing (with voices more to be pitied than scorned) the deadly popular songs of the day. My sister would warble at me, "Two little girls in blue - one was forty before the flood, the other was forty-two," and I would retaliate with, "But I'd rather have the Bowery - Bow-e-ry." Or she would gaily chant, "There's a name that's never spoken, there's a *something's* heart that's broken, and a picture that is turned toward the wall," and I would trill out in my turn - "Knows the secret, knows it well, but yet I dare not tell, Sweet Mah-ree." After which we would try to sing each other down in one terrific rousing chorus, she with the "Wild Man from Borneo" and I with "Her Golden Hair was Hanging Down Her Back," like the Cherry Sisters singing down an orchestra. (My sister and I might have made a hit in vaudeville at that time, could we but have known it - "The Dishmop Sisters in Their Refined Singing Skit" - something like that.) The consequence of all which was that eight, nine, ten, and sometimes eleven o'clock came, and went, and we were still washing and wiping and driving dull care away in the kitchen with "Girls, quit that nonsense and get through there," or "Whatever in the world are those crazy things about in there," coming ever and anon through the swinging doors. But on the other hand, on days when we coldly hated each other, we would begin our dinner dishes at seven o'clock and would go through with them in fifteen minutes. There was no dallying, no sounds of song, pun, backbiting, and revelry. We would quarrel in short, sharp staccato, the while washing and wiping with the passionate quickness of heated tempers. My sister would wash a cup or a plate with lightning rapidity, and I would snatch it up and wipe it almost before 'twas set down. I have seen a stream of saucers slip out of her hands and into mine almost without a pause, and forks and spoons and knives were literally caught and wiped on the fly. And I recollect how she would sort of push the tin pans at me, in a way that was in itself an insult, and I would jerk them from her in a manner that was another. But the crux of the matter was: we would do up those dishes in fifteen minutes. And it demonstrates my point. Lovingkindness made for dawdling and dalliance - hatred made for strength and achievement.

And it's ever thus. Five or six years later I, for one, became a young monument of discontent - I hated everything around me. And out of that mental condition I achieved an audacious and original bit of literary success, which meant a lot of money, a wealth of experience, and an entire and absolute change of the face of all my world. Had it not been for the hatreds and malcontents it never would have been.

Which brings me back to what I at first said and will maintain, that our individualities are founded on our hatreds and not on our loves. Which in its turn brings me back to the subject of the Litany in the red Mary-MacLane book. Next to the Tooth-brush chapter, I believe the Litany received the most comment and acclaim. I was portraying a personality in all the chapters, but the Litany, since it chronicled my dislikes, was a nearer view of it than any of the others. I use the Devil but as a makeshift in the following present-day Litany, and because I used him in the first one. The Devil served his turn very well in the book, but he has since mostly outlived his usefulness with me. He was a sort of shadowy love of mine at nineteen - but having since had a young succession of real ones, the Devil's hopelessly outclassed. But to our muttons: First of all, from cockroaches, beyond all things (except one which I can't mention, because the *News* has to go through the mails - but all my friends know it, anyway): Kind Devil, deliver me.

From union-suits; from red ink; from a black satin petticoat; from the kind of man who calls me cold-blooded because I refuse to sit holding hands with him after I've known him just four minutes; from the people with hankerings for "culture"; from spinach and dandelion greens with sand in them; from incorrect grammar; from the flat Western pronunciation of the letter "a"; from reckless rhetoric; from the hideous and disgusting old foul humor of Rabelais; from a bed or a cocoa nut cake that sinks in the middle; from human beings with malice and cruelty of heart in them: Kind Devil, deliver me.

From scarlet fever; from people who do their thinking on the outside of their heads; from slap-stick comedians; from bent pins and unsharpened lead-pencils; from pikers and hedgers; from a cocktail made with Italian vermouth; from bed-fellows who eat cookies; from cross-eyed butchers; from false teeth, tape-worms, floating kidneys, and glass eyes; from the odor of a dead rat behind a wainscoting: Kind Devil, deliver me.

From the feeling of blotting-paper on my finger-tips; from the sound and look of anyone else's finger-tips rubbing across rough paper; from the feeling of a cotton sheet on the tip of my tongue; from the feeling of granulated sugar in the palm of my hand; from the feeling of a bit of card-board against my teeth; from the feeling of a woolen string in the center of my neck; from the feeling of a Wilton carpet on the sole of my foot; from all feelings which horrify the exquisite nerves of me: Kind Devil, deliver me.

From fat men; from a fish in a platter that has been dead o'er long; from the dressmakers mentioned in my first Litany; from short-hipped corsets; from nice young men; from time-pieces that do not record the time; from women who entirely lack virtue and reserve; from women who are all-too virtuous; from cotton stockings; from intoxicated, soused, inebriated, pickled, and drunk men; from songs with monkeys in them; from tight-wads; from perfumed soap; from very curly hair: Kind Devil, deliver me.

From bed-rooms in Atlantic City and Saratoga hotels with too-thin walls; from men I don't care about who insist on kissing me good-night; from a cake flavored with benzine in mistake for rose-water; from Easter eggs; from photographs of corpses with their eyes pushed open; from a pillow-slip too tight for its pillow; from a pie with a sodden under-crust; from jealousy which takes the form of tears, poisoned candy, reproach, and dirk-knives; from Turks; from half-baked poets: Kind Devil, deliver me.

From butter-scotch that tastes of onions; from cake and people that are cloyingly sweet; from postage stamps with no gum on them; from dainty men; from embarrassing loves; from technical chewers of technical rags; from treachery in the guise of friendship; from the dawn of day before the night is over; from loosely-rolled cigarettes; from a cheap sport: Kind Devil, deliver me.

From cads, bounders, and men who whine; from waiting at an appointed place for a fascinating friend who is late; from things that are plain vulgar; from tiresome affections; from a dusty bedroom; from people who tell me the unpleasant things they hear said about me; from the gnawing pangs of hunger; from high hopes which come to nothing: Kind Devil, deliver me.

From faded violets, from faded orchids and faded daffodils; from the scene of a night's dissipation in the pale morning light; from visions of death among scenes of youth and gaiety; from the ashes of burnt-out fires; from the letters of friends lost and gone and fled away in the gloom; from the shadows of memory; from the ghosts of dead loves; from the lies which once were truth; from the always tragic slips 'twixt the cup and the lip: Kind Devil, deliver me.

From the corrodent, battering, destroying effects of too much emotion upon my slim young body; from the murderous, tormenting effects of grief and loneliness upon my over-wrought nerves; from a revealing of sorrows in my two gray eyes, and of mournfulness in the droop of my two lips; from the least look of resignation and defeat in the inert clasping-together of my hands; from all untoward and bitter things, and the look of them: Kind Devil, deliver me.

From delicate incongruities; from a hat that's been rained on; from a stove that smokes; from a mongrel puppy; from finger-nails too much manicured and finger-nails not manicured enough; from a large, deep, passionate dried-apple pudding; from tooth-brushes in the nude; from a wrinkled skirt; from a newly-prisoned bird; from a cab-driver in the throes of any emotion; from the evidences of a wife and children in a head-waiter; from the tenor in a male quartet; from silver dollars: Kind Devil, deliver me.

From beggar women with dirty faces; from a cape which obviously was plucked from an ash-barrel; from spongy radishes; from mangy muffs; from petty small-minded men; from men who have the unparalleled presumption to hand me advice; from the fuzzy dust that is under a bed; from New York janitors; from the odor of yesterday's cigarettes; from the lingering kiss of one who has been eating garlic; from people who've been hastily put together: Kind Devil, deliver me.

From a slippery bath tub; from Canadian coffee; from a strawberry short-cake with broken glass in it; from an impossible kind of young woman whose specialties are German philosophers, malice, lies, and gossip; from people whose limitations are too obvious; from a newsboy whose logic is that of a decadent hen; from young Italian champagne; from physical discomfort: Kind Devil, deliver me.

From a telephone bell which drags me out of bed at ten in the morning; from the men who are so sure of my moral calibre; from type-writers; from the odor of burning rubber, burning feathers, burning whalebone, and burning bird-seed; from wall-paper with spidery patterns; from false teeth in a glass of water; from people who are prejudiced against the Irish; from June-bugs; from the losing of cherished trinkets: Kind Devil, deliver me.

From the accumulated books which I stole in my youth from Sunday-school libraries; from owing anybody four dollars; from being reminded of letters I haven't answered; from having my days too much occupied to find time to revel in the fascinations of my own thoughts; from the loss of my youth: Kind Devil, deliver me.

From the astonishing assumptions of people anent me, my home life, my family, and my relationships toward my friends; from newspaper writers in the East who are so sure I hate Butte; from the peculiar likenesses of myself that I find in Duluth, Los Angeles, New Orleans, and Denver publications; from press-clipping bureaus: Kind Devil, deliver me.

From the growing cold of love; from the passing away of friendship; from the dying of "The Flower that once has bloomed"; and again, last of all, from cockroaches: Kind Devil, deliver me.

*

There may be other antipathies in my makeup - but if there are, they're but few. I don't dislike nearly so many things in this adorable world as I did in the crude young scorn of nineteen, and, at that, with not the same headlong intensity. Yet the foregoing antipathies are extremely real to me and some of them, times, have caused me exquisite agony. Never a pleasure in my life has so wrought upon those cruelly sensitive strings, my nerves, with an alternative pitch of madding joy to match the anguished quiver I have felt at the sudden happening on one of my aversions.

And I am not peculiar in it. We are all made that way, but almost nobody ever analyzes it. The coming of a new Affair of the Heart, in all its fascinating intricacies and cross-purposes and subtle delights, brings not one-tenth the emotions of pleasure which the same Affair, when lying withered and dead before us, brings of bitterness and desolation and heartbreak. And let nobody say the detailed antipathies are trifles. Believe me. There is sufficient power in my hatred of cockroaches to change the currents of my being and the tenor of my life. There are sufficient punishments in a day's business, for me, to make up, with usury, for all the forbidden fruits I have ever nibbled. And I must pay, heavily, even for the things which themselves punish me. The things I love and the things I hate - their effects, their battering, searing effects, upon my slim young body are all the same. So it's why, then, to ever refrain - from the Cup, for instance, which clears today of regrets and makes the lowering future to seem to bloom like a golden rose?

"The Borrower of Two-Dollar Bills - and Other Women"

Butte Evening News · 15 May 1910

I, of womankind and something-and-twenty years, have by this time con-cluded that those gay buccaneers, the citizens of Butte, whose victims are the set-apart individualities in their midst, are going to put their own peculiar con-struction upon every thing one writes, say what one may to prevent it, which being the case, it's only to let them go ahead and do it. When I find I can not stem a tide I instantly stop trying and move aside with as much of good grace and light-hearted contempt as may be - and I let the wild water rush upon its way. Even though it's a matter one cares about much - still, it's to give but the shrug of a shoulder and to let all effort in the contrary direction die at its birth. When you come right down to it, I am fond of those gay buccaneers, the citizens of Butte. I should prefer that they understood me, rather than to in some ways misunderstand so profoundly as they do. But they never will. No, they never, never will. It's to let it pass. They will in particular misunder-stand some things about this article and the side of me it reveals. I care about it, but, well - *un haussement de m'epaule,* and forever my love to the citizens of Butte. The men I have met and known more or less intimately in my seven years of experience have far outnumbered the women and have been far easier to know and classify and manipulate and manage. But for some inexplicable reasons the women I have known and loved have been the crucial incidents in my life, the real and informing events. They have been alike my staunchest friends and my worst and bitterest enemies - the stars of my night and the murky pools and the pitfalls and snares about my feet. Women have always been, since the days of the Anemone Lady, more interesting to me than men, because they're more complex, more subtle, fuller of delicate incongruities and illusions, harder to understand. Two-thirds of all the women in the world, some consciously and some unconsciously, have the same feeling toward their own kind. There are millions who conventionally marry some worthy and agreeable husband and are happy with him in a perfectly sane and bromidic way - but the while to their woman friends, possibly without knowing it, they give all their poetry, all their imagination, their subtlety, their intricate complexity, their mental concentricity and fascination, and their tenderness of heart. And there are many women who recognize and admit the charmed fact. It is not wonderful. What every woman knows is that each and all of us are cursed with vulnerable fragile bodies, and vulnerable sensitively-sincere hearts which together bring, often and often, an anguished durance so poignantly real as to be the dominating factor of life with us, and yet so remote as to be beyond thought and analysis - beyond everything but feeling, and of which men have not the most shadowy conception. In the plainest language women could tell it in, it will be to men as Greek and Sanskrit; not even the men poets (with - who knows? - the exception of that most wonderful of them all, Robert Browning) know the inner voice of women. Not even Elizabeth Browning, as deeply woman as poet, could write the thing itself, though in her life and in the feeling of her poems it speaks fatally, heartbreaking, albeit with a restrained passion-flower sort of quiescence. It is this thing that to two-thirds of all women is the silent unseen tie that binds.

At that I shall but picture a few hybrid women who have been my friends and half-friends and passing acquaintances in New York of the Treacherous Delights. Women do not come in types except physically and in other outward seeming - each of them is mostly a personality and an individuality unto herself. Outwardly two women, or a dozen, may be of the same type - their bodies may have the same kind of garnishment as to clothes and coiffures and grooming, but inwardly they differ as the poles. One may be a settlement worker and another a kept woman; one may be a cloak model and another a club woman; one may be a plain crook and another a trained nurse - and yet be of one physical and mental caste. Caste - which has nothing to do with class - is possibly the subtlest distinction by which we differentiate human beings, and at first blush we make the mistake of thinking it a matter of breeding and environment and education. It is a long mistake. Caste, as the people of the world are measured, is caste of our physical equipment and the effects of our subsequent lives upon it, combined with the much or little of mental adroitness, which is not mentality, we may develop. It's a fascinating bit of work to determine that subtle distinction of caste among the people one knows, particularly women, and particularly in New York where women are the pervading spirit - the duchesses, the town princesses, the Beloved of the Town; a little nation of Nell Gwynns.

I have not known so many of them as of men, but still, during my last two years in New York, life seethed with women. They were one's companions in the apartment houses where one lived, at matinees, in tea rooms, at the Cafe Martin, in the shops, on Fifth avenue at the ends of the afternoons, on Broadway always, at the apartments of friends - in all the highways and byways. If you're an unattached young woman living alone in New York, and markedly a free-lance, you'll meet up with a million other unattached women. They color up your life and mean adventure - in the day-light and the dark. During my last months in New York I had an apartment - four and a half green-and-white rooms - with a young woman with whom I had once been good friends, but with whom I then maintained but a semi-intimate aloofness suitable for the sharers of apartments. Experienced livers in New York apartments - it's probably of all modes of living the most checkered and highly-seasoned - will tell you that the unwisest thing you can do is to take an apartment with any one you're fond of. My friend, a girl a year or two younger than I, who looked like an angelic child, but was in reality a little demon for tempers and furies, and as variable and false as the shade of the light-quivering aspen, with two divorced husbands and a meteoric career in her offing - had her own friends and I had mine. And the women (to say nothing of the men) who were likely to ring our telephone bell at any hour of the day or night were variegated indeed. When the bell rang for me it might be the Borrower of Two-Dollar Bills, the Logical Thief, the Morose Manicure Girl, the Golden Weeper, the Literary Woman, the Chorus Girl, the Young Russian Anarchist, the High-browed Actress, the Piquant and Passionate Pursuer, the Devilish Sub-Editor of the *Woman's Home Companion*, the Red-Headed Fisher of Men, the Fluffy Slob, my Friend in the Face-Fixing Business, the Discontented Marryer of Husbands, the Pink-and-Blue Dilettante, - or one of many more. When you consider that they all lived their lives, not as we do in Butte, Montana, with a deadly thrall and a wild-sea-bird shyness upon us, but as they do in New York, with absolute freedom and abandonment of emotion and nerve - you may infer that at least one's life had color. Seventeen minutes being one's time on the stage, one can picture but a few of them.

The Borrower of Two-Dollar Bills I met first in the Cafe Martin. I was sitting alone one afternoon behind that interesting door labeled "Smoking-Room Pour les Dames," upstairs, when there ambled over to me a half-beautiful woman of perhaps seven-and-thirty, in a black princess gown of a swagger cut and a black turban of the *chicest,* but with an indefinable air of subtle vagabondage about her. She had a complexion and skin of a lustrous softness and large sea-green eyes, and dusky hair artistically done, and she was in that state of goodfellowship which betokens recent libation - not too much, but some. "Kiddo," remarked this personage, "do you happen to have an extra Milo on you? I'm dying for a puff." I didn't have a Milo, but I lassoed Felice, the maid, and got her a box - her personality promised entertainment. She sank down upon a divan with one black suede foot on a taboret, and "lit up" - and spoke with a certain lack of reserve. "You're probably thinking, 'Gee, what a crust!' but as I said, I'm dying for a puff, and between you and me I'm absolutely strapped - I haven't even the price of one of these." I expressed a proper regret, which led the conversation into how extremely easy it is to be "strapped" in New York. "My God!" said the subtle vagabond, "for eighteen years I've never been able to see an hour and a half into my future, and yet I've lived - and always within a cab-whistle of Forty-second street and Broadway, at that. Me for the Rialto. I started in vaudeville, when vaudeville was punk, and then I did the choruses, and then I understudied Edna May for three years. I've earned the living wage, all right - but what's a living wage in New York? Besides, I've always been too strong on the liquor. Gee, I'm never happy if I'm not half soused all over - and now I've got a profession that almost makes ends meet." "And what's that?" said I. "I live by borrowing two-dollar bills all over the island and Brooklyn and Jersey City, wherever I can. Some days a few and some days a lot, but always some." "But," said I, "I should think you'd soon get to the end of your tether, and the works shut down, sort of." "Oh, not at all," said the Borrower, airily. "New York is a big place. Everybody in New York at two dollars a throw would mean a fortune, wouldn't it? Of course I don't know quite everybody, but at that it's a fertile field. I almost make ends meet. New York's certainly a big place." "But why limit each touch to two dollars?" I inquired. "Kiddo," said the Borrower, "because I don't want the populace forever at my heels. If they threw good money after a bad lady, wouldn't they be apt to follow her up? But who's going to follow up a two-dollar bill? It's a real profession - and let me again remind you, New York's a big place. I'll tell you a lot about it - if you happen to have the price of a couple of drinks on you." Unfortunately I had. It led to an acquaintanceship and almost constant companionship which lasted seven weeks and led me into the twilit mazes of life as it's led by the genus parasite. The Borrower of Two-Dollar Bills was one who lived for her physical senses alone. She had no friendships, though plenty of companions, and her one heart-interest had been years in its grave. She lived but to pamper and satiate her senses - she was held in a desolate bondage of the body which made even me feel like an ethereal sprite from a higher plane. But her effect upon me was like that of a blasting devitalizing south wind. There are many like her in New York.

The Literary Woman - I just knew her in Boston - a friend of mine for years, a girl of about thirty, with a pallid husband who was a secondary interest, her first being her work, which was short stories, for which she had made a distinct market. She was rather beautiful in a foreign-looking way, with a small svelte body, a complexion of rose-and-bronze, and eyes like hazel-colored half-glacial windows to her mind. She had spasmodic warmths of heart (I was, and am, fond of her), but I should hate to be wholly dependent on one of her ilk for the light o' love. This her line of talk:

"MacTrey, I don't know just how you look at it, but to me the two most worthwhile things in God's world are Fame and Freedom. If I were to be granted three wishes this instant, this instant I should say: Fame, Freedom, and the ability I feel in me now to appreciate them absolutely to their last pitch. I know I'll never be free - I'll always be held down by a hundred fetters, because I'm afraid. But I fully intend to be famous, if it isn't till I'm fifty. I've made me a short-story reputation in four years, by just keeping on hammering my typewriter and bucking the literary game. As for you, MacTrey, I don't quite get your attitude, and perhaps you'll say it's none of my business, but I can't help thinking you're squandering and dissipating your life on these experiences of yours - you seem to pay so high and to such an insatiate piper. In your place, what wouldn't you do? You've proved you're not afraid of anything the world can hand you and you've got, at an age which seems to me just like being a little girl, your own particular niche of fame. With that you might do anything - you might make even this big flinty New York sit up and rub its eyes and stare till they dropped out - you could put it all over the two million other sulphites. But instead of that you madly flit about after silver-and-scarlet butterflies. For what you have only to stretch out a languid hand and take, I'd give my useless soul for." "Jane," said I, "don't be a bore. Let's go over to Keith's and see Yvette Gilbert, she goes on at three. She has an exquisite French sort of pathos about her which will take your mind off me." "Yes, I want to see her," she replied, "I want to study her type a little. It's distinctly European. But I'd like still more to give you a much-needed spanking." A good sort, the rose-and-bronze, but if you ask me, a sort which misses the pink honey of life. There are many like her in New York.

The Devilish Sub-Editor of the *Woman's Home Companion*. She and I were pals-at-arms, and occasionally at daggers drawn, for six months. She had black, dead-looking hair, wonderful Nile-green eyes, a battered young body - she was about eight-and-twenty - and a clever and cynical mind. I was first attracted toward her by the delicate incongruity of her being on the staff of the *Woman's Home Companion* - herself would have fitted into the home-and-fireside with the facility and appropriateness of a billy goat. She was one of the crookedest pals I've ever had (which is putting it strong). She never told the truth when she could get away with a lie, and she drank whiskey, she drank absinthe, she "shot" cocaine occasionally, she took a form of deadly nightshade, and she played fast and loose, not only with her own emotions but with other people's. At twenty-eight she looked all of forty, and she had a fancy for dressing like a Lithuanian peasant woman - in a dark green kirtle and skirt with a white bodice. She and I met every noon, on the corner of Thirty-fourth street and Sixth avenue, and walked over to a Turkish Restaurant and had luncheon. "I love this place," said the Devilish Sub-Editor, "for a variety of reasons, and though we discovered it together I shall keep on coming here alone, even after you have begun to hate me, cherie. There's so much about it that's satisfyingly decadent and suggestive of death. This mysterious salad, perchance, is made from the green things which grow on poets' graves, and those white hyacinths - Monsieur the Headwaiter surely purchased them early this morning from one who took them from the dead body of a snow-maiden who died in her innocence. To eat this white, white flesh of the suckling pig is like eating one's own baby garnished with sugared cherries. The coffee is a heavy drug, and this ridiculous wine, for its warm, mild taste and its fiery effects, might be the blood of Sappho. And the people - look at those at that corner table, five of them, with white faces - I'll lay you three bob that the pupils of their eyes almost overlap the irises and are blacker than night - fine people, sitting eating and yet, as they sit, dead - dead. Drink up, MacTrey, and we'll pledge their deadness in another pint." She filled me with mirth as long as her crookedness didn't turn in my direction. But still, as a human being she was not a complete success. There are many, very many, like her in New York.

The Golden Weeper - my friend and daily companion for several months, during which time I had more tears, reproaches, recriminations, threats, jealousies, tempers, and general uproar of emotion spilled over me, like a glittering cascade, than life has contained for me before or since. I was very fond of her, and am yet, for the game abandonment with which she threw herself into all her affections. She was a charming young thing, a year or two younger than I, with golden hair and golden eyes, a slim young body and lips of startling redness. She played a harp in vaudeville and sang in a voice sweet as jessamine, as a vocation, and for pleasure and pastime she made a fine art of friendship. She made it altogether too fine an art - she would split hairs and snatch at straws, and trifles as light as air were things to be argued over for half a week without sleeping. And I - I matched her at it - we waded together in a delightful river of silliness. She lived up at Eightieth street with a most ineffectual mother whom she had completely dominated at the age of two years, and ever after. The Golden Weeper was likely to come to call on me at any hour whatsoever, by preference three in the morning. A ring at our bell some rainy night and I would go to the door (three being the conventional hour than otherwise) to find her standing in the dim light of the apartment-house hall in a pale green evening frock and a white cloak. "You," said I - "all these blocks in the rain! Come in - what is it now?" "No, I can't come in," said the Golden one. "I've come to ask you if you still love me." "You know I do," said I. "In fact I told you so at eleven o'clock this morning." "But I saw you at four o'clock this afternoon and you didn't say so then, and you looked at me only twice, and your manner was cold at that," said the Weeper. "Because you spent too much time talking to that LeMonte woman," I made answer. "Well, what could I do - you were simply eating that little Lloyd - I had to talk with somebody," said the Weeper. "And I talked to Lloyd," I said, "which is different from eating her, because she was the only one there who was friendly toward me. The rest of them didn't like me, and you joined with them, and yet you call yourself my dearest friend." "I didn't join with them," said the Golden Weeper; "you always say that - but I tell you, once and for all, you'll not have another chance." And, presto! a flood of golden and temporary tears de luxe. "If you think to start anything in the sympathetic line, with me, by weeping," said I, "you're making a deep mistake. You weep a deal too easily and too often." "Have I said I wanted to start anything?" said the Golden one; "and tears of mine have nothing to do with you." And so on and on. The gray dawn crept in at darkling skylights and we would still be standing at the door of the green-and-white apartment engaged in what was to us a fascinating cross-purpose. An ardent child of impulse, the Golden Weeper, and in New York there are many, many like her.

There are many, many of all ilks in New York. They move in deep and shallow waters. But in the deeps or the shallows they are all, and with it all - just human: the same in Butte-Montana.

"A Waif of Destiny on the High Seas"

Butte Evening News · 22 May 1910

The thing I went in for during my all-too-brief sojourn in New York was not
to improve my erratic mind and my slim, young body, but to fill them both
to the gunwales with life, to have them beaten and tossed about and played
with by the long swishing waves and wild white-capped breakers which roll
over Manhattan with each sun's rising and setting. And if the cold gods had
conspired together to that end I could not better have had my wish. I was
borne along on the tumbling waves like an unmoored and rudderless catboat - a waif of destiny on the high seas. And all about were crafts of every
known shape, from light-riding white-sailed ships, aflutter with pennants, to
low rakish craft which flew the black flag. And 'twas many and many a one
of them that ran across my bows.

You can go to New York for a variety of reasons: to study something -
anything, from settlement work to the stock-broking game; to earn money
or to spend it (it's a particularly good place for the latter purpose); to market
your wares or to commit suicide; to turn your wits into money or to learn to
poetically poison your body by way of the delicate pallid-tinted vices of the
day. But my hope when I went there was that I might get local color - not
to write with, but to swathe myself in - I wanted to gather up great lumps
of it and throw it into my unquiet life, to make it of vermilion and indigo. I
wanted to mix with something seething and vast and human and detailed.
And as I always do what I want to do, if the road lies straight before me - or
even if it's crooked, yet accessible - I got what I wanted from little old New
York. The unhuman aloofness which once was mine New York knocked off
me in less than twenty flitting weeks, and for local color - my two perfectly
good hands and my slim, young body were fascinatingly stained with it, in
all the wonderful tints and tones, in a twelve-months' time. Here and yet,
in the fastnesses of Butte-Montana, I look at my finger-tips and I see a little
rose-glow of passion on them: the local color of the town of Treacherous
Delights. And it will not rub off. It will never rub off.

Of three elemental things which lure humanity, the lure of the wild,
the lure of the blood, and the lure of seething cities, it's the lure of seething
cities which is the last winner out. The lure of the wild - back to Nature,
and that - is strong, but at best a spasmodic thing. Our love for it hardly
outbids our love for beds to sleep in, looking-glasses to look in, and silver

forks and white serviettes at dinner. The lure of the blood is indeed passing strong - a pleasure of the chase (or the chased), an enchantment, a seduction, an intoxication, all washed in the same white-burning fire and born of the same red instinct. It moves the world, but at that, following forever at its heels, are tawdry emotions of remorse, regret, dark humors, malcontents - and always there's the fatal element of satiety, the drop too much which can make wormwood of gold honey. But the lure of seething cities we have always with us. Their civilizations are as down cushions between our slim, young bodies and the rough surfaces of the world. The uncounted variety in them forfends satiety, and their infinite humannesses are the all-magnetic thrall that, while we contemn it, leads us to them, and back to them, and holds us in a quiescent bondage. It were better, as everybody knows, to live in New York and be knocked about and battered and bruised and seared, and by those tokens to be gifted with one spark of charity for one's kind, than to be deadlocked in a remote New England town, hedged in by puritanic and subtly immoral precepts, and with a large distrust of things human, like a worm in the bud, gnawing forever at one's soul.

The women I knew in New York were not, for the most part, an elevat-ing influence - and all that tiresome stuff. They were something human to be liked, studied as piquant articles of *vertu*, loved, and made friends of. There are women in New York who go in for cults - religious, mental, psychological, scientific - what not? - till they're blue in the face, or at least in the vitals, but who have not reached so high a plane, from any viewpoint whatsoever, as a hash-slinger who meets misfortune gamely and is on the level with her pals. I associated with a lot of women, friends and half-fiends, whom I didn't in the least approve of, but at that I don't entirely approve of anybody - myself, or the citizens of Butte. If I like people, that's enough for me - approving of them be damned, as I used to say in my first book. (From people, by the way, of whom I do entirely approve, kind Devil deliver me.) But this article is to picture a few live ladies I have met, so it's to have at them - as many as one has space for, culled from among those captioned: the Logical Thief, the Morose Manicure Girl, my Face-Fixing Friend, the Discontented Marryer of Husbands, the Kind-hearted Landlady, the Fluffy Slob, the Pink-and-Blue Dilettante, the Red-Headed Fisher of Men.

The Fluffy Slob - a fat blonde person, with very white hands, very pink, shiny nails, very yellow hair, very glad clothes, and a very noticeable lack of brains - was my next-door neighbor in the last New York apartment-house but one that I lived in. She barely knew she lived. She had a white poodle, even fluffier than herself, and a black maid who regulated her life. It was the maid who put her to bed at night, hauled her up in the morning, sat her down to her food, and girded up her loins when she went forth on the highways. She was one of those vague people who float along on the high-tides of life without effort and without volition - to whom the whole scheme is naught but eating, sleeping, and the donning of gay raiment. She was a most lazy creature - too lazy even to pronounce her words correctly. And thus the Fluffy Slob: "But if you really wanta know a nice gen'leman, you wait till you meet my gen'leman frien'. My gen'leman frien', he comes Friday nights, and we have a good, quiet, comfortable time. On Friday night I don' care for the theater, and I don' care to stick around the restaurants, and I don' care to go out in a taxi - I just wanta sit down and have a talk with my gen'leman frien'. His manners are so restful - you hardly know you're entertainin' a gen'leman when he's there - he's that soothin'. You yourself seem to have such noisy frien's - I hear you in there sometimes. And so I just wantcha to meet my gen'leman frien'." And one Friday night I did meet the gen'leman frien'. He was, indeed, all that she had said. If the Fluffy Slob was barely conscious of living, her gen'leman frien' went her one better - he had all but passed away. He was pallid, white-haired, silent - a very ghost of a gen'leman frien'. Yet I dare say he had his uses in this bright world - he suited the Fluffy Slob right down to the ground. And there are many, many like her in New York.

The Red-Headed Fisher of Men was a half-friend of mine and a marked contrast to all fluffy slobs and other tame birds. She was a dazzler - a high-flier and a very beautiful woman - with slenderness and grace and hair like burnished copper shining in the sun. Her way of entering a room was like that of the duchesses of one's dreams, and her speaking voice was the most seductive I have ever heard. It rivaled Mrs. Fiske's, in Mrs. Fiske's great moments. And with all this equipment the Red-Headed Fisher was nothing more and nothing less than a blackmailer, and her prey was Wall Street brokers. She used occasionally to have a cup of tea and a cigarette with me, and an afternoon's visit. And thus the Red-Headed: "Well, it may not be ethics and it may not be morals, but if I see a man with a pair of eyes in his head and a large account in a bank, I've just naturally got to have my toll out of it. The easiest thing in the world, believe me, Mary MacLane, is to blackmail a broker. They seem to lose their heads and then you've got them. They always have wives and fearfully respectable families and that makes them insanely cautious - so cautious they defeat their own purpose. But after all, it isn't because they're so very respectable, or so very cautious, that I find them an easy prey - it's because I myself - I say it without vanity - am so very handsome. I have lived, and lived well, on my looks alone since I was twelve years old. There's hardly a broker in Wall Street who wouldn't object to it being known that I visit his office, simply because I'm good looking and so well got up that everybody who knew it would suspect the 'ulterior motive.' So, as I say, it's the easiest thing in the world - a half-hour's perfectly innocent conversation in a broker's office, and either he gives me as much money as I ask for - I'm wise enough not to demand too much - or I make things generally very nasty for him by simulating intimacy and telling a few wonderful lies. Of course," added the Red-Headed, "unless one is very, very beautiful it doesn't work. But I know I'm beautiful - I have to know it - just as you know you're brainy, and Maude Adams knows she's magnetic." "You're certainly a stunner," said I, "and awfully clever, and a good fellow and altogether delectable - a rose o' the world. But your business seems to me a very rotten business to be in - you must have terrible moments." "Oh, yes, of course," she replied, "but who hasn't terrible moments? They're all in the day's work. I also have a very good living. I make men pay even for the privilege of admiring me - and so they should, what?" Rose of the world she surely looked, but she surely looked also a fisher of men. And like her, too, there are very, very many in New York.

My friend in the Face-Fixing Business - a plump bit of flotsam-and-jetsam, aged about five-and-forty, upon whom the untoward fates had wrought their wandering will for all of thirty brazen years. The world was her oyster and she either was constantly opening it by the hard brass of her kind of philosophy or having her fingers pinched and snapped by the sharp-edged and strong-muscled bivalve when it proved beyond her. She was heavily built, smartly garbed in black tailored suit, and endowed with a strongly marked appetite for food. If of her own purchasing the food took the form, perchance, of low-browed pork-chops, of some one else's it covered a wide range, from mallard duck to Mumm's. In two thick-padded, patchouli-scented rooms in Twenty-third street, just off the Avenue, she conducted the business of putting anything from a thick layer of complexion to an entire new face on a large and somewhat shady clientele of female women. I first knew her in the life-time of her husband (who was the manager of Armless Wonders and Oriental Dancers and other unpleasing things) between whom and herself cups, plates, and saucers flew at meal-times with startling regularity and fury. Once a cup, which she aimed at her husband, went unusually wide of the mark and hit me beneath the ear with quite some force. From which time she and I were the best of friends. It was several years ago in Boston, and when I saw her again in New York her husband had been gathered to his long house and she was doing faces for a livelihood. She had an apartment up at Ninety-sixth street and thither I went every Monday night to take dinner with her. The dinner was sent in from a cafe and served by an antique deaf woman, "not quite all there," to quote popular rumor, who acted as intermittent hand-maiden for seven other apartments in the same building. And thus my Face-Fixing Friend: "Now, Mary MacLane, if I seem to chuck in the eats for awhile instead of talking to you, just you remember I'm a poor working girl with a pelican's appetite. If you'd all day been doing over the maps of the rankest lot of plucked fowl that ever blew home from a week-end up the country, you'd know what honest hunger is. Here's the viands, so go to it, 'bo. Bring along that drawn-butter, you devil" - to the antique who presently sauntered nonchalantly in with it. The edge of the pelican's appetite having been removed, she proceeded. "If you ever think, Mary MacLane, of throwing away your little old pen and going into the face-fixing business, take a tip from me and gently refrain. I've been in several lines, but this certainly has them all nailed to the mast for showing up the kinks in the characters of ladies. I was in the hair-shampooing business for a while - I went up and down the Island dragging a living out of the tangled heads of the populace - and some nifty menages did I get into, my word. But that was nothing to what I get in this business. While I'm busy with my little trowel, laying on complexions, they're busy handing me out their raw inside histories. Bring the salad, you vampire. Yes, they tell me everything they know, and I hate it. It makes me feel as if I got only the lungs and livers and gizzards of life, and none of the white meat. But they seem to think I like it. Today a woman, whose complexion looked as if it had been eaten off her by a wild-cat, came in to have it put on again, and if she didn't give me one bad hour then I never had one. She gave me the complete story of her past, dating from about a day and a half before her birth (which it seems was premature and not entirely unconnected with her father's having eloped with the parlor-maid) up to that hour. Her family seem to have been visited with about every known affliction from cholera infantum to delirium tremens, and from very weak minds to very strong passions - and your face-fixing friend had 'em spread all over her. And, of course, it's me for the sympathetic every time. If they don't get their money's worth of sympathy out of me, besides their complexions, they think they're cheated. If I could do one or the other alone, I would not mind. But when it comes to renovating maps badly damaged by Manhattan orgies and sympathizing all over the place besides - it would tell on a mule's constitution. Open another bottle, you jade. But there are three distinct advantages in the business, after all. It saves me the necessity of paying good money to the vaudeville theaters, the moving picture shows, and those phoney clinics 'for women only.'" Thus my Face-Fixing Friend like whom, even, there are several more in New York.

The Pink-and-Blue Dilettante: she was one of those astounding creatures to be met with, among the followers of the various arts, who strive madly to be original and unusual. The Pink-and-Blue was a girl of twenty-six, pretty, but rather colorless, with a yearly income of about three thousand dollars, which enabled her to be original up to the handle. She owned but two frocks at a time, a pink one and a blue one both made of liberty silk, which for some reason always looked appropriate. They looked like evening frocks in the evening, and yet at seven in the morning they seemed the nicest and girlishest of morning dresses. And at seven o'clock every Tuesday morning she came to call on me. She knew that that was as midnight to me, and she herself went to bed at any time between six in the evening and six in the morning. But seven o'clock and Tuesday morning invariably found her leaning over the foot of my little brass bed, in either her pink or her blue frock, and with her own special sort of conversation which she paid out without a smile and without a change of voice or face: "Daughter of Eve, I am come to drag thee from the arms of Morpheus back into this world of Pink Things. See, I have brought thee for breakfast a love apple," - laying a pale tomato on my white blanket - "rouse thee and eat it. I myself rose with the lark and performed three tasks: I made an inkwell out of a felt slipper; I killed my canary and ate it; I wrote an obscene letter to Lyman Abbott. Very presently I shall boil a ham. My grandfather's sister came an hour ago to visit me. I gave her the yellow bottle of salad dressing to play with and came away. A loathly object, she. But served in the form of veal pie she might pass. Once I wrote a monograph on how to make soup from corset-laces. Couldst do better, my pink pet, and write on how to make a veal pie from a great-aunt? Eternity itself might be fashioned out of a dead mouse, a rubber eraser, a postage stamp, and an umbrella. I crave a veal kidney. I must go. As I pass through your outer room I shall steal your brass snuff-box." Upon which I bounced out of bed and rushed after her to rescue my brass snuff-box - for the Pink-and-Blue quite meant what she said. A struggle for the snuff-box, and I was left gasping and bruised on the floor with the outer door closing on the Dilettante and the box. "That's the confoundest class of persons New York has to show," I thought to myself, as I crept back to bed. And New York can show many like her.

The Kind-hearted Landlady was a half-friend of mine who kept a lodging-house up-town and whom I liked to go and take a cup of tea with now and again, for being both kind-hearted and a landlady in New York struck me as being a very delicate incongruity indeed. She was a brow-beaten looking woman in a black wrapper, whom every ring at her front bell made start up like a frighted dear. She may have been laying up for herself treasures in heaven, but she assuredly laid up none in New York. Her kindness of heart, added to her being a landlady, meant a houseful of perpetually "broke" people who never paid their rent and were never turned out in the street. Consequently hers was an extraordinary little household, kept up on nothing a week, and with a very thick atmosphere of indebtedness always hanging over it. Said the Kind-hearted Landlady: "They not only can't pay their rent - they can't buy their food. So they want me to board them. I tried it for a week but, Lord, they ate me out of house and home - and me with nothing to show for it but a new sheaf of bills. And the gas-man came and threatened to jerk the gas range right out from under my pots and kettles - I was cooking dinner - if I didn't pay the gas bill. They own the stoves, you know. Well, he didn't do that, but he turned off the gas - and there was I with a half-cooked dinner, not a light in the house, not two coppers to buy a candle with, and a raft of hungry people sitting around in the dark. Just think of it - not the price of a tallow candle among twelve grown people." "Goodness," said I, in an inward spasm of mirth, "why on earth didn't you run out and pawn something?" "Pawn!" shrieked the Kind-hearted. "It's a pipe you don't really know what a New York lodging-house is if you suppose there was anything left to pawn with when we'd got this far. We'd have pawned our false teeth if we could. I thought I couldn't stay in this business when I started in, but I find I can't get out. I seem to have adopted eleven people, and I can't keep them and I can't throw them away. It's an awful life." Thus the Kind-hearted Landlady - and I believe there's not another in New York.

New York or Butte-Montana, as I have remarked before, they are all, and with it all, - just human: the fascinatingest thing in the world.

"Cigarette Smoking by Women"

Indianapolis Sunday Star · 5 March 1911

It's unlikely that those mild militants, the Christian Endeavorers, will ever consider it worthwhile to treat with me, M. MacLane of Butte, Mont., to the end of inducing me to stop smoking my morals away in the little white rice-paper-evander of reverie and peace. But, if they did, I fear - I fear 'twere useless. Not if all the Christian Endeavorers from Dan to Beersheba, and all the Epworth and Anti-Cigarette Leagues, and all the King's Daughters, and all the exponents of Carrie Nation (if she has any - almost it would seem she were in a class by herself) were to send me petitions de luxe neatly inscribed on vellum in inks of many colors would I sacrifice so much as one pearl-tinted puff. First of all because such petitions would be questioning one's rights as a human being and an American citizen, and that, and secondly, because smoking is one of the fascinatingest pastimes of one's life.

To women, more than to men, belike, there is in smoking a lure that is exquisitely sensuous, exquisitely subtle - a chaste and nebulous enchantment the which they all are conscious of, though but few analyze it. The gray rings which float from the lips of us are to us magic rings of primrose and poppy.

I have never yet known a man - and I have known quite a lot of men - to whom smoking was anything that could be called real capital D'd delight. To some it is at best tame-and-sleepy joy (which indeed is not faint praise), to some it is merely in the same class with the juice of the corn and rye, and to some it is on the vulgar level of a necessity. But to women - those who smoke because they like it, not those who do it in a mistaken notion of being "sports," nor those who smoke only when with others, for conviviality - to women because of their high-strung complexity of body and mind, which amounts to what in myself I call physical imagination, smoking is a mild rapture, a joy for goddesses. It might be that I have more physical imagination than another; it has been at once the making and the undoing of me at every crucial point in my life. But every woman I know, to whom her cigarette smoking is a conscious fascination, confesses to relatively the same feelings.

Probably the first temptation for women in the entire cigarette smoking thing, in America at least, is that it's something we are supposed not to do - a half-forbidden joy, an off-color pastime, a near vice. Were it not banned for women there are countless thousands of them, in whom the temperamentalism of our Mother Eve is rampant, who would never cultivate it. Which is one more argument - if you consider smoking an iniquity - in favor of the doctrine of absolute freedom. The customs and conventions of civilization, aided and abetted somewhat by nature, have spun around the genus woman a web of restriction - thin and slight, yet with a heavy price upon the overstepping of its demarcations - whose intricate warp and woof entangle her feet at every turn, entwine her fingers at every stretching forth of hands, and blur her vision at every eager gazing-outward. The web was begun when the mist first lifted and the centuries were young, and its meshes by now are minutely comprehensive. In every glittering place where pleasure waits, in every primrose pathway where genus woman fain would go forth and, unhindered and untrammeled, gather all the flowers of life, be they sweet wind-blossoms on the hillsides or the poison blooms of tropic growth - in those places the network confronts her. *Certes* there's many and many a one of us who has torn away the frail threads with passionate or reckless or protestant fingers and gone her wayward road regardless, but she has paid the reckoning. The piper and the devil exact instant due always from slender silken-shod feet that dance. But it's the fact that the web is there, woven by time and the world and the race of men, and spread ever between us and our mind's and heart's wishes, that makes us rend it, that keeps us in a chronic emotional restlessness, and augments the long "desire of the moth for the star."

Anti-Cigarette League Cause of the Habit

It's because there's an Anti-Cigarette League in the United States that Bryn Mawr College girls, as much as Broadway chorus ladies, make cigarette smoking a surreptitious habit. It occurs to them, not unnaturally, that if a thing is worth an "anti" from the middle-aged and virtuous it must be something quite worth their while to do. In most of the cloistered girls' colleges the unwritten law is "hop to it," whenever a particular ban is called to their notice. The more restrained of Eve's daughters regard a ban as a virtual challenge, a throwing down of gauntlets, and they respond to it instantly. Possibly every girls' boarding-school in the land has gained a glowing impetus in the cigarette smoking way, all unbeknown to vigilant preceptors, since the Christian Endeavorers began their crusade to suppress cigarette smoking and Mrs. Longworth and Miss Lucy Page Gaston started in to interfere with the rights of American citizens in that particular. When the leaves of the judgment book unfold, maybe that deadly race, the people with a mission - missions which would deny the world those things which they have no temptation for themselves, people of the Carrie Nation and Anthony Comstock breeds - will learn three things. That they themselves do the chiefest harm to their own causes; that they must first of all study and know human beings before they can hope to expurgate them; and that by their foolish and irrational old methods they defeat their own ends up to seventy times seven. But that time is a long, long way off and in truth by the time the people with a mission know that much they'll also know it's no use, and they'll throw up the sponge. Nothing but absolute freedom to follow where impulse and desire lead, though they may lead to ruin and desolation and despair and death, can teach the human race those high lessons of the denial of self which the "anti" leagues, forsooth, would teach by tying people down with cords and hammering away at their morals with iron sledges.

The anti-cigarette crusade is a thing of folly in more ways than one, for when all's said, cigarette smoking's but a harmless "vice." Its effect upon our innards, according to the profession which makes our innards, and the effects of our living upon them, their study is far less insidious than are the effects of our breakfast and after-dinner coffee; and yet there's no anti-coffee league going up and down the earth like a roaring lion seeking whose liberties it may interfere with. The medicos also assert that the girls of America can ruin their health much more efficaciously and handily by consuming from five to fifteen pounds of candy per week - as a surprisingly large percentage of them do (with the odds quite in favor of the fifteen) - than they could by merely smoking ten or twelve cigarettes each day. Mmes. Huyler and Allegretti, they say, worshiped in the drastic fashion of which only Americans seem capable, have got Mr. Philip Morris and Mr. Egyptian Deity, as a "green-eyed menace," skinned quite fifty ways. Moreover, the candy habit effects a clogging and a cloying result, not nice to contemplate, upon their young bodies which makes cigarette smoking by contest seem a pure and esthetic rite. Yet no anti-bonbon league has reared its crest in the garden of chocolates. The Christian Endeavorers view with complaisance or indifference the piquant panorama of countless well-to-do young ladies stuffing themselves to the very eardrops with surfeit sweets; and chorile with horror at the vision of one or two young ladies wafting aloft pallid smoke rings from their wan little cigarettes. Those "anti" things and their relations to the public-at-large are full of such little anomalies. They are sincere, doubtless - but they're to damnation silly.

Fat Old Lady Smokes and Morals Not Tainted

As for the pernicious effects of the cigarette upon our morals, it's oh, piffle, and again, oh, piffle! I know a fat old lady in New York who began to smoke cigarettes nearly thirty years ago and keeps it up to this day. She lives uptown in a Riverside Drive apartment and her morals appear excellent. She subscribes to *The Atlantic Monthly, The Outlook, The Review of Reviews*, and all those high-brow publications, and she fits herself neatly into a large leather chair after dinner with one of them and puffs away while she reads. On Sundays she goes to the Episcopal church which stands at the head of Wall street, and on communion Sundays you will always find her there even though she has the audacity to inhale the smoke of her regular morning cigarette before setting out for church. Pit her morals against those of the entire Anti-Cigarette League and they would know no confounding, believe me. To be sure, my fat old lady may have an exceptionally good brand of morals - they are the Grant-and-Greeley-and-Centennial Year brand, grown before the "anti" leagues came reforming and demoralizing their way through these limited United States. But admitting that, it would seem to be but a poor, feeble, weak-kneed, wobbling, broken set of morals that could be vanquished by even the utmost human capacity for consuming cigarettes. The effects of one rousing, ripping, all-around lie, for instance, delivered from the heart out, were far more comprehensively damaging to one's moral constitution than were the effects of the smoke of a thousand crimson-boxed Pall Malls inhaled in the space of one day - my word! As well say that that lowly horror, chewing gum, undermined one's morality. Moreover and withal, whether you're a cook or a countess, when you come to summing up and comparing the values of the human equation, morals, or the lack of them, are among the trivialities; sometimes picturesque, sometimes delightful, sometimes a bore, but always unimportant.

It's truth and untruth - only those - that count. Let the Anti-Cigarette League put that into their pipes, and eke, smoke it.

No, take it from me, barring some kinds of invalids, there's really but one sort of people to whom cigarette smoking is harmful, and that's children who have not yet attained to their physical growth. Newsboys and messenger boys and one type of the boarding-school girl would seem to be the chief cigarette consumers among the youth of the land, and it's without any doubt a deteriorating factor in the building of their bodies. 'Twould be well for them if their natural or unnatural guardians could hit upon some persuasive measure which would do away with it, and incidentally with whatever else which crass, thoughtless youth affects and is decadent in its result upon their physical being. But it's somewhat more than likely that neither guardians nor Lucy Page Gastons will ever succeed in diminishing any decadent youthful tendency by so much as one hair's breadth. Willy-nilly, the headstrong little army of the half-grown will go on its own way gaily over jonquil-grown pitfalls to its graves like all of us - like all of us.

For myself, M. MacLane, of Butte, Mont., I am neither a messenger boy nor a boarding-school girl, but indeed a more or less wicked woman in my seething twenties, and the four or three or the two cigarettes that I smoke in a day have no deleterious effects upon my slim young body. On the contrary, they fill it with plaisance and peace. They touch my much-wrought nerves with a languorous thrill. And my many faceted, my many tinted, my iridescent mind, they soothe it with quiescent mists of memory, or reverie and retrospect. To all the warring personalities in me they bring tranquility tinctured with a piquant, charmed stimulus. Woe betide the league that would rob me of it.

Tonight I sat by my window on the edge of a blue chair, in my little blue and white room, with an elbow on the window sill, and 'twixt thumb and finger a cigarette with tip of straw. Two of them did I send, in the form of thin, blue smoke and delicate ash, out upon the soft gathering dusk to the region of ghosts. A cigarette lends my imagination impetus and it's easy as I smoke to imagine dead-and-gone cigarettes. Cigarettes have ghosts - quaint, almost-nothing sort of ones, like the memory-haunting ghosts of one's derelict loves. But it was mostly reverie and retrospect which floated my plastic fancy hither and yon upon the world. Though I am now in the fastness of seething Chicago, they bore me back to New York, the Isle of Countless Treacherous Delights, where many and many a lady breathes daily the primrose and poppy by way of the cigarette. So lightly defiant of Anti-Cigarette Leagues, and "antis" of all descriptions, did I feel, that my insolent young memory recalled, as a particularly alluring picture, the smoking room "Pour les Dames" at the Cafe Martin. It's at Fifth avenue and Twenty-sixth, hard by and in the realm of the beautiful bronze Diana of St. Gaudens, whose name is absolute-and-unrecking-youth-and-freedom. Never have I slipped within the Martin's padded portals at its most color-ful time, 4 o'clock in the afternoon - without turning my two gray eyes a moment to the lithe grace of her, against the sky, and wafting her a votive tribute from my battered heart. And she was tonight, as I smoked, the center o' my dreams.

Martin's Smoking Room has Fascination its Own

The Martin woman's smoking room is upstairs and somewhat sequestered and remote, though one door, usually standing open, goes into a hallway, where an occasional garcon wanders, casting an ennuied and lackluster eye as he passes at the picturesque scene within. It may look uninteresting and ordinary to raw mercenaries such as French waiters, but to me - in it and of it - it's human and fascinating. Martin's during the ten-hour is a favorite haunt of women - they're to be found there in gay-harried throngs, women of many castes, a well-to-do and hybrid company. And on them usually is an unwonted mood of freemasonry and subtle abandonment. After their tea, and possibly their absinthe or chartreuse (I can see those things now in their tiny glasses on the white tables, the one with its death-white hue faintly shot with green, the other of the lambent gold), the various rainbow-barged groups wander upstairs into the smoking room. Among other interesting things therein contained are the two maids, Felice and Marie, who each day from noon till the small hours of the night run the entire gamut of feminine foibles as manifested by the New York woman, and to whom no form of ladylike or unladylike weakness is strange. They are skilled as lady's maids and attire women, if mentally rather stupid, and they maintain a definite French middle-class aloofness of attitude, made of mingled contempt and envy, toward the clever, high-voiced, smartly clad American women whom they serve. And they lend an added delicate incongruity to a scene which in all ways is delicately incongruous. When the Mesdames enter the smoking room the maids bring forward cigarettes, each to her kind - gold-tipped, cork-tipped, straw-tipped, and plain, with trays and match boxes. The room has a reading-roomish and libraryish air with its subdued tones and dark leather chairs, and on the walls are old-fashioned engravings of staid character, such as no "anti" league in the world could reasonably object to. And even when the room is full of chattering, vivid-toned women - women with slightly rouged lips and lightly darkened eyelashes, women with wide drooping hats and fluffy curls and smart gowns - exchanging talk in the latest idiom of the hour, and puffing smoke-clouds the while, even then, strange as it may seem to Lucy Page Gaston, the room has not an atmosphere of vice, it is extremely modern, somewhat reckless and disdainful, a bit dissipated, if you like, and only that. Not that it is an angelic gathering - oh, far indeed from it. But it's enthrallingly colorful and human. I have seen in that room all in the durance of one gold autumn afternoon young women followers of the arts, bachelor girl types, *litterateurs*, Broadway chorus girls, middle-aged dwellers in apartments, actresses - "legit and vaudeville" - women about town (the exact feminine counterpart of men about town - no more and no less), conservative women with husbands and children no farther off than the dinner hour, hangers-on and parasitical women who follow any lead, Russian, English, French and Austrian sojourners, elderly women of gold mien and leathern morality, comfortable old ladies of epicurean persuasion, Brooklyn spinsters carrying their own cases of leaf-covered, frightfully strong little near-cigars, truant girls of eighteen or thereabouts, women whose original habitat might be Pittsburgh or Providence, R.I. And because smoking is a publicly banned pastime this motley company sustains a certain half-friendly unreserve, one with another and each with them all as being companions in crime. Without quite hobnobbing with each other they exchange impersonal speech, now and again, and are conscious of a vague, daintily ribald sisterhood - strangers who in another moment belike will again be out and scattered into the mazes of Manhattan to meet no more. In other words, though birds of extremely diversified feathers for the nonce they "mix." It is not in the least uplifting (which is a word I have found painfully liable to be synonymous with tiresome) but it's a most satisfactory place in which to contemplate one's kind in the mixed aggregate. The adamant outer wall of reservation which guards the feminine personality and is the keynote of all personality in the seething city, is there beaten down. We become aware that at least we belong in the same natural kingdom, or even in rare instances to the same sex. I have myself often sat there cigarette in hand alone, or with a friend watching the kaleidoscopic groups, and the French maids, and listening to the fragmentary chatter, bits of which float back to me yet on the wings of countless cigarette ghosts.

Oh no, it's not uplifting, however you look at it. But, oh, marry-come-up if these morality leagues would but realize its harmlessness and the utter absurdity of forming a league to make a row about it. If they could be made to let go of trivial detail and to turn their energy into the channel of something bravely big and simple - There are young children working in the mills and mines in the land of the free. The cause of woman suffrage, which is the cause of honor and justice, has much need of all the strong hearts in all their depth and sincerity.

Seventy years ago Charlotte Brontë, a noble-minded, gentle-souled woman, wrote in a preface addressed "to that class in whose eyes whatever is unusual is wrong," "Conventionality is not morality." Seventy years ago - and countless times before and since, someone has said so. And still we don't know it. We don't know black from white, nor blue from green. And the funny part of it is we don't even know we don't know it. There are a whole lot of us who think we do, like Lucy Page Gaston - and, too, there are some few like me, who don't much care. The world is bright - there are some true things in it - and there's always, over which to dream and meditate: the Ever-Chaste Cigarette.

"Mary MacLane Says -"

Chicago Daily Tribune · 10 September 1911

To me there are several fascinating things about this year nineteen eleven. One of them is the ever advancing progress of aviation, which seems to bring nearer one of the idols of my dreams - that I may one day start across the Atlantic in a dirigible balloon with an eight cylinder engine and a small crew.

Another is the equally advancing progress of the moving picture craft, which, though - and possibly because - I recognize that it's hopelessly lacking in "class," has enduring charms and allurements for me, to the extent of separating me from countless dimes and encroaching on countless hours.

Another was the coronation of George V, which contemplated from the distance of Butte, Mont., to London, seemed a pageant full of medieval poetry.

And still another are the clothes, the coiffures, the general appareling and war paint of women as set forth in the modes of the spring and summer of nineteen eleven. I designate the time because the fashion may all be changed before I get this written, so recklessly sudden do the man milliners spring their surprises on us, and applied to what may be then the prevailing modes this would be an anachronism.

But let the fashions be what they will, there's always a fascination in clothes. They reflect not only the follies and fads, the trend of thought, even in a qualified degree the literature and art of their day. They reflect, too, the make and manner and moods of their own wearers in a way at once subtle and illuminating.

Fashion an Undisputed Master

It's as if fashion worked in its own despite. We all simply have got to follow the fashion, of course - or else be content to enjoy a popularity commensurate with that of corpses in coffins. But fifty women clad in exactly the same, perhaps delicately barbarous, mode of the hour, will wear it in fifty more widely differing ways, thus revealing their individualities, than if each were dressed regardless to match her temperament, morals, character, or brains. You might have to look them over more carefully in order to recognize this fact, but you would recognize it - if your intuition is in good working trim. For, look you, if there were no such thing as Fashion, with a big F, and we were each allowed to choose our own style, most of us would studiously affect clothes which would conceal as nearly as possible the trend of our minds. It's the tendency of human nature to try to appear what it is not.

The grande dame wishes to given an impression of simplicity of philosophy and life. The dairy maid inclines to the sheet iron corset and amber velvet school of thought. The fat shop woman would fain show herself a poetry fed sylph in, say, a hand embroidered Chinese coat. The so-called immoral woman of leathern conscience would dress in a way to convince the world that she is "all heart" - white India muslin and snowdrops at her breast. The literary woman, as a rule, would wear the panoply of the chorus girl. The chorus girl with - who knows? - a secret sign of relief, would don a frumpy blouse and a lop sided suit and a facial expression of sanity and sense. The 14 year old girl would wear anything which seemed to her sufficiently un-wieldy to feel grown up. Her revolutionary, youth-pursuing grandmother would climb into a harem skirt.

Men at Least Deceived

Absinthe drinking young women artists and literati would wear the school-girlishest of serge skirts and middy blouses, with fillets of pallid ribbon round their devoted heads. Thus it would run. We would each have our bluff to put up, and unconsciously, we would each mentally "call" our neighbor's bluff. But - we would deceive uncounted legions of men.

But with a single prevailing fashion for all of us we willy-nilly reveal ourselves. Night brings out the stars, as any high school senior will tell you. By the same token the man milliners in making a uniform fashion for an infinitude of feminine types make shift to bring out our temperaments. Since we must all dress alike, it devolves upon us to assert our individual style at least to the extent of wearing our gay garments different from - and better than - everybody else. And in asserting ourselves we reveal ourselves. In other words, a shop girl, if she makes a "noise" in the way of clothes, can only make a noise like a shop girl - be her modish million-times-duplicated frock ever so skin tight. But, in clothes of her own planning and designing as to line and texture and color, who shall say that she couldn't make, in the busy marts of men, a sound like a naiad, a Chinese band, a vision of Theophile Gautier, all in one? Who shall say she wouldn't be number one, class A in delicate incongruities?

Clothes Important Factor in Life

No, let nobody run away with the idea that clothes are unimportant, or a trivial factor. Never, never! Clothes make or mar us - men on ninety-nine and seven tenths per cent of life's occasions and women on all occasions. And the making or marring depends, precariously, on whether the clothes fit the occasions and the dates thereof. What boots it that a woman has talents and brains galore, a heart of gold and a voice like Tetrazzini, if she thoughtlessly wears a nineteen nine moyenage dress in nineteen eleven, the day of the tube skirt?

What would be her showing at a swagger reception in the spring of nineteen eleven clad in the bygone hobble skirt of nineteen ten and the remote peach basket hat of nineteen eight?

It is hardly a supposable contingency, I'm aware. A modern maid of Orleans or a lady Caruso could scarcely have the hardihood to put over eccentricities such as those. But, mark me, if they did, their heart of gold, their brains to burn, their fame, and all that would be set utterly and completely at naught, and socially their lives would be worth - not a tinker's curse. This may sound like a jest, but it is not a jest. It is true as the sun's risings and settings. It's the surest thing you know.

Every changing fashion as it arrives has always had its full measure of unintelligent and irrational condemnation and ridicule. Those of today are no exception to that rule, in spite of the fact that the nineteen eleven fashions for women are the most sane, the most artistic, the most beautiful that the man milliners have permitted us to wear for many a long season past.

Harem Skirt Sensible Garment

The hats, broad, drooping, be-rosed and be-violeted, pliant things, which rest Gainsboroughesquely on our heads and not on a "bandeau" (whose office was never to allow any hat, by any chance, to seem to fit its wearer), and the sweeping brimmed Panamas and the little deep crowned Robin Hood turbans, which lend jauntiness and esprit to all manner of coy faces; the harem skirt, which is almost too "sensible" to possess much prettiness or suggestion of romance, but still has the smartness which at times seems to transcend both; the narrow tube dress which (if it's not transparent) needs no petticoat, and therefore means long graceful lines, and which is easy to walk in, and is altogether a thing of seductive beauty in its snake-skin like scanty clingingness; the silk stockings and satin pumps - of substantial Cuban heel and walking sole - that go with the tube skirt and that have brought to light a hundred types of shapely ankles; the long corsets whose snugness, it has long been written, must be all about the hips, where it really belongs, and not about the waist line; the many modified models of princess frocks, in which everybody except that tragically doomed one, the very fat woman, can have "lines" and a "figure"; and then - praise be to Allah! - our hair, our own hair, has come back into fashion.

Not a rat, not a puff, not a false curl, not a fillet of gold or velvet, hardly even a coronet braid, all of which we wore by the bushel, the pound, the yard, the cubic foot, only a year ago, dares to show its face in nineteen eleven. Why they went out so suddenly 'twould be hard to say, unless it's that, having piled everything upon our heads that they possibly could hold, the only conceivable change lay in taking some off, so fashion in its radical extremeness decreed to take them all off, root and branch.

Present Coiffure Replica of Old Style

Be that as it may, they have indeed gone, and, as hereinbefore remarked, praise be to Allah! And the coiffure of nineteen eleven-twelve is the soft and demure and quietly fluffy parting in the middle, with the long smooth locks lying close to the head and the ends done in little "buns," one over each ear and one behind - an exact replica of a fashion which came in with the Dickens and Thackeray and Charlotte Brontë heroines, all of seven and seventy years ago.

It's occasionally varied by the parting being on the left side, with but two "buns" behind and a reminiscent fringe in front, left over from nineteen ten and refusing to grow. But its simplicity after the terrors of nineteen nine and nineteen ten coiffures is something exquisite and appalling. There are women who would as easily have contemplated, a year ago, appearing in the market place at noonday in an Annette Kellerman diving costume as appearing on their front verandas with naught on their heads save their own hair - who are now wearing the Jane Eyre and Florence Dombey coiffure and blushing to find it attractive.

This simplicity of the hair is the real keynote of the nineteen eleven fashions. As the outline of a woman's hair is now the outline of her head itself - and many a beautifully shaped head stands confessed thereby - so the outline of her body in the silky, snaky narrow gown is her real outline, au naturel. And the result is not a surprising amount of angularity, but, instead, a surprising amount of grace.

Sylphlike Women in the Majority

There are incomparably more of beautifully formed sylphlike women walking the earth than there are of bovine and shapeless ones, and the nineteen eleven scant and revealing frocks have brought forth the fact. They, too, are a revived fashion - both augmented and modified - of a bygone time, the long straight falling gowns of the first and second empires, the shorter robes being then as now narrowed toward the ankles and cut scant around the hips. And the period of the first and second empires (vogues lasted longer then) was a time when all over Europe romance, chivalry, gallantry, tragedy, passion - all the big warring organic emotionalisms of man and woman - were ripe and rife.

Napoleon reached his zenith and saw his sun set. Byron was in his darkling, iridescent heyday. Keats and Shelley were making human the music of the lark and the nightingale. The French woman, Rachel, somewhat later, lit the histrionic stage afresh with a glowing magic. All those things find expressive reflection in the lustrous dressing of that time, and it's to that period more than to any other that the modes of today hark back.

It's alack and alas that the harking back is all and only in the clothes of women. The present day clothes of men (which, if you try to read picturesqueness in them, are the absolute limit) seemed to settle down along the line of least resistance about the time when Horace Greeley ran for president and never to have got very far away from it since.

With the possible exception of the immense antebellum hoopskirts and the nineteen ten hobble skirts - both of which were short-lived - women have never been made to wear anything so ridiculous as the masculine high hat, with its vacuous crown, as unlike as possible in shape to any known brand of human head. The most reckless hats of women can hardly be reasonably compared with it. The dizzily balanced Merry Widow at least afforded shade, and the peach basket turban came down over our heads and was a covering and a protection.

No Parallel in Fashion Annals

There appears to have been, in 1875 or thereabouts, according to the prints and tintypes of that day, an ungodly bit of headgear for women, consisting of a small flat oval disc with one long feather at the side, which was worn on what may be termed the front edge of the head - it lay athwart the forehead and balanced the terrific cataracts and waterfalls of hair which adorned the rear of the feminine head at that time. But even that, if it lacked every attribute under the sun that is requisite in a hat, including beauty and art, had at least the wan merit of not presenting a vulnerable surface to the wind, and the masculine ever blooming high hat lacks even that.

In fact, as a head covering it is simply a monstrosity, and if men can wear them and "get away with it," as they do - some can even look handsome in them - then women surely can get anything "across."

Yet men have worn picturesque clothes, albeit in the long distant past. The Elizabethan age was a day of velvet doublets and silk hose and plumes, a costume not lacking piquance, if inclining too much to mere prettiness. The cavalier period, the regime of the Stuart kings, was characterized by still more effeminate clothes for men, with lace ruffles and long curls - they reflected, indeed, a degenerate and effeminatized age in England and France.

But the costume in which the uneasy conscienced pilgrim fathers landed at Plymouth in 1620, dark knickerbockered suits with broad white turn down collars and buckled shoes, had an austere grace of its own. The clothes of the early eighteen hundreds, the Dickens period, were a garb for poets and pensive philosophers - mad young Edgar Allan Poes and incipient Copperfields, a not undelectable race. But the Napoleon costume was the most picturesquely masculine and masterful looking one that men have worn since the flower of mailed knighthood withered.

Mystery of Blue Serge Suit

Why, out of all of them - a vista ranging from the leopard skins on the gleaming brown shoulders of pagan shepherd lads to evening clothes, and including everything, from Roman togas to Highland kilts - the surviving fashion should be the futile and inexpressive and fearfully impersonal blue serge suit is one of the ironic mysteries.

But so much the more can we rejoice in the nineteen eleven apparel of women. They bring nearer the fiction women of a hundred years ago - the Lady Dedlocks and Lorna Doons and Bella Wilfers - with all the nebulous witchery which clings around the oft read about and oft lingered over ones. They recall some real life women of romantic renown, like Theodesis Burr and Peggy O'Neill, the notorious lady of Andrew Jackson's administration. More, they even contain suggestions of the days of Salome and of Sappho, in a certain triumphant disregard of their own picturesqueness, a half insolent contempt for the physical revelations which they make.

I remember a woman I saw in a theater not long ago, on the stage. She wore a very narrow cut dress of chiffon cloth the color of an absinthe frappe, and she happened to be sitting on the corner of a table, with her arms folded, one silk slippered foot touching the floor a-tiptoe and the other foot curled around the svelte bit of leg which showed above it. The dress was rendered still scanter by a fold of it being caught and held between her knee and the table edge, which, together with the extreme nonchalance of her attitude and the pale color of her gown - though it was merely an uncollared, elbow-sleeved one - gave her a startling look of being in the "altogether." She was a slender, young, daintily built thing, with smooth flat hair. She looked like a mermaid. And why not? Mermaids are beautiful things.

Also, the other day, I happened to see a shop woman - a head milliner - in a long straight wisteria colored gown of thin silk, standing at a telephone in her shop. She rested her knee on a chair as she bent over the desk telephone, in a sort of weeping Magdalene attitude, which showed the strong drooping shoulders of her to advantage. Her hair was gathered into an abandoned looking knot at the back of her neck. She was tall, big boned, gracefully muscular without *embonpoint*. She looked a stunning Amazon as her dress, which hadn't one superfluous inch of silk in it, showed her up. And why not? The Amazons were beautiful.

And I have a friend, a little copper haired blonde, who anon upon the shank of a summer afternoon wheels her baby to and fro on the walk in front of her flat. She wears the while a princess frock of unrelieved plainest white linen, with pale, tan silk stockings and pumps of grasscloth. With it she wears a wide hat of close woven white straw with what seems to be a bunch of feathery green carrot tops at the side of the crown. Her beautiful thick hair hangs beneath the brim in three pear shaped pendants fastened with brass hairpins. The hem of the linen dress is about eight inches above the shoes and the hat is prodigious. As she saunters along - dragging the exquisite caught and tamed and domesticated younger goddess - something in the coppery fire of her hair, the faint flush of her skin, the unregarded plainness of her sheathlike white dress suggests the "eternal summer" of the ancient isles of Greece. Also it somehow typifies the perennial summer day's sunshine of all the world. It is not so much beauty that is there as it is the suggestion of beauty - a thing far more subtle, more compelling.

Unfailing Charm in the Suggestion

Therein lies the crux of many things - the nineteen eleven clothes included. The obviously beautiful people and things are an unfailing delight to all of us in our journeyings down the world. Yet it's those people and things that merely suggest beauty that possess that profound and informing loveliness which is food for the human heart. Beautiful things must themselves change and fade and pass away - those things which mean beauty is the rose of the world to the quick hearts which know its raptures and the blooming lips which tell it. It remains the rose of the world - fresh, fair in its poignant sweetness - to all of us, long, long after those hearts and those lips are dust.

'Tis an ancient truth, and it has a million ramifications. If nearly all women look beautiful in the clothes of the present day fashion it is because the human form divine is itself a factor in it. The smooth flesh, the swift coursing blood, the beating pulse, the supple mechanisms and mysteries of our bodies, and, in short, the simple fact that we are human beings, are the raison d'etre of these gowns which fit us like the lily's sheath. There is the pregnant suggestion of beauty in the face and form of every woman ever born to inherit the curse pronounced upon Eve. Triumphantly the present day clothes declare the fact. There still remains some cosmic thing in each of us superior alike to curses and to clothes. Inaudibly that fact declares itself when we are let to wear raiment which bespeaks the old fashioned beauties and graces of the physical human being. And that - be it music, poetry, or clothes - is a very high art.

Still, and after all, what's the use? We are completely at the mercy of the man milliners. With a blind and absolute submissiveness we wear whatever they plan, and sally forth in it, like lambs to the slaughter, though it work our undoing. And even now they may be planning monstrosities, whereof wigs and farthingales are but trifling adjuncts, to pay for having arrayed us like goddesses in the summer and fall of nineteen eleven.

In 1906, after some years of success as both artisanal bookmen and makers of popular hits, MacLane's publishers had sold their assets entire to Pitts Duffield (who had trained at prominent Charles Scribner's Sons) and R.K. Fox (formerly of the well-known house of R.H. Russell).

It may have been the wide interest that MacLane's syndicated articles aroused in 1910 or some other factor - in the 1920s she would be hailed as protean Flapper, and that particular female evolution was rising - which inspired Duffield & Co. to propose a new edition of I Await *(still under its 1902 published title) for 1911. For that purpose, they commissioned MacLane to write some new chapters. She wrote a long single piece, as she said to M.E. Stone, Jr. in a subsequent unpublished letter, "showing how the leopard had changed her spots - and all that."*

Markings newly-arranged or not, the leopard was still the leopard.

AFTERWORD TO

"THE STORY OF MARY MACLANE"

- 1911 -

I, of womankind and eight-and-twenty years, will now make a fleeting flash-light portrait, in high lights and half tones, of what is to me, when all's said, the most fascinating thing in the world, my own personality: for which, belike, the world contains no parallel.

I am not, I admit, quite convinced of that - for I know by experience of it that the world, in ways, is very, very wide. Still, contemplating myself dispassionately I know that I am odd - a thing of mystery, subtlety, and brains.

Insomuch, therefore, I am unusual. I care neither for right nor for wrong. My conscience is like a rotten ribbon bound lightly about the moral codes.

I am sane, broad-minded, level-headed, yet prone to all the crass little-nesses and narrownesses withal.

I am complex and inconsistent to the last degree.

I have somewhat remarkable gifts of analysis and intuition, and of expression by way of written English.

I have a sense of humor that is rarer than ether, deeper-reaching than clairvoyance, and infinitely more precious to me than would be the sure cognizance of a rose-grown Paradise after death.

I am extremely egotistic, but I contend that I'm not more so than is all the world: only more frankly. Yes, I am frightfully but frankly egotistic.

I have a superficially kind heart - and a heart that's full of the utmost abysmal folly; a heart that follows whither its loves lead, down rocky roads, through brambly pastures and tangled underbrush, passing by on the other side always the Gold and the Worldly advantage.

I am wrapped around in a sort of comprehensive personal vanity that is more enduring and more useful and necessary - it has saved me from many a slip 'twixt the cup and the lip - than any garment of righteousness.

I have no ambition of any sort whatsoever. The top of my desire is for a measure of inward peace. For I have none - none.

The sum of seven dollars is wealth to me always. One hundred and fifty dollars is a tantalization and an exasperation. For one thousand dollars I would murder anyone who was not my friend, if I saw a chance to do it painlessly and tidily: for I hate physical pain for myself or another, and I hate sloppy things like bleeding flesh.

My every-day mood is made of indifference, a deep joy of living, a most somber, melancholy, and reckless disregard of fortune, all of which are quite genuinely real.

The day's business for me always includes a flash of horror, a nameless terror, a sort of look-in at the mysterious delirium of Life, brief as the passing of the winds around a house-corner, but black as a bottomless pit.

I have the passionate-sensual gray eyes of a world-weary courtesan, and the virginal pink lips of a cloistered nun.

I have the capable hands of a strong-hearted and womanly woman, and the slim wanton feet of an undisciplined girl.

I have the brain of a highway robber, and the soul of a subtle child.

Life never bores me. I find always a deep thrall in it - in the simplest things, and in all others. But a little bit of death seems to lurk in all things for me. I feel myself literally wearing out against the hard surfaces of this great glittering world. My life is a conscious dead march, a slow, seductive journey toward my grave.

*

After all these years, and once more back in Butte, Montana, I, Mary Mac-Lane, of womankind and eight-and-twenty years, in the stillness of one Saturday night, take up a worn purple pen to add this afterword. For the first time in years I have looked into this little old book that once was so near, so vital, so real to me: so near as is, at this moment, the beating heart within me, so vital as the red blood it sends pulsing through my slim young body, and so real as my white fingers which write this and my two gray eyes which watch the pen moving upon the paper.

I am asking me if any of the things in the book are real to me now.

At first they seem real only as ghosts and spirits and memories are real, only as cherished dead flowers are real - the poor, poor little crumbled petals! - and as the ashes of once-glowing fires are real, and the traces of dried tears. But how those little ghosts can live again - in the stillness of a Saturday night. How real is young grief and young scorn, even to look back upon. How much bitterer, even, are the tears of nineteen slowly and reluctantly shed again at eight-and-twenty, mingled with a deep and comprehensive and subtle regret. I'm asking me, too, what are the loneliness and solitude of the lost little Mary MacLane of nineteen-two, whose pathway was but scantly marked by one or two vague footsteps, compared to this solitude of me in nineteen-ten with my devious path, reaching from Butte to New York and to Boston and Chicago, crossed, re-crossed, trampled upon, be-grimed by the prints of a thousand human feet. For every footprint I can trace and recognize upon my pathway I feel an added bit of loneliness. For every human being whose life has touched mine - whose lips and whose hands have pressed my two lips and my two hands - I feel in this moment of clear vision, upon a Saturday night, an added solitude. For I have just re-read, for the first time in years, some chapters from this little old book.

My life then - I know it so much better now even than I knew it then - was absolutely barren of human beings. My life was drawn all in the black and the white of its own thoughts. There were no myriad shadowings and glowings, and blues and crimsons and rose-tints, reflected from the facets of countless other human equations surrounding it and touching it. I have all those things now. They do not make for less solitude and less loneliness. They but accentuate one's aloofness. Doubtless I am not more aloof from all the world than is each other atom in it. There are hidden chasms to divide us all. But I have a realizing sense of my own aloofness upon a Saturday night like this - an overwhelming sense of it. It is a thing to dread, to fear, to contemplate death for, that one may escape it.

*

All of this that I now write I write in complete sincerity - a more complete sincerity, when all's said, than anything in the little old book itself. There are in that one or two picturesque lies. I was very young then. I did not quite know that there is more of thrall and witchery and enchantment in one almost ordinary bit of truth - that *is* truth - than can be imagined into ten poetic lies. I can tell easily in a day a hundred lies. Many days I do. Without the lies I tell daily, my life as it is would totter, crumble, fall like a ruined bell-tower. A delicate web of a marvelous falseness wraps me round like a veil. But because more lies than ordinary are my portion - so much the more clearly do I see Truth. Two things in me are like bits of divine fire: my analytic intuition and my sense of humor. If in all other ways I'm possessed of devils, by the truth of those two things alone I'm anon the companion of gods and angels. By these two things which are real, though I myself may be a liar of lies, I claim the right to be, in moments like this, upon a Saturday night, absolutely sincere and to deal in truths alone.

The first thing I think as I re-read my nineteen-year-old book is, "What a clever and ridiculous and wonderful child!"

A thousand taut-drawn cords have snapped in me since I wrote that book. A thousand half-formed ideals have withered and faded and blown down the winds since the day of the Gray Dawn, the Devil, the Anemone Lady, and the Red Line on the sky. At nineteen I was strong, full of the ardors of revolt, full of the revolts of adolescence, and at that exquisite pregnant moment of physical and mental awakening which comes but once. And I was possessed with what seems to me now an incomprehensible desire to be "Happy."

Oh, the treasured thoughts of youth - the stuff that dreams are made of! It may be - in middle life, in the dissolutions of age, or in the last hours when one's grave yawns - that they come again, they live again. But five or six or seven or eight years after they're first dreamed - they are dead, dead, dead. Absolutely they are dead.

My young dream of the phantom Happiness was real to me then as the breath upon my lips, and sweeter to all my senses than blooming rosemary. And now, Happiness - whatever it may be - might be a pool of stagnant water by a roadside for what interest I have in it, or for what I care.

Next after that, the first difference between the me of now and the me of then has to do with things of bone and flesh. At nineteen I had a strong young body with but an intermittent touch of languor upon it. I used to take long walks over the barren sand-dunes which surround this little town, rather thinly clad, and in all weathers - in cold November rainstorms and in the teeth of January gales and flying snow. And I thrived upon it. At eight-and-twenty my slim young body is as fragile a thing as ever found itself tossed and battered by this glittering world, preyed upon and consumed by countless emotions, racked by the oft-swept gamut of my nerves. Wrapped heavily in furs I shrink from the winter winds on street corners, and I shiver, as I lean upon my window-sill, at only the sight of the cold sky and the cold, beautiful hills.

To myself that explains much. It has always been as if the physical in me were connected by live wires with the mental in me. My slim young body is the half-sister of my erratic brain. They mourn together, they quarrel with each other, and one is calm but when the other is calm. When the light glows in one, the red flame consumes the other. When false emotions play upon my heart, a false vitality stimulates my body. And by that token, when those things are, as by natural and visible decadence I feel myself brought yet a little closer to the Narrow House which somewhere awaits me, wherein - who knows? - may be peace.

I daresay I am not peculiar in that. Indeed I have known many, many emotion ridden young women whose minds and bodies were strung like harps, with the sensitive strings reaching from the one to the other in perilous accord. But also I have known a fat woman with a body like a barrel of blubber - and a heart slowly consuming in its own bitternesses.

Therefore it's mostly because my slim young body has become fragile and quiescent to the ways of the conventional world, which it never was at nineteen, that my mind and my heart and my soul - for I still believe that I have all of those - no longer know those profound and passionate revolts and protests against the long-established Order of Things. At nineteen I combated the universe daily with the same mad young scorn which must have come into fashion when Eve was young, and is in truth the epic of Youth.

Other things besides the dreams in my nineteen-year-old book have changed and passed away. I'm so very different a person now! When I was writing that book I had had no book published - I was an obscure little girl buoyed up by a talent and a keen ambition. There was nothing in the world for me except the book I was writing and my hopes for it.

And now, well - the book has been published, and eight years have slipped away.

What a thing it was for me - what changes it brought into my life, and how well I recall all the events of that crucial kaleidoscopic summer of Nineteen-two! The book was published in April, nineteen-two, and never since that time - since the showery day when came the telegram of acceptance from the publishers - has anything been quite the same for me. My attitudes toward everything were changed, perforce, by the stress of a thousand new circumstances. I was yanked out of the obscurities of my life in Butte into a none-too-friendly limelight of far-reaching radiation - all by way of my mooted little book of the Devil, the Olive, the Tooth-Brushes, and the word "Damn." The notoriety which encompassed me was a bewildering thing. It reached from sea to sea, from Chicago to London - the yellow newspapers blazoned me from Dan to Beersheba and back again. My little girl's-diary drew instant blood from the public-at-large, the newspapers, Anthony Comstock, and the vaudeville stage. I had been far-seeing, marvelously so, inasmuch as I was quite without experience of either the world or the book-market or anything beyond my own quiet life. But I did not anticipate quite the breadth and the virulence of the storm which my little old book would raise. A talent of some brilliance combined with unlimited audacity and woven together in a warp and woof of personal confession was a thing that they *all* fell for. It brought me an astounding notoriety and much good gold money.

By way of the good gold money I was able to leave Butte behind me and to go forth. On the fifth of July, Nineteen-two, alone and in a mood of mingled eagerness and contempt, I went into the eastern cities. I remember my absolute lack of excitement or agitation as I felt myself borne rapidly farther and farther from the "sand and barrenness" and watched the landscape changing from aridness to green "middle-western" as the train rushed on. Seven years rolled away, as easily and naturally as a black eagle winging down the sky, before I came back again, to this shadowy Butte - one little year ago to-night.

With the eastern cities and all things thereunto pertaining, I have an old, long familiarity now. But in Nineteen-two they were all untried ground. And they were full of beckoning lights. They were colored and perfumed and garlanded with fair, sweet flowers - the lily and the rose, and eke with wolfsbane and nightshade. I was fain to go and gather them all. That was my eagerness.

But meanwhile the deadly yellow press of those same cities had poured a rancid venom, in a plethoric stream, upon me and my rash book with the utmost indiscrimination. If in the early weeks it hurt me like caustic upon young wounds, thereafter - and ever since - it raised up in me only an antagonistic scorn for the irrational cravenness of it all. It attacked the delights and delicacies of the book with the same thick ink it used on the obvious discords, the while it was unaware of the steel-bowed compliment it paid the book by the persistence of its philippics. Doubly was it unaware of the still surer compliment it paid in that 'twas vituperation always. Had it been praises and paeans, from the yellows: alas for me! And that was my contempt.

But whatever were my lesser attitudes there remained beneath it all a sweet and subtle sense of triumph that I, myself, aged only nineteen, had achieved the thing that had wrought a so radical change upon the face of all my world. I felt myself the master of my fate. Not in any intoxicating head-long victorious sort of way, truly, but with a cold and quiet sense of superior inward potence which could cause heavy-locked doors to open before me and iron gates to give way, and could make me free of the highway. I feared nothing - I reverenced nothing - I besought nothing. As, of a truth, I do not to this day. But I have now at least a callous quality for my protecting which I then entirely wanted. And there's a tragic pathos about the me that I look back to, standing alone at the beginning of the hardpaved road she had opened for herself, in the summer of Nineteen-two.

Well, then, I traveled the road and I paid the tolls. It has been worth even the price it exacted.

I encountered along the roadway what has proved more wonderful than any picture my lonely imagination ever conjured for me out of the sunset skies above the barren deserts, more wonderful even than the sudden success of my book, a thing I had before had no realizing sense of, namely, People. I had been a solitary woman-child in Butte with no other companionship than the phantoms of my own fancy. But in Chicago, Boston, New York, humanity in many phases seemed to sweep and break over me like the changing sea upon a floating buoy. The readers of my book were legion and most of them gave me of their best. I met and mingled with and rubbed up against human beings - the most excitingly enthralling thing the world contains. I have had Loves and Friendships to which I have given my heart's blood by the gallon, to which my worn nerves have paid their last and utmost tribute of thrilled tension. Oftener than not they have left me worsted, frazzled, wounded, but - they were worth the price. I at last felt that I, too, was a human being, one with the multitudes and masses. Not that I worship people - far, indeed, from it. Only there's a seduction for me in the personalities of my friends which is like a lyrical if intensely human poetry. It exhilarates and exhausts me like reading aloud the Shakespeare sonnets or playing upon a harp.

*

New York, damaging as it is to every attribute in me, is yet the Place of my Dreams. I lived there all by myself for two years. I know its vast and cruel sordidness. There is nothing in it gentler than the hard, gray cobblestones which pave the down-town streets. I know its infinite preoccupation. I know the treachery of its charm. But by those tokens it teaches you absolutisms which someway grow precious to you the more you know them - they're like diamonds and emeralds and rubies. By its million vanities and its billion weaknesses and its vampire's ethics it hurls truth - adamant truth - into one's teeth. Two years of by no means easy living and plaisance on the Isle of Manhattan, and one knows the human race like a book. One can distinguish true things from false things. It costs you your slim young body by the ounce and your mentality by the cubic inch - if you're made that way: but it's to know the cold truths as they are.

Then, too, allow for the treachery and lo, the charm, the human charm of it all. The Cafe Martin at Twenty-sixth and Fifth, at five in the afternoon of an April day, with that incomparable picture of Youth, the St. Gaudens Diana on the Tower hard by, opposite and overlooking one's gaiety; the Spring jonquils abloom on the little tables; the amber tea and the bit of lemon in the thin cups; the pallid absinthe in the slender glasses, the sensuous music, the throng of gay-clad women with the mark of a restless *joie de vivre* upon their brows and lips, the delectable friend sitting opposite oneself: there's a delight and a magic in it. And one knows one's New York and does not lose one's head.

Beneath all the pleasant things is the ceaseless cry of the cobblestones. It is a harsh sound and wherever in New York you are you hear it. It is hard as steel nails and it disciplines your personality and tears away your illusions.

At that, and with it all, New York is full of romance and poetry. The Flatiron at six o'clock on a late summer evening with the gold sunset lights upon its battlements - an exquisite gray stone castle! And in it and all about it, by thousands, *people*, no more and no less wondrous than those who lived and moved by the waters of Rome and Babylon, before Vikings were. Even the kingdom of heaven - *that* quaint conceit, which at first thought seems a so tiresome bore - must forsooth be an enchanting and enchanted place if real people are there.

My two years in New York were like a chain of beads of alternate pattern and color. They were of alternate luxury and hungriness, of comparative wealth and half-vagabondish but very real poverty, of padded comfort and all-too-wearing deprivation - the exigencies of fluctuating fortune. It would be hard to say which I enjoyed the more - now that it's all over. I tell over the beads daily in the far remoteness of this shadowy Butte, for New York is indeed the place of my dreams. And there's a memoried bewitchment in each of them - "my rosary, my rosary." The while I count them there's an echo in my brain of the voice of the cobblestones, and in my heart a certain exultation at its flintiness.

I look forward to the time when I shall again be afloat, like a little catboat with but one sail fending the varying winds, upon that sea of treacherous charm.

*

Yes, truly, the leopard, somehow, someway, has changed her spots.

At nineteen I wrote myself down a "genius" in every other page of my book. At twenty-eight the word and my use of it inspire in me chiefly an idle mirthfulness. I think now that I don't quite know what it means, and it seems an extremely uninteresting word in any case. I am so appallingly human that I doubt if the most transcendent "genius" could make headway in me, if I had it.

At nineteen I imagined I bore many resemblances to that singular Russian woman, Marie Bashkirtseff, and I even believed I outbashkirtseffed her at every point. At twenty-eight I think it highly unlikely that I ever had the slightest quality in common with her. She was analytical, but in a nebulous metaphysical sort of way, whilst my analyses are material and almost viciously detailed. My reading of the Bashkirtseff, now, is that she was a patrician, a highbrow, a Brahmin of the French type, with a very unusual breadth and cast of mind: and entirely lacking in the fascinating trivialities, the iridescent romanticnesses, the picturesque follies which chiefly go to make up the sum and substance of me. Also I think she must have lacked the subconscious sense of humor which I quite expect will bring me one day to the inner gates of paradise.

At nineteen I wrote coldly that I stole three dollars. (That, by the way, was one of the quaint lies which I told in the book.) Well, I daresay I might have been capable of it then. But at twenty-eight - there's a small vulgarness about the thieving of such a sum which absolutely turns my stomach. I would hold up a train, though, or a late-homing pedestrian, if I had the nerve and the verve, and if I wanted money that much. But as to that, one always wants money.

At nineteen I looked forward to a Future as to something wonderful and alluring and replete with treasure. I placed no faith in it, still there was a wealth of wavering anticipation in the thought of it and what it might bring me that made my days at times opalescent; and my nights, if I lay wakeful in the dark, were filled with rainbows and roses. At twenty-eight the future near and far off, inspires in me the feeling that is the nearest thing I know to fear. If I see a vision of my future it shadows a day for me. It is a vision from an underworld, dark, desolate, sinister, forlorn. So it will always look to me, let it bring what gifts it may, for the coming nearer of the future means the going farther of my youth - fleeting exquisite youth. I want nothing, *nothing*, that I must exchange for it. Rather the Narrow House.

At nineteen I "wanted to be loved" - poor child, poor child! At twenty-eight I look back to one resting, though she knew it not, between the devil and the deep sea - between the lack and the luxury of loves. Take it from me, at twenty-eight, that love of any kind (except the long-suffering affection of one's own family) is a thing of countless cross-purpose, of corroding and cankering self-torture and an endless chain of Jealousy - jealousy in every possible form and hue: so that each love that comes into one's life is like, despite its encompassing fascinations, a wan little bit of hell.

At nineteen I found a mental and physical fantastic rapture in the nibbling of the green and briny olive. At twenty-eight there seems to be nothing in the way of food that pleasures me sufficiently to engage a so minute analysis. Yet at this moment I could write a thousand words easily upon that thing of "pit-fall and of gin," the Dry Martini Cocktail - not twelve of them, and not six of them, and not two of them: just one. Pale melted gold in a cup of glass, how often has it brought my shivering soul back from the realm of ghosts and forebodings into the sweet sunshine of human things. Its effect upon all of me is delicately demoralizing - it is the undoing of my wits. But *n'importe* - since it marks my translation from damp cellars to bright, sparkling-aired roof-tops. - "The Cup that clears to-day of past Regret and future Fears." Also at twenty-eight, though the first eagerness of my palate is for the red meat of slain cattle, I sit eating it in a slim and languorous greediness with my mind and imagination fast asleep in limbo. But I could write three pages of lambent prose upon the subject of Orange Marmalade, whose bitter-sweet, deep-gold translucence I have dipped up upon the end of a silver spoon, and gathered in with my soft pink lips and my cruel red tongue, and crushed with my sharp white teeth, and swallowed, till I became all of a delectable surfeit with it. I used to sit in the Hotel Belmont restaurant at ten o'clock on a Sunday morning, at a little white table in the sun, and eat a chaste and dallying breakfast of Orange Marmalade. The while I held little conversations with myself, and addressed me as Marie-Marmalade. Itself is like sunshine - lumps of sticky sunshine - and it, too, lightly but really, betides and betokens lightness of heart.

At nineteen I waited and longed for the coming of a concrete Devil. (That extraordinary Devil! How useful he was as the foil-character, and how plausible did he render the book!) At twenty-eight, after years of experience with dozens of quasi and pseudo and imitation devils, my dictum is - May my path ever be quit of the breed! They themselves fancied they were devils, but they were only men - all kinds, from *litterateurs* to prize-fighters, with every known brand of philosophy or lack of it, and with every shade of subtlety or lack of it - mostly lack of it. And they all had the one crude purpose: the seducing of me - what in old-fashioned novels would be called "to lead me astray" (a most preposterous phrase). The folly and the assurance of them to even *think* they could, when the man who can really seduce even the simplest maid - regarding seduction, which it is, as a high art - is rare as the night-blooming flower of the moon!

At nineteen I cherished a friend I called the Anemone Lady. At twenty-eight I know it for but the pallid shadow of a friendship that it was. But it was a natural conceit at the time. I was at the age which hugs its delusions, especially the delusions of its own making, and bedecks shadows with its most precious gems. Her I called the Anemone Lady was the closest friend I had at nineteen, and I barely knew her. She would be now half a stranger. For I have since known *real* friendships - things to conjure with. My friendships are always affairs of the heart, as are those of anyone who has a soul above cakes and ale, to whom sentiment is real and vital. To exchange bits of one's personality for bits of another personality, to sweep with one's finger-tips the infinitely sensitive idealisms of another human equation, to happen upon and softly to open the tiny doors back of which lives the spirit-guest in one's friend - those things, in truth, make of friendship an Affair of the Heart. On my friendships I have bestowed, always, the votive offering of all that I had to give - quite all. They were worth it. But Friendship can lay waste oft-times, like the avenging gods. And oft-times the lees of Friendship are exceeding bitter.

At nineteen I wrote the chapter of the Six Toothbrushes and I fancied I meant it and all it symbolized. At twenty-eight it's chiefly for that chapter that I say as I read, "clever and ridiculous child!" It is, perhaps, the subtlest and the best written in the book - and the foolishest and the falsest. The words in it were sincere, I dare say, and certainly it makes a true-to-life picture of the discontented, restless girl - whose name is legion in the kingdoms of the world. But despite the passion of my mood there was an unconscious regarding beneath it of the enduring ties of blood. At twenty-eight the loyalty in me for my immediate kinfolk is the one ever-abiding, ever-glowing taper on the shadowed altar in my Room of Things Beloved.

At nineteen I inclined toward Sunsets and Gray Dawns. At twenty-eight all my desire is in the dusk of the day. I remember lingering, one nightfall, on the edge of a woods in Massachusetts. The dews were gathering on a crumbling stone wall which lay between it and the highway. The lonely cry of a whip-poor-will came from the woods. There was an ancient mournfulness all about. And I had a rare moment of rest and peace. I should like to go to a heaven of Always Nightfall.

*

From drunk people; from false teeth; from a fish too long dead; from the dread Mood of Discontent: "Kind Devil, deliver me."

*

Also, and herein lies the crux of the matter - for whatever else I may be I am first of all a woman and young - I was at nineteen a plain little thing with a child's rather than a girl's personality and with no feminine arts. And now - I say it in cold blood and with an assurance gained from the attitude toward me of countless men I have known - l am a comely and quite graceful young woman with a penchant and a fondness for beautiful clothes and all that that signifies: the crux of the matter without a doubt.

*

In scores of ways has the leopard changed her spots. And there are some spots, willy-nilly, that never change. Looking at myself disinterestedly - I think I can - I see that I am in truth an untoward character. Anarchism goes on within me all the time. And I can see no slightest sign of insanity. I am uncompromisingly sane.

*

So once more I take leave of myself and of those who run and read, in the stillness of a Saturday night. No telling how and when I'll next take up the Worn Purple Pen, but - sometime, I daresay. For believe me, there's a deal of scorn and insolence in me yet that have withstood the slings and arrows. And when you least expect it, belike - out 'twill come!

I can fancy me reading both this book and this afterword when another nine years have slipped away - and wondering within me which is the more weird.

Another thousand experiences will have alit, like a flock of a thousand blackbirds, upon the field of my living and moving.

Or these three things might happen:

I might be dead.

I might be in a convent.

I might be married.

All of which I have contemplated. But in my contemplating there was always this doubt:

If I were dead - would I stay dead? I have heard there are other worlds.

If I joined a veiled sisterhood - would I stay in it? For all on a Spring day I might remember the bronze Diana on the Tower: the call of Manhattan.

If I married - would I stay married? Which seems the unlikeliest thing of all.

The world, all told, is filled with things of beauty. There are the silken shadows of dusk which come back every evening.

There is the voice of Caruso which is now.

There are the grandeurs of the by-gone poets which we have always with us: and all of them - as much Mine as Yours.

Upon my neck, as I sit writing, rests a string of amber beads. My slim young body (how I love that phrase!) is clad in a little black serge princess frock of the utmost plainness and nicety of fit. And on my wicked, wicked feet - my scarlet shoes! - my scarlet Louis Quatorze shoes with the little buckles of brass. Take those three signs with you, runners and readers, and know by them: if I live, we shall meet again at Philippi.

*

MacLane's final book was her testament in every way and concludes the evolution begun in I Await. *She had vowed to explode out into the world from Butte, and now she turns within and ranges through her internal world. Taking the static and neutral-toned* Annabel Lee *as center, her three books balance neatly.*

Written from c. 1911 to 1917, I Mary *seems both impromptu and outside of time. Superficially emulative of the dated-entry format of* I Await, *it positions the reader in the most intimate contact MacLane would ever permit: we are with her inside herself, in - except for the first and, movingly, a later entry - an eternal tomorrow. The martial author of* I Await, *who stood off and upbraided the world, is absent;* Annabel's *two personae have evidently fused in order to problematize the inner world. Here, MacLane seems to say: watch my givens as they pass; below these I will not go, and they are neither good nor evil - they simply exist. Yet her humor - dry, sly, strongest at her (as she might say) seriousest - never deserts us.*

It is not known if MacLane read Nietzsche - her iconoclastic sometime supporter H.L. Mencken was an early American advocate, and he'd read Max Stirner - but if I Await *was an exercise in self-assertion,* I, Mary *ventures into a self-criticism probably entirely uninfluenced by Freud.*

This book was issued by Gertrude Atherton's publisher, Frederick A. Stokes Co., and an editorial challenge is presented by their abandonment of left-indention throughout. Although this echoes MacLane's holograph practices (her left-indents, always narrow, disappear by 1917), it renders one unable to ascertain after a flush-right full stop or sentence-terminal dash whether a new paragraph begins or not.

Pending discovery of the MS - no trace has yet been found - the editor has inserted paragraph starts where they seem called-for on logical, rhythmic, or stylistic grounds - but retained flush-left for all dash-enclosed asides (which he gives in italics, to further set off from running text). Readers who wish to view the text as originally published will find it available on the Internet at no charge.

I, MARY MACLANE

A Diary of Human Days

- 1917 -

To
M- T-

these Live Fruits
from the Withered Garden

*

A Crucible of My Own Making

It is the edge of a somber July night in this Butte-Montana.

The sky is overcast. The nearer mountains are gray-melancholy.

And at this point I meet Me face to face.

I am Mary MacLane: of no importance to the wide bright world and dearly and damnably important to Me.

Face to face I look at Me with some hatred, with despair and with great intentness.

I put Me in a crucible of my own making and set it in the flaming trivial Inferno of my mind. And I assay thus:

I am rare - I am in some ways exquisite.

I am pagan within and without.

I am vain and shallow and false.

I am a specialized being, deeply myself.

I am of woman-sex and most things that go with that, with some other *pointes*.

I am dynamic but devasted, laid waste in spirit.

I'm like a leopard and I'm like a poet and I'm like a religieuse and I'm like an outlaw.

I have a potent weird sense of humor - a saving and a demoralizing grace.

I have brain, cerebration - not powerful but fine and of a remarkable quality.

I am scornful-tempered and I am brave.

I am slender in body and someway fragile and firm-fleshed and sweet.

I am oddly a fool and a strange complex liar and a spiritual vagabond.

I am strong, individual in my falseness: wavering, faint, fanciful in my truth.

I am eternally self-conscious but sincere in it.

I am ultra-modern, very old-fashioned: savagely incongruous.

I am young, but not very young.

I am wistful - I am infamous.

In brief, I am a human being.

I am presciently and analytically egotistic, with some arresting dead-feeling genius.

And were I not so tensely tiredly sane I would say that I am mad.

So assayed I begin to write this book of myself, to show to myself in detail the woman who is inside me. It may or it mayn't show also a type, a universal Eve-old woman. If it is so it is not my purport. I sing only the

Ego and the individual.

So does in secret each man and woman and child who breathes, but is afraid to sing it aloud. And mostly none knows it is that he does sing. But it is the only strength of each. A bishop serving truly and tirelessly the poor of his diocese serves a strong vanity and ideal of the Ego in himself. A starving sculptor who lives in and for his own dreams is an Egotist equally with the bishop. And both are Egotists equally with me.

Egotist, not egoist, is my word: it and not the idealized one is the "winged word."

It is made of glow and gleam and splendor, that Ego. I would be its votary.

So I write me this book of Me - my Soul, my Heart, my sentient Body, my magic Mind: their potentialities and contradictions.

- there is a Self in each human one which lives and has its sweet vain someway-frightful being not in depths and not in surfaces but Just Beneath The Skin. It is the Self one keeps for oneself alone. It is the Essence of soul and bones. It is the slyest subtlest thing in human scope. It is the loneliest: tragically lonely. It is long, long isolation - beautiful, terrifying, barbarous, shameful, trivial to points of madness, ever-present, infinitely intriguing to oneself, passionately hidden: hidden forever and forever -

It is my aim to write out that in the pages of this Me-book: no depths save as they come up and touch that, no surfaces save as they sink skin-deep. Only the flat unglowing bloody Self Just Beneath My Skin.

I shall fail in it, partly because my writing skill is unequal to some nicenesses in the task, but mostly because I am not very honest even with myself.

I'll come someway near it.

*

Half Inevitably, Half by Choice

To-morrow

Half inevitably, half by choice, I write this book now.

I am at a lowering impatient shoulder-shrugging life-point where I must express myself or lose myself or break.

And I am quite alone as I live my life.

And I am unhappy - a scornful unhappiness not of bitter positive grief which admits of engulfing luxuries of sorrow, but of muffled unrests and tortures of knowing I fit in nowhere, that I drift - drift - and it brings an unbearable dread, always more and more dread, into days and into wakeful nights.

And writing it turns the brunt of it a little away from me.

And to write is the thing I most love to do.

And I myself am the most immediate potent topic I can find in my knowledge to write on: the biggest, the littlest, the broadest, the narrowest, the loveliest, the hatefulest, the most colorful, the most drab, the most mystic, the most obvious, and the one that takes me farthest as a writer and as a person.

I write myself when I write the thoughts smouldering in me whether they be of Death, of Roses, of Christ's Mother, of Ten-penny Nails.

One's thoughts are one's most crucial adventures. Seriously and strongly and intently to contemplate doing murder is everyway more exciting, more romantic, more profoundly tragic than the murder done.

I unfold myself in accursed and precious written thoughts. I cast the reflections of my inner selves on the paper from the insolent mirror of my Mind.

- my Mind - it is so free -

My Soul is not free: God hung a string of curses, like a little manacling chain, round its neck long and long ago. Always I feel it. My Heart is not free for it is dead: in a listless way and a trivial way, dead. And my Body - it is free but has a seeming of something wasted and useless like a dinner spread out on a table uneaten and growing cold.

- but my free Mind -

Though I were shut fast in a prison: though I were strapped in an electric chair: though I were gnawed and decayed by leprosy: I still could *think*, with thoughts free as gold-drenched outer air, thoughts delicate-luminous as young dawn, thoughts facile, seductive, speculative, artful, evil, sly, sublime.

You might cut off my two hands: but you could not keep me from remembering the Sad Gray Loveliness of the Sea when the Rain beats, beats, beats upon it.

You might admonish me by driving a red-hot spike between my two white shoulders: but you could not by that influence my Thoughts - you could not so much as change their current.

I am intently aware of my Mind from moment to moment - all the passing life-moments. The awareness is a troubled power, a heavy burden and a wild enchantment. -

Also what I feel I write.

I am my own law, my own oracle, my own one intimate friend, my own guide though I guide me to dead-walls, my own mentor, my own foe, my own lover.

I am in age one-and-thirty, a smouldering-flamed period which feels the wings of the Youth-bird beating strong and violent for flight - half-ready to fly away.

I am not a charming person. Quite seventy singly-used adjectives would better fit me.

But I have some charm of youth, and a charm of sex, and a charm of intellect and intuition, and some charms of personality.

I have a perfervid appreciation of those things in other persons. And my steel has sometime struck fire from their flint.

But always my steel has turned back drearily yet strongly to itself.

*

A Twisted Moral

To-morrow

If I should meet God to know and speak to the first thing but one I should ask him would be, "What was your idea, God, in making me?"

I can believe he had some Purpose in it.

I'm in most ways a devilish person. There's sevenfold more evil than good in me. It is evil of a mixed and menacing kind, the kind that goes dressed in brave and beauty-tinted clothes and is sane and sound. While the good in me is ill and forlorn and nervously afraid - a something of tear-blurred eyes and trembling fingers.

Yet God has made many things less plausible than me. He has made sharks in the ocean, and people who hire children to work in their mills and mines, and poison ivy, and zebras -

- and he has made besides a Wonder of things: Thin Pink Mountain Dawns, Young English Poets, Hydrangeas in the sudden Blue of their first Bloom, human Singing Voices, - more things, always more -

When I think of them all a joyous thrill breaks over me like a little frenzied wave. It is delirium-of-bliss to feel oneself living though shadows be pitch-black.

God has a Purpose in making everything, I think.

I am half-curious about the Purpose that goes with me. He might have made me for his own amusement. He might have made me to discipline my Soul with some blights and goads or to punish it for bacchanalian ease and pleasure in the long-distant centuries-old past. He might have made me to season or scourge other lives, as I may touch them, with Mary-Mac-Lane-ness. He might have made me to point a twisted moral.

I muse about it with doubts.

But if I knew my Purpose I belike would not swerve a hair's-breadth from my own course which is an unhallowedly selfish one.

If I could myself see a way of truth I would walk in it. I have it in me to worship. I long to worship. And I am game, wearily and coldly game: when I start I go on through to the end.

But I see no way of truth - none for me. And God is eternally absent and reticent. So I go on in the way where I find myself. And muse about it. And damn it faintly as I make nothing of it.

*

Everyday and To-morrow

To-morrow

Aloofly I live in this Butte in the outward rôle of a family daughter with no responsibilities.

This Butte is an incongruous living place for me.

And I have not one human friend in it - no kindliness. And Nature in her perplexingest mood would not of herself have cast me as a family daughter. Three things have kept me thus for four years past: that nothing has called me out of it: a slight family pressure like a tiny needle-point which pierces only if one moves: and to stay thus is presently the line of least resistance.

Unless impelled to violent action by a violent reason - like love or hatred or jealousy or a baby or humiliated pride or rowelling ambition - a woman follows the physical line of least resistance. I have followed it these years with outward acquiescence and inward rages - languid rages which lay me waste.

The years and acquiescences and rages have built up a mood which compasses me, drives me, damns me, and lifts me up.

It is a forceful mood, though I am not myself forceful.

This mood is this book. -

I live an immoral life. It is immoral because it is deadly futile. All my Tissues of body, soul, mind, and heart are wasting, decaying, wearing down, minute by minute, hour by hour, day by day: with no return to me or to my life, nor to anything human or divine.

It makes me dread my life and myself.

I do not quite know why.

But to be an ardent pickpocket or an eager harlot would feel honester.

My Everyday goes like this: I waken in the morning and lie listless some minutes with drooping eyelids. I look at a gilt-and-blue bar of morning light which slants palely in at one window and at a melting-gold triangle of sun which shows at the other window on the red brick wall of the house next to this. Then I say "another day," and I kick off bed-covers with one foot and slide out of my narrow bed, and into blue slippers, and out of a thin nightgown, and into peignoir or bathrobe. I twist and flatten and gather up my tangled hair and push some amber pins through it. And I go into a respectable green-and-gray bathroom and draw a bath and get into it. I splash in brief swift soapsuds, and go under a sudden heroic icy cold shower, and dry me with a scourging towel. Then I go back into the blue-white bed-room and get into clothes, feminine thin under-garments and a nunlike frock.

I look in my mirror. Some days I'm a delicately beautiful girl. Other days I'm a very plain woman.

One's physical attractiveness is a matter of one's mental chemistry.

I say to Me in the mirror, "It's you-and-me, Mary MacLane, and another wasting damning To-morrow.

To-morrow and to-morrow and to-morrow
Creeps in this petty pace from day to day."

A haunting decadence is in that To-morrow thought. And always the To-morrow thought comes out of my morning mirror.

I dwell on it awhile, till my gray eyes and my lips and my teeth and my forehead are tired of it, and make nothing new of it.

I jerk the flat scollop of hair at one side of my forehead and turn away. I open door and windows wider for the blowing-through of breezes. And I wander down-stairs. It is half-after nine or half-after ten. I go into the clean empty clock-ticking kitchen and cook my breakfast. It is a task full of hungry plaisance and pleasantness. I make a British-feeling breakfast of tea and marmalade and little squares of toast and pink-and-tan rashers of bacon and two delightful eggs. Up to the moment of broaching the eggs the morning has an ancient sameness with other mornings. But eggs, though I've eaten them every day for quite five-and-twenty years, are always a fascinating novelty.

They are delicious in my breakfast. So are the squares of toast and the bacon-rashers and the tea and marmalade. When I've done with them I lay down my napkin by my cup, light a cigarette, breathe a puff or two from it and feel contentedly aware that my brain has gone to rest in sweet tranquility with my breakfast. When my brain is in my head it analyzes the soul out of my body, the gleam out of my gray eyes, the savor out of my life, the human taste off my tongue. That post-breakfast moment is the only peace-moment I know in my day and in my life.

Having puffed away the cigarette and read bits of a morning paper I then prove me arrantly middle-class by contemplating washing my breakfast dishes.

I am middle-class, quite, from the Soul outward. But it is not specially apparent - one's tastes and aspirations flit garbledly far and wide. But a tendency to wash one's dishes after eating one's breakfast feels conclusively and pleasantly middle-class. Not that I do always wash them, but always I think of it with the inclination to do it.

I sit on the shaded front veranda in the summer noon day and look away south at the blue Highlands, ever snow-peaked: or east at the near towering splendid grim wall of the arid Rockies which separates this Butte from New York, from London, - the Spain-castles - the Pyramids - the Isle of Lesbos: or south-west beyond house-tops at some foothills above which hangs a fairy veil made by melting together a Lump of Gold and an Apricot and spreading it thin.

Then restlessly I go into the house and up to my room. I put it in order - in prim, prim immaculate order. One marked phase of mine is of some wanton creature - a mænad, a mental Amazon, a she-imp. But playing opposite to that is another - that of a New-England spinster steel-riveted to certain neat ferociously-orderly habits. A stray thread on my blue rug hurts, *hurts* me until I pick it up. Dust around my room gives me a nervous pain, a piteous gnawing grief-of-the-senses, until I've removed it. And my chastened-looking bed - after I've turned over its tufted mattress and "made" it, smooth and white and crisp and soft - how the fibers of me would writhe should anyone sit on it. But no one sits on it. And I myself sooner than press one finger-tip down into its perfectness would sell my body to a Balkan soldier for four dimes: it is that way I feel about it. My bed *must* be kept perfect till the moment I slip into it at night to float under the dream-worlds.

Then maybe I pull a soft black hat down over my hair and draw on gloves and go out into the gray-paved streets for a longish walk. Or maybe the day is humidly hot. Then I don't go but stay in the blue-white room and mend a bit of torn lingerie or a handkerchief or a silk stocking or a petticoat. Or I take books and dig out some Greek - Homer or a Sapphic fragment - very laboriously but marveling that I can do it at all: the first thing one forgets being the last things one learned at school. Or I read an English or a French philosopher, or a translated Tolstoy, or a bit of Balzac novel, or some bits of Dickens-books with which latter I am long familiar and long enamored for the restful falseness of their sentiment and the pungent appetizing charm of their villains.

And betweenwhiles I think and think.

Then it's dinnertime and I perhaps change into the other nunlike dress, and nibble some dinner with no appetite, and talk with the assembled small family in a vein and tone of life-long insincerity. When in family-circle-ness I've had to hide my true self as if behind a hundred black veils since the age of two years. It would be a poignant effort now to show any of it at the family dinners, which is the only meeting-time. The one easy way is to be comprehensively insincere at the dinners where with no appetite I nibble. None there wants my sincerity, and so in my Soul's accounting now it is eternally and determinedly No Matter. It is a little bell which stopped ringing long and long ago. If it rang now it would ring only No-Matter, No-Matter.

Then it's night and I go to take the walk I didn't take in the afternoon. I walk down long lonely streets. Long lonely thoughts pile into me and through me and wrap me in a nebula that I can feel around me like a mantle. I walk two or three miles of paved streets till I'm very tired. I am lithe but fragile from constant involuntary self-analysis. One may analyze one's life-experience and life-emotion till physical tissues at times grow frail, gossamer-thin. It is then as if - at a word, a whispered thought, a beat of the heart - one's Soul might flutter through the Veil, join light hands with the death-angel, and flee away.

- but I love my life even while I analyze it bit by bit and so hate it. I love it in its grating monotones and its moments of glow and its days of shadow and storm and bitterish lowering passion -

I walk back beneath a night sky of dusky velvet-blue decked with jewels of moon and star and flying bright-edged cloud. The night has a subdued preciousness, like an illicitly pregnant woman's. It is big with the bastard-exquisite To-morrow. The night air kisses my lips and throat. I pull off my gloves to feel it on my hands. It gives me a charmed and unexciting feeling of being caressed without being loved.

I come back to my blue-white room, take off my hat, ruffle my fingers through my hair, look at Me in the mirror and smile the melancholy wicked smile which I keep for Me-alone. It's an intimate moment of greeting - a recognition of my Familiar on coming back to her. Often when I walk I go without Me, and wander far from Me, and forget Me.

Then I sit at my flat black desk and write desultorily for two or three or four hours. Sometimes a letter, sometimes some verses or a hectic fancy in staid prose. But now mostly this.

Then I go downstairs to a refrigerator or a cellar-way to find food - a slice off an affable cold joint, some chaste-looking slices of bread, a slim innocent onion. And I eat them, not relishingly but voraciously, reminding myself of a lean foraging furtive coyote. It is two or three or four in the morning. I smoke a quiet cigarette in a cool night doorway and count the nervous gray-velvet moths outside the screen.

And all the while I think and think.

Then I come up to my room and sit on the floor by my low bookcase and read some last-century English poets - the Brownings and Shelley and the unspeakable John Keats. The Poets make me a space of incalescent magic and loveliness. They are the beings blest of a flaming Heaven. In the midst of soddenest earthiness their fiery wings "pierce the night."

Then I'm thrilledly tired. I close the books and make ready for my bed in a lyric-feeling languor. A soft soothing unsnapping of whalebone stays: a muffled rhythmic undoing of metal-and-silk-rubber garters: a pushing down and sliding out of daytime clothes and into a thin pale cool silk nightgown: a hurried brushing of hair: an anointing of hands and throat with faint-scented cream: a goodnight to Me in the mirror: a last wave of a fateful thing - my life-essence - casual and determined and contemptuous and menacing - sweeping down over me in an invisible shower: and I'm betwixt smooth linen sheets.

In twenty seconds blest, blest sleep.

Of such wide littleness is my day made. One day will differ from another in this or that volcanic mole-hill. And some days I not only wash a great many dishes but do a deal of housework neatly and self-satisfactorily and like a devilish scullery maid.

And some days as I move in the petty pace thoughts and feelings sweet or barbarous come and change my world's face in a moment.

Also a casual human being of rabbitish brain and chipmunkish sensibility may stray across my path and gently bore me and accentuate my own paganness.

But always the same days in restless dubious To-morrowness.

Always immorally futile.

And eerily alone.

A Mathematic Dead-Wall

To-morrow

I'm put to it to decide whether God loves me or hates me when he sets me down alone.

There are times when my Loneliness is a charmed and scintillant and resourceful Loneliness with a strange and ecstatic gleam in it. The miracle of being a person rushes upon and about and into me "with lightning and with music."

One loses that in a day of many friendships.

But oftener are times when the tired, tired heart and the weary, weary brain beat-beat, beat-beat to anguished torturing self-rhythms. The spirit of me closes its eyes in turbulent dusks of wondering and wishing and leans its forehead against a mathematic dead-wall. And it prays - blind useless unhumble prayers which leave it dry and destitute, arid, unspeakably lacking. But when it lifts its head and opens its eyes there are the melting mauves and maroons of a dead sun across the evening sky, and the small far wistful flames of always-hopeful stars.

- they make it matter less whether God loves or hates me, but still I wish I knew.

*

My Neat Blue Chair

To-morrow

I suppose there's nothing quite peculiar to even my inmost self in what I ponder and what I experience and what I feel.

My only elemental "differentness" is that I find it and write it.

But I used to think at eighteen - those thrice-fired adolescent moments - that only I suffered, only I reached achingly out into the mists, only I tasted new-bloomed life-petals intolerably sweet and bitter on my lips.

The egotism of youth is merciless, measureless, endlessly vulnerable. Youth plays on itself as one plays on a little dulcimer, with music as sweet, but with a crude cruel recklessness which jerks and breaks the strings.

I have got by that stage of egotism. But I've entered on another wilder, more lawless - farther-seeing if less be-visioned.

While I sit here this midnight in a Neat Blue Chair in this Butte-Montana for what I know a legion-women of my psychic breed may be sitting lonely in neat red or neat gray or neat any-colored chairs - in Wichita-Kansas and South Bend-Indiana and Red Wing-Minnesota and Portland-Maine and Rochester-New York and Waco-Texas and La Crosse-Wisconsin and Bowling Green-Kentucky: each feeling Herself set in a wrong niche, caught in a tangle of little vapidish cross-purpose: each waiting, waiting always - waiting all her life - not hopeful and passionate like Eighteen but patient or blasphemous or scornful or volcanic like Early-Thirty: the waiting-sense giving to each a personal quality big and suggestive and nurturing - and with it a long-accustomed feeling like a thin bright blade stuck deep in her breast: each more or less roundly hating Waco-Texas and Portland-Maine and Red Wing-Minnesota and the other places: and each beset by hot unquiet humannesses inside her and an old yearn of sex and the blood warring with myriad minute tenets dating from civilization's dawn-times.

But though I am of that psychic breed no little tenets war in me.

It's as if a prelate and a wood-nymph had fathered and mothered me: making me of a ridiculous poignant conscience and of no human traditions.

I am free of innate conventionalities, free as a wildcat on a twilight hill. I am free of them as I sit here, quiet-looking, in my plain black dress. The virile Scotch-Canadian curl is brushed and brushed out of my hair to make it lie smooth and discreet over my ears and forehead. My feet are shod daintily like a charming girl's. My nails are pinkly polishedly pointed. My narrow black eyebrows look nearly patrician in their sereneness. My lips are stilly sad. My eyelids droop like the sucking dove's. But my gray eyes beneath the lids - when I raise them to the glass, my own Essence looks out of them, tiredly vivid. It seems made of languor and barbaricness and despair: and vague guiltiness, and some pure disastrous heathen religion, and lust: and lurid consciousness of everyday things and smouldering melancholy and blazing loving hatred of life.

My gray eyes out-look the wildcat's on a twilight hill.

But - so far as the Sitting goes - I sit here in my Neat Blue Chair the same as they all sit in any-colored chairs in their Wichitas and La Crosses.

*

A Lost Person

To-morrow

I am wandering about, a Lost Person, wandering and lost.

Not magnificently lost in wide Gothic forest closes, with strong great blackish green trunks and branches all around overwhelming and thrilling me.

Not dramatically lost on desert reefs with breakers riding up like menacing hosts and joyously drowning me.

But lost surprisingly in a small clump of shoulder-high hazel-brush. In it are some wood-ticks, and a few caterpillars, and a few wan spiders which spin little desultory webs from twig to twig and then abandon them for other twigs. Underfoot are unexpected wet places at intervals that my high hard heels sink into exasperatingly.

I walk round and round and across in the hazel-brush groping and knowing I'm lost in it but knowing little else of it: knowing no way out of it.

The bushes bear green leaves - rather small ones and warped because the clump is in a half-shaded place back of a hill. And they bear hazel-nuts, but not very good ones - mostly shell.

*

A Thin Damnedness

To-morrow

I own two plain black Dresses and none besides.

And I need no more.

In which two sentences I touch the crux and the keynote and the thin damnedness of my life as it is set: of my life, not of myself, for myself lives naked inside the circle of my life.

But my outer life is spaced by my Two plain Dresses. My Two Dresses measure how far removed I presently am from the wide world of things.

In the world of things a woman is judged not specifically by her morals: not invariably by her reputation: not absolutely by her money: not indubitably by her social prestige: only relatively by her beauty: and as to her brain or lack of it - la-la-la! She is judged in the matter-world simply, completely, entirely by her clothes. It is tacitly so agreed and decreed all over the earth - wherever women are of the female sex and men pursue them.

It is no injustice to any woman. It is the fairest fiat in the unwritten code.

Only a few women, the few specialized breeds, can express the fire or the humanness in them by play-acting or suffragetting or singing or painting or writing or trained-nursing or house-keeping. But there's not one - from a wandering Romany gypsy, red-blooded and strong-hearted, to an over-guarded over-bred British princess - who doesn't express what she is in the clothes she wears and the way she wears them.

Her clothes conceal and reveal, artfully and contradictorily and endlessly. It is all a limitless field.

No actor could act Hamlet without that perfect Hamletesque black costume.

A nun's staid beautiful habit interprets her own meanings within and without.

A woman naked may look markedly pure: the same woman clothed conventionally and demurely may achieve a meanly ghoulishly foul seeming.

One either is made or marred by one's habiliments.

A woman by her raiment's make and manner can express more of her wit, her ego, her temper, her humor, her plastic pulsating personality than she could by throwing a bomb, by making a good or bad pudding, by losing her chastity, or by traducing her neighbor. The germ and shadow and likelihood of each of those acts is in the fashion and line and detail of her garments.

A jury thinks it tries a woman for a crime. Some of the twelve good and true may admit each to himself that they are trying the color of her eyes or the shape of her chin or the droop of her shoulders. But it's only her clothes they unwittingly try for murder or theft or forgery, or whatever has tripped her. It may be an alluringly shabby little dress that saves her from the gallows. It may be a hat worn at the wrong angle that is found guilty and sentenced to death. A glove in her lap, a fluttering veil, a little white handkerchief dropped to the floor by her chair - those are what the court tries for life or liberty. -

But it is I I tell about, I and my Two plain Dresses.

In me a smart frock or an unbecoming one makes a surprising difference. I impress my costume with my mixed temperament and it retaliates in kind.

One day I looked a beautiful young creature - one August Saturday in New York it was - in a tailored gown of embroidered linen. With it I wore such a good hat: its color was pale olive: its texture was soft Milan straw: its price was forty dollars. My shoes were gray silk. I so fancied myself that day that I feared lest my writing talent had gone away from me. For God takes away the beer if he gives you the skittles. And in ill-conditioned clothes - some days the weather, the devil, the soddenness of life get into one's garments and make even fair ones look ill-conditioned - I am plain-faced, plain all over - so plain that the villainies of my nature feel doubtful and I half-think I may be a good woman.

In a life full of people I would own varied delicate beautiful clothes since it is by them one is judged, and since I am quite vain. But no people are in my life. I feel deadlocked. I am caught in a vise made by my own analytic ratiocination. I am not free to live a world-life till I've someway expressed Me and learned if not whither I go at least where I stand.

So it's Two plain Dresses I own and none besides.

It may be I shall not ever again need more.

The Two Dresses are at present of serge and voile. Their identity changes with change of fashion and with wearing out. They are cut well and fit me well. But the Two does not change, nor the plainness. I change only from one Frock to the other and from the other to the one again.

I have various other clothes. A woman - whatever her traits and tempers - garners what she can of handmade under-linens and dainty nightgowns and silk hose and all such private panoply. They are the apparel of her sex rather than her individuality. The uncognizant world is unable to judge her by them. But the woman herself judges and respects herself by the goodness of her intimate garments.

My sex is to me a mystic gift. I marvel over it and clothe it silkenly.

Also I own a healthful-looking percale house-gown or two in which I do housework.

But my passing life, my eerie lonely life, is lived in my Two Dresses and none besides, and I need no more.

*

A Prison of Self

To-morrow

My Two Dresses tell me the scope of my present Mary-Mac-Lane-ness.

Every day they tell me things about myself.

They tell me I'm living in a prison of self, invisible and ascetic and somberly just.

They tell me I'm living an outer life narrow and broodingly companionless and that if I were not self-reliant by long habit a leprous morbidness would rot me in body and spirit.

They tell me because of outer solitude an inner fever of emotion and egotism and a fervid analytic light are on all my phases of self: mental, physical, psychical, and sexual.

They tell me my way of thought is at once meditative and cave-womanish.

They tell me I'm all ways the Unmarried Woman and profoundly loverless.

They tell me I'm like a child and like a sequestered savage.

They tell me I am having no restful unrealities of social life with chattering women and no monotonous casually bloodthirsty flirtations with men.

They tell me I walk daily to the edges of myself and stare into horrible-sweet egotistic abysses.

They tell me I'm grave-eyed and coldly melancholy.

They tell me there's a bereftness in the curves of my breasts and an unfulfillment in my loose-girt loins.

They tell me I am barren of sensation and fertile in feeling.

They tell me God has taken away the beer and also the skittles and left me only pieces of bread and drinks of water.

*

A Winding Sheet

To-morrow

The least important thing in my life is its tangibleness.

The only things that matter lastingly are the things that happen inside me.

If I do a cruel act and feel no cruelty in my Soul it is nothing. If I feel cruelty in my Soul though I do no cruel act I'm guilty of a sort of butchery and my spirit-hands are bloody with it.

The adventures of my spirit are realer than the outer things that befall me.

To dwell on the self that is known only to me - the self that is intricate and versatile, tinted, demi-tinted, deep-dyed, luminous, gives me an intimate delectation, a mental inflorescence, and sometimes an exaltation. It is not always so but it can be so.

But always to look back on the mass of outer events that have made my tangible life darkens my day.

Introspection throws a witching spell around me, though it may be a black one.

But retrospection wraps me in a Winding Sheet.

When the day is already dark from low-hanging clouds - and often when the sun is bright, bright, bright - I walk my floor and think of my scattered life-flotsam with a frown at the eyebrows: a coarse and heavy and twisted frown.

To-day was a leaden day. The air held a quality like the infernal breath of dead people. I leaned elbows on my dull window-sill and looked off at green and purple mountains. I tried to think of some reason - some reason tangible or poetic - for living.

I wore my brocade Chinese coat fastened down the left side with round flashing glass buttons and embroidered with blue bats and gardenias: and with it a crinkly crêpe-silk petticoat: and silk shoes and respectable white silk stockings. I felt righteous because in the forenoon I had done much housework. I worked thoroughly and well, swearing and repeating poetry softly to lend me impetus. And afterward I felt useful and good.

But having changed from Dutch cap and apron and domesticness to scented silk and my sad window I grew suddenly frail and vulnerable. Shadows stormed my wall and scaled it and entered in and sacked my castle. I lounged away from my window, folded my arms in my loose blue sleeves, and slowly walked my floor. I had no strength within to combat shadows.

I picked up two alien shreds, of lint and paper respectively, from the rug, but inside me undigested and indigestible memories had their own way.

They brought close an unsatisfying and dissatisfying vista of Mary MacLanes.

There was a stubborn baby in Winnipeg-Canada, as I've heard, a baby with a white skin, coldly pensive dark-blue eyes, no hair, no voice, hand-worked muslin frocks, and a fat lumpish mien.

It was this Mary MacLane.

There was a three-year-old child, as I dimly remember, still in Canada and still stubborn, with a stout keg-like pink-and-white body, baffling blue eyes, a tiny voice, thick sun-colored curls, cambric frocks, and short white socks and a morose temper. She had one love, a yellow tortoise-shell kitten which she hugged and hugged with violence until one day it died surprisingly in her arms.

It was this Mary MacLane.

There was a seven-year-old child in Minnesota, as I well remember, still stubborn and still often morose, with a thin bony little body, conscious gray eyes, a tanned face, weather-beaten hands, untidy frocks, beautiful fluffy golden hair, a tendency to secretiveness and lies, a speculative mind, fantastic day-dreams, and a free hoydenish way of life. She had playmates but no loves except an objective love for quiet greenwoods and sweet meadows and windy hills and hay-filled barns, and for the surface details of life. She had subjective hatreds for being fussed over, for being teased, and for relatives.

It was this Mary MacLane.

There was a thirteen-year-old person, as I well remember, in a windy Montana town, who was neither girl, child, nor savage but was a mixture of the three. She had a devilish contrary will and temper, the unenlightened inexpressive wholly unattractive face and features of early adolescence, a self-love that had not the dignity of egotism, and a devouring appetite for reading. She read everything she happened on - from Voltaire to Nick Carter: from *Lady Audley's Secret* to Fox's Book of Martyrs. She read Alexander Pope and Victor Hugo and John Stuart Mill. She read *Lena Rivers* by Mary J. Holmes: also Confucius: and the Brothers Grimm. She had a long-legged lanky frame, conscious gray eyes, lovely coppery-gold dark hair, and a silly headful of tangled irrational thoughts. She had pathetic impossible day-dreams. She had few companions and no loves but much hatred for most things sane, sensible, and honest.

It was this Mary MacLane.

There was an eighteen-year-old girl in this Butte, as I well remember, with the outward savagery tamed out of her by studiousness. She was slim but no longer lanky and owned a white-hot aliveness and a grace. She had repelling gray eyes and the beautiful coppery hair, and about her an isolation, a complete aloofness. Her spirit fed itself on wonderful and exquisite dreams alternated by moods of young passionate woe, analyzed and torn to shreds: all of it hid beneath a very quiet surface. She had outwardly a tense markedly virginal quality but was inwardly insolently *demi-vierge*. She had no companions, no friendships. She absorbed herself in digging knowledge out of her high school text books, studying and imagining over it, and wandering in the fascinating highways which it opened to her. She was at her moment of brain-awakening, soul-awakening, sex-awakening, life-awakening, world-awakening: it uncurtained windows of magic old sorrow for her to look from. She had no characteristic weaknesses - she was strongly and scornfully courageous. It and the need of self-expression, born of her teeming spirit and life-long suppression of it, led her to write herself out in a book, which was published. It was a poetic book and had insight and vision and a riot of color with youth as its keynote. And it was human and figuratively and literally full of the devil. The far-and-wide public in England and America read it, and the newspapers made a loud noise about it, and the lonely girl who wrote it found herself oddly notorious. It brought money which made her free of Butte and it brought human things into her life which changed her life forever. And it brought her no inner or outer excitement or elation.

It was this Mary MacLane.

There was a girl of six-and-twenty in Boston and in New York who had half-forgot her long-familiar Ego for several years. She lived and moved in folly and triviality and falseness. From having had too few companions she had too many who did her no good and no harm but helped her waste passing days and dissipate her moods and mental tissues. She had grown worldly in taste, weak in manner of thought, fragile in body from a mad irregularity of food and sleep, and in every attribute uncertain of herself. Her Soul lay sleeping: her Heart because it felt too keenly worked overtime: nothing engaged her Mind. But her analytic trend stayed by and with it she pulled to bits the varied fragmentary things she encountered. She learned New York town in human sordid enlightening disciplining ways. She learned people of many kinds in many ways. She learned other young women, which depressed and exhilarated and perplexed her. She learned men - a race whose make and motive toward women bears no analysis. She had not the usual defensive armor of the normal woman, for she was not a normal woman but certain trends of varying individuals gathered into one sensitive woman-envelope. She was careless toward men in their crude sex-rapacity in ways no "regular" woman would dare or care to be. No man could wring one tear from her, nor cause a quickening of her foolish Heart, nor any emotion in her save mirth. And there were women friends - There were some friendships whose ill effects she will never recover from, from having bestowed too much of herself on them in the headlong newness of knowing and owning friendship after her long young loneliness.

- she could not cherish anything sanely. She couldn't stand in her doorway and watch a pretty bird flying above a green hedge, and admire it for the gleam of its brilliant wings in the sun, and let it go. She must needs run out - leaving her door standing open and tea-and-cakes untasted within - and follow where the bird flew, through mire and brier, round the world -

From the odd notoriety were many letters and experiences and adventures. She met some famous persons - writers, actors, artists - of agreeable philosophic plaisances. She saw her book of youth burlesqued with artistic piquance in the Weber-and-Fields show of its season (with one Collier, adroitest of comedians, cast as her long-lost Devil). There was a hasty voyage to the edge of Europe - a voyage of terrific seasickness lying in her stateroom: a half-glimpse of Paris all gray and green in the rain: a whole glimpse of London, mystic, Dickensesque, and roundly British in its yellow-brown fog: and back again within ten days with more berth-ridden seasickness lasting from Cherbourg to New York harbor: the whole adventure grown from a Spring morning impulse. There were winters in Florida at sun-flooded resort towns full of gaudiness and gambling and surprising winter-resort people. Those were mongrel wastrel years empty of every realness, every purpose, every vantage: they filled her with a bastard wisdom.

It was this Mary MacLane.

There was a girl of seven-and-twenty worn to psychic fragments and returned on a winter's day in a mood of indifference to this Butte. It was her first return since she and her book had gone forth eight years before. She celebrated it by being brought low with a baleful blood-sucking demon of illness, what is called scarlet fever. Borne upon by the mountain altitude after sea-levels and getting in the way of epidemic germs, she had no chance. A strong feverish serpent wound itself around her, consuming and destroying. There were tortured dying weeks. She had never been ill before in all her life.

This was the most crucial bodily adventure she had known. It opened a new and dreadful world. There was no passing of time in those long, long weeks, no rational thinking, no day, no night, no dark, no morning, no memory. There was pain, and utter weariness, and a feeling of being hurried to her grave. There was an air of hurry in the stillness around, as if she and Death had made a date which she would be late in keeping unless she were urged on. There was a doctor, and a crisp white starched nurse, and there were interminable bitter drugs and tall narrow glasses of monotonous milk. She was endlessly disturbed by milk and medicine, and by cold spongings and changings of feverish bed-linens, and anointings with olive oil, and takings of her temperature, and sprayings of her throat: when she wanted only to sink down, down, forever and forever to the underworld. She almost sank. But God capriciously decided he had other plans for her - insomuch as decreeing she was not to be let go then. After seven weeks she tiredly rose from her bed and took stock of herself. Her rôle then was of a horrible yellow skeleton with negative gray eyes, a wreck of tissue and vitality such as only scarlet fever can achieve, and her beautiful thick coppery hair changed to a strange short mouse-colored tangle. She was a long time recovering. The scarlet demon changed her life and its meanings and energies and outlooks more effectually than if she had been trapped by a game-at-law and gaols and courts had had their toll of her. But after months, a year and a half of months, her health came back perfect if not vigorous, and her good looks - the few she ever had, and even the humanizing incongruous curls, though changed, grew long and covered her head again in a heathen frivol. A so magnificent mystery is this blood-and-flesh. It grows up again out of its ashes. Burn all of it but one cell in the scorchingest sickness and so that bones are still whole it will renew itself from that, perfect as the sweet-bay. But this mind, less magnificent and less mysterious and more delicate and dubious, rallies only by aid of the heart beneath it and the soul beyond it. Her mind came slowly out of darkened apathy. It lived in a high-walled cloister telling its languid beads by rote. But as if it sensed the sweet aura of her renewed body it at last woke strong and cold overnight and was aware again of itself and the mourning magic of being.

It was this Mary MacLane.

And after a year or two more it is this Mary MacLane.

It is I myself.

I walk my floor in leaden retrospect-days with a feel in my throat of damned and damning unfulfillment and at my eyebrows the twisted frown.

In it is dread and anguish and worriment: in it is hideous altering breaking prepollence of death.

- if my hair, just my hair, had not come back after that red fever I'd have decided - not capriciously like God but determinedly like myself - to have died by my own hand one night. It is no brave thought and it would have been no brave deed. Though it wants a lowering courage to leave life when, despite all, one loves its very textureless color, its bodiless air: not to speak of the yellow hot deathless sunshine that can not reach one in her dark grave -

But the look and feel of my hair are the look and feel of positive life, opposed to death.

To live up to my hair would keep me brave.

But the retrospects, which I can't escape, come and wrap me in the Winding Sheet.

*

The Dover Road

To-morrow

I lay down at noonday on my green couch and I had a quaint dream. I have just awakened from it in a flush of languor and comfort. And the dream is vivid in my mind. I dreamed I was married and it was pink-and-pearl dawn in my married bed-room. And in the bed one inch away from mine was not my married husband but "another man." It was no man I can recall having seen. As I look back into the dream he seems of the nowhere, a stranger. But in the dream he was no stranger. I had crudely admitted him to my night. And I had just awakened in the pink-and-white dawn and was sitting silk-gowned and ruffle-haired in my bed, cross-legged like a tailor with my elbows on my knees and my chin on my palms, idly contemplating him. And he was lying in the other narrow bed contemplating me and smiling a little. He had nice teeth and yellowish hair. The crux of the dream was the sound "off-stage" of the approaching footsteps of monsieur-the-husband. As it always is in the psychology of dreams the insistent thing in the situation was not the footsteps, nor even that they were approaching, but the sound: the elusive threat of their sound. He would presently discover us. Nobody appeared to care: not "another man" smiling so tranquilly: not I sitting musingly over-looking him who had overnight "enjoyed me": not the husband, because he never knew it - before he could open the guilty door I awoke.

A short-cut gently headlong dream. I was at once married, mixed adulterantly with an imperfect stranger, and awaiting in pleasant mild anticipation, to match the pink-and-pearl of the summer dawn, the climax in the approaching sound of my husband's footsteps. It was humorous and artistic. Unseemly preliminaries were done away with in that dream. I was given at once the one exciting worthwhile moment in it.

Having no data as to what were my husband's temper and tenor, what he looked like or who he was, I could not in the dream or out of it surmise what he would say or how he would act when he opened the door.

- a theme for idling speculation in a summer's day -

Also I wonder whence came that dream: so Unexpected: so Irrelevant to any thought in me: so Artistically Right: so Disgusting: so Dramatic: so quaintly Vulgar.

A question: to which the one answer is that unanswerable answer to all questions, propounded by Mr. F.'s Aunt - "There's milestones on the Dover road."

*

The Harp of Worn Strings

To-morrow

May I own no unleavened egotism.

May I own no egotism that is not sensitive and poignant and vibrant: a harp of Worn Strings.

The surprising world is full of non-analytic persons of ox-eyed vision and hen-headed mental calibre whose egotism is a stupendous impregnable armor: those who burned the Maid of Orleans: those who crucified the prophet of Nazareth: those who killed John Keats.

They inherit the earth, which is a Golden-Green earth, but never look at it.

They accept this life, which is Intoxicating life, but never feel its texture with their fingers.

They gather a Blue iris by a marsh-edge and let it die in their sweating hands, or let it fall to the ground as they walk, or throw it away when the Blue petals droop: without looking at it and breathing it and knowing it: without sensing the tremulous Blue to be lovelier in its wilting.

Theirs is the thick fat solidly-fierce egotism of an emperor or an infant whose main metaphysic concept is that *he* is alive, and will remain alive, and must be alive, though all around him bleed drop by drop to their death.

I have analyzed mine, and it is not so with me.

If I say I am enchanting or false or despicable it is because I know it's true. Not because I say it but because I have tested and proved it. I feel the textures of my life with the tips of my fingers. I turn my senses outward and let the old winds blow over them - icy, balmy, harsh, gentle, scorching, cooling. I suffer for it but I know those winds: songs of seas and stars and of little pebbles are in their thunderous-dim wailing: life is in the soft stinging perfume of their wings.

No breath of poetry and beauty comes to me that I do not pay for with the beating ache of my Heart, the nervous tensions of my Body, the fraying and shredding of my Soul. If any beauty or poet-thing comes easily and gives me pleasure and not pain, I know I have not yet got it and that it will come again.

It will come again: with the pain.

I can't eat cake and have it.

I can't make silk purses out of sows' ears.

Those things I learn nearly perfectly from playing on my harp with the Worn Strings.

*

A Strongly-Windy Saturday

To-morrow

It is a strongly-windy Saturday.

A thought achieves itself in my roiled-and-placid brain: that one half of me is Mad, but the other half is doubly Sane and someway over-Sane, so that in it all I break a little better than even.

*

A Someway Separate Individual

To-morrow

This body I live in is familiar and mysterious.

It is like a book of poetry to read and read again.

It has the owned sentientness of bone-and-flesh, and with it tremors fine as spirit-emotions.

My Body is more chaste than my Mind, my Heart, and my Soul. My Body if fragile is healthful, and is one with the woman-race. It moves with the sunlit cosmos. My Mind wanders in sex-chaos and muses on piquant impure things, enchanting villainies, odd inversions, whatnot. My Soul - a sweet and an exquisite Thing - its tired wings have borne it languidly down the dim stairways of many centuries, some leading in wilful perverted ways. And my Heart is a pagan Heart. Its essence is flavored with the day and lyric trail of the Sapphic students.

Bodily I am also pagan in the freedom of my owned sex feelings - as are all women. Most of them do not know it and those who do hide it in a tomb-like silence, except the brazen, the headlongly honest, and the artlessly frank. I come under none of those heads. I am myself. I live and ponder alone.

And my Body feels consciously aloof and as a someway separate individual: with inner organs as eternal hopes, smooth skin as emotion, and drops of blood as thoughts - little drops of sparkling red virile sweet blood for its thoughts.

I so *love* my Body as it lives and breathes and moves about, with me and close to me. It is my so constant companion. It is an attractive girl, a human being of some charm. I love it for the priceless air it breathes and the long jewel-days of sunshine it has known: for the tiny wears and tears of its daily life - the rending of its magic tissues with each going-up-or-down-stairs, each crossing of a door-sill.

I love it for that it must lie at last pale, pale and still - still - still - in its grave.

I love my Body for its woman-complexities of sex.

I love it for the lonely lyric poetry of its cell-adventures.

I love my Body for this long journey of woe and loveliness which it goes, from Birthday to Deathday, in wilding passions of subtle nervousness: each day a day of bodily beauty and intolerableness and fear and utter mystery: because life *is*, and because I own a white smooth-skinned Body, and because the strange, strange Air of Everyday breathes on it - touches it - always!

*

Sincerity and Despair

To-morrow

I am a true Artist, not as a writer but as a writing-person. I try to feel myself literarily a poet - finer-made than a god. But I fail as a poet-*litterateur* as I fail as a poet-person. A poet flies always on wings of fiery gold though it might be waywardly. But often I walk with my feet in odd gutters, and have some plaisance in them, and analyze their gutteriness absorbedly and own them as part of my portion.

- poet or no poet, it is best to be myself. In heights and murks and widths and trivial horrors, myself -

But as an Artist I am in the true. As a painter of words and maker of paragraphs which picture my phases and emotions, and in my conscious feeling anent it, I realize the artist *flair*, the artist temper.

It is not a literary but a personal art.

I have what goes with all artist-matter - long periods of dry-rot when having nothing ripe to write I write nothing. My Artist-spirit proves itself, justifies itself in my times of stagnation and reaction. Out of it something human and sad and lustrous grows in me, something which is half worldly but awaits its ripe time of expression with someway-divine scorn.

I once thought me destined to be a "writer" in the ordinary sense. And many good people visioned a writing career for me. It has a vapid taste, just to recall it. My flawed life has that to felicitate upon - that I have not spent it in fat lumps of writing, magazine tales and sex-novels. In the days, and later, when my *demi-vierge* book made its success I was besought by publishers to write others - to go on, to reap and garner. I pushed all that away with a preoccupied hand, not as part and parcel of my wastrel living but in my assured Artist-temper.

I should feel more true-to-form to earn my living by making linen roses in a shop, along with rows of pale women, than by my writing.

My writing to me is a precious thing - and a rare bird - and a Babylonish jade. It demands gold in exchange for itself. But though it is my talent it is not my living. It is too myself, like my earlobes and my throat, to commercialize by the day.

But I can not think of me as an Artist without thinking of me as a Liar. The two are someway related. I am an appalling, an encompassing Liar. I am a Liar by the clock. My life ticks out silent lies as my little clock ticks out seconds. It is a phase hard to put my finger on. I feel it on me the way I feel a headache. I write this book with seriousness and earnestness. It is all a mood of sincerity and despair. But except I give it some backgrounding of lies, though each thing in it is fair fact, I fail as an Artist.

It is strange about lies - any lies, all lies. They are muscularly stronger than truths. They come more readily to human tongues. They fit more easily into the games of this life. And in me they seem needful to my Artist mind.

I mean not the lies I may tell but the lies I think.

I mean not my falseness. That is a different thing, one I feel someway responsible for. But the thinking lies feel to be a heritage from ancient evil selves.

I lie to myself, to the air around me - I blow lies into space from my quiet lips. And one half of me knows them for lies and the other half of me *believes* them.

Those half-known lies, the *need* of the lies half-believed, are the realization of an essential Artist-spirit.

The oblique belief in them and the recognition of them as lies proclaim me to myself, as a writing-person: Liar and Artist.

*

It's Not Death

To-morrow

It's not Death I fear, nor Life.

I horridly fear something this side of Death but out-pacing Life a little: a nervousness in my Stomach - a very Muddy Street - a Lonely Hotel Room.

*

A Human Prerogative

To-morrow

It is a quiet deep of night. A bell has just tolled two.

I am clothed in cool bedroom negligeés and a softening sweetness of cold cream, from head to foot.

I am tranquil for to-day I had a walk that made me feel Sincere and Safe.

It is a comforting feeling: it is like a beef-sandwich.

It was a long walk south-east of Butte along an outskirting road where I used often to walk when I was sixteen - a broad gray desert. It was the same sand and barrenness. It was bare and withered as if a giant coyote had picked its rocky ribs.

The day was windy and dusty. The sunshine was thick and sweet and heavy like floating honey. The dust that blew against the white of my neck was like ground glass.

My feet ached as I walked.

My shoes were Cuban-heeled thick-soled pumps of corded silk, a kind easy to walk in. But the same feet which once readily bore me seven miles along that road ache now at three. All of me ached as I walked along. I cursed desultorily with a smooth whispered flow of curses, because the circumstances seemed to demand it. But I loved the walk - even the more for my tired feet and my aching knees and my irking drooping shoulders and the hot glazed sand against my throat.

My Soul tasted realness in it.

Quite close to me, in immense sad beauty, were the deep high heavy silent somber hills of Montana. To-day the nearer ones were a stately enchanted Blue: a Blue of all ages: a Blue of infinitude: a Blue with a feel of life and death in its Blueness. Above it the sky was not blue but a pale glimmering shimmering silver hung across with gray silk clouds soft as doves' plumage.

I sat on a flat rock and looked at all of it and at the desert around, and at my dusty shoes.

All of it felt overwhelmingly sincere: at one with the wide worn used earth.

My dusty shoes looked to be at one with it and could interpret it.

I felt my shoes could claim their human prerogative of getting dusty in any of this world's roads.

It gave me a feeling of human Sincerity: good-and-evil Safeness.

It is on me now, along with cold cream and strong memory of Desert and Sun and Blue.

It is as good as a beef-sandwich.

Better: I don't like beef-sandwich.

*

The Merciless Beauty

To-morrow

Sometimes the dusk is full of fire.

Some dusks I sit by my window looking out and hotly and coldly want a Lover: hotly with my Body and coldly with my Mind.

A dusk has just gone. I sat looking out at it.

A mist of dark cream tinged with heated violet came from nowhere and hung above the ground.

Suddenly came on me a sense of bewildering mysterious beauty.

In it was a feel of rippling warmth that crept into my bone-and-flesh from forehead to heel, from temples to soles, from crown to toe-tips.

It crept slow and suffocating like magic chloroform.

I leaned elbows on window-sill and chin on palms and sunk my gaze in the violet shades outside and straightway knew I wanted a Lover: not in delicate moonlit culmination like Juliet in her balcony: not denyingly like the timid young nun in her cloister assailed unaware by faint forbidden emotions.

I wanted a Lover like the jungle leopard leaping through the Springtime covert at nightfall to find her mate.

It is a subtle and an obvious feeling, made of a merciless beauty.

It is the tired urge of sex-tissues and nerve-cells: positive, furious, fiery as the bloodiest sun. It is the same which the heated leopard feels in her sharp immaculate lust. It is quite the same - but it could not move me as I sat alone loverless to the knitting of an eyebrow, to a change of posture, a movement of elbows on the window-sill or of palms beneath my chin. Nor could it, though the potential Lover had stood outside my window.

For any woman of any charm the world is full of Lovers: each and all to be had by the flutter of her finger, the droop of her white eyelids, the trembling of her pink-bowed lips. The world is full of them - facile Lovers, craven, potent, and pinchbeck. And it's that kind I want hotly with my Body, coldly with my Mind in dusks of rippling warmth - rippling, rippling warmth -

I want the Lover as the leopard wants hers. But I'm not a leopard: instead, a woman-person of keen sentientness and wild wistful imagination. So I wouldn't so much as crook a finger to call a Lover to me: a curious nervous inertia.

It's only I *want* the Lover with frantic blind cosmic ardors inside me.

I analyze it in my magic Mind and find I would call no Lover. I analyze farther and find I'd reject all but an impossible one-in-ten-thousand. But remains the desire, hot as live embers, cold as hail.

Sex is an odd attribute. It has been to me like a blest impediment and a celestial incumbrance and a radiant curse. -

When I was seventeen I stood on a threshold and peered curiously into a dim-lit strange-scented Room.

It was unknown to me then. My mind alone bespoke it. As I stood at its doorway the air it wafted out touched my sense with only the lightest frayed-cobweb contact, unintelligible and unenlightening. I had lived an emptily alone girlhood. I was icily virginal.

At five-and-twenty I crossed the Room's threshold. I breathed lightly the odd fragrance. I looked curiously around. I touched some amorous-looking grapes and some love-promising apples that lay about: I bit into one and burst a grape with my finger and thumb. I gathered a weak-petaled flower or two. I gauged the Room and its furnishings and was unthrilled by anything in it. Even bodily it left me unthrilled.

Those two memory-mists do not keep me in the now-dusk and in the strength and terror and fire of top-most youth from wanting a sudden Lover with all that's in my Body.

Love has naught to do with it. Love is a flame-winged Bird. I know it. I know the values of my life and of me. I do not mistake tapers for torches, ducats for louis d'ors, vicarious nepenthe for dreamless death.

In dusk-moments my bone-and-flesh is all of me I'm sure of. It begins and ends in this earth. It answers the violent summonses of this earth and its dusks.

In the just-gone dusk I felt the prickling blood flow to my finger-ends. A flood-tide, blinding red, surged and seethed and bubbled and pounded at my heart.

"I want a Lover - some Lover" - I murmured to the shadows beyond my window.

I grew breathless.

The spirit of my flesh rose like a wind-blown flame.

A loud cry rang in my nerve-wilderness.

That moment the variant analysis which always rides with me stopped dead.

There came instead sheer feeling - the merciless beauty.

- a man-person, maybe - the man of happy unanalytic brutality - to be suddenly there with me: to flash into my shadowy solitude like a lightning bolt and burst and break me

- a quarter-hour of exquisite wildness - restlessness, made of Star-flame and Lily-petal and Cloud-burst on Mountain-summits and Sea-waves purple in a Stormy Dawn - an intolerable hunger and ecstasy -

But just gone and I sit writing it in the pale cast of thought.

But breathlessly I recall the breathlessness of it.

*

My Shoes

To-morrow

I love my Shoes.

I love them because they so guard my feet.

I walk many a mile along the stone pavements and into distant odd streets and on open roads at the outskirts of this Butte.

And while I walk I think.

I think things of a great many kinds - potent and magic and mad. The act of walking starts an engine in my sparkling infernal mind. And the weight and the sting and the hurt and the fascination of my walking thoughts bear down on my slim feet as they carry me along. And the hard-beaten world beneath them feels resentful and uncomplaisant to my soles.

And then I look down at my Shoes with their trim tailored vamps and their walk-worthy soles and instantly my feet feel secure against evil, smartly protected from my thoughts and from the world's surface: my thoughts which shoot down on them out of my devilish brain and the world-hardness beneath them.

To-day I was walking along the road that leads up the ever-wonderful Anaconda Hill - a place of stones and sand-wastes and hoists and scaffoldings and mines with ten thousand digging men thousands of feet down in their metallic bowels. Close by were melancholy mulberry-toned mountains at the north-east. They were tragic, triumphant, grief-stricken, terrifyingly beautiful. Purple clouds hung around them like mourning veils. I can't look enough at those - it is as if there weren't enough looking-power in my human gray eyes.

Presently I came to a small open space as I walked, a toy desert. A toy desert is more like a desert than is a real one. The sand in it is grayer sand. The stones are abrupter. The sun is flatter-looking. The air is less willing to furnish breath to a human being. The best that could be said of this one is that it was intolerably desolate. I looked about and about it. And suddenly I was afraid. Afraid of many things: afraid of grief-stricken mountains: afraid of my life and of Me.

I leaned against a yellow ledge of rock with a subtle sickening faintish feeling. "I am afraid," I said inside me, "of this world and this life, and of all things little and large - nerves and Christmas days and poetry: toy deserts and all. How can I cope with it - I alone?"

Then I looked down at my Shoes of black soft dull leather and cloth, buttoned snugly around my ankles and with tough supple soles fit to take me to Jericho and back. Thus neatly armored I felt suddenly my blue-veined feet need fear nothing from sand and stone and hardness of ground. And if my feet are not afraid - my feet which bear weights of all-of-me - why should afraidness touch my spirit which is proud?

There will be always Shoes in the world: stout stylish serviceable boots, and pale delicate rat-skin pumps, and satin mule-slippers.

And always I shall have Shoes: in toy deserts I shall have black strong snug-buttoned ones.

I looked at them in this toy-desert and straightway I wasn't afraid.

It has been often like that.

So I love my Shoes.

An Eerie Quality

To-morrow

When I was Ten years old I played marbles "for keeps," smoked little pieces of rattan buggy-whip in the hay-scented barn and slid "belly-buster" down long winter hills on my sled. And I hammered and sawed ruinously with grownup tools, whistling happily. And I played with dolls absorbedly for hours on end.

I was not boyish and not girlish.

I was not childish except for an oddly hungry child-heart.

I was myself.

So long ago and longer I consciously owned an eerie quality which toppled over the edge of my humanness.

And still own it.

*

A Helliad

To-morrow

This noonday as I sat on the veranda two young lads stopped by the stone coping which borders this front yard, and conversed. One was eager-looking and about eleven years old. The other was perhaps thirteen and morose and he had a small rifle which he polished with a bit of waste, not lifting his gaze as they talked.

Said the younger boy: "Say-Frank, I could'a had that old shot-gun off my dad if I'd'a went after it to Rocker that time."

"Like hell you could," said Frank.

"Say-Frank, you know that Winchester o' Billy O'Rourke's? - he made six bull's-eyes and one inside ring with it day 'fore yesterday."

"Like hell he did," said Frank.

"Say-Frank, Mexicans and Indians can get a guy ev'ry time with a long-distance rifle without taking aim through the sight."

"Like hell they can," said Frank.

"Say-Frank, there's a kid down on South Arizona that's got a Colt automatic that'll hit without him aiming at all."

"Like hell there is," said Frank.

"Say-Frank, you know them little brass machine-guns the militia's got? - the bores o' them things're rifled just like this."

"Like hell they are," said Frank.

"Say-Frank, my grandfather in Illinois's got a bullet in him he got at the battle o' Fredricksburg in the Civil War."

"Like hell he has," said Frank.

"Say-Frank, it costs a hundred thousand dollars to make a Krupp gun and eighty dollars ev'ry time you fire it."

"Like hell it does," said Frank.

"Say-Frank, it ain't a felony to croak a burglar with a gun even if he's only breakin' into somebody else's house."

"Like hell it ain't," said Frank.

"Say-Frank, my mother goes huntin', too - she can shoot rabbits and ducks on the wing and once she got a deer with that big old .44 o' my Uncle Walt's."

"Like hell she did," said Frank.

"Say-Frank - listen, will you gimme your gun for my bicycle, both my catcher's gloves, and four dollars when I get paid?"

"Like hell I will," said Frank.

"Say-Frank - listen, will you gimme it for my bicycle, my two catcher's gloves, four dollars when I get paid, and my shepherd pup?"

"Like hell I will," said Frank.

"Say-Frank - listen, - and my artificial snake?"

"Like hell," said Frank.

"Say-Frank - listen, - and my half o' Ernest's camera?"

"Like hell," said Frank.

"Say-Frank - listen, - and my last year's shin-guards?"

"Like hell," said Frank.

"Say-Frank - *listen*, - and my *this* year's shin-guards?"

"Like *hell*," said Frank.

"Say-Frank, come right down to it I don't want a .22. If I get a gun this year it'll be a .32."

"Like he -" -

Which point I felt to be the top-note of the helliad, so I rose and came into the house.

I felt replete with rhythm and with a sense of surprising human attitudes remote from my own.

*

Swift Go My Days

To-morrow

Swift, Swift go my days.

By rights I think time should drag with me, for I am wasting my portion of life as I live it.

But my days pass Swift - Swift, Swift.

They come, they fly away - before I know.

I'm thinking it is Tuesday: but while I'm thinking - Wednesday has come: and gone: and Thursday is rushing in. Tuesday, blue-and-gold or gray-and-silver, with its mornings and nights and bits of food and openings of doors and thinkings: Wednesday with the same equipment: Thursday the same.

Each day comes and goes like a flash of filmed silvered garbled light.

But there is time in each for me to touch the enchanted Everydayness: time for the turbulent sly delight of tasting, smelling, feeling the eternal humors and romances in each small thing near me - my Clock, my Window, my Jar of Cold Cream, my Two Thumbs. There is time in each day for it to make me pay a wearing glimmering feverish homage to the mystic daily godhead.

My life exacts terrific homages from me.

I am wearing out - frailly, tiredly, from a desolate uneasy love of living.

It is why my days go Swift when by rights time should drag leadenly in punishment for barbarous futileness.

There is not time-space enough in any of the days sufficient to love the virile green and the murderous red and the sweet pale surprising purple in the sunset above the west desert: nor space to love the smell of a sudden August rain: nor the flaming delicate Idea of the poet John Keats.

While I'm starting to love each of those to its height of love-worthiness - the to-day is gone: and the to-morrow, which must see a new love-game started for each Thing, is come.

But while I say "is come": it's gone.

So Swift go my days - oh Swift, Swift!

*

By the Blood of Dead Americans

To-morrow

Since I wrote the beginning of this there has come the war in Europe: a war full of suffering brave women and dead children: full of German greed and cruelty and stupidity and of French gameness and cheerfulness, French splendor of valor.

It has an effect of some kind on each person who reads so much as its "headlines."

It has the effect on me of making me a jealously patriotic American.

It makes me think of Lexington and Gettysburg with an odd furious personal shame.

We are Americans not by accident but by the blood of dead Americans. But we assume it is by accident.

We lie down like a nation of bastards to let the pig-hearted Hun trample by proxy on our neck.

It was for America to declare war in the same hour the *Lusitania* passengers met murder. We were not "too proud" but afraid. Afraid and not ready.

Not ready has no right thing to do with it.

They were not ready at Lexington.

I long with some passion to exchange my two black dresses for two white ones with red crosses on the sleeves: to serve my country in a day of death and honor.

It too is all the time under my skin though I write along but in this flawed song of myself.

*

To Express Me

To-morrow

I suppose I'm very lonely.

It is luck - luck from the stars - not to be beset by clusters of people, people who do their thinking outside their heads, "cheerful" people, people who say "pardon me": all the damning sorts scattered about obstructing one's view of the horizons.

But for want of - other, *other* people - I am intensely lonely.

When I was eighteen I thought I must be the most lonely creature in this world. I analyzed my life then as now and it by itself had set me apart. But I stood then as it's given Youth to stand - on High Ground. I was strong to endure loneliness while viciously hating it.

There was unaware a hope-colored bliss in my inexperience which companioned me. I felt it then without knowing I felt it. I can see that plainly now.

Now also I see plainly and feel plainly that I stand on lower ground, at poorer vantage. As my bodily strength which was then robust is now slight. The metaphysic life-shadows reach me more easily. They have a feel of fatally shutting down, fatefully closing in. They are the mirages on the dun-colored worldly air near me of my own useless untoward selves. There is no more the hope-colored bliss.

At eighteen I said to me: "I'm lonely but some day I may be happily friendshiped and apprehended and it will be like paradise."

Now I say to me: "I'm lonely by fate and by nature and temperament. I've known some friendships of vivid alluringness and informingness - they await me now in the offing. And others. There *is* paradise in it - an odd sweet dubious paradise. But what's the use - ?"

It's that what's-the-use, born of the lower vantage-ground and the closing-in shadows, that chiefly makes me lonely - lonely to a desperateness and on through to a ruinous calm.

It is this metaphysic loneliness which breeds in me one constant reason-less restless urgent motif: to Express me: not of-the-past except desultorily, not of-the-future save indifferently: but of my low-toned, low-echoing now. Until I've Expressed me there's no setting open the gates of my spirit to a passer-by, though the passer-by should be a poet-in-the-flesh, a god, an angel with a torch.

Four-and-twenty turbulent moods may break over me in a day, or four-and-twenty passive ones, or four-and-twenty someway joyous ones. But like the theme in a fugue this loud tranquil recurrent need to Express me transcends them all.

It is a big voracious part-human bird of prey. Of it too I say what's-the-use. But it is a need without a use, a need scornful of use. It springs unconceived, unsourced from inside me. It rises from the ashes of blightingest moods and beats its bruising strong wings against my face.

It says: "Know me, defer to me, Slim-woman. Serve me, follow me, gather-in all your answers for me. Do this though I undo you, though I rend you, tear you with my sharp teeth so like a wolf's. When you've answered me I may let you go. Until then, turn to me. Tell me: tell me again and again. Utter yourself. Interpret. Unfold."

It makes my life-space someway sweet, someway heartbreaking, someway frightful - strewn with dust of broken stars.

I live long hours of nervous profound passionate self-communion. I discover strange lovely age-worn facets of my Soul. I discover the subtle panting Ego - the wonderful thing that lives and waits in its garbled radiance just beneath my skin.

To ask oneself and make answer out of oneself is the most delicious of this life's mental delectations. I might have missed it but for those beating bruising wings against my face, now and years ago: for expressing breeds the last Expressions.

I might have gone on through years and decades and lumps of months knowing at best a little of some rare person, a little less or more of another rare person, a little of a musician's soul in a nocturne, a little of a dead poet's splendors. But to Me and my own fine spirit-relationships to those things I could remain, but for my radiant flawed egotistic interpreting, eternally strange.

But for it I'd not have the wit to perceive the one human being in the world I may know with vitalness: my own Self. I should drop into my grave at last without a good-by to the glowing one who was locked just inside, whose hand I'd never clasped, whose sad prescient eyes I'd never looked in, who was then flitting out and on and away.

It is a being cruel and transfiguring and terrifying: terribly worth clasping close and breathing with.

And some days it sleeps, sleeps like the dead: it is delicater than rose-vapors before the dawn: a sun-blown faëry thing.

When it sleeps I'm left alone. Then comes a doubtful dreadful quiet, a hell of dumbness that only God could reach.

It is as if neither God nor I attempts to cope with it.

*

Bastard Lacy Valentines

To-morrow

The thing I admire most is strength. The thing I most hate is Weakness, of each and every kind.

All the reassuring things in the world are in and of the strong deeds done in it. All the mischief and despair come from human Weakness.

I would better strongly murder my foe than forgive him Weakly for my seeming advantage. I would be happier in my mind as a careful charwoman than as a loose-jointed poet. I would rather have a farthing's value as a faithful concubine than no value as a slattern housewife.

Strength repays itself with strength - and with magnificence.

Truth is strength nearly always: and *not* always. To cheat strongly in the life-game gets me more than does Weak easy honesty. By being a strong man Napoleon brought home the bacon. Being an honest one would have got him not one rasher of the bacon of *his* desire. The race is too ridden with "temperament" to let truth be its prevailing force. But strength plows its scornful way through temperament like a steam-shovel. The bacon Napoleon brought home he took from other people, causing them misery. They were Weak and let him take it, or they were strong and got killed trying to keep it. To get killed trying to keep your bacon is to be even stronger than the Napoleon who lives and takes it from you. Those who sit still and *let* Napoleon get their bacon are fit only to be themselves made into bacon.

Truth belongs with love, with friendship, with charity, with psychic lovingkindness: with all the altruistic graces and tendernesses.

But in the mere grinding livingness of things it is to be strong. I say to Me, "Mary MacLane, be strong: whether you're living joyous on a hill or mournful in a valley, make shift to be strong."

In which paragraphs I make an apologetic preamble to Me when about to dwell on my odd ironic element of Weakness. My Weakness is not an art nor a science nor a gift nor a trait but is a sort of ruinous trade touched with all of those, a trade at which I work and lose heavily from a viewpoint of personal economy.

In Atlanta-Georgia lives a man with whom I exchange semi-occasional letters. He is thirty-nine and clever and what is called a business man. He is a business man not only by circumstance but by nature. At a glance one would picture him in the setting of an office in a steel-and-brick building with a roll-top desk, a swivel chair, a cabinet full of files, a stenographer with an unregenerate vocabulary, and stationery neatly engraved with his name, his business, his cable address, and his telephone number. The look of the neat letterhead and the fibrous feel of the bond paper give one the idea that whoever went into a business venture with him would come out of it disadvantageously.

After another glance at himself one would infer that his leisure hours might be fancifully spent. In hours of ease some business men follow baseball, others golf, "tired" ones musical comedy. Others take up curio collecting or some personal phantasm. In the latter category is my acquaintance of Atlanta. He affects Mary MacLane and musings of her in his leisure hours. But what I am to him does not concern nor much interest me. What he is to me concerns me, for he - his letters - are a present source of my elaborated Weakness.

I feel a wave of conscious Weakness washing over me as I write about it. His letters make a soft buffer, a foolish pretty window, a tinted veil between me and my too-harsh actualities.

I met him when I lived in New York. He had read the book I wrote in the early nineteen-hundreds and at meeting me he conceived a thinly insistent admiration which someway went to his head. He has at intervals since then written me letters full of charmed and salubrious flattery and of appreciation and praise for traits and gifts and qualities which I do not possess. They appeal and cater remarkably to my vanity - and are pleasant and unreal and vain and fatuous and fond and piquant.

He is a clever man and does not make love to me. A butcher's-boy may write love-letters - and I'd prefer those of a butcher's-boy to those of a business man: they would be more sincere and less hopelessly discreet. But this business man is discerning and intuitive and writes me no love. His wife - a business man always has a wife - could not rationally object to what is in the letters, though she would irrationally and naturally object to the letters themselves. She is unloving and unloved - they always are - but whatever may be her caste (I know only that she is tall and blonde and named Bertha) she doubtless would find something superfluous in the idea of her husband's letters to me.

A letter comes from him in Georgia after I have written him a brief disquieting one with a latent human appeal in it to make him think the chief thing I need in life is his appreciation, his attitude toward me, to brace my spirit. Then his comes, written in his small slanting commercial hand. It is arresting from any angle and well thought, well couched.

In it he tells me that my brain, scintillantly brilliant though it is, needs the dim twilights of other brains such as his to catch the sparks it throws off.

Which is a lie. My brain is not scintillantly brilliant and it "needs" nothing. But the lie is agreeable to read. There is a gentle caressingness in its untruth which feels someway soothinger than any flattering fact.

And he tells me my chief attraction as an individual is my ability accurately to gauge another individual and to breathe myself graciously out to it and upon it while pretending to be immersed in my own ego.

Which is another lie. Immersed in my own ego is never a pretense with me, and I have not gauged - in the sense of weighing and measuring - another individuality except to hate it. But it is piquantly restful to hear that I am thus benign.

And he tells me that though several years have passed since he and I took leave of one another he has never forgotten that last parting because it was like the passing of a little weir-woman who brushed him lightly with her garments as she went.

Which is another lie. My association with him was in brief meetings at hectic studio tea-fights and two noisy dinners at Churchill's, at all of which I frowned impatiently at his tiresome conversation. And his leave-taking with me consisted in his sharpening a lead-pencil - beautifully he sharpened it - for me to write a telegram with. It was not until this correspondence that we established an unreliable intimacy. But to be told I seemed a weir-woman to a hard-headed business man who could doubtless cheat a client out of four thousand dollars easily in a half-day's maneuvering is oddly inspiriting.

And he tells me he is highly privileged to be permitted to gaze in at the mezzo-tinted windows of my soul, which are surely curtained against the passing proletariat.

Which is another lie. He has never remotely glimpsed my tired Soul in the firmly false little letters I've written him. As to its being a privilege if he had: it is the proletariat, it so happens, who have first chance at those windows, which are not mezzo-tinted but made of the plainest of plain glass. But the conceit tastes mellow and naif and bromidic and appetizing to me, like cream and raspberries in July.

And he tells me the most delightful thing in the world would be to live near me and have a season of daily meetings - meetings of astral selves upon a "higher plane" whereon we should exchange those flowers and fruits of the spirit which grow not from the soils but from the esoteric essences of life: - that sort of thing.

Which is another lie. No possible man (except a Poet whom I loved - or perhaps a scientist -) could find me delightful for more than two consecutive meetings - I develop something like temper - and I care for no higher planes except in airships. As for esoterics, I would fainer exchange musings anent over-shoes than over-souls. And my spirit bears in fertile earthy soil chiefly thistles from which men gather no figs. But it gives me a warmish feeling, similar to a hot-water bottle between my shoulders on a winter night, to read that picturesque palaver written to me in my slim scorn by him in his springy swivel chair.

Thus it goes. His letters are made all of softest quaintest lies which I know to be lies the moment my gray gaze falls on them. All his premises in regard to me and his deductions from them are roundly lightly mistaken. But I like that fluent flattery the more because it is so false. I am too vain a creature to want to cope often with truths even though they might be uplifting self-lauding truths. My vain peculiar Weakness demands as well semi-occasional collations of creamed lies upon which it feeds like a sleek cat on creamed fish. My humor enters into it, in no obvious way but eerily like a gay ghost. My humor is a strong influence in me. It is stronger than my pride and anger and fear and caution and reverence and self-love - stronger than most things I own.

And it's for reasons of pastime and vanity and oblique humor I let letters from the business man come, though not often, into my solitudes. And I spend hours of inert time-waste conning his fanciful ideas. And the letters I write him in reply, though brief and impersonal and done in my best false manner, consume a surprising lot of time and mental and physical force to write. It is the Weakness in it which is so devouring: it eats me hungrily and lingers about like a buzzard, picking my bones.

A spinelessly Weak game. I hate its Weakness more than I like its pleasant futility. I hate it and myself in it all the time I'm dwelling on it. I hate it as I'd hate a little drug habit fastened on my nerves.

Its influence is the same but more insidious than a drug would be, more demoralizing. As feeling fear makes one afraid, feeling more fear makes one more afraid.

Still once in a month, once in a two-month, I feel the hankering itch to be applauded for second-rate qualities I do not own, and I give way to it: in a particularly Weak way, after my sanest self has reduced it analytically to shreds, and after saying bosh! with all my selves.

After telling Me too that it is a common-tasting game. Life is a strange music-clangor of gold bells, some silent, some far-echoing. And the common-tasting thing cracks a bell-edge.

Then briskly I answer the last letter from Atlanta-Georgia and soon there comes a fresh sheaf of smooth velvetish lies to pad my way.

There may come no more if this I write now should find its way to Atlanta-Georgia. Or if fate or Bertha should intervene.

But always I know Weakness of me will find ways to work at its losing trade.

It is of the dubious inevitable side of human nature - like gold teeth and tinned salmon and bastard lacy valentines.

*

Sweet Fine Sweatings of Blood

To-morrow

Merely from the view-point of outward intellect this book of myself is oddly difficult to write.

My most-loved thing to do and my hardest thing to do is to write.

It is hard to catch and hold with mental fingers one's own emotions and then doubly hard to write them.

A feeling is something without the words and without even the thought. To put it into the thought and then into the words is a minuter task than would be the translating of a Francois-Villon poem into Choctaw.

It's a knowing person who realizes her own emotions and a knowinger who recognizes what is what, who is who, which is which among them. I look inward at Me and I see an emotion of World-Weariness and want to write it. I write it as nearly as I can. But when I have done - it's not World-Weariness that I wrote but its twin sister, Boredom-of-the-Moment, which happened to be next the other when I looked.

I am glad to have transcribed Boredom-of-the-Moment. It is the finer and thinner and more elusive of the two. But how and why did I fail of World-Weariness?

But sometime when I aim at Fear or Resentment or Surprise it may be World-Weariness I'll bring down unexpectedly with a clean wing-shot.

When I set out to write the Look-in-my-Eyes it may be the Feel-of-my-Fingers that comes out in my round writing. Another time I think I'm writing my Bad-Tooth: until I get it written when it turns out to be my little Eye-Wrinkles.

Having failed of the thought often I fail of the words.

When I have a particularly M.-Mac-Lane thought to express I review the top tier of my vocabulary of words to find proper ones for it. They are all very nice words in that top-tier - neatly washed and dressed and hair-brushed and tidied-up, like the children in a small private school: words like Necessary and Irresolute and Crockery and Inconvenience and Broth and Apprise: good words and useful if one's thought is radical or risky and wants conserving. I call some of them to me and question them and consider them and ponder a bit, and decide they will none of them suit. Then I go to the bottom tier, the unkemptest of words in the untidiest attire: words like Traipse and Nab and Glim and Hennery and Chape and Plash. And I at once reject those as too carelessly bred for my terse thoughts to associate with. (But for my uncombed ungroomed grimy-faced thoughts I turn to them.) Then I glance over a tier of mysterious words, spruce but with inde-finable vagabond faces: such as Whelk and Mauger and Frush and Gnurl and Yare and Hyaline. They are expressive but of a kind it's well to use with caution, the kind that may trip up thoughts that would make them their medium and lead to slips 'twixt cups and lips. So I dismiss them with a mental reservation of one or two to use if I fail to find right ones among the less mysterious. Then I turn to a tier that represents the virile middle-class in words, the lower-case words, the mob and riot words, the words for poets and anarchists and prophets: such as Adroit and Nightingale and Gallows and Gutter and Woman and Madrigal and Death. And I say, "Without doubt here are my words." But I use discretion. I know that tier of words to be of the nature of bombs, of strychnine, of a dynamic force resistible against all human and worldly substance. They also must be used cautiously and with a sparing hand. With caution one can handle a bomb, and sparingly one can eat strychnine, and one can control any dynamic force by studying its tendencies and keeping out of its direct road. It behooves one to heed those conditions in broaching the counter-mining counter-irritant words if one would avoid blowing oneself analytically broadcast.

So I may have found the right sort of words and measured their pos-sibilities and pitfalls. But again: it's a nerve-racking task to choose out one word from seven, one from five, one from two. I see two words which may be the only proper ones out of ten thousand to bear my thought. The two may be Echo and After-glow, each an unacknowledged half-sister to the other: meaning respectively something living and growing and vibrant in my spirit-ears and fading and dying and radiant before my spirit-eyes. But because my spirit-ears may glow bright and hot from what they heard, or my spirit-eyes may seem to themselves to gaze a moment at a soundless sound - an Unheard Melody of Keats, - I miss the raylike distinction and I write After-glow when my true word was Echo.

But another time I write Echo perfectly and masterfully to my own delight: having meant After-glow.

So it is. There's no plain sailing on this analytic sea. And if there were it would be not worth while. I want nothing, nothing, nothing that comes easily. What comes easily I distrust, be it love or language. It afterward proves dead-sea fruit. What I suffer to get I know to be life-food even if it drugs or pains or poisons me. It is one lesson I have learned.

Without doubt it is so with everybody, all around. One sees only surfaces, husks. Anyone looking casually at this Me sitting writing might say, - "How easily and smoothly and well she writes. How kind of God to give her so light a task in life. How complacently go her working hours." And I looking casually at, oh, Miss Lily Walker singing and swaying and glancing sideways in a gorgeous Broadway chorus - I might say, "How easy a task in life has *that* brainless gazelle. To work with her body, and not even with the sweats and sinews of it like a scrub-woman, and not with the facile shames of it like a lorette, but with the grace and suppleness and beauty and suggestions of it, aided by a soprano throat and a soprano face - with only the effort it wants to fling it all over footlights. And that pastime gets her her livelihood."

But whoever marks me writing as one doing an easy task because I write along rapidly enough considers nothing of my mental travail for the thought, my blind grope for the language, my little nervous anguish of choice among the double-edged and triple-pronged words: and the neat concise failure of the result.

And no, I do not thus comment on Miss Lily Walker. I have an appreciative pleasure in her charm and suppleness and bird-and-butterfly prettiness. But after a bit of contemplation and analysis of her surface I deduce the unconscious struggle it may be for Miss Lily Walker to be supple on nights when she does not feel supple, the thin agony of being sweet when she does not feel sweet, the neurotic torture of being seductive *regularly* - by the night: the more that perchance the struggle always *is* unconscious. Her brain being required in her body it's to be assumed there's none in her head. But I can deduce a nervous red heart beating illogically somewhere in her being protesting dumbly sometimes against one irking item, sometimes against another, sometimes against all the items in Miss Lily Walker's scheme of life, but beating and beating on, like a little automatic drum wound up tight and tossed into a maelstrom to beat itself out.

I'd like - like with breathless eagerness - to read the analyzed being just beneath Miss Lily Walker's skin.

Everybody - every human being - is wildly *Real*: radiant and desolate. -

With no amount of temperamental struggling could Miss Lily Walker analyze a psychic emotion of her own and then find the right word-combination to write it in.

With no conceivable effort of mine could I manage to be supple when I do not feel supple.

So Miss Lily Walker and I are quits at this game.

It totals up evenly, all ways around.

Nobody gets through one Real day - though it be a dayful of Real lies - without a demoniacal struggle of soul or a heavy blow on the personal solar plexus.

And I make not even the intellect side of this book, which is a Realness to me, without sweet fine sweatings of blood.

*

Instinct - A "First Law"

To-morrow

I long to do a Murder.

Despite my futile way-of-life and my rotting destroying half-acquiescence in it I have a furious positive Murder in me.

One near me in my daily life injures me and goes on injuring me in a way which is scourging and malicious and intensely petty. There is in it helpless humiliation for me - me self-loving, proud, and determinedly unsuppliant - and it makes maddening Murder rise in me.

I don't know why I do not do the Murder. I have nothing to lose by paying the law-penalty: nothing but my life, and my life is stripped bare - and was always barren by God's decree - of all that makes a life sacred or lovely or precious. For long years and years, since child-days, I have been lost.

I don't know why I do not do the Murder: except that I think of it and brood over it and turn it round and round smoulderingly in my Mind. From no choice. I have tried to push the feeling away as a common thing beneath me. It is beneath me, for I am not little but someway big. But my

Mind will take its toll of all that confronts me.

The humiliation and the helplessness to combat being humiliated in me who keep a casual proudness toward people is like a secret hot sword thrust, and kept freshly thrust, in my flesh. It makes me wild to do the Murder. But it makes me brood over it till the red act is lost in red brooding.

There come also thinkings.

Murder, any Murder, is in its essence cowardly, a slinking meanness. And I am not cowardly and I am not mean. I am above malice and retaliation - all such impoverished impoverishing emotions. A shrug of my shoulders and they are satisfied. The impulse to hit back after a bitter wound is not of vengeance. It is instinct - a "first law." But Murder is self-accusingly cowardly and sneakingly human. I can't get away from that. To take away a person's life is like setting fire to his house - an officiously stooping act. It's for me to live my life in aloof self-sufficience. No human malice should reach me in it. Then it's not for me to reach out of it and stain my good fingers with unpleasant sticky blood. I am always in a prison of radiance and gloom.

But the mere habit of being a human being is breakingly insistent - no matter how many or how few frocks one owns. Neither of my two dresses is a protection against humiliation. A thin black serge dress gives me to myself a melancholy cold inert air: but beneath the smooth-fitting breast of it comes too often a throbbing frightful to feel, frightful to know, made of fierce petty anger and abasing hurt. I hide it and me in my room and twist my hands together and walk my floor, and a hurricane of helpless bitter trifling woe shakes and wrenches me. Then Murder enters me.

What humiliates me is an obvious common thing that to any human one would mean hurt and more hurt. Though I am determinedly brave I am sensitive.

I do not write itself because this is the book of me and not of people.

It is a slight, a poor and vivid cruelness. There is the tie of blood in it which in all ways - from a deep heritage - I respect: and it rubs an added stinging poison in the wound.

It is an injury I do not deserve. What I deserve I accept. What I do not deserve pressed on me to humiliate me makes Murder in me. Regardless of the other one -

- it would be simpler and finer for me to do that Murder than to keep it in me. So many times in a week the trembling smothering longing to do that Murder beats, beats in my thin breast. To be so owned by a thing so small: - it is grief and despair and fury and wild nervous intolerableness. It strains my flesh - it wrenches my pulse - it blinds my eyes - it fills my throat -

- it would be a simpler and finer thing to do any Murder than to feel, even once, the strangling damnedness, rising, rising at my throat -

*

Loose Twos

To-morrow

I take it for granted God knows all about me.

If God should read this it would not be news to him.

But his knowledge of me is not immediate knowledge, nor immediately interesting to him. He knows my Twos-and-Twos but he does not make Fours of them.

I am formed of loose Twos which wait for God to make them Fours.

I can not do it myself. When I've tried the added Twos come out threes, seventies, nines, twelves - all the mysterious numbers. Never Fours.

Long ago I decided not to try but to wait for God.

I juggle with temperamental and psychic Twos and experiment in hysteric additions.

But it's no good my trying to make Fours.

If God does not take it up I shall be eternal Twos.

And I seem not greatly to care: whenever that comes home to me I merely light a carefree cigarette.

*

Knitting or Plaiting Straw

To-morrow

The things I know are jumbled and tangled into an indescribable heap inside me.

The things I Don't Know are separated and ranged of their own volition in long orderly rows in my conscious mentality.

The things I know glow with tints and gleams and will-o'-wisp lights and primal colors and waveringly with the blinding gold-purple lightnings of all-Time.

The things I Don't Know glow - each one separately - with a small precise lantern-brightness of its own.

Also in my wide background are things I don't know and am unaware of it: the mass of my luminous Ignorance - it shines with an earthy phosphorescence.

When I look at the things I know I get an undetailed perspective of me like a bird's-eye view of London.

When I look at neat formal rows of things I Don't Know I have a clear look, as if through an uncurtained window into a bare little room, at my quietest self sitting knitting or plaiting straw.

I reckon up and count up and check up lists of big and little things I Don't Know - like this, rapidly: I Don't Know what ink is made of, nor how to fire a Maxim gun: I don't know how to make a will: I don't know how to cook a prairie-chicken, nor what to feed a pet weasel, nor who invented the snarling-iron, nor what it is.

I Don't Know what food people eat in the Himalaya Mountains, nor how Lord Cornwallis felt when he surrendered: I don't know the color of a chicken's gizzard, nor of sand, nor of fish-scales, nor of mice: I don't know whether an English cabinet minister needs strength of mind or strength of will, or both, or neither.

I Don't Know how I hurt the true heart of my friend: I don't know astronomy nor solid geometry: I don't know what I think with: I don't know what ooze leather is, nor who pitched for the Tigers in nineteen-nine.

I Don't Know a good horse from a bad horse: I don't know why a bat sleeps head downward, nor what wasps live on: I don't know how to open oysters, nor how to milk a cow: I don't know the Latin for "whiskey."

I Don't Know whether friendship is a selfish or an unselfish thing, nor who discovered the medlar apple: I don't know what is a jab, fistically speaking, nor a punch, nor a hook, nor a wallop, nor the fighting weight of Packey McFarland: I don't know whether a moth "marries" or whether her eggs are impregnated like a fish's: I don't know why a clasp knife is called a jack knife, nor what to do for an aching foot.

I Don't Know how glass is blown: I don't know whether coal is vegetable or mineral: I don't know the chemical composition of the sunset vapors, nor how to play euchre: I don't know how many guns an armored cruiser carries, nor whether a gorilla meditates: I don't know whether I hate or greatly admire Catherine and Marie de Medici: I don't know a winch from a windlass.

I Don't Know where is the cinnamon bear's native haunt: I don't know how flint is mined, nor if wire is made of steel: I don't know who was the better man - William Wordsworth or the Duke of Wellington: I don't know the advantages of tariff revision downward: I don't know where ex-President Taft will go when he dies.

I Don't Know whether I feel more comfortable with or without my stays: I don't know the origin of the word "dogged": I don't know whether a "full house" is better than "two pairs," nor whether a right merry heart to-day is better than a wrong contented mind to-morrow: I don't know whether rabbit-pie is made of cats in Paris, nor how many sails has a sloop: I don't know what makes a dead body rot.

I Don't Know how to sharpen a carving knife, nor how to roll a cigarette: I don't know the real English meaning of the French noun "élancement": I don't know whether my sex is a matter of my genital organs or of my mental inwards: I don't know how to determine the contents of a circle in square inches, nor how to pronounce "zebra."

I Don't Know whether Edgar Allan Poe is big or little: I don't know how many soldiers fell at Shiloh: I don't know whether temperament or nature or circumstance makes one woman a happy kindhearted whore and another an unhappy cruel-hearted nun: I don't know how to grow artichokes: I don't know what brimstone is, nor how to play the accordion: I don't know what quality in me forms my handwriting.

I Don't Know what-like was my Soul in the Stone Age: I don't know whether cheese is good or bad for my health: I don't know what becomes of discarded hairpins, nor a tooth-brush's ultimate destiny: I don't know the *Fra Diavolo* opera, nor whether anyone ever uses the word "thwack."

I Don't Know whether my heart breaks from within or without: I don't know whether "good old Marie Lloyd" of the London "halls" has a brain like G.K. Chesterton or a dexterous individuality like a juggler: I don't know whether I feel spiritual bliss in my knees or in my spirit: I don't know why I breathe and go on breathing.

I Don't Know what became of the ten lost tribes of Israel: I don't know how to say how-do-you-do to a king: I don't know the exact meaning of my terror and despair: I don't know why I love - why I ever love -

I Don't Know whether laws of chance govern a spinning roulette wheel and ivory ball or whether chance is beyond law: I don't know what kind of missile a Krupp gun shoots: I don't know how a ground-and-lofty tumbler turns a triple-air-summersault: I don't know whether I really am the way I look in the mirror: I don't know whether the Russian language has Romanic roots: I don't know what is the wild power in poetry.

I Don't Know whether lust is a human coarseness or a human fineness: I don't know why death holds a so sweet lure since it would take away my Body: I don't know that I wouldn't deny my Christ, if I had one, three times before a given cockcrow: I don't know on the other hand that I would: I don't know whether honor is a reality in human beings or a pose: I don't know that I mayn't be able to think with my Body when it is in its coffin.

I Don't Know what makes each day a Day of dark Gold and life mournfully precious: I don't know where is God: I don't know how they make tea in Ireland: I don't know how to pronounce the word "girl": I don't know how to make lace: I don't know whether I hear a sound or feel it, nor why a spool of thread looks exactly like a Spool of Thread.

I Don't Know - I Don't Know - I Don't Know, rapidly, to the end of the mystic common-place infinitudes.

- those give me a clear look, as if through an uncurtained window into a bare little room, at my quietest self sitting knitting or plaiting straw -

*

A Life-Long Lonely Road

To-morrow

Fleeting times I wonder if it is my defect or others' that no human family tie holds and warms me.

There is none. I think about it with wistfulness.

The only tie-of-blood feeling that clings to me is of my warming and keeping-alive. And it is very feeble. It grows more feeble.

It is a trivial matter as I look at it universally.

But as I look at it earthlily: there would be an abnormalness, a lostness in one when the mother who bore her got from it at best but a small cool dislike.

It makes me feel humanly lost.

"Lost" is the shuddering life-long lonely word that brushes against me some nights and noons.

*

Their Voices

To-morrow

Every day at half-past ten and half-past two I hear the high shrill sweet choric Voices of hundreds of children shaking the thin clear air.

A public school is but a block from here. The children rush out of it, a hilarious noisy crowd, for a few mid-morning and mid-afternoon minutes. So those minutes, from hearing their Voices day after day, and day after day, have become lyric to my inner-listening.

Their Voices stir me, rouse me, speak to me with old very joyous, very woful meanings.

The children fairly leap out of the school-building through doors and down fire-escape stairways. And their Voices are at once hurled skyward, clamorous and chaotic.

The Sound they make is a roundly common sound yet "winged." It is an untrammeled Sound, uncultivated, only a little civilized.

It is world-music.

In it is the note beyond culture, higher than civilization, and older. It is brave as voices of the shrilling winds and warmer, viriler. It is liltinger than bird-songs and lustier than roarings of mountain cataracts.

Music of the world! -

A little door inside me opens to those Voices.

My little door opens at the first shriek of the first child out of doors, and I hear not only the hundreds of vivid piercing Voices but more - their far-off echoes.

They are the Voices of children, children light-held in crude cold innocence. The eyes of the children are clear - their impulses and instincts rule their little lives. They are yet untouched by the tiredness and terror and shame and sorrow of being human beings.

So the Sound of their Voices sweeps out resistless and regardless as the sea or the sun which makes nothing of its own strength or weakness. And through my little spirit-door I hear them, the poignant common little sweet Voices, echoing, flying away, farther and farther: along the roads: over plains and hills: through valleys long worldly distances from here: through streets: through stone buildings and dingy courts: through big rich houses: through homes of comfort and homes of misery and homes of desolate smugness: into lifeless social foyers: into learned places: into law-courts and cabinet-rooms of nations: into graveyards and churches and down into dead-vaults: into theatres: into clinics: into shops: into factories: into dives and stews and brothels and at lustful doorsteps: into hotels and on sport-courses: into market-places and across battle-fields, round monuments, and in towers and in forts and in prisons and in dungeons: - there along fly their Voices.

It is a brave, brave Sound, and an insistent: nothing stops it.

It is triumph.

The noise of the noisiest battle dies away in time. The pounding of ocean-surf on the rocks and of electric thunder in the clouds are lasting only with this earth. But brave wild Voices of children fly on and on, outlasting a million earths, silencing aeons of thunder, floating strongly back of the stars. The voices of men - wizards, monks, artisans, thieves - echo no farther than their talking conceits: even of poets except as they catch up into their sonance something to interpret a cool gay clamor of child-Voices. The voices of women - singing women, lovely women, angelic honest women - die with their bodies: even of mothers of the children except as they follow with their own echo, by dream and shadow, the thronging child-Voices as they go.

For the Sound of the child-Voices is more potent than wizards' - it is not cramped into thought-forms: more devotional than monks' because super-conscious; more menacing than thieves' because absolute. And it echoes, echoes, echoes in the market-place full-tongued, ringing, rising like the northern gale when all the other voices are long dead-silenced: and after.

Music of the world.

This moment I hear it for it is half-after two of a bright gold day. The air is emotional, nectareal, and mellow and yellow and hot-sparkling. The Voices pierce it like a storm of fine steel arrows. I at once set open my spirit-door and through it come the sweet shrill chorus and the marvel echo beginning and swelling and starting away. It wakes vision so that I see - quick, evil, terribly human, in the dazzlingest daytime colors - all those Places where the Voices go.

I go to a window and watch the children running about beneath the high tide of their Voices. And they and the school-building and the streets and stone walls show in duller colors than the Places where their Echo goes.

- small girls with clipped hair and bloused cotton frocks, taller girls throwing a basket-ball, thin-legged little girls playing hop-scotch, groups of varied sizes with rainbow ribbons in their hair, confused masses of knitted sweaters and fat white-stockinged legs and shiny leather belts and ankle-strapped shoes, and little young shoulders and knees and waistlines - restless and kaleidoscopic -

- and confused boy-groups - little fellows in suits misnamed Oliver-Twist, larger boys of serge-Norfolk persuasion, types of the generic knickerbocker at once motley and monotonous - all with the strong sturdy calves of their legs clad in a time-honored kind of black ribbed stockings, all with the same breed of ties and collars and short-cropped hair, all with the tacit air of confessing themselves the most serenely cruel of all animals -

A careless conscienceless happy mob.

It is the Sound of their Voices that invests them with the terrifying Power, the long world-sweeping Force as of spirit and matter merged, the human radioactivity not evil and not good, stronger than all evil and all good.

Those children I look at must cease to be children, and must lose their Voices and grow into monks and thieves and singing women - must turn into persons - "Romans, countrymen, and lovers."

But will come after those another chorus: the same chorus: the same Voices.

The brief yellow mellow minutes have passed and the last shout has been silenced and the hundreds of children, Rainbow Hair-Ribbons and Black Ribbed Legs, are again gathered into the McKinley School.

And my little door is shut again: that door opens but for those Voices.

The Voices: their echo flying everywhere flies here into my still room: and it stirs me, rouses me, speaks to me with the old joyous woe.

Music of the world.

*

My Damns

To-morrow

I bear the detailed infliction of being a person with a tired mixture of patience and indifference and scorn.

I say on Monday, Damn the ache in my left foot: on Tuesday, Damn that rattling window - I hate it: on Wednesday, Damn this yellow garter - it's too tight: on Thursday, Damn my futile life: on Friday, Damn the solitude: on Saturday, Damn these thoughts: on Sunday, Damn my two dresses.

But I pronounce each day's Damn in a half-perfunctory half-preoccupied tone, more from duty and fitness than from conviction. I intently mean each Damn, but the scornful indifferent patience which is my spirit-essence leavens each one. I swear at my life's perversities with only a fatigued contempt due partly to bodily fragileness but mostly to a cold continently reckless mood which is clasped on me like a strong stupefied devil-fish. In this mood I should murmur the same gelded Damn if I found myself penniless and foodless in strange streets: if I became suddenly deaf: if my Body were being lashed with whips or raped by a Mexican bandit. I should murmur the same worn Damn if I were this moment on a gallows with the rope around my neck and life were dearly madly precious.

I mark that with my musing regrets. I remember in the strong young furies of eighteen each new day of my life was filled with passionate poetic blasphemy, protests, and rebellions of youth. Those were not tired, not acquiescent, not indifferent to slings-and-arrows, but fiery-blooded quick-pulsed breathless brave young Damns.

There is splendor in being brave in a fighting attitude, but in being brave through indifference there is no splendor.

But it is only toward calamity and adversity and worldly untowardness that I feel indifferent. Fighting blood is stirred in me if not against the hated things then for the loved things. I could fight and I could die, and love it, to save poet-lusters, poet-fineness, poet-beauty from the world's flat griefs. In that, which I feel warm and real and sparkling in my blood, is some splendor for me.

- and also I could die for my country: and there is fighting hatred stirred in me against its foes -

But in poetry there is nothing that evokes a lusty curse against its vulgar adversaries. Poetry floats too high upon its dazzling wings. I get delicately drunk from watching it till I can see the wings' Gold Shadow touch its foes and magically split them into dust-atoms.

So then the morale of my Damns remains perfunctory.

But they are apt and useful. They fit into the nervous rhythms of my life. They mark time in my spirit's flawed action. I begin each day with a Damn of sorts. I end each day with a Damn of sorts. At midday sometimes it's "Damn the terrifying ignorance of people." In the dusk a deep-felt Damn of the blood. In the night another. And at my late eating time a negligible Damn.

A wonderful word, Damn. It means enough and not too much. It means everything in life, and roundly nothing.

Without Damn my day would lack tone. Damn richly justifies each pronouncement of itself in word-value, substance-value, and musical resonance. It harms nobody and it helps me. It destroys nothing and it strengthens me. It damages my annoyances and mends me somewhat.

But - perfunctory, desultory, tiredly, insolent, it would be thrilling to think the hot fire would sometime be back in my Damns. Better that than Youth's faith in my dreams. Better that than the *jeune-fille* beauty in my hair. Better than even Youth's ichor in my veins: Youth's fire in my Damns -

But there is dearness in this mood, which is indifferent and scornful and slightingly patient, though it wants splendor. Let my Damns be always brave, always contemptuous of disaster to me, and they will be first-water value though their kind alter never-so.

*

To God, Care of the Whistling Winds

To-morrow

This morning came a letter from a half-forgot friend in London. She is in vaudeville and has been booked for two months in the Music Halls. Her letter is of a tenor productive of a letter in turn. But I am somehow not free to write letters to friends while I'm living in my two plain dresses. So I wrote this letter to God instead:

19th November

Dear God:

I know you won't answer this letter. I'm not sure you will get it. But I have the feeling to write you a letter, though it should only blow down the whistling winds.

I haven't a thing to ask of you: no prayer to make. I am not suppliant nor humble nor contrite. Nor would I justify myself as a person in your eyes. I scorn to try to justify myself. What I am I am. If I am a bad actor I take the results of it without plaint. I comment on it - why not? - since cats may look at kings and each person inherits four-and-twenty hours a day. But I am bewildered and distraught and sad.

The best you do for me, God, when I think of you - you personally - is to make me bewildered and distraught and sad.

But I've imagined I could put myself to you as a proposition to take or to leave as you like: on my terms since I do not know yours.

There are some verses - the *Rubaiyat* - in which you are upbraided as if you might be the dealer in some gambling game who had the long end of all the wagers and still so protected his money that *he* could not lose however the cards turned. - "from his helpless creature be repaid pure Gold for what he lent him dross-allayed." - "thou who didst with pitfall and with gin beset the Road I was to wander in. -"

But to me that seems a cheap attitude toward you, God. I admit you are fair. If I thought you weren't my mind would not vex itself with you at all. I can not make you out a crooked dealer nor one who lends out bad money and demands good money in repayment.

But you are reticent and cold-tempered and uninterested. So it seems. The necklace which you gave me so long ago, made of little curses, I wear always round my spirit-neck. It serves some purpose, perhaps, and it answers as a keepsake: so at least I may not forget you whether or not you forget me. I don't ask any more of your attention nor anything more of you than I would be willing to give you in return. But I wish you would be willing to exchange attention with me. I am lonely. I am terrified. I am frightfully overshadowed by myself and my odd aloofness and my thronging solitary emotions and my menacing trivialities. I am always fearing not that I may be wicked or immoral or allied with evils - I don't really care a tinker's curse about that - but that I may be growing petty and trivial and weak. It is horrible, horrible to feel that I may be a weakling - you, God, may not know how horrible to me. It is like black annihilation for all eternity when my Soul longs frantically, desperately to live. I feel weakness to be the only immoralness - hateful and vile in whatever aspect. I want to be strong to endure and to live in noonday lights and to overcome my poorness. I want, though I'm far from it, to be brave and big. What I admire you for, though you're so far off and strange and inexplicable, is that you are strong. You are Strength, you are Light, you are the Solution and the Absolute. You'd hardly know what weakness is if it did not so crop out in this human race you made. This human race is a faërily beautiful thing: star-flaming poets have sung in it: lovely youth has breathed upon it: happy wild hearts have informed it. But the odd keynote of it all is weakness. And I have felt me tuned overmuch by that keynote.

- but I won't be weak, I won't be, I won't be, God! Whether you pay attention or not, whether I breathe only futileness, I will be strong, strong, strong in myself - strong if only in my falseness - strong and strong again -

This would be your chance with me if you cared to take it: because I own now just my plain two dresses. When I grow out of this quiet mood - (if ever I do: I begin to doubt it) - I shall have more dresses, and then I shall think about them, God, and the phases of life they'll build up around me, and not about you. It's not that pretty frocks would take my attention away from you if you once claimed it. Once you claimed my attention it would be yours forever. But pretty frocks would mean I am again walking in paved peopled roads. Being there without your attention I shall go where my garments may lead me forgetful of you. One's life is of the flavor of one's clothes: "the wine must taste of its own grapes."

Now feels like a fitting time for you to be personal with me, to give me a sign that you know I'm here. I know I am blind and ignorant about that. You may know a time that shall be more fitting, a time when my still mood and two dresses are long gone and my life is made of fluff and lightness so your sign will crash into it like a black two-ton meteor.

I only tell you how it seems. If you should come now and speak to me I should feel suddenly glad. To-day feels such a day-of-God. The sky is all wet silver and the air a thin cloud of gold. I sit writing you by my window, often looking out with my forehead resting against the cool pane. There is an ache in my forehead, in my insteps, in my backbone, and in my spirit. By stopping in here a moment you would gladden me. If you could give me, or show me - where it perhaps had always been - one true thing to have always in my life I should cling to it and ask nothing of it but that it remain true. If you'd make me one far-off promise of a dawn to come after this tired darkness I would take your word for it and would walk toward your dawn in a straight road from which I should not ever turn aside. In me is a small torch glowing though set in chaos. By its light I should keep in the road leading to your dawn. I should keep in it at any sacrifice to my merely human self: any sacrifice, believe me.

It isn't a bargain I would make with you. I don't like the thought of a bargain with you. I would rather take the chance and lose honestly: not in everything but in this matter with you. You show me the road and I take it for the sole reason that it's a true one. I should expect myself to pay the tolls - heavy ones since I'm innately a liar, a someway bad lot. I know, the same as I know one and one make two, that I've only to be square in the human business of living to get back a square deal, though I'll get badly battered, with it. But it isn't what I mean. Something inside me hungers for answeringness - a Gleam - to make me know the worldly squareness and the battering are worth while beyond themselves: but a detail in the game.

You mightn't guess it but I am diffident about broaching this much that may sound like a plea, so I'll say no more of it.

But before I close the letter I want to tell you that I'm not wanting in gratitude for the terrible beauty of this world. I feel with ecstasy the burning loveliness of the life you give the human race.

I want to tell you thank-you for some things in it. But all that they mean I can not tell in words.

Only yesterday a light at sundown lingered on the hill-tops and on the desert back of the School of Mines in tints of Olive and Copper and Ochre and Rose so delicate, so radiant, so dumbly forlorn that I closed my eyes against it all as I walked along the sand: its aliveness, its realness, its flawless golden dreadful peace tortured and twisted and too-keenly interpreted me.

And one summer-day in Central Park in New York I saw a little Yellow-Yellow Butterfly fluttering above a small plot of brilliant Green-Green Grass in the afternoon sunshine. To you, God, used to the purpling splendor of untold worlds that mightn't seem noteworthy. But to me - because I am half-sister to so many trivialities the Yellow-Yellow of those little wings and the sweet bright Green of the clipped velvet Grass beneath the sun suddenly fiercely entered in and beat-beat hard on my imagination. O the glare and the flare of that fairy prettiness! I shall never forget that picture though I should one day see those worlds. It made me think wildly of you, God, at the time - and ever since. It is there yet in Central Park, that particular plot of Grass, and if not that Yellow-Yellow Butterfly - happily, happily Yellow it was - then another!

And to-day and often other days I read this -

Heard melodies are sweet, but those unheard are sweeter -

- magic words: potent hushed wizardry of beauty.

It opens the doors of all the Inner Rooms and more blest, more precious, of the celestial brain of him who wrote it. In making the glimmering Purple of all your worlds, God, you have not surpassed the thing you made in the regal wistful glory of John Keats.

And two nights ago I went close to my glass and looked deep into my own dark gray eyes, and they were beautiful. Their color is the gray not of peace but of stormy sky and clouded sea. Their expression is alien and melancholy and they are never without circlings of fatigue or stress. And when I meet their glance they mostly accuse and condemn and confound me. But two nights ago they grew wide and deep and breathless-looking at realizing me human and alive. And presently I saw, back of their gray iris - my Soul: like a naked girl: like a willow in the wind: like a drowning star at daybreak: an inherent inexpressible grace - my Soul of many ages.

And this moment another little memory, God, of a tropic marsh a little way back from the sea on the island in the bay at St. Augustine, as it looked in the wane of one sun-flooded February day. In the marsh were tall waving feathery salt-marsh grasses, and little pools of murky water. And there were snail-shells and ancient barnacles and smooth beach pebbles. And bordering the pools were reeds and flags and tiny wax-petaled death-white lilies. By a mound of wet moss was a slim wild blue heron standing on one leg and staring about and preening its blue feathers. And over all the scene was a Pink-Pink Flush. The curving quivering tops of the long grass were Pink with it. The pools were dull Pink mirrors. The barnacles, the pebbles, the death-white lilies were as if a thin bloody veil had been flung down on them. Pink touched the heron's wings, its beak, its head, its glittering beady eyes and spindly leg. The sinking sun shot a Pink broadside of dream-dust all over the marsh: it lingered and hung and floated. Almost I could have reached out my two hands and gathered a bouquet of Pink Flush. The stillness, which was intense, was Pink stillness. O but it was pleasant, pleasant, pleasant, God - it wrapped me in a scarf of Pink sweetness: it filled my throat with Pink honey: it laid on me a gentle eager quiet covetous Pink spell.

Nobody knows how you do it, God. But it is all - Sunset Tint, Yellow-Yellow Moth, Conscious Soul, Poet-Flame - maddening and precious and terrifying and transfiguring to me who live among it. I cherish it as a lonely one may who loves it with passion and is never happy in it. And for it all I thank you, God.

Yours very sincerely,
Mary MacLane

I wrote the Letter on my long-unused monogram note-paper to please my whim, and put it in the envelope and addressed it to God, care of the Whistling Winds. He may receive it - what do I know - only *he* knows, and is reticent.

I only know he'll not answer it.

*

A Working Diaphragm

To-morrow

I am not Respectable nor Refined nor in Good Taste.

I take a delicate M.-Mac-Lane pleasure in those facts.

I doubt if they are anyway peculiar to me, but they feel like a someway delicious clandestine circumstance: something to enjoy all to myself.

It is difficult to imagine any woman really Respectable on her inner side, the side that is turned toward herself alone. And it's certain no woman is Refined: it feels not possible. (There are yet inland places where the word is used in its smug sense and believed in.) And no woman but a dead woman in her coffin is in complete Good Taste. Every live woman has for instance a working diaphragm: and in a diaphragm there is, in the final analysis, simply no taste at all.

(As for men - except poets - I mean *poets*: and perhaps scientists - they are so ungenuine: a race of discreet cautious puppets: wooden dolls who move as their strings are pulled: with nothing so real about them inside as even outside - what use to dwell upon them?)

Nearly all women are perplexingly interesting as human beings. And I am quite the most interesting human being I know: and with it the most appealing, the most sincere - in my own false fashion, and the most bespeaking.

It is much due to knowing and feeling me to be not Respectable nor Refined nor in Good Taste: particularly to being not in Good Taste.

One autumn evening in Boston I went to dine with a man in his apartment in Beacon Street. He is a mining engineer whom I have known since we were both children. He had bidden me to dinner in his off-hand engineering way, but when I arrived at his diggings he was not there. He did not come. Instead there was a dinner waiting, a Japanese boy to serve it, and a strange man who had happened in. The strange man had iron-gray hair, a brow like Apollo, a jowl like Bill Sikes, and much conversation. He said that he was newly from China, South Africa, and Egypt and that in his life he had been married seven times with book and bell. Together we ate the dinner, talking pleasantly in the light of colored Chinese lamp-shades. There were little birds to eat and Chinese wine to drink - *sam shu* distilled virilely from rice: always a little of it is too much. After the dinner we were standing by a teakwood sideboard and the strange man was holding me tightly in his arms against a large smooth evening panel of shirt-front, and he was kissing my mouth with a great deal of ardor. I did not like it. I thought of all the women he had married and wondered if they had liked it. And I mused in my placid brain, "As I was going to St. Ives I met a man with seven wives." It was the only thought in my mind as I waited boredly for him to have done. (It's no good struggling.) And that incident I know was not Respectable.

And one summer day I was riding horseback up a steep gorge in these Montana hills. It was hot dusty riding. I came to a mountain stream with a beautiful little white-and-blue cascade tumbling over a high rock upon smooth pebbles below. I got down from my horse, took off my dusty khaki suit and all my clothes and stood under the fall of the little tumbling cascade, whitely naked, without so much as a figleaf's covering. It was delectable and pagan, what with my quaint thoughts as I stood crouched beneath the sparkling splash. And I know there was nothing Refined in it.

And one evening between nine and ten, a week ago. I was walking across the broad desert valley east of this Butte. It is late November and the night was stormy. A strong high gale swept the Flat. Presently it rained. I was on my way back with a mile or two to go. It rained harder. Heavy sheets of black water whipped and whirled down on me and wrapped me in their wet wings. I love all weather when it is mild and more when it is rough except when it bears down too hard: then I feel indifferent to it. As I moved along the dark road not hurrying and not loitering I was saying inside me, "Why am I going to any shelter out of this heavy wet rain? Why am I not a houseless beggar-woman with nothing gentler in all my life than this November storm? It is not because I deserve gentler things -" And with a sudden heavy shudder I whispered, "I wish I were a beggar-woman! I wish I had no roof to cover me in this cold night-blackness. It would be honest: I should be stripped to my deserts. And I wish it were so - this drenching rain, this strangling wind - nothing but this - shelter, money, comfort, self-satisfaction, however seemingly earned, are dishonest - thieved. I ought to be - ragged beggar - bleared eyes - dirty petticoats - a foul ratty hole to creep into - hunger - bodily misery - all the portion of outcasts - As God may hear me - I'd eagerly tremblingly change lives this moment with a beggar-woman. I would - I would! -" It is a piece of clear inside truth about myself. And I know it proves me to be in poor Taste.

It is a matter of attitude. Each of those incidents might happen to any woman - except perhaps the last. I have known but one girl who agreed with me in such a feeling. And not quite that feeling. She had married a lot of money with a horrible old gentleman and had wearied of both. But the other two episodes could readily belong to any woman of *esprit* who might be on the outside both respectable and Refined: even a woman lawyer.

But my attitude in the incident of the strange iron-gray man, though in a bored way I could have viciously knifed him, was not a Respectable attitude. I was bored and fanciful when doubtless I ought to have been breathlessly angry. But my breathless anger is too rare and beautiful an emotion to waste on ridiculous strange iron-gray men. In the incident of the sparkling cascade my attitude was shameless: something of the sort. It is never reprehensible for a woman to take a cold shower-bath in solitude and health. But my spirit rose and rejoiced at my bodily nakedness and then grew nymph-like and figleafless on its own account. My sex exploited itself in mental visions, like of Leda and the Swan or of myself as a slim villainous Scotch Aphrodite conceived by a bold surprising Titian. And doubtless I ought to have felt timorous in the vast sunlit mountainside, or like a sexless child (or merely "hygienic" like William Muldoon and Bernarr McFadden). But the quick charm of the situation and the heavenly anguish of the icy water, and my lovely Body, and my odd moralless musings were too intriguing to expend themselves banalely.

The wet night road and the beggar-woman wish: it is drearily real to me. Though I wear two plain dainty dresses, in a house - in me, beating, beating, pounding down is a cold wild heavy rain: and under my feet a long lonely muddy road. If they belong to me - well. I love Me the more for feeling them.

And I feel them because I am not yet dead and in my coffin, but alive and with a working diaphragm: which diaphragms are in not Good Taste.

*

Lot's Wife

To-morrow

To-day in the afternoon I briskly manicured my fingernails, sitting by my gold-and-blue window, and I mused upon Lot's Wife.

So many persons and incidents and events and adventures and episodes there are to muse upon, in this mixed world, dating from when it began till now. There's something to charm any mood. Let me leave the doors of my mind open and anything at all may float in like an errant butterfly on a summer's day.

It is an entertaining world, by and large: a limitless vaudeville.

Lot's Wife is to me a fantasy from the antique, a bit of archaic frivol to beguile me.

When first I heard of her, from an acrid aunt of caustic humor who told me the tale tersely in explanation of a biblical print, I was seven years old. From that day to this my meditative thoughts have from time to time flitted backward to dwell interestedly upon Lot's Wife. Later when I went to an Episcopal Sunday-school I was pleased to find this adjuration in according-to-St-Luke: "Remember Lot's Wife." There seemed no special meaning attached to it. It seemed like Remember Lot's Wife in any way you like - as it might be with a card on her birthday, a useless gift at Christmas, in your prayers, or in retributive patriotism like Remember the Alamo, Remember the Maine.

But I remember her because I like her.

There's no name given for Lot's Wife in the brief biblical narrative, so I long ago named her Bella as expressive of the temperament and character that have grown around her image in my thoughts.

Poor Bella, I ruminated as I tinted and polished my nails. Her life in Sodom was not entirely satisfying to her. Sodom was a town completely given over to pleasure of the physical and outward sorts. The dwellers lived in and for their physical senses alone. And Bella had it in her to care for the foods of the spirit. Not that she longed for them - she was not so conscious of herself - but she had it in her to care for them had they been given her. Still, Sodom and its ways were the best she knew and she had known them all her life. The roots of her temperament had shot down into the Sodomesque substrata. She fondly loved the place.

Sodom was a prototype for Babylon or Pompeii, worshiping the hotness of the sun in moralless plaisance, with fetes and drinkings of wine from gold and silver cups, and bathings in warm scented marble-lined pools, and anointings with oils of olive and palm, and dwellings among flowers of thin bright petals and birds of vivid plumage and fountains of crystal and rainbow, and caterings to the sparkle and froth of human emotions, and browsings amid loves and lights o' love. Can Bella be wondered at for growing fond of it all, having known nothing substantialer? And can she rightly be blamed for hating the thought of leaving it for dry sage-brush wilds in the mountains? She did hate and dread that thought with all her soul from the moment it was made known to her that Sodom for its sins was booked for destruction. She had perhaps a fortnight in which to dread it, and a fortnight if given over to dread is long enough to damage stronger spirits than hers.

Bella was slender and svelte, with long straight soft beautiful silken pale red hair and white-lidded eyes of grayish green. She was thirty-eight - a young thirty-eight. There's an old thirty-eight which applies to greedy school teachers, gangrenous woman government-clerks, fading hard-hearted stenographers, over-righteous woman doctors; to all whose virtue is ever indecently on guard. But there's a glory-tinted sun-kissed young thirty-eight which applies to sensitive high-strung generously-emotional women like Bella Lot. She had smooth hands with supple tapering fingers, an irregular expressive-lipped mouth like a pimpernel-bloom, firm slim feet, and the quivering suggestive white knees of a wood-nymph. From any angle-of-view can she be blamed for hating to take that equipment away from the city-de-luxe which was its so proper setting and hiding it in the sage-brush?

Furthermore Bella had a lover in Sodom. It is beyond a sane effort of the imagination that she could have loved that unpleasing old man Lot. The best and worst that can be said of him is that he was a fit addition to the company of the old Patriarchs who were for the most part an exceeding craven crew. The martyrs, the sages, and especially the prophets had their splendors. But the lean old patriarchs - The sporting blood of all of them, in the sense of merest simplest courage - from Adam down, would hardly aggregate one drop. There are any number of reasons - as many as Bella had charms - to account for Lot's having married her. But what she could have seen in him to make her wish or even willing to be married to him is a deep mystery to me. It may have been his family. I believe Bella lacked family: she was just a person. And was he not nephew to Abraham? But even being niece-in-law to Abraham himself seems insufficient compensation for being Lot's Wife.

The Lots had two young daughters, one fifteen and one seventeen, it might be. I do not know their names - call them Ethel and Agnes. But they were of a recalcitrant temper and absorbed in their own racy pastimes among the younger youth of Sodom and they had no need of their mother. Besides, they "took after" their father. So Bella was fain to turn outward in search of nurturing matter whereon to feed her humanness. Had it been expected of her to play fair with the patriarch she would have played fair. But it was not expected of her by anyone in Sodom - far from it, and least of all by the patriarch. She was eight-and-thirty, and Lot - *he* was doubtless eight or nine hundred years old, after the surprising long-lived fashion of the period.

So Bella found a lover ready and awaiting her. She would have found a lover in the circumstances even without caring to. But she quite cared to, I think. Everything points that way, and when one remembers that good old man her husband one can not censure her but only pity her. Be it as it may she had one - one as real as anything could be in that town of sparkling froth.

Of the lover's identity - little is known, as the historians say. My fancy as I filed my fingernails failed me on the point. Suffice it to state that ever and anon as time passed in Sodom the gray-green eyes of Bella were gazed into with fondness, affection, adoration, and desire: the white eyelids of Bella had showers of light kisses bestowed on them, soft-falling as rose-petals shaken loose in summer winds: the tapering white hands of Bella were caressed and caressing with the oddly intense tenderness of physical love: the pale red hair of Bella was ruffled and fluffed and disarrayed by the fingers of love: the red-pimpernel mouth of Bella was touched, bruised, clung to by the lips of love: the svelte whiteness and nymph-knees of Bella glowed as she broached love's arms: - and all went much merrier than marriage bells. In short, Bella paid herself with usury for the deadliness of being Lot's Wife.

And there we have the crux of Bella's dread of leaving Sodom and its tempered sweetness for the arid sage-brush hills and the respectively cold and hectic companionship of the good old patriarch and the recalcitrant daughters.

It can not be claimed for Bella that any white poetic fires gleamed across her soul, that any limning beauty shone palely from within her. The air of Sodom was not conducive to suchlike matters and Bella was no finer than her breeding and generation. But she was gentle and wistful and kind of heart. She was lovely to look at and ingenuously lovable in her clinging affection and disarming naturalness. She was all one could want to imagine in the word "charming."

Came the night set for destruction and the Lot family fled according to schedule. They fled away in the early damps of an autumn evening through the outer city gates and along a rough road faintly lit by a dying moon. They had three separate reasons for fleeing. Lot fled because he was a patriarch and was given to doing craven Old-Testamentish things of that sort: Bella fled because she was Lot's Wife and obliged to act out the role: and Ethel and Agnes fled because they had true patriarchal blood in their veins and had therefore no marked inclination to remain in Sodom to be annihilated - "safety first" was one of their watchwords. They fled in the van. Lot came after them, being less swift of foot. Bella lagged behind. She didn't want to go. Every way she looked at it she didn't want to go. She hated that flight for a thousand reasons.

The ghastly moon shed a terror on her with its dim rays. The ground was hard and rutted with frosty mud and bruised her slender feet through her white buckskin sandals.

She wore a loose *ninon* gown of white silk and linen with a gold girdle around her narrow loins and a gold clasp at the left shoulder. Binding her long hair, so palely red in the moon, was a white-and-gold fillet. In one hand she carried a gold-and-enamel link bracelet, a gift but that afternoon from the lover. Suddenly she stopped and cried to herself, "I'm too lovely for this fate - I'm too lovely and beloved - the cruelty of God - : I'll not go on!" She thought of the gleams and colorings of Sodom. She quickly reckoned the cost and decided to pay it. She was a rare good sport, and a quaint. She looked back at the doomed city blazing in brimstone - "But his wife looked back from behind him, and she became a pillar of salt." - As I put away my chamois-skin buffer and glass paste-jar through my mind floated the pensive burden of a by-gone French song -

Oh, the poor, oh, the poor, oh, the poor - dear - girl -

She must have made a beautiful statue, all in glistening salt.

I wish I had a glistening little salty replica of it to set on my desk: a so unusual, a so dainty conceit, Lot's Wife!

*

My Echoing Footsteps

To-morrow

While I live so still in this life-space, while I muse and meditate and analyze everything I touch, while I walk, while I work, while I change from one plain frock to the other: in quiet hours roiled tumbling storms of vicarious unhopeful Passion whirl, whirl in me: Passion of Soul, Passion of Mind, Passion of living, Passion of this mixed world: in terror, in wild unease, in reasonless mournful joy.

I never knew real Passion, Passion-meanings, till I reached thirty. It's now I'm at life's storm-center, youth's climax, the high-pulsed orgasmic moment of being alive.

At twenty the woman chrysalid soul and aching pulses awaken in crude chaste Spring-cold beauty. At forty her fires either have subsided to dim-glowing coals or leaped to too-positive, too-searing, too-obvious flames

- her bones and the filigrees of her spirit may be alike dry, brittle-ish. But at thirty her Spring has but changed to midsummer. Poesy still waits upon her Passions.

My spring has changed, bloomed, burst to midsummer.

Soft electrical heat-currents of being swing and sweep around me. They touch me and enter my veins. But the liquid essences of youth still quell and compress them. I am at youth's climax - a half-sullen, half-smouldering youth which still is youth.

My rose of life is fragrant and aglow. Its sweet pink petals are uncurled and conscious in the wavering light.

Winds flutter and stir and rumple and twist those petals -

To-day is a To-morrow of countless unrests. Large and little Passions beat at me all the blue-and-copper day. I walked my floor with irregular lagging steps. I felt menacing, dangerous to myself, dynamic as nitro-glycerine: and smoothly drearily sane as a bar of white soap. I stood at my window and looked long at the circling range of mountains which skirt this Butte. Nothing else I have looked at, of sea or plain or hill, affected me like that chain of barren peaks. They are arid splendor and pale purple witchery and grief and lasting sadness and deathlike beauty and woe and wonder. Their color quietly stormed my eyes and blurred them with tears.

It was a mood in which any color or gleam or thought or strain of music or note of sad world-laughter or any un-sane loveliness of poetry could enchant or flay or transport me to my frayed last nerve.

There is terror in facing death on battlefields, on sinking ships, in black ice-floes, in blazing buildings. But to me no death, for I fear no death, could be so dreadfully pregnant with in-turning woe and frenzy and all intolerable feeling as facing starkly my futile life.

My life is a vast stone bastile of many little Rooms in which I am a prisoner. I am locked there in solitude on bread and water and let to roam in it at will. And each Room is tenanted by invisible garbled furies and dubious ecstasies. I run with echoing footsteps from Room to Room to escape them: but each Room is more unhabitable than the last. There are scores of little Rooms, each with its ghosts, each different.

In one Room silent voices in the air accuse my tired Spirit of wanton vacillations and barren lack of purpose and utter waste, waste, waste of itself. And they threaten death and destruction. I know that accusation and I hate it: I hate it the more for that it's wholly just. To escape it I run from that Room along a dim passage into another one. In it unseen fingers clutch my Heart. In their touch also is an accusation: of selfishness and waste and want of something to beat for: and in their touch is the savor of wild wishes and human longings and passionate prayers for something warm and simple and real to rest against: and in their pressing clutching turbulent touch is a tormenting half-promise, chance-promise, no-promise: and the hovering inevitable threat of death and destruction. That too I know and hate and half-love: and I can't bear it. So I run out of that Room along a passage and into another. I hear my footsteps echoing as I run.

- as a child when I ran in the early night through a dark leaf-lined tunnel-like driveway the sound of my own flying footsteps on the hardened gravel was the only thing that frightened me. I quite believed there were bears in the brush-wood on either side, but fear of them never struck to the core of my child-being like the unknown thing in my echoing steps. And it is fear I feel now from the ghost-sound of my ghost-footsteps running, running away from the little Rooms. It is realer to me now than were my child footsteps to my child-self long ago: it is more definite than my hand which writes this: it is hideous -

Out of a dim passage I run into another little Room. In it some gray filmy threads, like strands of loose cobwebs caught on ceilings, float about. They sweep gently against my cheeks and hands and neck, and cling and twine and lightly hold with the half-felt feeling peculiar to bits of cobwebs on the skin. And it torments my woman-flesh with calefaciant thrills fierce and goading and sweet. There also is the accusation, now against my Body; for tissues and strength wasted: for useless fires meant to warm human seeds to life, meant to make me fruitful, meant to make me bear dear race-burdens: accusation for the cosmic waste of hot objectless desire, for the subtle guilt of a Lesbian tendency, for an unleashed over-positive sex-fancy. With it too is the lowering promise of death and destruction. It also is just. But out of my borne-along helplessness in it comes no culpable emotion because of cobweb thrills and their arraignment but only a wearing wearying despair. I rush out of that Room in shrugging impatience, with only scorn for a threat of death, for a threat of destruction - but with a wild fear of my own flying steps. I hurry and hurry on from door to door: but it's no good. In some other Room my brain is anathematized from frowning walls as an impish demoniac power which I use with no good intent and therefore with bad intent: and again I shrink and run away. In another Room are all the lies I have ever told: I have told legions - my own peculiar lies, gentler on me than truths: they dart around me in the Room like black heavy-winged moths, clouds of them fluttering at my forehead. They drive me out shivering. In another Room four times when I was a not-good-sport confront me in a row like pictures and sting me and make me hide my eyes: I'd rather be a leper, a beast, a maniac than a not-good-sport (for my own precious reasons) - and I rush away again. In some other Room -

- the same galling torment in all the Rooms. Wherever I run with the echo-echo of steps there are Accusing voices and half-formed Prayer and uncertain Yearning and violent yet dumb and inexpectant Protest and the unfailing Threat of death and destruction: not earth-death but universe-death: death and death and death everywhere coming on and on: myself knowing the just note in it all and from it grown numb with some cold and restless terror. Also I know no door I run through with my panic-feet will ever set me free of the bastile except a death door: the earthly death of this tired life -

But it's from this maelstrom that the flashing burning sparkling mad magic of being alive leaps out brilliant and barbarous - and throbbing and splendid and sweet. A merely human hunger comes back on me. Then I want all I ever wanted with a hundredfold more voltage of wanting than I have ever yet known.

I am all unhopeful, all unpeaceful, all a desperate Languor and a tragic Futileness: I am an unspeakably untoward thing.

And already I have been seared and scarred trivially from standing foolishly near some foolish human melting-pots.

No matter for any of it. I want to plunge headlong into life - not just imitation life which is all I've yet known, but honest worldly life at its biggest and humanest and cruelest and damnedest: to be blistered and scorched by it if it be so ordered - so that only it's *realness* - from the outside of my skin to the deeps of my spirit.

It is not happiness I want - nothing like it: its like never existed since this world began.

I want to feel one big hot red bloody Kiss-of-Life placed square and strong on my mouth and shot straight into me to the back wall of my Heart.

I write this book for my own reading.

It is my postulate to myself.

As I read it it makes me clench my teeth savagely: and coldly tranquilly close my eyelids: it makes me love and loathe Me, Soul and bones.

Clench and close as I will the winds flutter and stir and crumple and twist my petals as *they* will: - as I sit here tiredly, tiredly sane.

*

A Comfortably Vicious Person

The blue-and-copper of yesterday is dead and buried this To-morrow in a maroon twilight.

I this moment saw darkly from my window the somber hills in their heavy spell of pale-purple and grief and splendor and sadness and beauty and wonder and woe.

But their color brings no tears to my wicked gray eyes.

The passion-edged mood is burnt out.

Gone, gone, gone.

I listlessly change into the other black dress for listless dinnertime and all my thought is that my abdomen is beautifully flat and that I must purchase a new petticoat.

I rub a little rouge on my pale mouth and I idlingly recall a clever and filthy story I once heard.

I laugh languidly at it and feel myself a comfortably vicious person.

I pronounce a damn on the familiar ache in my beloved left foot and turn away from myself.

I stick out the tip of my forked-feeling tongue at the bastard clock on the stairs. I note the hour on it with a fainness in my spirit-gizzard to dedicate Me from that time forth to a big blue god of Nastiness: Nastiness so restful, humorous, appetizing, reckless, sure-of-itself.

- these hellish To-morrows creeping in their petty pace: they bring in weak-kneed niceness, and they bring in doubts, and they bring in meditation and imagery and all-around humanness, till I'm a mere heavy-heeled dubious complicated jade

*

In My Black Dress and My Still Room

I have fits of Laughter all to myself.

The world is full of funny things. All to myself I Laugh at them. I lounge at my desk in the small night hours, and I finger a pencil or a box or a rubber or a knife and rest my chin on my hand, and sit on my right foot, and Laugh intermittently at this or that.

Ha! ha! ha! I say inwardly: with all my Heart: relishingly.

I laugh at the thought of a mouse I once encountered lying dead - so neat, so virtuous - though soft and o'er-long dead - with its tail folded around it - in a porcelain tea-pot: a strong inimical anomaly to all who viewed it. It had a look of a saint in effigy in a whited sepulcher. Looked at as a mouse it seemed out of place. Looked at as a saint it was perfect.

I Laugh at the recollection of a lady I once met who had thick black furry eyebrows incongruous to her face, which she took off at night and laid on her bureau. They were at once "detached" and detachable: itself a subtle phenomenon. She referred to her mind as her "intellects" and talked with a quaint bogus learnedness, and in remarkable grammar, of the Sweden-borgian doctrines. Looked at as a person she was inadequate. Looked at as a conundrum she was gifted and profound.

I Laugh at that extraordinary tailor in the Mother Goose rhyme - him "whose name was Stout," who cut off the petticoats of the little old woman "round about," herself having recklessly fallen asleep on the public highway. The tale leaves me the impression that such were the straitly economic ideas of the tailor that he obtained all his cloth by wandering about with his shears until he happened upon persons slumbering thus publicly and vulnerably. Looked at in any light that tailor is ever surprising, ever original, ever rarely delectable.

I Laugh at William Jennings Bryan.

How William Jennings Bryan may look to the country and world-at-large I have never much considered.

It is all in the angle of view: St. Simeon Stylites may seem rousingly funny to some: Old King Cole may have been a frosty dullard to those who knew him best.

To me William Jennings Bryan means bits of my relishingest brand of gay mournful Laughter.

The ensemble and detail of William Jennings Bryan and his career as a public man, viewed impersonally - as one looks at the moon - are something hectic as hell's-bells.

I remember William Jennings Bryan when his star first rose. It was before Theodore Roosevelt was more than a name: before the battleship *Maine* was sunk at Havana: before Lanky Bob wrested the heavyweight title from Gentleman Jim at Carson: before aeroplanes were and automobiles were more than rare thin-wheeled restless buggies: before the song "My Gal She's a High-born Lady" had yet waned: before one Carrie Nation had hewn her way to fame with a hatchet. I was a short-skirted little girl devouringly reading and observing everything, and I took note of all those. So I took note of William Jennings Bryan nominated for president by the Democratic convention in eighteen-ninety-six. The zealous Democratic newspapers referred to him, though he was then thirty-six, as the Boy Orator of the Platte. Looked at as a grown man, advocating free coinage of silver at sixteen-to-one, a daring dashing Democrat, he was a plausible thing and even romantic. Looked at as a Boy Orator he turned at once into a bald and aged lad oddly flavored with an essence of Dare-devil Dick, of the boy on the burning deck, of a kind of political Fauntleroy madly matured.

Long years later with the top of his hair and his waistline buried deep in his past he became Secretary of State: and at the same time a Chautauqua Circuit lecturer - entertaining placid satisfied audiences alternately with a troupe of Swiss Yodlers.

Of all things, yodlers. Politics makes strange bedfellows and always did. But never before has the American Department of State combined and vied with the yodler's art to entertain and instruct. Looked at as a monologist he might pass if sufficiently interpolated with ah-le-ee! and ah-le-o-o! Looked at as Secretary of State he is grilling and grueling to the senses: a frightful figure quite surpassing a mouse softly dead in a tea-pot, a pair of detachable fuzzy Swedenborg-addicted eyebrows, a presumptuously economical tailor.

And he entertained the foreign ministers at a state dinner, did this unusual man, and he gave them to drink - what but grape-juice, grape-juice in its virginity. Plain water might have seemed the crystalline expression of a rigid puritanic spirit. Budweiser Beer, bitter and bourgeois, might have been possible though surprising. But grape-juice, served to seasoned Latin Titles and Graybeards and Gold-Braid, long tamely familiar with the Widow Clicquot: that in truth seems, after all the years, boyishly oratorical, wildly and darkly Nebraskan. Looked at as an appetizing wash for a children's white-collared and pink-sashed party, or for anybody on a summer afternoon, grape juice is satisfactory. In the careless hands of William Jennings Bryan with his soul so unscrupulously at peace, the virgin grape juice becomes a vitriolic thing: a defluent purple river crushing one's helpless spirit among its rocks and rapids.

- a terrible American, William Jennings Bryan. He is for "peace at any price." There were some, long and long ago, who suffered and endured one starveling winter in camp at Valley Forge that William Jennings Bryan might wax Nebraskanly fat: and he is valiantly for peace: at any price -

For that my Laughter is tinged with fulfilling hatred.
Rich hot-livered Laughter must have in it essential love or hatred.
To William Jennings Bryan everything he has done in his political career must seem all right.

It is all right, undoubtedly. Just that.

- that Silver-tongued Boy Orator
those Yodlers
that Peerless Leader
that Grape-juice -

They come breaking into my melancholy night-hours with an odd high-seasoned abruptness.

I wonder what God thinks of him.

It might be God thinks well of him.

But I - in my black dress and my still room - I say inwardly and willy-nilly, and with all my Heart and relishingly: Ha! ha! ha!

*

Their Little Shoes

To-morrow

Often in windy autumn nights I lie awake in my shadowy bed and think of the children, the Drab-eyed thousands of children in this America who work in coal mines and factories.

Whenever I'm wakeful and the night is windy and my room is dark and I lie in aloneness - a long aloneness: centuries - then shadows come from far-off world-wildnesses and float and flutter dimly unhappy around my bed. They tell me tales of shame and tame petty hopelessness and trifling despair.

And the one that comes oftenest is the one that tells of those Drab-Eyed children distances from here, but very immediate, who work in coal mines and factories. I read about them in magazines and newspapers, but they aren't then one one-hundredth so real as when their shadow floats as close to me in the windy autumn night.

Once in Pennsylvania I saw a group of children, very Drab in the Eyes and very thin in the necks and legs, who worked in a mill. Their look made its imprint in my memory and more in my flesh. And it comes back as if it were the only thing that mattered as I lie wakeful in the windy night.

The children - unconscious and smiling their small decayed smiles - they are living and being crushed between greed and need as between two murderous millstones. Their frail flesh and their little brittle bones, their voices and their pinched insides, the sweet vague childish looks which belong in their faces are squeezed and crunched by two millstones - squeezed,

squeezed till their scrawny fledgling bodies are dry, breathless, and are gasping, strangling, striving frightfully for life: and still are slowly, all too slowly, dying between two millstones.

If it were their own greed or their own need - but it's the greed of fat people and the need of their own warped gaunt parents. Betwixt the two the children meet homelike hideous ruin. Placidly they are cheated and blighted and blasted, placidly and with the utmost domesticness.

The most darkling-luminous thing about the Drab-Eyed children is that they never weep. They talk among themselves and smile their little dreadful decayed smiles, but they don't weep. When they walk it's with a middle-aged gait: when they eat their noontime food it's as grown people do, with half-conscious economic and gastronomic consideration. They count their Tuesdays and Wednesdays with calculation as work-days, which should be childishly wind-sweptly free. Which is all of less weight than the heavy fact that they never weep.

They reckon themselves fairly fortunate with their bits of silver in yellow envelopes every Saturday. They are permitted to keep a bit of it, each child a bit for herself or himself, so that on Sunday afternoons they lose themselves for precious hours watching Charlie Chaplin. Many pink-faced inconsequent children whose parents nurture them and guard them and eternally misunderstand them are less worldlily lucky. But the pink-faced children often weep - loudly, foolishly like puppies and snarling furry cubs - and wet sweet salt tears of proper childishness are round and bright on their cheeks and lashes. It's a sun-washed blestness for them: they're impelled and allowed to weep. But the Drab Eyes shed no tears - they know no reason why they should. There's no impulse for soft liquid grief in the murderous philosophy of two grinding millstones. And there's no time - the lives of the work-children move on fast. Their very shoes are ground between the millstones.

- their little shoes are heartbreaking. The millstones grind many things along with little-little shoes of children: germs of potent splendid humanness that might grow bigly American in heroic ways or in sane round honesty: germs that might grow into brave barbaric beauty or warm wistful sweetness: germs that would grow into lips blooming tender and fragrant as jonquils or into minds swimming with lyrics: - what is strongly lasting and glorified in the forlorn divine human thing - crumpled - twisted forever when millstones grind children's little poor shoes -

The young Drab Eyes are endlessly betrayed: their very color thieved. There's no reason why they should weep.

But there's a far-blown sound as if ten thousand bad and good worldly eyes were weeping in their stead: with a note in it careless, compassionate, and jadedly menacing.

I seem to hear it in the wakeful windy night. And I hear no world-music pouring out of small throats of work-children shrill with woe-and-joy. The sound they make is a dumb sound, for they never weep: a ghost-wail of partly-dead children borne lowly across this mixed world on a stale hellish breeze.

*

The Sleep of the Dead

To-morrow

When I'm dead I want to Rest awhile in my grave: for I'm Tired, Tired always.

My Soul must go on as it has gone on up to now.

It has a long way to go, and it has come a long way.

My Soul first started on its journey somewhere in Asia before the dawn of this civilization. And it has gone on since through the centuries and through strange phases of Body, terrors of flesh and blood, suffering long. But it has gone someway on, each space of the journey taking it nearer to the journey's-End.

It is the dim-felt memory of those journeys that heaps the Tiredness on me now. Not only is my spirit Tired. Through my spirit my hands are Tired: my knees are Tired: my drooping shoulders: my thin feet: my sensitive backbone. When I lift my hand in the sunshine the weight of the yellow honeyed air bears down and down on it because I'm so Tired. When I start to walk on stone pavements the ache of them is in my feet before I set a foot on them because I'm so Tired. The pulse in my veins Tires my blood as it beats. My low voice, though I speak but rarely - it Tires my throat. My breath Tires my chest. The weight of my hair Tires my forehead and temples. My plain frocks Tire my Body to wear. My swift trenchant thoughts Tire my Mind.

It is not the Tiredness of effort though I strive to the limits of my strength every day.

It is not pain, Restful pain. It is Tired Tiredness.

So when I'm dead I want to Rest awhile in my grave. It *would* Rest me.

In the Episcopal Church they use a ritual of poetic beauty, full of Rest-ful things. One of them is the sleep of the dead. The crucified Nazarene slept three days. But all others of us when we go down into our graves are to sleep until a Judgment Day. "Judgment Day" is preposterous and evilly crude: there's no judgment till each can judge himself simply and cruelly in the morning light. But the sleep of the dead -

- the sleep of the dead. Its sound by itself without the thought is Restful -

And the thought is Restful.

I imagine me wrapped in a shroud of soft thin wool cloth of a pale color, laid in a plain wood coffin: and my eyelids are closed, and my Tired feet are dead feet, and my hands are folded on my breast. And the coffin is nine feet down in the ground and the earth covers it. Upon that some green sod: and above, the ancient blue deep sheltering sky: and the clouds and the winds and the suns and moons, and the days and nights and circling horizons - those above my grave.

And my Body laid at its length, eyes closed, hands folded, down there Resting: my Soul not yet gone but laid beside my Body in the coffin Resting.

- might we lie like that - Resting, Resting, for weeks, months, ages -

Year after long year, Resting.

*

Stickily Mad

To-morrow

It is damn-the-Smell-of-Turpentine!

Here I happen on a damn in me which is not desultory but bloodily strong and alive and alone.

The wood in my blue-white room has been newly painted. For a day and a night I intermittently encounter and go to bed in a spirit of Turpentine. It bears a cruel obscure abortive message to my nerves.

I lie wakeful in the dark and try to reason out a logicalness or poetry in a thing so artfully pestilential.

But I am hysterically lost in it and my heart beats hysterically in it.

I remember the inexpressible ingenuity of man: of white man as against bone-brained savage races. Every invented usefulness feels like divine witch-craft. A pen and a bottle of perfume and a doorknob and a granite kettle and an electric light: I have the use of each since white man is so ingenious. Were I a red Indian I should have only the awkward barbarous stupid tools my race had used a thousand years. I contrast the two as I lie wakeful, with a sense of richness and of detailed repletion and of material blestness.

But at once comes the Smell of Turpentine and announces itself something outside that and *different,* something stronger, something masterfuler than ingenuity and savagery together. It tortures my nerves: it burns my eyes: it lames my flesh: it jerks and flays and garbles my inner body.

The ingenuity of man has produced opium and cocaine which would combat and hide it all behind a heavy curtain of stupor, with effects equally damaging if less grievously subtle.

The Smell of Turpentine is a thing to bear since all its counter-things bring only solider evil.

The paint was put on the wood by a dirty little man whom I briefly inspected as something removed from my range of life. In return he covertly eyed me. I expected my wakeful hours would be punished by strong new paint and be-visioned by dirty little men. But it is all sheer Turpentine with a power suggesting nothing human nor super-natural nor divine. Just itself: a goblin virulence.

In all my Soul and bones and Mary-Mac-Lane-ness it is damn-the-Smell-of-Turpentine as a bastard murderous hurt.

I have an odd feeling God has no more power over it than have I.

It half-calls for a *different* Turpentine God.

I am shakily mad tonight, I believe, from a so slight sticky matter.

*

God Compensates Me

To-morrow

It's a Sunday midnight and I've just eaten a Cold Boiled Potato.

I shall never be able to write one-tenth of my fondness for a Cold Boiled Potato.

A Cold Boiled Potato is always an unpremeditated episode which is its chief charm.

It's nice to happen on a book of poetry on a window-sill. It's nice to surprise a square of chocolate in a glove box.

It's nice to come upon a little yellow apple in ambush. It's nice to get an unexpected letter from Jane Gillmore. It's nice to unearth a reserve fund of silk stockings under a sofa pillow. And especially it's nice to find a Cold Boiled Potato on a pantry shelf at midnight.

I like caviare at luncheon. And I like venison at dinner, dark and bloody and rich. And I like champagne bubbling passionately in a hollow-stemmed glass on New Year's day. And I like terrapin turtle. And I like French-

Canadian game-pie. And artichokes and grapes and baby onions. And none of them has the odd gnome-ish charm of a Cold Boiled Potato at midnight.

I can imagine no circumstance in which a Cold Boiled Potato would not take precedent with me at midnight. If I had a broken arm: if I had a husband lying dead in the next room: if I were facing abrupt worldly disaster: if there were a burglar in the house: if I'd had a dayful of depression: if God and opportunity were knocking and clamoring at my door: I should disregard each and all some minutes at midnight if I had also a Cold Boiled Potato.

I love to read Keats' Nightingale in my hushed life. I love to remember Caruso at the Metropolitan singing Celeste Aïda. I love to watch the bewitching blonde Blanche Sweet in a moving picture. I love to feel the summer moonlight on my eyelids. And it's disarmingly contented I am with a Cold Boiled Potato at midnight.

Content is my rarest emotion and I get it at midnight out of a Cold Boiled Potato.

Some things in life thrill me. Some drive me garbledly mad. Some uplift me. Some debauch me. Some strengthen and enlighten me. Some hurt, hurt, hurt. But I'm not thrilled nor maddened nor uplifted nor debauched nor strengthened nor enlightened nor hurt, but only fed-up and fattened in spirit by a Cold Boiled Potato at midnight.

I stand in the pantry door leaning against the jamb, with a tiny glass salt-shaker in one hand and the sweet dark pink Cold Boiled Potato in the other. And I sprinkle it with salt and I nibble, nibble, nibble. And I say aloud, "Gee, it's good!"

I liked Cold Boiled Potato at four-and-twenty. I liked it at seventeen. I liked it at twelve. At three I climbed on cake-boxes in search of one. And now in the deep bloom of being myself I am made roundly replete at midnight with a Cold Boiled Potato.

A Cold Boiled Potato - it tastes of chestnuts at midnight, the first frost-kissed chestnuts in the woods: and it tastes of rain-water and of salt and of roses: it tastes of young willow-bark and of earth and of grass-stems: it tastes of the sun and the wind and of some nameless relishingness born of the summer hillside that grew it: it tastes at midnight so *like* a Cold Boiled Potato.

A precious peach-colored orchid, an antique spider-web-like lace handkerchief, a delicate purple butterfly, an emerald bracelet: I'd strive for each of those in an eagerly casual way. But it's like an ogre at midnight I pounce on a Cold Boiled Potato.

A Cold Boiled Potato reminds me of the Dickens books in which so much food is eaten cold and tastes so savory - even the "wilderness of cold potatoes" portioned to the Marchioness by Sally Brass. And it reminds me of the Rip Van Winkle play - "give this fellow a cold potato and let him go." And it reminds me of Hamlet - funeral baked meats might include it. And it reminds me of Robin Hood's merry men, and Huckleberry Finn, and the Canterbury Pilgrims, and the Prodigal Son, and all the picturesque wayfarers. It reminds me of the poor as a colorful race wrapped around with hungry romance. It reminds me that life is full of life - rich and fruitful and evolutionary and cosmic: few things feel so cosmic as a Cold Boiled Potato at midnight. It makes me want as I nibble to plant a field of potatoes on a southern-exposed hill and hoe them and dig them all by myself: and give all but one to the poor and Boil that to eat Cold at midnight.

I have to be very hungry to crave a Cold Boiled Potato, but being hungry no possible morsel of food can so interest me at midnight. The same potato hot is domestic and tasteless. The same potato at ten in the evening lukewarm within and sodden with memories of dinner, is a repellent item. At midnight it is all unexpected magnetism.

At midnight my whole being is profoundly courteous, wooingly cordial toward a Cold Boiled Potato.

If I had only what I deserved my portion might well be a Cold Boiled Potato. Intrinsically it is rated low and I know me to be a sort of jezebel. But I'd wonder each midnight if whoever metes out the deserts in this surprising universe knew with what gust I rise at it - *would* I get it.

Nor am I satisfied like the meek and lowly with my midnight supper of Cold Boiled Potato: damn the meek and lowly. It's a satanic delight I take in it. It's a sly private orgie I make of it: a pirate's banquet, a thieves' picnic, a pagan rite, a heathen revelry, a conceit all and unhallowedly my own. My thoughts as I nibble are set mostly on my villainies. No food I eat brings me so broad a license of feeling - a sense of freedom - as a Cold Boiled Potato at midnight.

On a Cold Boiled Potato at midnight I am lightly valorous: call me a trickster and I'll call you a rotter: call me a liar and I'll call you a traitor: call me a coward and I'll call you another: not pugnaciously but gayly and serenely.

I am then in my most bespeaking mood. Anyone who met me standing nibbling in a pantry doorway at midnight would be charmed. I would talk with a dainty ribaldry and offer to share the feast.

For shadow-things piled too near God compensates me in unexpected midnights with a Cold Boiled Potato: along with it a pantry doorway to stand in and a little glass salt-shaker to hold in my other hand.

*

The Strange Braveness

To-morrow

If God has human feelings he must often have a burning at the eyes and a fullness at the throat at the strange Braveness of human people: their Braveness as they go on in the daily life, with aching dumbish minds and disgruntled bereft bodies and flattened pinched gnawed hearts.

The easy human slattern way would be to sink beneath the burden.

Instead, people: I and Another and all others - seamstresses and monotonous clerks and lawyers and housewives: sit upright in chairs and talk into telephones and walk fast and eat breakfasts and brush hair: all the while marooned in a morass of small wild unexciting tasteless Pain.

Of others - what do I know?

But I might say, "Look, God, I am not fallen on the ground, from this and that - utterly lost and down. But sitting, drooping but strong, in a chair, mending a lamp-shade - neat, orderly, and at-it in my misery."

*

Just Beneath My Skin

To-morrow

This I write is a strange thing.

So close to fact: so far from it.

So close to truth: so surrounded by lies.

It does not contain lies but is someway surrounded by a mist of lies.

A strange thing about it is that it is expressing the Self Just Beneath My Skin.

That Self is someways trivial and outlandish and mentally nervous, flightly, silly - silly to a verge of tragicness. I know that to be true from a long acquaintance with me. It is oddly intriguing to read over some chapters and find it *shown*.

Some unconscious exact photography aids my writing talent.

Some chapters are bewilderingly and mysteriously true to life.

My everyday self that casually speaks to this or that person is nothing like this book. My absorbed self that writes a letter to an intimate acquaintance is not like this book. My heartfelt self that deeply loves a friend, and gives of its depths, and thrills answeringly to other depths, is not like this book.

This book is my mere Hidden Self - just under the skin but hid away closer than the Thousand Mysteries: never shown to any other person in any conversation or any association: never would be shown: never could be.

How Another, any Other, would come out: what Another would show: photographed Beneath the Skin - what do I know?

Perchance ten times more trivial and inconsequent and mad than Me.

If Another thinks Me someway mad, let him look at Himself Just Beneath the Skin.

Perchance Another every day as he thanks a janitor for holding open a door, would much prefer to drive a long rusty brad-nail deep into the janitor's skull.

Perchance Another has a brain like Goethe, a Soul like a humming-bird, a Heart like a little round nutmeg.

What do I know?

I know what I am.

Another may know what he is.

But I can't tell Me to Another and Another can't tell Himself to Me.

I can tell Me to myself and write it.

Another if he reads will see Me: but not as I see Me. Instead, through many veil-curtains and glasses, very darkly.

*

God's Kindly Caprice

To-morrow

For twenty-five cents and one hour and twelve minutes one may get in this present detailed world a bit of unforgettable complete enchantment.

So I found to-day in a moving-picture theater. A Carmen, the real Carmen of Prosper Mérimée glowed, vibrated, lived, and died with passion on a white screen.

Of all prose writers I know Prosper Mérimée is the one - (intimate and sensitively alive as if I had lain against his shoulder as I read *La Guzla* and "Venus d'Ille" - he melts into my veins -) whom I would most eagerly see interpreted. Of all fiction characters - if she is fiction - the poignant Carmen is the one I would most eagerly see realized.

Carmen is one of those fictions which are truer to life than life is. Such fiction-things are all around, touching everybody: the spoken truths which grow false at being spoken: the thought lies which turn to truths the moment they touch words.

I have heard Carmen sung and seen her filmed by the lustrous Farrar, and I have seen her play-acted by some lesser lights. But Bizet's opera, a sparkling music-storm, creates a sonant objective Carmen, a beautiful bloody lyric, remote from Mérimée who made a Carmen intensely peculiar to his own subjective art. And the stage-Carmen has always been a stage-Carmen waiting in dusty draughty wings for her cues. It remained for the cinematograph, which is a true literal mirror of human expression, to make Carmen burst into violent physical life.

But it was less the scopes of the films which made Carmen animate than it was the virile woman who played her. It was acting - but acting in the sense of losing and sinking and saturating and dissolving herself in another woman's temperament: and by it she achieved some strong sword-keen shadings of the Carmen character - to the hair's-breadth.

And she *looked* like Carmen. It was not important to the vigorous fire of her acting but it made bewitchment in the portrait. No one I have before seen play Carmen fitted the elusive points of her description.

"Her eyes were set obliquely in her head but they were magnificent and large. Her lips, a little full but beautifully shaped, revealed a set of teeth as white as newly-skinned almonds. Her hair was black with blue lights on it like a raven's wing, long and glossy. To every blemish she united some advantage which was perhaps all the more evident by contrast. There was something strange and wild about her beauty. Her face surprised you at first sight but nobody could forget it. Her eyes especially had an expression of mingled sensuality and fierceness which I had never seen in any human glance. Gypsy's eye, wolf's eye -"

This (from the English translation of the story by Lady Mary Loyd) fitted to a charm the pictured vision of the foreign-looking woman - her name is Theda Bara - who flung a throbbing Carmen across the screen with inde-scribable heat and color and luster. It was comparable only to the muscular force of the original which that Mérimée rubs nervously and heavily into one's thoughts. I felt it someway satisfyingly unbelievable - an illusion more actual than actuality: a dream which outbore fact.

I suppose there's no other character like Carmen for flaming roundness in all fiction: filled with her treacheries yet purely true to herself, without fear, utterly game: fierce, coarse, ruthless, and reckless yet wrapped in a maddening unwitting pathos: strong and bold and cruelly poised yet capable of sudden complete surrender: ignorant and abandoned and criminal in every instinct yet beyond every littleness, every pettiness: sensual yet contemptuous and indifferent in it, a woman of essential chastity. Carmen is the one criminal conception in whom there is no vulgar evil, no personal maculateness though wrecking all the wildness of her temper in her tempestuous days'-journeys. She is a romantic murderous appeal to human superjudgment. It was this isolate quality of her which Theda Bara gave out with mystic masterful art. She gauged the personal odors and blood-pressures of Carmen. She slipped into Carmen's skin and first sucked in and then breathed out the irresistible menacingness and arresting ruination of her beautiful diabolic spirit. A little feverish artistic thrill ran in my veins as I sat in the dark watching.

"She had thrown her mantilla back," says Don José in the translated tale, "to show her shoulders and a great bunch of acacias that was thrust into her chemise. She had another acacia bloom in the corner of her mouth and she walked along swaying her hips like a filly from the Cordova stud farm. In my country anyone who had seen a woman dressed in that fashion would have crossed himself. In Seville every man paid her some bold compliment on her appearance. She had an answer to each and all with her hand on her hip -. 'Come, my love,' she began again, 'make me seven ells of lace for my mantilla, my pet pin-maker.' And taking the acacia blossom out of her mouth she flipped it at me with her thumb so that it hit me just between the eyes. I tell you, sir, I felt as if a bullet had struck me."

This first meeting of Carmen with the dragoon was pictured in a brilliant hot-looking plaza as if before the cigarette factory in Seville. This woman in throwing the flower at the soldier expressed wonderfully in one fleet moment, by hand and lip and eye, the savage sordid poetry and passionate freedom - that unearthly fragrance - which *is* Carmen.

The film version followed the scenes of the opera rather than the story, which took nothing from the headlong truth of the central figure.

But no picturing can equal the star-clarity of Mérimée's prose in Carmen's death-scene - a thing of a piercing pathos comparable to nothing I know in writing.

After we had gone a little distance I said to her, "So, my Carmen, you are quite ready to follow me, isn't it so?"

She answered, "Yes, I'll follow you to the death - but I won't live with you any more."

We had reached a lonely gorge. I stopped my horse.

"Is this the place?" she said.

And with a spring she reached the ground. She took off her mantilla and threw it at her feet, and stood motionless with one hand on her hip, looking at me steadily.

"You mean to kill me, I see that well," she said. "It is fate. But you'll never make me give in."

I said to her: "Be rational, I implore you, listen to me. All the past is forgotten. Yet you know it is you who have been my ruin - it is because of you that I am a robber and a murderer. Carmen, my Carmen, let me save you, and save myself with you."

"José," she answered, "what you ask is impossible. I don't love you any more. You love me still and that is why you want to kill me. If I liked I might tell you some other lie, but I don't choose to give myself the trouble. Everything is over between us two. You are my rom and you have the right to kill your romi, but Carmen will always be free. A calli she was born and a calli she'll die."

"Then you love Lucas?" I asked.

"Yes, I have loved him - as I loved you - for an instant - less than I loved you, perhaps. And now I don't love anything. And I hate myself for ever having loved you."

I cast myself at her feet. I seized her hands. I watered them with tears, I reminded her of all the happy moments we had spent together, I offered to continue my brigand's life, if that would please her. Everything, sir, everything - I offered her everything if she would only love me again.

She said: "Love you again? That's not possible. Live with you? I will not do it."

I was wild with fury. I drew my knife. I would have had her look frightened and sue for mercy - but that woman was a demon.

I cried: "For the last time I ask you, Will you stay with me?"

"No! No! No!" she said and she stamped her foot. Then she pulled a ring I had given her off her finger and cast it into the brushwood. I struck her twice over - I had taken Garcia's knife because I had broken my own. At the second thrust she fell without a sound. It seems to me that I can still see her great black eyes staring at me. Then they grew dim and the lids closed. - For a good hour I lay there prostrate beside the corpse. -

No play-acting could make the scene so pregnant and palpitant with human-stuff and alive in vision as that translucent jewel-prose of Mérimée. But so close as one art may counterfeit another, by drinking-up the fiery spirit essence which informs it, so close did this actor-woman compass and consummate the strong delicious unafraidness of Carmen's death-hour.

The scene was staged as in the opera - a court outside the bull-fighting arena, with Carmen richly bejeweled and dressed in the lacy smart-lady clothes of the Toreador's mistress. But that was nothing. The gypsy wildness of the written scene was in every insolently splendid bodily movement and each fateful loveliness of eyes and lips of the fulfilling Theda Bara.

I can still see the dark drooping-lidded dying eyes.

I sensed Carmen in conscious chambers of my Mind.

I felt her in my throat. It was Carmen herself living and breathing near me, the fearsomely adorable Carmen who has haunted the edge of my thoughts since I first read her.

There are some odd crudenesses in Theda Bara's acting which had the effect of making her un-stagey, unobvious. They made her humanly vibrant. And they added a devilish wistfulness to her Carmen and a surprising feel of genuineness to the whole masque.

The actor's art brings out the romance which is in human bone-and-flesh. And Theda Bara seems someway a master of its physical and spiritual subtleties. She expressed the swift emotion of Carmen by ringing slightest possible changes on her own virile and mobile body: insolence by kimboing an elbow: cruelty by the twitch of a wrist: sensual feeling by moving a knee and an ankle: murder in the twisting of her waistline: a fleet repressed animal tenderness by a posture of shoulder and breast: a heartbreak of mirth in her careless vivid lips: the desperate bravery of that death by the tilt of her potent chin: the hurricane-freedom of Carmen's soul by lifting her face and her arms in the night wind. She worked with an exquisite muscular sincerity, as if she strongly gave her best of brain and blood and mettle to the part.

I looked at photographs of her which decorated the lobby of the theater. She looks a beautiful and earnest-seeming girl of a mental rather than a physical caste, with melancholy dark eyes, a child-like mouth-profile and the slim patrician hands of a Bourbon duchess. She will live in my warmed memory as the star of all the Carmens.

A flood of life and color goes into the staging of a Carmen film: a throng of attractive faces and bodies of people, women and men and lovely children, move through it in a pulsating gay pageant: flowers and Spanish prettinesses of costume and country-side and street and café are all over it, bright as life: and sweet winds blow in it and leaves and grasses wave and flutter, and the sunshine melts and mellows the air - all as if one saw it thrice-enlarged through windows. It is not poetry - it is not in itself any art, but a dear delectable counterfeit of it, a miracle-*taste* of the outer-looking madly-peopled world.

For me it meant my long-adored Mérimée given sudden brief life, the haunting Carmen turned into flesh: a spell of silent human-music which glowed and burned upon me like gentle fire.

Often is God thus capriciously kind to me.

*

A Fascinating Creature

To-morrow

I am a fascinating creature.

I move in no stultifying ruts. There's no real yoke of custom on my shoulders. My round white breasts beneath their black serge are concurrent with nothing settled or subservient or discreet.

My Mind goes in no grooves made by other minds. It lives like a witch in a forest, weaving its spells, revelling in smooth vivid adventure. When I look at a round gray stone by a roadside I look at it not as a young woman, not as a person, not as an artist, nor a geologist, nor an economist, but as Me - as Mary MacLane - and as if there had not before been a round gray stone by a roadside since the world began. When I look at a chair with my somber eyes I say to the chair, "What other persons may see when they look at you, chair, I don't know - how could I know? But I well know what I see and that what I see is uninfluenced by other eyes that may have looked at you, were they Aristotle's or Galileo's or an archangel's." There may be equally egotistic viewpoints - in Waco-Texas, or Japan, or Glasgow-Scotland, or the Orkney Islands, where not? I don't know - I don't care. What is it to me? I know my own virile vision and that it thrills and informs and translates me as if crackling bright-jagged lightnings broke along my sky. -

It is a night of whispering breezes and little restless clouds, an endearing night. It makes solitude a delectation. I walked out in it, in the glimmering moonlight past buildings and houses and mines and mounds. My thoughts as I walked were all of Me: how fascinating is Me.

I came in at midnight and met Me in my mirror. I pushed my three-cornered hat backward off my head, slipped out of my loose coat, and dropped my squeezed gloves. I sank fatiguedly into a little chair before the mirror, tipped the chair forward on its front legs, rested my elbows on the bureau and my chin in my hands, and looked absorbedly at myself. Lovingly, tenderly, discerningly, marveling and absorbed and deeply fascinated I looked at Me in the mirror. "You enchanted one!" said I, "You Witch-o'-the-world! you Mary MacLane! - who you are *I* don't know - what you are I but partly know. You're my Companion, my Familiar, my Lover, my wilding Sweetheart - I love you! I know that - that's enough. I love your garbled temper, your aching thoughts, your troubled Heart, your wasted spirit. I know much, much, much of you and love you! I love your beauty-sense and your proud scornful secret super-sensitiveness. I love your Eyes and your Lips and your bodily Fire and Ice" -

- to know *oneself: apart from all the world!*

One looking at me sees a cold-poised young woman, reserved and aloof, slightly diffusing insolence and inspiring misgivings.

But I looking at Me see a woman standing high on flame-washed battlements of her life in whom burn and beat the spirits and lights and star-discords of uncounted tired lustrous ages. I see me forlorn and radiant, drab and brilliant. I see me wrapped in a fiery potentiality of pain and beauty and love and sorrow. I hear wild voices in Me like horrid-sweet wailing of ghost-violins, muted but crying loudly in frightful reasonless vital joy and in unspeakable terror and sadness. I see Me ragged-clothed, bleeding, with disordered tangled hair and bloodshot eyes, with coarse soiled hands, broken-nailed, like a criminal's: a woman of woes. And I see Me wistful in quiet pure garments like one seeking light. I see Me old as old sin and young as new Spring days. I see Me un-sanely sensitive and hardened over - closed in worldly cases: guarded antagonism round my thoughts, protecting indifference round my Heart, dead silence round my Soul. I see Me with brains to know, with prescient mind to grasp, with mobile sense to feel. I see Me all futile, all hopeless, all miserable. I see Me all poetry. I see Me all wonder, mystery, and beauty. I see Me! -

- *much more than that,* this *Me sitting here! my deep gray wanton dark eyes: my lips - like pink flowers - with the inscrutable expression: my white fingers - slim, strong, glossy-nailed, silken at the tips. My glass gives Me back to Me, sitting by it, languid of Body, tense of spirit and Mind, bathed in witcheries of Self -*

I love my Mary MacLane! Ah - I love her!

It is good - since I can't find God, since I can't find way-of-truth however I grope about.

Every human friendship I form throws me back more completely on myself. Whom then shall I love but myself?

I know my own human enchantments and that they never fail me.

I'll know them more! I'll love them more! - I'll love them in sane madness lest mad madness overtake and destroy Me, Soul and bones.

*

No Resonance

To-morrow

My life, myself, I know are nothing noble, nothing constructive.

There is no resonance in this analysis, but all Dissonance.

Something lives, lives muscularly in me that constantly betrays me, destroys me against all my own convictions, against all my own knowledge, against all my own desire.

It may be true of Everybody.

I don't know. I think about it but get nowhere.

It seems someway unlike God to make each person a something all of cross-purpose.

But I doubt that I am different from Everybody.

I doubt if I am anyway abnormal.

I am very sane.

A match-flame burns me the same as it burns Everybody: pins prick me and hurt.

Yet I look in myself and see, through harmonic details, the massed Dissonance.

I am dying in a pit.

*

Black-Browed Wednesdays

To-morrow

All my life I've liked the Back of a magazine.

Some black-browed Wednesday I purchase a magazine, a fifteen-cent one, and read it through. I read the stories and they deeply engage or lightly interest me. I read the "special articles" and if they tell about flying machines or wild birds or hospitals or woman-prisoners in penitentiaries they charm or absorb my thoughts. I look at the illustrations and try to decide whether they are art or science or mechanism. I read the verse and if it's poetry it exhilarates me as if closed shutters were opened to let Day into a gloomy Room.

Then I read the advertisements in the Back and they do all of those things to me in comforting life-giving oxygen-furnishing ways. Each advertisement is a short story with an eerie little "plot" in it: each is a special article full of purpose: each is fruitful poetry: and in my two hands I all-but have and hold those wonderful Things they exploit.

They make me feel it's my birthday and I'm presented a wealth of lavish gifts.

They make me feel it's all a world of playthings.

They make me feel like a baby with a rattle, a ball, and a hoop of bells.

I like *everything* in the Back of a magazine.

I like the Revolvers, handsome plausible short-barreled Revolvers with pictures of ordinary people in dim-lit midnight bedrooms, and ordinary expected-looking burglars climbing in windows - Revolvers of ten shots and of six, and of different calibers, and all of them gleamingly mystically desirable: I like the Soaps, smooth amorous appetizing Soaps, some in luxurious Paris packets, and others spread out in blue water and rosy foam, splashed in by athletic Archimedesque young men and fat creamy babies and slim beautiful ladies - Mary Garden Soap of pungent delicious scent, tar Soap for the long lovely hair of girls, austere Ivory Soap - it floats: I like the Rubber Heels of resilient charm so tellingly pictured and described that at once I desire them beneath my spirit-heels - springy and solid and thick and firm: I like the Tooth-pastes and Tooth-powders and Tooth-lotions in tubes and tins and bottles, each bearing beneficent messages to the human white teeth of this world - one unfailing kind coming lyrically out like a ribbon and lying flat on the brush: I like the foods - of miraculous spotless purity and enticement - Biscuits and Chocolate and Figs, and *Foie-gras* in thick glossy little pots, so richly pictured and sung that merely to let my thoughts graze in their pasturage fattens my Heart: I like the men's very thin Watches, and men's Garters - no metal can touch you -, and men's fluffy-lathered shaving sticks, and men's trim smart flawless tailored Suits, in none of which I have use or interest until I find them in the Back of a magazine - where at once they grow charming and romantic: I like the jars and boxes and tubes and glasses of Cold Cream, Cold Cream fit for skins of goddesses, fit for elves to feed on - a soft satiny scented snow-white elysium of wax and vaseline and almond paste, pictured in forty alluring shapes till it feels pleasantly ecstatic just to be living in the same world with bewitching vases of Cold Cream, Cold Cream, Cold Cream - always bewitching and lovely but never so notably and festively as in the Back of a magazine: and I like the Pencils: and Book-cases: and Silver: and Jewels: and Glass: and Gloves: and Shoes - beautiful Shoes: and Fountain-pens: and Leather things: and Paint - silkish salubrious Paints, house-Paints, and the panegyrics with them - they make me long to own a spirit-house and paint it liberally: and Rugs: and Varnish: and Clothes - wonderful Clothes: and Bungalows: and Phonographs - his master's voice: and Paper - fine-wrought Paper to write on - bond and linen and hand-pressed, pale-tinted - a vast virgin treasure: and Oranges: and Cigarettes - a shilling in London, a quarter here: and Water Bottles of powdery rubber: and Stockings - patrician Stockings which take me into realms of silk-looms and delicate dyes and slim ankles: and Candle-Shades: and Candle-Sticks: and countless Cosmetics - Cosmetics of tender colors for the outer woman: and Sealing-wax indescribably use-less and attractive: and Tennis-Racquets: and Ivory - smooth Vantine Ivory toys and trinkets polished softly bright as moonlight - and their lily-worded descriptions like restrained sonnets: and Washing Powders - let the Gold Dust twins do your work: and Shower-baths: and Evans' Ale: and Flying Boats: and Umbrellas: and Cameras - if it isn't an Eastman it isn't a kodak: and boxes of Candy - sweet wilderness of chocolates - their very makers' names have a melting gust - Allegretti, Huyler, Clarence Crane, Maillard - cloying courtiers all: and Diamond Dyes - a child can use them: and Veranda Screens - she can look out but he can't look in: and Cedar Chests: and Chartreuse from Carthusian monasteries: and Perfumes - Perfumes in their maddening-sweet pride, Perfumes from Paris, Perfumes bottled in thick crystal, enchantingly costly - each American dollar added to their price-by-the-ounce making them fragranter to my thoughts: and boxes of benevolent Matches, and captivating Brooms, and fascinating Scouring-powders - a Dutch girl on the can chasing dirt - all three luscious tempting things in the Back of a magazine: and Automobiles - ask the man who owns one: and Rifles - simple and formidable and fine: and restful Rat-poison - they die in the open air seeking water: and sacks of Flour - eventually, why not now - flour unusual and piquant in the Back of a magazine, flour novel and endearing: and Type-writers: and Mushrooms: and Monkey-Wrenches: and Rosaries: and Rock-salt -

- the Back, the Back, the Back of a magazine -

There's no sadness and no terror in the Back of a magazine.
And it is for Everybody, Everybody.
A million people read a story in the middle of the magazine and half the million readily miss its point. But a single tin of Talcum Powder in the Back - the whole million note that and miss nothing in it: it gets to them both on and under their skin.
Some of the million read a ten-line poem in *vers libre* in the front of the magazine - and nine-tenths of their number are hard-put to it: the mentalities of this human race being mostly shops shut down. It is something pregnant and prophetic to a poet, merely musical to a plain prose writer, arrant folly to a telephone girl, amusing nonsense to a butcher, a comic fantasy to a milliner, a form of insanity to a plumber, an unknown tongue to a milk-man, a kind of sin to a Baptist minister. But to each of those a Can of Soup in the Back of the same magazine has easily, exactly the same ox-tail-ish meaning: it reaches them where they live.
A thousand persons agree with an article about atavism in orang-outangs and ten thousand more quite refute it. But they all harmoniously commit suicide with the same make of Revolver - hammer the hammer - or get

rousing drunk to the same degree with the same brand of high-powered whiskey - Wilson, that's all.

A countess, a courtesan, and a convict-woman summarily pass over the front and middle of the magazine as containing nothing to their purpose. But like jungle denizens at their drinking pool the three of them meet hostilely on the common ground of a popular Cigarette featured in the Back - a blend to suit every taste - wherewith they unwittingly smoke away half their generic differentiations.

The Colonel's Lady and Judy O'Grady anoint themselves nightly into a state of shining invisible kinship from separated twin jars of the same bewitching Cold Cream.

I'm not sure myself and Miss Lily Walker of the Broadway chorus regard similarly a beauteous box of Rice Powder: she perchance would at once dash madly into it and powder herself o'er with it, whereas I would fain ponder about it awhile as a tiny be-violeted adventure. But pondering or powdering, equally exciting to each of us is its delicate pale lilac blazonment in the Back of a magazine.

The front of the magazine may mean little to you and the middle of the magazine may mean nothing to me: the Back of it none of us escapes.

It is for Everybody, Everybody.

Even Senegambians: they can look at the pictures and marvel over them.

I can there meet a Senegambian on the common ground of it might be a delicate transparent oval of Pears' Soap, pretty as a jewel of price: perchance we would each unconsciously feel we wouldn't be happy till we got it.

It's only as playthings I want the Things in the Back of a magazine.

To me they are toys, lyrics of matter, food of the senses.

The octroi would have no sympathy with my loiterings among their wares. It is a fete of my own, indolent and fanciful, unrecognized in commerce.

Any article I may put to its forthright use in actuality becomes an idyllic toy when I find it in the Back of a magazine. The desirable Revolvers are not firearms with which to shoot myself and burglars, but only bijous to have and handle and caress. The luxuriant vervain- and violet-scented Soaps are not for my toilet, but something to eat, for my astral body to feed on - nourishing food they make. The lush Cold Creams have no massaging possibilities in them - they are for my thoughts to gambol among, for my meddlesome spirit-fingers to touch and fuss with deliciously, blissfully, transcending all vulgar use. The men's thin Watches mean nothing to me as Watches: and their Garters - what's it to me whether no-metal-can-touch-you or no-metal-at-all? My thoughts merely revel and juggle with them, picture and legend - they are pastimes of my child-self. The cream-woven Note Papers are not to write on but wherewithal to imagine how cool and smooth they would feel drawn slowly across my flushed cheek. A sack of Flour - I feel only how I'd like to have it spilled out - eventually-why-not-now - in a thick warm-tinted heap on the blue-velvety floor of my room that I might roll and bathe in it and feel it feathery-fluffy on my skin.

So I play with my toys on black-browed Wednesdays.

Some Wednesdays even fail to be black-browed because there are Backs to magazines.

*

The Conscious Analyst

To-morrow

I don't know whether I write this because I wear two plain dresses or whether I wear two plain dresses because I write it.

My life fell into a lowering mood which calls for but two dresses: which mood compels me to write out these things that are in me as inevitably as heavy gathered clouds come raining to the ground. The mood having overtaken me I can not keep from writing this day after day, more than I can keep from brushing my hair every day, and eating lumps of food every day, and picking up tiny white specks from my blue rug.

I love this book and I fear and hate it. I love the writing of it though it is a finical unobvious task - more so than it looks. And often I fear to read it over lest I hurt my own feelings. And I hate it in ways. I am a particularly sane woman when all's said. And many things I come to in me are grating and inexplicable and incongruous. But also I love it. It is my companion "when the world is gone." I am as solitary as if I had no human place in this earth. My days are as silent as if I lived in it alone. The few voices that bespeak me in a day or a week stop at my ear-drums and are immensely alien. At times, for weeks on end, I am quite alone in this house and the silence then has a depth and a hollowness. From it I feel not alone in a house but alone in a world: and more when the family is in the house.

And it is what-should-I-do if I had not a writing talent to expend me upon from day to day, and so rest me. I feel God around some corner but that feeling is no rest, but only an odd terror which wants the dignity of terror.

Times I wonder if I shall have this published afterward for all to read and if so what colors it will paint on my world - and what else may befall.

But it's an aspect dim and remote now. I wearing but two nunlike dresses and face to face with me, have nothing to do with publishing books and with the beautiful noisy world and its befallings. It is easy to believe I shall never again have to do with any of that. This may be my death-mood. I am very tired. The weight of being a person is heavy on me as weights of lead. And still I know if I suddenly bloomed with beautiful frocks and went out to-morrow to lose myself among people, people, people I should at once achieve a veneer of the utmost frivol. I have an odd frivolous quality full of an ardor and strength, with all of my mental mettle in it. Also I know if I did that now it would be but postponing this analytic reckoning. Which would confront me again with the more rancor, the more futileness gathered into it from having been put off.

This book and the two dresses are my present portion. If I could escape them (I am not quite sure I want to - but - *hell!*) - it would be of no use. They would come back again in an unexpected ripeness of time and demand a hearing: an exquisite nervous tragic hearing.

They are such stuff as the conscious analyst is made of.

But though I'm the conscious analyst I can't quite tell whether I write the book because I wear two plain black dresses or I wear those because I write it.

*

Eye When I Mean Tooth

To-morrow

I write it, and it's a surprising book.

It is not what on the surface it looks to be.

I do not write what my clear Mind may want to say to the white blank paper.

I do not write what my thoughts are saying to me.

Those things are facile, uninformed - flat mental pictures, the writer's craft.

I write what still voices of life - voices trivially frightful in their secret pettiness - voices of all my life - merest living - say to my ancient Soul and my young present Body and what they two may answer.

I am in some sort a wonderful person - and in places I do that, nearly perfectly.

I am also tired and someway whelmed by self-conscious despair, and possessed of a talent imperfect and inadequate to reveal the radiances and shades my being perceives: and in places I fail.

I fail remarkably. I write Eye when I mean Tooth. I write Fornicate when I mean Caress. I write Wine when I mean Blood. For no better reason than that my writing hand is not sufficiently dexterous: the little flashing shutters open and shut so quick that the second ones are shut and the third starting to open before I have got written the things I saw through the first ones. Only not always.

*

A Wild Mare

To-morrow

Also I am dissatisfying to myself.

My thoughts smother me: they keep me from life.

I am a hundred times more introspective than most people, most women. Most women, even conventional ones, are lawless - the more conventional, the more lawless usually.

And so most women beat me to life. Where they yield to an impulse the moment they feel it - I, because an impulse itself is adventure-fabric - I feel of its quality, test it for defects, wash a little corner of it to see if the color will run - and conclude not to use it.

That I gaze inward at the garbled biograph of Me keeps me from several sorts of violent action.

I have violent action in me, chained in analysis.

Most women are secretly lawless on the old plan inaugurated by Eve - of inclining to do anything forbidden, of hugging everything they are unsupposed to hug, of determinedly kicking over the traces when coerced too much. The ban is the chief attraction.

It's but little like that with me. There would be point and purpose in my Action. But it is kept in stupor by analysis.

I am malcontent about that, though I live upon analysis. I hate the inaction and inertia that follow on its heels.

I could be an anarchist. I condemn anarchists but not as I condemn Me. I would respect me more were I this moment prisoned in a real bastile for having stuck a good knife into a bad king. I could feel, no matter how foolish and mistaken in itself the act, that I had done the strong and brave thing at sacrifice of my personal selves. The dry living-death of the prison would be compensated for each day when I said to Me, "It was a needful honorable act and *I* did it: for once in my life I was a Regular Person."

There would be a nourishment in being able to tell that to myself. There would be warming food in owning one so brave remembrance of myself.

But, my Soul-and-bones! - at the very moment of lifting the good knife a thought would come: "How is this king worse than another? What rotten rascal mightn't rise in his place?" And on with a lightning-trail of analysis till my pale hand dropped inert and the knife in it grew harmless as a lily-petal.

It isn't that I haven't the guts. I have.

I am a wild mare in foal: and unfoaling.

*

The Mist

To-morrow

Because I am to myself someways dissatisfying and exasperating often this thing I write is dissatisfying and exasperating.

It is a true account of what is inside me. "The wine must taste of its own grapes."

It would be easier to make it an untrue account, for fiction is the most effortless of writing. So I have found it. And I am very clever.

I could write myself as a pretty dainty harmlessly purring one - the leopard with claws clipped and fangs drawn.

When my dynamos rest I am like that, doubtless.

But the wears and tears of breathing and the influences of varied life-details and of clothes worn and food eaten start me moving devilishly.

Phases of a score of persons, men and women, come to light in me.

To be one human being means to be monstrously mixed.

I write me out not as I might be, nor as I should be - whatever that may be -: but merely as I am.

As, Just Beneath The Skin, I am.

So my written account must come out someways dissatisfying and exasperating. Logically dissatisfying and divinely and ethically exasperating.

- a passage in Virgil tells of a Mist that is all over and about this world from the human "tears that are falling, falling, falling always." Something, and it may be that Mist, makes one's view of everything - everything in life - a little blurred. It may even blur one's view of oneself. So it may be I do not see myself with entire clearness -

I only know I write me as clearly as I see me, considering the Mist.

*

A White Liner

To-day came the Finn woman and cleaned my blue-and-white bedroom.

She comes now and again and cleans excellently.

I would like to clean my room myself but lack the strength and skill to do it well.

But I stay with the Finn woman and show her how and I watch her work and muse upon her. She would be called in England a charwoman, but in this America of the vast mongrel heterogenesis she is an unclassified laborer.

I like to watch her and talk with her a bit and dwell on her mixed potentialities. She contrasts fascinatingly with me.

She is a human being and so am I, and beyond and with that there are odd parallels and similarities and distinctions between her and me.

Her name is Josephina and she looks as if it might be.

Mine is Mary MacLane but I don't look entirely like it.

She lives a lonely life and so do I, differing in sort and circumstance.

I am middle-class and American of Canadian reminiscence, and early-thirty.

Josephina is Finn and lower-class with a "foreign" look, and she is forty-five and looks sixty and is twelve years out of Finland.

I am tallish and slim and weigh nine wavering stone.

The Finn woman is short and solid and weighs all of a hundred and seventy pounds.

I am slender of flank and ankle, narrow through the loins and bony at the shoulders.

The Finn woman is thick everywhere, broad of girth and deep of chest like a Percheron stallion.

I am darkish with dusky gray eyes.

Josephina is dirty-blond with pale narrow blue eyes like a china doll's.

My sex feels to me like a mysterious sweetness.

Josephina's sex looks porcinely obvious and uninteresting like her large dubious breasts.

I am inwardly full of strong-flavored emotions.

The one positive outward feeling Josephina manifests is a dull but comprehensive hatred, peculiar to her nationality and station, for everything Swedish.

The Finn woman has a husband now and had a different one formerly.

I have none and never had.

Josephina is elemental primeval woman.

So am I but terrifically qualified by complexity, incongruity.

I have white smooth firm beautiful hands.

Josephina's hands are particularly ugly and have a menacing look.

I have quick intelligence.

Josephina is markedly stupid.

I live in a quiet clean bungalow.

Josephina lives in an unusually filthy unrestful little house.

I own two dresses whose personnel alters at intervals.

Josephina owns one unchanging dress, septic, maculate, and repellent.

I have a sense of humor vivid and intriguing to myself.

Josephina has no more sense of humor than a flat-iron.

I bathe foamily icily each morning.

Josephina would seem never to have had a bath.

She cleans windows and floors and rugs for thirty-five cents an hour. She would regard it as a fantastic waste of time and soap to clean herself for nothing.

I own in a still flawed life one phase which is an endless treasure of beauty and power and charm and light: my love for John Keats.

The Finn woman owns about the same thing in a life which may be more still and flawed than mine: her love for strong drink.

There begins a curious line of similitude between us.

I feel oddly joyous and light of heart on a solitary veranda corner with the John-Keats poetry book open in my lap.

And Josephina has been found many a time by Butte policemen sitting alone joyous and very drunk, in dark alleys with empty pint bottles strewn all about her.

In my un-Keats hours I am mostly mournful. And Josephina sober has all the melancholy of her race with an added gloom, as if the acetylene had run out of all her lamps. That my melancholy is more lustrous than hers I lay to her native dullness as against my native braininess, and to alcohol's having rotting effects on human mental tissues: whilst John Keats to those who drink his poetry is a starry savior.

I like to think there's the same ambrosial food in the Demon Rum for Josephina as in the Grecian Urn for me.

There seems no other pleasure in life for her.

The limit of her literary pursuit is the reading of a four-page Finnish newspaper full of obituaries.

The opalescent enchantments of her inner being mean nothing to her: she wouldn't know her entity from her duodenum.

Her body can bring her no delight: there's no lightness to it, no tang, no feminine charm, no consciousness to make her love it as the Dianas love theirs.

A sunset above the western peaks is less than a setting sun to her.

Her food is merely her fodder.

Love and Romance pass her by. She and the husband vie with each other for solitary possession of their little nasty house. And her personality is not conducive to lovers.

She has nor chick nor child to mother.

Her idea of a life beyond this vale is crude and uncomfortable. She went two Sundays to the Finnish church and had a surprising lusty doctrine of eternal fire rammed down her throat: she took the Finn minister's word for it and quitted the fold, preferring to live this life unhampered by flaming anticipation.

All her material treasure she works for with mops and scrubbing-brushes at thirty-five cents an hour.

Other roads being thus blocked it is sing-ho for King Alcohol in pint bottles.

Josephina is what is called a white liner. Which means that she has drunk so long, so much, so regularly that whiskey, rum, gin, and brandy have no or negligible effects upon her. To achieve her intoxicating aim she must drink pure alcohol.

By the same token I eschew many a tame poet: I must have John Keats. What the poetry of John Keats does to me I know.

What the distilled waters of her choice do to Josephina it pleases me to imagine while I watch her clean my walls and floor and windows.

She works strongly, steadily, quietly till I pronounce the room clean. Then she stops, carries the pails and other things downstairs to the kitchen, removes a big brass pin from the rear of her dingy skirt which had held it back and doubled over her darkling petticoat, re-dons an antique rain-coat and bad hat, ties her clinking silver into the corner of a decadent handkerchief, bids me good-evening with a grave blond Finn bow and goes out into the dusk. She takes her way through alleys and short-cuts to the side door of a "Finlander" gin-palace in the Finn quarter of the town. And there she lays out her day's wage in the pint bottles of her delight. As many pint bottles as her few dollars will buy, so many she buys. She ventures her all in the name of passionate thirst taking no thought of the morrow. She then seeks out some alley with a dark door-step and there she does her drinking. It would not do to go home with her alcoholic wealth because the husband might be there who, like the alphabetic vintner, would "drink all himself." So she drinks away in pint-bottle-ish peace, sitting alone in the gloom of the alleyway door-step, in her limp rain-coat and bad hat and her stolid

Finn self-sufficience.

Because I like Josephina it charms me to think of the happiness that must be hers as she sits emptying pint bottles into herself and the white strong firewater begins to work.

Before having her drinks she is unelated and uninformed like a corpse coldly electrified by a storage battery. As she drinks and drinks on she remains outwardly unchanged as the way is with her race - but within! The changes that come to pass in the heavy person of Josephina as the white flames wash down her walls!

Into her dull veins pours a hot stream like melted seething copper and it heats her knees till she knows she *has* knees and that they are white and very beautiful: and it heats her legs and her back and her breasts till they glow with the double-glow of an Aphrodite's in a reluctant Adonis' arms: it heats her eyes and temples and throat till she feels herself a radiant girl: it heats the crown of her head till she feels something like a brain there: it heats her heart and stomach till she's filled with a gay gust for life: it heats her imagination till she even imagines herself in love with her hard Finn husband since he is not by to beat her and so dispel the fancy: it heats a sense of humor into her till she laughs suddenly and heartily at some fugitive funniness that had lain long frozen in her memory: it heats a hundred little human carburetors in her which send a wreathe of vapors up into her drab being to flush it with misty golds and thin blues and rosy crimsons till her dormant involuntary soul awakes - a thing of old mellowed beauty, it may be - and is wafted on warm pretty vapory wings far from alleys, far from mops and scrubbing brushes, far from thirty-five cents an hour, far from doorsteps - to fair sweet Isles of the Blest!

Nearing the last of her pint bottles she reels sideways on the door-step: her bad hat cants forward: she sprawls about. The policeman on that beat to whom in that aspect she is a figure long familiar strolls toward her late in the night and looks at her with a lackluster eye. But Josephina is physically unaware of all this world. Her last pint bottle is gamely emptied, her inner sun's chromosphere burns like mad - but her body, unable to cope with the virile delectations new-risen within it, limply gives way.

A quaint picture, interesting to dwell on: her thick bathless body laid low in the darkened alley, with the empty pint bottles scattered on the paving-stones beside it - but her astral shape, lit by the subtle fires of alcohol, lifted high, high to remote elysiums. The policeman calls the "wagon" and Josephina is taken up by several ungentle hands and tossed into it like a sack of coal. They take her to the city jail and lock her in a cell. The next morning she stands jaded and morbidly intoxicated before a police judge who glances at her uninterestedly for the several-hundredth time and says five days.

The five days can not be pleasant days but Josephina owns a robust sporting spirit. She gives not so much as the shrug of a shoulder either at going into jail or coming out of it. A black eye from her husband, a broken arm from a drunken fall, a filthy sojourn in jail: all one to her. She accepts them as she accepts all of her life, with an immense psychic calm. But she takes strongly to drink to translate herself out of it. And let her drink.

I know how she feels for I take to John Keats.

I don't myself care much for strong drink. I drink a little of it at irregular intervals, but, by and large, I drink without éclat. In this mountain altitude whiskey makes me sick, champagne makes me dizzy, and gin is a pungent punishment. One morning after reading of Josephina's white-line distinction in a police-court column I tasted some alcohol, but it had a varnish flavor and had strangling effects on my throat. It made me marvel at Josephina's prowess. I like absinthe in its bitter strength mostly because to sit sipping it feels restfully forbidden. Port wine is a brackish medicine, I hate the stickiness of cordials, and a cocktail I like chiefly to contemplate. So much for me and strong drink.

Josephina on the other hand does not care for John Keats. I sounded her on poetry in some of its human aspects: there was nobody at home. Her own enlightened north-country has some poets of borealic iron and brain-brawn and beauty: to Josephina's wooden intellect their books are eternally closed.

But the Demon Rum looses a heated flood of poetry upon her, which I can but vision and not feel.

I am incapable of strong drink even as Josephina is incapable of John Keats. We are quits there.

I look on myself as the more fortunate. - John Keats!

A woman so drunk as to fall and reel about is always an exquisitely shameful thing. And when I think of how she's tossed into the wagon - to mention but one item -

But it's a matter of the human equation. Doubtless it is all relative. The Finn woman is not aware of how she is knocked about, and if she were she would not regard it with any of my imagination. So what matter?

A likeable and admirable person is Josephina. A so strong fine businesslike worker, a so thorough-bred sport, a so splendid drunkard, and asking no odds of God or man. In her stolid Finn fashion she likes me as she has proven, and I like her though she makes me feel inferior.

- if Josephina could and would write *her* inner isolated world of thoughts - the saga of her one horrid gown! There would be a book. All blacks and carmines - all stolidly sober and brilliantly drunk - all dingily bathless:

deeply savagely quietly human.

It would be a book savoring not of white alcohol but of the salty unshed Tears, the dry artistic Griefs of Josephina.

*

Beneficent Bedlam

To-morrow

I have been so long Sane it would be gay and sweet and resting to go Mad.

I would I could go Mad.

To a Mad-woman a Door is not a Door, probably: a Cat is not a Cat, belike: and To-morrow is not To-morrow at all - it may be week-before-last, it may be next year, it may be an exquisite jest. One can not tell *what* it is.

It is the thing one escapes by going Mad: Monotony.

It's all beneficent bedlam.

*

A Deadly Pathos

To-morrow

I love the sex-passion which is in this witching Body of me. I love to feel its portent grow and creep over me, like a climbing vine of tiny red roses, in the occasional dusks.

It is not shame or shadow or sordidness: but beauty and sweetness and light.

- no token of sin: a token of virtue.
- no thing to crush: rather to nurture, to garner.
- no thing to forget: to remember, to think about.
- no flat weak drawn-out prose: live potent clipped heated poetry.
- not common and loosely human: rare and divine.
- not fat daily soup: stinging wine of life.
- not valueless because born of nothing and nowhere: valuable, priceless, a treasure under lock and key.

Sex-desire comes wandering in dusk-time and gulfs me as in a swift violent sweet-smelling whirlwind.

It goes away sudden-variant as it came, out of a region of hot quick shadows.

And for that, for hours and days afterward, oranges and apples look brighter-colored to my eyes: hammocks swing easier as I sit in them: rugs feel softer to my feet: the black dresses lend themselves gentler to my form: pencils slide faciler on paper: my voice speaks less difficultly into telephones: meanings sound super-vibrant in Keats' Odes: sugar - little pinches of granulated sugar - are sharper, sweeter-sweeter in my throat.

And God grows less remote. And my wooden coffin and deep wet yellow clay grave move a long way back from me.

- all from fleeting ungratified wish of sly sex-tissues -

Also in it, and in my life from it, I sense some deathly pathos.

*

The Necklace

To-morrow

The necklace which God long ago hung round the white neck of my Soul is composed of little-seeming curses, like precious and semi-precious gems. They are polished smooth as if by age, as if by wear, as if by fingering, and as if by brisk industrious rubbing.

The Necklace is at once beautiful and ugly. The gems are in color chiefly blues and greens - with grays, lavenders, drabs, and mauves. But mostly blues and greens. They make a circlet of small stones strung at short intervals as if on a strong thin gold wire, with two large tawdry pretty pendants hung in front. One of the pendants is my fertile phase of Weakness and the other my odd encompassing Folly. The smaller stones are seventeen in number and their names and natures are these:

- the first is Dishonesty which makes ghosts of half my life.

- the second is Pretense, hard and genuine stone, which keeps me from being all-ways sincere even to anyone who knows me and whom I know: who loves me and whom I love.

- the third is Fear which makes me who scorn all leonine dangers cringe and crawl for trifles of life incredibly little.

- the fourth is Sensuality which burns and bursts across my Mind, half-missing my Body.

- the fifth is Anxiety, strange flawed green stone - by it I worry, tortured and wildly wavering, about the passing hours of my life: where they are going, where they are taking me.

- the sixth is Amativeness, extraordinary deep-tinted warm false gem -

it makes me love someway amorously some person I meet and fancy: an intimate tragedy, crucial and trivial.

- the seventh is Fatigue of the spirit itself, gray sad stone, meaning terrible sensations of age in my young flesh.

- the eighth is Incongruity, the sense and feeling of it, round blue stone - it kills what might be art and constructiveness and excellence in me.

- the ninth is Acquiescence, worn dull stone - it has kept me all the ages from the salvation of heated luminous strife.

- the tenth is Sensitiveness, pale-toned stone - by it the fingers of life touch me too suddenly, too sharply, too tensely to do me the good they might.

- the eleventh is Doubt, frail opalescent stone - by it my delight in the sunny Spring wind against my cheek is qualified with dubious surprise: by it I half-disbelieve in moon and stars and in long country roads stretched out solitary, lovely, drenched in sunset.

- the twelfth is Self-consciousness, blue-and-green stone - it robs me of the comfort and self-respect of feeling any motive in me to be un-ulterior.

- the thirteenth is Introspection, beautiful-beautiful blue-green stone - it pays for its place in beauty but by it I lose the building, the substance, the *matter* of living.

- the fourteenth is Intensity - too vivid vision, too vivid taste for some details of life - little hot-looking cool-feeling stone - by it I undervalue and overvalue, dwell upon surfaces, missing the serene feel and possession of precious solidness.

- the fifteenth is Isolation, pale purple stone - it makes me feel *never* at home, *never* at ease, *never* belonging - a subtle insulation - in this sheltered peopled world.

- the sixteenth is Bewilderment, mixed-tinted stone - by it I wonder *what* is truth with truth seeming that moment fluttering soft-plumed wings at my throat.

- the seventeenth is - it has no name - the *Feel-of-Me*, bright blue-green stone, lovely and loathesome - by it I've lost my way, I've felt all and only Me when I might have groped outward, hand and foot, and found a wind-swept path to go in: I was always blurred by Me.

A small Necklace, all dull gleams and unusual tints, strung finely and strongly and beautifully on shining gold. The sweet Soul droops like a wilted lily under even its slight weight. Strong fine rivets hold it firm-clasped and the weight of the two charming imitation pendant-stones keep it gracefully in place.

My loved and lovely Soul has worn it through the ages: manacle, shackle. How long more - God may know but does not tell me.

It's only a Necklace. And my Soul is a Soul!

Even under the frail galling burden of the flesh the Soul of me to-morrow could tear off that Necklace and crumble it to airless nothing.

It does not: but *could*.

*

Slyly Garbling and Cross-Purposing

To-morrow

At rarish intervals comes my Soul to visit me.

My Soul is light sheer Being.

My Soul is like a young most beautiful girl marked and worn by long cycles of time but not anyway aged. She comes dressed in something like gray-white de-soie muslin or fine-grained crêpe silk, a loose-belted frock reaching to her ankles.

My Soul is unmoved by the world and the flesh and their feeling, as befits a Soul. She looks on me with a chill faëry-ish contempt, as also befits a Soul.

The quality of her contempt is of weary understanding and is like a caress.

In the dusk of yesterday came my Soul to visit me - a dusk of a deep beauty. The last glow of the sun lay along the earth, and all was gentian blue.

I leaned against my window-pane watching it, and beside me sat her Presence. Her Presence makes me feel wonderfully gifted: it is *mine*, this Soul all Golden-Silk and Silken-Gold!

We talk on many topics, of many things: I in worldly nervous ignorance and with a wishfulness to reach and compass and know: the Soul with poise and surety of attitude, a wearied patience and the chill sweet contempt.

She answers me from her cool old tranquil view-point, which is near me yet remote.

We talked last of some bygone persons I have been, some shapes she wore.

Said the Soul: "Early in the sixteenth century you were a ragged Russian peasant girl living in ignorance and filth in a hut by a swamp-edge. You had parents both of whom beat your body black-and-blue from your babyhood. And at eighteen you were a coarsened hardy wench tending a drove of pigs and goats on the sunny steppe. I was there with you as presently as now - as sentient, as perceptive. But it is a question whether you or the little beasts you drove were the more beastly stupid. You and they were equal in outer quality, equal in uncleanliness, equally covered with vermin."

I have no ghost-memory of that time, but as the Soul told of it a nascent feeling came on me, as if some part of my Mind felt its way back to that.

I warmed to the thought of the Peasant Girl. I was quiescent to her filth and ignorance.

Said I: "Was she brave and fairly honest?"

Said the Soul: "You were a ready liar - you lied your way out of many a beating. But you were brave enough. You faced the roughnesses of your life uncringing, and you died game."

Said I: "How did I die?"

Said the Soul: "You were run neatly through the body by the short sword of a soldier whose lust-desire you had had the hardihood to refuse - and I fled away upon the instant."

Said I: "I half-knew it - she died a violent death. You - were you glad to be quit of her filthy flesh, her surroundings, her ignorance?"

Said the Soul: "Glad? Such things mean nothing to me. Your body, be it sweet or foul, has no bearing on my long journey. Motives - motif - back of your human acts make me glad or sorry at leaving you."

Said I: "Tell me about a time when I seemed someway fine, humanly fine."

Said the Soul: "In London, near the end of the seventeenth century, before and during the period of the Gordon Riots, you lived in a way of peace. From when you were fourteen until you were twenty-nine you lived alone with your little lame half-sister whom you cared for very devotedly, very tenderly."

My little half-sister - Until the Soul spoke of her there was no vision, no image like her. Then something of me remembered.

Said I: "What was she like? Who were our parents?"

Said the Soul: "Your mother died at your birth, hers at her birth. Your father was hanged at Tyburn for forgery. The sister was pale, large-eyed, long-haired, crippled from a dislocated shoulder and hip. When you were twenty-five she was eleven, a beautiful frail child. You lived in two rooms above a linen-draper's and you supported the two of you by weaving and calendering cloths for the shop-keeper, and by illuminating missals and manuscripts when you could get that work. For a very poor wage, but living was cheap. All the time you took zealous care of your sister. Your heart was bound up in her - you adored her."

Said I: "I know that. Tell me what we did - how we lived - how we loved each other."

Said the Soul: "In the summer evenings you often walked out along quiet London streets - the sister sometimes with a crutch and your arm about her, sometimes in a rolling chair, whilst you walked beside her pushing it. Your father had educated you in an erratic fashion. You had a deal of desultory knowledge - what is called knowledge - and you educated the young sister in the same manner. Often it was of the poets - Latin, English, Italian - and of histories and sciences and arts - what odd comprehensive bits you knew - that you two talked as you sauntered in the bright late English sunlight. Or you talked of the little details of your joint life. Sometimes you sat together - you holding her close in your arms - by a window in your darkening front room, and watched the children at play in the common opposite, and conversed and were quietly happy. You were maternal and the child was a mature old-fashioned yet childish innocent child."

My little sister - sweet - long gone - Would that I had her now!

Said I: "Tell me what we said."

Said the Soul: "You said to her, 'Our poverty and even our deprivations, dearest, which for your sake I feel deeply would not matter, not the least, to me if I could see you well and strong.' And the child replied, 'Sweet, just to rest like this in your arms each twilight makes me rich, rich - as rich as the smartest ladies in Piccadilly.' And you said, 'Rich reminds me, Darling, we shall have four extra shillings - four bright silver shillings - at the end of this week from the book-seller. So what shall we purchase for a treat? There'll be, if you like, prawns and crumpets for tea, for days to come - or if my Child prefers oranges or pineapples once -' And the child replied with her cheeks quite pink at the thought, 'O Sister-love, let us have the pines, just one day, and let us make-believe to be ladies that day, and comport ourselves like ladies, and take our tea - all like ladies.' And you pressed her close to your breast - you both wore caps and kerchiefs and stuff-gowns in the fashion of the lower-middle artisan class - and showered gentle kisses on her cheeks and eyelids, and promised her the pineapples and the tea like ladies."

I listened to this with vivid still pleasure. It felt like endearing fulfilling life - a day of tenderness -. And oddly familiar.

Said I: "What were we in the habit of having for our tea - that prawns and crumpets would make us a treat?"

Said the Soul: "Your tea was chiefly bran-bread and cress or perhaps lettuce, with a stone mug of milk for the child when you could afford it. The London of that day had no luxuries for the poor. And having had none you missed none. But the populace lived in starveling misery. The rabble rose and rallied to the Gordon as it would have to anyone who urged it to rioting. You were Protestants but you regarded him as a weakling visionary. You watched the rioting in the streets with little fear, but the linen-draper and all other shop-keepers kept barred doors. You two were venturesome and were yourselves of the masses, and when the mob stormed Newgate prison you both stood watching with many other householders on the outskirts of the crowd, in terror but secretly half in sympathy. You were safe enough from the rioters who were intent on wrecking the gaol and freeing the inmates. It was characteristic of you as you were then to be out looking on at a murderous night scene with interest, carefully protecting the child from contact with the throngs."

Said I: "How long did that life last?"

Said the Soul: "Four years after that your sister changed from her bare little bed to a coffin and you went on alone achingly suffering her loss for long years. You lived to be seventy, a thin old woman, working latterly as one of the night nurses in a public hospital. You lived an abstemious outwardly self-sacrificing life and died alone, from hardened arteries, one autumn night."

Said I: "And was there an informing beauty for you, for you and for me, in my life then?"

Coldly said the Soul: "You were self-centered, for all your self-sacrifice. You reckoned it your duty to care for your sister. It was also your irresistible delight. And after her death you took self-satisfaction in self-sacrifice: smug - smug. For me there was a laming distortion in it all."

Said I: "Tell me some other life."

Said the Soul: "You were once a little thief in the streets of a later London. You picked pockets, you stole bits of food in Covent Garden market, you pilfered shop-tills, you systematically worked the wealthy throngs as they came from the Opera at midnight. You were known to the police as the cleverest child-thief in London."

It warmed my vanity to think of myself as clever in so theatric a rôle as thief.

Said I: "How did that life like you?"

Said the Soul, with a shrug of her delicate shoulders: "I had little to do with it and that in a negative way. My part in you was to keep up your heart in hungry hunted days. You were neither a good thing nor a bad thing: perishingly passive. And you were dead in a potter's field before your sixteenth birthday."

Said I: "How did the little Thief look?"

Said the Soul: "You were sufficiently ugly - an undersized form, a gamin face, bastard features."

Said I: "And I daresay ignorant?"

Said the Soul: "Ignorant of everything rated useful, but wise to the undersides of human nature and in the sordid viciousness of London slums. And singularly shrewd - what is called philosophical."

Said I: "Pray tell me another life."

Said the Soul: "An earlier time - Paris, some century before the Terror -

saw you a slim *fille-du-pavè*, a prostitute of a low cheap type, but with more brain, more of what is termed character than you have ever possessed. You had wit, will, *esprit*, determination. From having been at seventeen most obscenely of the streets you were at thirty a wonderfully grand courtesan: no better in what are called morals but possessed of very much inner and outer strength and luster. You were *chère-aimée* to men of brain, men of importance to the state, whose acts were shaded by your influence. And you achieved unusual wealth chiefly by the powers and strategies of your character. You lived in the extreme of luxury of that time and of your type - a delicate luxury, almost high-bred. You were wanton in amour, being physically extremely passionate, but admirably straightforward and strong in each matter and aspect of your life."

Said I: "You admired her?"

Said the Soul: "I was serene and vividly alive within you. You were in all ways, simply and completely, an honest woman, and for the only time."

Said I: "How could she be honest, since she lived by exchanging treasure of much personal economic value for cheap cheapest gold, trash, and a besmirched name: and all through two sorts of greed?"

Said the Soul: "You were honest since you made no pretense of any kind to yourself. You took no gold that you did not logically, humanly, or shame-fully earn. You were consciously and unconsciously above all subterfuge. You wrought no ruin nor error nor darkness upon your own spirit or any other. You deceived neither yourself nor anyone about you. The tone of your life was of sun-shining simplicity and cleanness. There was no greed in you. You saw your way of life before you and lived it without degradation, with a positiveness of strength."

It is as if my Soul's view and mine were infinitely separate from being narrowly paralleled. The portrait was mystically familiar: but not by her light.

Said I: "Was she beautiful to look at?"

Said the Soul: "You were beautiful in a pallid saint-like French manner - an uncertain type of beauty which fatigue or depression turns to plain-ness. You had but little light charm of prettiness. But you had what counts for more than beauty: the nerve and verve of attractiveness, the force and fascination of physical being, the fragrance, the *flair* of the deeply-sexed woman. In one phase you were constantly preying and preyed upon, but with high valors of attack and endurance."

Said I: "Did she live in peace - had she no times of suffering?"

Said the Soul: "You had hours of violent bitter suffering. Paris has always accepted without countenancing the prosperous cocotte. And often you were infamously insulted at street-crossings by soldiers and *sergeants-de-*

ville as you drove out in your small bright-colored carriage. And you were hailed with opprobrious appropriate names by the ragged populace as they picked up silver pieces which you threw among them. Such things were stinging brands and lashes to you. But you bore yourself with entire courage. You gave much money to churches and charities but looked on such acts in yourself rightly as some slight weakness which would, however, be of benefit to the starving poor. I can not describe - so you could grasp it - the peace, the expansion, the freedom for me in that life and in that attitude."

The exact outlook of the Soul throws over me a veil of wistfulness, bewilderness, freedness, lostness which hides the material moorings of my life and casts me adrift on broad clouded seas.

Said I: "What was the end of that - how did she die?"

Said the Soul: "You died exquisitely, of syphilitic disorders. You were something past forty, badly broken - your looks were gone, your friends were gone, your money was not gone but it was of little use to you. But you smiled serenely and lived up personally and mentally to your smile. A surgeon and a fat mustached old woman saw you die in the beginning of that bodily rot - the just portion of the passionate whore - one sweet Spring dawn, with birds twittering in green branches outside your window and a great gold sun slowly breaking the mist. Then for once I left you with reluctance. I clung to you. The kiss of me was last on your fainting brain and your fast-cooling heart. For I was leaving, in an agony of my own, an *honest* person. And I knew not what might be my next petty prison."

Said I: "What was my next life?"

Said the Soul: "It was not so petty as were some others. You were next - about seventeen-fifty - a quaint extremely common little person. You were apprenticed as a child to a milliner in Liverpool, England. You grew out of that and became a dancer in a dingy theatre - a cheap bedraggled life. You were a cheap and bedraggled young woman. You wore odd gay tawdry frocks, hideous little shoes, ragged raveled silk hose, surprising bright bonnets. Your mind was a shallow pool filled with tales from shilling shockers and penny dreadfuls in which you believed implicitly. You were mentally degenerate, organically a fool, a wonderful snob. You wanted only wealth and place bitterly to deride and browbeat the low class to which you belonged - not from lack of heart but because you believed it to be the proper aristocratic manner. And what you wanted in mind you made up in temper. You quarreled, you came to blows, with your fellow-dancers in any of a half-score of small selfish daily disputes. Cleverness among you consisted in gaining any possible advantage over the others and in calling each other names. Also in maneuvering bits of money - as much as might be - from unpleasing men who hung about the dingy play-house. On holidays you were invariably half-drunk."

Said I: "And wherein was she not petty?"

Said the Soul: "You believed in yourself. You had not a doubt you belonged in worldly high places but were kept down by the malice and depravity of human nature, people about you. And you lived up to your vulgar ideal of ambition. There was a simplicity, an enlightening pathos in you then which was lacking in the linen-draper's lodger."

In my flawed way I saw that, but objected to the bygone Liverpool lady from many an angle.

Said I: "Had I no life of a sweetness and gentleness and with it something that buoyed and bore you on?"

Said the Soul: "Never once. You were many centuries ago a Greek girl of the aristocratic class, bred in an intellectual life. You read the philosophers in the cool retreats of an olive grove. The mental knowledge you have now compared to your learning then is a tangle of ignorance. But the Greek girl had no heart, no human flame, no active blood of personality. Those wanting I starved. The Liverpool dancer in her warming virile vulgarness bore me vastly farther on my way. You were a Greek woman in a still earlier time - of a type which murders all simplicity. Your body and mind were haunted by perfervid imagination and both ached with the weight of it. You were made of twisted fires. I grew in *that* day: grew burdenedly: grew distortedly."

Always those Greek visions are my "half-familiar ghosts." -

Said I: "Was I sometime a married woman?"

Said the Soul: "You were - in four separate ages. Which brought you and me singular solitude."

Said I: "Was I always woman?"

Said the Soul: "You were once a young lad of fierce temper and were at twenty a madman. And died mad. No male body and brain could withstand and outface merely the emotional besiegings of *you*."

Said I: "When I went mad, what of you?"

Said the Soul: "I fell asleep, and knew no rest, but dreamed."

Said I: "Of what?"

Said the Soul: "Things I always dreamed in your mad lapses - poetry served very conscious and very hot: the material Color of the Sunshine: the musical Softness of the Dawns: the pulsing Thoughts in Girls' Throats: the Scent of Water-Falls."

The Soul has an airless voice which tells her meanings, beside her words and in their rhythm.

Said I: "What do you, and how do you, with me now?"

Said the Soul: "I grow tired with you. Exasperated. Desperate. As if I too wore flesh. You are a deathly prison, a torture chamber. I turn everywhere and nowhere at all. You tire me - you wear me. I wait. I stay. Yet I move."

She looked lovely, my Soul - and quite in and of this bitter-ish lovely world in its bloody bitter wrappings of bone and flesh. Around her neck was the Necklace she wore in all the ages, showing greenish in a dusk of gentian blue. -

All of it slyly garbles and cross-purposes me a little bit more than usual.

I wish I'd been born a Wild Boar.

*

Not Quite Voilà-Tout

To-morrow

The clearest lights on persons are small salient personal facts and items about them and their ways of life.

To know that a woman is 'sensitive' is to have but a blurred conception of her as one easily impressed, easily hurt. But to know that she wears thick union-suitish under-clothes and uncompromising cotton stockings is to know much about her: by those tokens she is plain: she is stupid: she is smugly virtuous: she is poor: she is narrow-thoughted: she lacks imagination: she is prosaic: she has a defective sense of humor: she is catty: she is 'kind': she catches cold: she is a thoroughly good woman. To know that a child is 'bright' is to have no definite knowledge of the child. But to know she flies into rages and bites whisk-brooms, laces and her fragile grandmother is to have a wide-beamed far-reaching spirit-light upon her.

That I am 'thoughtful' means little or anything or nothing: that I love the odor of ink, that I hate the stings of conscience, that I never lounge untidily about the house or in my room but am always 'groomed,' those tell me to myself. Here for my enlightening I write a garbled list of my items and facts:

- I never see a soft new yeast-cake without wishing to squeeze it for the salubrious feeling of the tinfoil bursting facilely and the yeast oozing with its odd dry juiciness through my fingers.

- And I never see a shiny waxy green rubber plant without wanting to bite the leaves precisely and daintily with my sharp teeth.

- My luncheon each late midday is made of four radishes, three crackers, and a thin glass of water: an anchoretic feast which I eat with relish. The rhyme I murmur with it is: "what do you think, she lives upon nothing but victuals and drink."

- Whenever I look out my window at five in the afternoon I see a neat nice-looking strange black woman walking past. And the black woman glances casually up at my window and sees me. We are unknown to one another and have belike as much and no more in common as if we grew on different planets. But the black woman and I are someway dimly liking each other and dimly knowing it.

- I scent my belongings faintly with Houbigant's Quelques Violettes perfume.

- I like to light a box of matches at a twilight window-sill singly and by twos and threes and little bunches, and hold them till they burn out, and watch the little flames, and drop the burnt ends out the window: a pastime inherited from my child-self.

- Of living creatures that I know I most hate cockroaches.

- Of inanimate things that I know I most hate a loose shutter rattling at night in the wind.

- When I smoke after-dinner cigarettes downstairs I put flat round black records on a tall red Edison phonograph and I curl up in a leather chair in the dark to listen to the music which is soft and deep: "Che Gelida Manina" in a wistful tenor, and "Refrain Audacious Tar," and "Ah Quel Giorno," and "Scenes That are Brightest," and others and others - tantalizing, tawdry, artistic, cheaply pleasant, luring, whatnot. And by turns it makes me lighthearted, lightheaded, emotional, romantic, restless, evilly coarse. It is piquant debauchery. Music sweetly poisons me.

- My bureau-drawers I keep neatly in order - lingerie and other articles arranged convenient to my hand in white rows and fragrant tidy piles: with the exception of the upper left-hand drawer which is a bit of terrific snarled chaos. In it is an inky handkerchief of an old vintage: in it are several unmated crumpled gloves: in it are some olive-pits: in it is an empty sticky liquid cold-cream bottle with tufts of eider-down powder-puff stuck to it: in it is a tangle of smudged ribbons: in it are two pieces of pink rock-candy: in it is a spent yellow-silk garter: in it is a torn sponge: in it are blackened pieces of chamois-skin: in it is a broken scissors: in it are three twisted ragged black-net veils: in it is a brass curtain-ring: in it is a broken scattered string of coral beads: in it is a lump of wax: in it is a piece of knotted twine: in it are little bunches of cotton wool: in it is a spilled box of powder whitening everything: in it is a spilled box of matches: in it is a jet bracelet broken into small pieces: in it is a broken hand-mirror: in it are some crushed cigarettes: in it is a ruined blue plume: in it is a warped leather purse: in it is a damaged lump of red fingernail paste: in it is a stick of gum arabic: in it is a bisque kewpie defiled by wax, ink, paste, powder, and rock-candy: in it are some partly melted vestas: in it are other bits of rubbish: all in wildest disorder. Why I do not empty the drawer and burn the rubbish I don't at all know.

- I sometimes take one or two of the neighborhood children to a picture-show.

- Sometimes as I lean at my window I alternate looking at the distant deeply-blue mountains by looking at the near-by women who chance to pass on the stone pavement below - the smartly-clad and light-hearted-seeming ones. I look at their good shoulders in pastel-toned silk and at their trim silk ankles and proud flaring skirts and insolent beautiful hats - the buoy-ant worldly insouciance of their ensembles - as their owners walk along on happy errands. As I look I feel Me to be behind prison bars looking out in thin psychic jealousy: regret for a time when I also went thus buoyantly on happy worldly errands and an odd raging silent impatience for a time when I may again. But with it too the wavering acquiescence in this analytic-writing mood.

- "Pussy-cat-mieow," I ruminate, "can't have any milk until her best petticoat's mended with silk."

- One kind of man I impatiently scorn is the kind that looks bored if I mention Ibsen or ceramics or Aztec civilization but is interested instantly, alertly, if I mention my garters. Equally I abhor the type that begrudges me my own private phases of amorousness: not those who condemn me for them: not those who dislike them in me: not those who deplore them: but who *begrudge* me them.

- Always I come up a stairway softly. Always I close doors softly. I make no noise.

- The quaintest character I have met with in fiction is Huckleberry Finn's father, looked at as a father. Next in quaintness I place Sally Brass, regarded as a human being.

- I like a glass of very hot water and a dish of preserved damson plums on a sultry August day: and another of each on top of that: and another of each on top of that.

- I like the word addle: I hate the word redress. I would fain have my "wrongs" ever addled than redressed: merely for the word prejudice.

- I would rather that almost any physical disaster should befall me than that I ever achieve an "abdomen." When an abdomen comes in at the door life's romances fly fast out the windows: so it looks to me. May death overtake me haply before the menopause.

- The pictures I have crowded on a small side-wall space two feet from my eyes as I sit at my desk are: Theda Bara as Carmen: the late Queen Isabella of Spain: Marie Lloyd, loved of the London populace: a velvety-looking black-and-orange print of a leopard: Blanche Sweet, loveliest of film actors: John Keats, a small old print: Ethel Barrymore, a pencil drawing made by herself: Nell Gwyn, a photograph of a Lely portrait: Watts' "Hope": Stanley Ketchel, dead middle-weight fighter: "Jane Eyre" by a Polish artist: Fanny Brawn, the solitary extant silhouette print: Ty Cobb: two children: Charlotte Corday in the Prison de l'Abbaye: Susan B. Anthony: a Chinese lady: Andrea del Sarto: Queen Boudica: and Christy Mathewson.

- I am old-fashioned in many of my tastes - in all my reading and writing tastes. I do not like type-writers: they make fingertips callous in a poor cause. And I do not like fountain-pens which someway seem suitable only for business-letters, forgeries, book-keeping, and crude cursory love-letters. I like a steel pen in a fat glossy green enameled wood pen-holder with a thick pleasant-feeling rubber sheath at the lower end.

- I wear to-day a modest frock of black silk: beneath it a light silk petticoat: beneath that a white pussy-willow silk "envelope" and a pale narrow pink silk shirt chastened by many launderings: no stays: thick white silk stockings gartered above my knees by circles of mild mauve elastic: on my feet cross-ribboned bright-buckled black shoes: round my neck a jet necklace - all of it a costume that might be of a conventional woman, a plain-living woman, a good woman, a well-bred woman - saving only that beneath my left shoulder-blade the smooth new pussy-willow silk has a jagged two-inch rent where it caught on a drawer-handle: and the rent - in lieu of neatly mending it with the thread and needle of woman's custom - I caught up any way by its jagged edges and tied tight in a hard vicious heathen knot: the note of spiritual fornication, of Mary-Mac-Lane-ness: always there's some involuntary pagan touch to undo me, to arraign me, to betray me to God and to myself.

- I wear five-and-a-half A-last shoes: number twenty-one snug whalebone stays: and weigh a hundred-twenty-four pounds.

- I am fond of green peas, baseball, and diamond rings.

- I like violently to spoil a little charlotte-russe with a fork: it gives me the same feeling of lawless sweet-fiery lust which must belong to a Moslem soldier when deflowering a Christian virgin: and harms nobody.

- Sometimes when I'm dressing in the morning I glance down through my window and see two elderly Butte business men, one a lawyer and one a banker, going by on the way to their offices. And I wonder at how frightfully respectable they look in their tailored clothes and reproachless gloves and perfectly celestial-looking hats. I murmur: "Robin and Richard were two pretty men who lay in bed till the clock struck ten."

- I keep on my desk a little doll with fluffy skirts, blue eyes, pouting lips, and curly hair and named Little Jane Lee after an adorable child I have seen in moving pictures.

- I am five feet six inches tall in my highish heels.

- I wear number six gloves: the calf of my leg is a shapely thing.

- The six extant Americans I most admire are Thomas A. Edison, Harriet Monroe, Gertrude Atherton, Theodore Roosevelt, the remaining Wright Brother, and Amy Lowell.

- I think I'd learn to be a cook, a professional cook, if I were less easily fatigued.

- I love the sound of the clinking of two clean new white clay pipes, one upon the other.

- I crack nuts with my teeth.

Voilà!

But not quite *voilà-tout*.

*

A Damned Spider

To-morrow

To-day was one of the To-morrows of encompassing dissatisfaction when this seems all a nasty world and a nasty life.

A Spider drowned in my bath-tub this morning.

It was one of those long-legged spiders. It was in the tub when I went there - a small ovalish dark-gray pellet with seven ray-like legs as of an evil little sun lying flat on a white desert. It feels inconceivable that any creature should naturally have an odd number of legs: we are all, including spiders, laid out as with rule and compass. Perhaps it is inconceivable. But this Spider had seven legs. I counted them while I knelt, blue-peignoired, beside the tub with my elbows on the edge and watched the Spider and waited for it to go away. Whether it had lost a leg, or had one too many, or its kind is normally made like that: those things I vexedly wondered about. In either case it seemed a so much worse Spider. It did not go away so I touched it gently with an oblong of green soap. Then it moved and began to walk up the side of the tub. But the side is smooth as glass and always it slipped back. I went to my room and fetched a post-card.

With a post-card newly from Delaware I lifted the Spider out of the bath-tub. Then I scaled card and Spider to the farthest ceiling corner of the room. Then I drew the tub one-third full of tepid water. And there floating in it as if brought down by Black Art was the seven-legged Spider, drowned and ruined. It spoiled the atmosphere and anticipation of my morning tub. I shuddered miserably. I pulled out the rubber plug and water and Spider washed down and away into the dark sewer-wastes of Butte, into the bowels of the earth, through the gateways of hell, I hope. I took a hasty shower with a flavor of long-legged Spiders in it. I dressed, and combed and coifed my hair, with the clouded thought in me that throughout my life I shall inevitably encounter by eternal law a long-legged Spider from time to time. I know there'll be no evading it. Those who know statistics doubtless could tell me how many Spiders I shall encounter in so many or so many years: the exact percentage even to the division of a week and the half or the quarter of a Spider. There is something disconcerting and tragic in the thought.

The drowned Spider's ghost pursued me all day though its memory faded.

My breakfast, though it included an egg, seemed antagonistic, hostile toward me as I ate it. It made me melancholy.

I watched from my back window a slim boy painting a porch and singing in incipient tenor a rhythmic lullaby beginning "go to sleep my dus-ky ba-by." He painted silently for some minutes and then dipped his brush in the tin of paint. Whenever he left off painting to dip the brush he sang. Once he failed to sing when he dipped the brush but instead burst forth with it in the midst of painting a long mustard streak on his porch. Ordinarily that would not have mattered to me since I am innately keyed and pitched to expect the galvanically unexpected. But to-day it made me rackingly nervous.

In the afternoon I went for a walk. Down and down, seventeen squares from here, in a quiet neighborhood a strange woman accosted me. She was pale and smartly dressed and quite drunk. She said, "Listen - can you remember which of these corners I was to meet a friend at?" It made me feel annoyed and bewildered and sad and silly.

When I came back I read awhile - a story of Guy de Maupassant's about a little dog named Pierrot, whose owner loved him much but loved money more and could not bring herself to pay a tax of eight francs to make Pierrot's existence legal. So she threw him into a pit. As heartbreaking a tale as even de Maupassant ever wrote. It made all the loves in this world feel terrifyingly sordid. It made me unhappy.

Then I found a poetry-book and read about the Blessed Damozel leaning out from the gold bar of heaven. Always, by her loveliness alone, she stirs me to my still depths of tears. But to-day the song made me feel over-wrought and life-worn.

To-night I walked out to a little desert-space west of the town, a very pale, very gray desert, with a sweet wet mist like dissolving pearls swathing it.

The million placid stars looked down, remote and hard, as if each one had newly forsaken me. It made me afraid and cold around my heart.

Here I sit and nothing in all the world is pleasant and reassuring.

That damned Spider.

*

To Wander and Hang and Float About

To-morrow

My damnedest damningest quality is Wavering - Wavering -

I might say I prefer the dawn to the twilight or the twilight to the dawn. Neither would be true.

I love the dawn - I love the twilight.

What I unconsciously *prefer* is the long negative Wavering space-of-day between the two.

I might say I prefer heaven to hell or hell to heaven.

Neither would be true.

My garbled gyral nature, partaking uneasily of both, prefers to wander and hang and float about between the two.

I might say I prefer strength to weakness or weakness to strength.

Neither would be true.

What I prefer is a hellish hovering, an endless torturing Tenterhook between the two.

And that Wavering preference is against my will, against my reason, against my judgment, against my taste and liking - against my life, my welfare, my salvation: against the clear lights of my spirit.

I know I work intently and industriously at the articles of my damnation in the Wavering - Wavering -

I know it would be better to die at once: failing that, to live but to live positively as a beggar, a whore, a thief, or a milliner. Knowing that, I know also I Waver: I know I shall prefer to Waver: I know I shall constantly Waver.

I am constant - I am remarkably profoundly constant - in my Wavering.

In the morning as I dress I draw on a stocking - a long black or white glistening stocking. I know I do it only because the mixed big world, which refuses to Waver, is pushing - pushing me. I would choose if I could - though loathing my choice - to stay with my bare foot and my stocking in my hand, Wavering. Between drawing it on and pausing barefoot, Wavering. I prefer not to draw on the stocking: I prefer not to be barefoot: I prefer Wavering - Wavering -

When I'm hungry I choose: not to let food alone: not to eat it: to have it by me and Waver, Waver, emptily. Not to enjoy its anticipation: not to contemplate it. No - *no*! To *Waver*! I reach and take the food because the world in its pushing pushes me.

If the world stopped pushing -

One reason it will be pleasant to be dead: I can then no longer Waver.

Worms will eat me unwaveringly. Or they may then do the Wavering. But *I* shall no more pause with a bare foot and an empty stocking, a dish of food and a gnawing midriff.

Here I sit as yet, alive and Wavering.

The Wavering is not the pale cast of thought: it is not my way of analysis: it is only Wavering - Wavering -

Wavering is not among the blue-green Stones in my antique necklace: not by that name - not as one Stone.

It is a marked and hateful and hellish gift of this present Me who house my Soul.

It is half of this Mary MacLane - who is I -: and I know.

I am constant alone - noticeably tensely constant - in my Wavering: and less constant in Wavering than in the ghoulish preference.

An odd and subtle doom.

*

A Thousand Kisses

To-morrow

Among my other gifts I own also Wantonness. In proof of which I am wishing as I sit here for a Thousand careless kisses: eleven o'clock of still evening - a Thousand Kisses.

A wonderful, wonderful attribute, Wantonness: rich, rich luster in the conscious temperament which owns it, a Gift-thing delicate and gorgeous.

By it I want a Thousand Kisses: a Thousand - made all of Wantonness. Kisses come in differing kinds and only one is Wanton.

The kiss of a lover has an intense cosmic use: the kiss of a mother is tender fostering food: the kiss of a friend is vantage and grace of friendliness: the kiss of a child is cool charm of snowflakes and green springtime leaves.

And the kiss of Wantonness is not of use, nor of food, nor of gracing vantage, nor of childhood charm - but is restless essence of humanness and worldliness and mere sheer limitless encompassing liking: born of sweet lips, alien it might be, and secretly "unattuned," but warm and fond and *present*: answering the pathos of infinite jejuneness which flows, flows always in red human blood.

Through the race rides a long dread wistfulness, made of tears and lies and the barbaric distress and pitfall of everyday's journey: a crying wish for a cup of warmed drugged sweet ease to turn it all a moment away: but a moment away.

And through all the race is the measureless poetry, purling and mantling in its bowl of flesh. Each human one is made of the sun, and made of the moon, and made of the four winds and the seas and the last pink sea-foam on the crests of the twilit waves: and made of salt and of sugar and of lonesome calling of loons and quick song of skylarks: and made of sword-edges and of money and of dolls and toys and painted glass: and made of loose reckless shuffling of dry autumn leaves, and of nerves and of illusions and of broken food and hesitance: and made of Mother-Goose rhymes and of cigarette-ashes and of raveled silk: and made of layers and layers of mixed-up passionate colors and of gilded cakes and of strawberries and of temperamental orgasms and raw silvery onions and gaming and dancing and minute-by-minute inconsistency: all veiled in a thin gold veil - all in a thin gold veil.

Betwixt the wistfulness and the poetry - *hélas*, what chance has the human equation, unsought, unwarned, unchallenged of God to be straitly equable!

No chance.

Happily no chance.

Thus I, Mary MacLane, so conscious of Me and garbledly gifted, want a Thousand Kisses at eleven o'clock of a still evening.

No spirit-hands of Love are laid soft on my drooping shoulders in the passing days: no Love - no Love - in all my life.

No miracle Wonder and Gentleness stirs in and against my Heart: my Heart is strangely dead of a strange Realness, known and felt but unachieved: - no Love - no Love in my life.

And I can wish for no Love, for the listless Heart is listlessly dead.

I wish instead, in hastening present clock-ticking moments, for a Thousand present-warmed Kisses: a Thousand in Wanton response to a Wanton 'leven o'clock.

Dominating waving washing warmth of Wantonness, compassing me at eleven o'clock.

A Thousand careless insouciant Kisses: a Thousand gorgeous delicate Kisses: a round Thousand.

From what lips - whose lips - what do I know? -: so their Kisses are a Thousand.

From what lips - what do I care? -: so they be eager and live and tenderly false.

- come some of the Thousand glowing on my pink lips, and my white fingers, which were tense, relax -
- come more of the Thousand, and my rigid hard-riding thoughts grow drowsy and pliant and negligible -
- come more of the Thousand, and my knees and the marrow in my bones are gently aware of most logical opiate ease -
- come more of the Thousand, and my midriff is full of cream-and-chocolate casualness and my smooth arms are washed down with mists of custom -
- come more of the Thousand, and my seven senses start to melt at the edges -
- come more of the Thousand, and the palms of my hands wax merely pleasant-feeling and the soles of my feet fatly comfortable -
- come the last of the Thousand in a swirling silly lovely lightly-insane shower
- and I feel exactly like a woman in the next street who goes forth clad in mustard-and-cerise with a devilish black-and-white Valeska-Suratt parasol: and more - much more - I feel the way she looks -

For this Wanton-thing is not amour but psychology: in it I am less the mænad than the philosopher: less the Cyprian woman than the Muse.

I am a deeply gifted woman.

I am not prone on my green couch, frayed, frazzled, bowed-down in spirit from a day of frightful stress and cross-purpose.

Instead, hair-triggerishly alive, with definite desire beating hotly this moment in my throat: the wish for Kisses - Kisses far removed from Death and Graves and Coffins: Kisses of this present clock-tickingness, Kisses useless, meaningless, sweet - oh, *sweet!* -

- in number, a Thousand: in kind, Wanton.

*

A Fluttering-Moth Wish

To-morrow

A wish that God would come personally to see me flutters in my thoughts ever and anon like a restless moth.

I am in a prison-mood and coldly content to be in it. For how long content - content is not the word: despairingly acquiescent - there's no word to express that - I can noway tell. But now I live and breathe aloof and strange-mooded. And with it I wish God would visit me a moment.

It is not a strong wish. Yet restless and persistent. I want to be free from myself and away, loosed in the little broad big narrow World: but first and more I want God to visit me.

I want people again, those away from here who are my friends - some glowing-spirited ones who appreciate my Mind and cater to me: I want, I think, a poet to love me with some unobvious madness: but first and more I want God to visit me.

More than I want strength of spirit and flesh, more than I want a fat mental peace, more than I want to know John Keats in star-spaces: more than I want my dream-Child: I want God to visit me.

More than I wish this appalling tiredness would leave me: more than I wish this I write to be a realization, a *de-fait* portrait of the thin-hidden Me, my self-expression achieved: more than I want to be quit of my two black dresses and back in the wide sweet frivol of variegated clothes: I want God to visit me.

God must know all about that. He must have known it a long time. He still does not come.

If he would come and tell me one thing, one *certain* thing, it would be enough. It would show me a direction and I could keep on in it by myself. If God would tell me even a sheerest matter-of-fact, for *sure* - like What O'Clock by his time it really *is*: that would be a spark from which I could build an eternal fire for myself. Forever after I could dispense with God as a personality.

I am strangely weak. Strong of will, strong of mind, but weak of purpose: damnably, damnedly. I shall never be able to write in words one one-thousandth of the dramatic drastic weakness which is in me. But I hate weakness with so deep and strong a hatred, and to know one eternal certain thing would be so roundly restful, I could then go on: I could vanquish the potent pettinesses which beset me.

I do not want from God a passport, a safe-conduct into heaven. I don't want to get into heaven. I don't know what it is, but the word has sounds of finality, as if all winds, sweet nervous petal-laden winds, had stopped blowing forever. For cycles and centuries to come the Soul of me will be too restless to live where winds can not blow.

I love the journey: so that only I might have one dim torch to go by. I love the pitfalls and ditches - all the dangers - black-shaded woods and wolds, and lonesome plains and briery paths, and very wet swamps, and strong whistling gales which chill me: so that I could feel but one tiny bright-bladed truth, within and without, pricking and urging me to struggle on through it all till I might emerge at last like a human being, rather than linger indifferent and inanimate like a jaded wood-nymph in drearily pleasant spaces.

*

Twenty Inches of Ajarness

To-morrow

God might come to visit me on a Monday afternoon.

He would come in at the door of my blue-white room which had been left about twenty inches ajar: for I cannot imagine God, the aloof and reticent, opening a shut door to visit anyone.

It is as if God purposely lacks all initiative. If I wish to meet God I must first suffer deeps of terror and passion and loneliness to make the mood that wants it. Then I must train my life down to two plain frocks. And to crown all my room-door must be left ajar on the day he happens to come or he will not come in. That seems certain: but for twenty inches of ajarness at my door he will not come in.

In it God is quite fair. I do the reaching-out and I live out the despairs: he furnishes a fact to go upon: I go upon it, in some anguish doubtless: but then mine, not God's, are the lights and the translated splendor. It is a "gentleman's game" God plays. It is because I feel that to be true, more than for that he is the Dealer, that I would have a word with him.

On a Monday afternoon -

He might come in the figure of a precise mystic-looking little old man, punctilious of dress and manner like an English duke on the stage. He might wear overwhelmingly correct afternoon attire, with spats and a monocle on a wide ribbon. It someway fills my peculiar trivial concepts of God: mystic-seeming because he is the God of the dead dusty hosts of Israel, and punctiliously modern because he is also the God of new-poeted, radium-gifted Now. A God like a druid or like Aladdin's genie, such as I fancied as a child, or like Jove or Vulcan, would seem an inadequate and unsuitable God. What would such a one know of the shape and fashion of my two plain dresses, and of my shoes, and my breakfasts, and the charmed surface joy in the back of a magazine? God, to be God to me, must know all those things.

And if he only bespoke me in thunderous preludes touching souls' triumphant apotheoses - bold and intolerable ecstasies beyond heaven's last poignantest door - it would be nothing to my purpose. Those my poet-brain can make for me if I wish. But I'd like God to explain me the little frightful puzzles which thrive all around me in the wide daylight of this knife-and-fork-ness.

God might come walking lightly in and perhaps seat himself fastidiously in my chastest chair. He might cross one knee over the other. He might adjust his monocle and regard me through it speculatively or sadly or politely-wearily. I should be outwardly calm but I might feel an inward panic: lest he go away again without having told me a fact.

I might say to God: "God, if you please, this small blue vase on my window-sill - I see it and I touch it and I love it - will you tell me, you who *know*, is there a blue vase there or is there no vase?"

And God might merely glance at the vase through his glass and daintily hold his white handkerchief crumpled-up in his gray-gloved fingers and might merely say: "Madame, you have eyes with which to see the vase and hands with which to touch it and sentiments to lend it charm for you, no doubt. Then why not let them inform you as to its actuality?"

And then I might say, with a weariness equal to God's: "My senses are pleasant - they are sweet - but they do not inform me, or they inform me wrong. Because they don't plainly tell me whether it's a Blue Vase or a Blue Shadow - just for that I burn in little disconcerting hell-fires, and vulture-thoughts with beaks and talons come and tear me in the night, and I starve and decay trivially, and my life is a flattish ruin and a tasteless darkness and a slight shallow death, a death in the sunshine - I am fed-up with a sense of death because of pricking doubts as to my blue vase's realness."

To which, again, God might reply with his head tilted to one side, tranquil and impersonal: "As to that, Madame, there may be less death in doubt than in certainty about your vase. You might in discovering it discover in yourself no right whatever to the sunshine - no right to live in it, no right to die in it."

And I might answer, with some insolent feeling: "I should wish to discover the *fact* about it though it proved to me I don't exist and never existed - that I'm a dust on a moth's wing, and at that alien - not belonging there."

Upon which God, for what I know, might only shrug-the-shoulders.

In that identity he might shrug-the-shoulders or break-the-world with equal omnipotent plausibleness.

But I might try again. I might say: "One thing *feels* realer than my blue vase - this blue-and-green Necklace which my Soul wears. It is rare and recherché but my beautiful Soul is very tired from wearing it. Will you please unclasp it for me?"

And God might say, deprecatory: "Pray, Madame, do you consider what portion of the beauty you mention may be in the Necklace? Should I un-clasp it - it is doubtful whether you would recognize your soul without it."

To which I might answer, with more insolent feeling: "I don't know anything of that and I don't care for it. I only know I want the Necklace off. To wear it makes me languid and frenzied and worn - full of wild goaded saneness and the wish to go violently mad."

And God might answer: "Permit me to express my regrets for those senti-ments which, I should add, I neither concur in nor refute nor deny nor share."

There I might be: conversationally whip-sawed. -

God is full of works of beauty, serene and miraculous: Gray Lakes and Blue Mourning Mountains and Deserts beneath the Moon. Those have quietly ravished me many and many a night and day - and will again, and still again, in pacing To-morrows. But I can't tell What O'Clock it is by them. And if God were by me and I asked him the time the odds are all that he would look at the toy-face of my little ivory toy-clock, which sets on my desk where I can see it myself, and tell me the time by that. But though he is thus perplexing he knows the right time and could tell me it.

For that restlessly I wish God would make me one brief visit.

I wish that though he should so godlily baffle me and divinely bore me.

*

A Profoundly Delicious Idea

To-morrow

It is nineteen minutes after one on a summer night. And if only I felt a bit hungry this is what I should wish - spread out on a damask cloth before me in a few gold-medallioned Chinese dishes, with no forks or knives: first of all, two thin *foie-gras* sandwiches, four grilled snails, and maybe a little alligator pear: on top of those, two truffles: on top of those, two slim onions: on top of those, two thin salted biscuits: on top of those, a bit of Camembert cheese: on top of that, two cigarettes: on top of all a hollow-stemmed glass of sparkling Burgundy.

I'm not hungry, but it is comforting to think how delightful that supper would taste if I were. Food is a so magic rich gusty gift bestowed on the human race: and is besides a profoundly delicious Idea.

I like food better to imagine than even to eat. If I were hungry I think I could obtain that chaste supper item for item, and eat it: swallow it down magic and all, and thus vanquish it magic and all, and there an end. So I am glad I am not hungry. It is much more delectable to sit here and think that if I were -

- *if* I were -
- a Hollow-stemmed Glass of Sparkling Burgundy.
- two Cigarettes.
- a Bit of Camembert Cheese.
- two Thin Salted Biscuits.
- two Slim Onions.
- two Truffles.
- two Thin *Foie-Gras* Sandwiches: Four Grilled Snails: and maybe a Little Alligator Pear.

If I were a bit hungry: oh, the idea of a little supper! It would then be blestness, benediction - fruit of the very garden of Paradise!

*

A Mountebank's Cloak

To-morrow

I am so *Clever*. I am the Cleverest human being I know.

I have thought my Cleverness an outer quality, a mountebank's cloak, and as such not belonging in this book of my own self. But there are no outer qualities. Everything in and about me is my own self.

My Cleverness is of high quality - even supernatural, I have thought - and is of unobvious tenors.

To any essentially false nature, such as mine, a quick and positive Cleverness is its needfulest resource in coping with this pushing world. To any un-sanely sensitive nature such as mine Cleverness is its fender against human encounters and onslaughts.

There is no Cleverness in this I write. There is writing skill and my dead-feeling genius. But my Cleverness is beside those points.

I use Cleverness when I encounter people.

Sometimes I like people and wish to impress them.

Always I am vain and sometimes I wish my vanity catered to.

And I can get from people whatever tribute I choose.

I mostly choose to bewilder and half-fascinate, which is easiest: I talk about anything, nothing, everything with a tinsel-bright complexity which captures average intellects. And even very Clever people seem not Clever to me because I feel so exceeding Clever to myself. I am a little more intuitive, a little falser, a little lightning-quicker than the most artistically antic mentalities I have known.

I am a lady with the ladies, a woman with women, a highly intelligent writer with writers, a loosed fish with the loose fish: being all the time nothing but my own self, unspeakably incongruent. Having never found anyone remotely matching me in barbaric and devastating incongruity of nature I use in human encounters whatever phase makes the occasion most gently befit me. I cater, or I thrill some bastard dull brain, or I grow roundly versatile: all with a sudden coruscant Cleverness which is not in itself any of Me but is my mountebank's scarlet cloak.

But its main cause and reason is not vanity nor a fancy for piquant trickery, nor the wish to try my superior wings in glowing human atmospheres - the preponderant impulse to fly because I can fly. It's none of those, but a need of protection, of a bright armor to keep other people's superficialities from touching me. There's a human effluvium which I feel from people which would touch, wrap, enclose me in a harsh vapor - a half-froze, half-stinging worldly cloud. It hurts with thin cruelness like a corroding spray of acid on my skin: unless I send out the sudden air of my own Cleverness to keep it off and away.

It is long months since I have encountered people with any impulse save hastily to avoid them. But if I should meet, with an aggression of mettle and mood, some woman or man or little group of human sorts (except children of and for whom I have always a fear and a respect) I should then suddenly be casual and half-fascinating and phosphorescently glowing and insolent: being inside me haggard from solitude, wistful from a bereftness and a beauty-sense, suffering and lost.

Ah, I'm notably Clever!

I write a letter of Clever delicate surprisingness - it is the only Clever writing I do. There are twenty people, now long outside my life, to whom a Mary-Mac-Lane letter is the agreeably-vividest thing that could come into a day. The letter, which is an unapparent cater, is not real Me who am someway a strong and contemptuous spirit - but instead one tinsel facet. And it makes people - people! people! - admire and defer to me in a subtlest human aspect: an unwilling antagonistic homage. It stays me, buoys me for the time.

I am profoundly Clever in that I who am in reality so futile, so wavering, so sensitively lyingly artistic, can still show myself aggressively Clever to other persons. I must, being false, be Clever in order to get by.

It is at its best a trickster's quality: and so much the more am I Clever in stretching it out over my shaded life like a strong bright cloak-of-mail.

Just to be Mary MacLane - who am first of all my own *self*! - and get by with it - how I do that I can not quite make out.

I'm by odds the Cleverest human being I know: more than likely one of the Cleverest who ever lived in this world.

*

A Familiar Sharp Twist

To-morrow

I have - a Broken Heart -

It is nearly a year now.

It feels strange to be writing it. What *is* one's Heart? But it is a plain fact of me.

I have not had a Broken Heart in the years before. I have had silly fancies - I have wasted the outer tissues of my Heart, and it has been bruised and battered. But nothing pierced deep enough to break it till this.

My Broken Heart is the outstanding inner item of my life: and it still is a very small thing even in my own reckoning. It tortures me minutely all the minutes and moments and hours. And yet my all-round life moves on beside it and often passes it on the road.

My Broken Heart contributes nothing, no cause and no urge, to the writing of this song of my Soul and bones. It rather is a handicap. It makes me sit and brood. It makes my eyelids heavy and my head droop. It makes my shoulders ache. It makes me sit longish half-hours with my head on my lonely hands. It fills me with foolish wasting despair.

Its foolishness is the foremost thing about my Broken Heart. It is not a foolishness of worldly reasons nor of outer causes but of all the surprising folly of myself crowded into my Heart and into that which Broke it. The foolishness would not be so noticeable if the Brokenness were not so hideous and genuine and actual and matter-of-course. It was foolish to lay myself open, who am humanly starved, to the possible Breaking of my Heart: and doubly foolish to let it be Broken. And being left in possession of a Broken Heart I feel it to be a triply insanely foolish thing: but complete and absolute and natural.

I am so oddly a fool.

The proper price for such or such a thing in the Market might be one-and-twenty drops of red human blood. But I headlongly pay for it one-and-ninety drops: each one touched with fire, shot with purple, tinctured with hottest spirit-essence. The proper payment for Love is to pay back value received - which is enough. But I in addition dip my white bare foot into red world-and-hell flames by way of quixotic bonus. When other persons emerge from Love with the old-fashioned accustomed wounds and scars I emerge with besides an immensely useless futilely ruined foot.

It is wildest foolishness. Not merely folly. Folly is something picturesque - a bit romantic.

I am oddly a fool. It is that consciousness that rushes over me with each sad black thought of my Broken Heart.

My Broken Heart - it feels half-false to myself as I write it. And the written words look half-false to my eyes. But it is realer than my fingernails: than my palms: than my aching left foot.

My Broken Heart, besides being a triviality is a mistake, and will pass in time doubtless, but is long about it.

It is one thing I do not dwell upon in this book of me. A Broken Heart is sharply immediate like a newly-bitten tongue. It may bleed at a touch. To dwell on it connects me strainedly with the world around, and the world is really gone from me. This book is I as I breathe alone. I cannot write in it the silly shadowy Breaking of my Broken Heart. This writing is I Just Beneath My Skin. My Broken Heart is beneath bones and flesh. And though my M.-MacLane heart intact is wildly individual, my Broken Heart is merely human: made not alone by me and not alone by God. Its place in this I write is just outside the margins.

At times my Broken Heart feels far off while I'm feeling it hideous and wan inside my breast. Myself is Me, and much of Me had nothing to do with my Heart when it Broke: though I loved with all of Me, I loved with all of Me one who lives in New York - and I lost and lost, all the way. There was mere human ordinariness about which I built up a strangely sincere temple-of-grace which I looked to see shed light on my life like the new eternal beauty of a Day-break. I gave the best I knew to it, from the distance, and I lost. The day was a little day and broke at last only like my Heart. All was broken without so much as clasp-of-hands.

I am realest, strongest, passionately-sincerest in my essential known falseness -

It was all foolish and petty and someway false but I felt foolishly and shudderingly that I could live no more. But I am singularly brave from life-long custom. I have no pleas and surrenderings in me. I shudder but live on.

One Thursday I felt suddenly oppressed and beset and something in my throat cried out to the absent God to help me and guard me.

It was something in my throat which shrieked it dumbly in the deafening silence in my room. It was not I myself: for I am unsuppliant toward everyone human and divine though there often come such Thursdays.

Harder than Thursdays are Fridays and some other days when comes a familiar sharp twist beneath my chest-bones without the cognizance of my remembering thoughts: and when though I strive against it my Broken Heart makes me sit longish half-hours with my head on my hands.

*

A Dark Bright Fierce Fire

To-morrow

I am Lonely. I am so Lonely that I can feel myself rattle inside my life like one live seed in a hollow gourd.

I am on fire with Loneliness.

I am living this month alone in this house. The solitude is pregnant: Doors and Door-knobs and Curtains and Tables have silently come alive in it and have taken on identities like those of tamed wild beasts.

I do housework - I dust window-sills and water flowers. I gather up newspapers and brush the floors with a dust-mop. I wash my dishes. I cook my breakfasts. I look out of windows. I linger at screen-doors.

I answer the telephone: I say, "They're not at home."

I change my frock and put on a hat and a cloak and gloves and go softly out the door and front gate on an errand.

I meet people on the street whom I know, whom I may speak to, whom I may avoid: who may speak to me: who may avoid me: for I am at best well hated in this Butte.

I come back again, softly unlock the door, and come in. I come upstairs, take off the out-door things, give a hasty side-glance in my glass, and go downstairs.

I read awhile. To-day I read an old-fashioned short story whose soft wondrous prose cadences fed my senses - the Parable of the Prodigal Son. - for this my son was dead and is alive - was lost and is found -.

But I am very restless and cannot read long. I am on fire - dark bright fierce fire with Loneliness.

I move about again from room to room. I look out of windows and linger at doors.

I close my eyes and open my eyes.

My Soul-and-bones! I'm afire with Loneliness!

It is Loneliness not made of the Empty House and the tamed wild Door-knobs and Doors and Curtains and the Lonely Errands. Those are its small-fruits. Itself is my ancient daylight Loneliness dating from Three-Years-Old when I first began whisperingly analyzing things and finding little life-items to be of a fierce bitter importance.

If I were living among people, friendly people, then the Loneliness though unchanged would be disguised and vested with a padded muffling power - false, belike, and a mistake (but everything *is* false and a mistake: only there are wrong mistakes and right mistakes) - but made of the world-stuff that lets a human being get by in this nervous life.

But it would be of no use now. I must face Loneliness: and outface it. I do, and with no effort: for I am Lonelier than Loneliness' self. So it feels. This locked-in mood - soon it may be worn down and outgrown, and the husks blown away in the winds.

But may come after it a wilder Loneliness of being free, fearfully free: flavored with the heaviness of rain at night and draggledness of beggar-women's skirts. -

Meanwhile bright and black among Doors and Door-knobs and Curtains and Tables burns the fire of this Loneliness with strong, strong flame. It is mystic agony. There is no thinking in it. There is an utterly irrational wish, an aching yearning for people: not people to see, or listen to, or talk to, but - humanness I could *feel* with familiarity. I wish for hands and bodies near me: breath for mine faintly to mingle with: the feel of their human garments in the room around me: the feel of the pulsing blood in their veins remotely vibrant in the air: the feel of minds and spirits and throats and rich warm virile hair of human heads keeping me warmly company. I have heard one may step rarefied out of this living-place into the Fourth Dimension, where one feels everything without the efforts of feeling, and knows everything without the weights of knowing. It might be that I grope for in this black bright anguish.

Yet I feel rarely rarefied, heavily rarefied, wornly rarefied in this living-place where Loneliness burns me in strong fire and where I can shake my life like a hollow gourd and hear the eerie rattling sound I make in it.

*

Late Afternoon

To-morrow

Last night as I slept I dreamed a vivid dream.

I dreamed it was late afternoon and I was locked in a condemned cell, sentenced to die. I would be led out and hanged on a gallows the following morning at day-break. I dreamed I sat beneath a narrow window in the cell through which shone the light of the waning afternoon. The light was very pale, as of sunshine long dead. I dreamed I held on my knees a small block of paper which had a half-inch blue border at the top to mark a perforation, and in my hand I had a red pencil. And I dreamed I had cheated the gallows and was writing a little ballad about it in sudden rhymes and rhythms quite alien to my waking forms. When I awoke the song was still beating time in my brain. And with my black awake-time pencil I wrote, except for two words, the rhyme, title and all, as I dreamed:

Late Afternoon

They'll think when I pass through that door
To-morrow in the dawn,
I'll then be going to my death.
It's I've already gone.

They'll watch me walk serenely out,
Still-nerved and somber-eyed,
"So strong," they'll say, "to meet her death."
To-day it is I died.

There'll be my pulses quick with life,
My white sweet throat, my breath:
But flesh and bone are all will hang.
This noon I met my death.

For days I charmedly dwelt on death -
I raved at death - I swore -
Till vexedly death waived the date:
And came this Day-Before.

From being lured with artful thoughts
My life abortive grew.
From being broached in livid mood
My death aborted too.

To-morrow they'll remark my calm -
No fuss, no fright, no swoon.
They'll kill a wench to-morrow dawn
Was dead to-day at noon.

Three oddnesses are in that dream:

- that it is true to life in that I in my lightning Mary-Mac-Lane-ness *would* manage to cheat a gallows.

- that it is untrue to life in that instead of writing of it in the true twilit poetry of my own sufficient prose I wrote it in the shallow trick-phrasing of rhyme, a little serenade to the gibbet.

- that it catches and holds my Shadow-self who lives not *in*side me but *be*side me: the resembling dissembling shadow I cast when I stand between the daylights of the actual world and the quivering films of the region of dreams. -

My owned mysteries thrive apace. They are poetry and beauty and loveliness yet they bruise and batter me and split me to atoms. Withal are terrifyingly superfluous: they violently kill the wench to-morrow dawn who died restfully to-day at noon.

*

An Ancient Witch-Light

To-morrow

Also I am someway the Lesbian woman.

It is but one phase - one which slightly touches each other phase I own. And in it I am poetic and imaginative and worldly and amorous and gentle and true and strong and weak and ardent and shy and sensitive and generous and morbid and sweet and fine and false.

The Lesbian sex-strain as an effect is reckoned a pre-natal influence - and, as I conceive, it comes also of conglomerate incarnations and their reactions and flare-backs. Of some thus bestowed it makes strange hard highly emotional indefinably vicious women, turbulent and brilliant of mind, mystically overborne, overwrought of heart. They are marvels of perverse barbaric energy. They make with men varied flinty friendships, but to each other they are friends, lovers, victims, preyers, masters, slaves: the flawed fruits of one oblique sex-inherence.

Except two breeds - the stupid and the narrowly feline - all women have a touch of the Lesbian: an assertion all good non-analytic creatures refute with horror, but quite true: there is always the poignant intensive personal taste, the *flair* of inner-sex, in the tenderest friendships of women.

For myself, there is no vice in my Lesbian vein. I am too personally fastidious, too temperamentally dishonest, too eerily wavering to walk in direct repellent roads of vice even in freest moods. There is instead a pleasant degeneracy of attitude more debauching to my spirit than any mere trivial *trainant* vice would be. And a fascination in it tempers my humanness with an evil-feeling power.

I have lightly kissed and been kissed by Lesbian lips in a way which filled my throat with a sudden subtle pagan blood-flavored wistfulness, ruinous and contraband: breath of bewildering demoniac winds smothering mine.

Lesbian essence is of mental quality. There are aggressively endowed women whose minds are so bent that they instinctively nurture any element in themselves which is blighting and ill-omened and calamitous in effect. There are some to which the natural inhibition of their own sex is lure and challenge. There are some so solitary by destiny and growth that the first woman-friend who comes into their adolescence with sympathy and understanding wins a passionate Lesbian adoration the deeper for being unrealized. There are some so roiledly giftedly incongruous in trait that they are prone to catch and hold any additional twisted shreds afloat in human air-currents.

Each of those influences biases the Mind of me, which is none the less a clear-visioned mind which rates no thing a truth which it knows to be a lie: though it batten on the lie.

- often here and there around this human world the twisted and perverted and strongly false concepts are the strong actual working facts and the straight road is myth - myth - existent but in visions -

I don't understand why it's so: I know it is so.

Not only so with me: so with millions whose stars jangled.

Not always. But often. -

The deep-dyed Lesbian woman is a creature whose sensibilities are over-balanced: whose imagination moves on mad low-flying wings: whose brain is good: whose predilections are warped: who lives always in unrest: whose inner walls are streaked with garish heathen pigments: whose copious love-instincts are an odd mixture of mirth, malice, and *luxure*.

Its effects in me who am straight-made in nothing, but strongly crooked, is to vivify tenfold or a hundredfold or a thousandfold in my shaded vision the womanness of any woman whose inner or outer beauty arrests and stirs my spirit.

I see in some woman, some girl, any who attracts me - be she a casual acquaintance, or a Victorian poet dead fifty years whose poetry and portrait live, or an actor in a play, or a sweet-browed friend, or an Old Master - I see one such as if all her charm were newly painted and placed near me shining wet with delicate fresh paint. It is bewitching to look at: it has a deep seductive fragrance of smell: it is luxuriantly aromatic to all my known senses - and two senses unknown float from my deeps and rise at it. The Stranger becomes a dearly poignant fancy to dream over. My Friend turns into a vivid goddess whose fingers and hair I would touch tenderly with my lips.

Because of it a little flame, pale but primal, leaps from the flattest details of life. In such a mood-adventure a window-shutter blooms: a hair-brush glows: a sordid floor has gleams upon it. These bewildering frightful beautifulnesses in this life -.

- withal the same inherence which makes me someway Lesbian makes me the floor of the setting sun - strewn with overflowing gold and green vases of Fire and Turquoise - a sly and piercing annihilation-of-beauty, wonderful devastating to feel - oh, blighting breaking to feel - oh, deathly lovely to feel! -

It is the bewitched obliquities that run away with me: grind, gnaw, eat my true human heart like bright potent vitriol.

What God means me to do with such gifts and phases - I don't and don't understand. I never get anywhere as I think it out. I don't know shades of rights and wrongs since that ancient witch-light has found more trueness of human feeling in me than has any simplicity my life knows.

It began, they say, with Sappho and her dreaming students in the long-ago vales of Lesbos. It may be, I daresay. I know it did not stop there. And I know that - Greek, French, Scotch, Italian - Welsh - Japanese - *all* women sense its light lyric touch.

For myself, I only know it is part and parcel in my tangled tired coil.

I don't know whether I am good and sweet in it or evil and untoward.

And I don't care.

*

The Gray-Purple

To-morrow

Close at the east edge of this Butte is a barren ridge of Rockies that is sudden and big and breathing-looking, barbarously personal, touched with varying gifted color-moods and glowering morose color-passions: at the south the snow-topped Highlands lie long faëry solitary miles away, caressed at their summits by thin soft sun-rings and sun-vapors of salmon and sea-green and turquoise and mauve: at the west a gray-shadowed desert burns red-gold in the setting sun and sleeps in pearl-and-ashen stillness under midnight stars: at the north smaller spurs of the range break into foothills and bluffs and gulches, restful wastes of lonely stones and blurred radiances of tawny sand: on top of all the rarefied air of these plateau heights refracts the light into hot dazzling prisms at any vagrant flash of sun on a trailing storm-fringe. This Butte is capriciously decorated with sweet brilliant metallic orgies of color at any time, all times, as if by whims of pagan gods lightly drunk and lightly mad.

St. Paul-Minnesota looks a greenlier-prettier town: the Arizona Cañon looks vastly more fearfully beautiful: Wichita-Kansas probably looks more a regular town: Akron-Ohio doubtless looks more Americanly reassuring: Rome-Italy must have a more "settled" look: New York is much larger and much brighter-looking.

Only this Butte looks deeply and exactly like Butte-Montana.

Its insistent charm is that it goes on strongly resembling itself year after year.

There is love in me for this Butte.

I am profoundly lonely in it: my life-tissues are long familiar with the feel of it: its mournful beauty has entered like thin punishing iron into my Soul: and my love for it is made of those things. For no *reason* I feel love for this Butte.

As much as for the mountains in their mourning intimateness I feel love for all the outsides and surfaces of the town itself: the stone streets full of houses and shops and stores and brick walls and laundry-wagons and persons: the vacant lots where boys play ball: the school-buildings which for twenty years have needed the same green grass around them and the same playgrounds for schoolchildren to play in (and will go on twenty years needing them): the little mines in unexpected mid-town blocks with their engines and hoists and scaffolds and green coppery dumps: the big mines on the Hill busily working day and night, a bristling citadel of smoke-stacks and tall buildings above the treasure-drifts and tunnels that come down honeycombing the town under its streets and houses and yield up wealths of monthly millions: the desolate wind-swept cemetery on the Flat: the Timber Butte: the School of Mines: the Brophy grocery-window full of attractive grocery-food: the St. Gaudens statue of Marcus Daly: the few sweet green trees on North Montana Street by the court-house: the edge of Walkerville: Ex-Senator Clark's old-fashioned closed house in Granite Street: the stone Episcopal Church with the memorial windows: the surprising steep Idaho Street hill: the old Reduction Works reminiscent of the bygone Heinze and the bold buccaneering days: the Montana Street cemetery at last kempt and nurtured green as Beloit-Wisconsin: the little rocky Missoula gulch: the North Excelsior Street neighborhood where I wrote my Devil and Gray-dawn book: the Butte High School where I studied and meditated youngly: the old Library where I used to get a variety of books in my gangling girlhood: the electric ore-trains going to Anaconda: the vegetable Chinamen: the Post-Office News-stand: the Mexican tamale venders in the early night: the sweet green trees and other greenness in people's yards garnered and cherished in a way which would astonish Toledo-Ohio: the brilliant sparkling look of the town from far out on the Flat late in the evening, like a mammoth broken tiara of starry diamonds, twinkling points of blue and orange and cerise and violet, fired and flung against a mountainside of dark velvet, - an aspect intensely Butte: the cool mosquitoless summer nights: the *Anaconda Standard*: the sulphurous smoky deadly-cold winter mornings: the Cornish and Irish and Austrian and Finn miners: the little slim green onions in the markets: the noise and color and morale of the crowds on a Miner's Union day: the markets on the afternoon shade side of West Park Street full of crabs and lobsters from Seattle and shining fish from California, and mushrooms and froglegs and squabs and hothouse things from hereabouts: the Parrot smelter: the Chinese gardens at Nine Mile: the Italian village of Meaderville: the fortified battlemented look of the town at the east of South Butte: the mystic familiar sand-and-barrenness -

All of it has a feel of something aloof and metallic and distinctive and gray-purple and Butte-Montana.

Gray-purple is the color of the town, its spirit-tone. Its odor and fascination are gray-purple.

This Butte is bodily a young rich present-day city of a hundred thousand population, all told: miners who bulwark its foundations: masses who make and manage its business: millionaire-members who spend most of their lives and dollars in New York: all are Butte-made. But its soul is still the soul of the frontier mining-camp which sprang into copper being when the Comstock mine in Virginia-Nevada failed of its silver-ish promise.

A very few years ago - what one could count on one hand's fingers - there were no lids on in this Butte. Every summer bony thoroughbred horses from Juarez and Denver raced round the oval track on the Flat, watched by a shrieking betting throng of Butte citizens and citizenesses, ridden by silk-bloused black-booted jockies, their finish-spurts under the wire chaperoned by a flock of book-makers. Roulette and poker and faro were wide-open in the town and flavored the air with a taste of gray-purple hazard. Gin-palaces and mining-camp dance-halls, highly de-luxe'd, lent their tinted breath to the current. Noodle-ish and little bacchanalian dives flourished in unexpected nooks. The police court on a Monday morning resembled the debris from an alcoholic human volcano, a condemned but owned portion of this Butte in its Butte-Montana-ness. All of it was but one element in an isolated prosperous town of many elements, but it someway tinctured all.

No pagan-wild sunset burst above the west desert but suggested that the vague lid was off the town, and vaguely lost: a lost lid.

The gambling lid is fast on now - if they gamble they gamble under it. And no more do ribby horses and surprising-mixed crowds disport them at the deserted race-track.

But the setting Butte sun suggests the same wealth and wildness as if always its celestial chemistry were shot with essence of mining-camp: rich, generous, feverish, and virile.

Brophy's grocery-window and the Marcus Daly monument and the Parrot smelter and the Clark house and the Idaho Street hill - all of it - owns the gray-purple which is not St. Paul and not Wichita and not Pittsburgh and not Spokane: not anything except intensely Butte-Montana.

I have felt it since I first lived here in little young short-frocked days, and I felt it when I lived away from Butte: I feel it all these now-days to the roots of myself.

I have no reason: but the contrary: to love Butte as a townful of human beings.

I have no friends in it, no feel-of-friendship, no human friendliness.

And the sculpturesque poetry of the outlying deserts and buttes pushes and presses hurtingly upon the lonely and introspective gazer in Body and Soul: I knew it as child and girl and woman.

There is nothing benign, nothing enlightening - no gentleness, no pity - in its barren beauty. But its hard chaste influence on the sensitive spirit is beyond any analytic power to gauge.

Its wonderful Aridness starves human nerve-soil till the sad wide eyes of the Soul grow bright - fever-bright, light-bright, star-bright - from denial and unconscious prayer: involuntary worship: homage of the unsuppliant unhoping devotee.

Because of that - and because of all its long-familiar outsidenesses - mournful, beautiful, mystic, lavish, madly-mixed, gray-purple - a fascination beyond plaisance or pain - I feel love for this Butte.

*

The Subdivided Cell

To-morrow

When I was twenty I was one strong Cell firmly, primly closing many little cells different from each other but each greenly intact.

When I was thirty the Cell had burst in dusty worldly winds and loosed the little cells. Those in turn had subdivided, losing strength by the cellful but gaining in shadowed truth by a roundabout road. And they showed me my fates and inevitablenesses as in a broad wrecked field misty but plain to view. And thus I see me in the subdivided cells:

- a piece of a normal woman.
- a piece of a child.
- a piece of a poet.
- a piece of a Lesbian woman.
- a piece of a writer.
- a piece of a jester.
- a piece of a savage.
- a piece of something someway brave.
- a piece of a student.
- a patriotic American.
- a lump of tiredness.

My strength is in knowing the evil from the good and the false from the true in it.

My weakness is in wildly waveringly inclining toward the false.

Except for love of my country I am ardenter, determiner, stronger in my falseness than in any of my shadowy truth.

*

Food and Fire

To-morrow

The first beauty in my life is John Keats.

In John Keats is my faith in some resurrection.

Without John Keats human nature feels to be something broken, menacing, unspeakably despicable and lost - lost in the shade. With John Keats the lights break across it and reflect the blazing yellow sun again from eyes and foreheads and fingers and shining hair.

There are world-and-human things which it thrills me to think about and dwell on: Nathan Hale on the British gallows: the charge of Pickett's Confederate infantry at Gettysburg: Henry V, prince among kings and men, at Agincourt: Charlotte Corday in prison: Columbus with his felon crews sailing westward: Susan B. Anthony - a woman made in a strange still heroic splendor half-incredible: Alexander Hamilton: Arnold Winkelried: the sea-worn Pilgrim women disembarking into bitter Novemberness.

Those thrill me because they are brave persons and brave things full of idealistic terrific strife: but they still are made of very struggling-garbled world-stuff - they are mere human fabric - till I think of John Keats: and at once they grow informing and eternal.

In his light the detailed world burns and glows!

John Keats! John Keats!

Other poets have written Nightingales and Grecian Urns and Sonnets and Mirth-and-Passion things: but *he* wrote them in his glorious and wistful pain. He wrote the sweet headaches of his spirit into his delicate beaten-gold verse: the precious fevers of his mental veins: the bone-aches and muscle-aches of his thoughts: the darling skin-damps and palm-damps of his divine fancy: - all in the Song of his lilied youth.

There is no poet but writes his poetry out of inner travails and immense wistfulness. But they all write just beside their travail, not in it: just beside their wistfulness, not with it. A poet who feels the throat of his soul aching and swollen and inflamed writes - not just that astral diphtheria, not till another time: but instead the fine smothering of a hope, perhaps, the oblique suffocating of a love. A poet whose brain-hands throb with some horrible dulcet-ish tiredness from handling the heavy bright tools of his craft writes instead the throbbing of his brain-soles and brain-insteps from walking small odd hard rutted daily ways.

It rouses me - it heats my eyeballs with salty honeyed warmth as I read: but it is not John Keats: who writes his own immediate magic sickness in perfect sudden obvious blood-warm golden *Now!*

It is always old, old-fashioned ailment, worn of ages. The drowsy ache of the Nightingale goes a thousand years back and a thousand years to come: the restless ecstasy of a thousand thousand Nightingales, one for each who reads, in any age, all ages. Long, long after the jeweled English language is gone, dead as Homer's, Keats' Nightingale will flutter lyric-winged in the nervous jeweled lovely *Now*.

"Weep for Adonais," wailed the differently-lovely Shelley, "he is dead." But he isn't dead. He is terribly living, passionately living.

Each day of my life I feel him living. He breathes. He breathes close to me, pantingly, like a swimmer breasting waves or a playing child in a summer day. - John Keats!

Just Beneath My Skin he is my God-of-the-World, my Fetich, and my Lover. He has been my Lover for seven gold years.

He is the first beauty in my flawed futile life. He is the most beautiful thing in the living and dying world. John Keats - John Keats! -

In everyone else I can feel mixed motives, tough tangled silk threads of self woven into wonderful wefts of days and deeds: in *everybody,* from Iscariot to Toussaint l'Ouverture, from Jeanne d'Arc to Victoria Woodhull, from Paul of Tarsus to Aaron Burr.

Only John Keats stands out alone, a true-breathing Poet, an Inmost Heart bleeding outward.

The lyric poet is the true poet. The lyric poet achieves no end in his art. He turns fragments of light and life into terms of beauty and sends them flying forth on flaming word-wings which translate the smooth human flesh they brush-by into delicious flesh-of-gold, flesh-of-petals, flesh-of-fire! But he makes no morals, teaches no lessons, finishes nothing. It's as it should be. Nothing *is* finished. The mixed world is all unfinished, a glorified Mistake. The race is a millionfold Mistake: lives it, breathes it, battens on it - coarsely and finely and lamentably and musically and bravely. So that all poetry which wanders from the lyric is only a play or a picture or an airship or a cause which aims at *fait-accompli,* attaining an object: it is limited and man-made: its beauty is lopped off like boughs and branches after a storm: its wings are clipped. Its distanceless spaces, little and large, are visibly engineered by mathematic hands. But the lyric poetry is the true luminous and bloody interpreting of humanness.

John Keats wrote by the lights of his living and he lived all his days in joyous lyric anguish.

Once he wrote, "Ever let the Fancy roam, Pleasure never is at home." It is a factful of himself - lawless, radical, and non-civilized, agleam in the mixed world. It is everybody - poets, burglars, nurse-maids: everybody. He wrote it in a hundred other ways, but it is all in that: it is the lyric epitome of every day. Pleasure never *is* at home.

And "Heard melodies are sweet," he wrote, "but those unheard are sweeter -"

There spoke the wild delicate wiseness of his brain and the passionate delicate wonder of his heart. - John Keats! John Keats!

But everything he wrote, the Grecian Urn itself, is immeasurably less lyric than himself writing it and being it.

He is rich bright-wet living lyric for this Me in this Now though he has lain dead in Rome nearly the full hundred years.

My garbled life and my thinking hunger feed upon him.

He was the one human one who walked on in the way before him: not around the jagged little stones and icy little pools that were in it: but straight on through them all, though his lyric feet were quivering shuddering sensitive, sensitive beyond knowledge of commoner feet that walk around.

It fattens my leanest self to keep that in my constant remembrance.

The thought of his brave radiant loveliness reassures me to myself, by the hour.

I am futile: but *he* is mysteriously omnipotently useful and I catch some of it from him.

I am half-full of vanity: but he is of a lustrous priceless vanity himself that justifies mine and all the world's.

I am fearing and false: but he is so brave, so true to infinite form, that by it he leavens the lump of the whole world's mendacious cowardice.

My brain is full of wilding darknesses, snarled and knotted gifts and penchants: but into *his* strong brain the strong fresh yellow rain-washed sun shines straight down - through the wide twin-brightness of his Eyes. I look down his Eyes - twin public wells (he belongs publicly and privately to all this mixed mad world, and anyone may look! -) - I look into that titanic vibrant brain, and mine catches some of it: a blest and precious Disease, oh, a rare Disease!

My Heart - my Heart feels strange and tired and dead, a bit of dead-sea fruit: but his heart, warm and real and boundlessly unsatisfied, is always the deep quick fragrant Rose of this World.

A Hero! - a Poet-at-arms! - John Keats!

"He has outsoared the shadow of our night," wrote that Shelley, and wrote no truer word.

I have read so many of the strange and splendid things - bits of them: Virgil and Homer and Villon and Goethe and all the English poets, and prose writers like Carlyle who in places out-poet poets, - and moderner ones and the new poets, imagists and others: John Keats feels a noticeably braver thing, and always, always a little way beyond. He is purely lyric.

When he loved a woman he loved the dubious fascinating Fanny Brawn - sordid-brained, worldly: to him a mixed living devilish-glowing goddess. A higher-souled woman would neither have so tortured nor so held him. He was purely lyric. He cared truly nothing for the verdicts of critics and reviewers: and in the sweet-lipped boyish beauty of his youth they truly and easily killed him. It would be like that - it had to be. He was so purely lyric.

He died in the sweet fierce dazzling cause of Beauty.

I have so many thoughts and my thoughts are always my own. There are endless written thoughts deeper than mine - finer, stronger, anything-you-like. But mine answer for me: no written thoughts affect them, though they thrill my reading hours. Only John Keats' thoughts can enter in and crush and cripple mine.

Because everybody is a little bit like John Keats I have a starry thin edge of faith inside me. He is food for my hunger of thought, fire for my passion of life. - John Keats!

He is the resurrection and the life. -

From my desk he gazes at me in a frame of old-gold. Every day the sunset on the glass blurs his large mournful joyous eyes with strangest agonized sunset tears: he shows me the sweet, sweet intoxication of his lyric grief.

He died young, unfinished - and oh, but it's a shivering ecstasy to think of all those lyrics in him he never wrote! - the sweeter melodies - "Unheard."

*

The Edge of Mist-and-Silver

To-morrow

Hidden somewhere in the invisible unused air-plateaus is a little Child: mine: who has never been born.

A tenet in me is that a woman by every right and by old earthen law should, if she will, have her child - should be the warm-winged mother.

I am a devil and a fantasy, a jezebel and a wanderer in fields of inverted fungi: so I seem to me. I do not know my status - I but know my personal incidents as they happen. But I am also woman: a woman by inherence and by fact. Being woman I am the potential mother, mother of my Child who has not been born.

I feel myself a fitting mother.

I am bodily in good health - if not robust yet durable, as a mother should be: I am always tired as if from touches and weights of living as a loving mother should be: I am warm of blood, latently savage-toothed like a jungle-mother, deadlier than the male, as a brave mother should be. Though I have no child I have an ancient right in my Child, and I want my Child. My Child *is*, but has not been, born. Merely to want my Child makes me a fitting mother.

My Child often is realer to me than books I read and walks I take and the friend who writes me frequent letters.

Sometimes my Child is a soft pink baby smelling of rain-water, milk, and flowers: lying close to the curves of my breasts in the hollow of my arms: feeding soft insistent baby hunger and feeding soft strong living hunger of my kissing mother-lips -

More often my Child is a little happy-voiced fellow, my small brave boy three years old: he clings to my skirt with his sweet tiny hand as we hurry along a frosty pavement in an early December morning. We live in New York in a little common quiet apartment and are gratefully poor, and I work in a factory for a little weekly wage for the living of my little fellow and me. Every day in the early morning we go out to a corner bakery to buy a long crisp loaf of French bread for breakfast. And in the December morning my heart contracts with a sort of happiness and a sort of grief at the sound of little feet in stout shoes yet frail shoes pattering-pattering gaily along beside me on the frosty flagstones. We start out hand-in-hand - his small hand is wonderfully firm and virile - but presently I let go his hand as we hurry along, to feel it instantly clutch the folds of my work-skirt: it pulls and drags at my waistbands and my Heart together with twisted sweetness that makes me ache from head to foot. "Mother, wait" he says in his happy voice, "wait for me." But I hurry faster. Always I hurry faster when my happy brave little fellow cries "Wait, mother," for the sweet feel of that dragging at my mother-skirt -

More often my Child is the little girl six years old of the shy eyes and the sun-kissed hair and the firm child-mouth, full of high temper and strong will. All over her is need and demand of her mother to guard and adore and cherish her every moment of her life. We are together in a country field with oak-trees in it, and poplars, and daisies and bluebells and other field-flowers, and it is overgrown with long coarse fragrant wild grass. The noonday sun is bright-hot and I bring my Child there to dry her hair, for I have newly washed it with a square of white soap and a porcelain bluebird bowl: the feel of her small round wilful head was marvelously fulfilling in my cupped hands. She wanders around in the hot-brightness through the tall grass, gathering the hardy scentless field-flowers with her little brown fingers, and she shakes back her beautiful thick short damp curls. I sit on a flat stone like a Sioux squaw and watch her. The grass brushes her bare legs: the magic sun mixed with a faint cool breeze plays upon her head: the tragic delicate music of rustling poplar leaves comes down from tree-tops and catches her in a fairy song-net. She is always very new, very incredible, my Child. She looks toward me with her shy radiant eyes and she says, "Mother, look, my hair is nearly dry." Her hair is thick and heavy. In my experienced subdued mother-wisdom I know it will not be dry for an hour. I feel the damp of her hair rheumishly keen all over me: a menacingness for me to guard her from: a dear anxiety: an ancient mother-note in the long human gamut of sounds.

- it is precious wearing racking colorful romance to be her mother: each mother-day holds gold-and-blue foreboding: each mother-day holds thin insistent gold-and-purple sorrows: each mother-day holds deep gold-and-gray care, incessant and absolute: an aching wealth of beauty: no more but no less than the damp of

her hair in the noonday field. My Child! - herself incessant and absolute: warm pure palpitant gold-of-my-life -

Someway realer than books I read and walks I take my Child clamors to be born.

My Child will never be born to any other woman. While she hovers and flutters on the edge of Mist-and-Silver - a border edge - there are ten million fertile hot milk-teeming bodies of women each ready to gather her in and wrap her in delicate-sweet flesh. Ten million other children hovering on the edge will drop off into the ten million matrix-cups - each woman mysteriously a fitting mother so only she wants her baby - though she be, besides, a thief or a traitor or a weakling or a murderer or a harlot or a drunkard or a fool.

Let them come, the ten million. The chrysalid children are clamoring, clamoring always for their birth: a wide "melody unheard."

But my Child will never drop over the edge to any woman but me. She calls with veiled and dazzling flames of eagerness for her Birthday: but she will await my made-readiness through a long night, though it should last till the day-break of another age. Dimly I weep for her, my needing-me Child. I weep that she must come to this richly-cursed me. But I weep more that I have not got her in this sterile now, where is flawed passionate wealth of intangible life-stuff: but no small round wilful head of hair to wash: no little fellow's feet on December flagstones and sweet dragging at my skirt: no soft pink baby hunger -

It is hunger I feel from her. I feel her always *hungry* where she is and I can give her no nourishing - no warming *food* in all my strange unfertile passing life!

It is that less than my empty arms that makes blurred unrests and writhing in my Dreaming Womb.

*

A Right Shape and Size

To-morrow

Sometimes I fancy me married - a responsible wife, a housekeeping matron: with my window-sills full of potted plants.

I have a woman quality which seems uxoresque: I am someway a Right Shape and Size to be somebody's wife. My bodily and astral dimensions have outlines apparently suitable for something in the married-woman way.

The wild piquance of being myself - who but for extreme saneness would be mad - rises up and smashes that concept.

But being a Right Shape and Size I involuntarily imagine it.

Fleetingly I imagine a flat in the West Seventies in New York, or a bungalow on the Jersey side, or a middle-sized house in a middle-sized town in Middle-West Illinois - whichever might happen - with me set marriedly down in the midst of it like a suitable maggot in a suitable nut. Suitableness, diametrically opposed to Romance, is its keynote.

I fancy me walking about my married house mornings after breakfast in a neat linen dress and high-heeled satin slippers: snipping dead leaves off my window-sill plants, dusting bits of porcelain, giving my maid some tame household directions. My Body looks slender and supple and newly-married and in-the-drawing in the linen house-dress. The geometric gods regard me with immense satisfaction as being an exact proved theorem. I go to the telephone to order some Little Neck clams and some vermouth cocktails for dinner, and a roast and some Brussels sprouts and the assemblings of a salad: and in it I am ingrainedly domestic, dreadfully useful, a strong pillar of the vast good nice world.

Afternoons I go out to a modiste's to fit a gown, or to a mild bridge-party along with other suitable women, or to a matinee with a suitable neighbor. Everything is perfectly right in my insides and in my thoughts: my thoughts run in little troughs in which there is no leakage or deviation, thoughts of a dreadful niceness, thoughts which ever presuppose potted plants on my window-sills.

Evenings I go out with my husband, or sit around with my husband, or take leave of him for a few hours at the hall door.

My husband would be the sort of man that is called a Good Scout. And he would have married me not for my wistfulness or wickedness or weirdness but for that I am a proper Shape and Size, with a smooth proper covering of flesh, to make a suitable sizable wife. And he would be a heavy grappling anchor to hold me fast in an ocean of domesticness.

Men of the genus Good Scout are all fiercely alike. All women, no matter what their genus, are exceptions to the rule. But men - rich men, poor men, beggar-men, thieves: so only they are Good Scouts - are of marvelous sameness. It comes from the want of minute lifelong pinpricking care of petticoats and potted plants - a detailed intensely personal sort of pain which touches dull solid tones of individuality with vivid various spots of color.

Men are made in "job lots" like their own cravats. Their cravats will differ in texture and color and quality and price. But each one is innately necktie. Use it as a garter or a tourniquet or a strangler's noose: it still is a man's deadly necktie. Its use may be ruined but its necktique is deathless. Except poets - and perhaps scientists - men are themselves like that. They cannot get away from the Adam. Nor can women get away from the Eve. But Eve was not a type but a somewhat pleasant human ensemble. While Adam was a type and a sufficiently nasty one: a rotter and a welcher: doubtless the Good Scout type of his day.

A Good Scout is the sort of man who if a woman trusts him with one one-hundredth of her heart will take the whole heart and twist and batter it: and read the paper and smoke his pipe and pay the bills: serenely unaware.

Which is beside the point in this. For in this image all my marriedness is a thing of outer Shape and Size and Suitableness. The odd but natural sequence is that I make an excellent wife. Excellent is the word. I keep a neat house with no dust left in the corners and no dead leaves on the potted plants. My husband is well looked after as to breakfasts and dinners and bodily comfort, and I am rigidly square with him and chastely true to him.

If, some dinnertime, as I sit opposite him in a soft pretty chiffon gown, my secret thoughts overflow their troughs and I passionately forget the potted plants and the window-sills and want horribly to rise up and bloodily murder my husband for being such a Good Scout: that would be a genuinely powerless matter, a cobweb trifle, compared with my actual potent Shape and Size which are so suitable for a wife.

I make truly and simply an excellent wife.

- by God and my Soul-and-bones! it would be honester, finer, sweeter - more comfortable *to be the dirty beggar-woman in the wet slippery streets -*

But it's facilely fancied because I am of Right Dimensions to be some Good Scout's wife.

A curious subtly pitfalled world: in it my Shape and Size, and my Weight which is also Right, could betray me into being an excellent wife: and by that a lying chattel, an inexpressibly damaged woman.

*

Ice-Water, Corrosive Acid, and Human Breath

To-morrow

I have love for two towns. One is this Butte that I tiredly love inside me. And the other is New York that I smoothly love with all my surfaces.

It is some years - a little lump of years - since I have seen New York: and it is two thousand miles away. So I see and feel its hard sweet lurid magnetism now ten times sharper than when I lived in it. But I felt it sudden and sharp at every turn then. A surface emotion which hits one's flesh and spreads wide over one's area is more exciting than a spirit emotion which pierces inward at one tiny point: an ice shower-bath on the white skin is more anguishing than an ice-water drink down the red throat. The spirit emotion lives longer and works more damage and buries itself at last in proud shaded soul-reserves. The surface-emotion stays always on the surface and lives actively in the front of one's senses and musings.

The feel of New York is a mixture of ice-water, a corrosive acid, and human breath sweeping someway warmish against one's flesh.

It is immensely ungentle, New York: immensely human: immensely intriguing to all one's selves. It is too big to have prejudices and traditions of locality: so it leaves its dwellers free, by ones and multitudes, to be human beings.

In South Bend and Toledo and Beloit and St. Paul and all the tight-built inland towns they murder you with narrowness and harshness and rancorous ill-will: they are scowlingly annoyed with you for making them murder you.

In New York they murder you with a large soft wave of indifferent insolence - no annoyance, no friction. New York eats you as it eats its dinner, rather liking you.

And my love for New York is made of liking: a made of liking: a plaisance of liking.

I like New York with a charmed restfulness for varied things in it: subways, and Fourth Avenue, and the River, and Fifth Avenue on a sunny October afternoon, and the statue of Nathan Hale, and old cockroachy downtown buildings, and the soft rich whelming creamy boiling-chocolate fragrance from the Huyler factory in Irving Place. And mostly I like it for the people in it - People - Persons - People: they are human beings.

In the inland towns people are half-afraid of thoughts, half-afraid of spoken words, half-afraid of each other, half afraid of the fact of being human.

In New York they are not afraid of any humanness. Even when they are in themselves craven-cowardly, cowardly enough to turn their own stomachs, they still turn their humanness unfearfully face-outward like upturned faces of a pack of cards.

An Italian organ-grinder grinding out his loud fierce music in a long deep New York side-street is a human organ-grinder: he bestows his rasped melody widely on everybody in ear-shot, not individually - since all around him is a spreading world of strangers - but jointly. So it feels-like.

A beggar-woman at a subway entrance with a whine and a dirty face and the deadly black cape and chicken-coopish beggar-odor is a human beggar-woman. She throws out an inner savor of herself like a soiled aura on all collectively who pass her. Each-and-all of New York by tolerating and owning her partakes of her mean human essence.

A stout-hearted worn-bodied Jew factory girl working at a hard greasy little machine day after day gives all New York her bit of young virtue which is hardy and heroic and unaware: the whole Island of looseness and vice has an equal gift of impregnable surprising sordid purity thriving on sixes and sevens of poor dollars-a-week.

All of it is because New York is one Large Condition made of human breaths and the worn scrapings of tired Youth rather than one large town made of individuals and stone houses.

And in that is an odd enchantment for me who am born and grown in the places of Half-fear with an old isolated whole fear always on me.

In New York I am a partaker of that smooth manna of humanness as I am of the air and the sunshine and the little black specks of coal-soot: partly from choice, partly willy-nilly, partly in the sweeping unanalyzable pell-mell-ness of massed human nature.

And it is in New York I have those strangest things of all: human friend-ships. Not many friendships and not of spent familiarities: for I don't like actual human beings too much around me. But yet friendships made of the edges of thoughts and vivid pathos and pregnant odds and ends of nervous human flesh and fire.

It is in New York I go to the apartment of a Friend at the end of an afternoon. In the apartment are some persons having tea, men and women. The Friend greets me at the door. She wears maybe a dress of thin dark and light silk, shaped in the quaint outlandish fashion of the hour. And she has shrewd kindly eyes like a Rembrandt portrait, and a worn New-York-ish Latin-ish brain and heart both of which are made of steel, sparkle, and the very plain red meat of living. She says, "Hello-Mary-Mac-Lane," and clasps my hand, and we exchange a glance of no real understanding at all but suggesting warmed challenge of personality, and an oblique sweet call of depth to depth, and of friendship which by mere force of preference and of our separate quality and *calibre* is true rather than false. So close and no closer may friendship be. And friendship, with-all, is closer than any love. It is the closest human beings ever come to meeting. In a New York doorway I, made in broad loneliness of self, get suddenly companion-warmed at the little pleasant twisted fire of someone else.

It might be so in some other town, even Beloit, but it feels only like New York to me.

I go in the room where the others are and they say, "Hello-Mary-Mac-Lane," and I drink some tea and listen and talk in fragments of half-meanings. And I get warmed and half-warmed and cooled and slightly scorched in the easeful unevenly-heated humanness of the women and men sitting around.

In the inland towns they throw their thoughts and ideas at you at tea-time, inland thoughts and ideas, which hit and then drop off like little pebbles and nuts and hard green apples.

In New York they throw those things in the form of long ribbons, heated from being worn next their skin, which fly out and wrap around your skin: pleasantly or foolishly or fancifully.

The point of it is that nobody is afraid of that.

It is nothing fulfilling, nothing satisfying. It is merely human. It is half-lyric. It reassures me as a person: it makes me feel human in all my surfaces.

Which are harder to humanize, in everybody, than any deepest deeps.

And it is therefore with all my surfaces, smoothly and restfully, I love New York.

*

Rhythm

To-morrow

Now and again I think I catch some truth by the sweat of its Rhythm.

Often I read the Beatitudes in the Sermon on the Mount and feel their truth in the blood-sweating tone of their Rhythm - Rhythm unspeakable and ecstatic.

The prophet Christ believed himself divine and was all Rhythm in his utterances: and so sounds true as the scheme of digestion and the laws of hygiene. He said, Blessed are they that mourn: for they shall be comforted.

Everybody who has tried it knows that to be true with the flawless Rhythmic truth of health and illness.

Mourn frightfully a day and the next day will be a day of soothed warmth and quiet like a grateful pitiful heat current in the breast. Mourn a week and that will come the week following. Mourn a year and the next year will be the year of peace. For anguish: peace. For peace: anguish. It never fails.

The great thing lacking in Christ, the sense of humor, permitted his perfect personal Rhythm. Humor oddly wants Rhythm. The human race is made in Rhythm like its beating heart: but humor is an "extra." Everybody is so full of lies that humor, an "extra," always wonderfully appetizing and out of season, and inexplicably God-given, feels like a great keystone of the race.

So it is: but in a lying race. And Christ in his beautiful dual role would lack humor. As a God come among the human race to save it, knowing it as he did: his measureless worldly wisdom being paramount even to his gentleness: his mind and his personal tenor could be set only in intense terrific gloom.

The Rhythm in the Beatitudes is equal Rhythm of sense and Rhythm of sound: Rhythm of music and Rhythm of meaning. Equally, half and half.

The most Rhythm thing in it is: Blessed are the pure in heart: for they shall see God.

I feel it soft-prickling just under my skin. Rhythm - Rhythm and ecstasy!

I have read it many times since I was a child: till I know it in my brain, in my Soul, in my hands, in my breast, in my throat, in my forehead, in my gray eyes, in my aching left foot. I know it and feel it by its Rhythm. There is barbarous justice in it. It cuts everybody off from seeing God.

Pure in heart I take to mean pure in motive. A fool has an equal chance with a philosopher: a harlot with a horse-thief: a nasty rag-picker with a small sweet child. But none is pure in motive.

Of other persons I don't judge. But me I know to be murderously un-pure of heart.

If I could open a window or unlock a door with only the simple mechanical motive in the act - But I can't. There's a romantic impurity in even the look of my hand as it touches the window-sash or the door-key. There's a pervasive delicate infusion of impure motive all over me, Soul and bones, as I perform the act. It is one curse in the Necklace which God himself bestowed on me so long ago.

It is not my fault that I am un-pure in heart.

And it is not God's. It is a comfort to me that I can reason out that it is not God's fault. He knew I needed the Necklace and each blue-green stone in it to rhyme and balance me. In the wide surprisingness of the universe everything will be rhymed and balanced. In me, being savagely complex, that balancing took a bit of doing: hence my unusual Necklace. It comforts me that I can reach that analytic point. It leaves me a lightning conviction that God is worth seeing.

And if a day dawns for me when I can open a door with no ulterior motive: thinking only of the door and the fine small muscular power of smooth hand and supple wrist given me to open it: thinking only that I want to get the door open: then back of that door I know I shall see God!

It is so written in that barbarous blood-sweating worldly Rhythm on the Mount.

*

A Prayer-Feeling

So it is finished: and I have oddly Failed.

I have slyly Succeeded and oddly Failed in equal degree.

I have Failed because I am too cowardly and too weak and too dishonest to write certain bruised and self-accusing places in my Soul and in my Heart and in my Mind which rightly come in the scope of this: there are the Stern and Delicate Voices one closes one's ears against: there are the starry grimy Actualities one drops from one's hands: there are the Thoughts one Does Not Think. Yet and yet: they too are in it, hanging cobweb-ish on my wordings and colons.

It is not a strong tale, and that is very well. This book is less I-written than it is I-myself. And Just Beneath The Skin no person is strong: not Theodore Roosevelt, true fearless American: not Bonaparte, splendid tyrant: not Joan of Arc, titanic martyr. They are strong in their depths and strong on the outside. So are many others. So am I, I think. But just under the skin all who are human are roundly weak.

Roundly weak, every one.

And with that, in my case, False.

This primarily is the picture of one who is made-False: False from her fingertips to her innermost concept.

It is belike because of that that this, as itself, oddly Fails.

It is as if I have made a portrait not of Me, but of a Room I have just quitted. My Gloves are left on a chair: my Hat is left on a couch: my taken-off Shoes are left on the floor: my faint-smelling Handkerchief is dropped by the door: my round ribboned Garter is hanging on the door-knob: my Breath is in the air: my Grief is on the walls clinging like smoke: my flat Despair is on the petunia-leaves in the window: my fragrant Horridness lingers in the curtains. I am not there! But I - *I have just Quitted that Room!* -

Therein I have slyly Succeeded.

*

My feeling at my book's-end is a prayer-feeling, both frantic and quiet: God have mercy on me! but not unless you want to.

And I feel barbarous and utterly solitary, solitary from here to Jericho, solitary from here to the cool stars.

There comes off the grim gray east hills a soft whelming taste of Sunset, bloody and full of human marrows.

And I feel a need of great Pain or great Sin to make and break me, Soul and bones.

*

Having followed the muse through a trail of words back to Butte to write her last book, by mid-1917 she left the mining city - almost to the day that Butte's metals production crested and began to decline - to move to the place that would be her home for the rest of her life, the site of her discovery (and home to the sisters Monroe): Chicago.

The Flapper Era was beginning, the Vamp had been newly-established by Theda Bara in 1915, and while freshly-arrived in Chicago MacLane was approached by representatives of Essanay Studios with the idea of making a movie of one of her feature articles.

Essanay - home to such stars as Gloria Swanson, Charlie Chaplin, and Harold Lloyd - had, in 1908, created some of the earliest cartoon films, and in 1916 had issued America's first Sherlock Holmes movie. One of its founders, G.K. Spoor, had co-created the first workable 35MM projector for large audiences, the first newsreel, the first film miniatures for special effects, and would co-develop a 3D movie system in 1923 and a 65MM widescreen format in 1926. He produced only eight films himself - and MacLane's would be one of them.

The proposed movie was duly innovative: framed by short repeated scenes of the protagonist's reminiscing to her young, recently-married maidservant, the film's body is a re-creation of the author's memories in detailed, realistic interiors called by one trade paper the best yet seen.

Shot that fall by Sherlock Holmes' *director, ninety minutes long on seven reels, released in 1918, exhibited across the country, censored in its Midwest, still on display (to almost uniformly delighted reviews) a year later in Tasmania and mainland Australia, it would be her only movie: Mary MacLane as Mary MacLane - smoking while directly addressing her audience, musing to help a woman of the next generation when undistracted by demands of romance or action, asking at the very end if despite all love does exist (to which her maidservant answers, "Oui, mamselle") - in* Men Who Have Made Love to Me.

It is not known with certainty if it is lost or not.

LATE PIECES

1917 - 1918

"Mary MacLane on Marriage"

Chicago Herald · 24 June 1917

Not to let concealment, like a worm in the bud, prey longer on my damask cheek, here once more come I idly forth, purple pen in hand. This time to hand out to, or to rub into, as you will, my inward convictions anent marriage. I never have been married myself, but the woods, on either side my pathway, are full of people who are. And I'm free to contemplate their marriedness and to gather convictions therefrom, ad lib.

I have singular views, I'm aware, on several subjects in the gamut of human experience. I doubt if my views on marriage are more erratic than some others that are filed in the pigeonholed turrets of my mind. I only know that my opinions thereunto are considerably less likely to change and moderate than almost any others in me.

For marriage, as a condition and an institution, looks to me, when in theory I apply it to myself, something sinister and forlorn and as near the old-fashioned conception of hell as anything that's legal in all our world. Its entire end and aim, its alpha and omega, are restriction, limitation, tied-downness, and a desolate dependence of spirit. All of which are fatal to romance and to faithfulness of heart.

Romance, with lips abloom and magic finger tips, is marriage's one raison d'etre. But two can live cheaper than one, and the world wants populating; those are most people's reasons, if not for marrying, at least for hanging together afterward. And what have those to do with romance - with lips abloom? Nothing - nothing at all.

Marriage, like romance itself, should be woven in a warp and woof of absolute freedom. It's a game that wants no rules except those of ordinary honor, and no restrictions save those of love. To make marriage an ideal and an idyllic thing people should marry only because they want to, should stay married only because they want to, and should, when they want to, quit.

That it's a statutory institution is the topmost reason why in most marriages there's always the estranging rift in the lute. Marriage is by nature and tradition the most intimately personal of all relationships. But the statute books make it as airtight as an affidavit and as cold blooded as a mortgage. They would have us marry by the clock. As well have laws to govern the brushing of our teeth or the wearing of our gauds.

*

Not that one advocates for everybody Victoria Woodhull's doctrine of free love (of which she was herself its most - perhaps its only - courageous exponent). And not that one places faith in the so-called "affinity" thing (a foolish and futile word applied to anything but chemicals). Those things presuppose that we're angelic. And the human race, as almost any person will admit readily, is not a race of angels. It is more like a race of roaring lions and snarling tigers and whining jackals and squeaking ferrets.

To turn free love and the system of affinities loose among such a rabble would not mean that everybody would begin, in a large, liberal Good Samaritan sort of way, freely to love everybody else. Far indeed from that. 'Twould mean that women and men would lay siege to each other's hearts with the utmost indiscrimination, and would assault the tiny doors thereto with merciless battering rams, and would burn and pillage and plunder at will, and would leave ruin and desolation where before all had been spring-time and blooming florets.

Marrying should be always and only an affair of mutual agreement. But civilization and its conventionalities are not quite compatible, by and large, with idyllic marriage.

Human nature, since the days of Eve the Elemental, is well nigh syn-onymous with the law of contraries. It is the only law which really governs us. If the state legislatures could revise all their statute books so that each enactment might be founded on a comprehensive knowledge of humanity and a ruse of subtle contradiction, almost we could do away with penitentia-ries and the millennium, of a truth, would have begun. It's chiefly because we have laws that we break them. It's because we're not supposed to steal, more than our instinct of acquisition, that would impel nine-and-ninety one-hundredths of us to "lift" a diamond necklace or a heavy roll of bank notes wherever we saw it not nailed down. It's because the demon rum is bad for us that it seems to so many of us to be so well worth going after. And for that saffron tea is good for us, nobody's crazy about it.

So exceeding deep is our unconscious belief in this law of contraries that often we do the thing we don't want to do because we believe, since we don't want to do it, it must be good for us - so that, having done it, we can [carry] a large entry on the credit side of our account with the universe at large. It makes us as happy as if we had succeeded in cheating a Chinese laundryman or had beaten a waiter at his own game. And it's because the restrictions of marriage are made water tight by the hand of the law that they spring, without warning, so many leaks. It's because the law makes it compulsory, in marrying, to marry only one person at a time that we shortly go wandering after strange loves and envying other people theirs, though our own may be as good - or better. If there were no laws and no restrictions connected with marriage and the giving in marriage one [would, to a banker's certainty, be] in love on the tenth anniversary of one's marriage with the person one happened to marry. Applying the principle to marriage and reducing it to so many words, should any lady at the outset of her married life turn to her husband as they stood together in the midst of their Mission furniture surveying the newness of their flat and say, "Mine golden lad, the door is unlocked and the road lies straight before thee. If at any time I pall upon thee, if at any time the glint in another's eyes outglints mine, or the lilt in another's voice has thee going, remember, my first and last word to thee is, Away - thou'rt free! Madly as I might want thee, I want thee only when desire and love are rampant in us both," you can take it from me that lady would have her husband as good as nailed. Let her convince him that she meant just that and his passage would be booked - through.

*

And he possibly might nail the lady by the same method. BUT HE WOULD BEST NOT BANK ON IT. Feminine contrariness, unlike the crude masculine brand, is an infinite complexity of wheels within wheels. The balance is struck, however, by the fact that the ordinary woman, having once given her heart to any man not a complete idiot, will continue to bestow it on him daily until it is absolutely thrown back at her, a battered ruin.

But those, I'm aware, are aspects of marriage as applied to the human race in its less complex evolutions. There are large assortments of people in the world with whom even the ruse of subtle contradiction wouldn't work. There are countless people who cannot rest content with marriage, or with anything, unless they can be kept constantly guessing. When a woman and a man know each other's temperaments to their last gasp, in all their colors, and in their tricks, and their lights and shades, and sincerities and insincerities; when they are quite convinced that each has no longer any surprises for the other, then in every way but physically the marriage has ceased. It might take six days or six months, and they might live together fifty years, but all that once lived for each, in the other, is as Dead Sea fruit. They are but ships that passed in the night - they spoke each other for a time, and then went on, each by itself, in the dark.

*

Other temperaments, in the form of loves and friendships, will glow for them both ever and anon. But to each other they're the same as dead. Though there's an outward camaraderie between them, and their children are realities - without even death's romance to put glamour upon it - they're the same as dead.

It's a form of incompatibility too subtle for the divorce tribunal at Reno. And it would constitute, for me at least, a wan little bit of hell.

Speaking of the dying of the temperamental lights reminds me of my own private convictions - of which I have quite the courage - upon marrying as applied to myself. If at any time, under the influences of passing feelings of allurement, charm, fascination, what not, I should make the colossal mistake of marrying one of the neat young men who play around from [now to then] in my life, and if after two days I held his temperament in the hollow of my hand and there were no surprises left in it for me - then, of a truth, on the morning of the third day he would awake to find the bird flown and a note on the kitchen table couched, in my cold handwriting, in very succinct terms of a farewell. The neat young man might rave and rant (for, without egotism, I would take oath he couldn't run the gamut of my temperament in two days), my circle of acquaintances might talk (might? say rather they would: the one best bet); the papers might blazon it forth in flaming headlines, and I might find myself socially and sociologically on very thin ice. Much more than that might happen.

But foreseeing it all and measuring it all, and telling over each separate consequence like beads in a rosary - still for mine, freedom by the token and sign of the note on the kitchen table. I would say to myself: "As between forty years of deadly boredom with this neat young man - whose neatness and youth will simultaneously and yearly grow less, and who will frequently love another merely by reason of his being married to me, and whose temperament is lasting me but two days - between all that and a simple farewell note on the kitchen table, need one hesitate a moment?" And so I would not hesitate, I would write the note in cold young scorn and leave it on the kitchen table and go.

Oh, there's indeed a wide and deadly field of boredom and atrophy to contemplate along matrimony's line of least resistance. The name of the deadly marriage is legion. The other day I saw on a car, for the first time [in some years,] a young man whom old ma[...] kidhood, a [...] A year or two ago he "went and got married." I had analyzed him thoroughly in his young days as a youth in whom economy, in its most pronounced and virulent form, struggled for supremacy against such mild attributes as educational aspirations and slight tendencies toward watermelons and Daisy air rifles. The lad rose at daybreak to sell papers and every evening after school he sold more papers. And his every nickel was doubly earned by also being saved. And he worked his way into a clerkship in a bank.

*

When I looked at him the other day as easily as the simplest arithmetical deduction I worked out the plausible theory of his marriage: He met, belike, a nice looking and not very fluffy young woman sufficiently younger than himself to warrant him in a belief that he could subdue whatever luxurious tastes might crop out in her. And he said to himself (not in so many words, but in what may be termed a "straight flush" of thought): "Now, I've got a good position, but not too well paid, and if I want to get ahead I have to save like thunder. In the next fifteen years, if I don't marry, I'll probably be set back, do what I may, from $60 to $80 in gallantry toward the ladies - for even I am human. At the lowest calculation that would be $900, and with interest at 4 per cent, which is a conservative estimate and not counting the compound, it would be $36 more.

"Now, here's an awful nice looking girl - not stunning (she'd be no use to me if she were; that always calls for clothes) but, well, very attractive and very sweet. I'm living at home, so my board bill isn't so high as it might be, but I see a way of making it even less and at the same time doing away with this $60 to $80 a year gallantry. And I'll go to it right now. I'll combine business with pleasure straight away by marrying this very nice girl. I'll have the pleasure of her company; I'll teach her to run a household with the least possible waste and, above all, I'll save in the next fifteen years, with all my other savings, that $936."

So he married her - for the nice girl, not having known and analyzed him in his frankly close-fisted youth, saw in him but a good looking young man, in well-fitting clothes and neat coat shirts and collars, whom it would be pleasant to be married to by the Presbyterian minister. They have no children - probably the young man hastily catalogued children in a hypothetical ledger under the head of "expensive luxuries" and closed the book for good. And now the most romantic interest the nice girl's young life contains is planning each day what new disguises to throw over the remnants of the very tough "chuck" roast which she purchases on Saturday, at the instance of her lord, and serves, in serial form, every day for a week.

*

Into his subconsciousness will enter not the thought itself but the shadow of it, that his young wife, had she but a very tiny bit more imagination and a very tiny bit less niceness, would elope any day with a Finn bartender, a vaudeville virtuoso, a Swiss milkman - anyone at all who seemed poetically improvident, who threw his substance systematically to the dogs.

'Tis but one picture culled from matrimony's line of least resistance. There are countless thousands more - all different and all deadly.

But all that apart, in marriage looked upon as romance with lips abloom and magic finger tips, decked with amaranth and perfumed with myrrh, I believe with all my heart. To be bored, indeed, I should never submit. But having fallen in love with one, and he with me; having plighted and pledged troth in the subtle madnesses of fascination and witchery and intoxication and seduction of soul which come from nothing in the world but the meeting of two hearts, and in simple truth; so long as no cold, disillusioning breath blew over it and no blasting distraction of lies killed it - to marriage like that I should cling till the final fleeting breath passed my lips.

*

And even though the madness and the fascination and the thousand intoxications had faded out of it, one by one, and bright lights paled, and glowing fires died - if only simple truth remained it still would be the altar of my deep desire and worth all the world beside. It would not matter what manner of man he might be, so that he were true with me.

So far from being bored - though it might be in poverty and deprivation, in a tent on a hillside, a hut in a desert, or wandering afoot by country roadsides - I should pass my days in gaiety and peace and lightness of heart. My slim young body, being of a fragileness, would be quickly worn out. But all the better, I would reason, that it should die with the dying of the witcheries. I should have tasted at once rapture and truth; it would be worth even the passing of my life in its youth, and the losing of the great glittering world in its romance, garlanded with amaranth and perfumed with myrrh.

That is the picture which flits across my pagan mind, and it's the reality of my belief. It has nothing to do with the tenets of civilization. Belike it would require a most brazen courage, and there would be consequences and penalties such as no person might care to take on. Yet I know there are countless outwardly conventional women in the world whose feelings are equally pagan. In truth, many, very many, of the things, I, M. MacLane, say openly (and get slammed for) are the inward convictions of unconfessed thousands.

"The Movies - and Me"

Photoplay · January 1918

Any time I write my opinions and impressions of this moving picture thing in its varied phases and components, it is not in the least as a critic who carps, but purely as an ardent film fan who eats up the whole game relishingly from soup to nuts.

Everybody knows it is not the critics who keep that multi-colored ball rolling, but "us fans" who pay our fifteen cents and go in at the front door prepared to like every possible thing we see that's likeable and eat up every possible morsel of romance that slides Lillian-Gishfully across the screen.

Many a critic, if we are to credit their interesting dope sheets, has come away from a picture show sickened, nauseated to his hard heart's core by the tragic want of art, logic, continuity, and all those juggled-up things to be found in the whole film idea as is.

But nothing like that ever happens to me. In the first place, I don't attend picture shows in order to get nauseated. And in the second place, I usually grow so delightfully fussed up with charm, thrill, appreciation, and the general sense of human emotion and color that the demon art seems quite all out of it.

It is one of my theories that the true expression of the human equation never can be pure art, and pure logic and pure continuity. Human beings are not formed to that end - not while kaisers and cabarets still go on and beds continue to sag in the middle. And since - which is another of my theories - the cinematograph really does mirror human life as it really does daily happen, it can't possibly be pure art and pure logic and still be good moving picture stuff.

Charlie Chaplin is, in my opinion, the nearest thing to a perfect artist in the long gamut of film stars, and he is by that token a case in point: Charlie Chaplin does not in any way express any form of human life as it is lived in this present state of civilization.

He falls down flights of stairs nine times with the utmost abandon and runs around tables with surprising velocity and precision, but, strictly speaking, those things are unlikely to happen in most average households. The cook would leave too often, and besides it would wear out the rugs, and prove otherwise inconvenient. No, the nonchalant Charles, though I hand it to him as an artist and a very good one, is not a favorite of mine.

Nor is Mister Fairbanks, remarkable though he is for his ready mirth and his ability to jump over things. For, again, the following reasons: though indubitably great stuff it is not true to life. I have not yet known the host in any menage I've been in to go from room to room in leaps and bounds. It's all very intriguing to those who relish the bizarre and the highly improbable in pictures.

But for myself, I am the tamest, the least fiery, the most equable type of film fan. I like dramas where young people marry with lacy clothes, and a mob in the last few feet; romances where I can sit open-eyed and pensive, forgetful of passing time; and everydayish stories where I can watch Alice Brady walk and Robert Warwick frown and Valeska Suratt's back and Louise Glaum look balefully at her leading man.

Sometimes the mere look of a country hillside with the sunshine sparkling upon it, and leaves and grasses and wild flowers blowing in the breeze, to a gaze too long inured to farthest Butte or darkest Chicago, is plaisance and paradise enow.

Since nineteen-eleven when most of the stars who now bloom madly in electric lights were not even names and were in fact working humbly and anonymously for Biograph, the picture theater has been my main stand-by in moods of relaxation.

I spotted the lyric-looking Blanche Sweet as a coming star when I was totally unable to discover her name, so reticent was the screen in those days. And the famous Pickford was known but by her curls. And the artistic Walthall peered at the camera merely as a hard-working lead. And "legits" shied like frightened steeds at the mere mention of the films. And Theda Bara in her sleek darkling pride existed not.

I have trailed stars from their dawn to their be-limousined present. I have paid fifteen cents on several thousand afternoons in the far wilds of my native Butte in order to translate me from the somber colors of myself to the passionful prisms of life as presented by Mister Selig, Mister Fox, Mister World, Mister Essanay, Mister Blue Bird, Mister Paramount, Mister Triangle, et al. And I have never been disappointed.

There has always been something in every picture I have ever seen, though it might be but the single expression of some warmly-sexed lips or eyes, that registered at rather more than fifteen cents' value. I maintain there is more of sheer beauty - world beauty, life beauty, human beauty - in moving pictures than in any other popular expression of everyday life. If there's much that is crude in it all as yet, there is much more that is lovely.

And speaking of Mister Essanay reminds me of the most astonishing thing that ever happened to me. Without effort, without volition, without, in short, wanting to, I - I have become a "film star."

Such is fame.

Nay, more, a vampire. I had thought that it required a devilish lot of energy and pep and punch and stunningness to become one of those things. But not so. It requires languor and clothes and ease and loads of astonishingly yellow make-up. And a kindofa, sortofa vampish way with men. I have thought of myself, when it came to self-expression, purely and simply as a lit-ry woman.

But being gently induced to play the lead in a picturization of some of my own stuff I found I had all the requisites of the little old screen vampire.

I shall have a lot to write about the making of my picture when it is all over. But just at present my days are a wild maze of directors, camera men, extra people, heroes, sets, props, electricians, luncheon hours, and tumblings out of bed at six o'clock in the morning.

And they tell me I have a screen personality. Still I remain in my own accounting not a film actor, but a lit-ry lady. I am still deeply unused to grease paint. I may look like a vampire, but I continue to feel singularly unlike one. I am a fan and not a critic, and my secret hankering is to be an extra person, ad-lib-ing in a mob. *Voila*.

FURTHER READING

ACKNOWLEDGMENTS

NOTES

Atherton, Gertrude. *Perch of the Devil.* Frederick A. Stokes, New York, 1914, pp 37, 173.

‑‑‑‑‑‑‑‑. *Adventures of a Novelist.* Liveright, New York, 1932, pp 490-492.

Burlingame, Merrill K. and Toole, K.R. *A History of Montana.* Lewis Historical Publishing Co., New York, 1957, vol. II, p 286.

Brooks, Van Wyck. *The Confident Years.* Dutton, New York, 1952, pp 319-320, 469.

Brownlow, Kevin. *Behind the Mask of Innocence: Sex, Violence and Crime - Films of Social Conscience in the Silent Era.* Alfred A. Knopf, New York, 1990, pp 30-33, 514-515.

Canfield, Mary Cass. *Grotesques and Other Reflections.* Harper & Bros., New York, 1927, pp 48-60. (Essay on *I, Mary MacLane.* Orig. appeared as "Mary MacLane and the Apparent Agonies of Introspective Pathology," under the by-line "Peter Savage," in *Vanity Fair,* June 1917.)

Derleth, August. *Still Small Voice.* Appleton-Century, New York, 1940, pp 58-59. (Biography of MacLane's *New York World* interviewer, Zona Gale.)

Doran, George H. *Chronicles of Barrabas (1884-1934).* Harcourt-Brace, New York, 1934, pp 29-30.

Faderman, Lillian. *Surpassing the Love of Men: Romantic Friendship and Love Between Women From the Renaissance to the Present.* William Morrow, New York, 1981, pp 299-300.

‑‑‑‑‑‑‑‑. *Odd Girls and Twilight Lovers: A History of Lesbian Life in America.* Columbia University Press, New York, 1991, p 113.

Ferlinghetti, Lawrence and Peters, Nancy. *Literary San Francisco.* City Lights Books, San Francisco, 1980, p 92.

Foster, Jeannette Howard. *Sex Variant Women in Literature.* Vantage, New York, 1956. (Reprinted by Diana Press, Baltimore, 1975.)

Garland, Hamlin. *Companions on the Trail.* Macmillan, New York, 1931, p 147.

Hall, Dr. G. Stanley. *Adolescence: Its Psychology, and its Relations to Physiology, Anthropology, Sociology, Sex, Crime, Religion, and Education.* Appleton, New York, 1904, vol. I, p 559-560; vol. II, p 629.

Katz, Jonathan Ned. *Gay American History.* Meridian, New York, 1992. (Rev. ed.; orig. pub. Crowell, New York, 1976.)

Kittredge, William and Smith, Annick, eds. *The Last Best Place: A Montana Anthology.* University of Washington Press, Seattle, 1991. (Reprints passages from *I Await* and *I, Mary.*)

Kramer, Sidney. *A History of Stone & Kimball and Herbert S. Stone & Co.* University of Chicago Press, Chicago, 1940.

Mencken, H.L. "The Butte Bashkirtseff," in *Prejudices: First Series.* Alfred A. Knopf, New York, 1919, pp 123-128.

Richards, Dell. *Lesbian Lists.* Alyson Publications, Boston, 1990.

Ross, Ishbell. *Ladies of the Press.* Harper, New York, 1936, p 419.

Rudnick, Lois Palken. *Mabel Dodge Luhan: New Woman, New Worlds.* University of New Mexico Press, Albuquerque, 1984, pp 139-140.

Spacks, Patricia Meyers. *The Female Imagination*. Alfred A. Knopf, New York, 1975, pp 6, 166, 171-180, 182, 184, 189, 192, 205, 218, 250, 316, 317.

Truitt, Evelyn M. *Who Was Who on Screen*. R.R. Bowker & Co., New York, 1977, p 293.

Workers of the Writers' Program of the WPA in the State of Montana. *Montana - A State Guide Book*. Viking Press, New York, 1939, p 103.

-------. *Copper Camp: Stories of the World's Greatest Mining Town - Butte, Montana*. Hastings House, New York, 1943, pp 1, 257-258.

*

Grateful acknowledgment is made to the Newberry Library for permission to quote material from the Stone & Kimball and Herbert S. Stone & Co. archives and to the University of Chicago for permission to quote from the Harriet Monroe Papers at the Special Collections Research Center, University of Chicago Library.

M often refers to the prices of things; in place of a myriad of conversions, a list of 2013 values of single dollars during her flourish-years is offered: 1918 - $15.30; 1917 - $17.97; 1916 - $21.09; 1915 - $22.70; 1914 - $22.92; 1913 - $22.22; 1912 - $23.78; 1911 - $24.64; 1910 - $24.64; 1909 - $25.55; 1908 - $25.55; 1907 - $24.63; 1906 - $25.54; 1905 - $25.54; 1904 - $25.54; 1903 - $25.54; 1902 - $26.51; 1901 - $27.57; sources: *Historical Statistics of the United States* (USGPO, 1975) and *http://www.westegg.com/inflation/* (accessed 29 September 2014).

16. *To The Devil* - This dedication was cut by the publisher.

17. *peripatetic* - Ref. to Aristotle, whose thrust is akin to M's emphasis upon sense-experience, logical analysis, friendship, and self-realization. M plays upon the (now questioned) tracing of his philosophy's nickname to his known habit of strolling as he taught - *peripatein* means "to walk about."

17. Marie Bashkirtseff - Russian painter and diarist (1860-1884), died of tuberculosis in Paris. Bashkirtseff's posthumously-published diary was well-known in its day for the writer's unabashed egotism.

17. *Byron of* - His incomplete epic in the tragicomic *ottava rima* scheme was famed for its irony and vastness of scope. Goethe called it "a work of boundless genius."

20. *germs of intense* - Poss. from story in Cicero's *Tusculan Disputations* (orig. in Phaedo's *Zopyrus*): as rendered by Nietzsche, "A foreigner who knew about faces once passed through Athens and told Socrates to his face that he was a *monstrum* - that he harbored in himself all the bad vices and appetites. And Socrates merely answered: 'You know me, sir!'" (*Twilight of the Idols*, trans. Walter A. Kaufmann).

22. *sulphur smoke* - Smelters operated within Butte's city limits.

26. *ozone* - In this usage, archaic term for wind-freshened rural air; thus, Ozone Park, Queens, New York (*c.* 1882) and Ozone, Tennessee (1896).

26. *Bacchantes* - Female Dionysus-worshippers in Euripdes' play *The Bacchae.*

27. *of shade* - From the poem "The Meeting of the Waters" by the Irish musician, poet, popular entertainer (and friend of Byron's) Thomas Moore (1779-1852): *Sweet vale of Avoca! how calm could I rest / In thy bosom of shade, with the friends I love best, / Where the storms that we feel in this cold world should cease, / And our hearts, like thy waters, be mingled in peace.*

27. *memory is possession* - From the prelude to the poem "Regret" by the English novelist and poet Jean Ingelow (1820-1897): *It is true / That we have wept. But O! this thread of gold, / We would not have it tarnish; let us turn / Oft and look back upon the wondrous*

web, / And when it shineth sometimes we shall know / That memory is possession.

30. *blue* - Prob. *Pulsatilla patens* ("Eastern pasqueflower," "prairie smoke"), poss. *Anemone blanda* ("Grecian Windflower"), both of fam. *Ranunculaceae* (buttercup); *P. patens* (sometimes incl. in genus *Anemone*) is a Montana-area native (indeed, is Manitoba's provincial flower - a sub-species is S. Dakota's state flower) and prized for its blooming near Easter (whence "pasqueflower"); *A. blanda* is native to Lebanon, Syria, SE Europe, and Turkey, but is also known as "Blue Anemone" (as was *P. patens* in Montana in early 20th c.).

30. *to rejoice* - From the 1864 free-love novel *Victoire* by Mary Clemmer (1839-1884, also known as Mary Clemmer Ames): *Be faithful to thyself and to all that ever was thine. Thy friend is always thy friend. Not to have or to hold to love, or to rejoice in, but to remember.*

33. *when Omar* - From the third stanza of the introductory poem by the Irish politician and author Justin Huntly McCarthy (1859-1936) to his translation of *The Rubaiyat of Omar Khayyam* (1889): *Alas for me, alas for all who weep / And wonder at the Silence dark and deep / That girdles round this little Lamp in space / No wiser than when Omar fell asleep.*

33. James Whitcomb Riley (1849-1916) - American Midwestern writer, best-seller in his time, known as "The Hoosier Poet" and "The Children's Poet"; tended to the humorous or sentimental; contributed to the creation of regional literature in the US.

33. *tragedy to* - From aphorism attrib. to English antiquarian, litterateur, and politician Horace Walpole (1717-1797): *Life is a tragedy to those who feel, and a comedy to those who think.* (Attrib. at times to Molière.)

34. *vile dust* - Prob. from Sir Walter Scott's "Lay of the Last Minstrel" (pub. 1805): *High though his titles, proud his name, / Boundless his wealth as wish can claim; / Despite those titles, power, and pelf, / The wretch, concentred all in self, / Living, shall forfeit fair renown, / And, doubly dying, shall go down / To the vile dust, from whence he sprung, / Unwept, unhonoured, and unsung.*

35. Jacques - From Shakespeare's *As You like It* II:I (spoken by the First Lord at the Forest of Arden): *The melancholy Jaques grieves at that, / And, in that kind, swears you do more usurp / Than doth your brother that hath banish'd you.*

35. *dropsical* - From "dropsy," an archaic term for edema.

35. *of green* - From the poem "Afoot" by the Canadian author Sir Charles G.D. Roberts (1860-1943), known as "the Father of Canadian Poetry": *Comes the lure of green things growing, / Comes the call of waters flowing - / And the wayfarer desire / Moves and wakes and would be going.*

35. *Law of Compensation* - From Emerson's *Essays: First Series* (1841).

36. Anne "Ninon" de l'Enclos (1620-1705) - French courtesan and wit.

36. Olive Schreiner (1855-1920) - South African novelist and feminist; wrote *The Story of an African Farm* (1883) and *Woman and Labour* (1911).

37. *pathetic* - The modern contemptuous/ridiculing sense (which dates from the 1930s) must nowhere be applied to M's use of the term.

43. *Give thyself* - From Charles E. Norton's rendering (*c.* 1896) into English of J.B. Nicolas' French translation of *The Rubaiyat* (1867): *Give thyself to joy, for grief will be infinite. The stars shall again meet together at the same point of the firmament; but of thy body shall bricks be made for a palace-wall.* Paragraphing appears to be M's.

43. *this be* - From a song ref. to in, or a direct quote from, the novel *Sir Jaffray's Wife* by English author Arthur Williams Marchmont (1852-1923): *For answer, he kissed her again. / "Have I made you happy, Jaffray?" she asked, after a long pause. / By way of answer this time, he hummed the snatch of a song, "If this be vanity, vanity let it be," an old teasing trick of his, when she had seemed to look for a compliment from him.*

44. *conceiving but* - Poss. ref. to Descartes, specifically his argument that mind and body are two substances since they may be clearly and separately conceived. (If so intended, M ironically inverts and extends the argument in a passage of sensualism.)

44. *heart with* - From the final stanza of Wordsworth's poem "I Wandered Lonely As a Cloud" (pub. 1807): *For oft, when on my couch I lie / In vacant or in pensive mood, / They flash upon that inward eye / Which is the bliss of solitude; / And then my heart with pleasure fills, / And dances with the daffodils.*

44. *meeting of* - Where the rivers Avonmore and Avonbeg meet to form the Avoca is called the Meeting of the Waters.

44. *never to* - From Shakespeare and Fletcher's *Henry VIII* III:2: *There is, betwixt that smile we would aspire to, / That sweet aspect of princes, and their ruin, / More pangs and fears than wars or women have: / And when he falls, he falls like Lucifer, / Never to hope again.*

45. Henry James (1843-1916) - American-born writer, regarded as a central figure of 19th-century literary realism.

45. William Dean Howells (1837-1920) - American realist author and literary critic; nicknamed "The Dean of American Letters."

45. *"Goo-Goo Eyes"* - Ref. to song "Just Because She Made Dem Goo-Goo Eyes" (1900), lyr. John Queen, mus. Hughey Cannon.

45. Maria Louise Pool (1841-1898) - American author, pub. by M's publisher Herbert S. Stone's predecessor company, Stone & Kimball; M was unaware that Pool had died several years earlier; para. was del. in published ver.

46. Eugene Field, Sr. (1850-1895) - American writer best known for his children's poetry and humorous essays.

52. *plungers* - Gamblers.

52. *box rustlers* - Prostitutes who worked the curtained upper boxes of theatres.

52. *impossible women* - Prostitutes; there may also be some Lesbian signaling to the term.

52. *beer-jerkers* - Barkeeps who drew beer in saloons.

52. *biscuit-shooters* - Waiters or waitresses (incl. Harvey Girls, of the respectable railside dining establishments of Fred Harvey) or camp cooks.

53. *four-in-hands* - Ref. to carriage with four horses and a single driver.

54. *grass widow* - Euph. for a not-respectably-single woman: *e.g.* divorced, separated, an ex-mistress, mother of an illegitimate child, or parted from husband for a protracted time.

54. *of sprouts* - Difficult, prolonged course of instruction or treatment.

56. *stalled ox* - From Proverbs 15:17: *Better is a dinner of herbs where love is, than a stalled ox and hatred therewith.* (King James)

56. *among thieves* - From Luke 10:30, but M reverses gender: *And Jesus answering said, A certain man went down from Jerusalem to Jericho, and fell among thieves, which stripped him of his raiment, and wounded him, and departed, leaving him half dead.* (King James)

58. *little folding* - From Proverbs 6:10: *Yet a little sleep, a little slumber, a little folding of the hands to sleep* (King James)

60. Nora Perry (1831-1896) - American journalist, poet, writer of children's stories.

60. *with reluctant* - From Longfellow's poem "Maidenhood" (pub. 1842): *Standing, with reluctant feet, / Where the brook and river meet, / Womanhood and childhood fleet!*

60. *Hildegarde Graham* - Ref. to popular series of girls' novels (1889-1897) by Laura E. Richards (1850-1943) known as The Hildegarde Series; neither the series nor any volume in it bears the title that M gives.

60. *What Katy Did* - Girls' book by Susan Coolidge (pseud. of Sarah Chauncey Woolsey, 1835-1905).

67. *are heavy* - From Matthew 10:28: *Come unto me, all ye that labour and are heavy laden, and I will give you rest.* (King James)

67. *the waters* - From the first stanza of Charles Wesley's influential hymn "Jesus, Lover of My Soul" (pub. 1740): *Let me to Thy bosom fly, / While the waters near me roll, / While the tempest still is high. / Hide me, O my Saviour, hide, / Till the storms of life be past; / Safe into the haven guide; / Oh receive my soul at last!*

69. *little more* - From stanza 39 of Browning's "By the Fireside" (written 1853): *Oh, the little more, and how much it is! / And the little less, and what worlds away! / How a sound shall quicken content to bliss, / Or a breath suspend the blood's best play, / And life be a proof of this!*

69. *the people* - From Job 12:2: *No doubt but ye* are *the people, and wisdom shall die with you.* (King James)

72. *Cashmere* - Common archaic term for Kashmir. M poss. read in Byron's friend Thomas Moore (cf. n. 27 p 553): *Who has not heard of the Vale of Cashmere, / With its roses the brightest that earth ever gave, / Its temples, and grottos, and fountains as clear / As the love-lighted eyes that hang over their wave* (from "Lalla Rookh," pub. 1817) or the New England poet George Bancroft Griffith (1841-?): *With its cincture of snows lies the wonderful plain / That the paladin formed when the dragons were slain; / 'Tis the Hindoo's delight; and the poets endear / By their songs of its beauty, the Vale of Cashmere* (from "The Vale of Cashmere," apparent 1st pub. *Granite State Monthly*, Oct. 1881, p 17).

72. *Lethe* - In Greek mythology, Lethe was one of Hades' five rivers; those who drank of its waters forgot all.

72. Charles Kingsley (1819-1875) - British university professor, priest, historian, novelist; poem has variant texts - ver. given here is that in the orig. printing.

75. Archibald C[lavering] Gunter (1847-1907) - Popular American playwright and widely-read self-published author and magaziner.

75. Albert Ross (pseud. of Linn Boyd Porter, 1851-1916) - American novelist.

76. *mere vile clay* - Not, evidently, a literary quotation.

78. *two thieves* - Poss. ref. to a set of Rembrandt drypoints of the subject in various stages of finish.

80. *deferred and* - From Proverbs 13:12: *Hope deferred maketh the heart sick: but* when *the desire cometh,* it is *a tree of life.* (King James)

81. *servant a* - From 2 Kings 8:13: *And Hazael said, But what, is thy servant a dog, that he should do this great thing?* M may also have had the echo at 2 Samuel 9:8 in mind: *And he bowed himself, and said, What is thy servant, that thou shouldest look upon such a dead dog as I am?* (King James)

81. *song of* - Poss. from *A Modern Ideal: A Dramatic Poem* - an early work (1886) by Sidney Royse Lysaght (1860-1941), an Irish writer who also worked in the iron industry: *The kind and wonderful voices, / They speak the truth of existence, / Truth, the wonder of wonders, / They show us the soul of all things, / They touch the shadow and semblance, / And set the reality free; / They sing the song of the world that is / To the music of what might be.*

82. Charlotte Corday (1768-1793) - French patriot, assassinated revolutionary leader Marat while he bathed; was executed.

82. *If to do* - From Shakespeare's *Merchant of Venice* I:2: *If to do were as easy as to know what were good to do, / Chapels had been churches, and poor men's cottages / Princes' palaces.*

86. *gall and* - Wormwood and gall are paired at numerous points in the Bible, but in the King James that phrase appears only in Deuteronomy 29:18: *lest there should be among you a root that beareth gall and wormwood.*

87. *and Haidee* - Beautiful Moorish-Greek girl who found Don Juan cast ashore, restored him to animation, and became his lover.

88. *timothy-grass* - *Phleum pratense*; European perennial grass that has spread through the US since Colonial times; important in some nutritious animal feeds, *e.g.* for horses and rabbits.

89. *health and* - From the hymn "Sweet the Moments, Rich in Blessing" (orig. James Allen, 1757, ed. Walter Shirley, 1770): *Sweet the moments, rich in blessing, / Which before the cross we spend, / Life and health and peace possessing / From the sinner's dying Friend.*

89. *winds with* - From Milton's "Ode on the Nativity" (1629): *The winds, with wonder whist, Smoothly the waters kiss'd;* "whist" is an archaic form of "quiet" or "silent."

89. *blew, and* - From Matthew 7:25: *And the rain descended, and the floods came, and the winds blew, and beat upon that house; and it fell not: for it was founded upon a rock.* (King James)

90. *nearer my* - From the hymn "Nearer, My God, to Thee" (1841) by the English poet Sarah Fuller Flower Adams (1805-1848); based on Genesis 28:11-19.

91. *air was over* - From second stanza of the poem "Great, Wide, Beautiful, Wonderful World" by the English author, reporter, preacher, and renowned nursery-poet William Brighty Rands (1823-1882): *Great, wide, beautiful, wonderful World, / With the wonderful water round you curled, / And the wonderful grass upon your breast - / World, you are beautifully drest. // The wonderful air is over me, / And the wonderful wind is shaking the tree, / It walks on the water, and whirls the mills, / And talks to itself on the tops of the hills.*

93. *Dr. Johnson* - Samuel Johnson.

93. *Our Young* - Prominent children's magazine; it merged with *St. Nicholas* in 1874, so the volume M was reading was decades-old.

93. J[ohn] T[ownsend] Trowbridge (1827-1916) - American author and editor; his Jack Hazard novels (1870s) were a popular boys' series; one was *Doing His Best* (c. 1873).

94. *Lucy* - From Wordsworth's "Lucy Gray - Or, Solitude" (1888): *You yet may spy the fawn at play, / The hare upon the green; / But the sweet face of Lucy Gray / Will never more be seen.*

94. *are old* - Seventh stanza of Lewis Carroll's nonsense poem "You Are Old, Father William" in *Alice's Adventures In Wonderland* (1865): *"You are old," said the youth, "one would hardly suppose / That your eye was as steady as ever; / Yet you balanced an eel on the end of your nose - / What made you so awfully clever?"*

102. *the other* - From the refrain in the hymn "Rest for the Weary" by the Irish-born American professor and minister William Hunter (1811-1877): *There is rest for the weary, / There is rest for you. / On the other side of Jordan, / In the sweet fields of Eden, / Where the tree of life is blooming, / There is rest for you.*

102. *thorns* - From Matthew 7:16: *Ye shall know them by their fruits. Do men gather grapes of thorns, or figs of thistles?* (King James)

105. *the beasts* - From Psalms 49:12: *Nevertheless man being in honour abideth not: he is like the beasts that perish.* (King James)

105. *brave thing* - As the ed. has located no earlier appearances, this phrase appears

to be from *A Practical Grammar of the English Language* (1878) by Ohioan educator, schools commissioner, and writer Thomas Wadleigh Harvey (1821-?).

106. *cometh not* - A refrain in Tennyson's poem "Mariana" (1830) about the char. in Shakespeare's *Measure for Measure*.

106. *The Mill on the Floss* - 1860 novel by George Eliot.

108. *sweet-fern* - Deciduous flowering shrub, *Comptonia peregrina* (monotyp.); leaves give pleasing odor when crushed; tends to grow in dry, sandy areas, esp. amid pines; native to eastern North America, extending west to Minnesota.

111. *for bread* - From Luke 11:11: *If a son shall ask bread of any of you that is a father, will he give him a stone? or if he ask a fish, will he for a fish give him a serpent?* (King James)

115. *sweet-flags* - *Acorus calamus*, also known as "calamus"; lofty wetland perennial, used in fragrance-making and archaic medicine; native to areas in various continents, incl. the northern us and southern Canada.

116. *eats its* - Poss. from article "James Russell Lowell," *Southern Review*, Oct 1875 (no author given but employs editorial "we"): *It may be as a cause, or it may be as an effect; but falseness of expression, and falseness in principle, are indissolubly associated. Like sentimentality in feeling, cant in religion, affectation in manner, it is sure to be a superficial malady, which is either a sure indication of the unsoundness within, or else, after a time, it eats its way inward, poisoning, finally, the very springs of life.* All previous uses the ed. has located relate literally to fungi, larvae, etc.

117. *L'Envoi* - From older French poetry, in which a brief separate line or verse at the end states the theme or dedicates the piece to a specific person.

*

124. *weary* - Popular quot. of Walter Horatio Pater (1839-1894), English writer and critic, infl. upon the Aesthetics, esp. Oscar Wilde; from his seminal *Studies in the History of the Renaissance* (1st ed. 1873), re. da Vinci's *La Gioconda*: *Hers is the head upon which all "the ends of the world are come," and the eyelids are a little weary. It is a beauty wrought out from within upon the flesh, the deposit, little cell by cell, of strange thoughts and fantastic reveries and exquisite passions.*

124. *Phyllis* - At present, an untraceable ref.

128. *have only read* - An odd claim even if m were being provocative, in light of m's knowledge of Bashkirtseff's work in *I Await* and having two pictures of the Russian

diarist in her room (*cf.* p 98); ed. suggests a reporter's or shorthand recorder's mishearing of M's speaking in past tense: *I had only read two or three entries in her journal, but I knew that.*

129. *Cyrano* - Ref. to Edmond Rostand's play *Cyrano de Bergerac* (1897).

*

131. *and vanities* - M is incorrect: from the Catechism in the Church of England's 1689 *Proposed Book of Common Prayer.*

132. *sloe-eyed* - Having slanted or dark blue to purpling black eyes; from the small dark fruit of the blackthorn.

132. *vineyard* - From Isaiah 5:1: *Now will I sing to my wellbeloved a song of my beloved touching his vineyard. My wellbeloved hath a vineyard in a very fruitful hill.* (King James)

133. *flesh-pots* - From Exodus 16:3: *And the children of Israel said unto them, Would to God we had died by the hand of the* LORD *in the land of Egypt, when we sat by the flesh pots, and when we did eat bread to the full; for ye have brought us forth into this wilderness, to kill this whole assembly with hunger.* (King James)

133. *Solomon* - From the Sermon on the Mount.

133. *purchased sea air* - Ref. to charities that gave vacations to New York's poor youth, *e.g.* The Fresh Air Fund (founded 1877).

133. *equipages* - Ref. to a carriage inclusive of its horses and attendants.

134. *Bailey's* - Then as now an exclusive private beach club; owned by the Spouting Rock Beach Association.

135. *the brave* - From the first stanza of the poem "Alexander's Feast" (1697) by John Dryden: *None but the brave / deserve the fair.*

135. *small and old* - Trinity Church, constr. 1720s, Episcopal; attended by prominent families; Washington's having attended in 1781 is a local oral tradition.

136. *the little rift* - Ref. to Tennyson's poem "Merlin and Vivien," part of his large elegiac cycle *Idylls of the King* (pub. 1856-1885): *It is the little rift within the lute, / That by and by will make the music mute, / And ever widening slowly silence all.*

*

137. *all's right* - From Pt I of Browning's poem "Pippa Passes" (1841): *God's in his Heaven - / All's right with the world!*

138. *half-seas* - Sailors' expression for drunkenness; archaic.

139. *Villette* - Pub. 1853; features Gothic doubling.

141. *durance vile* - Older term for lengthy imprisonment.

*

143. *old, old* - From Dickens' *Dombey & Son* (serial pub. 1846-1848): *The golden ripple on the wall came back again, and nothing else stirred in the room. The old, old fashion! The fashion that came in with our first garments, and will last unchanged until our race has run its course, and the wide firmament is rolled up like a scroll. The old, old fashion - Death!* M alludes to this passage several times in her early work; the close of her second book, *My Friend Annabel Lee* (1903), is an extended homage.

143. *the ten-thousandth* - Prob. from Deuteronomy 7:9: *Know therefore that the* LORD *thy God, he* is *God, the faithful God, which keepeth covenant and mercy with them that love him and keep his commandments to a thousand generations* (King James)

144. *minds are they* - From Matthew 5:4: *Blessed* are *they that mourn: for they shall be comforted.* (King James)

144. *that soft tale* - A literary phrase which appears in several sources in the early 1800s, *e.g.* "The Lady of the Lake" by Sir Walter Scott (pub. 1810), M's likely source.

144. *mills of* - A widespread alteration of Longfellow's translation (1845) of Friedrich von Logau's poem "Retribution" (1654): *Though the mills of God grind slowly, yet they grind exceeding small.*

145. *bay-tree that* - Prob. from Psalms 37:35: *I have seen the wicked in great power, and spreading himself like a green bay tree.* (King James)

145. *duck* - Cotton linen fabric, classically unbleached white in color.

146. *Trinity* - Episcopal church at intersection of Broadway and Wall St. in lower Manhattan; first building const. 1698; third (and present) building finished 1846; 281-foot spire was city's tallest point until the New York World Building (finished 1890).

147. *lame, the* - Popular phrase based on Luke 14:21: *So that servant came, and shewed his lord these things. Then the master of the house being angry said to his servant, Go out*

quickly into the streets and lanes of the city, and bring in hither the poor, and the maimed, and the halt, and the blind. (King James)

147. William Andrews Clark, Sr. (1839-1925) - One of Butte's three "Copper Kings," politician; reputedly deeply corrupt; among the richest men in American history; de facto founder of Las Vegas, Clark County, Nevada.

*

148. *times* - Popular term of the time for "at times"; for earlier-yet use by M, *cf.* p 267.

149. *[content]* - Available newspaper source has section flaked off due to age; bracketed word is ed.'s speculative reconstruction.

150. *wot* - Archaic: "know," rel. to "wit."

151. *[sit]* - Available newspaper source has section flaked off due to age; bracketed word is ed.'s speculative reconstruction.

151. *Long Branch* - Seashore town in New Jersey, *c.* twenty-five miles by water from Manhattan's Battery.

152. *hand forget its* - From Psalms 137:5: *If I forget thee, O Jerusalem, let my right hand forget her cunning.* (King James)

156. *Abide* - From Scottish Anglican hymn "Abide with Me" (1847), lyr. Henry Francis Lyte, mus. by various.

157. *Obelisk* - Ancient Egyptian obelisk of solid granite, 68 feet high, dating from reign of Thutmose III (*c.* 1450 BC); a present to the US government from the Khedive for remaining neutral as European powers machinated to control Egypt; popularly, and misleadingly, called "Cleopatra's Needle."

157. *Claremont* - Genteel hotel-resort on the Hudson, famed for its location (Riverside Dr. and 125th St., just opposite Grant's Tomb), view, and dining; suffered fire in 1940s; demolished *c.* 1950.

158. *Pulitzer* - Alt. name for the New York World Building.

*

162. *Lucy Gray* - As elsewhere, M's nickname for Lucy Monroe; *cf.* also n. 94 p 559.

164. *but for* - "For" was a popular term of the time for "as for."

167. *world and* - From Tennyson's poem "Locksley Hall" (written 1835, pub. 1842): *When I dipt into the future far as human eye could see; / Saw the Vision of the world and all the wonder that would be.*

167. *sometime hedge* - From Shakespeare's *Hamlet* IV:5 (spoken by Claudius): *Let him go, Gertrude; do not fear our person: / There's such divinity doth hedge a king, / That treason can but peep to what it would, / Acts little of his will.*

168. *shawm* - Medieval and Renaissance woodwind; oboe's predecessor; notable for clear projection, thus suitable for use outdoors.

168. *jessamine* - Likely the familiar *Jasminum* genus comprising over 200 species; poss. *Cestrum nocturnum* (night-blooming, greenish-white flowers, heavy perfume).

168. *to the sea* - From Psalms 107:23: *They that go down to the sea in ships, that do business in great waters* (King James)

168. Pierre Puvis de Chavannes (1824-1898) - Well-known painter, co-founder of Société Nationale des Beaux-Arts; early Symbolist; particularly noted for murals, the Library's (1895-1896) prominent among them.

170. Lilian Whiting (1859-1942) - American author and newspaper editor; particularly connected to Boston.

170. *habitation among* - From Psalms 120:5: *Woe is me, that I am constrained to dwell with Meshech, and to have my habitation among the tents of Kedar!* (trans. *Book of Common Prayer*, 1660 ed. if not earlier); unusually, M does not quote the King James: *Woe is me, that I sojourn in Mesech, that I dwell in the tents of Kedar!*

170. *of spices* - From Song of Solomon 6:2: *My beloved is gone down into his garden, to the beds of spices, to feed in the gardens, and to gather lilies.* (King James) Again, M inverts gender.

177. *grouty* - Ill-natured, grouchy; US regional term.

177. *this Mr.* - From *His One Fault* by J.T. Trowbridge, Lee & Shepard (Boston), 1886. Orig.: *"...and he sold him to this Mr. Badger for seventy dollars." / "Seventy gimcracks!" ejaculated Uncle Gray, aghast. "Any fool might know he's wuth twice that." He was thinking of Brunlow, but Eli applied the remark to himself. / "I did know it," he growled. "That's why I bought him. And mighty glad I am I didn't pay no more." / "To be sure," said Uncle Gray. "But didn't it occur to you that no honest man would want to sell an honest hoss*

like that for any such price?" / "I didn't know," said Eli, groutily. "He told a pooty straight story. I got took in, that's all." / "I should say, took in!" exclaimed Uncle Gray. "I know the knave, and I'm amazed that any man with common sense and eyes in his head shouldn't 'a' seen through him." / "Mabby I haint got common sense, and mabby I haint got eyes in my head," Eli muttered, with dull fire in the place where eyes should have been, if he had had any. "But I didn't expect this." / Kit hastened to interpose between the two men.

178. *Three Grains* - From the poem "Give Me Three Grains of Corn, Mother" by Amelia Blanford Edwards (1831-1892), English travel writer, wide-selling novelist, Egyptologist, and lecturer; poem exists in variant texts.

183. Minnie Madern Fiske (1865-1932) - A leading American actress, champion of Ibsen; play was *Mary of Magdala* - opened in Boston in March 1903 after Broadway run.

184. *thirst after* - From Matthew 5:6: *Blessed* are *they which do hunger and thirst after righteousness: for they shall be filled* (King James)

185. *sweat* - From popular rendering - "the sweat of his brow" - of Genesis 3:19: *In the sweat of thy face shalt thou eat bread, till thou return unto the ground; for out of it wast thou taken: for dust thou art, and unto dust shalt thou return.* (King James) Pop. literary phrase at her time and before; again M inverts gender.

188. *Virgins* - From Matthew 25:1-13: *Give us of your oil; for our lamps are gone out* (King James)

191. *Shad* - River-dwelling fish, genus *Alosa* (various spec.), related to the herring; particularly valued as food in the 18th c.

192. *Peg of Limmavaddy* - Ref. to Thackeray's poem "Peg of Limavaddy" (pub. 1842), composed to honor an innkeeper's daughter.

193. *mother-hubbard gown* - Usually "Mother Hubbard dress": wide, lengthy, loosely-fitting dress with high neck and long sleeves; designed to cover the body as completely as possible.

194. *a l'huile* - With oil.

195. *Seaton* - From the ballad "Four Marys" (btwn. 1719-1764): *Last night there were four Marys / Tonight there'll be but three / There was Mary Seaton and Mary Beaton / And Mary Carmichael and me.*

196. *give her some* - Lines attached to the nursery poem "I Love Little Pussy" (pub. 1830); orig. poem is speculatively attrib. to English writer Jane Taylor (1783-1824),

author of "Twinkle, Twinkle, Little Star" (1806).

197. *slip betwixt* - English proverb: *There's many a slip twixt the cup and the lip* - poss. from Erasmus: *Multa cadunt inter calicem supremaque labra*, in *Adagia* Bk I, in turn poss. from epigram by Palladas (incl. in *The Greek Anthology* X, 32).

198. *mickle ... muckle* - Archaic terms of Northern English/Scottish origin: each means "large amount."

198. *nothing half so* - From first stanza of the poem "Love's Young Dream" by Byron's friend Thomas Moore: *But there's nothing half so sweet in life / As love's young dream.*

198. *the Assyrian* - From first stanza of Byron's poem "The Destruction of Sennacherib" (pub. 1815): *The Assyrian came down like the wolf on the fold, / And his cohorts were gleaming in purple and gold; / And the sheen of their spears was like stars on the sea, / When the blue wave rolls nightly on deep Galilee.*

198. *Iberian* - Ref. to saying attrib. Julius Caesar: "I would rather be first in a little Iberian village than second in Rome."

200. *wind tempered* - From trad. saying (sometimes wrongly attrib. to the Bible), "the wind is tempered to the shorn lamb."

202. *Devil's snuff-boxes* - Puffball mushroom, genus *Lycoperdon*.

204. *her wagon* - Ref. to popular quote of Emerson: "Hitch your wagon to a star"; M inserts a female gendering.

206. *adjutant-birds* - Sizable tropical storks of genus *Leptoptilos*; so called in English from a stiff, upright manner while walking.

210. *escheats* - Is transferred to or becomes a part of; often a legal term.

212. *sadness of* - Prob. ref. to third stanza of Tennyson's "Crossing the Bar" (1889): *Twilight and evening bell, / And after that the dark! / And may there be no sadness of farewell, / When I embark*; the poet requested this stand last in any collection of his poetic works.

217. *deal* - Prob. *Pinus sylvestris*, commonly "Scots Pine," less so "Norway Pine"; in timber form, called "yellow deal" or "red deal." In Dickens' time, more broadly, plank-made furniture; often suggested cheapness.

218. *bannocks* - Given M's Scottish preferences, likely scones; term covers wide variety

of flat, rapidly-preparable breads.

218. *tend my* - From Shakespeare's *3 Henry VI* II:5 (spoken by Henry): *So many hours must I tend my flock; / So many hours must I take my rest; / So many hours must I contemplate; / So many hours must I sport myself*

218. *oh, mine* - From 1 Kings 21:20: *And Ahab said to Elijah, Hast thou found me, O mine enemy? And he answered, I have found* thee: *because thou hast sold thyself to work evil in the sight of the* LORD. (King James)

220. *put up* - Heat-intensive method of canning; often used an open kettle.

223. *long, rubber* - Per pub. text.

235. *Mount Royal* - Hill in Montreal, directly west of downtown; source of city's name; Colline de la Croix, at 764 feet, is the Mount proper.

235. *adventurous* - Jacques Cartier (1491-1557), led to summit in 1535 by indigenous people; named the hill in honor of François I of France, his patron.

235. *Place d'Armes* - Square in Old Montreal quarter.

235. *statue* - In honor of Paul Chomedey de Maisonneuve (1612-1676), French military man and founder of Montreal; unveiled 1895.

235. *Romanism* - At the time, an often-derogatory term for Roman Catholicism.

237. Sir Hugh MacDonald (1850-1929) - Cabinet minister and, for a brief time, the eighth Premier of Manitoba.

237. *Dominion Day* - In Canada, holiday honoring its formation as a Dominion on 1 July 1867; renamed "Canada Day," 1982.

237. *Orangemen's Day* - Commemoration of July 1690 Protestant victory over Roman Catholics in Ireland; provincial holiday in Newfoundland and Labrador.

237. *Queen's Own* - Canadian militia based in Toronto; came to public note during Second Boer War (1899-1902).

237. *Lord Aberdeen* - Popular term for John Campbell Hamilton-Gordon, 1st Marquess of Aberdeen and Temair (1847-1934); Seventh Governor General of Canada (1893-1898).

237. *good king* - Ref. to the genial, sanguine Edward VII (1841-1910), namesake of the

Edwardian era.

237. Sir John Alexander MacDonald (1815-1891) - Canada's first Prime Minister (1867-1873); father of Sir Hugh MacDonald (*cf.* n. 237 p 567).

238. *marguerites* - Poss. ref. to *Leucanthemum vulgare*, one of the members of family *Asteraceae* to be called "daisy."

238. *Goneril* - Female char. in Shakespeare's *King Lear*; aggressive and focused upon power at all costs.

*

245. *hied* - Went rapidly.

247. *titivated* - Decorated or renovated.

247. *furbelow* - Showy ornamental item, spec. a garment's flounce or ruffle.

247. *toilet* - One's washing and aesthetic preparation for going out.

248. *of the Gods* - Hilly area featuring unusual rock formations in Colorado Springs, Colorado; public park since 1909.

*

249. *true, 'tis pity* - From *Hamlet* II:2 (spoken by Polonius): *Madam, I swear I use no art at all. / That he is mad, 'tis true: 'tis true 'tis pity; / And pity 'tis 'tis true - a foolish figure!*

250. *Lydia* - Ancient kingdom in Asia Minor; inside borders of modern Turkey.

250. *fretted palaces with music in the enameled walls* - A misquote of the novel *Captain January* (1891) by Laura E. Richards (*cf.* n. 60 p 557): *"Oh, that kind of princess!" said Star, loftily. "I didn't mean that kind, Daddy. I meant the kind who live in fretted palaces, with music in th' enamelled stones, you know, and wore clothes like these every day"*; M alludes to phrase on p 74 ("fretted palaces") and again misquotes it on p 311 ("fretted palace with music in th'enameled walls").

250. *asphodels* - Attractive flowering plant native to Europe, genus *Asphodelus*; often mentioned in pieces of lyric writing.

251. *that they may eat and drink* - Poss. 2 Kings 6:22: *And he answered, Thou shalt not smite them: wouldest thou smite those whom thou hast taken captive with thy sword and*

with thy bow? set bread and water before them, that they may eat and drink, and go to their master. (King James)

251. *long suit* - From games of cards: the preponderating suit in a hand.

*

253. *little red book* - Ref. to cover of *I Await*.

253. *of this great* - From Shakespeare's *Merchant of Venice* I:2 (spoken by Portia): *By my troth, Nerissa, my little body is aweary of this great world. Cf.* M's misattrib. on p 304.

*

255. *rum days* - Unusually favored days; poss. from old military custom of portion of rum on set days; also poss. term in rum-producing areas when trade was strong.

256. John Maguire (*c.* 1850s-?) - Pioneering Butte impresario; produced celebrity appearances by the likes of Mark Twain.

256. *iron dollars* - Colloq. for metallic money versus paper; suggested full, ready value, sim. to "cash on the barrelhead."

257. *Town Topics* - Once-respectable society arts paper; under ed. Col. William d'Alton Mann (1839-1920) had degenerated into scandal sheet used to blackmail high-society persons; M's widow ref. is to its fallen state.

258. *second little red* - Ref. to cover of *Annabel*.

*

263. *inst.* - The present ("instant") month.

264. *make interviews* - Ref. to press' practice of concocting interviews; a major plot point in Jack London's *Martin Eden* (1909).

265. Harriet Hubbard Ayer (1849-1903) - Well-known journalist and cosmetics entrepreneur.

266. Nelson Hersh (*c.* 1861-1902) - Editor of *The Sunday World*; would die in November in a carriage accident.

266. *yellow* - *The World* was a crusading "people's paper"; the paras. M mentions are

presumably those about Bailey's Beach.

267. MS - Ref. to *Annabel.*

269. *McPaine* - Vaudeville skit (1902- 1903) caricaturing *I Await.*

269. *Weber and* - Well-known Broadway music hall.

269. Samuel Sidney McClure (1857-1949) - Publisher of *McClure's*; a founder of muck-raking journalism; introduced the Montessori method to North America.

*

272. *Miss Monroe* - Here, Lucy Monroe.

273. *Fergus* - Fergus Falls, Minnesota; *cf. e.g.* pp 309-317.

273. *the cars* - Poss. Providence and Danielson Railway Company; its electric line to Scituate, about six miles distant, was opened in 1901.

*

274. Yone Noguchi (born Noguchi Yonejirō, 1875-1947) - Japanese writer who had substantial career in US; protege of Joaquin Miller, wrote first US English-language novel by a Japanese person - *The American Diary of a Japanese Girl* (pub. in instal. 1901, book pub. 1902).

275. Charles Warren Stoddard (1843-1909) - Bohemian, travelsome US editor and author.

*

276. *Four Years* - At least one newspaper announced forthcoming publication; copy has yet to be located.

277. Frances Brawne Lindon (1800-1865) - Keats' fiancee from 1818 to his death in 1821.

278. *hotel* - Ref. to Monroe's poem "The Hotel," pub. *Atlantic Monthly*, Mar. 1909, pp 324-325; begins: *The long resounding marble corridors, the shining parlors with shining women in them. / The French room, with its gilt and garlands under plump little tumbling painted Loves. / The Turkish room, with its jumble of many carpets and its stiffly squared un-Turkish chairs. / The English room, all heavy crimson and gold, with spreading palms lifted high in round green tubs. / The electric lights in twos and threes and hundreds, made into festoons and spirals and arabesques, a maze and magic of bright persistent radiance. /*

The people sitting in corners by twos and threes, and cooing together under the glare. / *The long rows of silent people in chairs, watching with eyes that see not while the patient band tangles the air with music*; one scholar maintains that it should be considered "a key text in the emergence of modern American poetry" - *cf.* Newcomb, John Timberman: "Poetry's Opening Door: Harriet Monroe and American Modernism," *American Periodicals*, Vol. xv, No. 1 (2005), pp 6-22.

278. *Seasons* - Prob. ref. to Monroe's poem "The Dance of the Seasons," pub. *Fortnightly Review*, May 1908, pp 914-920 (but in existence earlier, *e.g.* at author's reading at Art Inst. of Chicago, 15 Jan 1907, under title "Dance Symphony," with final title as subtitle); begins: *1 - Spring / Allegro / Wake! wake! / Out of the snow and the mist, / In rain-wet wind-blown gauze / Of amber and amethyst, / Cometh Spring like a girl. / Trembling and timorous / She peers through the thin white thaws, / Afraid of the winds that whirl / Down paths all perilous / Where her so tender feet are softly going, / Where the rich earth is awaiting her lavish sowing / Of green and purple and white / In the gardens of day and night*; this - said to have been the first poem by a US author accepted by the *Fortnightly Review* - has also been of interest to scholars; *cf. e.g.* William, Ellen: *Harriet Monroe and the Poetry Renaissance: The First Ten Years of Poetry, 1912-22*; Univ. of Illinois Press, Champaign (Il.), 1977, p 12.

279. *this book* - *Cf.* p 288.

279. *shrieking of* - Ref. to metal trolley wheels against metal flanges on curves.

*

280. *Bow-wows* - From Dickens' *Nicholas Nickelby* (serial pub. 1838-1839), Chapt. 64 (spoken by Mr. Mantalini, AKA Mr. Muntle): "He has gone to the demnition bow-wows."

281. ASMS - Associated Sunday Magazines syndicate.

282. *frenzied finance* - Popular phrase, further spread by *Frenzied Finance: The Crime of Amalgamated* (pub. in instal. 1904, book pub. 1905) by Thomas W. Lawson (1857-1925): insider's expose (with score-settling) of F. Augustus Heinze's battle against Amalgamated Copper in Butte; *cf.* n. 517 p 594.

283. *redeem* - In unpub. letters to Stone, M had spoken of a someday lunch she would pay for, eventually calling it "the Long-Deferred."

283. Arthur M. Brisbane (1864-1936) - Ed., Hearst's *New York Evening Journal*; Hearst assoc. until his death; called most powerful or greatest journalist of his day.

283. *Lares and Penates* - Guardian and household deities, respectively, in Ancient

Rome; often carried together; came to symbolize the home's center; analogically: one's central personal possessions.

283. Alice Lloyd (1873-1949) - English vaudeville and music hall performer; sister of Marie Lloyd.

283. Marie Lloyd (1870-1922) - English vaudeville and music hall performer; sister of Alice Lloyd; called "Queen of the Music Halls."

285. *New Thought* - 19th c. American spiritual-religious movement, emph. metaphysical power of consciousness or mind.

285. Kate Elinore (*c.* 1874-1924) - Brooklyn-born vaudevillian; perf. (1884-1909) with her Brooklyn-born sister May Elinore (*c.* 1877-?).

285. James Stetson Metcalfe (1858-1927) - American author, prominent theatrical reviewer for *Life* (1888-1920) and other major publications; apparent anti-Semite; article is "Vodeville as It is Vawdvilled," *Life*, 3 June 1909, pp 774-775; *cf.* M's use of "vodeville," p 321.

285. Evelyn Thaw *née* Nesbit (1884-1967) - American chorus girl and model, object of notorious love triangle murder of architect Stanford White by her husband, Harry K. Thaw; the Thaws ran into White at M's haunt, the Cafe Martin, a few hours before the murder at Madison Square Garden; M's claim of invitation is credible: Nesbit was a known alcoholic and morphine addict in later years.

285. *Pell* - Street in New York's Chinatown; in early 20th c. known as "Red Street" because of ongoing Tong wars.

*

291. *of my stocking* - Prob. money, poss. secreted high-value cards.

291. *jade* - Slang for nag, old woman, or prostitute - here, prob. cocky or disreputable.

292. *accouchement* - Fr.: confinement, esp. laying in, before childbirth.

292. *shocked Butte* - Ref. to various unlikely rumors of her behaving with shocking rudeness to Butte high society ladies at a tea, luncheon, or evening party; Atherton (1932, p 491) repeats one such.

293. *plaisance* - Fr.: pleasantness.

293. *rounder* - Slang, several meanings; here, prob. one who "makes the rounds" from drinking establishments to prisons to flophouses and then repeats the cycle; term is colored by other meanings: itinerant worker on railroads (thus unprosperous and work-worn, of the lower class), and a criminal or hustler.

293. *swissesse* - Briefly-fashionable hairdo with one or several curls dangling behind the ear.

293. Thomas Joseph "Sailor Tom" Sharkey (1873-1953) - Irish-born heavyweight boxer active 1893-1904; considered one of the sport's great punchers; his eponymous bar on 14th St. was famous for a time.

293. *of a deadlock* - Ref. to price of Butte's then-primary export, copper, being down; copper's tonnage price is illuminating: 1906 - $524; 1907 - $441; 1908 - $291; 1909 - $289; 1910 - $284; 1911 - $277 (per *http://minerals.usgs.gov/minerals/pubs/historical-statistics/ds140-coppe.pdf*, accessed 30 September 2014).

293. *cabs* - "Sea-going cab" was slang for: a yacht, a small launch, and recklessly or rapidly driven taxi; "deep" seems M's addition - perhaps for "deep in(to) the night."

293. *roadhouses* - Slightly disreputable drinking establishments located just outside city limits on secondary or primary roads, thus often unmolested by authorities; some offered gambling and, at times, prostitutes.

293. *Mercury* - Center of Butte's prostitution district.

294. Carrie Nation (1846-1911) - Teetotaler; famed for carrying an axe wherewith to wreck bars.

295. Ann O'Delia Dis (or Diss) Debar - (born Ann O'Delia Solomon, var. Salomon, 1849-?) - Notorious American spiritualist/con artist with numerous pseudonyms; influenced by Theosophy; served several sentences in prison.

295. Elinor Glyn (1864-1943) - English screenwriter and novelist; wrote the successful sex novel *Three Weeks* (1907); popularized the concept of "It" - magnetic appeal of a charismatic personality.

295. Cecilia Loftus (1876-1943) - Scottish music hall performer/vaudevillian.

295. Vesta Victoria (1873-1951) - English music hall singer.

295. *'alf* - Ref. to trad. English drinking mixture of any two of ale, beer, and twopenny (the strongest, so called because 18th c. cost was two pence per quart).

*

298. *dead-sea fruits* - Trad., something of apparent but illusory value; used by *e.g.* Dickens in Chapt. 4 of *A Tale of Two Cities* (serial pub. 1859); also in Moore, "Lalla Rookh": *Like Dead Sea fruits, that tempt the eye, / But turn to ashes on the lips!*

298. *belike* - Archaic: perhaps, probably.

298. *ferulity* - Syn. for fruitfulness; usage very rare.

298. *hop-fiends* - Ref. to habitual drug users.

298. *Three-and-a-Half-Mile House* - Butte roadhouse; such were often named for the distance from town or town limits.

299. *be filled with* - From eleventh stanza of Longfellow's poem "The Day is Done" (1845): *And the night shall be filled with music, / And the cares, that infest the day, / Shall fold their tents, like the Arabs, / And as silently steal away.*

300. *gudgeons* - Several species of freshwater fish used as bait.

301. *contemn* - Treat or view with scorn.

301. *run and read* - From Habakkuk II:2 *And the* LORD *answered me, and said, Write the vision, and make it plain upon tables, that he may run that readeth it.* (King James)

302. *that clears* - From Edward FitzGerald's translation (5 ed., 1859-1889) of *The Rubaiyat*: *Ah! my Beloved, fill the Cup that clears / To-day of past Regrets and future Fears / To-morrow? - Why, To-morrow I may be / Myself with Yesterday's Sev'n Thousand Years.*

302. *for mine* - Affirmative slang of the time; roughly, "for my part"; sim. "me for" - roughly, "I have chosen/am wholly committed to" - *cf* p 341 ("Me for the Rialto"), also p 347 for ironic/exasperated "me for the sympathetic."

*

303. *eke* - Archaic: also.

306. *and that* - Slang of the time; meant "all of that" or "and so on"; *cf.* p 352.

308. *ignis fatuus* - Lat. "foolish fire": will-o'-the-wisp.

308. *the Grape* - Ref. to *The Rubaiyat*; alcoholic products and their source in the fruiting berry have deep meaning in other Sufi poets, *e.g.* the in-turned, complexifying Rumi and the extroverted, senses-celebrating Hafiz.

*

309. *what boots it* - Archaic phrase: "what profits it"; appears in, *e.g.* FitzGerald's translation of *The Rubaiyat*: *Ah, fill the Cup: - What boots it to repeat / How time is slipping underneath our Feet. / Unborn* TO-MORROW, *and dead* YESTERDAY, */ Why fret about them if* TO-DAY *be sweet?*

309. *anent* - Regarding, about.

309. *Gramercy!* - From Old Fr.: *grand merci* - "great thanks."

309. Anthony Comstock (1844-1915) - Crusading United States Postal Inspector, founder of the New York Society for the Suppression of Vice.

310. *fields and running* - Poem, and eponymous volume of poems (pub. 1893), by James Whitcomb Riley.

311. *grew the* - Prob. ref. to folk song "Green Grew the Rushes, O."

311. *glengarry-bonneted* - Ref. to trad. Scottish hat.

311. *four-flushing* - From poker: one who boasts emptily or bluffs failingly.

312. Benjamin Harrison (1833-1901) - 23rd US Pres. (Mar 1889-Mar 1893).

312. *straw ... hay* - *Cf.* p 92 - M appropriates from Thackeray.

314. *teetotum* - Spinning top used in gambling; mentioned in Lewis Carroll's *Through the Looking-Glass.*

314. *little one* - George W. Frankberg (1882-1937); in 1910, was lawyer in Fergus Falls; late in decade would be elected Mayor and in 1932 would be a delegate from Minnesota to Republican National Convention.

315. *horned-pout* - North American fish (*Ameiurus nebulosus*); also known as brown bullhead or mud cat.

315. *rew* - Syn. for "row" - in v. form, "to raise a scandal or conflict over."

315. *peck* - US and British dry measure equivalent to 8 dry quarts.

315. *pelican* - Slang term of various meanings; one is "a hearty eater"; another (from Fr.) "a dressy courtesan"; here, poss. a non-specific term of opprobrium.

316. *butch - er's-boy* - A text highly variant to known versions of the old ballad "A Butcher's Boy," which itself has numerous variants, *e.g.* in first lines: *In Jersey City where I did dwell / A butcher's boy I loved so well* and *In London city, where I did dwell. / A butcher boy I loved right well.* The version M gives is abbreviated, suppresses the suicide of the abandoned maiden, and has lines not recorded elsewhere. *Cf. http:// en.wikipedia.org/wiki/The_Butcher_Boy_(folk_song)* (accessed 30 September 2014).

316. *desire of* - From second stanza of Shelley's poem "One Word Is Too Often Profaned" (pub. 1822): *I can give not what men call love; / But wilt thou accept not / The worship the heart lifts above / And the Heavens reject not: / The desire of the moth for the star, / Of the night for the morrow, / The devotion to something afar / From the sphere of our sorrow?*

316. *time has* - From FitzGerald's translation of *The Rubaiyat: Come, fill the Cup, and in the Fire of Spring / The Winter Garment of Repentance fling: / The Bird of Time has but a little way / To fly - and Lo! the Bird is on the Wing.*

316. *who's kissing her* - Ref. to song "I Wonder Who's Kissing Her Now" (1909), lyr. Hough *&* Adams, mus. Howard *&* Orlob: *I wonder who's kissing her now, / I wonder who's teaching her how, / Wonder who's looking into her eyes, / Breathing sighs, telling lies; / I wonder who's buying the wine, / For lips that I used to call mine. / I wonder if she ever tells him of me, / I wonder who's kissing her now.*

*

318. *in bought* - Ref. to corruption in Senatorial appointments prior to 17th Amendment (1913); Senator Clark (*cf.* n. 147 p 563) was one of the Amendment's major inspirations.

319. *soul, like* - Ref. to American marching song about famous abolitionist; lyrics have many variants.

319. *Coeur* - Ref. to Richard I (1157-1199).

319. Elizabeth Cady Stanton (1815-1902).

319. Victoria Claflin Woodhull (1838-1927).

319. Tennessee Celeste Claflin (1844-1923).

320. Julia Ward Howe (1819-1910).

320. Lucy Stone (1818-1893).

321. *Fourteenth* - Area, fashionable in 1890s; had become degenerate center of brothels and streetwalkers; 1910s crackdowns only partly-successful.

321. Ida Husted Harper (1851-1931) - American author, journalist, early historian of suffrage movement.

321. Carrie Chapman Catt (1859-1947) - American suffrage leader.

321. Emmeline Pankhurst (1858-1928) - Militant English suffrage leader.

322. *hook-worm* - Intestinal parasite assoc. with improper sanitation; in N. America, *Necator americanus*; particularly injurious to children, pregnant women.

322. *poets say* - Ref. to arriving at happy occasion in carriage or sleigh with bells on the horse-harnesses.

322. *young sovereign* - Wilhelmina (1880-1962).

322. *her tiny* - Juliana (1909-2005).

322. *his* - Alfonso XIII (1886-1941).

322. *girlish queen* - The Queen Consort, Princess Victoria Eugenie of Battenberg (1887-1969).

322. *certes* - Archaic: "with certainty" or "truly."

*

325. Trixie Friganza (born Delia O'Callaghan, 1870-1955) - American musical comedienne and vaudevillian.

326. *vertu* - Alt. spelling of "virtu": objects of art or art-knowledge.

326. *tea-fight* - Slang: a party.

328. *Port Arthur* - Chinese restaurant on Mott St.

329. *Green God* - Absinthe was called "The Green Fairy" or "The Green Goddess"; was often thus visually depicted.

329. *Misericorde* - Two meanings, here apparently fused by M: dispensation from monastic discipline (as with the waiver of a fast) and a dagger used to deliver a merciful death to a badly wounded medieval knight.

329. *be again* - "Thy portion" is a recurrent phrase in the King James.

330. *this vaudeville* - Seventeen minutes was a standard act length (if on the long side) in vaudeville; *cf.* p 340.

331. *whence, and* - From FitzGerald's translation of *The Rubaiyat*.

*

332. *giant powder* - Nitroglycerine-based blasting compound.

332. *tent scene* - Ref. to Shakespeare's *Julius Caesar* IV:3.

333. *before the* - Song appears to be undocumented; the line "Two little girls in blue" does appear in a song thus-titled, said to have been written *c.* 1893 by Charles Graham; *cf.* Randolph, Vance: *Ozark Folksongs - Vol. IV - Religious Songs and Other Items*, Univ. of Missouri Press, 1980 (orig. pub. 1949), p 338; the remainder of the song bears no textual or thematic resemblance to the fragment given by M; the later Broadway musical thus-titled - lyr. Ira Gershwin, mus. Lannin & Youmans (1921) - appears unrelated to either song.

333. *rather have* - Song appears to be undocumented.

333. *never spoken* - From the song "The Picture That is Turned Toward the Wall" ("Descriptive Pathetic Song and Chorus," 1891), lyr. & mus. by Charles Graham.

333. *the secret* - From the song "Sweet Marie" (debuted in music show *Africa* in 1893); lyr. Cy Warman, mus. Raymond Moore; first stanza: *I've a secret in my heart, Sweet Marie - / A tale I would impart, Love, to thee. / Every daisy in the dell / Knows my secret, knows it well, / And yet I dare not tell Sweet Marie.*

333. *Borneo* - Poss. ref. to music piece "Wild Man from Borneo" or "The Wild Man from Borneo Has Just Come to Town" by John W. Schaum (poss. piano arranger); same song poss. ref. to by Joyce in *Ulysses*; *cf.* Thornton, Weldon: *Allusions in* Ulysses: *An Annotated List*, UNC Press Books, Chapel Hill (N.C.), 1982, p 321.

333. *Hanging* - From the song "And Her Golden Hair Was Hanging Down Her Back" (1894); lyr. Monroe H. Rosenfeld, mus. Felix McGlennon.

333. *Cherry* - Infamously bad vaudeville act of several Iowa sisters; active early 1890s-1903; toured nationally; famed for being as void of talent as they were rigid in morality; *Cherry v. Des Moines Leader* is landmark affirmation of press' right to critical comment.

333. *Lovingkindness* - Word in Coverdale Bible (1535) for Hebrew word *hesed*; in the Vulgate, translated as *misericordia* (*cf.* n. 329 p 578); also used in Theosophical texts, early English renderings of Buddhist sutras.

334. *to our muttons* - Trunc. of "return to our muttons": to return to the subject or matter at hand; English rendering of still-current Fr.: "revenons à nos moutons"; from 15th-c. *La Farce de Maître Pierre Pathelin*, wherein a thieving shepherd speaks in court about everything but the sheep he had stolen; the judge repeatedly orders him back to the point using that phrase.

334. *Wilton* - A carpet woven in loops that form a velvet-like, cushioning pile.

335. *dirk* - Short thrusting dagger; worn with trad. full Scottish Highland dress.

335. *chewers ... rags* - Ref. to "chew the rag" - slang: talk or chat lengthily; M's addition of "technical" suggests a lengthy fix on minutiae.

335. *cheap sport* - Slang: man who lives extravagantly (by way of drinking, attending parties, dressing well, etc.) without necessary funds, and so borrows.

337. *the lowering* - From FitzGerald's translation of *The Rubaiyat*.

*

338. *un haussement de m'epaule* - Fr.: "a shrug of my shoulders."

339. *cloak* - A live model of feminine attire for purchases in stores; strict standards of proportion and fitness were enforced.

339. *caste of our* - The ed. has changed the original's "a waste" to "caste" as a likely compositor's error.

339. Eleanor "Nell" Gwyn (alt. Gwynn, Gwynne, 1650-1687) - Comic actress of Restoration England, Charles II's long-term mistress, mother of two of his sons.

340. *Milo* - Popular "Egyptian"-style cigarette made in US.

341. Edna May (born Edna May Pettie, 1878-1948) - American musical actress in Edwardian era, noted for comedy; as May was pretty, often featured on postcards, the Borrower indicates her attractiveness in youth.

342. *MacTrey* - An otherwise-unexplained nickname; *cf.* p 343; *cf.* Pruitt, Elisabeth (ed.): *Tender Darkness: A Mary MacLane Anthology*, Abernathy & Brown (Belmont, Calif.), 1993, pp 193-194 for extended discussion.

342. *sulphites* - *Cf. ibid.*, p 194.

342. *Yvette Gilbert* - Ref. to Yvette Guilbert (name usu. Americanized with dropped "u," 1865-1944); French actress and cabaret singer; as M indicates, noted for working pathos into her acts.

342. *Woman's Home Companion* - Highly successful US magazine (1873-1957); shared publisher with *Collier's* and *Farm and Fireside*; M may be alluding to the latter with "the home-and-fireside."

342. *kirtle* - Middle Ages garment, sim. to a tunic.

343. *than night* - Ref. to mydriasis, either due to cocaine use or withdrawal from opioids, *e.g.* morphine or heroin.

344. *LeMonte* - Untraceable ref.; poss. pseud., or poss. ref. to woman connected with singer Signor Lemonte [*sic.*], part of traveling troupe Ferullo and His Band (AKA Ferullo's Band); for Sig. Lemonte as band member *cf. Racine Daily Journal* (Wisconsin), 12 Oct 1908, p 2; for Ferullo's Band in New York City *cf.* Joseph Gigante Coll., Wisconsin Music Archives listing at UW-Madison, at *http://music.library.wisc.edu/wma/papers/gigante/gigante.htm* (accessed 30 September 2014).

344. *that little* - Alice or Marie Lloyd.

*

345. *settlement* - Movement (1880s-1940s) begun in Great Britain aimed at overcoming class divisions by creating integrated community residences containing people of lower and middle classes that were funded by upper class people; Jane Addams' famed Hull House in Chicago was inspired by earlier British examples.

346. *hash-slinger* - Cook in cheap restaurant.

346. *captioned* - M's articles on women bore captions prominently listing her monikers for the women she would portray.

348. Maude Adams (born Maude Ewing Kiskadden, 1872-1953) - American stage actress who had immense success, particularly with J.M. Barrie's plays; was the first Peter Pan on Broadway.

348. *rose o' the world* - Prob. ref. to Yeats' poem "The Rose of the World" (1893); first stanza: *Who dreamed that beauty passes like a dream? / For these red lips, with all their mournful pride, / Mournful that no new wonder may betide, / Troy passed away in one high funeral gleam, / And Usna's children died.*

348. *a fisher of men* - Ref. to Matthew 4:19 and Mark 1:17.

349. *go to it, 'bo* - Popular phrase; evidently alludes to having set a plate of food before a hungry hobo.

350. *silk* - Printed by firm founded by Arthur Lasenby Liberty (1843-1917); noted for fresh floral designs.

350. Lyman Abbott (1835-1922) - American clergyman and religious writer.

*

352. *Christian Endeavorers* - Ref. to Young People's Society of Christian Endeavor - famed US evangelical movement, founded 1881; poss. first youth ministry.

352. *Dan to Beersheba* - Ref. to northernmost and southernmost cities of ancient Israel, thus the entire kingdom, *i.e.*, a vast expanse or everywhere; phrase (and "from Beersheba to Dan") appears in several places in Old Testament.

352. *Epworth* - Ref. to Epworth League: American Methodist youth and young adult association, founded 1889.

352. *Anti-Cigarette* - Ref. to The Anti-Cigarette League, successful American advocacy group, founded 1899.

352. *Daughters* - Prob. ref. to The King's Daughter's Society: nonsectarian youth service group, founded 1880s in New York State.

353. *Cause of the* - Section-titles likely contributed by newspaper; in an unpub. letter to M.E. Stone, Jr., M objects to their paragraphing of the article.

353. *Mrs. Longworth* - Poss. ref. to Alice Roosevelt Longworth (1881-1980), Theodore Roosevelt's eldest child; odd if so, as Mrs. Longworth was flamboyantly in favor of women's smoking.

353. *Lucy Page Gaston* (1860-1924) - Founder of The Anti-Cigarette League.

354. *seventy* - From Matthew 18:21-22: *Then came Peter to him, and said, Lord, how oft shall my brother sin against me, and I forgive him? till seven times? / Jesus saith unto him, I say not unto thee, Until seven times: but, Until seventy times seven.* (King James)

354. *Huyler ... Allegretti* - Well-known candy manufacturers; M's female gendering of the co.s is notable: Huyler was the enterprise of John S. Huyler (1846-1910), "the candy king."

354. *chorile* - From Germ.: in, or like, hymn tones.

355. *Grant-and-Greeley-and-Centennial* - Ref. to period (1869-1877) of Pres. Grant (1822-1885), famed editor Horace Greeley (1811-1872), and the US Centennial (1876).

357. *legit and vaudeville* - Evidently a then-common phrase; recorded here and there.

358. *marry-come-up* - Archaic exclamation of shock or outrage.

358. *eyes ... not morality* - From Preface to 2nd ed. of *Jane Eyre* (1848).

*

399. *serge* - A both-sides-ridged twill fabric; in worsted (durable, somewhat scratchy) and silk types.

360. Pierre Jules Théophile Gautier (1811-1872) - French critic, dramatist, novelist, journalist; famous for attacking the bland male dress of the day; the deliberately bizarre excess of the outfit he wore to the premiere (1830) of Hugo's *Hernani* set the tone for the Romantics' Bohemian clique.

361. Luisa Tetrazzini (1871-1940) - Italian coloratura soprano; had tremendous international career.

361. *moyenage dress* (usu. "moyen age") - Dress fitted through the waistline with a set-in band or belt around the hips.

361. *maid of Orleans* - Joan of Arc.

361. Thomas Gainsborough (1727-1788) - English painter, some of whose society paintings of women (*e.g.* of the Duchess of Devonshire) feature his subjects' outsized hats.

362. Annette Kellerman (1887-1975) - Australian vaudevillian, professional swimmer,

movie star, author; pioneer in wearing one-piece bathing suits; believed to have invented synchronized swimming.

362. *Florence Dombey* - Char. in Dickens' *Dombey & Son* (serial pub. 1846-1848).

363. *empires* - Napoleonic Empire (1804-1814/15) and French Empire (1852-1870), respectively.

363. Elisabeth Rachel Félix (stage name Mademoiselle Rachel, 1821-1858) - French actress, lover to a number of highly-placed men; never married; died of tuberculosis.

364. *incipient* - Ref. to eponymous protagonist of Dickens' *David Copperfield* (serial pub. 1849-1850).

364. *Lady Dedlock* - Char. in Dickens' *Bleak House* (serial pub. 1852-1853).

364. *Lorna Doon* - Eponymous protagonist of *Lorna Doone: A Romance of Exmoor* (1869) by Richard Doddridge Blackmore (1825-1900).

364. *Bella Wilfer* - Char. in Dickens' *Our Mutual Friend* (serial pub. 1864-1865).

364. Theodosia Burr (married name Theodosia Burr Alston, 1783-1813) - Daughter of US Vice-Pres. Aaron Burr; a prodigiously learned young woman for her day.

364. Peggy O'Neill - Ref. to Margaret O'Neill Eaton (popularly "Peggy," 1799-1879) - vivacious hotel-keeper's daughter; in time married Sen. John H. Eaton, who became Sec. of War under Andrew Jackson; Eaton resigned when the cabinet-members' wives refused to cease disdaining her; situation became known as the Peggy Eaton Affair.

365. *embonpoint* - Fr.: "stoutness."

365. *"eternal summer"* - Phrase in Shakespeare's *Sonnet 18* (pub. 1609); appears also in Milton's maske *Comus* (1634).

366. *farthingales* - Skirt-shaping hoop-structures.

*

378. *rosary, my* - From widely popular song "The Rosary" (1898); lyr. Robert Cameron Rogers, mus. Ethelbert Nevin; first stanza: *The hours I spent with thee, dear heart / Are as a string of pearls to me / I count them over, ev'ry one apart / My rosary, my rosary*

379. *pit-fall and of gin* - Ref. to Shakespeare's *Macbeth* IV:2 (spoken by Lady Macbeth):

Poor bird! Thou 'dst never fear the net nor lime, / The pitfall nor the gin. Cf. also p 438.

379. *n'importe* - Fr.: of no matter or import.

380. *soul above* - Ref. to Shakespeare's *Twelfth Night* II:3 (spoken by Sir Toby Belch): *Art any more than a steward? Dost thou think because thou / art virtuous there shall be no more cakes and ale?* - A parallel in British slang is "skittles and beer," for which *cf.* pp 327, 399, 401.

382. *three signs* - Poss. ref. to mystical sign, *In hoc signo vinces*, seen by Constantine at the Battle of the Milvian Bridge against Maxentius.

382. *we shall* - Ref. to *Julius Caesar* IV:3: *Brutus: Why comest thou? / Ghost: To tell thee thou shalt see me at Philippi. / Brutus: Well; then I shall see thee again? / Ghost: Ay, at Philippi. / Brutus: Why, I will see thee at Philippi, then. / Exit Ghost*

*

386. The identity of M- T- is unknown.

387. *devasted* - Old variant of "devastated."

388. *winged word* - Orig. an Homeric phrase, later taken up by Carlyle; sometimes poetically rendered "wing'd word."

391. *rowelling* - Mid. English: a wheel with sharp teeth inserted into a spur's shank-end.

392. *To-morrow and* - Spoken by Macbeth (V:5): *To-morrow, and to-morrow, and to-morrow, / Creeps in this petty pace from day to day, / To the last syllable of recorded time, / And all our yesterdays have lighted fools / The way to dusty death. Out, out, brief candle!*

395. *incalescent* - Growing intenser or hotter.

395. *pierce the* - Poss. ref. to stanza 33 of Shelley's poem "The Revolt of Islam" (pub. 1818): *But more he loathed and hated the clear light / Of wisdom and free thought, and more did fear, / Lest, kindled once, its beams might pierce the night, / Even where his Idol stood; for, far and near / Did many a heart in Europe leap to hear*; less likely, poss. ref. to anon. (prob. because near-treasonous) English poem "America, An Ode" (pub. 1776) II:3: *Heaven her blazing portal spreads; / Shafts of glory pierce the night; / Lo! the bright van the royal patriot leads, / Founder of laws, and arbiter of right*

395. *stays* - Ref. to a corset.

396. *put to it* - Phrase used in law courts: a pointed issue to be heard or decided upon.

396. *lightning and* - From stanza 12 of Shelley's poem "Adonais, An Elegy on the Death of John Keats" (1821): *And pass into the panting heart beneath / With lightning and with music: the damp death / Quenched its caress upon his icy lips*

397. *sucking dove's* - From Shakespeare's *A Midsummer Night's Dream* 1:2 (spoken by Bottom): *But I will aggravate my voice so that I will roar you as gently as any sucking dove. I will roar you an 'twere any nightingale.*

399. *voile* - Fr.: "veil"; a lightweight, shear, soft cotton or cotton-blended fabric.

402. *hoyden* - Roisterous girl; orig. a rude youth; from Dutch *heiden*: heathen, boor.

402. *Nick Carter* - Dime-novel detective; first appeared in 1886 in *The Old Detective's Pupil; or, The Mysterious Crime of Madison Square* by John R. Coryell (story by Ormond G. Smith).

402. *Lady Audley's Secret* - Early true-crime-based novel (1862) by English novelist Mary Elizabeth Braddon (1837-1915); centers on socially-climbing bigamous female criminal; sensation in its time; features three secondary female chars. distinguished respectively by tomboyishness, social restraint, and loneliness.

402. *Lena Rivers* - Novel (1856) by prolific popular writer Mary Jane Holmes (1825-1907); centers on spunky orphan displaced to live with family members who don't know what to do with her; the grandmother is heavily oppressive of all concerned.

403. *demi-vierge* - Fr.: "half-virgin" - One who has been partway sexually active but not to the point of intercourse; also sometimes a young person whose thoughts are no longer chaste.

404. William Collier (born William Morenus, 1864-1944) - Light comedian noted for a natural, understated manner, said to have influenced Noel Coward; after long career in vaudeville, moved to motion pictures.

405. *prepollence* - Quality of being dominant, supererogatory.

406-407. *Dover* - Line spoken by Mr. Finching's grimly oracular aunt in Dickens' *Little Dorrit* (serial pub. 1855-1857); the line's enigmatic quality has been much commented-upon.

409. *inversions* - "Inversion" would have unambiguously suggested homosexuality, then called (and thought of as) "sexual inversion"; *cf.* also p 524: "a wanderer in fields

of inverted fungi."

413. *pinchbeck* - Spurious, as replacement; M curtails the imaginary lovers' potency by indicating they, as counterfeits, won't be kept around for long.

413. *incumbrance* - Uncommon variant of "encumbrance."

413. *nepenthe* - Mythical drug of Ancient Greece: inducer of forgetfulness (of pain or sorrow esp.); attempted actual prep.s believed to have been opioid in nature.

415. *vamps* - Section of shoe's "upper" between the toes and the ankle-break.

416. *Rocker* - Suburb of Butte, about 3 miles west of town.

419. *song of myself* - Poss. ref. to Whitman's epic poem.

423. *Churchill's* - One of Broadway's great mid-town "lobster palaces"; famed for vast dining room (1200 seats, 300 waiters) and cabaret entertainment; owned by ex-NYPD Capt. Jim Churchill (1863-1930); popular with Theatrical District people; *cf.* p 307.

424. *naif* - Variant of "naive."

424. *over-souls* - Prob. ref. to Emerson's neo-Platonic concept of a single transcendent soul of mankind.

425. François Villon (birth name uncertain, *c.* 1431-poss. 1460s) - French thief, itinerant, poet; at once thematic and formal innovator, writer about the lower classes, and includer of thieves' argot into poetry; *cf.* p 523.

426. *Glim* - A light-source, or light given by such.

426. *Chape* - A buckle's metal tongue or a scabbard's metal trim or tip.

426. *Plash* - A spatter or gentle splash.

426. *Whelk* - A sea snail, often but not always member of family *Buccinidae*.

426. *Mauger* - Despite, regardless.

426. *Frush* - To crush (or disintegrate) by battering; appears in Shakespeare's *Troilus and Cressida* v:6 (spoken by Hector): *I like thy armour well; / I'll frush it and unlock the rivets all, / But I'll be master of it: wilt thou not, / beast, abide?*

426. *Gnurl* - A grippable knob or other small protuberance; usually, one of a series of small grooves or ridges on a metal object's edge(s) or surface(s).

426. *Yare* - Quick, ready, nimble.

426. *Hyaline* - Any glasslike substance; has specific affine meanings in entomology, ichthyology, histopathology.

427. *Melody of* - Ref. to poem "Ode on a Grecian Urn" (1820) by John Keats, specifically its famous lines 11-14: *Heard melodies are sweet, but those unheard / Are sweeter; therefore, ye soft pipes, play on; / Not to the sensual ear, but, more endear'd, / Pipe to the spirit ditties of no tone*

427. Lillian Walker (1887-1975) - American vaudeville actress, moved to silent movies in 1911; extremely popular in 1910s.

427. *lorette* - Courtesan.

429-430. *simpler and finer* - These may be variations on one of Blake's "Proverbs of Hell": "Sooner murder an infant in its cradle than nurse unacted desires" (from *The Marriage of Heaven and Hell*, writ. c. 1789-c. 1793).

434. *woful* - Variant of "woeful."

435. *Oliver* - Boy's suit-style: featured short trousers and prominent buttons; was often paired with a string-tie.

435. *serge-Norfolk* - Single-breasted pleated jacket or suit including same, worn loosely and with belt or half-belt; in blue, a serge Norfolk suit was the predominant nurses' uniform in World War I.

436. *countrymen* - From Brutus' pulpit-speech in *Julius Caesar* III:2: *Be patient till the last. Romans, countrymen, and lovers! hear me for my cause, and be silent, that you may hear: believe me for mine honour, and have respect to mine honour, that you may believe: censure me in your wisdom, and awake your senses, that you may the better judge.*

436. *devil-fish* - Poss. *Mobula mobular*, also "giant devil ray"; species of eagle ray, family *Myliobatidae*, found in Mediterranean, less commonly in Atlantic.

437. *the whistling winds* - Poss. from Pope's trans. of Homer's *Iliad* (install. pub. 1715-1720) and (collab. Broome & Fenton) *Odyssey* (pub. 1726), in both of which the phrase recurs.

438. *cats* - Ref. to familiar phrase (origin unknown): "A cat may look at a king."

438. *from his ... wander in* - From FitzGerald's translation of *The Rubaiyat*; first quote omits a beginning poetic "What!"; second omits a beginning "Oh."

439. *wine must* - From Sonnet 6 of Elizabeth Barrett Browning's *Sonnets From the Portuguese* (written c. 1845-1846, pub. 1850): *And what I dream include thee, as the wine / Must taste of its own grapes. And when I sue / God for myself, He hears that name of thine, / And sees within my eyes the tears of two.*

443. *"Bill" Sikes* - Char. in Dickens' *Oliver Twist* (serial pub. 1837-1839); a vicious criminal and, in time, murderer.

443. *book and* - Indicates religious ceremony; orig., method of excommunication mentioned in Shakespeare's *King John* III:3 (spoken by the Bastard): *Bell, book, and candle, shall not drive me back / When gold and silver becks me to come on*; appears in Bk XXI, Chapt. I of Malory's *Le Morte d'Arthur* (pub. 1585): *I shall curse you with book and bell and candle.*

443. *sam shu* - Alt. "samshoo" or "samshu" - burningly intense Chinese liquor; distilled from rice or sorghum.

443. *to St.* - Trad. English nursery rhyme.

444. William A. Muldoon (1852-1933) - Prominent physical culture advocate, sometime actor; undefeated in Greco-Roman wrestling in his time.

444. Bernarr MacFadden (1868-1955) - Prominent physical culture advocate; focused on nutrition and bodybuilding; wrote over 100 books, touted sexual intercourse for health and pleasure; publ. text misspells his name.

448. *back from* - Genesis 19:26 (King James).

448. *Oh, the* - Song quoted in Guy de Maupassant's short story "The Viaticum" (English trans. 1903).

450. *calefacient* - A substance that causes a sensation of warmth.

452. *pace* - Cf. n. 392 p 584.

453. *Goose* - The rhyme is "The Old Woman And The Pedlar."

453. St. Simeon Stylites (*c.* 390-459) - Known for living for 39 years on a small platform atop a pillar in Syria; subj. of eponymous poem by Tennyson (pub. 1842).

453. *Lanky Bob ... Carson* - Ref. to Corbett-Fitzsimmons boxing match at Carson City, Nevada (1894); British boxer Robert J. Fitzsimmons (1863-1917) wrested heavyweight title from Irish-American James J. Corbett (1866-1933) in a surprise win; subj. captured in a documentary film - at 100 minutes, the longest to that date; only fragments remain.

453. *Gal* - M misquotes title of song: "My Gal is a High-Born Lady" (1886), lyr. & mus. Barney Fagan.

454. *Dare-devil Dick* - 19th c. boys' adventure stories, sold in some printings for a penny per.

454. *Chautauqua* - Nationwide adult-educating movement of the time; featured touring groups of lecturers and entertainers; often performed in tents; "entertain and instruct" was a common phrase ref. to them.

454. *Widow* - Ref. to Champagne wine innovator Barbe-Nicole Cliquot *née* Ponsardin (1777-1866), widow (Fr. "veuve") of Philippe Clicquot-Muiron; the house her husband founded (and she controlled after his death) is Veuve Clicquot Ponsardin

458. *bone-brained* - A reminder that even highly individuated persons may remain in the offensive group-think of their time; while such refs. in M's work are rare (and are contradicted by other statements and her life-course), they do exist - *cf.* p 320 on race.

459. Inez Haynes Irwin (*née* Gillmore, 1873-1970) - Author, feminist, member of the National Women's Party.

460. *to read* - Ref. to "Ode to a Nightingale" (pub. 1820).

460. *Celeste Aïda* - Act I romanza in Verdi's *Aïda* (sung by Radamès).

460. Sarah Blanche Sweet (1896-1986) - American actress; noted for independence and strength.

460. *Marchioness ... Brass* - Chars. in Dickens' *Old Curiosity Shop* (serial pub. 1840-1841); M's quote is incorrect; actual (Chapt. 36): *"Go further away from the leg of mutton, or you'll be picking it, I know," said Miss Sally. / The girl withdrew into a corner, while Miss Brass took a key from her pocket, and opening the safe, brought from it a dreary waste of cold potatoes, looking as eatable as Stonehenge.*

461. *this fellow* - From *Rip Van Winkle* (1859) by renowned American actor Joseph Jefferson (1829-1905); M's quote is incorrect; actual (Act IV, spoken by Derrick): *Here, give him a cold potato, and let him go.*

461. *baked* - From *Hamlet* 1:2 (spoken by Hamlet): *Thrift, thrift, Horatio! the funeral baked meats / Did coldly furnish forth the marriage tables. / Would I had met my dearest foe in heaven / Or ever I had seen that day, Horatio!*

461. *Canterbury Pilgrims* - Presumably Chaucer's; a group of emigrants to New Zealand were known thus, but bore no substantive relationship to potatoes.

463. *Instead, through* - Ref. to 1 Corinthians 13:12: *For now we see through a glass, darkly; but then face to face: now I know in part; but then shall I know even as also I am known.* (King James)

463. *La Guzla* - 1827 hoax poetry-collection by Mérimée; passed off as translation from Serbo-Croatian; had a strong influence in Russia.

463. *Venus* - Ref. to "La Vénus d'Ille" (1837), a fantasy horror piece.

463. Geraldine Farrar (1882-1967) - Well-regarded American soprano and actress; upon her 1922 retirement and after, her large and passionately devoted following among young women would be called "Gerry-flappers"; at least one writer has speculated on a homoerotic quality of the fan reaction; *cf.* Castle, Terry: *The Apparitional Lesbian: Female Homosexuality and Modern Culture*, Columbia Univ. Press, New York, 1995, Chapt. 9.

464. *sonant* - Having the quality of being voiced (as opposed to surd or asonant).

464. *Theda Bara* (born Theodosia Burr Goodman, 1885-1955) - One of the cinema's first sex symbols; the archetypal Vamp.

464. *maculate* - Contrary of "immaculate."

471. *shilling* - Slogan of Pall Mall cigarettes; straight-Turkish blend, marketed as a high-society item.

471. *Vantine* - Ref. to A.A. Vantine *&* Co., a major exotics importer; "The Oriental Store"; had a large building at Fifth Ave. and Thirty-Ninth St. in Manhattan.

472. *an Eastman* - A slogan adopted by the Eastman Kodak Co. to combat the uncapitalized "Kodak"'s having become a generic term; M's "k" subverts the intent.

472. *Clarence Crane* - Innovative candy manufacturer from Cleveland, Ohio; invented Life Savers (1912); maintained a Chocolate Studio.

472. *Maillard* - American candy manufacturer; of high-class repute.

473. *octroi* - Authorities (orig., and generally, taxation authorities).

474. *world is* - Poss. from posth.-publ. (1694) *Journal of George Fox*; lived 1624-1691, founded Religious Society of Friends; phrase appears in journals several times.

476. *biograph* - Pop. term for a movie, derived from very early firm American Mutoscope *&* Biograph Company (parent co. founded 1895).

477. *Mist* - Apparent ref. to line in Virgil's *Aeneid* (1.462): *Sunt lacrimae rerum et mentem mortalia tangunt*; the translation M gives does not correspond to any found; however, as this was a standard (if difficult) assignment in Latin studies, M may be recalling her own.

478. *wavering* - Nine stone exactly would be 126 pounds.

480. *alphabetic ... 'drink all himself.'* - Untraceable ref. and quote; ed. speculates poss. ref. to Shlomo Yitzhaki (known as Rashi, 1040-1105), father of Talmudic and Tanakhic commentary, said (by Rabbi Zalman of Liadi) to have pressed "the wine of Torah"; the characters of the Hebrew alphabet in which his commentaries are printed are a special semi-cursive font.

482. *éclat* - Fr.: brilliant effect, result; connot. verges on flamboyant display.

482. *restfully* - Bans on absinthe had spread through Europe; by 1912 it was prohibited in the US.

486. *de-soie* - A fine or thin silk (or, later, rayon); can be to the point of gauziness.

487. Lord George Gordon (1751-1793), Pres. of the Protestant Association.

487. *riots* - London-convulsing uproar (1780) over 1778 Act that had partly loosened anti-Catholic laws; M's century is incorrect.

487. *Tyburn* - A Middlesex village known almost exclusively as the site of execution by hanging of London criminals (c. 1196-1783).

487. *illuminating* - An anachronism unless M means producing fake goods for the bookseller.

490. *being narrowly* - Likely an allusion to Euclid's fifth postulate.

491. *shockers ... dreadfuls* - Anachronisms; they emerged only in the 19th c.

492. *half-familiar ghosts* - An untraceable quotation.

493. *anchoretic* - In the manner of a self-denying religious recluse (*i.e.*, an anchorite).

493-494. *upon nothing* - From Mother Goose rhyme "A Strange Old Woman": *There was an old woman, and what do you think? / She lived upon nothing but victuals, and drink; / Victuals and drink were the chief of her diet, / And yet this old woman could never be quiet.*

495. *vestas* - Ref. to brand (Swan Vesta after 1906, orig. intro. 1883) of wax-soaked safety match with a shank of treated threads; its short length and damp-proof, wind-resistant qualities made it "the smoker's match"; in time, any waxed safety match was a "vesta" (*sans* capital), and some such appear in the Sherlock Holmes story "Silver Blaze" (1892); named for Roman goddess of home and hearth.

495. *petticoat* - From Mother Goose rhyme "Pussy-cat Mew": *Pussy-cat Mew jumped over a coal, / And in her best petticoat burnt a great hole. / Poor Pussy's weeping, she'll have no more milk / Until her best petticoat's mended with silk.*

496. Stanley Ketchel (1886-1910) - Widely-admired American middleweight, famed for fearlessness; would fight heavyweights, at times victoriously; got his start in a 1904 match in Butte.

496. Andrea del Sarto (1486-1530) - Florentine painter who straddled High Renaissance and very early Mannerist periods.

496. Boudica (?-*c.* 61) - Queen of the British Iaceniae, who uprose against Roman occupation; said to have been of Amazonian character.

496. Christopher Mathewson (1880-1925) - Prodigiously talented American pitcher; some of his statistics remain records (*e.g.* third-best all time wins, third-best shut-outs, eighth-best ERA).

496. *charlotte-russe* - Trad. holiday dessert of creamy consistency; made of eggs, whipping cream, and whiskey.

496. *lay in* - From Mother Goose rhyme "Robin and Richard": *Robin and Richard were two pretty men, / They lay in bed till the clock struck ten; / Then up starts Robin and looks at the sky, / "Oh, brother Richard, the sun's very high! / You go before, with the bottle and bag, / And I will come after on little Jack Nag ..."*

497. Jane Lee (1912-1957) - Scottish-born American child actress.

497. Amy Lawrence Lowell (1874-1925) - Distinguished New England poet, winner of posthumous Pulitzer Prize (1926).

498. *sleep* - From "Go to Sleep, My Dusky Baby" (1915), lyr. Frank Reader Rix (1853-1919), mus. Antonin Dvorak arr. Rix.

498. *tax* - Ref. to "Pierrot" (1882) by Guy de Maupassant (1850-1893).

498. *leaning* - Ref. to "The Blessed Damozel" (1st vers. pub. 1850) by Dante Gabriel Rossetti (1828-1882); written in Keats' manner - depicts a woman in Heaven looking down upon her lover on Earth and longing for reunion; it would mark Rossetti's career and be the subject of several of his paintings.

500. *unattuned* - Reason for quotation marks is unknown; the word was used at the time and before and not under proscription. A contemporaneous meaning seems to have been "in psychic or mental sympathy or connection"; *cf.* Beach, Rex: *The Ne'er-Do-Well* (ser. pub.), *Everybody's Magazine*, May 1911, p 678: *Promptly at seven o'clock on the following evening he returned to his post, and before he had been there five minutes knew that his presence was noticed. This was encouraging, so he focused his mental powers in an effort to communicate telepathically with the object of his desires. But she seemed unattuned, and coyly refrained from showing her face. He undertook to loiter gracefully, knowing himself to be the target of many eyes, but found it extremely hard to refrain from sitting on the curb - a manifestly unromantic attitude for a lovelorn swain.*

501. *purling* - A river or stream's flowing swirlingly and with babbling sound

501. *mantling* - The hunching of a bird of prey over a kill to protect from competitors.

502. Valeska Suratt (1882-1962) - American actress and early Vamp (known as the screen's "Vampire Woman"); noted for the great hauteur of her garb.

502. *mænad* - A female disciple of Dionysus.

502. *Cyprian woman* - Euph. for prostitute; ultimately derived from an epithet for Venus ("the Cyprian goddess").

504. *gentleman's* - A general term for more refined games of chance (*e.g.* baccarat); here, poker is more likely meant.

505. *recherché* - Fr.: of refined, elegant appearance or manner; slight connot. of tending to the sumptuous.

506. *there an end* - Shakespearean phrase, *e.g. Macbeth* III:4, *Two Gentlemen of Verona* I:3.

515. *trainant* (properly "traînant") - Fr.: dragging, trawling; implicitly, disreputable.

515. *straight* - The term as a contrapositive to homosexuality would not be seen in print until *c.* 1941 (by 1868, however, it had appeared as a term for a chaste woman); the image-complex, however, is already present in M's thought: *direct repellent roads ... twisted ... straight ... straight-made* (pp 514-515).

517. *Timber* - Prominent mountain a few miles south of the city of Butte.

517. Fritz Augustus Heinze (1869-1914) - One of Butte's "Copper Kings"; ruthless competitor with Daly's Amalgamated Copper - bought judges, reduced miners' hours, ran as Anti-Monopoly Party candidate for Mayor; eventually was paid $12,000,000 by Amalgamated to leave Butte; moved to New York, where with his brothers had central role in causing the Panic of 1907, which became central argument for the Federal Reserve system.

518. *Noodle-ish and little* - Prob. ref. to small food and alcohol providers near Venus Alley behind Butte's famed Dumas Brothel on E. Mercury St. (*cf.* pp 293, 294, 300), held to have been the country's longest-operated house of prostitution (1890-1982); prostitutes who had not made it into the Dumas or one of other houses received customers in cribs in the Alley which featured telephone lines to noodle parlors and bars for rapid deliveries.

519. *lid* - Ref. to statewide gambling prohibition, begun in 1910.

520. *Pickett's* - A futile charge against Union forces at Gettysburg (1863); though immensely costly in Southern casualties, considered by some the Confederacy's most-bravely fought; M refs. to battlefield valor to the point of death (*cf.* n. 520 p 594).

520. Arnold Winkelried (14th c., poss. legendary) - Swiss hero; charged into the pikes of Hapsburg Austrian troops at the Battle of Sempach (1386); his action, eventually fatal, opened the way for eventual Swiss victory; his name would come to be invoked for heroic bravery unto death in aid of a cause.

521. *Fetich* - Variant of "fetish."

522. *wefts* - From weaving: yarn drawn through the warps to form cloth.

522. François-Dominique Toussaint Louverture (1743-1803) - Leader of the Haitian Revolution; deported to France, where he died.

522. *pleasure* - From "The Realm of Fancy" (sometimes simply "Fancy") by Keats (pub. 1820).

523. - *outsoared* - From Shelley's "Adonais."

523. - *imagists* (usu. cap.) - Early-1910s group that coalesced around Ezra Pound, H.D., and Richard Aldington; favored compression and sharp-lined imagery; "Imagism" made its bow in Harriet Monroe's magazine *Poetry*, which Pound served as foreign correspondent (and to which M undoubtedly subscribed, likely from inception).

524. *deadlier* - From Kipling's poem "The Female of the Species" (pub. 1911) - *But the Woman that God gave him, every fibre of her frame / Proves her launched for one sole issue, armed and engined for the same; / And to serve that single issue, lest the generations fail, / The female of the species must be deadlier than the male.*

526. *uxoresque* - From Latin *uxor*: "wife"; still found in older English-language legal documents, sometimes abbrev. "ux."

527. *maggot ... nut* - "A maggot in a nut" is an old English expression; became prominent in 18th c.

527. *in-the-drawing* - Ref. to gambling: in the game, being in play.

529. *Hale* - Ref. to MacMonnies statue (1890); still stands in City Hall Park; *cf.* p 156.

530. *sixes and sevens* - Very old English phrase for chaos or disarray; connot. frazzledness.

533. *Jericho* - Poss. ref. to 2 Kings 2-4: *And Elijah said unto him, Elisha, tarry here, I pray thee; for the* LORD *hath sent me to Jericho. And he said, As the* LORD *liveth, and as thy soul liveth, I will not leave thee. So they came to Jericho.* (King James)

*

539. - *the bud* - From Shakespeare's *Twelfth Night* II:4: *Orsino: And what's her history? / Viola: A blank, my lord. She never told her love, / But let concealment, like a worm i' the bud, / Feed on her damask cheek: she pined in thought, / And with a green and yellow melancholy / She sat like patience on a monument, / Smiling at grief.*

539. - *ideal [marriage]* - Phrase used here and there - in 1928 would be title of famed sex manual.

540. *free love* - Woodhull and other 19th c. reformers advocated for freely-chosen, readily-dissolvable sexual relationships; in some cases this was extended to statutory marriage and even parental relations.

540. *affinity* - Marriage (or, still less conventionally, relationship) founded not upon

familial or social approval but upon personal, esp. sexual, compatibility; like companionate marriage, a much-discussed issue at the time; in Goethe's novel *Elective Affinities* (pub. 1809), the chemical metaphor is made almost non-metaphoric.

540. *millennium* - Ref. to belief, usu. religious, that after a coming upheaval a healthier or more just society or world will emerge.

540. *carry* - Available newspaper source has sections flaked off due to age; bracketed word is ed.'s speculative reconstruction; some alternatives are "have" or "bear."

541. *banker's* - Bracketed phrase is ed.'s entirely-speculative guess; some alternatives are "to a fine certainty" or "to a nice certainty," but they fit less well into spacing of the missing section.

541. *spoke* - Ref. to nautical trad. of ships that catch sight of one another on the high seas pulling alongside and exchanging goods, news and information, poss. mail-items, then parting.

542. *now to* - Bracketed phrase is ed.'s speculative guess.

542. *kidhood* - Approx. two sentences are lost; as M was still in Butte at the time of writing, the sentences gave some background to their acquaintance, perhaps to do with his family.

*

545. *dope sheet* - Usu. a sheet listing news, statistics, and/or odds, as with football or horse-racing; more generally, an information-rich publication about a specific field.

545. *demon art* - Ref. to "the demon Rum" fulminated against by, *e.g.*, Carrie Nation.

545. *cinematograph* - Lit., an integrated camera/developer/projector, as with the Bouly-Lumière system of the earlier 1890s; here is meant, almost certainly, the projector-and-screen combine.

546. Douglas Fairbanks, Sr. (1883-1939) - American actor, famed for his dashing, physically-adventurous roles.

546. *last few feet* - Ref. to a film's final seconds.

546. Alice Brady (1892-1939) - American actress; would win Best Supporting Actress Oscar in 1937 for *Old Chicago*.

546. Robert Warwick (born Robert Taylor Bien, 1878-1964) - American actor; noted for handsomeness.

546. Louise Glaum (1888-1970) - American actress, considered one of the best of the Vamps; also played two-gun-slinging heroine in 1917's *Golden Rule Kate*; went into vaudeville in the 1920s; would be well-reviewed for her starring turn in the problem play *Trial Marriage* (1928); became a drama instructor.

546. Mary Pickford (1892-1979) - Canadian-born actress, called "America's Sweetheart," later co-founded United Artists; married for some years to Douglas Fairbanks, Sr.

546. Henry Brazeale Walthall (1878-1936) - American actor, worked with D.W. Griffith and, in early years, Mary Pickford.

*

THIS
BOOK HAS
BEEN SET IN
ADOBE GARAMOND
PRO, A FONT BY ROBT.
SLIMBACH SPECIFICALLY
FOR DIGITAL TYPESETTING.
PERSONAL INSPECTION OF C.
GARAMOND'S ORIGINAL PUNCHES
INSPIRED A DESIGN FAITHFUL TO THE
ORIGINAL ROMAN TYPE, WHICH
TRADITIONALLY HAS BEEN
PAIRED WITH THE MORE
SLOPED, ENERGETIC
ITALICS CUT BY
R. GRANJON.

*

BOOK
DESIGN
HAS, IN YEARS
RECENT, DEPARTED
FROM CLASSICAL STRICTURES
AGAINST TYPOGRAPHICAL WIDOWS
AND ORPHANS. GIVEN THE NATURE
OF THIS TEXT, THE DECISION WAS
MADE TO HOLD RIGIDLY TO
PAGEBLOCK GEOMETRY
AND PERMIT WIDOWS
AND ORPHANS
FREELY.

*

* COMING NEXT *

Mary MacLane - a 19-year-old diarist from the early 20th century, still influential today - was the first of the modern media personalities. Now, her whole story is being told in a series of books from Petrarca Press.

We are proud to announce 2015 release of two new books in our Mary MacLane Series: *Mary in The Press: Miss MacLane & Her Fame* and the first-ever complete study of MacLane's life, career, and influence, *A Quite Unusual Intensity of Life: The Lives, Works, and Influence of Mary MacLane.*

Mary in The Press provides, for the first time, more than one thousand pages of interviews, news stories, reminiscences, attacks, opinions, plaudits, personal letters, cartoons, photographs, and more - almost all unseen for a century. With a detailed introduction and lengthy footnotes and bibliography, this mammoth two-volume edition unfolds for the first time the enormous controversy - and adoration - over the writer a forthcoming PBS documentary calls "The First Woman of the Twentieth Century."

A Quite Unusual Intensity of Life goes beyond the usual biography to unfold Mary MacLane's inner and outer worlds; the people she knew and loved; her influences, and her influence on the future; her life outside of writing as a gambler extraordinaire and silent film writer star; the inner secrets of her unique, still-compelling literary style - and much more.

Michael R. Brown, foremost MacLane scholar in the world today, says of these two books: "This is the other half of Mary's story, and it's taken decades of research to tell it. She gave herself totally in her writing, and the world's slowly remembering now. These are the books I wish I'd had at my side when I read those first words, thirty years ago."

Check http://marymaclane.com for exclusive content, updates, and all news about the ongoing discovery of Mary MacLane. For publication information and pre-ordering for *Mary in The Press* and *A Quite Unusual Intensity of Life*, email groupmail@petrarcapress.com or dial 530-566-6615. ISBN and SAN information forthcoming.

*

Adobe Garamond Pro * Body: 11.5 pts, lead: 12 pts. * Notes: 10 pts, lead: 11.175 pts. * Page: 6in. x 9in. * Margins: top 1 in., bottom 1.375 in., inner 0.91 in., outer 0.7213 in. Text width 4.3687 in. * Normal indent: 0.1667 in.

www.ingramcontent.com/pod-product-compliance
Lightning Source LLC
Chambersburg PA
CBHW032252020726
47495CB00001B/71